DISCOVERING PSYCHOLOGY

Study Guide

to accompany *Psychology: Science, Behavior and Life*, 3rd edition
(Richard Ettinger, Robert L. Crooks and Jean Stein, Harcourt Brace College Publishers, 1994)

By Ellie Goldberg and Morton P. Friedman

Funded by
The Annenberg/CPB Project

Harcourt Brace College Publishers
Fort Worth   Chicago   San Francisco   Philadelphia
Montreal   Toronto   London   Sydney   Tokyo

ISBN: 0-15-502092-7

PRINTED IN THE UNITED STATES OF AMERICA

4 5 6 7   095   9 8 7 6 5 4 3 2 1

Harcourt Brace College Publishers
The Dryden Press
Saunders College Publishers

This book was developed for use by students enrolled in the *Discovering Psychology* telecourse. The telecourse consists of twenty-six half-hour public television programs, the Study Guide, and an introductory psychology textbook selected by the instructor. Selected short portions of the programs have been excerpted and are available as video modules. *Discovering Psychology* was produced by WGBH-TV, Boston, Massachusetts. Major funding was provided by the Annenberg/CPB Project. This series is closed captioned for the hearing impaired.

For further information about the print components of the course or the video modules, contact:

Harcourt Brace College Publishers
301 Commerce Street
Suite 3700
Fort Worth, TX 76102
(817) 334-7500

For information about *Discovering Psychology* videocassettes, print materials, video modules, off-air taping and duplication licenses, and other video and audio courses from the Annenberg/CPB Collection, contact:

Discovering Psychology
The Annenberg/CPB Project
c/o Intellimation
P. O. Box 1922
Santa Barbara, CA 93116-1922
1-800-LEARNER

For more information about telecourse licenses and off-air taping, contact:

Discovering Psychology
PBS Adult Learning Service
1320 Braddock Place
Alexandria, VA 22314-1698
1-800-ALS-ALS-8

ACKNOWLEDGMENTS

The distinguished members of our Advisory Board, listed below, provided invaluable assistance in developing both the programs and the print materials for this telecourse.

Philip Zimbardo
Chief Academic Advisor
Professor of Psychology
Stanford University

W. Curtis Banks
Professor of Psychology
Howard University

Ludy T. Benjamin, Jr.
Professor of Psychology
Texas A & M University

Tom Bond
Professor of Psychology
Thomas Nelson Community College

Freda Rebelsky Camp
Professor of Psychology
Boston University

Daniel Goleman
Behavioral Science Reporter
New York Times

James B. Maas
Chairman and Professor of Psychology
Cornell University

Margaret S. Martin
Associate Professor of Professional Development
   and Health Sciences Administration
Medical University of South Carolina

Joe L. Martinez, Jr.
Professor of Psychology
University of California, Berkeley

Wilbert J. McKeachie
Professor of Psychology
University of Michigan

Fay-Tyler M. Norton
President
Colleague Consultants in Higher Education

Michael Wertheimer
Professor of Psychology
University of Colorado, Boulder

Special thanks also go to Robert Arkin, Dean of Undergraduate Studies at Ohio State University and the project's chief print advisor, who carefully reviewed the manuscript at several stages in its development and suggested many valuable improvements. The print materials also benefited greatly from the editing and fine-tuning provided by Naomi Angoff. Winifred Dunn deserves considerable credit for developing the faculty test bank as well as review questions for students. Researchers Tamra Pearson and Susan Kopman spent many hours in the library to locate anthology readings, citations for studies, additional resources, and other information necessary to complete the project. Patricia Crotty was the editorial assistant for the project and, with Deborah Paddock, oversaw photo research. Karen Barss was the permissions editor, and the manuscript was copyedited by Margo Shearman.

WGBH Educational Foundation
Boston, Massachusetts

PROJECT DIRECTORS

Brigid Sullivan
Manager of Special Telecommunications

Kim Storey
Project Director

PRINT DEVELOPMENT

Ann Strunk
Director of Print Projects

Beth Kirsch
Coordinator of Print Projects

PRODUCTION TEAM

Thomas Friedman
Executive-in-Charge/Executive Editor

William C. Brennan
Executive Producer

Tug Yourgrau
Senior Producer

CONTENTS

COURSE OVERVIEW AND GOALS

The first psychology laboratory was established in Leipzig, Germany, just 100 years ago. Yet despite its relative youth as an empirical science, psychology has made an indelible mark on our culture. We have become a psychology-oriented society, especially in the last half-century. Psychological research has changed many of our views on mental illness, learning, perception, motivation, sex and gender, aging, decision making, and health. Today researchers and clinicians worldwide continue to investigate the puzzles of human behavior, studying questions of great interest not only to psychologists but to all of us as we strive to unravel the mysteries of mind and body—why we think, act, and feel as we do.

Discovering Psychology, an introductory psychology course consisting of 26 half-hour programs, an introductory psychology textbook, and this Study Guide, will help you understand the variety of approaches to the study of human nature. The series will expose you to leading researchers and the latest developments in the field, from new ways of treating anxiety and depression to the psychological factors involved in space travel. Important psychological concepts and principles are brought to life by documentary footage, interviews, demonstrations, classic experiments, simulations, computer graphics, and animation.

GOALS

Discovering Psychology:

- Explores the major psychological approaches to the study of behavior, including their history, contributors, methods, research findings, terminology, and current directions

- Promotes the development of scientific values and skills, a recognition of individual bias in experimentation, and the ability to evaluate generalizations

- Encourages personal development through increased understanding and tolerance of the behavior of others and a curiosity about the forces that make us behave as we do

- Integrates new developments with classic research findings

- Challenges some traditional perspectives in light of new knowledge

- Illuminates the decision-making processes used by researchers

- Interweaves the theme of psychology as a scientific enterprise with that of psychology as a course of knowledge and practice that can improve the quality of life

THE HOST

Philip G. Zimbardo is Professor of Psychology at Stanford University. Internationally applauded for his vibrant teaching talent, he is the recipient of distinguished teaching awards from New York University, Stanford University, and the American Psychological Association. He has published more than a dozen books and more than 100 articles on a wide range of topics, including aggression, shyness, animal and human behavior, individuals, groups, and culture. The chief academic advisor for the *Discovering Psychology* television course, Professor Zimbardo has been teaching introductory psychology for more than 30 years.

COURSE COMPONENTS

Discovering Psychology includes three components:

1. 26 half-hour television programs, corresponding to the 26 units of the telecourse
2. Textbook: *Psychology: Science, Behavior and Life*, by Robert Crooks and Jean Stein, 1st edition, Holt, Rinehart and Winston, 1988 (or another textbook assigned by your instructor)
3. Study Guide

THE TELEVISION PROGRAMS

1. Past, Present, and Promise

An introduction to psychology as a science at the crossroads of many fields of knowledge, from philosophy and anthropology to biochemistry and artificial intelligence.

2. Understanding Research

An examination of the scientific method and the ways in which data are collected and analyzed—in the lab and in the field—with an emphasis on sharpening critical thinking regarding research findings.

3. The Behaving Brain

The structure and composition of the brain: how neurons function, how information is collected and transmitted, and how chemical reactions determine every thought, feeling, and action.

4. The Responsive Brain

How the brain controls behavior, and conversely how behavior and environment influence the brain's structure and functioning.

5. The Developing Child

The nature versus nurture debate, and how developmental psychologists study the contributions of both heredity and environment to the development of children.

6. Language Development

The development of language, and how psychologists hope to discover truths about the human mind, society, and culture by studying how children use language in social communication.

7. Sensation and Perception

How visual information is gathered and processed, and how our culture, previous experiences, and interests influence our perceptions.

8. Learning

The basic principles of classical and operant conditioning, and how renowned researchers—Pavlov, Thorndike, Watson, and Skinner—have influenced today's thinking about the nature of animal and human learning.

21. Psychopathology

The major types of mental illness, including schizophrenia, anxiety, affective and manic-depressive disorders, and the major factors that influence them—both biological and psychological.

22. Psychotherapy

The relationships among theory, research, and practice, and how treatment of psychological disorders has been influenced by historical, cultural, and social forces.

23. Health, Mind, and Behavior

How research is forcing a profound rethinking of the relationship between mind and body—a new biopsychosocial model is replacing the traditional biomedical model.

24. In Space, Toward Peace

New horizons in psychology, including the ways in which psychologists are preparing astronauts for space travel and insight into the psychology of peace, from the complexity of arms negotiations to our responses to the possibility of nuclear war.

25. A Union of Opposites

A review of some of the most significant insights and principles regarding human nature and animal behavior, and how a yin-yang set of opposites has contributed to our understanding of them.

26. New Directions

The speculations of prominent psychologists on the future of the field, new directions in research, theory, and application, and how psychology can contribute to improving the quality of our lives.

THE TEXTBOOK

A variety of introductory psychology textbooks can be used with this telecourse, but this Study Guide has been developed for use with the textbook *Psychology: Science, Behavior and Life,* by Richard Ettinger, Robert L. Crooks and Jean Stein 3rd edition, Harcourt Brace College Publishers, 1994. The textbook is an integral part of this television course. The assigned textbook readings for each unit will expand upon the television programs and present new information. The review questions and tests for this course will include questions from both the programs and the textbook readings.

You may find that the television programs present certain concepts or topics somewhat differently from the way the textbook does. Sometimes the information is presented in a different order, or the textbook may provide different examples and illustrations. The Study Guide will help you link the programs with the textbook.

THE STUDY GUIDE

The 26 units of the Study Guide correspond directly to the 26 television programs. The Study Guide previews, reviews, and applies the concepts and information from the television program. It also integrates program themes and concepts with the textbook. Each unit of the Study Guide includes the following elements:

- Objectives—concepts, facts, and themes from both the program and the textbook that you should be able to define, identify, explain, or apply

- Reading Assignment—identifies the page numbers in the textbook *Psychology: Science, Behavior and Life* that correspond to the themes and topics of the television program; your instructor may also assign the anthology selections that accompany each unit

- Key Terms and Concepts—lists important terms and concepts introduced in the textbook reading and defines new terminology from the programs

- Program Summary—a narrative description of the themes and highlights of the corresponding television program

- Review Questions—self-test items that enable you to evaluate your understanding of the program and textbook reading to prepare for exams (answers are included in the Appendix)

- Questions to Consider—open-ended questions to promote critical thinking (suggested answers are included in the Appendix)

- Optional Activities—a variety of optional projects, writing assignments, or experiments to help you gather evidence, raise issues, apply basic concepts, and review important information

- Anthology—a selection of items from professional and popular sources chosen to illustrate concepts related to each unit, to show relationships among unit concepts, and to stimulate critical thinking

- Additional Resources—an annotated bibliography of related books, articles, and films

TAKING
DISCOVERING PSYCHOLOGY
AS A TELECOURSE

Find out the following information as soon after registration as possible:

- What books are required for the course

- If and when an orientation session has been scheduled

- When *Discovering Psychology* will be broadcast in your area

- When examinations are scheduled for the course (mark these in your calendar)

- Whether any additional on-campus meetings have been scheduled (plan to attend as many review sessions, seminars, and other meetings as possible)

To learn the most from each unit:

1. Before viewing the television program, read the corresponding unit in the Study Guide, paying particular attention to the Objectives, Key Terms and Concepts, and Program Summary.

2. View the program, keeping the Objectives in mind. *Be an active watcher.* Some students find that taking notes while viewing the programs is helpful. If your area has more than one public television station there may be several opportunities for you to watch the program. Many public television stations repeat a program at least once during the week it is first shown. The programs may also be available on videocassettes at your school, or you can tape them at home if you own a VCR. If you don't have a VCR, you can make an audiocassette of the program for review.

3. Read the textbook sections listed in the Study Guide and any anthology selections assigned by your instructor. As you do these readings, pay particular attention to the Key Terms and Concepts identified in the Study Guide. In addition, chapter outlines, headings, summaries, and terms in bold type will help you identify the important information.

4. Do the Review Questions and any other questions, activities, essays, or experiments assigned by your instructor.

5. Keep up with the course on a weekly basis. Each unit of the Study Guide builds on knowledge gained in previous units. Stay current with the programs and readings. Make a daily checklist, and keep weekly and term calendars, noting your scheduled activities such as meetings or examinations as well as blocks of time for viewing programs, reading, and doing assignments.

6. Keep in touch with your instructor. If possible, get to know him or her. You should have your instructor's mailing address, phone number, and call-in hours. Your instructor would like to hear from you and to know how you are doing. He or she will be eager to answer any questions you have about the course.

A NOTE FROM PHILIP ZIMBARDO

© Sydney R. Goldstein

Welcome to the start of an exciting and challenging adventure in *Discovering Psychology*. I am delighted that you are about to join in this unique exploration into the nature of human nature. Through the medium of television, we will leave the confines of the traditional classroom to go where the action is, has been, or soon will be in psychology's scientific study of behavior and mental processes.

Our journey will take us to research laboratories throughout the United States to observe experiments in progress that are unraveling the mysteries of how the brain works, how animals and humans develop and change, and how the mind guides us through life's mazes. We will also visit mental hospitals, clinics, and therapists' offices where the pathologies of human functioning are studied, diagnosed, and treated. And we will venture out into the field where other researchers observe behavior in its natural habitat, whether it is stress among African baboons, shyness among chimpanzees, healing practices of Native Americans, competition in the classroom, or the destructive power of cult leaders over their followers.

This introduction to the state of the art of psychological knowledge is shaped by interviews with many of its most distinguished contributors. We will meet more than 70 researchers, theorists, and practitioners, all offering their individual perspectives on why they have devoted their talents to trying to solve the puzzles that brain, mind, and behavior continually present to the curious explorer. In addition to new interviews with Nobel Prize winners David Hubel and Herbert Simon, we will hear from psychology's most prominent figures, among them B. F. Skinner, Neal Miller, Noam Chomsky, Carl Rogers, Erik Erikson, Albert Bandura, and Eleanor Maccoby. To get an inside view of the "cutting edge" in psychological knowledge, we will turn to the new generation of psychologists who present ideas that are influencing the directions psychology is taking and charting the course it is likely to follow in the future.

We will do more than just talk about psychology, we will show it in action: through documentary footage, laboratory re-creations of experiments, case studies, and live demonstrations of perceptual illusions, hypnosis, memory, biofeedback, lie detection, and many other topics of vital concern to today's—and tomorrow's—psychologists.

We shall travel back in time to see the actual archival footage of some of the most significant experiments and demonstrations in the history of psychology: Ivan Pavlov's monumental discovery of the laws of conditioning, John Watson's research on infant emotional reactions, Kurt Lewin's study of democratic and fascist leaders, and Stanley Milgram's provocative look into the conditions that foster blind obedience to authority.

Throughout our series, we will discover that *what* we know about the content of psychological inquiry is influenced by *how* we know it. So we shall look behind the facts and principles to examine the methodology used to collect the data on which our conclusions are based.

For the most part, the selection of the programs and their sequence of presentation follow what has become traditional in introductory psychology courses. The flow is from the areas considered to be the "hard core" or foundation disciplines of psychology—such as brain processes, development, perception, learning, memory, cognition, motivation, and emotion—to those that are somewhat more complex, broader in scope, or more recent, or that involve applications of basic psychological knowledge. The latter topics include consciousness, the self, testing and assessment, sex and gender, social psychology, psychopathology, therapies, and health psychology. Finally, our journey, which started by looking inside a single nerve cell in the brain, ventures up and outward to travel in outer space and toward emerging research on the prevention of nuclear war and the maintenance of peace.

An important goal of this series is an increased understanding and tolerance of the behavior of others, along with a fuller appreciation of the complex set of influences that determine our own actions, from the genetic, cultural, and environmental to the political and economic. Just as we as individuals are always part of a broader array of overlapping contexts, so we will see that psychology too is at the crossroads of many other disciplines.

Psychology is a unique field of study, a social science that draws from sociology, anthropology, economics, and political science. But it is ever more akin to the biological sciences, especially to the neurosciences, the study of brain processes. For many, the new core of psychology is what it shares with the cognitive sciences, artificial intelligence, computer science, and applied mathematics. And because one of the distinguishing features of psychology is its concern for improving the quality of individual and collective existence, it is also a health science, brimming with ties to education, law, medicine, and the environment.

While this remarkable breadth and depth of modern psychology is a source of attraction to those who become psychologists, it is also what makes the field a difficult challenge for the first-time explorer. As an undergraduate, I certainly found it tough to integrate all that diverse information in my Psych 1 course; my only college C grade in that course represents an enduring testimonial to that difficulty. But the excitement of being able to contribute to our understanding of human nature as a researcher and to communicate it to others as a teacher has since been a continual source of joy to me. I have taught introductory psychology for more than 30 years now, in seminars as small as 10 students and in lectures at more than 700 colleges. With equal delight I have also shared psychology with high school students, ghetto kids, elders, and teachers and professionals in other disciplines.

Discovering Psychology presents the best of contemporary psychology in a format that is interesting and intellectually stimulating. In a half hour's time, an enormous amount of knowledge is conveyed because television can compact information through fast-moving images, graphics, and tightly packed commentary.

Of course each video program highlights only a limited number of major points, introduces a few major contributors, touches on some historical background, and presents a brief view of current research or practical applications in a given area. But the hope is that by adding this unique visual component to the wealth of information in the textbook and the exercises and activities in this guide, psychology will come alive as never before.

DISCOVERING PSYCHOLOGY

Study Guide

UNIT 1

PAST, PRESENT, AND PROMISE

Science is the attempt to make the chaotic diversity of our sense-experience correspond to a logically uniform system of thought.

Albert Einstein

Unit 1 introduces psychology as the scientific study of behavior and mental processes. It looks at how psychologists work from a variety of theoretical models and traditions, record and analyze their observations, and attempt to unravel the mysteries of the mind.

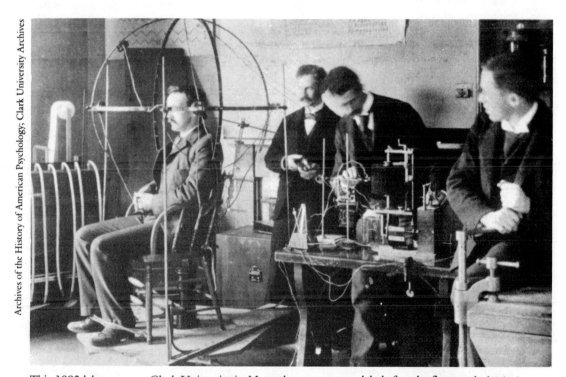

This 1892 laboratory at Clark University in Massachusetts was modeled after the first psychological laboratory, established in Leipzig, Germany, in 1879 by Wilhelm Wundt, the "father" of modern psychology.

OBJECTIVES

After viewing the television program and completing the assigned readings, you should be able to:

① Define *psychology*

② Explain the difference between common knowledge and the scientific investigation of behavior

③ Summarize the history of the major theoretical approaches to psychology

4. Explain the importance of both internal and external factors in understanding behavior

⑤ List and define the fields of specialization in psychology

6. Identify major subfields of psychology and describe what psychologists in each of these subfields do

⑦ Briefly describe and state the central idea of each of the following: behaviorism, Gestalt psychology, psychoanalytic psychology, humanistic psychology, and cognitive psychology

The whole 4— [handwritten annotations] *→Freud* *→selfactualization & free will* *thought process affects behavior*

8. Understand the difference between the micro, molecular, and macro levels of analysis

READING ASSIGNMENT

After viewing Program 1, read pages 3–21 in *Psychology: Science, Behavior and Life*. Your instructor may also assign the anthology selections for Unit 1.

KEY TERMS AND CONCEPTS

As you read the assignment, pay particular attention to these terms, which are defined on the given pages in the text.

psychology (4)

functionalism (10)

behaviorism (11)

Gestalt psychology (12)

psychoanalytic approach (10–11)

humanistic psychology (13)

cognitive psychology (14)

counseling psychology (16)

clinical psychology (16)

experimental psychology (15)

biological (physiological) psychology (15)

educational psychology (16–17)

school psychologist (16–17)

industrial/organizational psychology (17)

engineering psychologists (17)

developmental psychology (14)

social psychology (14)

personality psychology (15)

forensic psychology (18)

health psychology (17)

The following terms are used in Program 1 but are not defined in the text.

dispositional factors—a person's internal characteristics and potentials

ERP (Event-Related Potentials)—variations in brain waves as recorded by the electro-encephalograph (EEG) which are triggered by specific internal or external events

micro level—the smallest unit of analysis in psychology; for example, studying P-300 brain waves or other neural or biochemical changes

molar level—the analysis of larger units of behavior of the whole person in complex situations, taking into account cultural background and social experiences

molecular level—the analysis of discrete, observable behaviors such as body language, crying, or laughing

nonverbal communication—communication between people omitting all of the words

psychophysics—measuring mental reactions to physical stimuli

situational factors—characteristics which come from the environment in which a behavior takes place

PROGRAM SUMMARY

Psychology is a field that asks questions about the relationships among the mind, brain, and behavior. Why do people laugh and cry? What is intelligence? Are we molded more by heredity or experience? What makes us fall in love? And how can we cure mental illness?

Psychologists are people who ask questions about the puzzles of human nature. Like most of us, they are people watchers who make assumptions about their observations. But as scientists, they test their ideas under special, controlled conditions.

During the next 26 programs we will see psychology in action and discover that it has a lot in common with many other fields of study. From understanding the smallest chemical reaction in the brain to recognizing the special needs of astronauts in space, psychology constantly seeks to answer this fundamental question: What is the nature of human nature?

Professor Philip Zimbardo, the host for the series, will introduce psychologists who work in many different settings: laboratories, classrooms, clinics, hospitals, and prisons. They study animals and people asleep and awake, healthy and ill, alone and in groups. But no matter what their field of expertise, all psychologists are dedicated to gaining a better understanding of behavior. We'll see how they observe behavior and attempt to describe it objectively, using their knowledge to predict behavior, and sometimes to control it.

Psychologists assume that our behaviors—our brain waves, gestures, eye movements, and word choices—are external signs of an inner reality. Even our slightest reaction can raise a host of questions about our underlying perceptions, expectations, feelings, and ideas.

Whatever type of behavior psychologists choose to study, they try to make sense of it by relating the behavior to certain aspects of the individual and to elements of the situation. They ask what it is about the person—gender, cultural background, past experiences—that could account for a particular reaction. By looking at the situation and the environment, they try to identify the elements that could have influenced the response.

But not all psychologists work in the same way. In 1975 a psychologist named Emanuel Donchin discovered that our brains register surprise even before we are aware of it. By recording the brain's electrical activity, he discovered that events trigger specific brain wave patterns. When psychologists focus on a small unit of behavior such as a brain wave, they are working at the micro level of analysis.

Most psychologists operate on the molecular level. They study larger units of behavior such as body language. Psychologist Robert Rosenthal has shown that our body language can reflect much of what we're thinking and feeling. Rosenthal describes how we can predict behavior in certain situations but emphasizes that the same gestures can have very different meanings in different situations.

At the molar level of analysis, researchers investigate the whole person in complex situations, focusing even more on cultural background and social experiences. Psychologists working at the molar level might study sexual attraction, worker morale, or the nature of prejudice. Because psychologists are scientists, they must always be aware of the limits to their powers of observation and assessment and to their ability to be truly objective.

Like all disciplines, psychology can be better understood in its own historical context. Modern psychology began in 1879 when Wilhelm Wundt founded the first experimental psychology laboratory in Germany. There he designed studies to collect data on such behaviors as reaction times to sensory stimuli, attention, judgment, and word associations.

The history of psychology took another step forward when G. Stanley Hall founded the first American psychology lab in 1883. Hall became the first president of the American Psychological Association, and he introduced Sigmund Freud to the United States through his translation of Freud's *General Introduction to Psychoanalysis*.

Then in 1890 Harvard professor William James published *Principles of Psychology*, considered by many to be the most important psychology text of all time. And James found a place in psychology for human consciousness, emotions, the self, personal values, and religion.

But James's methods—observation, introspection, and reasoning—were rejected by the Wundtian psychologists as too soft for science. They insisted on patterning psychology on the physical sciences, focusing on such areas as sensation and perception, and adding studies on learning, memorization, and conditioning later on.

Since its inception, the field of psychology has included people with very different ideas about what to study and how to study it. Although the field has changed and expanded dramatically, the very ideas that originated over a century ago form the basis of psychological inquiry today.

REVIEW QUESTIONS

Program Questions

1. What is the best definition of *psychology*?

   a. The scientific study of how people interact in social groups
   b. The philosophy explaining the relation between brain and mind
   c. The scientific study of the behavior of individuals and of their mental processes
   d. The knowledge used to predict how virtually any organism will behave under specified conditions

2. The program shows a woman who is suffering from multiple personality disorder. Which statement about these different personalities is true?

   a. Each is unaware of the others.
   b. Each has its own biology.
   c. Each is rather similar to the others.
   d. All began functioning at the same time.

3. What is the main focus of Donchin's research involving the P-300 wave?

   a. The relation between brain and mind
   b. The role of heredity in shaping personality
   c. The development of mental illness
   d. The role of situational factors in perception

4. What is the main goal of psychological research?

   a. To cure mental illness
   b. To find the biological bases of the behavior of organisms
   c. To predict and in some cases control behavior
   d. To find out how people think

5. The reactions of the boys and the girls to the teacher in the "Candid Camera" episode were essentially similar. Professor Zimbardo attributes this reaction to

   a. how easily adolescents become embarrassed.
   b. how an attractive teacher violates expectations.
   c. the way sexual titillation makes people act.
   d. the need people have to hide their real reactions.

6. What do EEGs measure?

   a. Heart rate
   b. Changes in hormone levels in the body
   c. Energy expended in overcoming gravity
   d. Brain activity

7. According to Robert Rosenthal's research, you are most likely to detect a liar by

   a. observing eye movements.
   b. listening to tone of voice.
   c. considering cultural factors.
   d. looking at body language.

8. Which cluster of topics did William James consider the main concerns of psychology?

   a. Reaction times, sensory stimuli, word associations
   b. Consciousness, self, emotions
   c. Conditioned responses, psychophysics
   d. Experimental design, computer models

9. What do we learn from our misreading of the "Paris in the spring" sign?

   a. We are accustomed to an artist's use of perspective.
   b. Experience disposes us to respond in a particular way.
   c. Unexpected events trigger P-300 waves in the brain.
   d. We laugh at those things that violate our expectations.

10. Christine Hall is conducting research on group behavior. She is particularly interested in how behavior varies based on

    a. the relative status of those present.
    b. the type of task the group is working on.
    c. how recently the group was formed.
    d. how many people there are in the group.

11. In her research, Christine Hall factors in the individual's cultural background and social experiences. Such research is being conducted at the

    a. micro level.
    b. molecular level.
    c. organic level.
    d. molar level.

12. Who founded the first psychology laboratory in the United States?

    a. Wilhelm Wundt
    b. William James
    c. G. Stanley Hall
    d. Sigmund Freud

13. How did Wundtian psychologists such as Hall react to William James's concept of psychology?

    a. They accepted it with minor reservations.
    b. They expanded it to include consciousness and the self.
    c. They rejected it as unscientific.
    d. They revised it to include the thinking of Sigmund Freud.

Textbook Questions

14. Psychology is defined as

    a. the study of human behavior only.
    b. the study of the mind.
    c. the study of organisms.
    d. the scientific study of the behavior and mental processes of humans and animals.

15. Why do psychologists study animals?

    a. To aid those majoring in animal psychology.
    b. Veterinarians need the information.
    c. Because so many household pets are present in our society.
    d. Psychologists can experiment with animals in ways that would be unethical or unlawful if humans were used.

16. Scientists studying neurological processes which underlie behavior may use an animal or an insect in their studies because

    a. the insect's nervous system is more complex.
    b. we need to get rid of as many insects as possible.
    c. of a need to begin with a simpler model than a human.
    d. insects or animals are inexpensive to purchase.

17. Psychology has its historical roots in

    a. the study of ancient medicine.
    b. philosophy and physiology.
    c. early religious writings.
    d. prehistoric man's quest for knowledge.

18. "Experimental self-observation" is also known in psychology as

    a. psychoanalytic disclosure.
    b. introspection.
    c. contemplation.
    d. functionalism.

19. Edward Titchener thought the proper goal of psychology was to

    a. emphasize the functional, practical nature of the mind.
    b. observe stimuli and behavior.
    c. specify mental structures.
    d. understand the unconscious mind.

20. William James is the founder of the concept of

    a. functionalism.
    b. structuralism.
    c. behaviorism.
    d. Gestalt psychology.

21. The _____ concluded that consciousness evolved because it served a purpose.

    a. behaviorists
    b. Gestaltists
    c. structuralists
    d. functionalists

22. J. B. Watson is the founder of

    a. Gestalt psychology.
    b. Introspection.
    c. Behaviorism.
    d. Structuralism.

23. The contemporary approach of "emphasizing the whole person" is a
    _____ approach in psychology.

    a. behavioristic
    b. psychoanalytic
    c. cognitive
    d. Gestalt

24. Sigmund Freud is considered to be the father of

    a. humanism.
    b. cognitivism.
    c. behaviorism.
    d. psychoanalysis.

25. Psychoanalysis has been widely criticized in part because

    a. Freud is considered to be a "quack."
    b. it is too expensive to study.
    c. Freud did not reveal enough theoretical information.
    d. its assertions cannot be tested in a laboratory.

26. You act impulsively, then wonder why. Freud would tell you that your behavior
    was influenced by your

    a. irritation.
    b. unconscious mind.
    c. immaturity.
    d. inability to think fast.

27. Humanistic psychology tends to focus on such concepts as

    a. motivation, emotion, and perception.
    b. love, feelings, and self-esteem.
    c. habits, sensations, and images.
    d. unconscious processes.

28. Humanists emphasize the role of _____ in our lives.

    a. environmental influence
    b. Gestalt perception
    c. unconscious motivation
    d. free choice

29. A psychiatrist differs from a clinical psychologist in which important way?

    a. He has a Ph.D. degree.
    b. He has a medical degree.
    c. He sees more severe cases of mental disorders.
    d. He is a Freudian.

30. If you were thinking of improving the workplace in your factory by increasing the
    lighting, reducing noise, and piping in music, a good psychologist to consult
    would be a(n)

    a. social psychologist.
    b. community psychologist.
    c. environmental psychologist.
    d. industrial psychologist.

31. _____ psychologists are concerned with changes in behavior throughout the life span.

    a. Clinical
    b. Developmental
    c. Community
    d. Personality

QUESTIONS TO CONSIDER

1. Although psychologists are involved in many different kinds of research and professional activities, there are certain fundamental issues that form the basic foundation of psychology. What are they?

2. Why do some people believe that psychology is only concerned with abnormal behavior?

3. Why are critical thinking skills important?

4. How do your culture, age, gender, education level, and past experience bias your observations about events, your own actions, and the behavior of others?

5. Is thinking a behavior? How can it be studied?

OPTIONAL ACTIVITIES

1. Start a personal journal or a log. Make a daily practice of recording events, thoughts, feelings, observations, and questions that catch your attention each day. Include the ordinary and the unusual. Then analyze what you observed, first listing as many questions as you can about the event. Speculate on the possible forces causing your behavior. As you progress through the course, review your notes and see how your observations and questions reflect what you have learned.

2. The two comic strips below illustrate common thoughts and feelings about everyday events. Analyze each situation and make inferences about the characters' behavior. What is happening? Why do people behave that way? What are the characters feeling? What gestures and expressions reveal their feelings? How might a psychologist evaluate and test your inferences?

Rose is Rose   By Pat Brady

For Better or For Worse®   **by Lynn Johnston**

ANTHOLOGY

Today, psychologists practice their profession in many settings. They are called on to apply their expertise to solve a host of personal and social problems. As you read the following selections, ask yourself what special concepts and terms you must know in order to understand the information and approach it as a critical reader. What insights have you gained into the thoughts and feelings of others? Has the information challenged your own ideas or opinions?

Reading 1

Whether or not we are aware of it, body language is an important aspect of successful communication. Studying communication problems between American and Japanese executives involves understanding cultural roles and relationships as well as the cultural meaning of specific mannerisms. As you read this article, consider the immediate and long-term benefits of this kind of research—for business, interpersonal relations, and international relations.

Striking the Right Trade Posture

By John Pfeiffer

East meets West across the bargaining table: two Americans and two Japanese conferring at Toyota's American headquarters in Torrance, California. The Americans want to set up a Toyota sales company in Brazil and have just suggested the establishment of four production plants. The Japanese spend several minutes talking it over, in Japanese of course. Now they arrive at a decision, but they say nothing. Hands resting on the table, eyes lowered, they sit tight in complete silence. Things become increasingly uncomfortable as both sides wait for some response—and wait and wait and wait. Finally, one of the Americans blurts out: "I don't think this is getting us anywhere!" The meeting ends soon thereafter.

To see the tension mounting, to feel the silence getting thicker and thicker, you would never guess that this was an elaborate simulation. The participants, real-life Toyota executives, had been hard at it for more than a month, playing an experimental trading game designed by John Graham of the University of Southern California's Graduate School of Business. The game is one phase of an extended study of national bargaining styles, a study that has already involved observation and testing of more than 750 foreign and American students and executives.

The current focus on Japanese-American relations is for good reason: Americans are getting murdered at the bargaining table.

Last year the U.S. bought more than $60 billion worth of Japanese products but managed to sell Japan only about $23 billion worth of American products. There is no simple explanation for the formidable trade gap—which continues to widen—though Japan's aggressive competition and restrictive import policies have a lot to do with it. On the basis of his observations, however, Graham stresses that Americans' notably inept bargaining results from a failure to understand Japanese culture.

To start with, not bothering to learn your competitor's language puts you at a serious disadvantage. Graham estimates that of a few hundred American business executives in Japan, only a fraction speak Japanese, while 10,000 Japanese businessmen living in the U.S. speak English. Even allowing for the language imbalance, which is considerably greater than the trade imbalance, there are further barriers to communication. Take that awkward silence at Toyota headquarters, for example. As measured on video tape, it lasted 26 seconds, and pauses as long as 45 seconds have been recorded.

"Silence drives Americans crazy," Graham reports, "but it is part of the game and can be dealt with." Centuries of living close to one another have made the Japanese extremely reluctant to cause offense by saying no straight out. They have evolved a fine art of indirect naysaying, and silence is one of their main ploys. An appropriate American response: light your pipe, study your notes, sit back, and above all, keep cool. If you decide to break the silence, suggest putting the problem off until tomorrow, or better yet, ask what the objection is. (When in doubt, it's good policy to ask a question.)

Keeping cool is also called for when it comes to the preliminaries. Although Americans are well aware of the importance of establishing rapport with some social chit-chat, they generally come to the bargaining table with a short fuse. The immediate deal is primary. That is how they have been trained and what they are rewarded for back home. The Japanese recognize this in the Americans, but they have their own deeply rooted bias. Namely, they take their time and concentrate on establishing relationships good for a decade or more. While five or 10 minutes of small talk is just about the limit for most American businessmen, the Japanese are perfectly comfortable with 20 minutes, half an hour, or even longer.

Indeed, if the guest is sufficiently important in Japan, several days of getting acquainted are in order—tours of factories, golf in the afternoon (it's practically impossible to lose to your Japanese host; Graham once shot over 100 and still came out ahead), visits to nightclubs, restaurants, geisha houses. Americans rarely go to such lengths. The board chairman of a major Korean investment firm recently received special treatment in Tokyo but not in New York: "They didn't even give me a cup of coffee." According to one estimate, entertainment expenses for Japanese businessmen amounted to 1.2 percent of the gross national product, or about $12 billion in 1981, as compared to about 0.9 percent for national defense. This is trade warfare with a vengeance.

The video tape catches many mannerisms and nuances—most of them unconscious and yet to be fully analyzed. There is the dance of the eyes, seen most clearly in one-on-one bargaining. The American looks up, trying to establish direct eye contact, at which point the Japanese lowers his gaze, only to raise his eyes again when the American looks down at his notes. This seesawing may go on for a minute or two. By habit, the Japanese limit direct eye contact, which may indicate aggression or pushiness; Americans, in turn, interpret looking away as evasiveness. Ac-

tually, it's mainly a matter of upbringing. "Look at me when I'm talking to you," American parents tell their offspring, while Japanese children learn to look down as a mark of filial respect.

The exalted position of the buyer is crucial to the Japanese. If the buyer is king everywhere, he is considerably more so in Japan. When Japanese bargain with one another, the buyer ranks several notches above the seller, who assumes a suitably deferential posture. The buyer is expected to go after a favorable deal, but good form demands that the seller go away satisfied—a delicate operation anticipating successful dealings in the future. This tradition puts the American buyer in a fine position to drive a hard bargain. But the American rarely goes out of his way to make the Japanese seller feel good about it. Graham notes a common complaint among Japanese sellers after their encounters with American buyers: "We took a beating."

In the reverse position, the Japanese buyer expects a measure of humility, but the American seller goes by his own rule of equal status. The situation is ripe for conflict. A typical clash occurred in a video-taped game involving citrus fruits, products in high demand among the Japanese. After some amicable small talk, the Japanese buyer asserted his top-dog position with a low initial offer, the lowest price the game permitted. The American seller, no kowtower, was shocked at the buyer's greed: "Not possible at all. . . . There's no way we can negotiate." Now it was the Japanese negotiator's turn to be shocked; he had never encountered such an aggressive seller. They finally reached a reasonable agreement but at the price of ruffled feelings and poor prospects for the future. Real-life observations suggest that this sort of misunderstanding might help explain why Americans buy much but sell little to the Japanese.

Congress has recognized the problem. With the aid of Department of Education funds and Japanese volunteers, Graham and other investigators are conducting special classes designed to help American executives sell more effectively to their overseas peers.

In the meantime, it looks like we haven't come too far since Commodore Matthew Perry's gunboat diplomacy opened up Japan to foreign traders in 1853. Samurai returning from a subsequent visit to the United States, Japan's first diplomatic mission to the United

States, recorded in their diaries that a Spanish warrior named "Korunbus" had discovered America, that every four years the natives "hold an auction to see who will be president or Shogun of America," and only after special attempts at understanding would the Americans "respect us and abandon their intention of plunder."

Reading 2

Research on the risks and benefits of child care has important economic, political, social, and personal implications. Writers often extract information from professional journals and interpret it for the popular media. As you read this article from Working Mother, *think about the following questions: Does it seem objective? Might the information influence your opinion about funding day care in your town, sending your own child to day care, or lobbying for a day care plan for employees in your company?*

What Is Best For the Children?

By Susan Seliger

All mothers ask themselves the same question: "Am I doing what's best for my child?" For women who work outside the home, the question raises acute anxiety—they're trying something new and they don't know how it will turn out.

Recent research brings reassurance. "The main concern among people who say that mothers should not go to work is fear that there will not be true bonding and rapport between mother and child—but no studies have shown any difference between employed and nonemployed mothers in the security of the attachment relationship between mother and child," says Lois Wladis Hoffman, a psychology professor at the University of Michigan, whose research focuses on the effects of child-rearing patterns on development.

As for children's later achievement in school, here, too, the findings are promising. "If the children are in a day care center with *any* structure to it, then their social and intellectual development tends to be somewhat more advanced than that of children who stay home with their mother," says Alison Clarke-Stewart, a psychology professor at the University of California at Irvine.

In a soon-to-be-published study of 150 children aged two to four, in the Chicago area, Clarke-Stewart found: "The day care children were more advanced in language skills, knowledge of the world, ability to get along with other kids and confidence in meeting someone new.

"The only negative thing we found is that because these kids tend to be advanced, they tend to be more aggressive with other kids and assertive in general," says Clarke-Stewart. "They're less compliant—even with their parents. That's the price you pay."

Despite the current furor over whether mothers should work, it turns out that a mother's employment status is merely one factor in determining how well adjusted and successful a child will become—and not the most powerful factor, at that.

The quality of the child's care during his waking hours may prove more influential than who provides that care. "You can predict a four-year-old's adjustment better from knowing what kinds of experiences the child had with the caregiver than knowing whether the caregiver was the mother, the babysitter or the day care teacher," says Judith Rubenstein, associate research professor of psychiatry/psychology at Boston University School of Medicine and author of *Infant and Environment* (1975). "On the average," Rubenstein says, "studies have not found mothers any better than day care providers in stimulating infant and toddler intellectual and social development."

The child's sex also plays a part—boys and girls respond differently to a mother's employment. In general, girls from all social classes seem to benefit more from having a working mother than one who stays home. Boys, however, respond differently, depending on the family's socioeconomic status. Boys from economically deprived families tend to do better if the mother works outside the home; boys from blue-collar families show mixed results, in some studies doing a bit better with a working mother, in others doing the same whether the mother works or stays home. Middle-class boys, however, tend to benefit most from a mother who stays home.

But no one can explain exactly why. "One suggestion is that nonworking mothers invest a lot in their sons," says Clarke-Stewart. "To get psychoanalytic about it, a nonworking mother is living out her ambitions through her son and focusing intense attention on him." It isn't that those mothers aren't attentive to their daughters too, Clarke-Stewart adds. But society's age-old bias favoring sons is slow to fade. "And it isn't so much that daughters of stay-at-home mothers are disadvantaged as the fact that daughters of working mothers gain an advantage by having the active role model of a working mother," Clarke-Stewart says.

Perhaps the most significant influence on children's welfare is not whether the mother has a job or not, but how she feels about what she does. "When the mother is satisfied with what she is doing, the children seem to fare better," says Hoffman, who has published a number of studies on this subject. "If she's working and she prefers that arrangement, the children score higher on adjustment scales than if she's working and doesn't want to be, or if she's staying at home and doesn't want to be."

The timing of the mother's reentry into the work force surely affects the child—but it is still too early to pinpoint "the best time" to go back to work. There is nothing magical about four months, but that is the time Dr. T.

Berry Brazelton and other child care experts have settled on: They are campaigning for a federal law requiring four months' maternity leave. In their choice of timing, the experts were considering the welfare of the mother as much as that of the child. Further research also needs to be done on how the father's participation affects the child's development.

What makes it so hard to predict how the children will turn out is that we are entering a new era in parenting. We don't do quite the same things parents in previous generations did. And the changes aren't restricted to working mothers of young children. The mothers who stay at home have changed too. With smaller families and the availability of high-tech household aids, full-time mothers have an unprecedented amount of time and energy to devote to their children.

"The nonemployed mother today may represent a more intense parent-child interaction than we have ever had before," Hoffman says. "It is important to keep in mind as employed-mother families are compared with nonemployed-mother families, that *neither one represents the traditional pattern*."

The world is not the way it was in the easygoing Eisenhower fifties—and there is no going back. Today we are all breaking new ground, mothers who stay home or go out to work, alike. And instead of fanning the flames between us, it would help to remember that, in the end, we are all struggling for the same thing: what is best for our children.

ADDITIONAL RESOURCES

Books and Articles

Cantril, H., and C. H. Bumstead. *Reflections on the Human Venture*. New York: New York University Press, 1960. This book weaves together quotes from a wide range of literature in an effort to examine the human venture.

Stanovich, Keith E. *How to Think Straight about Psychology*. Glenview, Ill.: Scott, Foresman, 1986. This "consumer's guide" to psychology sketches out what the behavioral science is—and is not.

Wilson, J. R., ed. *The Mind*. Morristown, N.J.: Silver Burdett, 1969. A beautifully illustrated book that introduces you to psychology now and will help you review what you have learned later.

UNDERSTANDING RESEARCH

Whatever knowledge is attainable must be attainable by scientific method; and what science can not discover, mankind can not know.

Bertrand Russell

Unit 2 demonstrates the hows and whys of psychological research. By showing how psychologists rely on systematic observation, data collection, and analysis to find out the answers to their questions, this unit reveals why the scientific method is used in all areas of empirical investigation.

Tufts Educational Media Center

Rats are put through a series of tests in a radial maze at Tufts University to help researchers better understand memory processes.

OBJECTIVES

After viewing the television program and completing the assigned readings, you should be able to:

1. Discuss why the scientific method is important in psychology
2. List the characteristics of the scientific method
3. Define and explain the importance of an operational definition
4. Discuss the role of the concept of hypothesis in scientific research *prove it wrong*
5. Define observer bias and discuss the steps that can be taken to eliminate it
6. Discuss the limitations of the experimental method
7. Discuss the case study, survey and naturalistic observation methods of research and list the advantages and disadvantages of each *detail of one individual   no cause & effect*
8. Define correlation and understand why it is incorrect to say that correlation indicates a causal relationship
9. Compare the uses of descriptive and inferential statistics *lets you draw conclusions*
10. Discuss the considerations to be made in selecting a sample for research
11. Define dependent and independent variables. Define experimental and control groups *effect   cause*
12. Define mean, median, mode, range, and standard deviation *not to much*

READING ASSIGNMENT

After viewing Program 2, read pages 33–55 in *Psychology: Science, Behavior and Life.* Your instructor may also assign the anthology selections for Unit 2.

KEY TERMS AND CONCEPTS

As you read the assignment, pay particular attention to these terms, which are defined on the given pages in the text.

hypothesis (34)	observias bias (43)
replication (35)	observer effect (43)
experimental research (45)	case study (38)
independent variable (46)	correlational method (44)
dependent variable (46)	coefficient of correlation (44)
experimental groups (46)	statistics (50)
control groups (46)	descriptive statistics (51)
representative sample (40)	mean (52)
random sample (40)	median (52)
observational method (42)	mode (52)
naturalistic observation (42)	normal distribution (51)

skewed distribution (52)   standard scores (53)
range (52)   inferential statistics (53)
standard deviation (52)   operational definition (54)
percentiles (53)   statistical significance (54)

The following terms are used in Program 2 but are not defined in the text.

double-blind procedure—an experimental procedure in which neither the researcher nor the subject knows which particular subjects are receiving the various treatment and control conditions

field study—research carried on outside the laboratory where naturally occurring, ongoing behavior can be observed

placebo effect—a significant response to an experimental treatment that occurs simply because the subject believes that the treatment will work and not because of any specific power of the treatment itself

subjective reality—the perceptions and beliefs that we accept without question

PROGRAM SUMMARY

Tune in to any television or radio talk show, and you are likely to find someone peddling psychic powers, astrology, ESP, or mind reading. Because psychology is so often sensationalized and misrepresented, it is difficult for the average person to distinguish science from pseudoscience, fact from fiction.

Program 2 demonstrates how psychologists separate superstition and irrational beliefs from fact and reason. Understanding how ideas are tested enables us to become skeptical consumers of media information and to develop critical thinking skills to protect us against deception and fraud.

Psychologists are guided by a set of procedures for gathering and interpreting evidence using carefully controlled observations and measurements. This is called the scientific method and requires that research be conducted in an orderly, standardized way. Then the results are published so that others can review and perhaps repeat the process.

Scientists employ a variety of study methods. They conduct experiments in laboratories, administer surveys, and take measurements in the field where they observe people and animals in natural settings. Seeing how scientists try to eliminate error and bias from their work helps us avoid some of the faulty reasoning in our own lives.

One factor that scientists consider is the placebo effect. In medicine, a placebo is a substance that is chemically inert, such as a sugar pill. It may nevertheless have a therapeutic effect. The placebo effect complicates the job of a researcher because the mere suggestion of a believable treatment will make many people feel better. Some researchers have found that despite different settings or tactics, the power of any change agent relies on the person's absolute belief in the change agent's power.

Any medical or psychological treatment can only be considered successful if it demonstrates a level of effectiveness beyond the placebo effect. To do this, researchers use the double-blind procedure in which neither the participant nor the experimenter knows who is getting the real drug and who is taking the placebo. That information is held by another researcher who has no contact with the experimenter or subjects.

In order to analyze a miracle cure or a magic trick, we must evaluate all kinds of beliefs and theories. It is important to test hypotheses, define success, account for chance, and establish controls. Consider the case of Norman Cousins, the respected editor of the *Saturday Review* who had a form of spinal arthritis that is usually incurable. Unsatisfied with traditional medicine, he designed his own treatment based on a regimen of laughter. He claimed that 10 minutes of laughter gave him at least two hours of pain-free sleep. He has since recovered completely.

But was laughter the sole cause of his cure? The scientific method requires that we separate its effects from all the other possible sources of influence on Cousins's state of mind and health. When several factors (in this case, Cousins's optimism and high doses of vitamin C) might be responsible for the outcome, we must try to determine which one deserves the credit. It may be that Cousins's cure was influenced by the combination of these factors.

We must resist the temptation to conclude that things that merely occur together necessarily have a cause and effect relationship. There may be a third factor that causes the other two. Consider a report that suggests that when the time spent watching TV goes up, grades go down. Should we conclude that watching TV causes poor grades? In fact, students who watch a lot of TV might spend less time on their homework. But students who get bad grades might watch more television because they don't like homework. They would get bad grades whether they watched TV or not.

When interpreting data, we have to make sure that the subjects in an experiment are a representative sampling of the population they are meant to represent. Shere Hite's controversial report on women's attitudes about sex and marriage highlights a sampling problem. Her conclusions were based on only 4 percent of all the people who had received her questionnaire. She had taken no steps to ensure that her sample would be representative of the age, education level, and race distribution in the general population. Hite's sample method was too flawed to be useful (see Figure 1).

Shere Hite Study	ABC News and *Washington Post* Study
4% of sample responding	random sampling
98% dissatisfied with some aspect of their relationship	93% *satisfied* with their relationship
75% involved in extramarital affairs	7% involved in extramarital affairs

Figure 1: Comparison of Sex and Marriage Studies
Shere Hite's study of women's attitudes toward sex and marriage did not include a representative sampling since only 4 percent of the women she contacted responded. A similar study conducted by ABC News and the *Washington Post*, which included a random sampling of women, found very different results.

Professionals as well as the general public can be taken in by pseudoscientific technology. The polygraph, or lie detector, for example, measures changes in physical arousal, such as heart rate or the galvanic skin response. But these machines are fallible. Research has shown that innocent people who believe they might be mistakenly identified may show anxiety. And guilty people may fool the machine by taking drugs or purposely tensing and relaxing their muscles. This so-called lie detector can play a crucial role in people's lives; sometimes it is used to help make decisions about hiring and firing employees.

Getting at the truth about psychological phenomena is difficult, but there are guidelines that help us avoid common pitfalls: Don't assume that two things that occur together are cause and effect. Seeing isn't always believing. Question data that aren't collected using rigorous procedures. Keep in mind the power of placebos. Restrain enthusiasm for scientific breakthroughs. Beware of people claiming absolute truth and of attempts to persuade rather than educate. And remember that conclusions are always open to revision.

REVIEW QUESTIONS

Program Questions

1. In the science section of a newspaper, there is an article about recent psychological research on differences between men and women. According to Professor Zimbardo, how should you approach such articles?

   a. With a skeptical attitude
   b. With complete disbelief
   c. With a willingness to accept them completely
   d. Such accounts are not worth reading at all.

2. The scientific method is defined as a set of

   a. theories.
   b. truths.
   c. procedures.
   d. statistical methods.

3. What is the main reason that the results of research studies are published?

   a. So researchers can prove they earned their money
   b. So other researchers can try to replicate the work
   c. So the general public can understand the importance of spending money on research
   d. So attempts at fraud and trickery are detected

4. Why does the placebo effect work?

   a. Because researchers believe it does
   b. Because subjects believe they are receiving a treatment
   c. Because human beings prefer feeling they are in control
   d. Because it is part of the scientific method

5. What is the purpose of a double-blind procedure?

   a. To test more than one variable at a time
   b. To repeat the results of previously published work
   c. To define a hypothesis clearly before it is tested
   d. To eliminate experimenter bias

6. If you had been one of the subjects in the lie detector study, what information would have helped you earn some money?

   a. The results depend on the skill of the person administering the lie detector test.
   b. Lie detectors only measure arousal level, not lying.
   c. The polygraph is used to make millions of decisions each year.
   d. The placebo effect works with lie detectors.

7. What suggestion does Jerome Frank make that would help explain why Norman Cousins's method worked so well?

   a. People need a sense of mastery.
   b. Laughter makes us feel good.
   c. Psychotherapy has much in common with faith healing.
   d. A healing saying is an important feature of a cure.

8. A report on children's television watching found that children who watch more TV had lower grades. What cause-effect conclusion are we justified in making on the basis of this study?

   a. TV watching causes low grades.
   b. Poor school performance causes children to watch more TV.
   c. Cause-effect conclusions can never be based on one study.
   d. Cause-effect conclusions cannot be based on correlation.

9. What was the major weakness of the Hite report on women's attitudes toward sex and marriage?

   a. The sample was not representative.
   b. Hypotheses were not clearly stated beforehand.
   c. Experimenter bias arose because the double-blind procedure was not used.
   d. No control group was used.

10. A prediction of how two or more variables are likely to be related is called a

    a. theory.
    b. conclusion.
    c. hypothesis.
    d. correlation.

11. Imagine a friend tells you that she has been doing better in school since she started taking vitamin pills. She urges you to take vitamins too. On the basis of the program, what objection might you make?

    a. You remember reading somewhere that healthy people don't need vitamins.
    b. You realize that if a person believes something will help, there's a good chance it will.
    c. You will believe her only if she takes a polygraph test.
    d. You think that she would be doing well in school in any case.

12. Why can't psychologists do a controlled experiment on the effect a mother's use of cocaine has on her baby?

    a. The placebo effect would be too strong.
    b. Causation could not be established.
    c. It would be unethical.
    d. People who use drugs make unreliable subjects.

Textbook Questions

13. Tentative explanations for relationships or events designed to be tested by research are called

    a. theories.
    b. problems.
    c. laws.
    d. hypotheses.

14. When psychologists publish new research findings they do so in great detail so that others may

    a. repeat the experiment for verification.
    b. appreciate the hard work put into the research.
    c. evaluate the researcher's skills.
    d. find the truth.

15. One advantage of experimental research is that it allows the experimenter to

    a. observe subjects in a natural way.
    b. directly control the subjects to determine results.
    c. prove his or her hypothesis.
    d. go into depth with one person's case.

16. In scientific study, the variable that is manipulated so that its effects may be observed is called a(n)

    a. population.
    b. hypothesis.
    c. dependent variable.
    d. independent variable.

17. Ideal experiments use experimental and control groups. The _____ group receives the treatment and the _____ group does not.

    a. experimental; control
    b. control; experimental
    c. experimental; population
    d. population; experimental

18. A _____ group is a group of subjects who experience all the same conditions as subjects in the experimental group except for the key factor the researcher is evaluating.

    a. experimental
    b. control
    c. population
    d. single-blind

19. An experimenter administered a different amount of alcohol to each of four different groups in order to test its effect on hand coordination. The independent variable in this study was

    a. the amount of alcohol administered.
    b. the method by which the alcohol was administered.
    c. how much food the subjects ate before taking the alcohol.
    d. the subjects' coordination after taking alcohol.

20. Which of the following is a limitation of the experimental method?

    a. Too few psychologists are capable of doing research.
    b. The laboratory setting is somewhat artificial.
    c. All research questions should be investigated by experimentation.
    d. Limited laboratory space is available.

21. Subjects selected from a population make up a group called a(n)

    a. experimental group.
    b. control group.
    c. sample.
    d. general population.

22. A representative sample assures researchers that

    a. everyone has a chance to participate.
    b. subgroups are represented proportionately.
    c. a random sample has been achieved.
    d. the sample is ethical.

23. A researcher should generalize findings only to

    a. the sample studied.
    b. the population from which the sample was drawn.
    c. the individuals in the sample who are closest to the sample average.
    d. none of the above.

24. Questionnaires have an advantage over interviews because questionnaires are

    a. more anonymous.
    b. more flexible.
    c. more expensive.
    d. given face-to-face.

25. The *Literary Digest*'s telephone survey of voters in the 1936 presidential election was not a true random sample because

    a. they had only the "yellow pages."
    b. they telephoned only men.
    c. only higher socioeconomic status Americans had telephones.
    d. they published their results too early.

26. When the presence of another person alters behavior it is called

    a. observer bias.
    b. expectation.
    c. observer effect.
    d. a placebo effect.

27. A major limitation of the case study method is

    a. the researcher's lack of control of the variables.
    b. the lack of in-depth information obtained.
    c. that generalization is too broad.
    d. control group contamination.

28. A method of scientific investigation that studies the relationships between variables is called

    a. correlational.
    b. case study.
    c. survey.
    d. experimental.

29. The most common mistake made when interpreting correlational studies is to conclude that

    a. a survey may have been better.
    b. one variable causes the other.
    c. there is no cause-effect relationship.
    d. correlational studies are of no use.

30. There are essentially two kinds of statistics, _____ and _____ .

    a. descriptive; correlational
    b. variable; range
    c. descriptive; inferential
    d. inferential; correlational

31. A measure of variability which indicates the difference between the highest and lowest score is called

    a. the range.
    b. skewed.
    c. the mean.
    d. a standard score.

32. The standard deviation (S.D.) is a better estimate of the variability of a distribution than the range because the S.D. is

    a. easier to compute.
    b. about the same as the mean anyway.
    c. not as confusing to readers.
    d. less influenced by extreme scores.

33. The smaller the standard deviation between two groups, the more likely that the difference of the means is

    a. statistically not significant.
    b. statistically significant.
    c. statistically nil.
    d. in error.

QUESTIONS TO CONSIDER

1. If some people really get healed by faith healers, why condemn the practice of faith healing?

2. Would you like to be graded on a curve? Why or why not?

3. What are some of the objections to studying mental processes?

4. Why is there so much uncertainty in psychology?

5. If the placebo effect can make a person feel better, do you think a person's disbelief can undermine the effects of drugs known to be effective?

6. Are animals adequately protected by the APA's guidelines? Why or why not?

7. Why is a study that uses only volunteers likely to be biased?

OPTIONAL ACTIVITIES

1. Write operational definitions of the following:

   success   intelligence
   love   power
   affection   wealth
   attractiveness   learning
   aggression   hunger
   anger

2. Design a study that would test the validity of one of the following proverbs:

   Birds of a feather flock together.
   Spare the rod and spoil the child.
   You can't teach an old dog new tricks.
   Actions speak louder than words.
   A stitch in time saves nine.
   If it ain't broke, don't fix it.

ANTHOLOGY

Unit 2 emphasizes that understanding the basic principles of psychological research will help you think critically about what you see, hear, and read about psychology in the media. The following selections illustrate the problems of collecting information and interpreting data. As you read, consider the sources of error in gathering data, drawing conclusions, and reporting results. Think about how you can become a wiser consumer of information and advice.

Reading 3

The popular media are filled with reports on new treatments for allergies and illnesses. This selection emphasizes the importance of objective evaluation of anecdotal evidence. As you read, consider the following questions: Why isn't a person's own experience considered proof? What can we learn from a double-blind placebo controlled study? What course of treatment would you be inclined to follow if you or your child were suffering from asthma?

Ask Dr. White

By Dr. Martha White

Dear Dr. White,

I am the mother of a 13-year-old boy with allergies and asthma. He was tested at 2 and put on shots, medication and a breathing machine with Cromolyn.

The reason I am writing is I made a change in our treatment of Ross when he was 9 years old and I really feel I'd like to tell you about it. Some friends of ours asked us if we had ever tried vitamins. We listened to their ideas and felt we had nothing to lose as Ross was up every night 2 or 3 times wheezing. We started him on vitamins and I began reading various books and started to learn how important vitamins are.

To sum it up, within a week Ross was sleeping through the night for the first time in 7 years! I slowly took him off his medication and his shots. He uses his Proventil inhaler if he has trouble and has had to go on an antibiotic and Metaprel or Theophylline only 2 or 3 times in four years. Before he had to be to the doctor every 2 months. If he's having trouble I up his vitamins, especially now when he's playing football or when he wrestles. I would much rather put vitamins in his body than the medications with their side effects.

This is a field that I feel needs to be looked into more. My pediatrician thought I was crazy and told me so, so I changed to a doctor who understood where I was coming from because it worked. Ross is *not* cured nor has he grown out of it, he just has it under control because we are now giving his body help naturally to fight his asthma.

We aren't crazy or strange—people look at me like that—we are a normal family of four: school teacher husband, wife at home, 2 children ages 10 and 13 and a dog! We have just looked into giving your body and your health a lot of help with good vitamin supplementation.

Linn Schueller
Jenison, MI

Dear Linn,

Congratulations! You decided to play an active role in your child's asthma management and it paid off. I was happy to see your letter, which provides anecdotal (not scientifically proven) evidence for the effectiveness of vitamins in the therapy of asthma, because it gives me the opportunity to address the question of how to evaluate anecdotal reports. Most of us have read similar anecdotal reports, usually dealing with the use of vitamins or mineral supplements for a variety of illnesses, and it's difficult for most non-research people to objectively evaluate such reports.

The best way to prove that a medication is effective is to perform a double blind placebo controlled study. This means that some subjects (patients) receive the real drug, while others receive a dummy look-alike, or placebo. Neither the researcher nor the subject knows who's receiving what. At the end of the study, the responses of the group receiving the active drug are statistically compared to those of the placebo group. You might wonder what's the point of putting a group of subjects on a placebo. After all, you can easily tell the two groups apart since nobody could be expected to improve while taking a placebo, right? Wrong.

On average, 15 percent of subjects respond to placebo with symptomatic improvement. I used to think that was crazy until I conducted my first clinical study on an anti-asthma drug. At least initially, everybody in the study got better and I was able to wean almost everyone to lower doses of their pre-study medications. One subject receiving the placebo was even able to be weaned off all of his pre-study medications, leaving him only on an inactive placebo.

So why did the placebo patients improve? As part of the study, they used a peak flow meter, kept daily symptom diaries and had frequent office visits. As a result, all the subjects had the opportunity to learn more about asthma and their particular triggers. This knowledge plus input from the doctor could lead to subtle behavior changes which reduce exposure to triggers, thus reducing the severity of the asthma. Another explanation is that asthmatic subjects may have gotten better even without the study. The take home message is that improvement after starting a new medication or nutritional supplement cannot necessarily be attributed to the new drug or supplement unless the new agent has been proven in well controlled trials to be effective. This doesn't mean that the unproven agent is not effective. It simply means that there's no proof and some other overlooked factor could have caused the improvement.

Linn, your efforts are commendable and I think you may not be giving yourself enough credit for influencing your son's asthma management. I've read a number of placebo controlled studies examining the use of various vitamins in asthma and none have proven to be more effective than the placebo.

Therefore, I do not recommend that parents rush to put their children on special vitamin supplements in search of asthma control.

You comment that in addition to starting vitamins, you started reading a lot. I suspect that you learned more about asthma and good health in general, were better able to monitor your son's triggers and early warning signs and you were probably able to project a more positive attitude about his asthma and its management.

All of this would result in improved self management skills with improvement in your son's condition. These are the same techniques we advocate so strongly in this newsletter. A skilled physician or asthma specialist should have been able to provide this same relief. Nobody could say for sure whether the vitamins actually played a role in your son's improvement, but I suspect that other factors were largely responsible.

Now that he's doing so well, you may be able to cut your costs and wean him from some of his vitamins. Keep up the good work and good luck.

Reading 4

This article illustrates how statistics are used to argue public policy and sway public attitudes. Do you agree with the writer's categories and definitions of child abuse? What is your operational definition of child abuse? Consider the public policy implications of using statistics to build a case about the nature of such a problem. Can you identify the writer's point of view about funding programs to protect children from abuse? Compare your reactions to Besharov's article with your reactions to Daniel Kagan's piece, which follows.

The Child-Abuse Numbers Game

By Douglas J. Besharov

In the past 20 years, programs to protect abused and neglected children have expanded enormously. In 1986, according to the American Humane Association, about 2.1 million children were reported to the authorities as suspected victims of abuse and neglect. This is 14 times the estimated 150,000 children reported in 1963.

In state after state, and community after community, the exploding number of reports is used as proof that there is a child abuse "crisis." But most experts will agree that there probably is no real increase in child abuse—only in its recognition. Although many cases still go unreported, years of public-awareness campaigns and professional education have had their intended effect. Americans are much more sensitive to the plight of maltreated children, and are more willing than ever to report suspected cases.

Grossly Misleading

A comparison of the two large-scale, federally funded studies of the incidence of child abuse and neglect confirms this conclusion. The first study, conducted in 1979 and 1980, reported a rate of 10.5 maltreated children per thousand children. The second study conducted in 1986 and released this June, round a rate of 16.3. Some have seen the difference as an indication that child maltreatment increased by more than 50% in six years. However, as the later report is careful to note, the increase "probably reflected an increase in the likelihood that professionals will recognize maltreatment rather than an increase in the actual occurrence of maltreatment."

Moreover, raw reporting statistics are grossly misleading. National reporting statistics from the American Humane Association indicate that, since the early 1980s, about 60% of all reports have proved to be "unfounded"—that is, they were dismissed after investigation. This is in sharp contrast to 1975, when only about 35% of all reports were "unfounded." Thus, of the 2.1 million reports, only about 40% are substantiated. This is about 840,000 children.

Furthermore, since many children are reported simply because they are the siblings of apparently maltreated children, it is illuminating to think in terms of the number of families who are reported. An average of 1.8 children are named in each report, so the actual number of substantiated family cases is about 470,000. The 1986 federal study found about 20% of these to be repeat reports on the same child, so that the unduplicated count of families in which substantiated maltreatment occurs is about 375,000 per year.

Approximately 1,100 children die under circumstances suggestive of parental maltreatment each year, according to the 1986 study. This would make it the sixth-largest cause of death for children under age 14.

Between 25% and 45% were previously reported to child protective agencies, according to a recent federal study by Jose D. Alfaro, head of research for the New York City Children's Aid Society. Many thousands of other children suffer serious injuries after their plight becomes known to the authorities.

Program advocates tend to blame these deaths on inadequate funding. Certainly, more staff and treatment resources are always needed. However, the current flood of unfounded reports is a more immediate culprit. Unfounded reports are consuming the limited resources of child protective agencies. For fear of missing even one abused child, workers perform extensive investigations of more than 500,000 families for what turn out to be unfounded reports.

Even when a home visit based on an anonymous report turns up no evidence of maltreatment, workers usually interview neighbors, teachers and day-care personnel to make sure that the child is not abused. And even repeated anonymous and unfounded reports do not halt a further investigation. All this takes time.

Forced to allocate a substantial portion of their limited resources to unfounded reports, child protective agencies are increasingly unable to respond promptly and effectively when children are in serious danger.

The word "maltreatment" encompasses much more than the brutally battered, sexually abused, or starved and sickly children that come to mind when we think of child abuse. Both federal studies found that only about 30% of all "maltreated" children are physically abused, and only about 10% of these children (3% of the total) suffer an injury severe enough to require professional care. Thus, nine-tenths of the cases labeled "physical abuse" are really situations of excessive or unreasonable corporal punishment that, although a matter of legitimate government concern, are unlikely to escalate into a dangerous assault against the child.

Sexual abuse makes up about 14% of the total. This is probably a low figure, and major efforts are being made to increase the reporting of suspected child sexual abuse.

Physical neglect makes up less than 20% of all cases. The three largest categories are failure to provide needed medical care (8%); abandonment and other refusals of custody (9%); and failure to provide food, clothing and hygiene (2%). Physical neglect can be just as harmful as physical abuse. More children die of physical neglect than from physical abuse. But, again, the number of cases where serious physical injury has occurred is low, perhaps as low as 4% of all physical neglect cases.

Educational neglect and emotional maltreatment constitute about half of all maltreatment cases. (Percentages cannot be exact because about 15% of the children suffer more than one form of maltreatment.) Educational neglect, at 28%, is the single largest category. Emotional abuse, mainly "habitual scapegoating, belittling and rejecting behavior," accounts for 17% of the total. And various forms of emotional neglect, defined as "inadequate nurturance" and "permitted maladaptive behavior," add an additional 5% to the total. While some forms of emotional maltreatment are deeply damaging to children, most cases do not create the need for aggressive intervention that cases of serious physical abuse or neglect do.

Therefore, about 80% of all substantiated cases of "child maltreatment" involve excessive corporal punishment, minor physical neglect, educational neglect, or emotional maltreatment. These are forms of emotional or developmental harm to children that pose no serious physical danger. Children living under such conditions need society's help and protection, but they should not be lumped together with cases of brutal battering. Failing to recognize the difference makes it many times more difficult to provide them with long-term, supportive services they need while providing immediate and forceful intervention to children in life-threatening situations—like Lisa Steinberg in New York City.

Reducing Hysteria

Moreover, the overwhelming bulk of these cases are really forms of social deprivation with roots in the family's poverty. Almost all of these families fall below the poverty line. Half receive Aid to Families With Dependent Children. Compared to the general population, families reported for maltreatment are four times more likely to be on public assistance and almost twice as likely to be black. Protecting these children means lifting them from the grinding poverty within which they live.

Recognizing how statistics are badly misused would go a long way toward reducing the current hysteria about child abuse. It also would make people less likely to believe that every bruised child is an abused child. Up to now, though, most child welfare officials—in federal, state, and local agencies—have been reluctant to correct the public's misconceptions about the size of the problem, because they fear that such honesty will discredit their efforts and lead to budget cuts.

Child maltreatment is a serious national problem. It shouldn't be exaggerated in order to gain public and political support.

ADDITIONAL RESOURCES

Books and Articles

Agnew, N. M., and S. W. Pyke. *The Science Game: An Introduction to Research in the Behavioral Sciences*. 2d ed. Englewood Cliffs, N.J.: Prentice-Hall, 1978. Explores the basic methods, procedures, and tools of behavioral scientists.

Cousins, Norman. *The Healing Heart*. New York: Norton, 1983. Determined to take charge of his recovery from heart failure, Norman Cousins developed his own health plan, which included not only proper diet and exercise but also hobbies and humor.

Huff, D., and I. Geis. *How to Lie with Statistics*. New York: Norton, 1954. An entertaining and informative introduction to the use and potential misuse of statistics and graphs.

Moroney, M. J. *Facts from Figures*. Baltimore: Penguin, 1963. Describes the statistician's tools and how they are applied to a wide range of problems.

Page, Jake. "Dilutions of Grandeur." *American Health* (November 1988): 78–82. The placebo effect can make even quack treatments look good. Jake Page takes a critical look at flawed research and scientific fraud.

Randi, James. *Flim Flam: The Truth about Unicorns, Parapsychology and Other Delusions*. New York: Lippincott & Crowell, 1980. Randi exposes individuals who claim paranormal, occult, and supernatural powers. He shows how scientific procedures can reveal the truth behind illusions.

Sibbison, Jim. "Covering Medical Breakthroughs." *Columbia Journalism Review* (July/August 1988): 36–39. Too many reporters—and editors—are suckers for the miracle cure story.

Tierney, John. "Fleecing the Flock." *Discover* (November 1987): 50–58. James Randi, an expert on scientific quackery, has debunked TV faith healer Peter Popoff, but true believers are hard to dissuade.

THE BEHAVING BRAIN

There is no scientific study more vital to man than the study of his own brain. Our entire view of the universe depends on it.

Francis Crick

Psychologists who study the structure and composition of the brain believe that all our thoughts, feelings, and actions have a biological and chemical basis. Unit 3 explains the nervous system and the methods scientists use to explore the link between physiological processes in the brain and psychological experience and behavior.

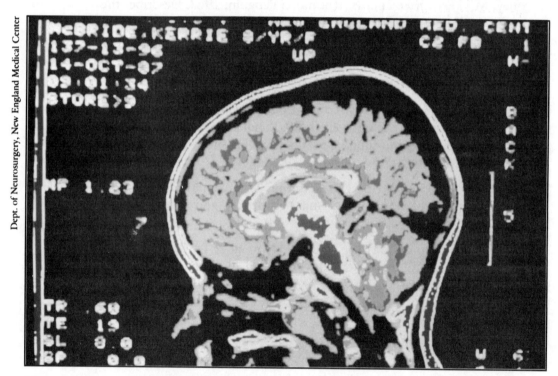

Dept. of Neurosurgery, New England Medical Center

Magnetic Resonance Imaging (MRI) creates detailed, three-dimensional color images of the brain in action—and can provide key information about the differences between psychologically healthy and unhealthy individuals.

OBJECTIVES

After viewing the television program and completing the assigned readings, you should be able to:

1. Identify the major parts of the nervous system and their functions

2. Identify the main structures and specialized functions of the brain

3. Describe the structure of a neuron

4. Explain the mechanism of neural transmission

5. Discuss how the endocrine system effects mood and emotion

6. Explain the functions of the sympathetic and parasympathetic divisions of the nervous system

7. Describe the various methods used to study the brain and give examples of research findings associated with each

8. Explain how neurotransmitters may be directly related to certain psychological disorders

9. Indicate the major function of endogenous opiates and explain how they might be involved in the beneficial effects of acupuncture

READING ASSIGNMENT

After viewing Program 3, read pages 61–106 in *Psychology: Science, Behavior and Life*. This textbook reading covers Units 3 and 4. Your instructor may also assign the anthology selections for Unit 3.

KEY TERMS AND CONCEPTS

As you read the assignment, pay particular attention to these terms, which are defined on the given pages in the text.

central nervous system (CNS) (62)
peripheral nervous system (PNS) (62)
neurons (62)
sensory (afferent) neurons (64)
motor (efferent) neurons (64)
interneurons (64)
cell body (soma) (64)
dendrites (64)
axon (65)
terminal buttons (65)
graded potential (66)
resting potential (66)

action potential (66)
all-or-none law (67)
glia cells (68)
myelin sheath (68)
synapse (68)
neurotransmitters (69)
endorphins (72)
Parkinson's disease (72)
cerebral hemispheres (76)
medulla (78)
cerebellum (78)
reticular activating system (RAS) (78)

limbic system (79)
amygdala (80)
hippocampus (80)
septal area (80)
hypothalamus (81)
thalamus (81)
localization of cortical function
   (84)
sensory cortex (84)
motor cortex (84)
association cortex (84)
frontal lobe (84)
Broca's area (85)
parietal lobe (85)
occipital lobe (86)
temporal lobe (86)
auditory cortex (86)
Wernicke's area (86)
lateralization of function (87)
corpus callosum (87)

lesion production (lesioning) (90)
brain stimulation (91)
electroencephalography (92)
computerized axial tomography
   (CAT) (92)
positron emission tomography
   (PET) (93)
magnetic resonance imaging (MRI)
   (93)
somatic nervous system (74)
autonomic nervous system (74)
sympathetic nervous system (74)
parasympathetic nervous system
   (74)
endocrine system (94)
hormones (94)
pituitary gland (94)
thyroid gland (95)
adrenal glands (96)
gonads (97)

The following terms are used in Program 3 but are not defined in the text.

agonist—a chemical or drug that mimics the action of a neurotransmitter

Alzheimer's disease—a currently incurable condition of aging that destroys the capacity to remember, think, relate to others, and care for oneself

antagonist—a chemical or drug that blocks the action of a neurotransmitter

Neurometrics—a technique developed by E. Roy John and his colleagues to quantify patterns of brain electrical activity associated with different psychological states

PROGRAM SUMMARY

All information that we receive, process, and transmit depends on the functions of the brain, the most complex structure in the known universe. Program 3 describes the brain's biological and chemical foundation for all our thoughts, feelings, and actions.

There are about 10 trillion nerve cells in the brain. These cells, called neurons and glia, use a combination of electrical and chemical messengers to perform their specialized functions. Dendrites, or receptor fibers, gather incoming messages and send them to the cell body, or soma. Then the messages are sent on as electrical discharges down the axon to the neuron's terminal button, which releases a chemical message to adjacent neurons.

Some chemicals generate a nerve impulse by exciting nearby receptors; others reduce or block nerve impulses and regulate the rate at which neurons fire. These nerve impulses are the basis for every change that takes place in the body, from moving our muscles to learning and remembering our multiplication tables.

Although the brain works in a holistic way, some of its parts specialize in particular jobs (see Figure 2). The brain stem, which connects the brain to the spinal cord, controls breathing, heartbeat, waking, and sleeping. The cerebellum coordinates body movement and maintains equilibrium. The amygdala, part of the limbic system, seems to control sensory impulses, such as aggressive urges. For example, a mouse receiving electrical stimulation to the amygdala will attack a cat. And suppressing the amygdala will stop a bull in his tracks. The hypothalamus is the liaison between the body and the rest of the brain, releasing hormones to the pituitary gland. The thalamus acts as a relay station, sending signals from the body to the brain.

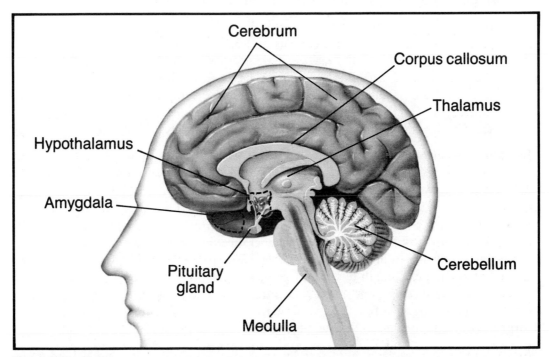

Figure 2: The Brain

The cerebrum translates nerve impulses into higher-level cognitive processes, using images and symbols to form ideas and wishes. Its outer layer, the cerebral cortex, is the center of conscious thought and action. The cerebrum's two halves, or hemispheres, are connected by a bundle of millions of nerve fibers called the corpus callosum, which acts as a conduit of messages between the right and left sides of the brain.

Scientists use a variety of methods to understand better the structure and functions of the brain. In the past, autopsies revealed how impaired abilities might be the result of damaged brain tissue. Later, experimenters purposely destroyed specific parts of animal brain tissue so they could observe what sensory or motor losses occurred. Researchers also stimulated specific regions with electricity or chemicals. Today we can get actual pictures of the brain's inner workings using a technique called imaging. Scientists can also record nerve signals from a single neuron or electrical wave patterns from the entire brain. This brain wave pattern is known as an electroencephalogram, or EEG.

But how do scientists know what constitutes normal electrical activity in the brain? By analyzing and comparing brain wave patterns from people all over the world, they have concluded that all healthy members of the human species have similar brains. Variations in electrical patterns may reveal environmental influences such as poor nutrition or even living at unusually high elevations. This methodology helps scientists identify structural or chemical causes for thought, mood, and behavioral disorders, thus making it easier to evaluate different therapies.

Other neuroscientists study the brain's biochemical activity. They look at many groups of neurotransmitters and hormones which affect brain functions and behavior. Nerve cells manufacture opiatelike molecules known as endorphins, part of the complex system of neurotransmitters. Endorphins can affect our moods, emotions, and perception of pain. Some long-distance runners report a feeling of euphoria, or "runner's high," after a strenuous workout. This may be the result of exercise's increasing the body's endorphin activity.

Endorphins are only one of many chemical influences on the brain. Some scientists investigate the influence of brain chemicals on learning and memory. By comparing the performance of experimental rats given drugs that block or mimic specific neurotransmitters with that of untreated animals, scientists hope to discover which changes in the brain produce specific actions. So, by learning how the brain works or fails to work, they can begin to prescribe new drug therapies to prevent, minimize, even cure diseases, such as learning deficits or memory losses, and Alzheimer's disease.

In addition to better understanding the brain, scientists are also improving how it works. Some researchers are actually designing new ways to overcome brain damage. In one lab, a scientist grafts healthy brain tissue into dead or damaged brain areas and finds that the tissue can survive and grow. Rats have gained learning and memory abilities following tissue transplants from aborted fetuses. These results may eventually help people with Parkinson's disease, a degenerative disorder caused by a loss of dopamine-producing brain cells, which affects more than a million people in the United States alone. Though fetal brain tissue transplants in human patients raise many ethical questions, scientists seek to understand whether successful transplants result from a strong placebo effect, some actual release of dopamine caused by the surgery, or the adjustment of medication before or after the surgery.

Although research involving human tissue transplants is highly controversial, even in the scientific community, scientists are continuing to uncover the biochemical mechanisms that underlie the complexities of behavior in an effort to prevent, control, and cure disease, and to improve the quality of life.

REVIEW QUESTIONS

Note: Review Questions for Units 3 and 4 are provided in Unit 4.

QUESTIONS TO CONSIDER

1. What is the advantage of knowing that mental illness is caused by neurochemical problems if we don't know how to correct them?

2. There are millions of people who will try just about anything to control their weight. They buy diet pills and nutritional supplements that claim to alter the chemistry of their appetite. Some are so desperate that they have their mouths wired shut. Why don't doctors treat people with eating disorders by placing electrodes in their brains?

3. Why should you be suspicious of studies claiming that high doses of vitamins or nutritional supplements are necessary for preventing physical or mental disorders, maintaining health, or curing diseases?

4. Different technologies for measuring brain activity help psychologists view structures and functioning of the brain. What advantages do these advanced techniques offer?

5. How does knowing about the workings of the brain help to make you a better student?

OPTIONAL ACTIVITY

1. Can you feel the effects of your hormones? Try this: Imagine yourself falling down the stairs, stubbing your toe, or suddenly losing control of your car on a busy highway. Did your heart skip a beat? Did you catch your breath or feel a tingle up your back? Did the hair on your neck stiffen? Your imagination has caused a biochemical reaction in your brain, and you are feeling the effect of the hormones it produces. Can you name the hormones involved?

ANTHOLOGY

The following readings illustrate concepts from Unit 3 and stimulate critical thinking. As you read, consider the relationship between the brain and behavior. How does understanding the brain's chemistry influence the way you view mental illness and behavior problems? Does knowing something about biochemistry shed light on some of your own behaviors?

Reading 5

Alcoholism is defined as a chronic dependence on alcohol. Society has mixed feelings about alcoholics, who often consume alcohol to the point where it produces mental disturbances. Is alcoholism a sin or a disease? Are people responsible for the death and damage they cause while under the influence of alcohol? Do you consider alcoholism a legitimate excuse for misbehavior?

When Alcoholism Is the Excuse

By Ellen Goodman

I don't know when the town drunk was officially transformed into a victim of alcoholism. It is still only 30 years since the American Medical Association first declared that chronic drunkenness wasn't a sin. It was, rather, a disease.

Now, according to polls, 87 percent of us accept alcoholism as a sickness. But our attitudes toward the "ism" of alcohol are not as clear as this figure suggests.

We may no longer want to condemn alcoholics for their addiction. On the other hand, we don't want to excuse them from responsibility for their behavior.

This ambivalence about the semantics and social policy of alcohol abuse is now coming before the Supreme Court. Next week, the court will hear the cases of two men, both veterans, both recovered alcoholics, both suing the Veterans Administration.

The two men missed the VA deadline for college benefits. They were drunk during their eligible years. They complain that under the VA guidelines, disabled veterans would have had longer to apply for these benefits.

But VA doesn't call alcoholism a disability. It calls alcoholism "willful misconduct." So these two have accused the VA of illegally discriminating against them on the basis of their handicap: alcoholism.

The case may finally turn on some minor point, but it raises major questions. Is alcoholism a disease? Is an alcoholic disabled in the sense that, say, a paraplegic is? Does he or she deserve an extra hand from society, an extension of benefits, a special ramp into life?

Must we then agree that alcoholism is a legitimate excuse for misbehavior, even for a crime?

In a curiously parallel case, the president's friend, Michael Deaver, is using alcoholism as a defense against charges of perjury. He was too sick to know what he was saying. The disease, not the man, done it.

These lines between sick behavior and bad behavior are not always clear. Leonard Glantz of Boston University's School of Public Health offers another example: "If you have a brain tumor and attack me because of this tumor, is it fair to send you to jail? Most people would think not. But if you ran me down with a car because you were in the throes of alcoholic delusion should you go to jail? Most people would say yes."

Our ambivalence toward alcoholism may be entirely appropriate, even accurate. We are often comfortable labeling alcoholism as a disease. There is medical evidence to match the terminology. We know alcohol can be addictive. We read that people can inherit a susceptibility to addiction. There may be a genetic link.

The semantics also fit our current social-policy desires. If alcoholics are "sick" instead of bad, they need, indeed deserve, help. This attitude has destigmatized the addiction, and put into place a vast array of programs on alcohol abuse.

At the same time, we know that alcoholism has an element of choice. You can't just say no to cancer. But you can say no to a drink. The cure is not in the hands of a surgeon. It is in the hands of the "victim." Indeed, part of the cure is getting people to take responsibility for their actions.

Ultimately, says Glantz, "we must make choices about how people are handled." Choices for the whole of society, not just a 'sick' individual.

Most of those choices are made in the courts, not the medical lab. Today, even a sociopath—someone who has no regard for the life of others—is not considered mentally ill for the purposes of criminal prosecution.

We can label alcoholism a disease to help those who are in need. But we shouldn't accept it as a defense, when the alcoholic's behavior threatens the rest of the community.

If Michael Deaver had blacked out on the highway and slammed into another car, we would not have forgiven his behavior on account of drunkenness. Nor should we forgive perjury on these grounds.

As for the veterans demanding their handicapped rights, I don't think we should extend benefits to alcoholics that are denied to the sober. Remember that these two veterans have recovered from their disease. They didn't do it by making excuses.

Reading 6

People are often quick to label personal and social difficulties as psychological or emotional problems. This article points out that parents are likely to worry that personality or behavior changes are responses to psychological stress. To what do you attribute your own changes in temper or mood? Do you consider such factors as poor diet, inadequate sleep, or illness? As you read, consider the complex interactions of chemicals in the brain and body. Should diagnostic procedures for behavior or psychological problems include investigations of diet, hormone levels, and brain structure and functioning?

When the Body Affects the Mind

By Julius and Zelda Segal

Ann Barnes is a bright and charming six-year-old. Last year she became melancholy, unmotivated, and unable to concentrate. Her sleep was fitful, and her appetite was failing. She rarely chose to play with friends, and her usual enthusiasm was gone.

Ann's parents were sure that their daughter's difficulties were due to family tensions—and indeed that's what a child psychiatrist they consulted first thought. But before Ann started on therapy, her pediatrician suggested blood tests—and his suspicions were confirmed. Ann's problems stemmed not from emotional turmoil, but from *iron-deficiency anemia*, a readily treated blood condition resulting in depletion of the blood's iron stores. In the end, it was a regimen of iron pills—not psychotherapy—that led the way back to emotional health.

Hidden medical problems. Ann's case highlights an aspect of childhood that is too often poorly understood by professionals as well as parents: not every dramatic change of personality or behavior has an emotional basis. Doctors and psychiatrists have long recognized that stress and conflict can affect our physical well-being. But now it is clear that the reverse is equally true. Many psychological problems—even severe ones like anxiety, depression, phobias, and delinquent behavior—can arise from the body rather than from disturbing life experiences.

Studies by Richard C. W. Hall, a psychiatrist at Florida Hospital Medical Center, in Orlando, show that about 10 percent of patients treated in psychiatric clinics are found to suffer from hidden medical conditions that cause or worsen their psychological complaints. With appropriate medical treatment, their symptoms usually clear up. Says Hall: "A similar situation may be the case with children."

Hypoglycemia. One mother recently described her six-year-old son, Paul, as a "disturbed and disturbing child." He was irritable and fretful, given to unaccountable outbursts of anger and episodes of confusion and agitation. Paul was being treated by a psychologist but with no success. A routine medical exam eventually showed that Paul's "emotional" problem, like Ann's, was due to a physical condition. In his case, it was *hypoglycemia*, or an abnormally low level of blood sugar. The condition, correctable through diet, can cause abnormal behavior and is more common than even many doctors suspect.

Equally difficult personality problems can arise from glandular malfunctions. One example is *hypothyroidism*, in which too low a level of hormone is produced by the thyroid gland. This can cause dramatic changes in behavior ranging from lethargy and language difficulties to depression. The opposite condition—*hyperthyroidism*—occurs when the level of thyroid hormone is too high rather than too low. Studies of children with this problem have revealed a startling array of symptoms, including nervousness and restlessness, difficulties with school work, crying spells, and irritability.

Remember the connection. The examples described here are admittedly extreme, but keep in mind that psychological complaints can arise from physical conditions that are more common as well. Children recovering from even minor surgery, for example, may experience a period of depression, sometimes as a result of anesthesia. Viral infections, irregularities of metabolism, and vitamin deficiencies can affect mood and well-being as well.

Most children find it difficult to recognize or talk about their internal physical feelings. Thus parents are often slow to suspect that something going on in the young bodies may be affecting their children's moods and behavior. For parents whose children are experiencing emotional problems, an important first step, therefore, is to have a doctor look carefully for possible physical causes. More often than is generally supposed, appropriate medical treatment—without the need for psychotherapy—is the key to restoring the child's mental health.

Reading 7

This article reports on the high incidence of neurological problems and head injuries in a study of juveniles on death row and adults convicted of violent crimes. As you read, consider the brain's role in coping with stress and frustration. What are the personal, social, and legal implications of the information in the article? What are your thoughts about the death penalty?

Head Injuries Found In Young Killers

By Alison Bass

In the first psychiatric study ever done of juveniles on death row in America, researchers found that every one of the 14 youths they studied had suffered serious head injuries during childhood and almost all had been brutally beaten and abused as children. Many also had psychiatric disorders serious enough to justify hospitalization.

The findings may play a key role in an imminent US Supreme Court decision on whether to abolish the death penalty for juveniles in the United States, the only industrialized nation that still executes people under 18.

The court's decision is likely to determine the fate of all 33 juveniles currently under death sentence in 14 states. The youths, all of whom were between 15 and 17 when they committed their crimes, were tried as adults because of the extreme violence of the acts, which ranged from the rape-murder of a 78-year-old woman to the stabbing and shooting death of a close relative. In most states, youths under 18 are tried in the juvenile courts, in which there is no death penalty.

The results of the study were provided to the court last November, when attorneys representing some of the juveniles on death row argued that no juvenile is socially and morally mature enough to be held accountable "to the highest degree of responsibility"—the death penalty. The study was published in the May issue of the American Journal of Psychiatry.

"This study demonstrates that people who are on death row for committing crimes as juveniles have major psychiatric problems, neurological problems and educational and learning problems," said Steven Pincus, a New York attorney who worked on the case. "The law says that if someone's capacity is diminished—and the capacities of these juveniles clearly are—that needs to be considered in any calculation of moral blameworthiness."

Dr. Dorothy Otnow Lewis, a New York University psychiatrist who spearheaded the study, said she undertook the investigation after finding a consistent pattern of neurological problems and childhood abuse among adults facing execution.

"A year after that study, I was asked to evaluate a young adult on death row in the South and I started wondering whether this pattern might be even more clearcut among juveniles," said Lewis, who has been studying violent children 17 years.

While a history of deprivation and brain damage would ordinarily militate against the death penalty, Lewis discovered that much of the information she and her colleagues unearthed had never been brought to light. Most of the adult and juvenile convicts they examined had not even received medical and psychiatric evaluations prior to trial.

The 14 juveniles in the study were chosen because they were incarcerated in states that would allow the researchers into prisons. Lewis and her colleagues conducted extensive neurological, psychiatric and educational examinations of the 14 juveniles, all of them males. They also interviewed each convict and obtained corroborating information from records and, in some cases, from family members.

The team included psychiatrists, psychologists and neurologists at Georgetown and New York universities, together with educators from Central Connecticut State University.

"Every single juvenile in these four states was examined," said Lewis. "We believe they are representative of the juvenile death row population in general."

Their most dramatic finding was that all 14 juveniles had suffered a head injury in childhood, nine of them severe enough to require hospitalization and cause major brain damage.

One was hit by a truck at age four. He was comatose for days and then hospitalized for 11 months. Another was hit by a car at age 10 and still carries the scar: an indentation in his forehead.

The researchers also found that 12 of the 14 had been brutally abused physically or sexually as children. Five had been sodomized by older male relatives. One boy had been sexually abused by his stepfather and grandfather throughout his childhood, and had been hit on the head with a hammer by his stepfather.

Another had been forced to sit on the burner of a hot stove (the scars still show). That child had been sodomized by his stepfather and his stepfather's friends and compelled to participate in child pornography movies.

"You read this stuff and it curdles your blood," one of the researchers said.

The researchers also found that the majority of the young men were afflicted with episodes of psychotic thinking, such as distorting reality and extreme paranoia. Some suffered from other serious psychiatric disorders. One had tried to kill himself when he was 11. Another—the one who had been struck by a truck—had been hospitalized when he was 15 and diagnosed as psychotic.

The researchers reported that only two of the juveniles had IQs above 90 (which is below normal), and only three could read at the appropriate grade level. Three had not learned to read until they were jailed. Alcoholism, drug abuse and psychiatric hospitalization were common among their parents.

"Given what happened to these kids, it raises questions about whether these are the individuals that society should sentence to death," Lewis said. "The study showed these juveniles are different from adults—in their maturity and ability to judge the consequences of their actions accurately."

To protect the youths' confidentiality, Lewis would not disclose any names or backgrounds. However, attorneys for William Wayne Thompson, whose appeal was the basis of the pending Supreme Court ruling, confirmed in an interview that Thompson was one of the subjects. Information about Thompson and the others on death row is available in trial records.

Wayne Thompson, as he is known, was convicted in Oklahoma for killing his sister's former husband. Fifteen at the time, he was one of three people, including his older brother, convicted of the crime.

"The whole story is replete with violence," said Pincus, one of his attorneys. "From reading the record, it is clear the man who was killed had inflicted incredible violence on Wayne's sister and on Wayne himself and was seen by the family as a very serious problem."

The record also shows that when Thompson was younger, he had been beaten by his older brother and whipped by his mother. At age 11, he was kicked in the head by the brother-in-law, while trying to stop him from beating his sister. The same man had taught Thompson as a young child how to get high by sniffing paint, said Harry F. Tepker, a professor of law at the University of Oklahoma who argued Thompson's case before the Supreme Court.

Lewis and her colleagues also learned that Thompson had fallen from a tree at age 7 and had run into a car while bicycling at age 13. These accidents caused brain damage severe enough to produce abnormal results on a neurological test that measures brain wave activity. They had also left clear-cut signs of head injury (a prominent bump on his forehead and a scar behind his left ear).

"[Thompson] has been exposed to a constellation of psychological and environmental disturbances which have impeded his natural growth and development," attorneys wrote in a brief filed with the Supreme Court. "He suffers from serious cognitive and intellectual limitations, educational deficiencies and immature judgement. He is thus typical of the subgroup of adolescents who commit capital offenses."

Despite this history, Thompson's original attorney made no effort to provide him with a clinical evaluation during his trial in 1983. He was not the only juvenile in this study to receive an inadequate defense, the study concluded.

The researchers noted that the youths themselves had tried to hide their educational, psychological and family problems.

In some cases, attorneys didn't bother to obtain clinical evaluations for their clients, the researchers reported. In other cases, the families, out of shame and fear, conspired to conceal sexual and physical abuse.

"That's the real scandal in this country: These kids don't get an adequate defense,"

said Tepker. "The families can't afford to pay for an attorney and the public defenders are often unwilling conscripts."

"If there are resources in the family or community, the probability of getting the death sentence is so low as to be almost zero," said Victor Streib, a law professor at Cleveland State University and an authority on juvenile executions.

No one disputes the fact that the juveniles on death row commited vicious crimes—in Thompson's case, his brother-in-law was stabbed and shot and thrown in a lake with a cement block tied to his leg. The question before the Supreme Court is whether the juveniles had the maturity, capacity for self-control, and the sense of right and wrong to be held accountable with the ultimate punishment—death.

Some prosecutors, however, argue the question can only be answered on a case-by-case basis. David Lee, who argued before the Supreme Court for retaining the death penalty for juveniles, said age alone should not be a mitigating factor.

"Juveniles have varying levels of maturity—some 15-year-olds have the maturity of much older people and vice versa," Lee said in a telephone interview. "If you just use chronological age as the sole determinant in death penalty cases, we think that would be arbitrary and inappropriate.

Tepker and other attorneys who have represented juveniles on death row disagree.

"These are just not the kind of individuals who should be held fully accountable for their acts—not like the cold, calculating hit man or the husband who blows up his wife for the insurance," Tepker said. "This [psychiatric] study is really eloquent about the fact that these adolescents, although they have committed terrible crimes, are also victims."

ADDITIONAL RESOURCES

Books and Articles

Diamond, M., A. Schneibel, and L. Elson. *The Human Brain Coloring Book*. New York: Harper and Row, 1985. An entertaining, illustrated guide to the human brain.

Gazzaniga, Michael S. "The Social Brain." *Psychology Today* (November 1985): 28–38. Are our brains divided into independent units that often work apart from our conscious and verbal selves? This article, like Gazzaniga's book of the same name, discusses a new theory of brain organization.

Restak, R. *The Brain*. New York: Bantam Books, 1984. Chapter 1, "The Enlightened Machine," is a good, clearly written introduction to brain structures and functions.

Scientific American, 241: 9 (September 1979). This issue, devoted to the study of the brain, offers a good review of topics in the unit. Articles focus on various aspects of brain organization, chemistry, and functions.

Sinclair, J. D. "The Hardware of the Brain." *Psychology Today* (December 1983): 8–12. Will computers ever think the way humans do? Sinclair looks at how computers and human beings store and process information.

Valenstein, Elliot. "Science Fiction, Fantasy, and the Brain." *Psychology Today* (July 1978): 28–39. Examines how the psychological experiments of science fiction compare with actual research.

THE RESPONSIVE BRAIN

The Human Brain is a most unusual instrument of elegant and as yet unknown capacity.

Stuart Lyman Seaton

Chris Hetzer

Unit 4 takes a closer look at the dynamic relationship between the brain and behavior. We'll see how the brain controls behavior, and conversely how behavior and environment can cause changes in the structure and the functioning of the brain.

For premature infants, touch can mean the difference between sickness and health, even life and death, according to a study by psychologist Tiffany Field of Miami University.

OBJECTIVES

After viewing the television program and completing the assigned readings, you should be able to:

1. Explain how environment and experience can influence the functioning and structure of the brain

2. Cite examples of the brain's capacity to adapt to environmental change

3. Describe the mechanism by which touch deprivation is related to stunted growth

4. Explain how early experience can affect brain mechanisms that influence stress tolerance in later life

5. Cite research studies that contribute to an understanding of the role enriched environments play in brain development

6. Explain how individual maturation is controlled by social needs and group behavior

7. Explain the value of observation studies of animals in their natural habitats and how these studies complement laboratory research

READING ASSIGNMENT

After viewing Program 4, read pages 61–106 in *Psychology: Science, Behavior and Life*. Your instructor may also assign the anthology selections for Unit 4.

KEY TERMS AND CONCEPTS

To review textbook terms, refer to Key Terms and Concepts in Unit 3.

The following term is used in Program 4 but is not defined in the text.

cholesterol, HDL, LDL—blood chemistry factors important in understanding cardiovascular disease

PROGRAM SUMMARY

The brain is the place where an endless stream of electrical nerve impulses, chemical transmitters, and hormone messengers get transformed into experience, knowledge, feelings, beliefs, and consciousness. Learning how it functions helps us better understand human and animal behavior.

The reciprocal relationship between the brain and behavior is the subject of Program 4. The brain controls behavior, and behavior feeds back information to influence the brain. The brain can even alter its own functioning and structure. This capacity for internal modification makes it one of the most dynamic systems on Earth.

Several studies demonstrate the responsiveness of the brain's neurochemical system. In one, we learn that humans and animals thrive when they get adequate contact and suffer when they do not. For some infants, especially those born prematurely, touch can mean the difference between illness and health, even life and death.

Psychologist Tiffany Field explains her study in which some premature infants received gentle massages and others received routine care. Those in the massaged group gained more weight, were able to leave the hospital earlier, and showed long-term developmental advantages over the babies who received routine care. This research clearly demonstrates the therapeutic value of touching and suggests a way to save millions of dollars in hospital costs.

Psychologist Saul Schanberg, who conducted research with touch-deprived rats, demonstrated that maternal deprivation can stunt growth. But he also demonstrated that retarded growth can be reversed. Placing the stunted baby rats with their mothers or stroking them with a wet paintbrush restored normal growth.

Lack of touching also seems to affect the production of human growth hormones. When researchers removed touch-deprived, growth-stunted children from their unloving homes and placed them in more affectionate families, they grew dramatically.

Another study demonstrates that early experiences can cause permanent alterations in the structure of the brain. Rats raised in stimulating, visually enriched environments had a thicker cortex and were superior learners compared with rats raised in ordinary or deprived environments. The stimulated rats had more neurotransmitters, more enzymes in the glial cells, and more and larger spines on the dendrites.

Other research studies on early experience and the brain also show long-term effects of touching. Newborn rats who had regular handling were better able to cope with stress throughout their lives. They also showed signs of slower aging and of reduced learning and memory losses.

Developmental psychologist Michael Meany investigates how early experiences can change the brain and behavior. He explains that when an individual faces a threat, the adrenal glands release hormones called glucocorticoids, which prepare the body to handle stressful situations. But repeated exposure to stress hormones inhibits the glucocorticoid neurons in the hippocampus, a part of the brain that regulates stress and plays a key role in learning and memory. Handling the baby rats in the first three weeks of life seems to reduce the loss of glucocorticoid cells and improves the hippocampus's ability to turn off the stress response.

Field research is just as important as controlled experiments performed in the laboratory. Russell Fernald of the Institute of Neuroscience in Oregon studied the African Chiclid fish as an example of how the brain is altered when behavior changes. He observed that dominant male Chiclids have brightly colored patterns and dark eye bars. When these fish acquired territory, changes in the Chiclid's brain caused the fish to grow rapidly and colorfully. When they lost territory, they lost their coloration and sexual maturity.

Another study, conducted by Stanford biologist Robert Sapolsky, demonstrated that in baboon colonies, social rank is the most important principle of social organization. When baboons attained high social rank, they also became healthier and more physically resistant to wear and tear. With reverses in status, they showed a corresponding loss of health and tolerance for stress.

All these studies contribute to a better understanding of the interplay of environment, behavior, and biology. In the controlled setting of the laboratory, researchers can look more closely at how the brain changes. In the field, they can observe how animals naturally respond to demands from the environment.

REVIEW QUESTIONS

Program Questions

1. What section of a nerve cell receives incoming information?

   a. The axon
   b. The terminal button
   c. The synapse
   d. The dendrite

2. In general, neuroscientists are interested in the

   a. brain mechanisms underlying normal and abnormal behavior.
   b. biological consequences of chemicals produced by the body.
   c. comparison of neurons with other types of cells.
   d. computer simulation of intelligence.

3. Which section of the brain coordinates body movement and maintains equilibrium?

   a. The brain stem
   b. The cerebellum
   c. The hippocampus
   d. The cerebrum

4. Where in the brain are emotions centered?

   a. In the cortex
   b. In the brain stem
   c. In the limbic system
   d. In the cerebellum

5. Which method of probing the brain produces actual pictures of the brain's inner working?

   a. Autopsies
   b. Lesioning
   c. Brain imaging
   d. Electroencephalograms

6. E. Roy John cites the example of the staff member responding to a personal question to show how imaging can detect

   a. abnormal structure in the brain.
   b. abnormal biochemical activity in the brain.
   c. abnormal but transient states.
   d. pathological states such as alcoholism.

7. If a scientist were studying the effects of endorphins on the body, the scientist would be likely to look at a subject's

    a. memory.
    b. mood.
    c. ability to learn new material.
    d. motivation to compete in sports.

8. Joseph Martinez taught rats a maze task and then gave them scopolamine. What effect did the drug have on brain functioning?

    a. It enhanced the rats' memory.
    b. It made the rats forget what they had learned.
    c. It enabled the rats to learn a similar task more quickly.
    d. It had no effect.

9. Research related to acetylcholine may someday help people who

    a. have Alzheimer's disease.
    b. have Parkinson's disease.
    c. suffer spinal cord trauma.
    d. suffer from depression.

10. In research conducted by Fred Gage, what effect did neuronal transplantation have on the performance of aged rats in the hidden platform task?

    a. The rats could no longer perform the task.
    b. The rats performed better than young rats did.
    c. The rats could then perform the task.
    d. The rats performed at the same level as before.

11. When we say the relationship between the brain and behavior is reciprocal, we mean that

    a. the brain controls behavior, but behavior can modify the brain.
    b. behavior determines what the brain will think about.
    c. the brain and behavior operate as separate systems with no interconnection.
    d. the brain alters behavior as it learns more about the world.

12. Before an operation, men and women were gently touched by a nurse. What effect did this touch have on the patients' anxiety levels?

    a. It decreased anxiety in both men and women.
    b. It increased anxiety in both men and women.
    c. It decreased anxiety in men, but increased it in women.
    d. It increased anxiety in men, but decreased it in women.

13. A group of people comfortable with touching others is compared with a group uncomfortable with touching others. Those comfortable with touch were generally higher in

    a. self-esteem.
    b. social withdrawal.
    c. conformity.
    d. suspicion of others.

14. What long-term effect did Tiffany Field find massage had on premature infants?

    a. Massaged infants had better social relationships.
    b. Massaged infants were physically and cognitively more developed.
    c. Massaged infants slept and ate better.
    d. There were no long-term effects noted.

15. What is the relationship between the results of Saul Schanberg's research and that of Tiffany Field?

    a. Their results are contradictory.
    b. The results of Schanberg's research led to Field's research.
    c. Their results show similar phenomena in different species.
    d. Their results are essentially unrelated.

16. What area of the brain seems to be affected in psychosocial dwarfism?

    a. The hippocampus
    b. The cerebellum
    c. The brain stem
    d. The hypothalamus

17. What physical change did Mark Rosenzweig's team note when they studied rats raised in an enriched environment?

    a. A thicker cortex
    b. More neurons
    c. Fewer neurotransmitters
    d. No physical changes were noted, only functional changes.

18. In Michael Meany's research on aged rats' performance in a swimming maze, the rats that performed best were those that

    a. had received doses of glucocorticoids.
    b. had been subjected to less stress in their lives.
    c. had been handled early in life.
    d. could use spatial clues for orientation.

19. In his study of Chiclid fish, Russell Fernald found that there was growth in a specific area of the brain following

    a. improved diet.
    b. social success.
    c. gentle handling.
    d. loss of territory.

20. In Robert Sapolsky's study of stress physiology among baboons, what is the relationship between high status and "good" physiology?

    a. Animals attain high status because they have good physiology.
    b. Attaining high status leads to good physiology.
    c. Lowering one's status leads to improved physiology.
    d. Animals with poor physiology acquire low status.

Textbook Questions

21. The brain and spinal cord are two divisions of the

    a. peripheral nervous system.
    b. central nervous system.
    c. somatic nervous system.
    d. skeletal nervous system.

22. The nervous system that is made up of the somatic and autonomic nervous systems
    is the _____ nervous system.

    a. central
    b. skeletal
    c. peripheral
    d. sympathetic

23. The basic unit of the nervous system is the

    a. neurotransmitters.
    b. glia cells.
    c. neuron.
    d. axon bundles.

24. Motor neurons are otherwise known as

    a. afferent neurons.
    b. efferent neurons.
    c. glia cells.
    d. reflex arcs.

25. Afferent nerves send messages _____ the spinal cord and brain.

    a. away from
    b. toward
    c. within
    d. slowly away from

26. Neurons that transmit messages from the central nervous system to muscles or
    glands are

    a. sensory neurons.
    b. motor neurons.
    c. interneurons.
    d. glia cells.

27. The nucleus of a neuron cell is located in the

    a. axon.
    b. dendrite.
    c. myelin.
    d. soma.

28. The dendrite functions to

    a. transmit chemical messages.
    b. receive chemical messages.
    c. block chemical messages.
    d. hold chemical messages.

29. Axons end in smaller bulblike structures called

    a. somas.
    b. dendrites.
    c. terminal buttons.
    d. myelin sheaths.

30. The progress of a neural message is from the

    a. axon to the soma to the dendrite.
    b. dendrite to the soma to the axon.
    c. dendrite to the axon to the soma.
    d. dendrite to the terminal to the soma.

31. The process by which neural impulses are transmitted within the central nervous system is

    a. not chemical in nature.
    b. seen only in the brain.
    c. electrochemical in nature.
    d. the same as electricity through a wire.

32. An electrical signal or action potential that flows along the length of the neuron is generated when the

    a. sum of graded potentials reaches a sufficient magnitude.
    b. concentrations of neurotransmitters reach a threshold.
    c. voltage across the synapse is at its maximum strength.
    d. size of the synaptic cleft is reduced to a minimum.

33. Each time a neuron fires, it transmits an impulse of the same strength and is known as the

    a. action potential.
    b. threshold level.
    c. all-or-none principle.
    d. refractory time.

34. Glia cells wrap around axons forming an insulating cover called

    a. a node of Ranvier.
    b. synapse.
    c. a myelin sheath.
    d. a terminal button.

35. In terms of speed, neural impulses travel about

    a. 2 to 225 miles per second.
    b. 2 to 225 miles per hour.
    c. 186,000 miles per second.
    d. 186,000 miles per hour.

36. The neural impulse jumps across the fluid-filled gap (cleft) between neurons, much like the spark from a sparkplug in an automobile.

    a. Yes, that is the way it functions.
    b. Yes, but much faster.
    c. No, more like a short in a wire.
    d. No, chemicals are released; it is not a spark.

37. Neurotransmitter chemicals are contained and released from the

    a. axon end knobs/bulbs.
    b. dendrites.
    c. myelin.
    d. soma.

38. Insufficient levels of norepinephrine and serotonin may be linked to

    a. schizophrenia.
    b. depression.
    c. sleeplessness.
    d. narcolepsy.

39. The _____ contains nuclei that help control respiration and facial expression.

    a. thalamus
    b. medulla
    c. hypothalamus
    d. pons

40. The reticular formation plays a role in

    a. life-supporting functions such as breathing and heartbeat.
    b. the fine-tuning of motor messages.
    c. coordinating and regulating motor movements.
    d. controlling levels of arousal and alertness.

41. Electrical stimulation of the _____ awakens sleeping animals.

    a. reticular activating system
    b. pons
    c. medulla
    d. hypothalamus

42. The portion of the brain most closely associated with emotional expression is the

    a. cerebellum.
    b. limbic system.
    c. reticular formation.
    d. thalamus.

43. A limbic system structure which seems to be important for memory is the

    a. septal area.
    b. amygdala.
    c. hippocampus.
    d. hypothalamus.

44. The _____ is a small structure below the thalamus that plays an important role in motivation, emotional expression, and controlling the neuroendocrine system, and maintaining the body's homeostasis.

    a. hippocampus
    b. cerebellum
    c. cerebrum
    d. hypothalamus

45. Sensory input from the eyes is relayed to the visual cortex by the

    a. thalamus.
    b. hypothalamus.
    c. pons.
    d. reticular activating system.

46. The thin outer layer of the brain's cerebrum (sometimes called the "gray matter") that is responsible for higher mental processes, including perceiving, thinking, and remembering, is the

    a. cerebellum.
    b. cerebral cortex.
    c. medulla.
    d. reticular formation.

47. The wrinkles, convolutions, and fissures in the cerebral cortex

    a. have no known purpose.
    b. indicate higher intelligence.
    c. allow more nerve cells to be packed into the brain.
    d. contribute to emotional stability.

48. If a patient had severe damage to the frontal lobe, you might predict he could also have

    a. impaired decision-making and problem-solving abilities.
    b. difficulty in identifying visually complex forms.
    c. difficulty in identifying objects by touch.
    d. severe loss of memory.

49. The primary function of the temporal lobe is for

    a. sight.
    b. hearing.
    c. emotional control.
    d. taste.

50. The right and left cerebral hemispheres are connected by a thick nerve-fiber bundle called the

    a. corpus callosum.
    b. cortex.
    c. cerebral cortex.
    d. limbic system.

51. What part of the brain is severed in the split-brain operation?

    a. Frontal lobes
    b. Hindbrain and midbrain
    c. Pons and medulla
    d. Corpus callosum

52. The dominant (usually left) hemisphere seems to be more involved with

    a. language production and comprehension.
    b. fantasy.
    c. music appreciation.
    d. depth perception.

53. A technique for studying the brain that involves surgical damage to a precise region of the brain is called

    a. brain stimulation.
    b. electrical recording.
    c. axial tomography.
    d. lesion production.

54. The autonomic nervous system has two branches or divisions called the

    a. somatic and skeletal.
    b. sympathetic and parasympathetic.
    c. cranial and spinal.
    d. peripheral and central.

55. If you hit your thumb with a hammer, which nervous system sends the message to your brain?

    a. The peripheral nervous system
    b. The central nervous system
    c. The autonomic nervous system
    d. The corpus callosum

56. The portion of the autonomic nervous system that is most active during times of relaxation and restfulness is the

    a. sympathetic system.
    b. parasympathetic system.
    c. basal ganglia.
    d. limbic system.

57. Endocrine glands secrete substances called

    a. amino acids.
    b. myelin.
    c. hormones.
    d. transmitter substances.

58. The body's metabolism is affected by the _____ gland.

   a. pancreas
   b. adrenal
   c. thyroid
   d. limbic

59. The testes produce the male hormone

   a. testosterone.
   b. progesterone.
   c. estrogen.
   d. thyroxin.

QUESTIONS TO CONSIDER

1. Many different factors influence your performance on a test: your study habits, recollection of the material, familiarity with the test format, and confidence. Given the choice, would you take a drug that might improve your performance? Would you take a beta-blocker that interferes with the effects of adrenaline (used by some actors and musicians to reduce stage fright) or a drug that enhances retention and recall of information? Would taking a drug give you an unfair advantage over other test takers? Is there any danger in taking drugs for this purpose?

2. What are the biological benefits of touching? Program 4 suggests that children raised with significantly different patterns of physical contact and touching will develop different behavioral, social, and personality characteristics. What differences would you expect to observe between children from undemonstrative families and those from families whose members touch each other frenquently?

3. Consider the roles that biologically determined factors such as your health and looks, play in your life. How might social or environmental conditions influence your health and looks? How might your health and looks influence social and environmental conditions?

4. Considering what is known about the damaging effects of poor nutrition, drugs, cigarettes, and alcohol on the fetus, what can be done to protect a baby from the effects of its mother's activities? Should any legal action be taken?

OPTIONAL ACTIVITY

1. Interview a few parents from different generations about the infancy of their children. Did they read books on child development or follow an expert's advice? Did they sleep with their babies? How did they comfort them? Which early experiences do they believe were most influential in their children's future development?

ANTHOLOGY

Unit 4 focuses on the interplay between brain and behavior which continues throughout our lives. As you read the following selections, consider the implications of the concept of the responsive brain on such factors as individual temperament, intelligence, and physical and mental health.

Reading 8

This article discusses the changes in the number, complexity, and quality of neural connections that relate to specific visual and linguistic skills. As you read, think about the following questions: What is the role of early experience in fine-tuning the brain? What are the best times for preserving important neural connections? Are there phases of development during which the brain is especially receptive to certain experiences? What are the implications for childrearing and early education?

Making of a Mind

By Kathleen McAuliffe

"Give me a child for the first six years of life and he'll be a servant of God till his last breath."

—Jesuit maxim

A servant of God or an agent of the devil; a law-abiding citizen or a juvenile delinquent. What the Jesuits knew, scientists are now rapidly confirming—that the mind of the child, in the very first years, even months, of life, is the crucible in which many of his deepest values are formed. It is then that much of what he may become—his talents, his interests, his abilities—are developed and directed. The experiences of his infancy and childhood will profoundly shape everything from his visual acuity to his comprehension of language and social behavior.

What underlies the child's receptivity to new information? And why do adults seem to lose this capacity as they gain more knowledge of the world around them? Why is that the more we know, the less we *can* know?

Like a Zen koan, this paradox has led scientists down many paths of discovery. Some researchers are studying development processes in infants and children; others search the convoluted passages of the cortex for clues to how memory records learning experiences. Still others are studying the degree to which learning is hardwired—soldered along strict pathways in the brains of animals and humans.

Another phenomenon recently discovered: Long after patterns of personality have solidified, adults may tap fresh learning centers in the brain, new nerve connections that allow intellectual growth far after fourscore years.

Although much research remains to be done, two decades of investigation have yielded some dramatic—and in some instances unexpected—insights into the developing brain.

An infant's brain is not just a miniature replica of an adult's brain. Spanish neuroscientist José Delgado goes so far as to call the newborn "mindless." Although all the nerve cells a human may have are present at birth, the cerebral cortex, the gray matter that is the seat of higher intellect, barely functions. Surprisingly, the lower brain stem, the section that we have in common with reptiles and other primitive animals, dictates most of the newborn's actions.

This changes drastically in the days, weeks, and months after birth, when the cerebral cortex literally blossoms. During this burst of growth, individual brain cells send out shoots in all directions to produce a jungle of interconnecting nerve fibers. By the time a child is one year old, his brain is 50 percent of its adult weight; by the time he's six, it's 90 percent of its adult weight. And by puberty, when growth trails off, the brain will have quadrupled in size to the average adult weight of about three pounds.

How trillions of nerve cells manage to organize themselves into something as complex as the human brain remains a mystery.

But this much is certain: as this integration and development proceeds, experiences can alter the brain's connections in a lasting, even irreversible way.

To demonstrate this, Colin Blakemore, professor of physiology at Oxford University, raised kittens in an environment that had no horizontal lines. Subsequently, they were able to "see" only vertical lines. Yet Blakemore had tested their vision just before the experiment began and found that the kittens had an equal number of cells that responded to each type of line.

Why had the cats become blind to horizontal lines? By the end of the experiment, Blakemore discovered that many more cells in the animals' brains responded to vertical lines than horizontal lines.

As the human brain develops, similar neurological processes probably occur. For example, during a test in which city-dwelling Eurocanadians were exposed to sets of all types of lines. They had the most difficulty seeing oblique lines. By comparison, the Cree Indians, from the east coast of James Bay, Quebec, perceived all orientations of lines equally well. The researchers Robert Annis and Barrie Frost, of Queens University, in Kingston, Ontario, attributed this difference in visual acuity to the subjects' environments. The Eurocanadians grow up in a world dominated by vertical and horizontal lines, whereas the Indians, who live in tepees in coniferous forests, are constantly exposed to surroundings with many different types of angles.

The sounds—as well as the sights—that an infant is exposed to can also influence his future abilities. The phonemes *rah* and *lah*, for instance, are absent from the Japanese language, and as might be expected, adults from that culture confuse English words containing *r* and *l*. (Hence the offering of steamed "lice" in sushi bars.) Tests reveal that Japanese adults are quite literally deaf to these sounds.

Infants, on the other hand, seem to readily distinguish between speech sounds. To test sensitivity to phonemes, researchers measure changes in the infants' heartbeats as different speech sounds are presented. If an infant grows familiar with one sound and then encounters a new sound, his heart rate increases. Although the evidence is still incomplete, tests of babies from linguistic backgrounds as varied as Guatemala's Spanish culture, Kenya's Kikuyu-speaking area, and the United States all point to the same conclusion: Infants can clearly perceive phonemes present in any language.

The discovery that babies can make linguistic distinctions that adults cannot caused researchers to wonder at what age we lost this natural facility for language. To find out, Janet Werker, of Dalhousie University, in Nova Scotia, and Richard Tees, of Canada's University of British Columbia, began examining the language capabilities of English-speaking adolescents. Werker and Tees tested the subjects to see whether they could discriminate between two phonemes peculiar to the Hindi language.

"We anticipated that linguistic sensitivity declines at puberty, as psychologists have commonly assumed," Werker explains.

The results were surprising. Young adolescents could not make the distinction, nor could eight-year-olds, four-year-olds, or two-year-olds. Finally, Werker and Tees decided to test infants. They discovered that the ability to perceive foreign phonemes declines sharply by one year of age. "All the six-month-olds from English-speaking backgrounds could distinguish between the Hindi phonemes," Werker says. "But by ten to twelve months of age, the babies were unable to make this distinction."

The cutoff point, according to Werker, falls between eight and twelve months of age. If not exposed to Hindi by then people require a lot of learning to catch up. Werker found that English-speaking adults studying Hindi for the first time needed up to five years of training to learn the same phoneme distinctions any six-month-old baby can make. With further testing, Werker succeeded in tracking down one of the learning impairments that thwarted her older subjects. Although there is an audible difference, the adult mind cannot retain it long enough to remember it. "The auditory capabilities are there," Werker says. "Its the language-processing capabilities that have changed."

Even a brief introduction to language during the sensitive period can permanently alter our perception of speech. Werker and Tees tested English-speaking adults who could not speak or understand a word of Hindi, although they had been exposed to the language for the first year or two of life. They found that these adults had a major advantage in learning Hindi, compared with English-speaking adults who lacked such early exposure.

Werker and Tees's studies show that there is an advantage in learning language within the first year of life. But when it comes to learning a second tongue another study has revealed some startling findings: Adults actually master a second language more easily than school-age children do.

For four years Catherine Snow, of the Harvard Graduate School of Education, studied Americans who were learning Dutch for the first time while living in Holland. "When you control for such factors as access to native speakers and the daily exposure level to the language," Snow says, "adults acquire a large vocabulary and rules of grammar more quickly than children do. In my study, adults were found to be as good as children even in pronunciation, although many researchers contend that children have an advantage in speaking like natives."

Obviously not all learning stops when the sensitive period comes to a close. This observation has led some researchers to question the importance of early experiences. What would happen, for example, if a child did not hear a single word of any language until after one year of age? Would the propensity to speak be forefeited forever? Or could later exposure to language make up the deficit?

Because of the unethical nature of performing such an experiment on a child, we may never know the answer to that question. But some indications can be gleaned from animal studies of how early deprivation affects the development of social behavior.

In *An Outline of Psychoanalysis*, Sigmund Freud refers to "the common assertion that the child is psychologically the father of the man and that the events of his first years are of paramount importance of his whole subsequent development." At the University of Wisconsin Primate Laboratory, the pioneering studies of Harry and Margaret Harlow put this belief to the test on our closest living relative—the rhesus monkey.

"Our experiments indicate that there is a critical period somewhere between the third and sixth month of life," write the Harlows, "during which social deprivation, particularly deprivation of the company of [the monkey's]

peers, irreversibly blights the animal's capacity for social adjustment."

When later returned to a colony in which there was ample opportunity for interacting with other animals, the experimental monkeys remained withdrawn, self-punishing, and compulsive. Most significantly, they grew up to be inept both as sexual partners and parents. The females never became impregnated unless artificially inseminated. We don't know whether humans, like Harlow's monkeys, must establish close bonds by a certain age or be forever doomed to social failure. But an ongoing longitudinal study, the Minnesota Preschool Project, offers the encouraging finding that emotionally neglected four-year-olds can still be helped to lead normal, happy lives. To rehabilitate the children, the teachers in the project provide them with the kind of intimate attention that is lacking at home.

Perhaps one of the Harlows' observations sheds light on why the project was successful: During the critical period for social development, the Harlows found that even a little bit of attention goes a long way. During the first year of life, for example, only 20 minutes of playtime a day with other monkeys was apparently sufficient for the animals to grow into well-adjusted adults. L. Alan Sroufe, codirector of the Minnesota Project, tells the story of one four-year-old boy who was constantly defiant—the kind of child who would hit the other children with a toy fire truck. Instead of sending him to a corner, the teacher was instructed to remove him from the group and place him with another teacher. The message they hoped to impart: We are rejecting your behavior, but we're not rejecting you. Within a few months, the antisocial little boy learned to change his behavior.

If children aren't exposed to positive social situations until adolescence, however, the prognosis is poor. Like any complex behavior, human socialization requires an elaborate series of learning steps. So by adolescence, the teenager who missed out on many key social experiences as a child has a tremendous handicap to overcome.

Researchers are finding that each stage of life demands different kinds of competencies. This may be why sensitive learning periods exist. "When a baby is born it has to do two things at the same time," says biochemist Steven Rose of England's Open University. "One is that it has to survive as a baby. The second is that it has to grow into that very different organism which is a child and then finally an adult. And it is not simply the case that everything the baby does is a miniature version of what we see in the adult."

For example, the rooting reflex, which enables the baby to suckle is not a preliminary form of chewing. There's a transitional period in which the child must begin eating solid foods. And then other sorts of skills become necessary—the child must learn to walk, talk, form friendships and when adulthood is reached find a sexual partner. "But the child does not have to know all that at the beginning," Rose says. "So sensitive periods are necessary because we have to know how to do certain things at certain times during development."

During the course of a sensory system's development, several sensitive periods occur. In the case of human vision, for example, depth perception usually emerges by two months of age and after that remains relatively stable. But it takes the first five years of life to acquire the adult level of visual acuity that allows us to see fine details. And during that prolonged period, we are vulnerable to many developmental problems that can cause this process to go awry. For example, a drooping lid or an eye covered by a cataract—virtually anything that obstructs vision in one of the child's eyes for as few as seven days—can lead to a permanent blurring of sight. This condition, known as amblyopia is one of the most common ophthalmological disorders. Treatment works only if carried out within the sensitive period, before the final organization of certain cells in the visual cortex becomes fixed. After five years of age, no amount of visual stimulation is likely to reorganize the connections laid down when the young nervous system was developing.

Like molten plastic, the nervous system is, at its inception, highly pliable. But it quickly settles into a rigid cast—one that has been shaped by experience. Just what neurological events set the mold is not known. Some suggestive findings, however, come from the research of John Cronly-Dillon, a professor of ophthalmic optics at the University of Manchester Institute of Science and Technology, in England.

Working with colleague Gary Perry, Cronly-Dillon studied growth activity in the visual cortex of rat pups reared under normal light conditions. To measure growth, researchers monitored the rate at which certain cells synthesized tubulin, a protein vital for forming and maintaining nerve connections. The researchers found that tubulin production in the visual cortex remained at a low level until day 13, which marks the onset of the sensitive period for visual learning. It coincides with the moment when the animal first opens its eyes. At that time, tubulin production soars, indicating a rise in growth activity.

Cronly-Dillon and Perry found that the rat's visual cortex continues to grow for the next week and then declines. By the end of the critical period, when the pup is roughly five weeks old, tubulin production drops to the level attained before the eyes open.

To Cronly-Dillon the surplus of tubulin at the beginning of the critical period and its subsequent cutback have profound implications. "It means that an uncommonly large number of nerve connections can exist at the peak of the critical period, but only a small fraction of them will be maintained at the end," he says. "So the question, of course, is which nerve connections will be kept?"

If Cronly-Dillon is correct, experience probably stabilizes those connections most often used during the sensitive period. "So by definition," he says, "what remains is most critical for survival."

Cronly-Dillon's work elaborates on a theory Spanish neurophysiologist Ramon Y. Cajal advanced at the turn of the century. According to this view, which has been gaining broader acceptance in recent times, brain development resembles natural selection. Just as the forces of natural selection ensure the survival of the fittest, so do similar forces preserve the most useful brain circuits.

The beauty of this model is that it could explain why the brain is as exquisitely adapted to its immediate surroundings, just as the mouthparts of insects are so perfectly matched to the sexual organs of the flowers they pollinate. The textures, shapes, sounds, and odors we perceive best may have left their imprint years ago in the neural circuitry of the developing mind.

There is also a certain economic appeal to this outlook. Why, for example, should

Japanese adults keep active a neural circuit that permits the distinction between *r* and *l* sounds when neither of these linguistic components is present in their native tongue?

Yet another economic advantage of the theory is that it would explain how nature can forge something as intricate as the brain out of a relatively limited amount of genetic material. "It looks as though what genetics does is *sort of* make a brain," Blakemore says. "We only have about one hundred thousand genes—and that's to make an entire body. Yet the brain alone has trillions of nerve cells, each one forming as many as ten thousand connections with its neighbors. So imagine the difficulty of trying to encode every step of the wiring process in our DNA."

This vast discrepancy between genes and connections, according to Blakemore, can be overcome by encoding the DNA the specifications for a "rough brain." "Everything gets roughly laid down in place," Blakemore says. "But the wiring of the young nervous system is far too rich and diffuse. So the brain overconnects and then uses a selection process to fine-tune the system."

The brain of an eight-month-old human fetus is actually estimated to have two to three times more nerve cells than an adult brain does. Just before birth, there is a massive death of unnecessary brain cells, a process that continues through early childhood and then levels off. Presumably many nerve connections that fall into disuse vanish. But that is only part of the selection process—and possibly a small part at that.

According to Blakemore, many neural circuits remain in place but cease to function after a certain age. "I would venture a guess," he says, "that as many as ninety percent of the connections you see in the adult brain are nonfunctional. The time when circuits can be switched on or off probably varies for different parts of the cerebral cortex—depending on what functions they control—and would coincide with the sensitive period of learning. Once the on-off switch becomes frozen, the sensitive period is over."

This doesn't mean, however, that new circuits can't grow. There appears to be a fine-tuning of perception coinciding with these developmental events. And as the brain becomes a finer sieve, filtering out all but a limited amount of sensory input, its strategy for storing information appears to change.

"Studies indicate that as many as fifty percent of very young children recall things in pictures," says biochemist Rose. "And by the time we're about four or five, we tend to lose our eidetic [photographic] memory and develop sequential methods of recall."

To Rose, who is studying the neurological mechanisms that underlie learning, this shift in memory process may have an intriguing logic. "To be a highly adaptable organism like man, capable of living in a lot of different environments, one must start out with a brain that takes in everything," Rose explains. "And as you develop, you select what is important and what is not important to remember. If you went on remembering absolutely everything, it would be disastrous."

The Russian neurologist A. R. Luria had a patient cursed with such a memory—the man could describe rooms he'd been in years before, pieces of conversations he'd overheard. His memory became such an impediment that he could not hold even a clerk's job: while listening to instructions, so many associations for each word would arise that he couldn't focus on what was being said. The only position he could manage was as a memory man in a theatrical company.

"The crucial thing then," Rose says, "is that you must learn what to *forget*."

Some components of the brain, however, must retain their plasticity into adulthood—otherwise, no further learning would be possible, says neuroscientist Bill Greenough, of the University of Illinois, at Urbana-Champaign. While the adult brain cannot generate new brain cells, Greenough has uncovered evidence that it does continue to generate new *nerve connections*. But as the brain ages, the rate at which it produces these connections slows.

If the young brain can be likened to a sapling sprouting shoots in all directions, then the adult brain is more akin to a tree, whose growth is confined primarily to budding regions. "In the mature brain," Greenough says, "neural connections appear to pop up systematically, precisely where they're needed."

Early experience, then, provides the foundation on which all subsequent knowledge and skills build. "That's why it's extraordinarily difficult to change certain aspects of personality as an adult," says neuroscientist Jonathan Winson, of Rockefeller University.

"Psychiatrists have an expression: 'Insight is wonderful, but the psyche fights back.' Unfortunately, one of the drawbacks of critical-period learning is that a lot of misconceptions and unreasonable fears can become frozen in our minds during this very vulnerable period in our development."

Greenough acknowledges that the system isn't perfect; nevertheless, it works to our advantage because you can't build on a wobbly nervous system. "You've got to know who your mother is, and you've got to have perceptual skills," he explains. "These and other types of learning have to jell quickly, or all further development would halt."

Can these insights into the developing brain help educators to devise new strategies for teaching?

"We're a very long way from being able to apply the work of neurobiologists to what chalk-faced teachers are trying to do," says Open University's Rose.

But he can see the rough outline of a new relationship between neurobiology and education, which excites him. "We can now say with considerable certainty that there are important advantages to growing up in an enriched environment," he says. "That does not mean that you should be teaching three-year-olds Einstein's theory of relativity on the grounds that you will be turning them into geniuses later on. But it's probably fair to say that if you want bright kids, you should cuddle them a lot as babies because that increases the number of neural connections produced in the brain."

Although early learning tends to overshadow the importance of later experience, mental development never ceases. Recent studies indicate that our intellectual abilities continue to expand well into our eighties, provided the brain has not been injured or diseased. Most crucial for maintaining mental vigor, according to Greenough, is staying active and taking on new challenges. In his rat studies, he found that lack of stimulation—much more than age—was the factor that limited the formation of new neural connections in the adult brain.

As long as we don't isolate ourselves as we grow older one very important type of mental faculty may even improve. Called crystallized intelligence, this ability allows us to draw on the store of accumulated knowledge to provide alternate solutions to complicated problems. Analyzing complex political or military strategies, for example, would exploit crystallized intelligence.

There is a danger in believing that because the brain's anatomical boundries are roughly established early in life, all mental capabilities are restricted, too. "Intelligence is not something static that can be pinned down with an I.Q. test like butterflies on a sheet of cardboard," says Rose. "It is a constant interplay between internal processes and external forces."

To be sure, many types of learning do favor youth. As violinist Isaac Stern says, "If you haven't begun playing violin by age eight, you'll never be great." But in the opinion of Cronly-Dillon, the best time for learning other types of skills may be much later in life. Although he will not elaborate on this until further studies are done, he believes we may even have sensitive periods with very late onsets. "There's a real need," Cronly-Dillon says, "to define all the different types of sensitive periods so that education can take advantage of biological optimums."

It is said that the ability to learn in later life depends on the retention of childlike innocence. "This old saw," insists Cronly-Dillon, "could have a neurological basis."

Reading 9

This article discusses the impact of early hearing loss on important processes in the brains of chicks. It demonstrates the importance of laboratory research in helping scientists to understand the complex relationship between the environment, behavior, and the nervous system. Can you speculate on how sound may affect developing humans? Based on what you have learned, would you recommend limiting the use of sonograms on pregnant women? (Some physicians have suggested that the sound waves are like sonic booms inside the womb.)

Early Hearing Loss and Brain Development

By J. Greenberg

Severe damage to an infant's or fetus's inner ear can trigger damage to certain areas of the brain and impede brain development, according to studies with chicks and chick embryos by researchers in Seattle. Exposing adult chicks to the same type of ear damage—roughly equivalent to that induced by extremely loud noise—results in no such brain damage, reports Edwin W. Rubel, professor of otolaryngology at the University of Washington School of Medicine.

While he says it is premature to directly extrapolate these findings to humans, Rubel nevertheless suggests that "human fetuses and infants also may be hypersensitive to certain types of noises and that this sensitivity changes during the course of early development." He reported his results recently in Chicago at the annual meeting of the American Association for the Advancement of Science.

In a series of experiments, Rubel and his colleagues surgically destroyed inner-ear cells in chick embryos and in baby chicks up to 6 weeks of age. (The same type of destruction could be triggered by "high-intensity" sound, he says, equivalent to that found in some industrial settings or "on a jet runway.") Left intact were neurons that projected from the inner ear into the brain.

As little as two days later, the researchers discovered "dramatic cell loss" in the cochlear nucleus of the brainstem, Rubel reports. In addition, the brain cells that did remain in the affected regions had atrophied. "We found fewer and smaller neurons in areas of the brain corresponding to the areas where inner ear cells had been destroyed," he says.

In addition, he and his colleagues found that the affected brain areas displayed no protein synthesis and had retarded levels of certain enzyme metabolism. These changes were not seen in chicks older than 6 weeks.

"This tells us that early in life, [brain cells] not only receive information from the periphery [the ear] but are metabolically dependent on stimulation from the periphery," Rubel said in an interview. "At some point in life—at least in the chicken—there is a metabolic uncoupling, although the information coupling remains the same."

Rubel's latest work is based on a number of previous studies, including his own, suggesting that the inner ear's cochlea codes for sound differently in the infant than in the adult. Those studies found that whereas in the adult, the base of the cochlea responds to high-frequency sounds and the apex of the cochlea to low-frequency sounds, the opposite is true in infants and embryos.

Whether or not these shifts in sensitivity are involved in protecting the adult from ear-damage-induced brain damage is not known.

"The question is," Rubel says, "can we find out how adults are protected and can we provide this protection for young children?" Although there are conflicting views regarding fetal hearing, Rubel says, "we do know that a lot of low-frequency sound gets into the uterus from the external environment and that the baby is hearing." And though he cautions against jumping to conclusions from his chick studies, he adds, "If it were my wife, I certainly wouldn't let her use a jackhammer."

Reading 10

The use of fetuses and fetal brain tissue in medical research and treatment of disease raises many ethical questions. Clearly, some troubling dilemmas accompany modern medical advances. Should researchers be allowed to continue research on fetal tissue while ethicists and doctors sort out the problem? Who should regulate the use of fetal tissue? Doctors? The government? As you read this article, think about your own attitudes and feelings regarding this very delicate issue.

A Balancing Act of Life and Death

By Christine Gorman

After years of research, doctors feel they are ready to try to alleviate many incurable conditions, ranging from congenital heart defects to degenerative nerve diseases, through the transplanting of organs and tissues. Their pioneering triumphs, however, have created a Faustian dilemma. Each year in the U.S. hundreds of infants die who could have been saved by a new heart; literally millions of people with diseases like Parkinson's and Alzheimer's may eventually benefit from tissue implants. Should physicians manipulate the definitions of life and death to meet this growing demand for donor tissue? The question is taking on a new immediacy as doctors begin transplanting tissue from once unimagined sources: aborted fetuses and anencephalic newborns.

Surgeons at Loma Linda University Medical Center in California only last October transplanted a heart into newborn Paul Holc. What made the transplant different was that the donor, a Canadian infant known as Baby Gabriel, was born anencephalic, that is, without most of her brain. Like virtually all anencephalics, she could not have survived more than a few days outside the womb; unlike most, Gabriel died before her healthy organs deteriorated. Then, early in January, surgeons in Mexico City announced that for the first time, they had successfully grafted tissue from a miscarried fetus into the brains of two Parkinson's victims, who have since improved dramatically.

To many, the fetal-tissue transplant raised a troubling question: Should doctors be allowed to use tissue from intentionally aborted fetuses to alleviate an otherwise hopeless condition? The Baby Gabriel case focuses on even knottier dilemmas: Should laws defining death be rewritten to allow the "harvesting" of anencephalic donors? Should their existence be prolonged solely to enable doctors to take their organs?

Such issues are not academic. In the past few months, TIME has learned, Baby Gabriel's Canadian physicians kept three other anencephalic children on respirators in order to use their organs for transplantation. "I can't imagine a time when there have been so many advances in medical research that have raised such serious issues," says Neonatologist Lawrence Platt of the University of Southern California. Declares Arthur Caplan, director of the Center for Biomedical Ethics at the University of Minnesota: "Our fear is that somehow reproduction has shifted away from an act that creates a family into an arena in which money, profit and benefit for others start to enter."

Parents of anencephalics have been in the forefront of the campaign to make use of their infants' organs, as a way of making their brief, tragic lives meaningful. Such babies are often born with no skin or skull above their eyes. They have only an exposed bud of a brain and a brain stem that keeps their heart and lungs working erratically. Under current state laws, death occurs when all brain activity has ceased. Anencephalic infants are technically alive until their brain stem stops functioning. By then, however, the increasingly insufficient oxygen supply has ruined any potentially useful organs.

For some doctors, the respirator is an ideal solution: it assures a proper oxygen supply while putting off the infant's inevitable death. "There is no ethical problem with using the organs after the child is dead," says George Annas, professor of health law at Boston University School of Medicine. "The problem lies in the process of getting the child from alive to dead." There are certainly precedents for keeping donors alive artificially for the benefit of others. Accident victims, for example, are frequently kept on respirators to keep their organs fresh.

But the problem with anencephalics is starkly different: Doctors frequently do not know when death has legally occurred. Conventional measures of brain death are useless. Ethicist Caplan suggests that doctors rely on an older standard: that death occurs when the infant's pulse and breathing have stopped. Thus anencephalics would be taken off the respirator at set intervals to see when spontaneous breathing had ceased. When it stopped, the infants would be pronounced dead and their organs taken. The few medical centers like Loma Linda that handle anencephalic transplants currently follow similar protocols.

The principal difference between using anencephalics and aborted fetuses as sources for organs, Caplan says, is a matter of parental motive. Few doctors have problems with using the tissues of miscarried fetuses. But in the weeks since the Mexican tissue transplant, a handful of women have considered the possibility of getting pregnant for the purpose of providing tissue to treat themselves or a family member. Ray Leith, a young woman whose aging father has Parkinson's disease, declared her willingness to do so on national television early this year; her father refused the offer. Others have raised even broader fears that, as Feminist Author Gena Corea puts it, "women will be pressured by doctors and families or by economic need, to become fetal factories."

To prevent such abuses, doctors and ethicists suggest banning the sale of fetal tissue worldwide and prohibiting women from designating who would receive their fetus'

organs. Once such safeguards are in place, however, they believe that physicians can properly use tissue from abortuses for research and treatment. Except in the case of miscarriages, Dr. John Willke, president of the National Right to Life Committee, vehemently disagrees. "The abuse is not in the sale of those tissues," he says, "but in killing the baby in the first place." Janice Raymond, professor of women's studies at the University of Massachusetts at Amherst, is concerned that such attitudes, as well as practices like surrogate motherhood, have already begun to erode women's control over the childbearing process. "No one is holding a gun to any woman," she says. "But I think it's important to look at the entire context in which this issue of fetal tissue is arising." That may be easier said than done.

Reading 11

This article offers advice on how to understand and "talk back" to the automatic reactions recognized as stress. Can you think of examples of good stress and bad stress in your own life? Can you identify a potentially dangerously stressful situation? What changes could you make in your behavior that might alter the way you (your brain) responds?

Stress Can Be Good For You

By Susan Seliger

Every weeknight in New York, thousands of people remain hunched over their desks until well past the dinner hour. They leave the office with stuffed briefcases, unwind with a couple of drinks and a late meal, and finish their day's labors with a few hours of reading in bed. In the morning, they crowd into buses, trains, and cars and inch their way back to the office. Noontime finds them waiting on line to get into overpriced, understaffed restaurants. And when the sun sets on the city, once again those thousands of desk lamps will shine on in almost empty offices.

Stress? Of course.

A sure prescription for an early grave? Nonsense.

It's not that stress can't be harmful. It's been linked to every disease from asthma to heart disease to ulcers. But a number of recent studies have turned upside down the prevailing wisdom about who is most at risk. More important, these studies have found that stress is not always harmful, that it is in fact a crucial, often productive part of life—in

short, that stress can actually be good for you. A person who feels in control of his life can channel the stressful energy that accompanies both the drive to achieve and city living and can make himself healthier than those who avoid cities, conflict, and competition altogether. And this new research raises serious questions about the multi-million-dollar anti-stress industry, with its 72-million annual tranquilizer prescriptions and its hundreds of stress clinics and counseling businesses—most often aimed at exactly the wrong people.

According to the latest research, the ability to control stress is within each person's power. It is the perception of and attitude about both self and environment that most influence whether a person will be hurt by stress. What researchers are finding is that bad stress is triggered not by the pressures of decision-making but rather by the feeling that one's decisions are useless, that life is overwhelming and beyond personal control.

Those people making the decisions, the high-powered, high-pressure executives that many have believed are most vulnerable, turn out, therefore, not to be. And it is not that they are genetically more fit to cope that accounts for their rise to the top. It is their attitude. Yet, the notion that they are at risk has been perpetuated by those selling stress services to employers who are all too willing to spend money for stress counseling for their top people. Unfortunately, it's the underlings these managers supervise who are at far greater risk, people the employers pay little attention to.

"An executive who makes a lot of decisions is better off than his secretary," says Dr. Kenneth Greenspan, director of the Center for Stress Related Disorders, at Columbia-Presbyterian Medical Center. "Secretaries—along with assembly-line workers—are at a great deal of risk from stress because all their decisions are predetermined: when they start work, when they stop, what they do. They fear that they can be easily replaced; they see themselves as victims. And that produces bad stress."

When she came to New York from the Midwest to be a nurse, Joanna Sedgwick* never imagined she would experience stress. She thought stress only affected higher-level people, like doctors. Sedgwick moved into an apartment on the Upper West Side and soon found a job. She also found bedpans, bureaucracy, and belittling treatment by doctors. By the end of a workday, she invariably had a migraine.

Seeking relief, Sedgwick went to the Center for Stress Related Disorders. The biofeedback treatment she was given eased her pain, but it didn't stop the migraines from coming on. With encouragement from Dr. Greenspan, she came to realize that what was wrong with her were her feelings about her work.

"I got no respect; I couldn't make any decisions. Doctors looked down their noses at me and the other nurses," Sedgwick recalls. She ended up returning to school and became a research nurse. One year later, she was appointed head administrative nurse. She gets respect; her headaches are gone.

"I'm under a lot more stress now than I was as an ordinary nurse, and I work harder, but it's different," Sedgwick says. "I decide about treatment; I supervise other nurses. I no

longer feel as if everyone is running my life. And I don't get those migraines anymore."

Nor does Joe Carter get his workday headaches anymore, or the dizziness and anxiety he felt as he headed home at night. Joe works for a utility company, managing about 60 people and answering to several bosses. Unlike most of the middle managers around him, he has no college education, and that disparity worried him. Whenever some minor thing went wrong at work—and there were often emergencies that made him work more than 24 hours straight—he used to worry that he'd lose his job. His supervisors were much quicker to point out his mistakes than to pat him on the back.

And no relaxation awaited him when he got home at night. His wife always seemed to have some chore for him to do, and he found himself constantly worrying about earning enough money to put his teenage children through college.

Finally, Carter decided to undergo biofeedback and relaxation training at the Center for Stress Related Disorders, and that led to a more important decision: to talk to his bosses about their assessment of his work. He found that they regarded him as a more valuable employee than he had thought. His symptoms began to fade. Soon he found his confidence had increased enough to allow him to feel comfortable telling his wife he wanted to spend time at home just relaxing with her. If not as dramatic as Joanna Sedgwick's, Carter's recovery proved the same point: An increase in his self-confidence led to an increase in his sense of control over his life and eliminated the chronic stress he was undergoing.

Dr. Greenspan himself could be considered a stress case. Having squeezed three interviews into the morning, he rushes to the deli around the corner and wolfs down a sandwich so that he can race back to the center, see more patients, and then buzz over to another wing of the hospital to check on his latest research project. He talks fast; he walks fast. By most objective standards, he is under a great deal of stress. "But it isn't *bad* stress," insists Greenspan. "I love what I'm doing, and I know how and when to ease up. That makes all the difference."

So does success. In 1975, the Metropolitan Life Insurance Company examined 1,078

*The patients' names have been changed.

men who held one of the three top executive positions in Fortune 500 companies and found that their mortality rate was 37 percent lower than that of other white males of a comparable age.

The explanation may come in a study of 259 executives at Illinois Bell conducted by Suzanne Kobasa, Ph.D., a psychologist at the University of Chicago. She found that certain people seemed to be particularly able to handle stress—their health was not affected no matter how intense their job pressures or how ominous their family medical history. Based on her research, Kobasa concluded that if people felt a sense of purpose, viewed change as a challenge and not a threat, and believed that they were in control of their lives, they were not adversely affected by stress.

Executive women—presumably under a great deal of stress to make it in the corporate world—must feel some of this sense of control. Recent studies show no signs that their push into the upper ranks is causing them bad health. Metropolitan Life's 1979 study of 2,352 women listed in *Who's Who* showed their annual death rate to be 29 percent lower than that of their contemporaries. Indeed, the groups of women who have the highest rates of heart disease are secretaries and saleswomen—"women in jobs with little security, status, or control," explains Suzanne Haynes, Ph.D.

Another myth is that city life is bad for mental health. Back in 1954, Dr. Leo Srole, now professor emeritus of social sciences at Columbia University's Center for Gerontology, did a study of Manhattan residents that seemed to confirm that "stressful" living conditions in the city were driving people crazy. Dr. Srole reported that 23.4 percent of his white midtown Manhattan sample were suffering some kind of "emotional impairment" that interfered with their daily lives. That percentage seemed high until 1975, when Dr. Srole matched it with the findings of a similar Cornell University sample of a rural county in Nova Scotia. His conclusion was startling: New Yorkers had a "significantly lower" incidence of mental impairment than did the rural folk. According to Dr. Srole, one reason may be that "cities have resources for satisfaction that rural communities don't have."

These findings are reinforced by a 1978 report by the President's Commission on Mental Health that found that "rural communities tend to be characterized by a higher-than-average rate of psychiatric disorder, particularly depression... by restricted opportunities for developing adequate coping mechanisms for facing stress... by an acceptance of conditions as being beyond individual control."

Researchers have come to believe that there are actually three kinds of stress: normal stress; distress, or bad stress, which is normal stress that has become chronic; and eustress, or good stress.

Each of these kinds of stress is basically a three-stage series of reactions within the body that enable it to adapt to change. Since life is constant change, such reactions are obviously important; without them the body cannot survive. These reactions are most extreme (and thus easiest to monitor) under acute stress, a form of normal stress that one feels when threatened—a car swerving toward you; a child about to put his hand into a fire; the sound of footsteps behind you on a dark, lonely street.

The first stage of any stress reaction is alarm. The endocrine glands release hormones, including adrenaline; the heartbeat speeds up, as does breathing; oxygen-rich blood is directed away from the skin to the brain and the skeletal muscles for fast action. Pupils dilate to take in more information; hormones enter the blood to increase its coagulating ability in case of injury; and digestion slows so that more of the body's energy can be devoted to fighting or fleeing. The surge of energy, concentration, and power that comes with the stress alarm enables people to perform in a crisis—sometimes beyond their normal physical capacities.

Once the alarm stage of stress has passed, the body enters the second stage, one of recuperation in which it repairs any damage caused by the demands of the fight-or-flight response. This is the stage where one can say "Whew!" The third stage is a return to the body's normal state of relaxed alertness.

A diagram of this process would look something like this:

These large sawtooth jags of acute (or normal) short-term stress are part of regular living and are necessary for it. "A certain amount of stress is needed to tune you up for action and keep you on your toes," writes Dr. Hans Selye, the granddaddy of stress research.

Bad stress is normal or acute stress that becomes chronic, continuing for weeks and months so that the body never gets much time to say "Whew!" and recuperate. This kind of stress means trouble.

A normal, healthy life pattern might look like this on the stress diagram:

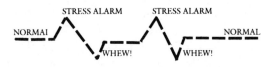

On the other hand, chronic stress might look like this:

One person who found herself in a chronic-stress cycle was Leslie Friedman, who ran a personnel department in a bank, overseeing the careers of about twenty employees. Friedman worked more than 50 hours a week, and when she went home at night, she had a second job: helping her husband with his business. Friedman didn't think her bosses appreciated her efforts, and by noon each day she'd have a splitting headache and a backache too. But at the end of the evening, although she was dead tired, she couldn't fall asleep. In the morning she would drag herself out of bed and begin the punishing cycle all over again.

Friedman was able to break out. She discovered that her boss didn't expect her to do all that she was doing and that that was the reason she didn't get the appreciation she thought she deserved. So she quit and found another job, where her skills at managing people were put to good use. She also convinced her husband that he had to hire an assistant. Going home doesn't mean going to a second job anymore, and, although Friedman still works very long hours, she says that the challenge of the new job seems to be energizing rather than enervating her.

Chronic stress can inflict real bodily harm. First, it can lower resistance to disease. According to Dr. Paul J. Rosch, an internist and president of the American Institute of Stress, in Yonkers, "interferon, a non-specific polypeptide which is one of the basic defenses against virus infections and is now being investigated in the treatment of cancer, is also suppressed under some conditions of emotional stress." If acute stress is occasional, the body's immune system is thrown out of whack.

Second, repeated and unremitting episodes of acute stress mean repeated release of adrenaline. If the problem prompts no physical exertion to use up the adrenaline—and most stresses in modern life are of a mental rather than a physical nature—then excess adrenaline will remain in the system and can play a part in the buildup of cholesterol in the arteries that can lead to heart disease.

There are early, recognizable signs that can allow a person to avoid entering a cycle of long-term, chronic stress. In addition, people can actually increase their capacity to cope with potentially stressful events.

"Knowing the danger signals can help you operate successfully at much higher levels of stress," says Dr. Sidney Lecker, director of Corporate Stress Control Services, in Manhattan. Once you become aware of the symptoms, there are definite steps you can take (see box on page 67) so that, as Dr. Lecker puts it, "you can go back into the thick of things and operate on the ragged edge of disaster—safely."

The flip side of the stress coin is eustress. It comes from successfully rising to a challenge, feeling confidence and a sense of control over one's destiny. Dr. Rosch believes that people who thrive on stress might die without it. "I take care of patients who are recuperating from heart attacks," he says. "Now, the ideal prescription for one guy is to lie on a beach in the Bahamas, but for another kind of patient that same prescription would be lethal.

"I'm convinced that good stress is healthy," continues Rosch, who began his stress research three decades ago with Selye. "Look at symphony conductors. They undergo physical exertion, deadlines, traveling, dealing with prima donnas in the orchestra. But, on the other hand, they have pride of accomplishment, the approbation of their peers, the plaudits of the audience.

"Look at the life and health records of conductors and you'll see it's outstanding. they live forever. Look at them." Waving his arms enthusiastically, he checks off their names: "Stokowski, Fiedler, Toscanini." He pauses. "The real secret to a long and healthy life is to enjoy what you're doing and be good at it. It's not to avoid stress."

One of the leading popular advocates of the theory that good stress may have the power to heal is Norman Cousins, the former editor of *Saturday Review*. Cousins says that laughter is one of those forms of good stress—and, as he wrote in *The New England Journal of Medicine* and in his book *Anatomy of an Illness*, he's convinced it saved his life.

Laughter? Yes, laughter. It might seem to be just another form of physical exertion, making the body respond much as it does under any kind of acute stress: The oxygen supply to the brain increases; the heartbeat speeds up, rushing oxygen-rich blood to the muscles; the pupils dilate; and so on. But recent brain research indicates that something far more powerful is at work on a biochemical level: Endorphins, the body's natural painkillers, are also being released. What the researchers do not yet know is whether endorphins, which may actually reverse some of the damage of the distress reaction, are secreted in equal amounts under all kinds of stress or in greater quantities during eustress.

"We're just on the frontier of discovering the nature of the biochemical reactions of stress, such as the release of endorphins," says Dr. Lorenz Ng, former chief of the Pain Studies Program at the National Institute on Drug Abuse, in Bethesda, Maryland, and medical director of the Washington Pain Center. "It's the newest thing in stress research, and it may lead us to understand the differences between good and bad stress," says Ng.

Dr. Rosch believes that the biochemical effects of eustress may actually reverse the course of various diseases, including cancer. He's written on this subject in a chapter of *Cancer, Stress and Death* for the "Sloan-Kettering Institute Cancer Series." "Cancer and other diseases set in when the immune system weakens," Rosch says. "There is evidence that on the cell walls of lymphocytes responsible for mediating the immune response there are receptor sites for ACTH, which is the prime hormone released under stress, endorphins, metenkephalin, and other brain hormones. This implies that the brain can talk directly to the immune system and that the immune system talks back. The intriguing possibility is that people may be able to tune in to that conversation—and even influence it, just as they can be trained to influence other systems, like pulse rate and skin temperature, through biofeedback. People may have the ability to cure themselves."

Actually, the idea of stress's being healthy has been around for a long time. In *Stress Without Distress*, published in 1974, Selye explained that this was possible, but no one in the stress field paid much attention. They were too busy making a living convincing people that stress was affecting their health. They wanted people to continue popping down their daily anti-stress pill and to spend $1,500 per week at anti-stress clinics. "Stress has become so popular that a variety of entrepreneurs and charlatans have capitalized on it," says Rosch.

The medical profession is also campaigning against stress, acknowledges Rosch. For example, Dr. Theodore Cooper, the dean of the Cornell University Medical College, headed a three-year program called "The Consequences of Stress: The Medical and Social Implications of Prescribing Tranquilizers." The program's message went by closed-circuit television lectures to nearly 20,000 physicians in 26 cities and 100,000 more physicians through similar tape recordings. The financier for all this was Hoffmann-LaRoche, Inc., makers of Valium, which is the biggest-selling tranquilizer in the world.

Yet, there is still great dispute in the medical community over the usefulness of tranquilizers for dealing with stress. Many doctors are convinced that they can do more harm than good. "Avoidance of stress has led to abuse of tranquilizers," says Dr. Nelson Hendler, the head of Mensana, a pain clinic in Baltimore, and a psychiatric consultant at Johns Hopkins Hospital's Pain Treatment Center. Valium doesn't help stress, insists Hendler. It inhibits the release of serotonin, which stimulates sleep naturally. And it may interfere with stage-three sleep—perhaps the most restful stage in the sleep cycle, in which REM (rapid eye movement) sleep occurs—and stage-four sleep, which is the deepest.

"One in three people who goes to a doctor about stress gets a prescription for a tranquilizer," Hendler says. "Most people should not fill it."

The anti-stress brigade has also been joined by hundreds of companies that provide counseling on stress, alcoholism, and other problems. Millions of workers are now eligible for such benefits. For instance, Isidore Lefkowitz Elgort, an advertising agency in New York, pays for employees to attend T.M. sessions to help them handle stress.

Many of these efforts may indeed be useful. However, a good number are misguided—aimed at the people under the least stress, the executives, instead of at their underlings. Other anti-stress efforts seem to cause more problems than they cure.

"Most organizations buy one-shot educational packages—a lecture on stress," says James Manuso, Ph.D., creator of the in-house biofeedback stress-counseling center at Equitable Life in New York. "Someone goes in there and tells the employees how much stress they're under, scares the hell out of them, and then leaves. That just *adds* to the stress."

Even Dr. Roy Menninger, president of the Menninger Foundation, in Topeka, Kansas, which charges New York corporation executives up to $2,300 each to learn, among other things, how to handle stress, believes the view that "stress is bad" has gone too far. Dr. Lecker is more emphatic: "Stress is essential for meeting challenges. If you didn't have stress, you'd be dead."

How to Convert Bad Stress Into Good

There are certain physical signals that provide a warning that the body's habitual response to stress is becoming destructive. People can learn to recognize these signals and to change their characteristic responses to daily tensions. They thus can endure higher levels of stress and perhaps even profit from them.

The telltale signals:

☐ Cold hands, especially if one is colder than the other.

☐ Indigestion, diarrhea, too frequent urination.

☐ Being susceptible to every cold or virus that goes around (which could mean that the physical strains of distress are weakening the immune system).

☐ Muscle spasms or a soreness and tightness in the jaw, back of the neck, shoulders, or lower back.

☐ Shortness of breath.

☐ Headaches, tiredness, sleeping too much or too little.

☐ Becoming suddenly accident-prone.

When someone recognizes any of these signals, he should stop what he is doing—if only for two or three minutes—take several deep breaths, and try to relax. If the tension also shows itself through tapping toes or drumming fingers, he should stand up and do a few jumping jacks or take a brisk walk around the office or the block, trying to look at everything as if for the first time.

The most important key to defusing distress is to become conscious of that inner voice each person has. Human beings are constantly assessing themselves and their environment and reporting silently to themselves: "This looks threatening; I don't think I can handle it. I certainly can't handle it without a cigarette. . . ."

Many people are not conscious of this internal commentator, but if a person learns to listen to the way he talks to himself, he may find that he is usually not being as encouraging as he could be—that he is actually making matters worse for himself.

Instead of standing on the line at the bank checking his watch and listening to his inner voice computing how long it has taken "those incompetent tellers" to handle each transaction, worrying about how late he will be to his appointment, and wondering why he didn't get cash for the weekend yesterday, he should make his inner voice be soothing: "I don't like waiting on this line, but there is nothing I can do about it now, so I might as well relax. Look how tense everyone else is getting. It's actually kind of funny."

Another trick is to stop thinking about the time. It may be slipping by, but counting the seconds only fritters away energy and activates the stress response. Dr. Meyer Friedman and Dr. Ray H. Rosenman, the authors of *Type A Behavior and Your Heart*, found that time consciousness, or "hurry sickness," was a key personality trait of the heart-attack-prone Type A personality. One stress researcher says she found that simply removing her wristwatch for several weeks greatly reduced the time pressures she felt.

To convert bad stress to good, remember the following:

Before an event expected to be stressful, visualize what may take place. Such a rehearsal will make the actual event seem familiar, helping one to relax and handle the situation with confidence.

During a tense situation, such as taking a test or meeting a tight deadline, talk nicely to oneself, don't harp on poor preparation or performance. Instead, one should make one's inner voice offer praise for what one did accomplish, and reassurance that the situation isn't so bad after all.

Afterward, luxuriate in the relief of the burden's being lifted. Even if things didn't go well, avoid puritanical self-criticism. This refreshing interlude can help strengthen the system to better resist the wear and tear of future distress.

"Any bad stress can be turned around," insists Dr. Kenneth Greenspan, "if you take steps that make you feel that you are controlling your life and it isn't controlling you."

ADDITIONAL RESOURCES

Books and Articles

Alper, J. "The Chaotic Brain: New Models of Behavior." *Psychology Today* (May 1989). Seemingly chaotic patterns of electrical activity of the brain are being better understood, thanks to the new "science of chaos." Chaotic models help link such patterns to changes in behavioral states.

Dawkins, Richard. *The Selfish Gene*. New York: Oxford University Press, 1976. A discussion and critique of sociobiology, the controversial science tracing such traits as aggressiveness to human genes.

Gardner, Lytt I. "Deprivation Dwarfism." *Scientific American* (July 1972): 76–82. Emotional deprivation can be damaging to a child's physical as well as psychological development. In some cases, a lack of love and support even leads to stunted growth and childhood balding. This article looks at the processes behind deprivation dwarfism.

Wartman, Richard J. "Nutrients That Modify Brain Functions." *Scientific American* (April 1982): 50–59. Nutrients in our food can act like drugs. Certain nutrients give rise to significant changes in the brain's chemical makeup, changes that affect how we think and feel.

THE DEVELOPING CHILD

When we hear the baby laugh, it is the loveliest thing that can happen to us.

Sigmund Freud

Unit 5 looks at how advances in technology and methodology have revealed the abilities of newborn infants, giving researchers a better understanding of the role infants play in shaping their environment. In contrast to the nature versus nurture debates of the past, today's researchers concentrate on how heredity and environment interact to contribute to the developmental process.

Research has shown that genetics, culture, and environment all play a role in child development.

OBJECTIVES

After viewing the television program and completing the assigned readings, you should be able to:

1. Discuss the nature vs. nurture controversy

2. Summarize the results of research on critical periods in human development

3. Explain the difference between genotype and phenotype and how genes control heredity

4. Describe the different research methods used to study development and explain the strengths and weaknesses of each

5. Describe the influence of heredity and environment on motor development and on personality characteristics

6. Define the Piagetian concepts of schemas, assimilation, and accommodation

7. Describe Piaget's four stages of cognitive development. Explain why Piaget underestimated the cognitive skills of young children

8. Relate the concept of attachment to "separation anxiety" and "stranger anxiety." Discuss attachment deprivation and the effects of secure and insecure attachment

9. Describe Diana Baumrind's three styles of parenting and indicate the influence that each may have on the personalities of the children

READING ASSIGNMENT

After viewing Program 5, read pages 403–448 in *Psychology: Science, Behavior and Life*. Your instructor may also assign the anthology selections for Unit 5.

KEY TERMS AND CONCEPTS

As you read the assignment, pay particular attention to these terms, which are defined on the given pages in the text.

prenatal (417)	dizygotic twins (410)
nature-nurture controversy (403)	concordant (410)
quantitative (404)	genotypes (410)
qualitative (404)	phenotypes (410)
critical periods (405)	heterozygous (410)
imprinting (406)	homozygous (410)
cross sectional design (407)	dominant gene (411)
longitudinal design (407)	recessive gene (411)
cross sequential design (408)	multifactoral inheritance (411)
birth cohort (408)	sex-linked inheritance (411)
gametes (408)	Huntington's disease (412)
germ cells (408)	recombinant DNA technology (413)
zygote (408)	phenylketonuria (414)
genes (410)	Down syndrome (414)
DNA (deoxyribonucleic acid) (410)	genetic counseling (414)
monozygotic twins (410)	karotype (414)

artificial embryonation (415)   object permanence (424)
amniocentesis (415)   preoperational stage (424)
chorionic villi sampling (416)   centration (426)
genetic engineering (416)   decentration (426)
embryo (417)   conservation (427)
fetus (417)   egocentrism (426)
cephalocaudal (421)   concrete operations stage (426)
proximodistal (421)   attachment (431)
schemas (423)   formal operations stage (428)
sensorimotor stage (424)   permissive (436)
assimilation (423)   authoritative (436)
accommodation (423)   authoritarian (436)

The following term is used in Program 5 but is not defined in the text.

stage theory—a theory that describes development as a fixed sequence of distinct periods of life

PROGRAM SUMMARY

Historically, the debate about the true essence of human nature was defined as "nature versus nurture." Empiricists, like John Locke, gave all credit for human development to experience and believed that we arrived in this world as blank tablets devoid of knowledge or skills. Nativists sided with Jean-Jacques Rousseau, arguing that what we bring into the world at birth most affects our development. This debate was sharpened by the discovery of "The Wild Boy of Aveyron" in 1800 and the attempts by Dr. Itard to educate him. Today, developmental psychologists focus on how heredity and experience interact from the beginning of life throughout the life span.

In the field of child development, the subject of Program 5, there have been many important changes in attitudes about the capacities of newborns. Advances in technology and methodology have rapidly expanded our ability to read the silent language of infants. The growing ability to test for and map their psychological states has led scientists to conclude that infants are born ready to perform many feats and are able to participate in shaping their environment.

Psychologist William James depicted the infant as totally helpless in confronting the world. But today researchers have powerful evidence that a newborn's behavior is meaningful. Newborns come ready to eat, turn away from bad odors, make friends, and mimic our expressions. We know that newborns can follow a moving face and express a preference for sights, sounds, tastes, and textures.

Researchers infer what newborns are thinking, seeing, and feeling by using techniques that measure how long they look at something or how intensely they suck when presented with stimuli. Researchers can also record and measure electrical responses in the brain, the degree of pupil dilation, and changes in heart rate. Using such indicators, it is possible to determine a baby's preferences and abilities, such as whether a baby is more interested in stripes or spots and whether it recognizes its mother.

One of the first researchers to use a baby's ability to express distinct preferences was Robert Fantz. He was able to show that babies preferred complexity and whole faces over jumbled parts of faces, thus demonstrating their cognitive capacities.

But it is the Swiss psychologist Jean Piaget who has contributed most to understanding the cognitive development of children. Piaget posed a variety of problems for children to solve, and after comparing their responses he demonstrated that understanding of the world varies with age. Piaget theorized that each child passes through four distinct levels of understanding in a fixed sequence, or stages— some children more slowly than others.

Despite his major contribution to psychology, Piaget vastly underestimated what children could do and overestimated the ages at which abilities emerged. Today, researchers are careful to design tasks that distinguish a child's ability to perform a task from the ability to explain or understand a concept. The results convince us that infants and children know more than we think they know—and they know it much earlier.

Researcher Reneé Baillargeon of the University of Illinois demonstrates that even six-month-old infants understand the concept of object permanence. Her colleague Judy DeLoache shows that changes in children's ability to use symbols occur between ages two and a half and three. Another well-known experiment that uses the visual cliff clearly shows that infants develop a fear of heights at about eight and a half months old, around the time they learn to crawl.

Researchers have identified activity level and shyness as the personality traits that show the most genetic influence. Harvard psychologist Jerome Kagan, who specializes in the study of inherited behavioral differences between timid and bold children, has found that being born shy does not necessarily mean a lifetime of shyness. Even inherited tendencies can be modified by learning, training, and experience. Researcher Steven Suomi explains how shyness decreased when he placed shy baby monkeys with extremely nurturant foster mothers, demonstrating that both nature and nurture play a significant role in many complex behaviors.

REVIEW QUESTIONS

Program Questions

1. Imagine that someone familiar with the last 20 years of research on babies was able to converse with William James. What would this time traveler probably say to James?

   a. "You were ahead of your time in understanding babies."
   b. "Babies are more competent than you thought."
   c. "Babies' senses are less sophisticated than you said."
   d. "Babies' perceptions actually depend on their cultures."

2. Which smell do newborns like?

   a. The smell of a banana
   b. The smell of shrimp
   c. Newborns can't smell anything.
   d. Newborns can smell, but we have no way of knowing what smells they prefer.

3. What task of infancy is aided by a baby's ability to recognize its mother's voice?

   a. Avoiding danger
   b. Seeking sustenance
   c. Forming social relationships
   d. Learning to speak

4. A toy company wants to use Robert Fantz's research to design a new mobile for babies to look at in their cribs. The research suggests that the mobile should

   a. be as simple as possible.
   b. use soft colors such as pink.
   c. be made of a shiny material.
   d. have a complex design.

5. Which of a baby's senses is least developed at birth?

   a. Hearing
   b. Taste
   c. Sight
   d. Touch

6. Jean Piaget has studied how children think. According to Piaget, at what age does a child typically master the idea that the amount of a liquid remains the same when it is poured from one container to another?

   a. Two years old
   b. Four years old
   c. Six years old
   d. Eight years old

7. A baby is shown an orange ball a dozen times in a row. How would you predict the baby would respond?

   a. The baby will make the same interested response each time.
   b. The baby will respond with less and less interest each time.
   c. The baby will respond with more and more interest each time.
   d. The baby will not be interested at any time.

8. Dr. Baillargeon and other researchers have investigated object permanence in babies. How do their results compare with Piaget's views?

   a. They show Piaget's age estimates were too high.
   b. They contradict Piaget's concept of object permanence.
   c. They support Piaget's timetable.
   d. They indicate that babies show more variation than Piaget found.

9. When Dr. DeLoache hid the small and large toy dogs, what was she investigating?

   a. Stranger anxiety
   b. Activity level
   c. Conservation of volume
   d. Symbolic representation

10. In a discussion of the nature-nurture controversy, who would be most likely to cite Steven Suomi's research on shyness in monkeys to support his or her point of view?

   a. Someone arguing that nature is primary
   b. Someone arguing that nurture is primary
   c. Someone arguing that nature can be modified by nurture
   d. The research does not support any of these viewpoints.

11. At what stage in their development do babies refuse to cross the visual cliff?

   a. As soon as their eyes can focus on it
   b. When they develop conditioned fears
   c. Just before they are ready to walk
   d. About a month after they learn to crawl

12. What conclusion has Jerome Kagan come to about shyness in young children?

    a. It is inherent but can be modified by experience.
    b. It is created by parents who misunderstand their child's temperament.
    c. It is an inherited trait that cannot be changed.
    d. It is normal for all children to be shy at certain stages.

13. How does Steven Suomi modify shyness reactions in young monkeys?

    a. By putting them in an enriched environment
    b. By providing highly supportive foster mothers
    c. By placing a shy monkey with other shy monkeys
    d. By administering drugs that reduce the level of social anxiety

Textbook Questions

14. The controversy over whether individual personalities and traits are a result of genetic endowment or of learning, is called the

    a. behavior modification controversy.
    b. psychoanalytic-humanist controversy.
    c. mind over matter controversy.
    d. nature-nurture controversy.

15. Konrad Lorenz (1937) is noted partially for his work concerning

    a. maturation.
    b. imprinting.
    c. stage theory.
    d. the tabula rasa.

16. Which research design evaluates the behavior of the same group of people at several points in time over a long term?

    a. Quasi-experimental design
    b. Cross-sectional design
    c. Cross-sequential design
    d. Longitudinal design

17. Genes are composed of large, complex molecules of

    a. ribonucleic acid.
    b. chromosomes.
    c. deoxyribonucleic acid.
    d. autosomes.

18. If you are heterozygous for a trait, that means that your genotype contains _____ genes for that trait.

    a. recessive
    b. dominant
    c. identical
    d. different

19. Geneticist James Gusella has discovered a genetic marker on chromosome 4 for

    a. Huntington's disease.
    b. Phenylketonuria.
    c. Down's syndrome.
    d. color blindness.

20. The inability to metabolize phenylalanine is a genetic disorder known as

    a. hypoglycemia.
    b. Down's syndrome.
    c. phenylketonuria (PKU).
    d. fragile X syndrome.

21. The approximately 9 months of prenatal development takes place in three stages in the following sequence:

    a. germinal, embryonic, fetal.
    b. germinal, fetal, embryonic.
    c. embryonic, fetal, germinal.
    d. fetal, germinal, embryonic.

22. The pattern of development normal to humans in which infants gain control over areas that are closest to the center of their bodies (for instance, control is gained over the upper arms before the fingers) is called

    a. accommodation.
    b. assimilation.
    c. cephalocaudal.
    d. proximodistal.

23. The psychologist who has contributed significantly to an understanding of children's cognitive development is

    a. B. F. Skinner.
    b. Sigmund Freud.
    c. Konrad Lorenz.
    d. Jean Piaget.

24. A child sees a cow and remarks, "Look Mommy, at the big doggie." According to Piaget, he or she is using a mental process known as

    a. conservation.
    b. centration.
    c. assimilation.
    d. accommodation.

25. Piaget hypothesized that _____ is the creation of new ways of looking at the world.

    a. accommodation
    b. assimilation
    c. centration
    d. animism

26. Piaget theorized that children's cognitive processes develop in

    a. an orderly sequence.
    b. regard to the socioeconomic status of the father.
    c. response to modeling and imitation.
    d. a random fashion.

27. According to Piaget, children first show object permanence during the

    a. sensorimotor stage.
    b. preoperational stage.
    c. concrete operational stage.
    d. formal operational stage.

28. A seven-year-old generally can express the correct answer when given Piaget's water glass test because he or she has developed

    a. object permanence.
    b. centration.
    c. decentration.
    d. egocentrism.

29. Abstract, symbolic thought is characteristic of the _____ stage of Piaget's theory.

    a. concrete
    b. preoperational
    c. formal
    d. sensorimotor

30. Piaget's theory has been criticized for

    a. placing too much emphasis on the maturation of biologically based cognitive structures.
    b. overstating the importance of environment.
    c. emphasizing individual differences.
    d. overstating the role of learning.

31. Fathers, as compared to mothers, tend to interact differently with their children by

    a. reading to the child.
    b. playing children's games.
    c. boisterous play rather than nurturing.
    d. nurturing rather than play.

32. Keven, who plays with cars and trucks, knows that he "is male." Lauren and Taylor play with dolls and know they "are female." Each has established

    a. gender consciousness.
    b. sex knowledge.
    c. gender identity.
    d. gender role.

33. Two-year-old Kevin wants to do things himself, put on his own clothes, feed himself, even try to drive his father's car. He is in the stage Erikson refers to as

    a. trust versus mistrust.
    b. autonomy versus doubt.
    c. initiative versus guilt.
    d. industry versus inferiority.

QUESTIONS TO CONSIDER

1. What are the advantages and disadvantages of being bold? Does boldness imply the same thing when used to describe both boys and girls? How might training and experience lead boys and girls to express boldness in different ways?

2. Consider different theories of infant abilities, and contrast the influence of both Gesell and Watson on developmental psychology and childrearing practices.

3. How might the knowledge of developmental norms affect a parent's response to a child? Speculate on what would happen if parents raised their children following inaccurate or out-of-date theories of child development.

4. Is reading the body language of an adult different from reading the body language of a child? How can some of the measures used to detect an infant's interest or learning be used to measure adult cognitive functioning?

5. Do you think it is possible to "spoil" an infant by holding it too much?

OPTIONAL ACTIVITIES

1. Recall your earliest memory. Speculate as to why you recall it and what effects the event has had on your development.

2. Compare yourself to your siblings. What traits, abilities, and interests do you share? Speculate on the roles of genetics and environment in the development of your similarities and differences.

3. Get permission from a day care center to observe two different age groups of children. Observe their play and social interactions. At approximately what age does it appear that children engage in cooperative play? Can cooperative play be taught?

ANTHOLOGY

The following readings illustrate concepts from Unit 5, particularly the interplay of biology and environment in the development of young children. As you read, consider how advances in research have led parents, psychologists, and educators to reevaluate long-standing theories that have played a role in childrearing and education.

Reading 12

Can development be 100 percent genetic and 100 percent environment? Daniel Freedman suggests using the concept of "reaction range" to understand how heredity and environment interact. As you read, consider how Freedman builds his argument. Do you think it is valid? How would you describe your own development, taking into account your cultural background and interaction with your environment?

Ethnic Differences in Babies

By Daniel G. Freedman

The human species comes in an admirable variety of shapes and colors, as a walk through any cosmopolitan city amply demonstrates. Although the speculation has become politically and socially unpopular, it is difficult not to wonder whether the major differences in physical appearances are accompanied by standard differences in temperament or behavior. Recent studies by myself and others of babies only a few hours, days, or weeks old indicate that they are, and that such differences among human beings are biological as well as cultural.

These studies of newborns from different ethnic backgrounds actually had their inception with work on puppies, when I attempted to raise dogs in either an indulged or disciplined fashion in order to test the effects of such rearing on their later behavior.

I spent all my days and evenings with these puppies, and it soon became apparent that the breed of dog would become an important factor in my results. Even as the ears and eyes opened, the breeds differed in behavior. Little beagles were irrepressibly friendly from the moment they could detect me; Shetland sheepdogs were very, very sensitive to a loud voice or the slightest punishment; wire-haired terriers were so tough and aggressive, even as clumsy three-week-olds, that I had to wear gloves while playing with them; and finally, Basenjis, barkless dogs originating in Central Africa, were aloof and independent. To judge by where they spent their time, sniffing and investigating, I was no more important to them than if I were a rubber balloon.

When I later tested the dogs, the breed indeed made a difference in their behavior. I took them, when hungry, into a room with a bowl of meat. For three minutes I kept them from approaching the meat, then left each dog alone with the food. Indulged terriers and beagles waited longer before eating the meat than did disciplined dogs of the same breeds. None of the Shetlands ever ate any of the food, and all of the Basenjis ate as soon as I left.

I later studied 20 sets of identical and fraternal human twins, following them from infancy until they were 10 years old, and I became convinced that both puppies and human babies begin life along developmental pathways established by their genetic inheritance. But I still did not know whether infants of relatively inbred human groups showed differences comparable to the breed differences among puppies that had so impressed me. Clearly, the most direct way to find out was to examine very young infants, preferably newborns, of ethnic groups with widely divergent histories.

Since it was important to avoid projecting my own assumptions onto the babies' behavior, the first step was to develop some sort of objective test of newborn behavior. With T. Berry Brazelton, the Harvard pediatrician, I developed what I called the Cambridge Behavioral and Neurological Assessment Scales, a group of simple tests of basic human reactions that could be administered to any normal newborn in a hospital nursery.

In the first study, Nina Freedman and I

compared Chinese and Caucasian babies. It was no accident that we chose those two groups, since my wife is Chinese, and in the course of learning about each other and our families, we came to believe that some character differences might well be related to differences in our respective gene pools and not just to individual differences.

Armed with our new baby test, Nina and I returned to San Francisco, and to the hospital, where she had borne our first child. We examined, alternately, 24 Chinese and 24 Caucasian newborns. To keep things neat, we made sure that all the Chinese were of Cantonese (South Chinese) background, the Caucasians of Northern European origin, that the sexes in both groups were the same, that the mothers were the same age, that they had about the same number of previous children, and that both groups were administered the same drugs in the same amounts. Additionally, all of the families were members of the same health plan, all of the mothers had had approximately the same number of prenatal visits to a doctor, and all were in the same middle-income bracket.

It was almost immediately clear that we had struck pay dirt; Chinese and Caucasian babies indeed behaved like two different breeds. Caucasian babies cried more easily, and once started, they were harder to console. Chinese babies adapted to almost any position in which they were placed; for example, when placed face down in their cribs, they tended to keep their faces buried in the sheets rather than immediately turning to one side, as did the Caucasians. In a similar maneuver (called the "defense reaction" by neurologists), we briefly pressed the baby's nose with a cloth. Most Caucasian and black babies fight this maneuver by immediately turning away or swiping at the cloth with their hands, and this is reported in most Western pediatric textbooks as the normal, expected response. The average Chinese baby in our study, however, simply lay on his back and breathed through his mouth, "accepting" the cloth without a fight. This finding is most impressive on film.

Other subtle differences were equally important, but less dramatic. For example, both Chinese and Caucasian babies started to cry at about the same points in the examination, especially when they were undressed, but the Chinese stopped sooner. When picked up and cuddled, Chinese babies stopped crying immediately, as if a light switch had been flipped, whereas the crying of Caucasian babies only gradually subsided.

In another part of the test, we repeatedly shone a light in the baby's eyes and counted the number of blinks until the baby "adapted" and no longer blinked. It should be no surprise that the Caucasian babies continued to blink long after the Chinese babies had adapted and stopped.

It began to look as if Chinese babies were simply more amenable and adaptable to the machinations of the examiners, and that the Caucasian babies were registering annoyance and complaint. It was as if the old stereotypes of the calm, inscrutable Chinese and the excitable, emotionally changeable Caucasian were appearing spontaneously in the first 48 hours of life. In other words, our hypothesis about human and puppy parallels seemed to be correct.

The results of our Chinese-Caucasian study have been confirmed by a student of ethologist Nick Blurton-Jones who worked in a Chinese community in Malaysia. At the time, however, our single study was hardly enough evidence for so general a conclusion, and we set out to look at other newborns in other places. Norbett Mintz, who was working among the Navaho in Tuba City, Arizona, arranged for us to come to the reservation in the spring of 1969. After two months we had tested 36 Navaho newborns, and the results paralleled the stereotype of the stoical, impassive American Indian. These babies outdid the Chinese, showing even more calmness and adaptability than we found among Oriental babies.

We filmed the babies as they were tested and found reactions in the film we had not noticed. For example, the Moro response was clearly different among Navaho and Caucasians. This reaction occurs in newborns when support for the head and neck suddenly disappears. Tests for the Moro response usually consist of raising and then suddenly dropping the head portion of the bassinet. In most Caucasian newborns, after a four-inch drop the baby reflexively extends both arms and legs, cries, and moves in an agitated manner before he calms down. Among Navaho babies, crying was rare, the limb movements were reduced, and calming was almost immediate.

I have since spent considerable time among the Navaho, and it is clear that the traditional practice of tying the wrapped infant onto a cradle board (now practiced sporadically on the reservation) has in no way induced stoicism in the Navaho. In the halcyon days of anthropological environmentalism, this was a popular conjecture, but the other way around is more likely. Not all Navaho babies take to the cradle board, and those who complain about it are simply taken off. But most Navaho infants calmly accept the board; in fact, many begin to demand it by showing signs of unrest when off. When they are about six months old, however, Navaho babies do start complaining at being tied, and "weaning" from the board begins, with the baby taking the lead. The Navaho are the most "in touch" group of mothers we have yet seen, and the term mother-infant *unit* aptly describes what we saw among them.

James Chisholm of Rutgers University, who has studied infancy among the Navaho over the past several years, reports that his observations are much like my own. In addition, he followed a group of young Caucasian mothers in Flagstaff (some 80 miles south of the reservation) who had decided to use the cradle board. Their babies complained so persistently that they were off the board in a matter of weeks, a result that should not surprise us, given the differences observed at birth.

Assuming, then, that other investigators continue to confirm our findings, to what do we attribute the differences on the one hand, and the similarities on the other? When we first presented the findings on Chinese and Caucasians, attempts were made to explain away the genetic implications by posing differences in prenatal diets as an obvious cause. But once we had completed the Navaho study, that explanation had to be dropped, because the Navaho diet is quite different from the diet of the Chinese, yet newborn behavior was strikingly similar in the two groups.

The point is often still made that the babies had nine months of experience within the uterus before we saw them, so that cultural differences in maternal attitudes and behavior might have been transferred to the unborn offspring via some, as yet unknown, mechanism. Chisholm, for example, thinks differences in maternal blood pressure may be re-sponsible for some of the differences between Navahos and Caucasians, but the evidence is as yet sparse. Certainly Cantonese-American and Navaho cultures are substantially different and yet the infants are so much alike that such speculation might be dismissed on that score alone. But there is another, hidden issue here, and that involves our own cultural tendency to split apart inherited and acquired characteristics. Americans tend to eschew the inherited and promote the acquired, in a sort of "we are exactly what we make of ourselves" optimism.

My position on this issue is simple: We are totally biological, totally environmental; the two are as inseparable as is an object and its shadow. Or as psychologist Donald O. Hebb has expressed it, we are 100 percent innate, 100 percent acquired. One might add to Hebb's formulation, 100 percent biological, 100 percent cultural. As D. T. Suzuki, the Zen scholar, once told an audience of neuro-psychiatrists, "You took heredity and environment apart and now you are stuck with the problem of putting them together again."

Navaho and Chinese newborns may be so much alike because the Navaho were part of a relatively recent emigration from Asia. Their language group is called Athabaskan, after a lake in Canada. Although most of the Athabaskan immigrants from Asia settled along the Pacific coast of Canada, the Navaho and Apache contingents went on to their present location in about 1200 A.D. Even today, a significant number of words in Athabaskan and Chinese appear to have the same meaning, and if one looks back several thousand years into the written records of Sino-Tibetan, the number of similar words makes clear the common origin of these widely separated peoples.

When we say that some differences in human behavior may have a genetic basis, what do we mean? First of all, we are *not* talking about a gene for stoicism or a gene for irritability. If a behavioral trait is at all interesting, for example, smiling, anger, ease of sexual arousal, or altruism, it is most probably polygenic—that is, many genes contribute to its development. Furthermore, there is no way to count the exact number of genes involved in such a polygenic system because, as geneticist James Crow has sum-

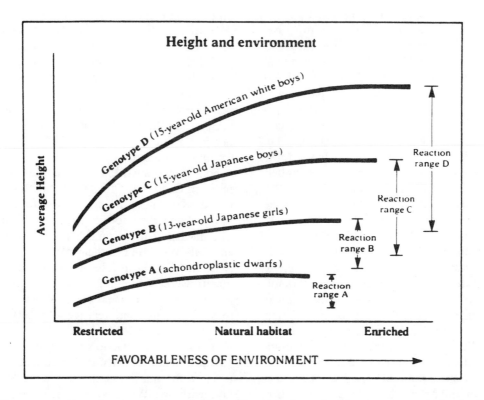

Height and environment

Average Height

Genotype D (15-year-old American white boys)

Genotype C (15-year-old Japanese boys)

Genotype B (13-year-old Japanese girls)

Genotype A (achondroplastic dwarfs)

Reaction range D

Reaction range C

Reaction range B

Reaction range A

Restricted   Natural habitat   Enriched

FAVORABLENESS OF ENVIRONMENT ⟶

The concept of reaction range shows clearly in this comparison of adolescent groups: the better the environment, the taller the person. Although some groups show considerable overlap in height, no matter how favorable the environment, height cannot exceed the possible reaction range.

marized the situation, biological traits are controlled by one, two, or *many* genes.

Standing height, a polygenic human trait, can be easily measured and is also notoriously open to the influence of the environment. For this reason height can serve as a model for behavioral traits, which are genetically influenced but are even more prone to change with changing environment.

There are, however, limits to the way that a given trait responds to the environment, and this range of constraint imposed by the genes is called a *reaction range*. Behavioral geneticist Irving Gottesman has drawn up a series of semihypothetical graphs illustrating how this works with regard to human height; each genotype (the combination of genes that determine a particular trait) represents a relatively inbred human group. Even the most favorable environment produces little change in height for genotype A, whereas for genotype D a vast difference is seen as nutrition improves.

When I speak of potential genetic differences in human behavior, I do so with these notions in mind: There is overlap between

most populations and the overlap can become rather complete under changing conditions, as in genotypes D and C. Some genotypes, however, show no overlap and remain remote from the others over the entire reaction range, as in genotype A (actually a group of achondroplastic dwarfs; it is likely that some pygmy groups would exhibit a similarly isolated reaction range with regard to height).

At present we lack the data to construct such reaction-range curves for newborn behavior, but hypothetically there is nothing to prevent us from one day doing so.

The question naturally arises whether the group differences we have found are expressions of richer and poorer environments, rather than of genetically distinguishable groups. The similar performance yet substantial difference in socioeconomic status between Navaho and San Francisco Chinese on the one hand, and the dissimilar performance yet similar socioeconomic status of San Francisco Chinese and Caucasians on the other favors the genetic explanation. Try as one might, it is very difficult, conceptually and actually, to get rid of our biological constraints.

Research among newborns in other cultures shows how environment—in this case, cultural learning—affects reaction range. In Hawaii we met a Honolulu pediatrician who volunteered that he had found striking and consistent differences between Japanese and Polynesian babies in his practice. The Japanese babies consistently reacted more violently to their three-month immunizations than did the Polynesians. On subsequent visits, the Japanese gave every indication of remembering the last visit by crying violently; one mother said that her baby cried each time she drove by the clinic.

We then tested a series of Japanese newborns, and found that they were indeed more sensitive and irritable than either the Chinese or Navaho babies. In other respects, though, they were much like them, showing a similar response to consolation, and accommodating easily to a light on the eyes or a cloth over the nose. Prior to our work, social anthropologist William Caudill had made an extensive and thorough study of Japanese infants. He made careful observations of Japanese mother-infant pairs in Tokyo and Caucasian pairs in Baltimore, from the third to the twelfth month of life. Having noted that both the Japanese infants and their mothers vocalized much less to one another than did Caucasian pairs, he assumed that the Japanese mothers were conditioning their babies toward quietude from a universal baseline at which all babies start. Caudill, of course, was in the American environmentalist tradition and, until our publication appeared, did not consider the biological alternative. We believe that the mothers and babies he studied were, in all probability, conditioning each other, that the naturally quiet Japanese babies affected their mothers' behavior as much as the mothers affected their babies'.

With this new interactive hypothesis in mind, one of my students, Joan Kuchner, studied mother-infant interactions among 10 Chinese and 10 Caucasian mother-infant pairs over the first three months of life. The study was done in Chicago, and this time the Chinese were of North Chinese rather than South Chinese (Cantonese) ancestry. Kuchner started her study with the birth of the babies and found that the two groups were different from the start, much as in our study of newborns. Further, it soon became apparent that Chinese mothers were less intent on eliciting responses from their infants. By the third month, Chinese infants and mothers rarely engaged in bouts of mutual vocalizing as did the Caucasian pairs. This was exactly what the Caudill studies of Japanese and Caucasians had shown, but we now know that it was based on a developing coalition between mothers and babies and that it was not just a one-way street in which a mother "shapes" her infant's behavior.

Following our work, Caudill and Lois Frost repeated Caudill's original work, but this time they used third-generation Japanese-American mothers and their fourth-generation infants. The mothers had become "super" American and were vocalizing to their infants at almost twice the Caucasian rate of activity, and the infants were responding at an even greater rate of happy vocalization. Assuming that these are sound and repeatable results, my tendency is to reconcile these and our results in terms of the reaction-range concept. If Japanese height can change as dramatically as it has with emigration to the United States (and with post-World War II diets), it seems plausible that mother-infant behavior can do the same. On a variety of other measures, Caudill and Frost were able to discern continuing similarities to infant and mother pairs in the old country. Fourth-generation Japanese babies, like babies in Japan, sucked their fingers less and were less playful than Caucasian babies were, and the third-generation mothers lulled their babies and held them more than Caucasian American mothers did.

A student and colleague, John Callaghan, has recently completed a study comparing 15 Navaho and 19 Anglo mothers and their young infants (all under six months). Each mother was asked to "get the attention of the baby." When video tapes of the subsequent scene were analyzed, the differences in both babies and mothers were striking. The Navaho babies showed greater passivity than the Caucasian babies. Caucasian mothers "spoke" to their babies continually, using linguistic forms appropriate for someone who understands language; their babies responded by moving their arms and legs. The Navaho mothers were strikingly silent, using their eyes to attract their babies' gaze, and the relatively immobile infants responded by merely gazing back.

Despite their disparate methods, both

groups were equally successful in getting their babies' attention. Besides keeping up a stream of chatter, Caucasian mothers tended to shift the baby's position radically, sometimes holding him or her close, sometimes at arm's length, as if experimenting to find the best focal distance for the baby. Most of the silent Navaho mothers used only subtle shifts on the lap, holding the baby at about the same distance throughout. As a result of the intense stimulation by the Caucasian mothers, the babies frequently turned their heads away, as if to moderate the intensity of the encounter. Consequently, eye contact among Caucasian pairs was of shorter duration (half that of the Navaho), but more frequent.

It was clear that the Caucasian mothers sought their babies' attention with verve and excitement, even as their babies tended to react to the stimulation with what can be described as ambivalence: The Caucasian infants turned both toward and away from the mother with far greater frequency than did the Navaho infants. The Navaho mothers and their infants engaged in relatively stoical, quiet, and steady encounters. On viewing the films of these sequences, we had the feeling that we were watching biocultural differences in the making.

Studies of older children bear out the theme of relative unexcitability in Chinese as compared to Anglos. In an independent research project at the University of Chicago, Nova Green studied a number of nursery schools. When she reached one in Chicago's Chinatown, she reported: "Although the majority of the Chinese-American children were in the 'high arousal age,' between three and five, they showed little intense emotional behavior. They ran and hopped, laughed and called to one another, rode bikes and roller-skated just as the children did in the older nursery schools, but the noise level stayed remarkably low, and the emotional atmosphere projected serenity instead of bedlam. The impassive facial expression certainly gave the children an air of dignity and self-possession, but this was only one element effecting the total impression. Physical movements seemed more coordinated, no tripping, falling, bumping, or bruising was observed, nor screams, crashes or wailing was heard, not even that common sound in other nurseries, voices raised in highly indignant

moralistic dispute! No property disputes were observed, and only the mildest version of 'fighting behavior,' some good-natured wrestling among the older boys. The adults evidently had different expectations about hostile or impulsive behavior; this was the only nursery school where it was observed that children were trusted to duel with sticks. Personal distance spacing seemed to be situational rather than compulsive or patterned, and the children appeared to make no effort to avoid physical contact."

It is ironic that many recent visitors to nursery schools in Red China have returned with ecstatic descriptions of the children, implying that the New Order knows something about child rearing that the West does not. When the *New Yorker* reported a visit to China by a group of developmental psychologists including William Kessen, Urie Bronfenbrenner, Jerome Kagan, and Eleanor Maccoby, they were described as baffled by the behavior of Chinese children: "They were won over by the Chinese children. They speak of an 'attractive mixture of affective spontaneity and an accommodating posture' by the children: of the 'remarkable control of young Chinese children—alert, animated, vigorous, responsive to the words of their elders, yet also unnervingly calm, even during happenings (games, classroom events, neighborhood play) that could create agitation and confusion. The children were far less restless, less intense in their motor actions, and displayed less crying and whining than American children in similar situations. We were constantly struck by [their] quiet, gentle, and controlled manner . . . and as constantly frustrated in our desire to understand its origins.' "

The report is strikingly similar to Nova Green's description of the nursery school in Chicago's Chinatown. When making these comparisons with "American" nursery schools, the psychologists obviously had in mind classrooms filled with Caucasian and Afro-American children.

As they get older, Chinese and Caucasian children continue to differ in roughly the same behavior that characterizes them in nursery school. Not surprisingly, San Francisco schoolteachers consider assignments in Chinatown as plums—the children are dutiful and studious, and the classrooms are quiet.

A reader might accept these data and observations and yet still have trouble imagining how such differences might have initially come about. The easiest explanation involves a historical accident based on different, small founding populations and at least partial geographic isolation. Peking man, some 500,000 years ago, already had shovel-shaped incisors, as only Orientals and American Indians have today. Modern-looking skulls of about the same age, found in England, lack this grooving on the inside of the upper incisors. Given such evidence, we can surmise that there has been substantial and long-standing isolation of East and West. Further, it is likely that, in addition to just plain "genetic drift," environmental demands and biocultural adaptations differed, yielding present-day differences.

Orientals and Euro-Americans are not the only newborn groups we have examined. We have recorded newborn behavior in Nigeria, Kenya, Sweden, Italy, Bali, India, and Australia, and in each place, it is fair to say, we observed some kind of uniqueness. The Australian aborigines, for example, struggled mightily against the cloth over the nose, resembling the most objecting Caucasian babies; their necks were exceptionally strong, and some could lift their heads up and look around, much like some of the African babies we saw. (Caucasian infants cannot do this until they are about one month old.) Further,

aborigine infants were easy to calm, resembling in that respect our easy-going Chinese babies. They thus comprised a unique pattern of traits.

Given these data, I think it is a reasonable conclusion that we should drop two long-cherished myths: (1) No matter what our ethnic background, we are all born alike; (2) culture and biology are separate entities. Clearly, we are biosocial creatures in everything we do and say, and it is time that anthropologists, psychologists, and population geneticists start speaking the same language. In light of what we know, only a truly holistic, multidisciplinary approach makes sense.

For Further Information

Cauldill, W., and N. Frost. "A Comparison of Maternal Care and Infant Behavior in Japanese–American, American, and Japanese Families." *Influences on Human Development*, edited by Urie Bronfenbrenner and M. A. Mahoney. Dryden Press, 1972.

Chisholm, J. S., and Martin Richards. "Swaddling, Cradleboards and the Development of Children." *Early Human Development*, in press.

Freedman, D. G. "Constitutional and Environmental Interaction in Rearing or Four Breeds of Dogs." *Science*, Vol. 127, 1958, pp. 585–586.

Freedman, D. G. *Human Infancy: An Evolutionary Perspective*. Lawrence Erlbaum Associates, 1974.

Freedman, D. G., and B. Keller. "Inheritance of Behavior in Infants." *Science*, Vol. 140, 1963, pp. 196–198.

Gottesman, I. I. "Developmental Genetics and Ontogenetic Psychology." *Minnesota Symposia on Child Psychology*. Vol. 8, edited by A. D. Pick. University of Minnesota Press, 1974.

Reading 13

In this article, researcher Janet K. Black questions Piaget's description of egocentrism in children. She suggests that researchers are now providing evidence for what teachers, caregivers, and parents have known all along—that children are not as egocentric as Piaget suggests. As you read, recall how Piaget defined egocentrism. Consider the implications of using new, more appropriate test procedures.

Are Young Children Really Egocentric?

By Janet K. Black

Recently a friend decided it was best if she gave away her dog. After screening responses to an ad she had placed in the newspaper, three-year-old Julie and her parents were invited to visit Zoe. Upon becoming satisfactorily acquainted with Zoe, Julie's mother and father asked her if she would like to take Zoe home. Julie replied in a concerned tone, "But if we take Zoe, she (Zoe's owner) won't have a dog."

Another child, two years of age, accidentally knocked off his grandmother's glasses

while she was reading to him. Marc patted her and said, "Sowy Grandma." This behavior was repeated several times throughout the afternoon.

Five-year-old Jonathan asked his mother how many quarters there were in a football game. After internalizing her explanation he said, "Five quarters would make one game and one quarter, and eight quarters would make two games."

The above behaviors are typical observations that parents, teachers, and caregivers have made while interacting with young children. These behaviors pose some questions about theories of child development which suggest that young children are totally egocentric. According to Piaget, egocentric behavior prevents young children from conserving and from acting altruistically. However, there is a growing body of research evidence that indicates even young children are not always egocentric.

Piagetian and Recent Research on Egocentrism

Yarrow and Zahn-Waxler (1977) conducted a detailed study of children's altruistic behavior between the ages of ten months and two-and-one-half years. After analyzing some 1,500 incidents, Yarrow and Zahn-Waxler conclude that children, from at least the age of one, have a capacity for compassion and various kinds of prosocial behavior. Pines (1979) discusses Flavell's conclusions about young children's egocentric behavior. As a result of his research, Flavell concludes that Piaget overestimated how egocentric young children are. His investigations with three-year-olds indicate that they behave in a consistently nonegocentric manner. Flavell believes that some of the role taking exercises used in earlier research may have been too complicated for young children, while simpler, more relevant tests are more reliable indicators of their true ability. For example, if children are shown a card with a dog on one side and a cat on the other, they will be able to tell you correctly what animal you see and ignore the one that faces them. Flavell concludes, "Though young children may not completely understand, they can pay attention to how other people feel" (Pines 1979, p. 77).

One of Piaget's best known experiments which allegedly documents young children's inability to decenter is the mountain task. Piaget used a three-dimensional model of three mountains (Piaget and Inhelder 1967) which are distinguished from one another by color, as well as the presence of snow on one mountain, a house on another, and a red cross on the third.

A child is seated at one side of the table upon which the above model is placed. The experimenter then stands a doll at varying positions around the mountains and asks the child, "What does the doll see?" Because it is hard for the child to give a verbal description, she or he is given a set of ten pictures and is asked to choose the one that shows what the doll sees. Generally, children up to the age of eight or nine cannot successfully do this task. Piaget (Piaget and Inhelder 1967, p. 212) concluded that these responses indicate that young children are unable to decenter.

Donaldson (1979) states:

> We are urged by Piaget to believe that the child's behavior in this situation gives us deep insight into the nature of the world. This world is held to be one that is composed largely of "false absolutes." That is to say the child does not appreciate that what he sees is relative to his own position; he takes it to represent truth or reality—*the world as it really is*. . . . Piaget believes that this is how it is for the young child: that he lives in the state of the moment, not bothering himself with how things were just previously, with the relation of one state to those which came before or after it. . . . The issue for Piaget is how the momentary states are linked or fail to be linked in the child's mind. The issue is how well the child can deal conceptually with the transitions between them. (pp. 12–13).

A task, similar to yet different from Piaget's mountain experiment, designed by Hughes (1975) demonstrates that there are important considerations in the experimenter's, as well as in children's, behavior which Piaget failed to take into account. After acquainting the child with a square board divided by barriers into four equal sectors, a doll was put in each of the sectors one at a time and a policeman was positioned at points of the sectors. The child was asked if the policeman could see the doll. Then another policeman was introduced and the child was told to hide the doll from both policemen. This was repeated three times so that each time a different sector was left as the only hiding place. Thirty children between the ages of three-and-one-half and five were given this task with 90 percent of their responses correct. Even the ten youngest children (average age, three years nine months) achieved a success rate of 88 percent. Thus, it seems that young children are capable of considering and coordinating two different points of view.

Donaldson (1979) explains the differences in children's behaviors on the mountain and policeman tasks from an experiential perspective. In short, "the mountain task is abstract in a psychologically very important sense: in the sense that it is abstracted from all basic human purposes, feelings, and endeavors"

(p. 17). However, "young children know what it is to try to hide. Also they know what it is to be naughty and to want to evade the consequences" (p. 17).

In the policeman task, the motives and intentions of the characters are comprehensible even to three-year-olds. If tasks require children to act in ways which make human sense, that is, are in line with very basic human purposes, interactions, and intentions, children show none of the difficulties in decentering which Piaget maintained. Thus, while adults, as well as children, are egocentric in certain situations throughout life, the extent to which young children are egocentric seems to be much less than Piaget suggested.

Related to the issue of basic human purpose and feeling is the nature and context of the language used by the experimenter. Once again Donaldson raises valid questions about various Piagetian class-inclusion tasks. In one of these tasks a child is presented with four red flowers and two white flowers and asked: Are there more red flowers or flowers? Children of five usually respond that there are more red flowers. Donaldson (1979) states:

> There is not much doubt about what a child *does* when he makes the standard type of error and says there are more red flowers than flowers; he compares one subclass with the other subclass.... The question is why does he compare subclass with subclass? Is it because he *cannot* compare subclass with class as Piaget maintains? Or is it because he thinks that this is what he is meant to do? Is there...a failure of communication? (p. 39)

In discussing a variety of task-inclusion experiments in which there was perceptual and/or language modification, Donaldson (1979) concludes that the questions the children were answering were very often not the questions the experimenter was asking. In short, the children's interpretations did not correspond to the experimenter's intentions. The children either did not know what the experimenter meant, what the language meant, or had expectations about questions or the experimental material which shaped their interpretation. In other words, when children hear words that refer to a situation which they are at the same time perceiving, their interpretation of the words is influenced by the expectations they bring to the situation. While Piaget was aware of the differ-

ences of what language is for the adult and what language is for the child, he failed to keep these differences in perspective in using language for studying children's thinking (Donaldson, 1979).

Gelman (1979) believes that if researchers stopped using incorrect assumptions and inappropriate measures, they would learn that the cognitive skills of younger children are far greater than has been assumed. She developed a magic task which does not ask a child to distinguish between more or less but rather to designate a winner or loser in number conservation activities. "According to the results of the 'magic task,' preschoolers know full well that lengthening or shortening the array does not alter the numerical value of a display" (p. 903).

Conclusions

There is a growing body of evidence which indicates that young children are not as egocentric as Piaget suggested. If children are in contexts where they can use their knowledge of very basic human purposes, intentions, and interactions, they show no difficulty in decentering. Likewise, children's interpretation of the language of others is dependent upon (1) their knowledge of language; (2) their assessment of the experimenter's, caregiver's teacher's, and parent's nonverbal intentions; and (3) the manner in which children would represent the physical situation if the adults were not present.

Because Julie had had very basic human experiences of relinquishing prized possessions or opportunities, she understood how people might feel if they had their pets taken away. Because Mac had had the very basic human experience of being hurt and comforted, he understood how his grandmother felt and what he could do to comfort her. Because Jonathan had had the very basic human experience of acquiring desired possessions with his allowance frequently given to him in four quarters, he readily indicated his ability to decenter when discussing the quarters in a football game. Contrary to Piaget, these three children's behavior indicates that they are not completely egocentric if the context is meaningful to them. While Piaget's vast contribution to the understanding of young children's cognitive development cannot be denied, no theory is final. Early childhood researchers and practitioners need to add to and clarify the roots of later cognitive and prosocial competence.

Implications

Astute and observant adults can renew their faith in their abilities to observe and know children in ways that researchers often misinterpret. Perhaps there should be more action research on the part of early childhood teachers or more dialogues between teachers and researchers.

Providing situations in which young children can demonstrate their knowledge of very basic human purposes and interactions is necessary to make a more accurate assessment of their competencies. Young children demonstrate varying competencies in different environments. There are contexts in which children indicate they do not know, when, in fact, they do (Black, 1979a, 1979b; Cazden 1975).

A third implication concerns the language adults use with children. Teachers and parents constantly need to be aware of young children's knowledge of language, of our nonverbal behavior, and children's probable understanding of physical situations.

By acknowledging that children in basic human situations and meaningful communicative contexts are more capable than previously thought, teachers, caregivers, and parents can obtain more accurate information about children's abilities. An awareness of these competencies facilitates provision of more appropriate experiences for young children.

Finally, researchers need to become cognizant of inappropriate methodology in studying young children. Conclusions and recommendations emanating from misguided research do not help practitioners provide appropriate experiences for young children. In fact, practices based on misinformation may actually impede children's development. Gelman (1979) cautions professionals about continuing to measure children with tasks that are more appropriate to older children (and even adults): "The time has come for us to turn our attention to what young children can do as well as what they cannot do. We should study preschoolers in their own right" (p. 904).

References

Black, J.K. "Formal and Informal Means of Assessing the Competence of Kindergarten Children." *Research in the Teaching of English* 13, no. 1 (1979a): 49–68.

Black, J.K. "There's More to Language Than Meets the Ear: Implications for Evaluation." *Language Arts* 56, no. 5 (1979b): 526–533.

Cazden, C. "Hypercorrection in Test Responses." *Theory into Practice* 14 (1975): 343–346.

Donaldson, M. *Children's Minds*. New York: Norton, 1979.

Gelman, R. "Preschool Thought." *American Psychologist* 34 (1979): 900–905.

Hughes, M. "Egocentrism in Pre-School Children." Unpublished doctoral dissertation, Edinburgh University, 1975.

Piaget, J., and Inhelder, B. *The Child's Conception of Space*, New York: Norton, 1967.

Pines, M. "Good Samaritans at Age Two?" *Psychology Today* (June 1979): 66–77.

Yarrow, M.R., and Zahn-Waxler, C. "The Emergence and Functions of Prosocial Behaviors in Young Children." In *Readings in Child Development and Relationships*, ed. R. Smart and M. Smart, New York: Macmillan, 1977.

ADDITIONAL RESOURCES

Books and Articles

Asher, Jules. "Born to Be Shy." *Psychology Today* (April 1987): 56–64. Some recent studies indicate there may be a genetic basis for shyness, but research also suggests that children "born to be shy" can learn to overcome their shyness.

Bettelheim, Bruno. *The Uses of Enchantment: The Meaning and Importance of Fairy Tales*. New York: Vintage Books, 1976. Stories help children make sense of the world and themselves, as well as reflect struggles children face growing up. A renowned child psychologist looks at Cinderella, Snow White, and other classic fairy tales.

Coles, Robert. *Uprooted Children: The Early Lives of Migrant Farmworkers*. Pittsburgh, Pa.: University of Pittsburgh Press, 1970. Constantly moving from place to place, the children of migrant workers face even more struggles in development than does the average child. Coles explores both their fears and strengths.

Fraiberg, Selma. *The Magic Years*. New York: Scribners, 1968. A celebrated exploration of emotional development in childhood.

Gibson, Eleanor J., and Richard Walk. "The 'Visual Cliff.'" *Scientific American* 202 (1960): 64–71. Classic study of the development of depth perception and the emotion of fear in children.

Itard, Jean. *The Wild Boy of Aveyron*. New York: Appleton-Century-Crofts, 1962. Itard's early nineteenth-century memoir tells of his attempts to educate and socialize a child reared in the wild.

Singer, Dorothy G., and Tracey A. Revenson. *How a Child Thinks: A Piaget Primer*. New York: New American Library, 1978. No one has influenced contemporary understanding of how children think more than Jean Piaget. This illustrated guide offers easy access to Piaget's ideas about how children learn language, perception, and morality.

Trotter, Robert J. "Profile: Tiffany Field." *Psychology Today* (January 1987): 27–34. Psychologist Tiffany Field is an expert on "child's play." This article profiles her life and work, including her study of how touching affects infant development.

Films

Child's Play: Prodigies and Possibilities. NOVA #1209, Time-Life Video. 1985. This film introduces us to prodigies who excel in several fields and to current research hoping to uncover more about the nature of giftedness.

The Wild Child. Directed by François Truffaut. 1969. Dr. Jean Itard, a nineteenth-century scientist, adopted and attempted to socialize a 12-year-old boy found in the wild. This film, based on Itard's memoirs, explores how children learn language and bond with others. It also shows how the values and expectations of scientists direct their research and may bias their conclusions.

The following popular films capture various aspects of children's perceptions of themselves, adults, and the world around them.

Big. Directed by Penny Marshall. 1988.

E.T. the Extra-Terrestrial. Directed by Steven Spielberg. 1982.

Fanny and Alexander. Directed by Ingmar Bergman. 1983.

My Life as a Dog. Directed by Lasse Hallström. 1985.

Small Change. Directed by François Truffaut. 1976.

LANGUAGE DEVELOPMENT

The birth of language is the dawn of humanity. The line between man and beast—between the highest ape and the lowest savage—is the language line.

Susanne K. Langer

Peter Vandermark/Stock, Boston

Unit 6 examines how children acquire language and demonstrates the methods psychologists use to study the role of biology and social interaction in language acquisition. It also looks at the contribution of language to children's cognitive and social development.

"Motherese," or "parentese," a special form of speech used by adults all over the world when speaking to babies, plays an important role in language acquisition.

OBJECTIVES

After viewing the television program and completing the assigned readings, you should be able to:

1. Give the current definition of language

2. Explain Chomsky's hypothesis of an innate biological capacity for language acquisition

3. Discuss the importance of social interaction in the development of language abilities

4. Describe the early stages of communication in infants and young children

5. Discuss the universal aspects of "motherese"

6. Cite evidence of children applying grammatical structure as they learn their native language

7. List and discuss the necessary elements of a conversation

8. Discuss research on communication in chimpanzees and indicate why the topic is important and controversial

READING ASSIGNMENT

After viewing Program 6, read pages 373–387 in *Psychology: Science, Behavior and Life*. Your instructor may also assign the anthology selections for Unit 6.

KEY TERMS AND CONCEPTS

As you read the assignment, pay particular attention to these terms, which are defined on the given pages in the text.

psycholinguistics (373)	nativistic perspective (375)
phonemes (374)	language acquisition device (375)
morphemes (374)	holophrases (378)
syntax (374)	condensed speech (378)
semantics (374)	overgeneralize (379)
learning perspective (375)	oversimplification (379)

The following terms are used in Program 6 but are not defined in the text.

parentese—modified speech that parellels children's level of language development

universal adaptability—the ability to distinguish sounds of any language and reproduce them, which is present in infants until they are about one year old

PROGRAM SUMMARY

Learning language, the subject of Program 6, is one of the most amazing of all human accomplishments. How a baby learns to talk so quickly with so little help stimulates intense scientific interest and debate. Until the late 1950s, linguists assumed that children learned to speak by imitating their parents. But observations of young children reveal that early language patterns are unique, and parents rarely try to teach their children to talk.

In 1957 Noam Chomsky revolutionized the study of language when he suggested that babies were born with a built-in language acquisition device. He claimed that babies have the innate capacity for extracting meaning from the words and sentences they hear.

Ideas about the biological capacity for language gave rise to a new field: developmental psycholinguistics. Some psycholinguists, like Jean Berko Gleason, concentrate on the role of social interaction in language development. Gleason explains that environmental and hereditary factors contribute to the process of language acquisition. Communication depends on the ability of both speakers to decode and express their intentions, and includes the use of words and formats with shared meanings.

Research has shown that biology does play a role in language acquisition. Children all over the world follow the same steps as they learn the sounds, words, and rules of their own language. All babies have a built-in preference for voices and can pick out their mother's speech within the first few days of life. The fact that every child goes through the same sequences suggests that learning depends on some form of biological maturation. Scientists believe that a developmental timetable regulates the maturation of the brain and the muscles in the mouth and tongue that are needed for communication.

Although true language develops later, communication begins at birth. All normal babies cry and coo and can imitate facial expressions. After a couple of months, they begin babbling and make many varied sounds. By the end of their first year, they tend to specialize in those sounds that have meaning in their own language.

Using words as symbols represents an advance in thinking skills and a new kind of relationship with objects and people. Children increasingly use words as tools for achieving their goals as they move from one- to two-word utterances and simple sentences. Later, they use language for abstract purposes, such as discussing past events.

Just as the first steps in language development are universal (see Figure 3), so is the tendency for parents everywhere to use simplified, high-pitched, melodic baby talk. Anne Fernald explains that people everywhere speak to babies in this adapted style that linguists call motherese, parentese, or child-directed speech (CDS).

Parentese is typically slow, with longer pauses and shorter utterances than the speech used with older children and other adults. It seems to help babies understand units of speech and conveys an emotional content. Researchers observe that caregivers typically adapt to the child's level of language as language skills grow more complex.

Age	Language Skills
first few days of life	cry, coo, recognize mother's voice
2 months	babbling, varied sounds
1 year	specialized sounds in own language
18 months	babbles, knows some words
2 years	two-word phrases, knows more than 50 words
3 years	knows more than 1,000 words
by age 6	understands grammar and syntax

Note: The ages in this chart are approximations. Not all children acquire language at the same rate.

Figure 3: Language Development
Language development occurs in a regular pattern, leading some researchers to think that language is biologically innate.

The biggest task before age six is discovering the underlying regularities of language—the rules of grammar and syntax. Berkeley psychologist Dan Slobin explains that regularities in children's words and word combinations show that they use a system of grammatical rules that is not based on imitation. For example, children say "foots" and "mouses," although adults do not use those words or reinforce them. The children are using the right rules but in the wrong places.

The complicated social and linguistic strategies of children are part of the language development process. Children need to learn multiple uses of language, how to ask a question, and how to begin and end a conversation. Parents and caregivers teach children the rules of dialogue by asking questions, then teaching them the proper response, like "Thank you" and "Yes, please." These lessons not only help children learn how to use language but also prepare them for more advanced social interactions.

REVIEW QUESTIONS

Program Questions

1. Lori's parents are thrilled that their daughter has just said her first word. Based on this information, how old would you estimate Lori is?

    a. Three months
    b. Six months
    c. 12 months
    d. 18 months

2. Before Chomsky's work, what assumption was generally made about language acquisition?

    a. Babies have an innate capacity for extracting meaning.
    b. There is a built-in language acquisition device.
    c. Language development varies widely, depending on culture.
    d. Language is a skill learned by imitating parents.

3. What sounds do very young babies prefer?

    a. Ocean sounds
    b. Human voices
    c. Other babies
    d. Soft music

4. How does an infant react when its mother's voice is paired with the face of a stranger?

    a. By becoming upset
    b. By laughing
    c. By paying closer attention
    d. An infant is not capable of noting any discrepancy.

5. What kind of sentences does a mother use in talking to her baby?

    a. One-word commands
    b. Short, simple sentences
    c. Telegraphic sentences that lack function words
    d. Sentences that violate standard English word order

6. How does the development of language competence compare from culture to culture?

    a. It varies greatly.
    b. It is remarkably similar.
    c. Certain cultures are similar, while others are very different.
    d. This topic is just beginning to be explored by researchers.

7. Jean Berko Gleason has studied mothers and their babies. Her major focus is on the role of

    a. neurological maturation in language development.
    b. melodic patterns used by mothers in different cultures.
    c. social interaction in language development.
    d. parental patterning of conversational conventions.

8. One difference between cooing and babbling is that babbling allows a baby to

    a. say real words.
    b. express discomfort.
    c. develop its vocal cords.
    d. vary intonations.

9. A seven-month-old American child with American parents is babbling. The sounds that the child produces include

    a. sounds from many different languages.
    b. only sounds used in English.
    c. only sounds found in Western languages.
    d. sounds unlike those of any language.

10. When Anne Fernald says "the melody is the message," she means that

    a. babies take meaning from pitch contours.
    b. mothers need to sing to their babies.
    c. babies need to learn the intonation patterns of their native language.
    d. mothers speak slowly and clearly to their babies.

11. If you heard a mother using a rise-fall pattern with a high pitch and a sharp peak, what would you guess the mother would be saying?

    a. "Don't do that."
    b. "That's a good baby."
    c. "See the dog."
    d. "Are you hungry?"

12. What mental ability must a child have developed in order to use words as symbols?

    a. Storing and retrieving memory codes
    b. Recognizing the letters of the alphabet
    c. Composing questions
    d. Recognizing the spatial relationships between objects

13. If you hear a child saying "Go store," what is a good estimate of the child's age?

    a. One year old
    b. One and a half years old
    c. Two years old
    d. Three years old

14. What is the typical word order in English?

    a. Object, Action, Actor
    b. Actor, Object, Action
    c. Object, Actor, Action
    d. Actor, Action, Object

15. What does a sentence such as "I bringed the toy" show about how children acquire language?

    a. They imitate their parents, including the parents' errors.
    b. They have no interest in grammar and need training.
    c. They acquire grammatical rules on their own.
    d. They make errors based on watching television and listening to their peers.

16. What has Dan Slobin's research shown about children's language acquisition?

    a. Children are persistent in building regularity.
    b. Correct word order is difficult for children to grasp.
    c. Children learn conversation conventions at an early age.
    d. Some languages are easier than others to learn.

17. Which of the following is *not* one of the essential features of dialogue?

    a. Signaling the willingness to converse
    b. Understanding rules for taking turns
    c. Using proper forms of address
    d. Closing conversations by mutual agreement

Textbook Questions

18. All languages are made up of individual sounds called _____ that are recognized as distinct and different.

    a. phonemes
    b. morphemes
    c. extensions
    d. syntax

19. Morphemes are the smallest units of _____ in a language.

    a. sound
    b. meaning
    c. word order
    d. pronunciation

20. A TV station repeats a critical football play for the viewers at home. It is called a *re*play, not a play*re*, because

    a. phonemes must always precede a word.
    b. morphemes have fixed positions in language structure.
    c. the English language must be different from other languages.
    d. the word has always been used that way.

21. The rules for placing words in proper order to form meaningful sentences is called

    a. phonology.
    b. semantics.
    c. syntax.
    d. inflection.

22. _____ concerns the meaning of language.

    a. Phonology
    b. Semantics
    c. Syntax
    d. Telegraphic speech

23. That children sometimes produce sentences spontaneously emphasizes the fact that

    a. children learn language by classical conditioning.
    b. children learn language by operant conditioning.
    c. learning theory only partially explains language development.
    d. language is not learned.

24. The _____ theory emphasizes the innate tendency to acquire language.

    a. classical learning
    b. observation learning
    c. nativistic
    d. operant learning

25. In the genetic or nativist perspective, the "prewiring" that gives humans the innate ability to learn language is called the

    a. psycholinguistic drift.
    b. instinctual set.
    c. neural network.
    d. language acquisition device.

26. When young children use a single word to express complex meanings and thoughts, it is called a

    a. two-word utterance.
    b. holophrase.
    c. coo.
    d. surface structure.

27. Speech in which only the essential words are used is called

    a. baby talk.
    b. overextension.
    c. condensed speech.
    d. displaced speech.

28. When children form the plural of goose by saying "gooses," they are engaging in

    a. overextension.
    b. overgeneralization.
    c. inadequate semantics.
    d. inadequate symbolization.

29. The Premacks consider their work with Sarah (a chimpanzee) as a demonstration of the role _____ plays in language acquisition.

    a. the language-acquisition device
    b. classical conditioning
    c. operant conditioning
    d. observational learning

30. The criticism that apes' use of language may be a result of the "clever Hans effect" means that the apes

    a. learn language by operant conditioning.
    b. learn language by classical conditioning.
    c. are responding to subtle cues from their trainers.
    d. learn many fairy tales.

QUESTIONS TO CONSIDER

1. Is human language unique? Is language unique to humans? Although chimps and gorillas lack the vocal apparatus for spoken language, they can use symbols and signs for communication. Consider your textbook's definition of language. Why is there so much resistance to the idea that animals use language?

2. How closely tied are language and thought? Is language ability necessary for thought?

3. What role does nonverbal communication play in language development? How is it learned?

4. Why do people talk to animals? Why do people often use baby talk when they talk to their pets?

5. If a parent does not use "parentese," what implications might that have for an infant?

6. If most children acquire language before the age of six, why is grammar instruction such an important part of the school curriculum?

OPTIONAL ACTIVITIES

1. Watch television with the sound turned off. How much speech and sound is necessary to understand what is happening? Compare a familiar show with one you have never watched. Does familiarity make it easier to interpret the action? Compare a news program with a situation comedy or commercial. How much information depends on language? Visual cues? Listen to a show without watching the picture. How much content is verbal? Do you think young children and adults respond to program and advertising content in the same way?

2. Arrange to do an observation in a home or day care center. Observe a one-year-old and a two-year-old conversing, one at a time, with an adult, preferably their own mother. For at least 15 minutes, write down everything each child and the adult say to each other. After you have observed both adult-child pairs, analyze your transcripts. Describe and compare each child's word choices and language skills. Describe the adult's word choices, intonations, and voice and speech patterns. How well did they fit the child's level of language?

ANTHOLOGY

The following selections illustrate aspects of language as part of an interactive social system, as well as a complex communication process affecting cognitive and social development. Can you remember how and when you learned to talk? Did you begin talking early or late? Does your style of talking today bear any resemblance to your communication style as a child?

Reading 14

In the past, many children who could not communicate in traditional ways were doomed to silence, unable to express their thoughts and feelings. But advances in computer technology are helping disabled children overcome their inability to write, communicate, and express themselves. As you read this article, consider the benefits of these new communication tools for disabled children, and think about what these devices might offer all *children.*

Word Processing: A New Route Around Old Barriers

By Anne Meyer and David Rose

"He refuses to do anything in school that involves writing," Peter's mother explained. "Since the stroke, he just hasn't been able to control a pencil the way he used to."

Peter is a twelve-year-old student with a learning disability. He suffered a stroke at the age of seven and, as a result, Peter has trouble controlling the smaller and more precise movements of his body. Like most of us, Peter is sensitive about his performance and is intensely frustrated by the difference between the way he wants his papers to look and the way they turn out.

When Peter tries to express his ideas in writing, he encounters difficulties faced by every writer. Writing effectively is hard work. A writer must devote attention to the sequence of ideas, effective phrasing and his or her purpose in writing.

In addition to the usual complexities, Peter's disabilities make writing an even greater task. He has trouble holding the pencil steady. He forms letters incorrectly and they often drift above and below the line. The spaces between the letters are uneven and he sometimes fails to leave a space between words. Peter is not an accurate speller. Sometimes when he produces legible letters, they are not the correct ones.

Because Peter is paying so much attention to forming letters and spelling words correctly, he doesn't concentrate on the content of his work. He often leaves out words or whole sentences, or puts words into the wrong order. By the time his paper is finished, he has struggled long and hard. Nevertheless, his paper looks a mess. Unfortunately, his labors have become a source of disappointment, not an accomplishment he can take pride in. Since the writing process has been so painful and exasperating, Peter refuses to write. He has begun to fail in school because he cannot and will not write. He has the potential to write effectively, but his prior experiences have prevented his progress. Peter is literally incapable of writing effectively without special tools.

Just as a visually impaired person cannot, through sheer effort, improve his eyesight, Peter cannot overcome his disabilities by working harder or by being taught differently. Just as a visually impaired person needs corrective lenses, Peter needs a "prosthetic" device for writing—a personal computer equipped with word processing software and a printer. These tools will serve as a substitute for a "normal" ability that he has lost and his classmates still have.

Using the powerful tools personal computers make available to writers, children with disabilities can overcome physical, intellectual, emotional and attitudinal barriers that have hindered their self-expression and independence. Computers can be used or adapted to help overcome the barriers to writing.

Overcoming Physical Barriers

A large number of children with disabilities have mild and severe impairments affecting their motor coordination and control. Even the most minor difficulty can make forming letters a slow and painful process, severely impeding writing.

Word processing equipment is a necessity, not just an efficient alternative to handwriting or typing, for children and adults with motor disabilities. Word processors enable writers to fix errors, edit and change text and to make corrections on the computer screen before a printed copy can be viewed by others. If rewriting is necessary, only the parts to be changed require keystrokes and then a brand new, perfect-looking copy can be printed. Many writers praise the use of personal computers with word processing programs.

Children and adults with disabilities who are not able to use a regular keyboard can gain access to word processing software through "alternative keyboards." A variety of alternative keyboards have been designed to accommodate individual needs. Expanded keyboards feature large, recessed keys and larger spaces between the letters on the board. Recessed keys enable the user to rest a hand on the keyboard without unintentionally striking a key. A greater distance between the keys makes it easier to pick out the target key.

Some people with disabilities are physically unable to access a word processor through the use of any keyboard. In such cases, a single switch, which can be activated by whatever muscle groups can be reliably controlled, will provide access. For example, if the user can reliably control the movement of their foot, a switch will be mounted so that it can easily be reached by the foot. Switches vary in size, texture and pressure sensitivity depending on the needs of the person.

To assist users limited to access with a single switch, other adaptations are available. Scanning programs are used in conjunction with the switch to scan the letters of the alphabet and the function keys on the screen. The user chooses a group of letters by activating the single switch when they appear. Then, the letters are scanned one by one, until the target letter is chosen and inserted into the text.

Word processing with a single switch can be a dramatically empowering experience. Some children, who are nonvocal, may be able to use a word processor with a speech synthesizer to literally "talk" for them. Those who have lost motor function through accident or illness are able to regain the power of writing.

Overcoming Intellectual Barriers

Many children are impeded from writing because of disorders affecting memory, planning, spelling, and organization. These problems are pervasive and resistant to even the most systematic of remedial efforts.

There are many software programs that help students plan or outline a composition. *Brainstorming*, from Milliken, is one example. With this program, students pick a subject, then type in a series of words or phrases. Next, they group the ideas and name the groups, forming the basis for a series of paragraphs. This program helps students who have trouble starting and organizing their compositions by structuring the steps and making each step small and manageable. This process is simply creating an outline with the aid of a computer. With this tool, children no longer need to sit and stare at a blank page, with their anxiety increasing, until someone else comes to give them an idea.

Computer software also serves as a proofreading aid to the age-old problem of spelling. Children with disabilities, like many youngsters, even if they are active writers, do not pay enough attention to spelling. Built-in spellcheckers, available with some software programs, will identify words that are not found in dictionaries; the writer must check the identified word for accuracy. Spellcheckers do not, however, find all the errors. For example, the program will not identify common errors such as using "here" instead of "hear." These tools help students gain the power to start monitoring the correctness of their own work, "look up" spellings on the screen when they are not sure, and keep track of their own errors.

Overcoming Emotional Barriers

Emotional disabilities can evolve out of failure and frustration. Children whose best efforts yield disappointing products eventually learn a destructive and unintended lesson: That trying hard does not yield results, that they are unable to bring about change. As was the case for Peter, these children may become unwilling to invest more effort where it seems to do no good.

Word processors and printers are tools that can help a child re-engage in writing. First of all, the computer is a new medium. The keyboard and screen are often free of the negative associations that have become attached to the pen, paper and book.

Using word processors enables children to produce quickly written work in which they can take pride. The very first line of text they write and print looks professional—even if the spelling isn't right, they can have a new feeling about their work, a sense of promise. Their disabilities no longer keep them dependent nor limit their expression; instead they find independence and power.

At The Center for Applied Special Technology (CAST), we have seen repeatedly the beneficial effects of this powerful device. When Peter began using the word processor, we discovered how much he had to say. Now he writes for long periods in front of the screen. He seeks advice when he wants to improve the effectiveness of a particular phrase, to give it more "punch." When he's ready to read over his work or show it to someone else, he tells the printer to produce a copy on paper. With one keystroke, he has produced a professional looking document, every letter is formed and spaced correctly. When he wants to revise or edit, he fixes only those parts of the paper that need to be changed, then prints another perfect copy. It is not an exaggeration to say that the word processor and printer have changed Peter's life.

The 'Right' to Tools

The ability to write is critical to academic and vocational success, to effective communication, and to self esteem. As children progress through the grades, instruction relies increasingly on writing as a means of demonstrating knowledge and developing ideas. Without word processors, children with disabilities that affect their ability to write do not have equal access to education and opportunity. Students with disabilities need three things—appropriate prosthetic tools, adequate access to those tools, and training in their use.

Like those who need powered wheelchairs for mobility or glasses for effective vision, students with disabilities need "prosthetic" devices for writing. Selection of appropriate tools should be based on careful individual assessment of a child's needs so that the tools provided are correctly chosen for individual needs.

Tools, even powerful ones, are ineffective unless full access to their use is provided. The presence of computers in the school does not ensure accessibility; frequently the actual time available on the machine is extremely limited. Imagine a child who needs corrective lenses being told that he can use his glasses once a week for fifteen minutes when his class goes to the "glasses lab." Or that he must wait his turn to use the one pair of glasses in the back of the classroom. Meanwhile, we encourage him to work on learning to see better!

Finally, children must be carefully taught to use prosthetic writing tools. Word processing and related programs are powerful, but they are not easy to learn. They are not a replacement for good teaching and good parenting. Helping children and adults to use the new tools requires the same sensitivity, imagination, and persistence that the effective teaching of anything important requires.

Many schools do not provide students with disabilities with the right tools, accessibility to those tools and the proper instruction to use them. It is surprising (and dismaying) to find how rarely the computer is being used in special needs settings. A survey conducted by Mokros & Russell, published in *The Journal of Learning Disabilities*, indicated that in a sample of "sophisticated," computer-using, special needs teachers, only one quarter were using word processing. In order to bring about change for our children, we must make accessibility to the power of computers a priority in their schools. Set an early deadline for your school; start today!

Reading 15

Every time we find ourselves in an unfamiliar situation in which we need to negotiate shared meanings with others, we use language in a new way. This article discusses the problem of exchanging medical information when communication is complicated by cultural barriers as well as by medical jargon. Imagine yourself trying to get medical care in a hospital where no one knows your language. As you read, note the elements of language and communication that interpreters must consider. Could a computer or translation machine provide this type of service?

Advice from An Interpreter

By Ozzie F. Díaz-Duque

There is a widespread misconception that being bilingual automatically qualifies a person to be an interpreter. This notion leads health care professionals to recruit the patient's family, friends, and even other patients to interpret—a practice that should be relegated to the category of "last resort."

For one thing, friends and relatives do not have a health care background, and therefore lack, in either language, a knowledge of medical terminology; nor are they familiar with hospital policies, procedures, and routines. In addition, many patients have complained that their rights of confidentiality have been violated by the relative or friend who served as a translator.

We therefore strongly urge care givers to rely either on a bilingual member of the health care team or on a trained interpreter who is familiar with interpreting techniques, patients' rights, and the way the health care system functions. At the University of Iowa Hospitals and Clinics we have had an interpreter program and staff since 1975, and there is general agreement that is has proved useful in facilitating understanding between health care provider and patient.

For health professionals to work effectively with interpreters, they need to know the kinds of problems interpreters have, as well as what to expect from them. The principles upon which good translations are based stem from a thorough knowledge of both the language and the culture of the patient, since barriers to communication can arise from either source.

Register. All languages have several registers, defined generally as the social/intellectual level at which the language is placed. The translator must be able to determine the patient's register and communicate with him or her on that level. Otherwise, the interpreter runs the risk of alienating the patient or precipitating the "nodding syndrome"— that is, the patient who nods in agreement out of fear of embarrassment because he doesn't understand. Also, if the interpreter speaks in too learned a register, the patient may fear that the interpreter will find his speech amusing or unpolished.

Health professionals (and interpreters) need to be aware of the quick nod, because many of the questions they ask require yes or no answers. For example, are you in pain? Did you have a BM today? Are you allergic to any medications? It may take the staff a long time to realize that even though a patient gives an affirmative nod, he has really not understood much of what was said.

Some patients may have a complete absence of register with regard to certain subjects. If the problem is a gynecologic one, for instance, the conversation often deals with highly personal matters. Many Hispanic women have never given names to such body parts as the vagina or such aspects of sexual response as orgasm. The interpreter must therefore transmit messages as clearly as possible, while maintaining decorum and diplomacy. Even under these circumstances though, the patient may still provide the wrong information, none at all, or simply succumb to embarrassment.

On the whole, it is usually better for the interpreter to include anecdotal information in the translation. Health professionals who try to prevent patients from relaying such information run the risk of alienating them. Since a *curandero* never isolates the patient's illness from his or her social environment, the patient may lose confidence in a practitioner who does.

Health professionals should also realize that Hispanic clients may expect immediate results, including returning home with a medication and a rapid cure for their ailments. They expect this because most folk healers diagnose the problem and offer an immediate cure or treatment. What they offer may be only a placebo, but something is done and this gives the patient satisfaction and may provide psychological reinforcement that may indeed speed recovery.

Fear. One factor that can and does interfere with a person's ability to communicate and receive a message is fear. Thus, the mere fact that a non-English speaker is ill and in a hospital can interfere greatly with that person's ability to communicate.

We have also noted that patients who otherwise have a basic command of English often request interpreting services when they come to the hospital. This is particularly true in such specialties as gynecology, urology, obstetrics, and psychiatry, or in relation to such services as abortion, venereal disease screening, and family planning services. Because of the delicate nature of the conversation on these subjects, the patient may feel more comfortable talking through an interpreter.

Nonverbal behavior. Interpreters who provide only a literal translation of the patient's words may not be as effective as those who take into consideration such nonverbal aspects of communication as nuances, intonation patterns, and facial expressions. These tell their own story, and it is important for everyone involved in the interview to be able to see, as well as to hear each other. Interpreters who "act out" their message—through intonation, facial expression, or gestures—are likely to be more effective in getting their message across. They need to be similarly expert in interpreting the patient's gestures and movements.

Even when every effort is made to insure effective translations, neither the health professional nor the interpreter can be completely sure that accurate communication has been achieved. Even when two people speak the same language, misunderstandings can occur. Communication through a third party compounds the problem, and one may discover, a few hours later, that the patient hasn't really understood. Even when patients are asked to repeat what was just said, they tend to add to or edit the material. This is especially likely to happen when the patient has had little or no formal education.

It is true that there are problems in communicating with the non-English-speaking patient, even with an interpreter, but it is possible to break down some of the barriers. We would recommend, first, that efforts be made to educate clients about modern health care practices, in order to demystify medicine and to bring it closer to the people in *their own language*. Second, health care personnel should learn something about popular beliefs, folk medicine, and sociocultural barriers that interfere with the delivery of health care. Third, health care facilities providing services to large non-English-speaking populations should consider establishing interpretation and translation services.

The need for *trained* medical interpreters will continue, however, and both the health care providers *and* patients should be made familiar with the role of the interpreter, an important—and sometimes crucial—member of the health care team.

ADDITIONAL RESOURCES

Books and Articles

Hockett, Charles F. "The Origin of Speech." *Scientific American* (September 1960): 89–96. Human languages share similarities with the communication systems of bees, fish, and other creatures. Hockett examines these similarities and sketches out the possible evolution of human speech.

Miller, G. A. *Language and Speech*. San Francisco: Freeman, 1981. This basic text examines language and its development in the individual and in the human species.

Moskowitz, Breyne A. "The Acquisition of Language." *Scientific American* (November 1978): 92–108. Children learn to speak in a highly methodical way. This article looks at the methods and rules children use to acquire language.

Motley, Michael T. "What I Meant to Say." *Psychology Today* (February 1987): 24–28. Freud believed slips of the tongue exposed actual thoughts and desires. Some psychologists and linguists disagree.

Pines, M. "The Civilizing of Genie." *Psychology Today* (September 1981): 28–34. In 1970 the discovery of a "wild child" in California stirred up many old and new questions about language development.

SENSATION AND PERCEPTION

We are told about the world before we see it. We imagine most things before we experience them. And those preconceptions, unless education has made us acutely aware, govern deeply the whole process of perception.

Walter Lippmann

Unit 7 explores how we make contact with the world outside our brain and body. We'll see how biological, cognitive, social, and environmental influences shape our personal sense of reality, and we'll gain an understanding of how psychologists use our perceptual errors to study how the constructive process of perception works.

The slanted walls, ceiling, and floor of the Ames Distorted Room in San Francisco's Exploratorium museum illustrate how visual clues influence perception.

OBJECTIVES

After viewing the television program and completing the assigned readings, you should be able to:

1. Describe the relationship between sensation and perception

2. Describe the different parts of the human eye and explain the functions of each in the transduction of light

3. Describe the main principles and theories of color vision

4. Outline the main processes involved in transducing physical sounds into auditory perception

5. Outline the main processes involved in taste and smell

6. Outline the processes involved in transducing physical stimuli for the skin and body senses

7. Describe and give examples of the main principles of perceptual organization

8. Describe stimulus characteristics that determine selective attention

9. Describe the binocular and monocular cues for distance perception

10. Define perceptual constancy and outline different sorts of constancy

11. Explain how perceptual illusions provide clues to perceptual rules

READING ASSIGNMENT

After viewing Program 7, read pages 111–162 in *Psychology: Science, Behavior and Life*. Your instructor may also assign the anthology selections for Unit 7.

KEY TERMS AND CONCEPTS

As you read the assignment, pay particular attention to these terms, which are defined on the given pages in the text.

sensation (111)	hue (121)
perception (111)	saturation (121)
psychophysics (112)	accommodation (122)
transduction (112)	retina (122)
sensory threshold (112)	rods (122)
absolute threshold (113)	cones (122)
difference threshold (114)	dark adaptation (123)
just noticeable difference (jnd) (114)	light adaptation (124)
Weber's Law (114)	additive color mixing (128)
attention (115)	subtractive color mixing (128)
adaptation (116)	Young-Helmholtz theory (128)
brightness (121)	

The following terms are used in Program 7 but are not defined in the text.

distal stimulus—a stimulus that lies in the world outside us

proximal stimulus—the stimulus that acts directly on the sensory receptors

bottom-up processing—the processing of sensory stimuli that proceeds from the receptors to the brain without taking the context of stimulation into account

top-down processing—the processing of sensory stimuli that uses contextual information stored in the brain to recognize the stimulus

subjective contours—a perceptual illusion illustrating closure principles. See Fig. 4.31 on p. 149 in the textbook.

PROGRAM SUMMARY

Can we believe our eyes? For centuries, magicians and artists have entertained, deceived, and delighted us because we tend to believe what we see. Most of the time our perceptions are remarkably error-free. They have to be; survival in our ever changing, complex environment depends on accurate perception.

Although psychologists study all sensory processes, including hearing, smell, touch, and taste, Program 7 focuses on visual perception and the processes we rely on to create meaning out of the world's myriad objects and events.

To sense, perceive, and understand the world, we use two different processes. When our eyes, ears, and other sensory apparatus detect stimulation and send the data to the brain, it is called "bottom-up" processing. Then "top-down" processing occurs, adding in what we already know and remember.

First, the raw sensory data is relayed to the thalamus, which analyzes and directs it to specialized areas in the cortex, the outermost covering of the brain. The cortex processes this information and, scientists believe, combines it with old data stored in the memory.

Visual perception takes place in three different areas: the retina, the pathways through the brain, and the visual cortex. It is in the visual cortex that flashes of light are broken down and decoded, enabling us to distinguish one object from another.

In addition to identifying objects, the brain has to compute size, distance, and boundaries. It must make these decisions almost instantaneously so we can go about our daily routines safely and smoothly.

Memories, expectations, culture, and language also influence how we derive meaning from sensory information. Unlike a camera, which merely copies an image, our perceptual process is actively processing the world by selecting, classifying, and judging. Consider that a simple curve and a line in the right place on a sheet of paper may look like a nose and a mouth. But when we put these same lines in another context, they may look like random, meaningless marks, or even like some different object.

The brain also must work to eliminate confusing signals and fill in the blanks. We know that a railroad track doesn't converge and disappear in the distance when we look toward the horizon. And if a shadow falls on our newspaper, we know that the paper isn't really turning black. Perception goes beyond sensory information to impose stability on a constantly changing flow of information.

Figure 4: What Do You See?
Do you see a young woman or an old woman in this image? Researchers have found that younger people tend to see a young woman and older people tend to see an older woman, because we expect to see what we're familiar with.

Psychologists have learned a great deal about how perception works from studying illusions—the perceptual traps we fall into because we use perceptual principles as shortcuts to deal with a flood of sensory input. Fortunately, these shortcuts work most of the time. For example, even when a stop sign is partially obscured by leaves, we still "see" the sign. Although we understand only about 70 percent of the words we hear, we can make sense out of a spoken message because our minds fill in the rest from context.

Have you ever failed to recognize people you knew when you encountered them in a place where you didn't expect to see them? The reason is that our expectations and personal biases have a powerful effect on perception (see Figure 4). We may fail to see something because we don't expect or want to see it, which is one reason why people are often unreliable eyewitnesses to an accident or crime.

All of our senses put us in touch with the world around us. But it is our brain that organizes our perceptions, letting us know what's out there and how we should react.

Because the perceptual process is the basis for everything we learn, think, and do, scientists and laypersons alike are interested in finding out more about how this extremely sophisticated system works.

REVIEW QUESTIONS

Program Questions

1. Imagine that a teaspoon of sugar is dissolved in two gallons of water. Rita can detect this level of sweetness at least half the time. This level is called the

   a. distal stimulus.
   b. perceptual constant.
   c. response bias.
   d. absolute threshold.

2. What is the job of a receptor?

   a. To transmit a neural impulse
   b. To connect new information with old information
   c. To detect a type of physical energy
   d. To receive an impulse from the brain

3. In what area of the brain is the visual cortex located?

   a. In the front
   b. In the middle
   c. In the back
   d. Under the brain stem

4. What is the function of the thalamus in visual processing?

   a. It relays information to the cortex.
   b. It rotates the retinal image.
   c. It converts light energy to a neural impulse.
   d. It makes sense of the proximal stimulus.

5. Dave Hubel discusses the visual pathway and the response to a line. The program shows films from an experiment where the response to a moving line changes dramatically with changes in the line's

   a. thickness.
   b. color.
   c. speed.
   d. orientation.

6. Misha Pavel is using computer graphics to study how

   a. we process visual information.
   b. rods differ from cones in function.
   c. we combine information from different senses.
   d. physical energy is transduced in the visual system.

7. Imagine that a psychologist equips a male baseball player with special glasses that shift the player's visual field up 10 degrees. When he wears these glasses, the player sees everything higher than it actually is. After some practice, the player can hit with the glasses on. What will happen when the player first tries to hit with the glasses off?

   a. He will think the ball is higher than it is.
   b. He will think the ball is lower than it is.
   c. He will accurately perceive the ball's position.
   d. It is impossible to predict an individual's reaction in this situation.

8. Imagine that a dog is walking toward you. As the dog gets closer, the image it casts on your retina

   a. gets larger.
   b. gets darker.
   c. gets smaller.
   d. stays exactly the same size.

9. You want to paint your room yellow, so you get some samples at the paint store. When you hold the sample against your white wall, it looks different from the way it looks against the green curtain. A psychologist would attribute this to

   a. perceptual constancy.
   b. visual paradoxes.
   c. contrast effects.
   d. threshold differences.

10. Because perception must work quickly, it relies especially on information about an object's

   a. color.
   b. relative size.
   c. edges.
   d. central point.

11. The program shows a drawing that can be seen as a rat or as a man. Subjects were more likely to identify the drawing as a man if they

   a. were men.
   b. had just seen pictures of people.
   c. were afraid of rats.
   d. looked at the picture holistically rather than analytically.

12. When we see a visual paradox such as the Escher picture, why do we have difficulty interpreting it?

   a. There is too much difference between the proximal stimulus and the distal stimulus.
   b. The difference threshold is the same as the absolute threshold.
   c. What we know contradicts what we see.
   d. There is too much unfamiliar information to take in.

Textbook Questions

13. The mechanical stimulation of sensory receptors and the transmission of sensory information to the central nervous system is known as

    a. hyperperception.
    b. innervation.
    c. perception.
    d. sensation.

14. The ability to distinguish sensations does not depend on differences between sense organs, but rather

    a. on the part of the brain activated by the sensory messages.
    b. on the particular sense that is activated.
    c. on the just noticeable difference.
    d. on transduction.

15. The minimum physical intensity of a stimulus that can be perceived by an observer 50 percent of the time is the

    a. difference threshold.
    b. just noticeable difference.
    c. refractory threshold.
    d. absolute threshold.

16. Weber's Law states that the size of the just noticeable difference is

    a. constant for all values of the standard stimulus.
    b. constant for all values of the comparison stimulus.
    c. a constant proportion of the absolute threshold.
    d. a constant proportion of the magnitude of a standard stimulus.

17. The _____ of visible light determines its hue, or color.

    a. intensity
    b. wavelength
    c. angle
    d. duration

18. The weakest amount of light a person can see is called the

    a. difference threshold.
    b. amplitude.
    c. absolute threshold.
    d. just noticeable difference.

19. The film or image surface of a camera corresponds to the _____ of the eye.

    a. lens
    b. retina
    c. fovea
    d. pupil

20. Rods and cones are

    a. bipolar cells.
    b. ganglion cells.
    c. photoreceptors.
    d. color receptors.

21. In very dim, low-intensity light, vision is diminished. If we look directly at an object we may not see it because we are focusing the available light onto the

    a. fovea, where there are only cones.
    b. fovea, where there are only rods.
    c. blind spot.
    d. peripheral part of the fovea.

22. Color vision is possible because of the _____ in the retinal tissue.

    a. fluid
    b. rods
    c. blind spot
    d. cones

23. The fact that we never perceive such shades as greenish-red or bluish-yellow supports which theory of color vision?

    a. The opponent-process theory
    b. The trichromatic theory
    c. The Young theory
    d. The Young-Helmholtz theory

24. Alternate expansion and compression of air molecules produces

    a. light.
    b. sound.
    c. sense of smell.
    d. sense of touch.

25. The quality or richness of a sound differing among instruments is known as

    a. overtone.
    b. decibel.
    c. pitch.
    d. timbre.

26. The thin membrane which vibrates in response to sound waves is the

    a. tympanic membrane.
    b. oval window.
    c. outer ear.
    d. cochlea.

27. According to the frequency theory of sound, the frequency with which receptor cells fire determines the _____ of a sound.

    a. pitch
    b. timbre
    c. loudness
    d. location

28. _____ and _____ are used by the individual to locate sounds.

    a. Loudness; timbre
    b. Loudness; time delay
    c. Pitch; loudness
    d. Time delay; timbre

29. There are four qualities of taste: sweet, sour, _____, and _____ .

    a. bitter; spicy
    b. bitter; salty
    c. salty; spicy
    d. salty; hot

30. The Gate-Control theory of pain suggests that

    a. pain is inevitable.
    b. acupuncture does not work.
    c. chemicals induce the perception of pain.
    d. competition from other sensations may block our perception of pain.

31. The Rubin vase is used by psychologists to demonstrate rules of

    a. perceptual organization.
    b. perceptual constancy.
    c. depth perception.
    d. visual illusions.

32. If you are listening to a TV announcer report an important event and a friend begins to talk to you at the same time, but you continue to listen to the TV, the TV becomes the

    a. figure.
    b. ground.
    c. closure.
    d. similarity.

33. The difference in the retinal image of an object as seen from each eye provides an important cue for depth which is called

    a. interposition.
    b. convergence.
    c. linear perspective.
    d. binocular disparity.

34. Artists use _____ cues to create an illusion of depth on a two-dimensional surface.

    a. monocular
    b. binocular
    c. perspective
    d. interposition

35. An important depth cue, based on the fact that objects that are highest on one's view appear to be farthest away, is

    a. interposition.
    b. convergence.
    c. linear perspective.
    d. height on a plane.

36. When an object is recognizable to us regardless of its distance, shape, or angle of perspective, we experience

    a. a perceptual constancy.
    b. depth perception.
    c. an illusion.
    d. a binocular cue.

37. When sensations give rise to misrepresentations, psychologists refer to this as

    a. a constant.
    b. perceptual organization.
    c. disorganization.
    d. an illusion.

QUESTIONS TO CONSIDER

1. As the population ages, adapting the environment for people with a range of sensory abilities and deficits will become increasingly important. Architects will need to improve access and safety of buildings, taking into account that older people need about three times as much light as young people in order to distinguish objects. They also need higher visual contrasts to detect potential hazards such as curbs or steps. Evaluate your home environment, and identify some changes you could make to create a safer, more comfortable environment for a disabled, or visually or hearing impaired person.

2. Investigations of people who claim to have extrasensory perception reveal that the better controlled the study, the less likely it is to support claims of ESP. Does it do any harm to believe in ESP? Why do most psychologists suggest that we should be skeptical of people who claim to have extrasensory perception?

3. Gestalt rules of organization are evident in any good page layout. Related items are often placed together or have some design similarities. Magazine advertisers know that it is not only the design but the positioning of the ad that is crucial for grabbing and holding the reader's attention. Analyze several page layouts in a popular magazine. How are color, size, copy, and pictures used? Are Gestalt principles used to convey ideas? If so, how?

4. Describe how film and television directors use sight and sound techniques to create meaning and feeling. As you watch a television commercial, program, or film, notice the way the camera frames the image, and how angle and motion create a mood or point of view. Notice the use of sound. Consider how these elements shape viewers' needs, expectations, and feelings.

OPTIONAL ACTIVITIES

1. Closure and continuity of line are organizing principles that we use to make sense out of stimuli. Make line drawings of familiar objects by tracing pictures from the comics, children's coloring books, or magazines. Leave out sections of the drawing, and ask family members or friends to identify the objects. See how incomplete the line drawing can be and still be identified.

2. Blindfold yourself. (Have someone standing by to prevent injury or damage.) Contrast the experience of moving about in a familiar room such as your bedroom or kitchen, with the experience of moving about a room in which you spend little time. Note the expectations and significant sensory cues you depend on to avoid tripping and bumping into things. How relaxed or tense were you in each room?

ANTHOLOGY

These readings illustrate aspects of the sensory and perceptual process. As you read, think about your own perception of reality and the roles biology, expectations, experience, and language play in shaping your world.

Reading 16

Separating what is real from what is not is the major task of perception. When do we begin to distinguish appearances from reality? According to this article, most children don't show a well-developed abstract understanding of the appearance-reality distinction until the age of 11 or 12. As you read, consider the following questions: How might a child's level of language acquisition influence the findings of the studies? What other factors might interfere with obtaining accurate data? Was the study design successful in overcoming these factors?

Really and Truly

By John H. Flavell

It looks like a nice, solid piece of granite, but as soon as you squeeze it you know it's really a joke-store sponge made to look like a rock. If I ask what it appears to be, you say, "It looks just like a rock." If I ask what it really is, you say, "It's a sponge, of course." A 3-year-old probably wouldn't be so sure. Children at this age often aren't quite able to grasp the idea that what you see is not always what you get.

By the time they are 6 or 7 years old, however, most children have a fair grasp of the appearance-reality distinction that assumes so many forms in our everyday lives. Misperceptions, misexpectations, misunderstandings, false beliefs, deception, play and fantasy—these and other examples of that distinction are a preoccupation of philosophers, scientists, artists, politicians and other public performers and of the rest of us who try to evaluate what they all say and do.

For the past half dozen years, my colleagues and I have been asking children questions about sponge rocks and using other methods to find out what children of different ages know about the difference between appearances and reality. First we give the children a brief lesson on the meaning of the appearance-reality distinction by showing them, for example, a Charlie Brown puppet inside a ghost costume. We explain and demonstrate that Charlie Brown "looks like a ghost to your eyes right now" but is "really and truly Charlie Brown," and that "sometimes things look like one thing to your eyes when they are really and truly something else."

We then show the children a variety of illusory objects, such as sponge rocks, in a straightforward fashion and ask questions in random order, about the reality and appearance of the objects: "What is this really and truly; is it really and truly a sponge or is it really and truly a rock?" "When you look at this with your eyes right now, does it look like a rock or does it look like a sponge?"

Or we show a 3-year-old and a 6-year-old a red toy car covered by a green filter that makes the car look black, hand the car to the child to inspect, put it behind the filter again and then ask: "What color is this car? Is it red or is it black?" The 3-year-old is likely to say "black," the 6-year-old "red." We use similar procedures to investigate the children's awareness of the distinction between real and apparent size, shape, events and the presence or absence of a hidden object.

In all these tests, most 3-year-old children have difficulty making the distinction between appearance and reality. They often err by giving the same answer (appearance or reality) to both questions. However, they rarely answer both questions incorrectly, suggesting that the mistakes are not random; the children are simply having conceptual problems with the distinction. By the time they are 6 or 7, however, most children get almost all the questions right.

Among 3-year-olds, certain types of illusory objects tend to elicit appearance answers to both questions (what we call a phenomenism error pattern), while others usually produce reality answers to both (an intellectual realism error pattern). The latter is the more surprising pattern because it contradicts the widely held view that young children respond only to what is currently most noticeable to them.

When we ask children to distinguish between the real and apparent properties of color, size and shape, they are most likely to make phenomenism (appearance) errors. If, for example, we use lenses or filters to make an object that is really red or small or straight look black or big or bent, most 3-year-olds will say the object really is black or big or bent.

But if we ask them what object or event is really present or has really occurred, most make intellectual realism errors. For example, children say the fake rock looks like a sponge. When they are shown a display consisting of a small object blocked from view by a large one, they say the display looks like it contains both objects rather than only the one they see. When they are shown someone who appears from the child's viewing position to be reading a large book but who the child knows is really drawing a picture inside the book, most children say it looks like the person is drawing rather than reading.

We also find that children make more phenomenism errors when we describe the same illusory stimuli in terms of their properties ("white" versus "orange" liquid) rather than in terms of the identities ("milk" versus "Kool-Aid"). Exactly why the appearance usually seems to be more important to young children in the first case and the reality more important in the second case remains a mystery.

Understanding of the appearance-reality distinction seems so necessary to everyday social life that it is hard to imagine a society in which normal people would not acquire it. To see if our findings applied in other cultures, we repeated one of our early experiments with 3-to-5-year-olds from Stanford University's laboratory preschool with Chinese children of the same age at Beijing Normal University's laboratory preschool. Error patterns, age changes and even absolute levels of performance at each age level proved to be remarkably similar, suggesting that our results were not due to a simple misunderstanding of the English expressions "really and truly" and "looks like to your eyes right now." Instead, it seems that 3 or 4 years of age is the time when children of both cultures begin to acquire some understanding of the appearance-reality distinction.

We have not yet found effective ways to test for possible precursors of the appearance-reality distinction in children younger than 3, but we have tried to find out whether 3-year-olds really and truly lack competence in this area or only appear to. If there is one lesson to be learned from the recent history of developmental psychology, it is that the mental abilities of young children are often seriously underestimated simply because researchers at first fail to come up with accurate ways to measure those abilities.

To avoid this mistake, we devised a number of what we thought were easy appearance-reality tasks to be administered to groups of 3-year-olds. We used the same object-identity (fake objects) and color (objects placed behind colored filters) tasks as in our previous investigations, but we tried to make them easier for very young children. The tasks still demanded some genuine, if minimal, knowledge of the appearance-reality distinction but came closer than the standard tasks to demanding that knowledge.

In one easy color task, for example, we left a small part of an object uncovered by the filter so its real color was still visible to the children when the appearance and reality questions were asked. In another one, we took milk, whose real color is well known to young children, and used a filter to change it to a different color that they never see it have in reality. We thought this might help the children both keep the real color in mind and recognize the bizarre apparent color as mere appearance.

And since the repeated linking of questions about appearance and reality might confuse 3-year-olds, we further simplified matters by avoiding appearance and reality questions on some tasks. For example, at the beginning of the testing session, prior to any talk about appearances and realities, we asked the single "is" question about the toy car's color. Is it red, or is it black?

Similar strategies were used to create what seemed to be easier object-identity tasks: After a brief conversation about dressing up for Halloween in masks and costumes, the children were questioned about the real and apparent identity of one of the experimenters who had conspicuously put on a mask. We assumed that young children would be more knowledgeable about this sort of appearance-reality discrepancy through Halloween and play experiences than with those created by the fake objects and filters we had used in previous experiments.

Our use of easier-looking, less demanding tasks to study appearance-reality competence was surprisingly unsuccessful. Some of the children did perform slightly better on the easy tasks, but as a group their level of performance was almost the same as on the standard tasks. The results suggest that the typical young preschooler cannot think effectively about appearances and realities even when the tasks are deliberately made "child-friendly."

In a final test for hidden competence on appearance-reality tasks, we selected 16 3-year-olds who performed very poorly on such tasks and trained them intensively for five to seven minutes on the meaning of real versus apparent color.

We demonstrated, defined terms and repeatedly explained that the real, true color of an object remains the same despite repeated, temporary changes in its apparent color due to the use of a filter. We fully expected that this training would help the children, but when we retested them, only one showed any improvement, and that was slight. The difficulties 3-year-olds have with the appearance-reality distinction are apparently very real indeed.

Things soon begin to change, however. In both the United States and the People's Republic of China we found that performance on our appearance-reality tasks improves greatly between 3 and 5 years of age. This is consistent with the reported increase, at around 4 years of age, in the ability (probably related) to talk with playmates about pretend play.

While 6- and 7-year-olds are almost consistently error-free on these simple appearance-reality tasks, their development of knowledge about the distinction is not yet complete. We found, for example, that even though 6- and 7-year-olds answer the questions correctly, they continue to have trouble with the concept and find it difficult to talk about appearances, realities and appearance-reality distinctions.

Most don't show a well-developed abstract understanding of the appearance-reality distinction until about the age of 11 or 12. In fact, it may not be until the time they reach adulthood that most people have a sufficiently rich and creative understanding of the concept that they can not only identify appearance-reality discrepancies but also reproduce them, change them to create new ones.

Our studies of how the appearance-reality distinction develops may shed light on a larger development—the child's understanding that mental representations of objects and events can differ both within the same person and between persons. I can be simultaneously aware, for example, that something appears to be a rock and that it really is a sponge. I can also be aware that it might appear to be something different under special viewing conditions, or that yesterday I pretended or fantasized that it was something else. I know that these are all possible ways that I can "represent" the same thing. In addition, I may be aware that you might represent the same thing differently than I do, because our perspectives on it might differ.

Knowledge about the appearance-reality distinction is but one instance of our more general knowledge that an object or event can be represented in different ways by the same person and by different people. The development of our understanding of the appearance-reality distinction, therefore, is worth studying because it is part of the larger development of our conscious knowledge about our own and other minds. And that's an area of development worth investigating—really and truly.

Reading 17

The case of Madeleine J. is a remarkable example of a woman, blind since birth, who had not used her hands for 60 years. Although the sensory capacity of her hands was intact, she had absolutely no perceptual awareness of her hands. Some animal studies have suggested that deprivation during critical stages of development damages perceptual capacities. Human studies suggest that the first two years are particularly crucial. How did Madeleine maintain tactile sensory capacity? Do you think other experiences compensated for years of sensory deprivation?

Hands

By Oliver Sacks

Madeleine J. was admitted to St. Benedict's Hospital near New York City in 1980, her sixtieth year, a congenitally blind woman with cerebral palsy, who had been looked after by her family at home throughout her life. Given this history, and her pathetic condition—with spasticity and athetosis, i.e., involuntary movements of both hands, to which was added a failure of the eyes to develop—I expected to find her both retarded and regressed.

She was neither. Quite the contrary: she spoke freely, indeed eloquently (her speech, mercifully, was scarcely affected by spasticity), revealing herself to be a high-spirited woman of exceptional intelligence and literacy.

'You've read a tremendous amount,' I said. 'You must be really at home with Braille.'

'No, I'm not,' she said. 'All my reading has been done for me—by talking-books or other people. I can't read Braille, not a single word. I can't do *anything* with my hands—they are completely useless.'

She held them up, derisively, 'Useless god-forsaken lumps of dough—they don't even feel part of me.'

I found this very startling. The hands are not usually affected by cerebral palsy—at least, not essentially affected: they may be somewhat spastic, or weak, or deformed, but are generally of considerable use (unlike the legs, which may be completely paralysed—in that variant called Little's disease, or cerebral diplegia).

Miss J.'s hands were *mildly* spastic and athetotic, but her sensory capacities—as I now rapidly determined—were completely intact: she immediately and correctly identified light touch, pain, temperature, passive movement of the fingers. There was no impairment of elementary sensation, as such, but, in dramatic contrast, there was the profoundest impairment of perception. She could not recognise or identify anything whatever—I placed all sorts of objects in her hands, including one of my own hands. She could not identify—and she did not explore; there were no active 'interogatory' movements of her hands—they were, indeed, as inactive, as inert, as useless, as 'lumps of dough'.

This is very strange, I said to myself. How can one make sense of all this? There is no gross sensory 'deficit'. Her hands would seem to have the potential of being perfectly good hands—and yet they are not. Can it be that they are functionless—'useless'—because she had never used them? Had being 'protected', 'looked after', 'babied' since birth prevented her from the normal exploratory use of the hands which all infants learn in the first months of life? Had she been carried about, had everything done for her, in a manner that had prevented her from developing a normal pair of hands? And if this were the case—it seemed far-fetched, but was the only hypothesis I could think of—could she now, in her sixtieth year, acquire what she should have acquired in her first weeks and months of life?

Was there any precedent? Had anything like this ever been described—or tried? I did not know, but I immediately thought of a possible parallel—what was described by Leont'ev and Zaporozhets in their book *Rehabilitation of Hand Function* (Eng. tr. 1960). The condition they were describing was quite different in origin: they described a similar 'alienation' of the hands in some two hundred soldiers following massive injury and surgery—the injured hands felt 'foreign', 'lifeless', 'useless', 'stuck on', despite elementary neurological and sensory intactness. Leont'ev and Zaporozhets spoke of how the 'gnostic systems' that allow 'gnosis', or perceptive use of the hands, to take place, could be 'dissociated' in such cases as a consequence of injury, surgery and the weeks- or months-long hiatus in the use of the hands that followed. In Madeleine's case, although the phenomenon was identical—'uselessness', 'lifelessness', 'alienation'—it was lifelong. She did not need just to recover her hands, but to discover them—to acquire them, to achieve them—for the first time: not just to regain a dissociated gnostic system, but to construct a gnostic system she had never had in the first place. Was this possible?

The injured soldiers described by Leont'ev and Zaporozhets had normal hands before injury. All they had to do was to 'remember' what had been 'forgotten', or 'dissociated', or 'inactivated', through severe injury. Madeleine, in contrast, had no repertoire of memory for she had never used her hands—and she felt she *had* no hands—or arms either. She had never fed herself, used the toilet by herself, or reached out to help herself, always leaving it for others to help her. She had behaved, for sixty years, as if she were a being without hands.

This then was the challenge that faced us: a patient with perfect elementary sensations in the hands, but, apparently, no power to integrate these sensations to the level of perceptions that were related to the world and to herself; no power to say, 'I perceive, I recognise, I will, I act', so far as her 'useless' hands went. But somehow or other (as Leont'ev and Zaporozhets found with their patients), we had to get her to act and to use her hands actively, and, we hoped, in so doing, to achieve integration: 'The integration is in the action,' as Roy Campbell said.

Madeleine was agreeable to all this, indeed fascinated, but puzzled and not hopeful. 'How *can* I do anything with my hands,' she asked, 'when they are just lumps of putty?'

'In the beginning is the deed,' Goethe writes. This may be so when we face moral or existential dilemmas, but not where movement and perception have their origin. Yet here too there is always something sudden: a first step (or a first word, as when Helen Keller said 'water'), a first movement, a first perception, a first impulse—total, 'out of the blue', where there was nothing, or nothing with sense before. 'In the beginning is the impulse.' Not a deed, not a reflex, but an 'impulse', which is both more obvious and more mysterious than either . . . We could not say to Madeleine 'Do it!' but we might hope for an impulse; we might hope for, we might solicit, we might even provoke one . . .

I thought of the infant as it reached for the breast. 'Leave Madeleine her food, as if by accident, slightly out of reach on occasion,' I suggested to her nurses. 'Don't starve her, don't tease her, but show less than your usual alacrity in feeding her.' And one day it happened—what had never happened before: impatient, hungry, instead of waiting passively and patiently, she reached out an arm, groped, found a bagel, and took it to her mouth. This was the first use of her hands, her first manual act, in sixty years, and it marked her birth as a 'motor individual' (Sherrington's term for the person who emerges through acts). It also marked her first manual perception, and thus her birth as a complete 'perceptual individual'. Her first perception, her first recognition, was of a bagel, or bagelhood'—as Helen Keller's first recognition, first utterance, was of water ('waterhood').

After this first act, this first perception, progress was extremely rapid. As she had reached out to explore or touch a bagel, so now, in her new hunger, she reached out to explore or touch the whole world. Eating led the way—the feeling, the exploring, of different foods, containers, implements, etc. 'Recognition' had somehow to be achieved by a curiously roundabout sort of inference or guesswork, for having been both blind and 'handless' since birth, she was lacking in the simplest internal images (whereas Helen Keller at least had tactile images). Had she not been of exceptional intelligence and literacy, with an imagination filled and sustained, so to speak, by the images of others, images conveyed by language, by the *word*, she might have remained almost as helpless as a baby.

A bagel was recognised as round bread, with a hole in it; a fork as an elongated flat object with several sharp lines. But then this preliminary analysis gave way to an immediate intuition, and objects were instantly recognised as themselves, as immediately familiar in character and 'physiognomy', were immediately recognised as unique, as 'old friends'. And this sort of recognition, not analytic, but synthetic and immediate, went with a vivid delight, and a sense that she was discovering a world full of enchantment, mystery and beauty.

The commonest objects delighted her—delighted her and stimulated a desire to reproduce them. She asked for clay and started to make models: her first model, her first sculpture, was of a shoehorn, and even this, somehow imbued with a peculiar power and humour, with flowing, powerful, chunky curves reminiscent of an early Henry Moore.

And then—and this was within a month of her first recognitions—her attention, her appreciation, moved from objects to people.

There were limits, after all, to the interest and expressive possibilities of things, even when transfigured by a sort of innocent, ingenuous and often comical genius. Now she needed to explore the human face and figure, at rest and in motion. To be 'felt' by Madeleine was a remarkable experience. Her hands, only such a little while ago inert, doughy, now seemed charged with a preter-natural animation and sensibility. One was not merely being recognised, being scruti-nised, in a way more intense and searching than any visual scrutiny, but being 'tasted' and appreciated meditatively, imaginatively and aesthetically, by a born (a newborn) artist. They were, one felt, not just the hands of a blind woman exploring, but of a blind artist, a meditative and creative mind, just opened to the full sensuous and spiritual reality of the world. These explorations too pressed for representation and reproduction as an external reality.

She started to model heads and figures, and within a year was locally famous as the Blind sculptress of St. Benedict's. Her sculptures tended to be half or three-quarters life size, with simple but recognisable features, and with a remarkably expressive energy. For me, for her, for all of us, this was a deeply moving, an amazing, almost a miraculous, experience. Who would have dreamed that basic powers of perception, normally acquired in the first months of life, but failing to be acquired at this time, could be acquired in one's sixtieth year? What wonderful possibilities of late learning, and learning for the handicapped, this opened up. And who could have dreamed that in this blind, palsied woman, hidden way, inactivated, over-protected all her life, there lay the germ of an astonishing artistic sen-sibility (unsuspected by her, as by others) that would germinate and blossom into a rare and beautiful reality, after remaining dormant, blighted, for sixty years?

ADDITIONAL RESOURCES

Books and Articles

Cobb, Vicki. *How to Really Fool Yourself: Illusions for All Your Senses*. New York: Lippincott, 1981. Offers do-it-yourself demonstrations to trick your own senses and explains how each illusion works.

Gregory, R. L. *Eye and Brain: The Psychology of Seeing*. 2d ed. New York: McGraw-Hill, 1973. An illustrated introduction to the fascinating psychology of visual perception.

Keller, Helen. *The Story of My Life*. Garden City, N.Y.: Doubleday, 1954. World-famous autobiographical account of a deaf and blind woman's struggle to learn to communicate with others and to live with severe handicaps.

Monmaney, T. "Are We Led by the Nose?" *Discover* (September 1987): 48–54, 56. Odors trigger memories, help rats find mates, and save us from eating toxic foods. Monmaney explores these and other fascinating functions of smell.

Sacks, Oliver. *The Man Who Mistook His Wife for a Hat and Other Clinical Tales*. New York: Summit Books, 1985. Perception of the outside world and of oneself can be distorted in bizarre ways by neurological disorders. Fascinating accounts of actual case histories.

Schwartz, Tony. *The Responsive Chord*. New York: Anchor Press/Doubleday, 1973. An expert explains how the media shapes our experiences and takes advantage of our perceptual biases.

Sekuler, Robert, and Randolph Blake. "Sensory Underload." *Psychology Today* (December 1987): 48, 50–51. Understanding how senses age can help older people and their families fight back.

Winter, Ruth. *The Smell Book: Scents, Sex, and Society*. Philadelphia: Lippincott, 1976. An entertaining book that puts the sense of smell into biological, historical, and cultural context.

Films

Houdini. Directed by George Marshall. 1953. A fictional screen biography of the master magician and escape artist Harry Houdini. Includes faithful recreations of dozens of Houdini's tricks and illusions and his efforts to expose mediums and spiritualists as frauds.

Roshomon. (In the Woods.) Directed by Akira Kurosawa. 1950. A murder is recounted by four people, including the victim. Each point of view and each story is different, illustrating how people can experience and interpret the same event in different ways. The audience must determine what is real.

The Thin Blue Line. Directed by Errol Morris. 1988. A remarkable and true detective story showing the limits and distortions of perception. Errol Morris calls it "a movie about how truth is difficult to know—not a movie about how truth is impossible to know."

LEARNING

Effective learning means arriving at new power, and the consciousness of new power is one of the most stimulating things in life.

Janet Erskine Stuart

Photo Courtesy of Canine Companions for Independence

At Canine Companions for Independence in San Diego, dogs are trained to push wheelchairs, pick up objects—even call for elevators—for those who can't.

Learning is the process that enables humans and other animals to profit from experience, anticipate events, and adapt to changing conditions. Unit 8 explains the basic learning principles and the methods psychologists use to study and modify behavior. It also demonstrates how cognitive processes such as insight and observation influence learning.

OBJECTIVES

After viewing the television program and completing the assigned readings, you should be able to:

1. Describe Pavlov's discovery of classical conditioning and the four key events in classical conditioning

2. Define the processes of acquisition, extinction, spontaneous recovery, generalization, and discrimination. Explain the importance of timing relationships in acquisition

3. Describe the contributions of Thorndike, Watson, and Skinner to operant conditioning

4. Describe the process of operant conditioning and the concepts of positive and negative reinforcement

5. Outline the effects of different schedules of reinforcement

6. Describe the key differences between operant and classical conditioning

7. Discuss the concept of punishment and its limitations in eliminating unwanted behavior

8. Explain the cognitive learning perspective and apply it to classical conditioning, insight, and latent learning

9. Define observational learning and the four key steps in the process described by Bandura *can learn from observing other people*

10. Discuss Skinner's views on the importance of operant conditioning in human behavior

11. Discuss applications of learning principles to everyday life such as the training of animals, the learning of fears and phobias, and behavior therapy

READING ASSIGNMENT

After viewing Program 8, read pages 197–228 in *Psychology: Science, Behavior and Life*. Your instructor may also assign the anthology selections for Unit 8.

KEY TERMS AND CONCEPTS

As you read the assignment, pay particular attention to these terms, which are defined on the given pages in the text.

learning (198)
associative learning (198)
classical conditioning (198)
unconditioned stimulus (UCS)
 (201)

unconditioned response (UCR)
 (201)
conditioned stimulus (CS) (201)
conditioned response (CR) (201)
acquisition (202)

The following terms are used in Program 8 but are not defined in the text.

reflex—an automatic, inherited response to a particular stimulus

fixed-action pattern—an automatic, inherited sequence of responses shown by all members of a species

agoraphobia—an irrational fear of public places

behavior therapy—the application of classical and operant learning principles to the treatment of psychological disorders

PROGRAM SUMMARY

Learning is the process by which people and all other animals profit from experience. During the process of learning, behavior is modified. Individuals acquire new skills that ultimately help them survive because they find new ways to anticipate the future and fine-tune their ability to control their environment. In Program 8, we will learn the basic principles of learning along with two methods, developed more than fifty years ago, that psychologists still use today to study behavior, help people to overcome old patterns of behavior, and learn new ones.

One method is called classical conditioning or signal learning. It takes advantage of our ability to anticipate what will happen. The second method is called instrumental conditioning, which takes into account the influence of consequences on future behavior.

Research on learning dominated American psychology for most of the twentieth century. It began around the turn of the century when the Russian scientist Ivan Pavlov noticed that the dogs in his digestion experiments began salivating before they even touched their food. In fact, anything they associated with food caused them to drool—the sight of the food dish, even the sound of Pavlov's footsteps. Pavlov decided to find out why and thereby discovered the basic principles of classical conditioning. He demonstrated that by presenting any stimulus, such as a light or a bell, before the food, the dogs would drool when the stimulus was presented without the food.

Pavlov and others also studied the extinction of such conditioned responses. They found that it was possible for a subject to learn over time that the stimulus no longer elicited the desired event (food, in the dogs' case), so the light or bell no longer elicited drooling. These simple experiments led to an important conclusion: any stimulus an animal can perceive can elicit any response the animal is capable of making.

While the Russians were working on classical conditioning, the American psychologist Edward Thorndike was studying how humans and animals learned new habits and skills. He observed and measured trial and error behavior and discovered that actions that brought a reward became learned—that, in fact, learning is controlled by its consequences. This became known as instrumental conditioning.

John B. Watson, another American psychologist influenced by Pavlov, studied observable behavior. He believed that he could use conditioning and environmental control to train any infant to become anything, regardless of talents or preferences.

Watson's famous test case involved eight-month-old Little Albert. In an experiment that today's ethical guidelines would prohibit, Watson conditioned the boy to fear a white rat by pairing the rat with the sound of a loud gong. Albert learned to fear not only the rat but anything that resembled it—even a fur coat. Years later, Watson's associate, Mary Cover Jones, developed a way to remove conditioned fears.

Then, by focusing only on observable events that precede and follow behavior, Harvard psychologist B. F. Skinner refined instrumental conditioning. His basic experimental device, the Skinner box, has become the symbol of radical behaviorism. In Skinner's simplest experiments, a pigeon learned to control the rate at which it received a reward (food) by pecking a disk. Because the rate of response varied directly with the reinforcing consequences, the behavior could be changed by changing the consequences. Skinner's version of instrumental conditioning is called operant conditioning.

Although Skinner's view that any behavior can be stripped down to its antecedents and consequences is controversial, it also has many practical applications. Dogs and monkeys have been trained to help disabled people lead more independent lives. Behavioral principles are also the basis for token systems used to reward healthy behaviors in disturbed patients and criminal offenders. Behavior therapy is also used to help people lose weight, quit smoking, and overcome phobias.

Behavioral principles are very powerful—so powerful that they can actually affect our body's immune system. Current research studies that have grown out of these basic learning theories may even shed light on how to enhance our ability to fight off disease.

REVIEW QUESTIONS

Program Questions

1. Which of the following is an example of a fixed-action pattern?

   a. A fish leaping at bait that looks like a fly
   b. A flock of birds migrating in winter
   c. A person blinking when something gets in the eye
   d. A chimpanzee solving a problem using insight

2. What is the basic purpose of learning?

   a. To improve one's genes
   b. To understand the world one lives in
   c. To find food more successfully
   d. To adapt to changing circumstances

3. How have psychologists traditionally studied learning?

   a. In classrooms with children as subjects
   b. In classrooms with college students as subjects
   c. In laboratories with humans as subjects
   d. In laboratories with animals as subjects

4. In his work, Pavlov found that a metronome could produce salivation in dogs. Why?

   a. It signaled that food would arrive.
   b. It was the dog's normal reaction to a metronome.
   c. It was on while the dogs ate.
   d. It extinguished the dog's original response.

5. What is learned in classical conditioning?

   a. A relationship between an action and its consequence
   b. A relationship between two stimulus events
   c. A relationship between two response events
   d. Classical conditioning does not involve learning.

6. What point is Professor Zimbardo making when he says "Relax" while firing a pistol?

   a. There are fixed reactions to verbal stimuli.
   b. The acquisition process is reversed during extinction.
   c. Any stimulus can come to elicit any reaction.
   d. Unconditioned stimuli are frequently negative.

7. What point does Ader and Cohen's research on taste aversion in rats make about classical conditioning?

   a. It can be extinguished easily.
   b. It takes many conditioning trials to be effective.
   c. It is powerful enough to suppress the immune system.
   d. It tends to be more effective than instrumental conditioning.

8. What is Thorndike's Law of Effect?

   a. Learning is controlled by its consequences.
   b. Every action has an equal and opposite reaction.
   c. Effects are more easily determined than causes.
   d. A conditioned stimulus comes to have the same effect as an unconditioned stimulus.

9. According to John B. Watson, any behavior, even strong emotion, could be explained by the power of

   a. instinct.
   b. inherited traits.
   c. innate ideas.
   d. conditioning.

10. In Watson's work with Little Albert, why was Albert afraid of the Santa Claus mask?

    a. He had been classically conditioned to fear the mask.
    b. The mask was an unconditioned stimulus creating fear.
    c. He generalized his learned fear of the rat.
    d. Instrumental conditioning created a fear of strangers.

11. What was the point of the Skinner box?

    a. It kept animals safe.
    b. It provided a simple, highly controlled environment.
    c. It set up a classical conditioning situation.
    d. It allowed psychologists to use computers for research.

12. Skinner found that the rate at which a pigeon pecked at a target varied directly with

    a. the conditioned stimulus.
    b. the conditioned response.
    c. the operant antecedents.
    d. the reinforcing consequences.

13. Imagine a behavior therapist is treating a person who fears going out into public places. What would the therapist be likely to focus on?

    a. The conditioning experience that created the fear
    b. The deeper problems that the fear is a symptom of
    c. Providing positive consequences for going out
    d. Reinforcing the patient's desire to overcome the fear

Textbook Questions

14. A relatively enduring change in potential behavior that results from experience defines

    a. learning.
    b. stimulus.
    c. memory.
    d. motivation.

15. What type of learning had taken place with the woman described in the textbook who could not return to her biology lab class?

    a. Classical conditioning
    b. Operant conditioning
    c. Cognitive learning
    d. Motor-skill learning

16. Assuming you have eaten sour pickles before, imagine eating a large, juicy sour pickle. If thinking about it causes your mouth to water, then your salivation would be referred to as a(n)

    a. conditioned stimulus.
    b. conditioned response.
    c. unconditioned stimulus.
    d. unconditioned response.

17. In classical conditioning, the process of learning to associate a CS with a UCS is known as

    a. operant learning.
    b. extinction.
    c. acquisition.
    d. generalization.

18. After extinction had occurred in Pavlov's dogs, the bell could cause salivation when presented again at a later time. This phenomenon is called

    a. an unconditioned response.
    b. a conditioned stimulus.
    c. spontaneous recovery.
    d. backward conditioning.

19. A dog taught to salivate when shown a circle also salivates when shown a square. This behavior is referred to as

    a. generalization.
    b. discrimination.
    c. stimulation.
    d. unconditioned response.

20. A child is knocked down by a large friendly dog and is frightened. Later he sees the neighbor's dog and is frightened. The fear has been

    a. suppressed.
    b. generalized.
    c. discriminated.
    d. natural.

21. Instrumental conditioning or learning is also referred to as

    a. operant conditioning.
    b. classical conditioning.
    c. backward conditioning.
    d. musical conditioning.

22. When an organism learns to engage in behavior because the behavior is reinforced, the learning is called

    a. classical conditioning.
    b. operant conditioning.
    c. social learning.
    d. vicarious learning.

23. When a behavior is followed by a stimulus which increases the frequency of that behavior, the stimulus is called

    a. an operant.
    b. a reinforcer.
    c. instrumental.
    d. learned.

24. A reinforcer is

    a. always food.
    b. always primary.
    c. a change in the environment.
    d. anything, so long as it increases the possibility that the response preceding it will be repeated.

25. When Mom tells her daughter, "If you don't clean your room, you are grounded next week," Mom is using

    a. positive reinforcement.
    b. negative reinforcement.
    c. punishment.
    d. aversive conditioning.

26. Which of the following is a *primary* reinforcer?

    a. A soft drink
    b. A coupon
    c. A pat on the back
    d. A paycheck

27. Extinction will occur in operant conditioning when operant behavior is

    a. reinforced on a ratio schedule.
    b. repeated without reinforcement.
    c. reinforced on an interval schedule.
    d. the same as classical behavior.

28. When an experimenter reinforces every correct response, it is called

    a. partial reinforcement.
    b. discriminative reinforcement.
    c. continuous reinforcement.
    d. classical conditioning.

29. A slot machine or "one-armed bandit" increases gambling behavior by

    a. continuous reinforcement.
    b. partial reinforcement.
    c. discriminative stimuli.
    d. classical conditioning.

30. Behaviors that are acquired through partial instead of continuous schedules of reinforcement are

    a. slower to be established, but more resistant to extinction.
    b. slower to be established, but less resistant to extinction.
    c. more quickly established, but more resistant to extinction.
    d. more quickly established, but less resistant to extinction.

31. A worker receives $1.00 for every unit he assembles. He is being paid on a _____ schedule.

    a. fixed-interval
    b. fixed-ratio
    c. variable-interval
    d. variable-ratio

32. Teaching a rat to run a maze requires reinforcing successive approximations, which is called

    a. observation learning.
    b. shaping.
    c. latent learning.
    d. classical conditioning.

33. In operant conditioning, reinforcement is contingent upon the

    a. learner's behavior.
    b. type stimulus used.
    c. punishment sequence.
    d. age of the learner.

34. Which of the following is desirable regarding the use of punishment?

    a. It does not suggest alternate behavior.
    b. It may be modeled as a way of solving problems.
    c. It reduces undesirable behavior.
    d. It can create anger and hostility.

35. Which of the following statements about punishment is true?

    a. B. F. Skinner believes punishment is a desirable technique to use.
    b. Punishment cannot be effectively modeled.
    c. Punishment may create anger and hostility.
    d. Punishment will not generalize to other similar situations.

36. Punishment works best when it is

    a. administered by more than one person.
    b. administered by the father.
    c. consistently applied.
    d. psychological rather than physical.

37. Today, learning theorists believe that the _____ of a relationship between the CS and UCS is probably more important than timing or frequency.

    a. predictability
    b. strength
    c. quality
    d. severity

QUESTIONS TO CONSIDER

1. Approximately 2 percent of Americans are hooked on gambling, which experts claim can be just as addictive as drugs or alcohol. Is compulsive gambling a disease or a learned behavior? Consider the kind of reinforcement gamblers get. What techniques do you predict would work best to help compulsive gamblers change their behavior? Which would be a better goal, controlled gambling or no gambling at all?

2. You are the city manager of a medium-size city. In an effort to reduce traffic congestion and improve air quality, you encourage workers to form car pools or choose alternative ways of traveling to work. What kinds of incentives might be effective for getting people to change their habits?

3. What role does intention play in classical and operant conditioning?

OPTIONAL ACTIVITIES

1. Design your own behavior change program based on the learning principles described in Unit 8. First identify a specific behavior. Instead of setting a broad goal, such as losing weight, design a strategy to reinforce a desired behavior—eliminating second helpings, cutting out midnight snacks, or choosing low-calorie foods. Analyze the specific behavior you would like to change in terms of Antecedents-Behavior-Consequences. Then get a baseline measurement of the target behavior, try out your plan for a predetermined amount of time, and evaluate the results.

2. Have someone teach you something new, such as how to juggle, iron a shirt, roller skate, or serve a tennis ball. Analyze the teacher's method. How does it apply principles of theories of learning?

ANTHOLOGY

These selections raise questions about learning in a school setting. As you read, think about the following questions: How should teachers motivate and reward students? Is it ethical to use behavioral methods in the classroom? Think about your own school experiences, and try to recall how rewards and reinforcers were used to teach, motivate, and control students.

Reading 18

This article draws a distinction between behavior influence and behavior modification, citing some of the problems, ethical concerns, and misuses of behavioral principles. Do you think an elementary school classroom is an appropriate setting for a token system? Is it possible to overcome the disadvantages of the token system?

The Token Economy: An Affirmative Perspective

By Thomas M. Stephens and John O. Cooper

When the present interest in applied behavior analysis began—around 1960—questions of its effectiveness were raised. During the 1960s and 1970s, principles of behavior were used successfully in hospitals, prisons, special education classes, and even with "normal achieving" school children.[1] Ample research evidence has laid to rest most of the early questions of effectiveness. Today, critics have moved from questioning the relative effectiveness of behavior modification practice to issues of ethical nature.

Consider these events from everyday life. A waiter provides good service; consequently, the diners leave a twenty percent tip. Had the service been poor, they would have left less. As a woman enters the airport terminal, she notices that the person behind her is carrying two large suitcases. She holds the door for him until he passes through, and he thanks her for her kindness. In a junior high school classroom, a student contributes an insightful comment during a discussion on current events; the teacher follows with a remark that clearly indicates recognition of the student's contribution. You have called a friend's office and home several times, leaving messages for him to return your calls but he does not. Consequently, you discontinue calling the person. Each of these events are typical behaviors which occur in the course of people's lives. All involve some schedule of reinforcement: tokens were used by the diner, while the airport and classroom scenes involved social reinforcement, and an extinction sched-ule was applied by your friend, i.e., he did not return your calls.

The root of applied principles of behavior (e.g., behavior modification, directive teaching, responsive teaching, operant conditioning, behavioral engineering, and applied behavior analysis) is determinism. Yet, this does not imply the conditioning processes described in *1984* or *Clockwork Orange*. Behavior is a function of its consequences. However, people do think, introspect, and control their actions.[2] Operant behavior is voluntary. To illustrate with our previous example: diners are expected to tip for good service in our society; the common courtesy of door holding for a stranger is an empathetic response (I have been in similar need); teachers' desires to encourage students; and a "friend's" continued discourtesy will have a natural consequence.

The question is, however, "Where do these expectancies, courtesies, and desires come from?" Behaviorism suggests they are the result of our past interactions within the environment. In short, it is reasonable not to question the sincerity of those who engaged in these acts. Conversely, when behavior modification programs occur in a planned, purposeful way, some may raise critical issues. Particularly if these programs are implemented in classrooms, charges of unethical practices are sometimes bandied about.

The charge of unethical practice may be justified when directed toward people who use techniques which have been classified incorrectly as behavior modification or some individual teachers who are incompetent in applying or who misuse the techniques.

Stolz, Wienckowski, and Brown distinguish between behavior influence and behavior modification. They state:

> *Behavior influence* occurs whenever one person exerts some degree of control over another. This occurs constantly in such diverse situations as formal school education, advertising, child rearing, political campaigning and other interpersonal interactions.
> *Behavior modification* is a special form of behavior influence that involves primarily the application of principles derived from research in experimental psychology to alleviate human suffering and enhance human functioning. Behavior modification emphasizes systematic monitoring and evaluation of the effectiveness of the applications. The techniques of behavior modification are generally intended to facilitate improved self-control by expanding individuals' skills, abilities, and independence.[3]

Behavior modification has been said to include psychosurgery, electroconvulsive therapy, and the administration of drugs. These techniques clearly influence behavior but are not consistent with the use of the term behavior modification. For example, justly or unjustly, a program attributed to behavior modification has been cited as abusive. Reimringer, Morgan, and Bramwell punished prisoners by administering the drug, succinylcholine chloride, which produced a brief paralysis.[4] This procedure is more related to *behavior influence* than behavior modification.

"Timeout" or "standout" could be used to illustrate how some individuals may be incompetent or who misuse the techniques. Timeout is effective in applied settings only with the removal of the opportunity to earn additional reinforcement for short durations of time (e.g., three to ten minutes), but some programs have involved extended time in isolation.[5] Clearly, ethical and legal issues should be raised in such situations.

In summary, most critics have been concerned about some procedures mislabeled as behavior modification and about individual competence in judgment, not good professional application of behavior modification tactics.

A token economy is a contingency package in which application is subject to the same rules of application as other reinforcement procedures (e.g., contingent, consistent, or relevant).[6] A token is any tangible symbol that can be given immediately after responses then exchanged later for known reinforcers. Examples of tokens used in applied settings include coupons, poker chips, tally marks, holes punched in a card, Peabody Kit tokens, and strips of paper.

Often token economies are misused by teachers. Too often teachers have established a token system in their classroom because of fad or custom, rather than basing the system on systematic objective evaluation. Token systems are intrusive in most school systems. Whenever a token system is employed, it should be because less intrusive reinforcers such as grades, praise, or high interest materials do not work well or fail completely. Other major difficulties include inadequate assessment for appropriate identification of activities and objects for token exchange, presenting tokens noncontingently, and failing to specify what students must do to earn tokens.

Token economies are not a cure-all; they are not an end in themselves. Token systems are a handy way to start increasing appropriate academic and social behaviors when nothing else (e.g., right answers, teacher approval) has worked. Token systems should be started after advantages and disadvantages are balanced. Listed are some advantages and disadvantages.

Advantages

1. Tokens can be given immediately after responses.
2. Tokens can be "saved" for larger reinforcers than would be practical after discrete responses (seeing a movie).
3. Tokens can be "saved" for reinforcers that would interrupt the progress of an educational task (getting a drink of water).
4. Tokens can be saved for events to be available at some time later (being Santa at the Christmas party).
5. Tokens force the teacher to attend to particular responses and to assure that many reinforcers are available in the classroom.
6. Tokens can be given for many discrete responses within a task with little danger of satiation.

7. Tokens can be given for many different kinds of tasks using the same system (for example, same system for math and reading).
8. Token systems provide practical experience in the economic activities of the "real" world.
9. Tokens may be exchanged for a variety of reinforcers.
10. Sometimes "saving" or piling up tokens can be reinforcing ("Ha, ha, look at MY bank balance!").
11. Contingencies can be individualized so that a student who is learning to discriminate "B" from "D" can earn the same amount as the student who is learning to write complete sentences.
12. Tokens are a concrete symbol of "I did a good job."
13. Tokens encourage students to set goals.

Disadvantages

1. Teachers can be so reinforced by the results of a token system that they may forget to "fade out" the system so students will continue working for reinforcers that are normally available in the regular classroom.
2. Fiddling with tokens or the process of token exchange may become so time consuming that time spent on academic tasks suffers.
3. Token systems can become so cumbersome that the teacher throws up his or her hands in despair.
4. Token systems can become so all-inclusive that it pays the student to spend more time on tasks which that person already does fairly well to the neglect of tasks with which he or she really needs help.
5. Fading out or removing token systems is not easy.
6. Tokens can be lost or stolen.
7. If the teacher has not sequenced student skills appropriately, no number of tokens will generate "learning."

8. Tokens, just like money, can generate competition and rivalry, which may not be *all* bad.
9. If the teacher has not thoroughly specified the plan, token systems can reinforce arguing and disputing.

Finally, a token system in school settings should be viewed as a temporary arrangement; it should be started only after teachers know how and plan to remove the system. Books and the things learned from exciting teaching maintain interest, not the tokens.

Summary

In recent years several legal and ethical issues have arisen concerning the use of behavioral tactics in schools and in other settings. There is little doubt that, because behavioral tactics are effective in teaching, steps must be taken by professional educators for proper ethical uses. First, all school personnel should be prepared to use behavioral applications correctly by competent trainers. Second, schools should have carefully devised and publicly known human subject guidelines to make certain that informed parental consent and other safeguards are incorporated into classroom procedures. Teachers now have a technology which does exchange behavior. It is incumbent upon all of us to use it wisely and in the best interests of students.

Notes

1. *Journal of Applied Behavior Analysis*, 1968–1979.
2. P.J. Champagne and C. Tausky, "Behavior Mod: A Short Reply to the Critics," *The Behavior Analyst*, Fall 1979, pp. 16–19.
3. S.B. Stolz, L.A. Wienckowski, and B.S. Brown, "Behavior Modification: A Perspective on Critical Issues," *American Psychologist*, November 1975, pp. 1027–48.
4. M.J. Reimringer, S.W. Morgan, and P.F. Bramwell, "Succinylcholine as a Modifier of Acting Out Behavior," *Clinical Medicine 77* (1970): 28–29.
5. E.M. Opton, Jr., "Psychiatric Violence Against Prisoners: When Therapy is Punishment," *Mississippi Law Journal* 45 (1974): 605–44.
6. B. Sulzer-Azaroff, and G.R. Mayer, *Applying Behavior-Analysis Procedures with Children and Youth* (New York: Holt, Rinehart and Winston, 1977).

Reading 19

The principles of behaviorism can be misused and overused. This author thinks her children's elementary school incentive programs have gone too far. Do you agree? What problems has the reward system created?

The Prizes of First Grade

By Paula Skreslet

In the first 10 days of the school year my triplets brought home the following from their first-grade classes: one candy bar, one peanut-butter-and-chocolate-chip cookie, two bags of popcorn, two "Very Important Person" badges, three "Constitutional Knowledge" stickers, one "I Know the Alphabet" award, two drawing prizes, 31 Nature Trail tickets, nine Lincoln play dollars, several music awards and innumerable Scratch N Sniff stickers, stamps, stars and smile faces. What an introduction to the Lincoln School's positive-incentive program!

It's unusual, I know, for one family to have three six-year-olds, and perhaps that's why the prizes seem so excessive. But I'm troubled by the fact that well-behaved, attentive children are being bombarded with rewards for doing what schools routinely expect. My children are bewildered by the riches they've earned merely for being themselves.

My husband and I have taught them that politeness, learning and order are good things, and something good is to be desired and developed for its own sake. But at school they learned, and very quickly, that children earn Nature Trail tickets for running the quarter-mile track during lunch recess. Or Lincoln Dollars for picking up trash on the playground or for helping a younger child find the bathroom—deeds that used to be called "good citizenship." Furthermore, the school keeps score. The children can redeem trail tickets and play dollars for group prizes, like a free recess. Thanks to the involvement of local merchants, students can also earn a free order of french fries or free admission to the roller-skating rink.

Why is it necessary to buy the minimal cooperation of children with rewards and treats? Our school is no detention chamber. It is a bright, tidy building surrounded by acres of lawn where pupils follow their teachers into classrooms in a line like little ducks. And Caldwell, Idaho, is so homogeneous a town that we still teach kindergartners the story of Jesus at Christmas time, and nobody thinks twice about it. What is new to me, what I question philosophically, is the idea that good behavior must be reinforced so systematically—that without tangible incentives, first graders won't return their library

books when due. Or that they won't learn the alphabet without stickers, stars and candy bars.

An inner-city high school in Cleveland received a lot of press attention recently when it began to experiment with a program for paying students for their grades. Each student is to receive $40 for an A, $20 for a B and $10 for a C. The amount earned will be credited toward a scholarship fund that students can apply to college tuition or for vocational training. In that respect financial aid based on performance is no shocking innovation. But the commercialism of paying for *each* notch on the grade-point average seems a bit much. It shamelessly assigns a dollar value to levels of learning that can scarcely be measured symbolically, much less in coin. It also says that students are so materialistic, so unmotivated and lazy that they will not learn without a bribe. I find that an insulting idea.

What I think we're seeing in Cleveland and at the Lincoln School is the well-meant but distorted application of a current business principle—the vogue that stresses "excellence" and its corollary, "competitiveness." We've convinced ourselves that the way to safeguard America's position in commerce and science is to appeal to young people's hunger for the rewards the marketplace can provide. Thomas J. Peters, in his influential book, "In Search of Excellence," writes: "Get the incentives right and productivity will follow. If we give people big, straightforward monetary incentives to do right and work smart, the productivity problem will go away."

Widget factories: Peters lists McDonalds, AT&T, Tupperware, IBM as companies that use "pins, buttons, badges and medals" to boost performance. He especially applauds programs that reward the majority of workers who can be tempted to perform a bit better than before. I don't know enough about the application of this principle in the business world, but I do know it's inappropriate in the first grade. Public and nonprofit institutions are not widget factories. Learning involves developing the intellect and character of a child—it's not a productivity problem that can be solved solely by a particular performance.

What I'm trying to do with my children is to teach them how to respond to challenges, how to contribute to the community even at their own expense. Secretary of Education William Bennett visited Caldwell last year and presented Lincoln with a plaque for being an exemplary school—an honor given to just 270 grade schools in the United States. Yet I'm afraid that with the best of intentions, the school may be my adversary instead of my ally. If children are taught to behave decently because they will profit from it, I wonder what principle will guide them as adults when they see how easy it is to profit from wrong behavior.

Some children at the Lincoln School have already discovered that they can skip running the quarter-mile track and simply pressure younger children into handing over their Nature Trail tickets. It isn't the ideal of healthy exercise that's motivating them. I believe that's what happens if we are taught to value a prize, a payoff, rather than a good that is to be sought without any accessory advantage—such justice, or honor.

I've lost count of the prizes my triplets have earned so far. They are well on their way to coming out winners in this scramble of enhanced self-interest. But I can't forget about the little boy who didn't remember to return his book and kept the whole class from getting its library star or the girl who talked in line so the class didn't get a playground award. The winners will also suffer if they don't discover for themselves that they can gain the pleasure of health and strength from exercise, the joy of music from songs, the power of mathematics from counting and all of human wisdom from reading. I'm going to do my utmost to teach my children about these rewards.

ADDITIONAL RESOURCES

Books and Articles

Burgess, Anthony. *A Clockwork Orange*. New York: Norton, 1963. In a nightmarish world of the future, authority figures attempt to reform, though conditioning, a violent young thug.

Cialdini, R. B. *Influence: How and Why People Agree to Things*. 2d ed. New York: Morrow, 1988. Looks at how people can be persuaded to do dangerous and unlikely things.

Gilbreath, Frank B., and E. G. Carey. *Cheaper by the Dozen*. New York: Crowell, 1949. A light-hearted novel about a time-management expert's use of behavioral techniques to organize and educate his large family.

Harris, B. "Whatever Happened to Little Albert?" *American Psychologist* 34 (1979): 151–60. Examines Watson's famous case in which fear was conditioned in a young child.

Hitz, Randy, and Amy Driscoll. "Praise or Encouragement? New Insights into Praise: Implications for Early Childhood Teachers." *Young Children* (July 1988): 6–13. Taking a position contrary to the popular one promoting praise in classrooms everywhere, the authors show how praise can work as a negative reinforcer because many students experience it as intrusive and controlling.

Kinkade, K. *A Walden Two Experiment*. New York: Morrow, 1972. B. F. Skinner proposed that operant conditioning could help create a utopian society. This book describes one attempt to set up such a community.

Miller, N. E. "Rx: Biofeedback." *Psychology Today* (February 1985): 54. Biofeedback techniques are helping to treat patients with scoliosis, low blood pressure, paralysis, and a host of other disorders.

Skinner, B. F. *Beyond Freedom and Dignity*. New York: Knopf, 1971. A reflection on the philosophical implications of behaviorism. Skinner discusses, in particular, the issue of determinism versus free will.

———. *Walden Two*. New York: Macmillan, 1976. Skinner's famous vision of utopia built from the principles of operant learning.

Films

A Clockwork Orange. Directed by Stanley Kubrick. 1971. In the film based on the novel, Malcolm McDowell plays a young thug conditioned to become sick when he thinks of sex or violence.

The List of Adrian Messenger. Directed by John Huston. 1963. Based on Philip MacDonald's novel, this detective film includes some fancy murder methods that illustrate themes of the unit.

The Manchurian Candidate. Directed by John Frankenheimer. 1962. The power of hypnosis plays a central role in the plot of this sophisticated political satire and thriller.

REMEMBERING AND FORGETTING

Memory is not just the imprint of the past upon us; it is the keeper of what is meaningful for our deepest hopes and fears.

Rollo May

Unit 9 explores memory, the complex mental process that allows us to store and recall our previous experiences. It looks at the ways cognitive psychologists investigate memory as an information processing task and at how neurobiologists study how the structure and functioning of the brain affect how we remember and why we forget.

San Francisco artist Franco Magnani painted this scene of the Italian town where he was born from memory—after a 30-year absence. The photo below shows the town as it stands today.

OBJECTIVES

After viewing the television program and completing the assigned readings you should be able to:

1. Describe the fundamental memory processes of encoding, storage, and retrieval

2. Describe the characteristics of sensory, short-term, and long-term memory

3. Discuss the concept of memory as a constructive process

4. Distinguish between the different kinds of knowledge stored in memory: procedural, declarative, episodic, and semantic

5. Discuss the use of mnemonic devices as aids to memory

6. Discuss the factors that distort the accuracy of eyewitness recall

7. Outline the various explanations for forgetting

8. Outline the different sorts of memory deficits due to organic factors

9. Discuss recent evidence on the physical basis of memory

READING ASSIGNMENT

After viewing Program 9, read pages 233–268 in *Psychology: Science, Behavior and Life*. Your instructor may also assign the anthology selections for Unit 9.

KEY TERMS AND CONCEPTS

As you read the assignment, pay particular attention to these terms, which are defined on the given pages in the text.

memory (234)
encoding (234)
storage (235)
retrieval (235)
sensory memory (SM) (235)
short-term memory (STM) (236)
long-term memory (LTM) (236)
iconic (visual) memory (237)
echoic (auditory) memory (238)
chunk, chunking (240)
procedural memories (243)
declarative memory (243)
episodic memory (243)
semantic memory (244)
dual-code model of memory (244)
mnemonic devices (245)
clustering (mnemonic) (245)

method of loci (mnemonic) (245)
narrative story (mnemonic) (245)
peg-word system (mnemonic) (246)
acrostics (mnemonic) (246)
acronyms (mnemonic) (246)
maintenance rehearsal (247)
elaborative rehearsal (247)
association networks (247)
recall (249)
recognition (249)
relearning (250)
serial position effect (258)
state-dependent memory (256)
flashbulb memory (256)
constructive process of memory (251)

schema (252)
memory trace (257)
retroactive interference (258)
proactive interference (258)
motivated forgetting (259)
repression (259)
organic amnesia (260)

retrograde amnesia (260)
anterograde amnesia (260)
consolidation (261)
engram (262)
Korsakoff's syndrome (264)
electroconvulsive shock (264)

The following term is used in Program 9 but is not defined in your text.

functional amnesia—forgetting caused by psychological factors. See "dissociative amnesia" on p. 580 in your text

PROGRAM SUMMARY

When we misplace our keys, forget a name, or go blank in the middle of an exam, we become acutely aware of the complexities of memory. Forgetting can be mildly irritating, or it can be a major frustration. Chronic forgetfulness can even be a symptom of disease. Program 9 explores memory, the basis for all learning and a process that enables us to survive, by linking the past to the present and the present to the future. To psychologists and neuroscientists, the memory is an essential tool for studying the functions of the mind and the structures of the brain.

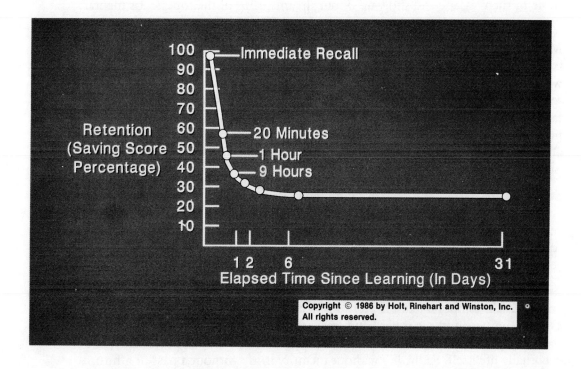

Figure 5: The Ebbinghaus Curve of Forgetting
In 1885 German psychologist Hermann Ebbinghaus published a systematic study of memory retention. He memorized lists of nonsense syllables and found that, after an initial rapid loss, the rate of forgetting slowed, making the 31-day retention rate about the same as the 6-day rate.

The early experimental study of memory began 100 years ago when German psychologist Hermann Ebbinghaus attempted to memorize random, three-letter combinations in meaningless series. But his memory faded quickly; he had no frame of reference or familiar context for the nonsense syllables. Because they had no meaning, order, or organization, he forgot them (see Figure 5).

With the advent of the computer in the 1960s, psychologists were able to create a working model of the memory. Their approach depicted the mind as an information processor that could be divided into its component processes: selecting, encoding, storing, retaining, and retrieving knowledge.

Today we know that there are two kinds of memory: long-term and short-term. Long-term memory contains everything we know about the world and ourselves. It has infinite capacity and stores concepts, smells, words, movements, and all our personal experiences in a complex network of associations. It functions as a passive storehouse, not as an active dispatcher.

The short-term memory holds information currently in use but only for a very brief time. When we talk with friends, read, or take in the sights and sounds of our environment, we are using our short-term, or working, memory. But without active attention and rehearsal, all items in short-term memory are quickly forgotten and lost forever—unless we transfer them into long-term memory where they become permanent.

Sigmund Freud was the first to recognize that what we remember and forget can help us maintain our personal integrity and sense of self-worth. He labeled this process repression. But even when we push these unacceptable ideas into the unconscious, some of them escape and show up in our dreams, slips of the tongue, or mental preoccupations.

Memory is not an exact record of our experience. What we select, retain, and retrieve is influenced by many factors. Our attitudes, expectations, interests, and fears affect what we remember and how we remember it. A student assigned to read a book that seems boring will not retain as much as another student who finds the book fascinating. A witness may provide a distorted report of an accident because of personal expectations or preconceptions. Our schemas—that is, our own set of beliefs about people, objects, and situations—often cause us to ignore some details and add or alter others.

Scientists are learning more about how the memory actually works. When something is remembered the brain changes physically. In fact, every bit of information we remember is encoded in our brains. These traces, or engrams, form the biological foundation for everything we know and do.

Clearly, memory is essential to individuality and personal identity. But sometimes people do lose their memories. The best known type of memory loss is functional amnesia. It is temporary and is often restored through hypnosis or psychotherapy. Organic amnesia, on the other hand, may well be the result of injury to the brain, disease, or alcohol addiction. As the memory fades, so does the personality, and eventually life itself. Sadly, life without memory is life without a past or a future.

REVIEW QUESTIONS

Program Questions

1. What pattern of remembering emerged in Hermann Ebbinghaus's research?

   a. Loss occurred at a steady rate.
   b. A small initial loss was followed by no further loss.
   c. There was no initial loss, but then there was a gradual decline.
   d. A sharp initial loss was followed by a gradual decline.

2. The way psychologists thought about and studied memory was changed by the invention of

   a. television.
   b. electroconvulsive shock therapy.
   c. the computer.
   d. the electron microscope.

3. What do we mean when we say that memories must be encoded?

   a. They must be taken from storage to be used.
   b. They must be put in a form the brain can register.
   c. They must be transferred from one network to another.
   d. They must be put in a passive storehouse.

4. About how many items can be held in short-term memory?

   a. 3
   b. 7
   c. 11
   d. An unlimited number

5. Imagine you had a string of 20 one-digit numbers to remember. The best way to accomplish the task is through the technique of

   a. selective attention.
   b. peg words.
   c. rehearsing.
   d. chunking.

6. According to Gordon Bower, what is an important feature of good mnemonic systems?

   a. There is a dovetailing between storage and retrieval.
   b. The acoustic element is more important than the visual.
   c. The learner is strongly motivated to remember.
   d. Short-term memory is bypassed in favor of long-term memory.

7. According to Freud, what is the purpose of repression?

   a. To protect the memory from encoding too much material
   b. To preserve the individual's self-esteem
   c. To activate networks of associations
   d. To fit new information into existing schemas

8. In an experiment, subjects spent a few minutes in an office. They were then asked to recall what they had seen. The subjects were most likely to recall those objects that

    a. fit into their existing schema of an office.
    b. carried little emotional content.
    c. were unusual within that particular context.
    d. related to objects the subjects owned themselves.

9. The paintings Franco Magnani made of an Italian town were distorted mainly by

    a. repression causing some features to be left out.
    b. a child's perspective altering relationships.
    c. sensory gating changing colors.
    d. false memories of items that were not really there.

10. What was Karl Lasley's goal in teaching rats mazes and then removing part of their cortexes?

    a. Finding out how much tissue was necessary for learning to occur
    b. Determining whether memory was localized in one area of the brain
    c. Discovering how much tissue loss led to memory loss
    d. Finding out whether conditioned responses could be eradicated

11. What has Richard Thompson found in his work with rabbits conditioned to a tone before an airpuff?

    a. Rabbits learn the response more slowly after lesioning.
    b. Eyelid conditioning involves several brain areas.
    c. The memory of the response can be removed by lesioning.
    d. Once the response is learned, the memory is permanent despite lesioning.

12. What is the chief cause of functional amnesia?

    a. Alzheimer's disease
    b. Substance abuse
    c. Traumatic injury to the brain
    d. Severe anxiety or hysteria

Textbook Questions

13. The process of perceiving, organizing, and categorizing information in some meaningful way for memory is called

    a. sensory memory.
    b. retrieval.
    c. encoding.
    d. storage.

14. The major factor affecting retrieval of memory is

    a. age.
    b. whether encoding and storage of the information was adequate.
    c. sex.
    d. education.

15. A very primitive type of memory storage, in which no organization or categorization of information takes place, occurs in the

    a. auditory memory.
    b. long-term memory.
    c. short-term memory.
    d. sensory memory.

16. The amount of information registered in sensory memory is

    a. seven plus or minus two chunks.
    b. up to a "lifetime's worth."
    c. the entire visual or auditory or olfactory panorama.
    d. any of the above depending on the person's attention span.

17. The short-term memory is called our working memory because

    a. it never stops.
    b. it is the largest memory system.
    c. it is so fast.
    d. it functions to store as well as retrieve information.

18. Most information placed in the STM is held there in a(n) _____ form.

    a. random, disorganized
    b. semantic
    c. acoustic
    d. iconic

19. Which statement is true of the long-term memory?

    a. Information is "displaced" by new information.
    b. It is limited to several hundred items.
    c. Information is stored by rote practice only.
    d. There is no evidence for any limit to the amount of information that can be stored in long-term memory.

20. You know that E. L. Thorndike stated the law of effect. The memory came from your _____ long-term memory.

    a. episodic
    b. semantic
    c. procedural
    d. declarative

21. The _____ memory represents essentially autobiographical facts concerning a person's experiences.

    a. episodic
    b. semantic
    c. procedural
    d. iconic

22. The _____ memory is equivalent to an encyclopedic collection of facts about our world.

    a. procedural
    b. laconic
    c. semantic
    d. episodic

23. The method of encoding which helps us organize material for more efficient storage and retrieval in LTM is known as

    a. dual-code memory.
    b. mnemonic device.
    c. chunking.
    d. the modality effect.

24. A mnemonic device to remember through forming mental associations between items you wish to recall, and specific locations along a designated route you may travel, is called

    a. method of loci
    b. clustering.
    c. chunking.
    d. acronyms.

25. Simply repeating words without any attempt to find meaning to them is known as

    a. maintenance rehearsal.
    b. elaborative rehearsal.
    c. mnemonic strategy.
    d. acrostics.

26. A superior method of remembering, which involves looking for meaning and organizing and clustering information, is called

    a. maintenance rehearsal.
    b. elaborative rehearsal.
    c. repetitive review.
    d. none of the above.

27. In a list of words, we would probably remember

    a. the first and middle words of the list.
    b. the first and last words on the list.
    c. the middle and last words on the list.
    d. just the middle words on the list.

28. A visit to our elementary classroom might help us remember more of the names of some of our classmates because

    a. we are in the same context where we first learned them.
    b. we are using the serial-position effect.
    c. we are using flashbulb memory.
    d. mental schemas come easier.

29. Vivid recall of earlier events associated with extreme emotion has been called

    a. eidetic (photographic) memory.
    b. dual-code memory.
    c. flashbulb memory.
    d. state-dependent memory.

30. Neiser (1982) believes that remembering is a(n)

    a. search of the LTM for a perfect copy of the event.
    b. accurate representation of what happened.
    c. reconstruction of an event.
    d. process which is 80 percent inaccurate.

31. When people try to remember information that is not consistent with their schema, they tend to

    a. distort facts to make it fit their schemas.
    b. change their schemas to make the facts fit.
    c. exert more effort to organize their schemas.
    d. focus on the inconsistencies.

32. The theory that explains forgetting in terms of deterioration of neuro-chemical and/or anatomical changes in the brain that encode memories is the

    a. memory trace decay theory.
    b. interference theory.
    c. motivation theory.
    d. distortion theory.

33. A person who must remember a new bank number frequently mixes the two numbers and can't remember the new one. This type of forgetting is an example of

    a. trace decay.
    b. motivated forgetting.
    c. proactive interference.
    d. retroactive interference.

34. To avoid the problems of interference forgetting when you must study more than one subject, you should

    a. study dissimilar subjects.
    b. take a nap after studying each subject.
    c. take breaks every hour.
    d. observe all the above procedures.

35. Freud's concept of repression parallels the _____ theory of forgetting.

    a. trace decay
    b. motivated forgetting
    c. interference
    d. distortion

36. In cases of amnesia, newer memories are more susceptible to loss than older ones, suggesting that amnesia reflects a temporary loss of

    a. the memory itself.
    b. a blood supply to memory areas.
    c. consciousness.
    d. access to information rather than destruction of a memory trace.

37. Chronic alcoholism may cause _____ amnesia.

    a. episodic
    b. anterograde
    c. repression
    d. retrograde

38. Extensive research over the last few decades indicates that

    a. each memory does not have one location but is spread over wide neural networks in the brain.
    b. each of our memories resides in specific neurons in the brain that can be precisely identified and localized.
    c. procedural memories are localized and declarative memory is spread over a wide neural network.
    d. the data is ambiguous and no generalization can be made.

QUESTIONS TO CONSIDER

1. What memory strategies can you apply to help you better retain the information in this course?

2. What is your earliest memory? Can you recall an experience that happened before you could talk? If not, why not? How does language influence what we remember? How do photographs and other mementos aid memory?

3. Learning the ABCs by singing them is almost universal. Why does singing the ABCs make it easier to remember them?

4. Many quiz shows and board games like Trivial Pursuit are based on recalling items of general knowledge that we do not use every day. Why is it so much fun to recall such trivia?

5. As a member of a jury, you are aware of the tendency to reconstruct memories. How much weight do you give to eyewitness testimony? Is it possible ever to get "the whole truth and nothing but the truth"?

OPTIONAL ACTIVITIES

1. Do you have an official family historian? In individual interviews, ask family members to recall and describe their memories of a shared past event, such as a wedding or holiday celebration. Perhaps a photograph or memento will trigger a story. Compare how different people construct the event and what kind of details

are recalled. What are different people revealing about their personal interests, needs, and values when they describe the experience?

2. Without looking, try to sketch all the features on the front or back face of a quarter or a dollar bill. Make the sketch as detailed as possible. Evaluate your sketch for accuracy. Did you include and locate the features correctly?

ANTHOLOGY

The following selections illustrate different aspects of memory, exploring the methods that psychologists use to study the process of remembering and forgetting. As you read, think about your own memories. Are you conscious of the strategies you use to remember things? Do you simply read and observe? Or do you make an effort to organize and encode information for retention? What would you life be like if you suddenly had no memory of your past, your friends and family, books you read, or major life events?

Reading 20

Some people fear that a decrease in their ability to remember is a sure sign of Alzheimer's disease, while others assume that memory automatically deteriorates with age. However, in many cases memory loss can be attributed to environmental factors. This article demonstrates the relationship of memory loss to health, sensory loss, medication, and other life changes.

Sometimes Memory Can Be Recalled

By Sy Montgomery

It started with difficulty remembering people's names. Then the 70-year-old retiree—we'll call him Russell Howard—began to forget to pick things up at the market. Finally, he would forget to go to the market at all. For three years, he tried to hide his memory loss, certain he had deadly Alzheimer's disease and would be forced into a nursing home if anyone found out.

But his daughter noticed, and she persuaded him to see a doctor. It turned out his memory loss was indeed severe. It was also completely reversible—with some changes in his lifestyle and the medication he was taking.

According to Dr. Martin Albert, professor of neurology at Boston University Medical School, this may be the case for many seniors who silently suffer from memory problems, resigned to the belief that they are inevitable and incurable.

"My own feeling is that more of the mild memory changes of aging are treatable than are not treatable," said Albert, who is also director of behavioral neurosciences and geriatric neurology at Boston University Medical School and at the Boston Veterans Administration Medical Center.

Fewer than 25 percent of seniors develop memory problems that interfere with their daily lives, according to neuropsychologist Stanley Berent, of the University of Michigan Hospital. And even if they do suffer memory loss, it doesn't have to mean they're losing their minds. They may have a problem that can easily be fixed, as in the case of retiree Howard.

When Berent first interviewed Howard, he took a careful medical history. He discovered that the patient was taking a variety of medications—tranquilizers to help him sleep, drugs to combat high blood pressure, aspirin for arthritis, a laxative—as well as drinking two glasses of wine each night.

"Each medication contributed to defects in memory, enhanced by alcohol," said Berent. "As soon as his medications were changed, and he cut out the tranquilizers and alcohol, his memory cleared up. And this is very common."

Indeed, most elderly people are taking more than one kind of medication, specialists say, and even some nonprescription medicines can interfere with memory, especially when they interact with other drugs.

"Anything that affects blood flow, concentration, or emotions will affect the brain and may affect memory," said Berent. Besides drugs, the list includes alcohol, conditions such as diabetes, heart disease and breathing disorders, sleep disturbances and psychological problems such as depression. Nutritional deficiencies—common among older people who live alone—can cause memory to fail, and a balanced diet will restore it.

To be sure, older people are more prone to many of the diseases, such as Alzheimer's, Parkinson's disease, and stroke, which are not treatable and do affect memory, says Dr.

Marlene Oscar-Berman, professor of neurology and psychiatry at Boston University School of Medicine and research psychologist at the Boston VA center. But "It's also possible to affect all sorts of thinking abilities by lots of environmental factors," she said.

For instance, she points out, you have to see well and hear well in order to process the sensory information that will form a memory. Many older people may think they are losing their memories when they merely need a hearing aid.

Often to a society that equates aging with deterioration, seniors may think they have a problem when in fact their memory is fine, doctors say. Albert gives this example: A 65-year-old woman is boiling some eggs when the doorbell chimes. She answers the door but just then the phone rings. She answers the phone, returns to the door. And then when she goes back to the kitchen, she finds her pot boiled dry and wonders if she's losing her mind.

On written memory tests, says Albert, she'd probably score fine. Often what looks like memory loss is really only a mild attentional deficit, a decline that is normal as people age. As people age, focusing attention on more than one task or problem at a time becomes more difficult.

Many mild memory impairments can be compensated for, stresses Oscar-Berman. You can write things down more often, buy a wrist watch that beeps to remind you of an appointment.

Although many older people worry about memory loss, researchers estimate that only 15 to 25 percent of people over 65 actually have a problem for which they should seek a doctor's help. The trick is knowing when, or whether, the problem is serious. The experts suggest you ask yourself a few questions:

Are you fearful, anxious or uncomfortable because of memory loss? Do you lose track of time or where you are? (It's OK to forget it's Tuesday when you're on vacation, but if it's July and you think it's September you should see a doctor.) Are your friends or family worried about your memory loss? Is the problem affecting your job, spoiling a favorite hobby, or interfering with your role as parent or grandparent?

Sometimes a simple medical history will reveal the cause of a memory problem, such as drug interactions; a routine physical can uncover some underlying health problems that affect memory. With results of written questionnaires, memory specialists can determine what type of memory—spatial, verbal, auditory, etc.—is affected, and how severe the loss is. More specialized procedures—including techniques such as CT scans—can look inside the brain and spot damaged areas; for example, an area impaired by stroke.

Even when memory loss is caused by irreparable brain damage, such as stroke, people can often learn ways to overcome it with a therapist's help, Oscar-Berman stresses. If, for instance, a stroke impairs the right side of the brain, one can lose visual and spatial memory. But if tests show the left side of the brain, where verbal memory is primarily stored, is undamaged, a therapist can help the person learn and remember directions and locations even though he or she can no longer read a map. The information just needs to be presented in words instead of pictures.

Although some kinds of memory decline with age, there is some evidence that other mental skills, including problem solving and vocabulary, actually improve with age—and, presumably, practice. In problem-solving, for instance, older people may not be as fast as young people, but they're more accurate, and therefore more efficient, says neurologist Norman Foster, head of the Cognitive Disorders Program at the University of Michigan Medical Center.

"The normal changes of aging are much less severe than people fear," said Albert. "Normal aging of the brain does not imply deterioration, and a healthy person in a healthy environment should be able to maintain an active, independent life."

Reading 21

This article analyzes some of the theories about why we remember or fail to remember early childhood experiences. The author, a therapist interested in the role of self-concept, explains some of the factors that influence how children perceive and interpret experiences and how that affects our personal histories as adults. Recall some of your childhood memories, and consider how your experiences might be reconstructed using your new insights into the memory process.

My Memory/Myself

By Anne Bernstein

The first years of life are packed with the most fascinating and absorbing experiences. An infant's discoveries of the sights and sounds, tastes, smells, and textures of the world around him rival those of Columbus and Marco Polo in their strangeness and novelty. Yet for all their richness, these early experiences are virtually inaccessible in later life. It is hard for most adults to remember, or even imagine, the experience of the young child, but the memories children carry of these early years shape their lives in many ways.

In fact, Sigmund Freud tells us—and most psychological thinkers agree—that our earliest experiences leave "ineradicable traces in the depths of our minds." But as influential to our behavior as these traces are, we are not necessarily conscious of them.

The popular explanation of why we don't remember so much of our early childhood is that we reject unacceptable memories. Freud theorized that to avoid pain we automatically block out the unpleasant or traumatic aspects of our early lives and prevent them from becoming conscious. This concept is called *repression*, and it is the basis of the worrisome question, "If I don't remember, does that mean something terrible happened?" The comforting answer to that question is no. Credible alternative explanations for lapses in memory abound.

The Process of Remembering

To understand why we remember or fail to remember early-childhood experiences, it is important to look at the way we store and retrieve memories. To begin with, what we pay attention to and what we think important at any particular age influence what we select to be remembered. Moreover, the way in which we search for hidden memories may determine what we find.

Attention is a key factor. We do a great many things without paying attention—breathing, crawling, and running, for instance, and even many activities we've had to learn consciously, such as skating, cleaning, and driving. We don't always realize, however, that what we do without paying attention may not be stored in memory. Consciousness does not occur without need, and we don't need to become conscious of an action if it succeeds. This is why many children and adults, when asked to crawl and then questioned about the movements they have made, cannot describe their own actions accurately. Things we do automatically are hard to remember.

On the other hand, a dramatic change in routine or an unusual occurrence is likely to make an impression on the memory of a child—but it is not always possible for an adult to predict exactly what a child will find dramatic or unusual. Breaking a doll may matter more to him than the outbreak of a war. Hitting a catsup bottle against a table to get it unstuck and having the catsup hit the ceiling, being carried under Mother's fur coat on a cold day, and getting lost in a supermarket for a few minutes are all events that may find their way into a child's memory.

Emotional arousal intensifies attention—which is one reason so many of our early memories are of fear, shame, physical pain, deaths, fires, and the births of siblings. One example of how this works is provided by the detail with which most of us who are old enough can recall where we were and what we were doing the day President Kennedy was assassinated.

Meaning is in the eye of the beholder. Although we may feel our memory is objective. In fact we all remember our own comprehension of events, not just simple perceptions of what happened. And what is meaningful to us is more likely to be remembered.

Even more than adults, children remember their interpretation, rather than the full range of sensory data that gave rise to it. Children's drawings depict what they know to be there, rather than what they see. For example, a face drawn in profile will still show two eyes and two ears. So even at the point of entry into memory, what is stored is a reconstruction of the world based on interpretation, not a copy of the world as seen by a camera.

My own earliest memory, as distinguished from anecdotes told to me by my parents, is of a long train trip taken at age two. I remember thinking how funny it was that my daddy had to sleep in a crib (the upper berth with its guardrail), while I, who shared the lower with my mommy, did not. A complete reversal of the world as I knew it, this seemed very important at the time.

After I told this to a friend, she remembered her own experience on a long train trip she took with her mother and sister, from Chicago, Illinois, to Birmingham, Alabama. It was the late forties, and in southern Illinois her family, being black, was required to change to a segregated car. As a three-year-old she did not comprehend the full meaning of racial discrimination, but the disruption and her mother's emotional response to it marked this event as meaningful and, therefore, potentially memorable.

Confusion about meaning is another way in which attention is heightened. Knowing one's understanding is incomplete is an irritant that keeps the mind working to know more. A twelve-year-old recalling his earliest memory tells of the puzzling discrepancy between what he thought was happening and his mother's reaction. She was expecting a visitor and very much wanted her two-year-old son to go to sleep. Yet each time she put him to bed, he would crawl out, put his head through the beaded curtain that hung in the doorway of his room, and grin at her. The twelve-year-old recalls this as a delightful game and also remembers his bewilderment at her angry lack of appreciation of the fun. The intensity of his mother's response, which she recalls as the angriest she had ever gotten at him, may have made this an occasion for heightened attention.

Mental development influences how memories are shaped. Researchers have widely observed that children younger than six or seven have trouble remembering events from their lives as complete stories. Memories that originate earlier than that are brief and fragmentary—images, feelings, or incidents, rather than narratives that develop from a beginning through a middle to an end.

In fact, the child's idea of himself as a separate person who has the same identity throughout his life span develops only gradually. Memory of personal experience depends on this growing understanding of identity and on the understanding that events that happened in his lifetime can be located with respect to other events to form a personal history.

How Memories Are Retrieved

Retrieving memories occurs in two ways. The first is involuntary. The smell of bread baking, the sensation of going down a slide, the sight of a red plaid skirt, call forth memories of other times and places where these smells, sensations, and sights have occurred. Spontaneous rather than purposive, these recollections are generally not triggered by words. Most of our earliest memories are retrieved in this way.

The alternative route to remembrance is voluntary, involving an organized search, and is dependent on language and rational connections. These more adult ways of thinking are not suitable receptacles for childhood experience. Although a young child's clearest memory of President Kennedy's assassination might be that it caused his mother to cry, an older child might attach special significance to the words "sniper" and "Dallas."

Our personal histories are reconstructed piecemeal from past events, built on the fragmentary images that arise unbidden and supplemented by a deliberate search. So much is lost (and found) in the process that it seems more accurate to talk about memories "relating to" childhood, rather than memories "from" childhood. What we remember is actually created at the moment of its revival; it does not emerge fully formed from the recesses of memory, even if it seems to.

Why We Remember
What We Remember

Motives for selecting the raw material for our autobiographical memories and weaving the strands into a narrative thread need not include historical accuracy. While memory may depict the past, it occurs in the present and serves its current employer's needs. Faithful to current interests, it reconstructs the past to fit the stories we tell ourselves about who we are and how we got that way. Facts that do not fit prevailing theory are discarded; those that support our present notions are embellished, embroidered, and set in relief.

One way that early memories are created is through the anecdotes parents tell their children about what they were like and what happened to them when they were little. Jean Piaget, noted Swiss psychologist of mental development, told of an incident from his own life that made him skeptical of childhood memories.

"I was still in a baby carriage, taken out by a nurse, and she took me down the Champs-Elysées. . . . I was the object of an attempted kidnapping. Someone tried to grab me out of the buggy. The straps held me in, and the nurse scuffled with the man, who scratched her forehead; something worse might have happened if a policeman hadn't come by just then. I can see him now as if it were yesterday . . . and the man fled. That's the story. As a child I had the glorious memory of having been the object of an attempted kidnapping. Then—I must have been about fifteen—my parents received a letter from the nurse, saying that she had just been converted and wanted to confess all her sins and that she had invented the kidnapping story herself, that she had scratched her own forehead, and that she now offered to return the watch she'd been given in recognition of her courage. In other words, there wasn't an iota of truth in the memory. And I have a very vivid memory of the experience, even today. I can tell you just where it happened on the Champs-Elysées, and I can still see the whole thing."

Family folklore, told or overheard, had been the basis for Piaget's reconstructing a memory that felt real. As Piaget's story shows, visual images are no guarantee of accuracy; the pictures in our memories can be created like the pictures in our dreams.

Hypnosis and Memory

Hypnosis is popularly given credit for recovering completely forgotten memories. What hypnosis does do, according to experimental psychologists Elizabeth and Geoffrey Loftus, is to encourage people to relax, cooperate, and concentrate. A good hypnotic relationship leads the subject to try to please the hypnotist; rather than being more *able* to remember, he may be merely more *willing* to remember. This is also the case with the free association employed by psychoanalytic psychotherapy. In informal conversations, therapists have observed that Freudian patients tend to have Freudian dreams, while Jungian patients dream in images that support Jung's psychological theories. These memory-retrieval techniques lead people to relax their standards for certainty. The resulting wealth of remembrances

need be no more accurate or complete than ordinary waking recall. Indeed, according to Geoffrey Loftus, several experiments have shown that people under hypnosis "confidently recall events not only from the past but from the future as well."

Knowing that substitutions in memory can occur helps us to understand how our memories are constantly being updated. Like Piaget, we may substitute what we have been told about events for our own experience. Parents' accounts of their children's early years form a large part of the memories later available to their offspring. Photographs strengthen the recall of the scenes they record; do we then remember the snapshot or the time itself? Any memory that includes "seeing" yourself as a child playing with other children or sitting on your father's lap—or in any tableau seen from the point of view of an observer outside the situation—is proof that the memory has been pieced together from scraps of reality but is not itself a record of that time gone by.

Targeting Memories

Another influence on early memory is that we are *taught* to remember, to target for later recall the events that people agree are memorable. Most families pull out the camera at birthdays, weddings, graduations, demonstrating to all concerned that this is "an affair to remember." Psychoanalyst Ernest Schachtel discusses how memory leans toward the conventional: more than ordinary thinking, memory can be dictated by social pressure because there is no immediate evidence of the senses to counterbalance the stereotypes. In other words, since our memories are based on experiences that are distant in time, we tend to organize them in conventional categories. According to Schachtel, "The memories of the majority of people increasingly come to resemble the stereotyped answers to a questionnaire, in which life consists of time and place of birth, religious denomination, residence, educational degrees, job, marriage, number and birthdates of children, income, sickness, and death."

However, not all the selection that goes into memory is dictated by social convention or other people. Memory, like other mental activity, tends to look for patterns and to cut the cloth of the past to piece together a costume that suits the characters we have become.

Reconstructing Our Own Dramas

For example, the daughter of an alcoholic father who frightened her with his rages and a mother who was the family mainstay may remember only good of her mother and ill of her father. Her images of her parents may have been oversimplified, but they helped her feel she could predict how each would behave, giving her some feeling of security in an often scary and chaotic home. Her initial impressions of each parent made her more alert to times when each ran true to form. Behavior that did not conform to her images of her parents failed to register, so in later life she may have no recall of her mother's self-righteous blaming and her father's helpless eagerness to please. She will explain her own fears, needs, and interests in terms of her father's alcoholism and her mother's courage, not relating her own eagerness to please to her father or her tendencies to be overcritical to her mother.

Who we are is a complex blend of intrinsic traits, experience—and an evolving self-concept. Our self-concept is based, among other factors, on what we choose to remember of our experience. Who I think I am influences how I see the world and what I do; in turn, what I do and how it is received determine what I think of myself. This dialogue between self-concept and experience is a lifelong process, continually—and selectively—building on what went before.

A feeling of being loved as a child is remembered "in one's bones" even without specific memories of cuddles and kisses. Having been appreciated encourages a child to approach other people with the expectation of being well received. His openness influences others to respond in kind. If early attempts to reach out for affection were rebuffed, however, one need not recall specific incidents when outstretched arms were met with ridicule or withdrawal to continue to feel discouraged about finding a welcoming embrace. Repeatedly called upon to stop the urge to reach out, the shoulder muscles may be permanently held back, so that extending the arms feels awkward and uncomfortable and evokes sadness. Wilhelm Reich called this accommodation of the body to early experience "character armor." Designed to protect the child from repeated frustrations, these "body memories" prevent the adult he will become from finding satisfactions that may have been unavailable earlier. Even with a child too young to remember, abuse and neglect leave their marks, as do love and protection.

As a therapist I am less interested in excavating the past for buried fragments than in helping the people I work with to rethink their life stories. This does not mean corseting memories to fit the arbitrary shapes of fashion but rather adding new dimensions of meaning. Knowing that memories are distorted and flattened versions of our early experience, we can attempt to round out the fragments of memory to recreate a complexity that is both more charitable and more realistic to who we are today. The child punished for making her parents anxious by her explorations can come to think of herself as a clever adventurer rather than a no-good troublemaker; the child who is pushed to be brave in the face of danger would benefit by relabeling fear as a useful signal of hazard rather than as damning evidence of cowardice.

As adults, we can help our children develop more benevolent memories. Without falsifying and without contradicting a child's feelings about his own experience, we can add a dose of generosity to a memory that might otherwise be a bitter medicine. In choosing to retell anecdotes about the child's early years that present him as lovable, smart, kind, and competent, rather than those that depict him as unworthy, stupid, mean, or clumsy, we are building a store of memories that will help him begin to piece together a past that will enrich his future.

ADDITIONAL RESOURCES

Books and Articles

Bower, Gordon H. "Moods and Memory." *Psychology Today* (June 1981). Our feelings act as a selective filter for perceptions and memory. This article describes Bower's hypothesis on the state-dependent effect and discusses its implications for other mental processes: learning, judgment, and imagination.

Loftus, E. F. *Eyewitness Testimony*. Cambridge: Harvard University Press, 1979. Recall is influenced by a number of factors, including suggestion and delay. Loftus discusses a number of eyewitness reports that demonstrate this, as well as their legal implications.

Luria, A. R. *The Mind of a Mnemonist*. Cambridge: Harvard University Press, 1968. A remarkable story of a young man with a seemingly limitless memory.

Neisser, U., ed. *Memory Observed: Remembering in Natural Contexts*. San Francisco: Freeman, 1982. A collection of papers on practical aspects of memory, such as flashbulb memories, eyewitness testimony, memory for poetry and prose, and memory aids.

Squire, L. R. *Memory and Brain*. New York: Oxford University Press, 1987. Examines the physiological study of memory.

Welty, Eudora. *One Writer's Beginnings*. Cambridge: Harvard University Press, 1983. Memories of childhood through the voice of the gifted writer.

COGNITIVE PROCESSES

I think, therefore I am.

René Descartes

The Bettmann Archive

The study of mental processes and structures—perceiving, reasoning, imagining, anticipating, and problem solving—is known as cognition. Unit 10 explores these higher mental processes, offering insight into how the field has evolved and why more psychologists than ever are investigating the way we absorb, transform, and manipulate knowledge.

If we are not aware of our own thoughts, reasoned seventeenth-century philosopher René Descartes, we would have no sense of personal identity.

OBJECTIVES

After viewing the television program and completing the assigned readings, you should be able to:

1. Define thought and outline the components of thought

2. Discuss the use of the computer model of cognitive functioning

3. Discuss the formation of concepts and distinguish between natural and formal concepts

4. Describe the use of prototypes, schemas, and mental pictures in understanding conceptual thinking

5. Outline the stages of problem solving

6. Discuss the various strategies for problem solving

7. Differentiate between inductive and deductive reasoning

8. Describe some common causes of reasoning errors

READING ASSIGNMENT

After viewing Program 10, read pages 349–368 in *Psychology: Science, Behavior and Life*. Your instructor may also assign the anthology selections for Unit 10.

KEY TERMS AND CONCEPTS

As you read the assignment, pay particular attention to these terms, which are defined on the given pages in the text.

thought (350)
subvocal or implicit speech (350)
concepts (352)
basic level concept (353)
subordinate level (353)
superordinate level (353)
association theory (354)
hypothesis-testing theory (354)
exemplar theory (354)
prototypes (354)
problem solving (356)
stages of problem solving (356)
trial-and-error strategy (359)

testing hypotheses (359)
algorithm (359)
heuristics (360)
means-ends analysis (360)
working backwards (361)
mental set (362)
functional fixedness (363)
confirmation bias (364)
deductive reasoning (365)
inductive reasoning (365)
syllogism (366)
belief-bias effect (367)

The following terms are used in Program 10 but are not defined in the text.

cognition, cognitive processes—usually refers to the "higher mental processes" such as thinking, deciding and problem solving. See also the discussion of cognitive psychology and information processing on pages 13 and 14 in the text

hierarchies—an ordered arrangement or ranked series of items

schema—conceptual framework used to organize and interpret information. See page 231 in the text

PROGRAM SUMMARY

Cognition is the term we use for all forms of knowing—remembering, reasoning, imagining, anticipating, planning, problem solving, and communicating. In Program 10, we'll find out how psychologists study these mental processes and what they have learned about how people think.

In 1958 British psychologist Donald Broadbent used a flow chart to demonstrate how people receive, process, and store information as words, pictures, and patterns in the memory. His model interpreted the workings of the mind as if it were a computer. Using the information-processing model, many cognitive psychologists today, including Nobel Prize winner Herbert Simon, are beginning to answer questions about how our experiences are transformed into knowledge that guides our actions.

One of the basic functions the mind performs is categorizing. We sort, label, and store all stimuli based on common features, similar functions, or other resemblances. The categories we form in our minds are called concepts. Although some concepts are simple and some complex, our minds link virtually all elements into coherent relationships.

Scientists have speculated that we store concepts in our minds by including a representation of the most typical member of a category: a prototype. For example, most people in our culture have in mind a prototype of a bird that looks like a robin, rather than a turkey or flamingo. Using this prototype allows us mentally to organize objects in an efficient way.

Complex concepts are known as schemas. They require us to organize a body of knowledge around prior experience, related events, and expectations. When we hear the word *picnic*, for example, we can immediately imagine what items go into a picnic basket, what to wear to a picnic, and in what environment the picnic is likely to take place. The more something fits into an established schema, the more it will make sense to us. If something doesn't fit our expectations or doesn't belong to our mental picture of the world, we may not even notice it.

Our concepts are formed not only as words or labels, but also as mental pictures. Evidence of visual thinking comes from laboratory experiments in which subjects' delayed responses indicate that they are mentally rotating or scanning images. Psychologists can also measure changes in brain wave activity or blood flow to areas of the brain to show how the brain reacts to surprises.

Visual thought builds on our experience of spatial or geographical relationships. We use mental maps to give directions, decide on an alternate route to work, and get around the house without turning the lights on. But cognitive maps also reflect our experience and values and may distort information. For example our mental map of the rest of the world might enlarge nearby or familiar places and foreshorten faraway places.

While some researchers try to understand how the mind functions, others examine the brain's chemistry and architecture in an effort to find out how we reason, learn, and remember. Psychologist Michael Posner uses sophisticated brain scanning equipment to look at the chemical and electrical processes that occur when a person is reading or solving a problem. Then there are scientists like Robert Glazer who try to use cognitive knowledge to understand better how we learn. His research may help to improve formal education and everyday learning in the years to come.

REVIEW QUESTIONS

Note: Review Questions for Units 10 and 11 are provided in Unit 11.

QUESTIONS TO CONSIDER

1. Where does the poem "Jabberwocky," by Lewis Carroll, get its meaning? Read the excerpt below and consider the concepts and rules of language and underlying structure that help you make sense of it. Can you paraphrase it?

   'Twas brillig, and the slithy toves
   Did gyre and gimble in the wabe;
   All mimsy were the borogoves,
   And the mome raths outgrabe.

   Beware the Jabberwock, my son!
   The jaws that bite, the claws that catch!
   Beware the Jubjub bird, and shun
   The frumious Bandersnatch!

2. What does the expression "Act your age" mean? Do you have a script that applies to someone in your age group? Do you have different scripts for someone 10 years older? Twenty years older? How does your script influence your behavior?

3. What is the symbolic power of political cartoons? How do people understand them?

4. What is common sense? Can a computer have it?

5. Can language and knowledge be separated? How do children acquire knowledge before they are able to use verbal labels?

OPTIONAL ACTIVITIES

1. There are many variations on the game Ghost. This version challenges players to manipulate concepts by using words in different contexts. Players may find it easier to think up new word pairs as time goes on. What might explain the change? How would you measure it?

   To play: The first player starts off by offering a pair of words that are commonly used together. They may be compounded, hyphenated, or entirely separate. The next player must come up with another pair of words, using the last word of the previous pair as the first word of the new pair. (Example: Baseball, ball game, game show, show girl, girlfriend, friendship.) Players keep the chain going until someone cannot come up with a word pair. He or she gets the letter *g* in *ghost*. The game resumes. A player is out of the game when he or she gets all the letters of the word *ghost*.

2. All of us tend to categorize the world into convenient units and to use common labels for our categories. Often those labels become permanent, and we tend to view our world in a rigid or stereotypical way. When this stops us from producing new ideas it is called functional fixedness. Can you overcome it?

   Try this: How many uses can you think of for an empty milk carton, a brick, a sock with a hole in it, a paper clip, a bandana, or another ordinary household object? After you feel you've exhausted all possibilities, list as many attributes of the object as possible. Draw a picture of the object from various points of view. Then see if you can generate any new uses.

ANTHOLOGY

How does the mind take in information and use it in adapting to life? The following selections illustrate the importance of categories and concepts for structuring the world. As you read, consider what role concepts play in our ability to be open-minded, creative, or prejudiced.

Reading 22

There has never been a practical typewriter or an efficient typesetting system for handling the 50,000-plus unique characters of the Chinese language. But not long ago an American engineer named James Monroe had a flash of insight that led to an amazing breakthrough. As you read this article, consider the combination of factors that helped him solve a problem that has puzzled the experts for decades. Are there other problems that require this uniquely human insight and creativity?

Finally, a Fast, Simple Chinese Keyboard

By David L. Chandler

The Chinese artisan Picheng invented movable type in 1041 A.D., and it was used to print newspapers in China four centuries before Gutenberg. But despite that headstart, the Chinese have never had a practical typewriter or an efficient typesetting system or computer keyboard.

Until now.

In a revolutionary development that could give a fourth of the world's people the ability to leapfrog into the computer age, a San Diego company has developed a simple, efficient and fast keyboard for Chinese characters. The first products using the keyboard could reach the marketplace as soon as this fall.

This time, the inspiration came not from China but from an American engineer, James Monroe, who decided to learn Chinese late in life. As he painstakingly learned to write Chinese characters he had a flash of insight that, after three years of hard work, resulted in a working typewriter and pending patents in more than a dozen countries.

If the invention lives up to its promise, it could produce "a major transformation" in China, said Dennis Simon, professor of international business and technology at Tufts University. "One of the major problems China is having right now," he said, "is finding a standard system for inputting characters" into a computer system.

The problem is that Chinese has no alphabet. It consists of more than 50,000 unique characters, or ideograms, each representing an entire word. Chinese typewriters and typesetting keyboards in the past have consisted of huge, cumbersome arrays of thousands of keys, each bearing a unique character.

As crammed as they are, such keyboards are limited to just a fraction of the characters in the Chinese language. And because of the difficulty of remembering the positions of so many characters, typing is very slow.

At a recent demonstration of a prototype of a Monroe system typewriter, with its 81 blank keys arranged in a nine by nine square (a simple English typewriter has about 50 keys), a typist entered Chinese characters at the unprecedented rate of about 50 words per minute—comparable to a competent touch-typist in English. And that was with just three months of practice.

M. Burdett (Det) Merryman, president of Sino Business Systems, the company that developed the keyboard, said in an interview that the system is based on principles so fundamental to the language that anyone who can write Chinese can learn to type on the keyboard in 10 minutes, and acquire a good working speed in two weeks of practice. Most characters, he said, can be typed with just five keystrokes—about the same as the average English word.

It's not that Chinese characters have never been typed before, it's just that the existing systems tend to be slow, cumbersome and inefficient. There have been four basic methods:

• Whole-character keyboards. These monsters contain up to 2000 keys, each for an individual character. Some also have as many as five "shifts," allowing five characters to be produced by one key. The prodigious feat of memorization required to learn the positions of the characters severely limits the number of people who can use them and their typing speed.

• Number codes. A unique number is assigned to each character, and just the numbers are typed in and converted to characters by computer software. Because the numbers bear absolutely no relation to the characters, memorization is even more difficult than for whole-character systems.

• Character parts. This breaks down all written characters into about 200 basic forms that are combined in different ways. Each part, or radical, is assigned to a key, and they are combined to produce an ideogram. But many different characters use the same radicals and some parts of many characters are made up of strokes that are unrelated to the radicals. Because this method bears no relation to the sequence of strokes by which characters are actually drawn, it is tedious to learn, slow to use and prone to errors.

• Phonetic. Systems using phonetic transliterations of Chinese words, called Pinyin, are perhaps the most widely used for computers, but they are severely limited because they require the user to be fluent in three areas: Mandarin, Chinese, which although it is the official dialect in China, is one of hundreds of dialects and the native tongue of only a small minority; the Roman alphabet, which most Chinese do not know; and English rules of pronunciation, which form the basis for the phonetic spelling. Even for those with a good command of Pinyin, these systems tend to be very slow. And because Chinese contains so many homonyms (there are, for example, 24 unrelated words that are all pronounced *lian*) that would be typed the same way but produce completely different characters, the system is highly ambiguous.

The Monroe keyboard, Merryman explained, is based on a system used by Chinese schools to teach the writing of Chinese characters, a method called the Box of Nine.

The Box of Nine is basically a tic-tac-toe board inscribed in a square, and is used to teach the correct positioning and proportions of the strokes (as few as one or as many as 36)

that make up a character. Each character has a very specific sequence of strokes that must be followed, and the combination of this sequence and the precise positions of strokes within the box are the keys to the Monroe system.

Its inventor, James Monroe, explained that the "method is based on the precept that the written Chinese language has a logical order, and is more than a series of random strokes."

Monroe is not Chinese, and until his mid-60s did not know anything about the language. But he learned fast and made what may be the crucial breakthrough.

An optical engineer, Monroe had read a lengthy Chinese text on engineering in an English translation. Fascinated by the book, and by China's history of major inventions, he decided to learn Chinese so that he could read the work in the original.

"I knew the Chinese written language was more sophisticated and involved than the Western world understood," Monroe said, "and that by studying Chinese, I might have a better understanding of what had been created."

In learning the new language, Monroe was "a sophisticated scientist in the environment of a kindergarten," said Merryman, and thus he had an insight that had eluded others. While Chinese experts may have been too close to the trees, Monroe, approaching from a distance, caught a glimpse of the forest.

"In a way, I think it's the only way it could have been done," Merryman said. "Experts have become so familiar with the intricacies they might overlook the simplicities of the language."

Monroe saw that while the characters were made up of many strokes, usually just a few characters were sufficient to distinguish between one character and any other. He found that almost any character could be uniquely identified by just five of these "disambiguating characteristics."

This insight has been transformed into the new keyboard system, which Merryman said can type 95 percent of the characters in a typical text with five keystrokes or fewer per character. The prototype is already programmed to accept and print 10,500 characters—considered more than enough for most normal use.

The first product using the new keyboard, "could be on the market in 60 days" from the time a licensing agreement is signed with a manufacturer, he said. But the negotiations could take six months or more, so it "might well be spring" before a Monroe system typewriter or computer is available.

When that happens, said Timothy Cheek of the Fairbanks Center for modern Chinese history at Harvard, it could have a great impact "for the greatest Chinese computer market: the Chinese."

In China, the system could have a great impact because it is "the nearest approximation to alphabetizing Chinese."

One of the great virtues of written Chinese is its independence from the regional dialects. With Chinese characters, Cheek said, "everybody can read them and understand them even though they pronounce them differently." It's something like the use of Arabic numerals in the Western world, he explained: We all recognize the symbol 3, although different languages may pronounce it three, *trois*, *drei* or *tres*.

"The value of a Chinese keyboard" such as Monroe's, he said, "is that everybody can use it."

Merryman noted that "the Western world tends to think other kinds of language are primitive," but in fact Chinese characters have some real advantages over Western alphabets.

For one thing, he said, written Chinese has remained virtually unchanged despite the evolution of the spoken language. "If I go back and try to read Chaucer, I have trouble. But in Chinese, someone can go back and read a document 2000 years old and have no trouble."

In addition, he said, because the Chinese ideograms are perceived instantly as a single "gestalt," a skilled reader of Chinese can read much faster than we can in English.

There has been periodic pressure in China, said Tufts' Simon, to abandon Chinese characters and substitute a Roman-alphabet system like Pinyin. But, he added, "only the very educated Chinese know Pinyin," so the effort would require a tremendous—perhaps unachievable—feat of re-education.

That would be ironic, since China already has one of the highest literacy rates in the developing world—about 90 percent among those who entered school since 1949. In urban areas of mainland China, as well as in all of Taiwan, said Chinese history professor Merle Goldman of Boston University, there is probably "very close to 100 percent literacy"—well ahead of US standards.

"To ask a society to abandon its mother tongue is a pretty big step," Merryman said. "It's not a practical approach."

With the Monroe keyboard, no change in the written language would be needed. "It bridges a cultural gap," said Merryman, "because it doesn't try to alter the language to fit our computer system. We've found a way to adapt the computer system to the language, which is the way the solution has to come ... I really think that we've built a better mousetrap."

Reading 23

Understanding and explaining scientific phenomena is often difficult—for children and adults. What does this article reveal about the way children see the world? Which statements reveal the schema the children are using? How do their views differ from yours? Do any of their responses make more sense than the rational explanations you have come to accept?

'Lime Is a Green-Tasting Rock'

By Ben Stewart

Take one class of elementary school students, mix it thoroughly with several pounds of scientific facts, then shake it up with an examination and you have the perfect formula for instant "youngsterisms" about science.

The beguiling ideas about science quoted here were gleaned from essays, exams and classroom discussions; most were from fifth- and sixth-graders. They illustrate Mark Twain's contention that the "most interesting information comes from children, for they tell all they know and then stop."

Question: What is one horsepower? Answer: One horsepower is the amount of energy it takes to drag a horse 500 feet in one second.

You can listen to thunder after lightning and tell how close you came to getting hit. If you don't hear it you got hit, so never mind.

Talc is found in rocks and on babies.

The law of gravity says no fair jumping up without coming back down.

When passing through Missouri, a typhoon is really not a hurricane but a tornado.

Scientists have found that when a toadstool is not a mushroom it is poison.

When they broke open molecules they found they were only stuffed with atoms. But when they broke open atoms, they found them stuffed with explosions.

Clouds are high flying fogs.

When people run around and around in circles we say they are crazy. When planets do it we say they are orbiting.

Rainbows are just to look at, not to really understand.

While the Earth seems to be knowingly keeping its distance from the sun, it is really only centrificating.

Some day we may discover how to make magnets that can point in any direction.

South America has cold summers and hot winters, but somehow they still manage.

Most books now say our sun is a star. But it still knows how to change back into a sun in the daytime.

One-hundred humidities equal 1 rain.

Question: In a free fall, how long would it take to reach the ground from a height of 1,000 feet? Answer: I have never performed this experiment.

Water freezes at 32 degrees and boils at 212 degrees. There are 180 degrees between freezing and boiling because there are 180 degrees between north and south.

A vibration is a motion that cannot make up its mind which way it wants to go.

Hard mud is called shale. Soft mud is called gooey.

There are 26 vitamins in all, but some of the letters are yet to be discovered. Finding them all means living forever.

There is a termendious weight pressing down on the center of the Earth because of so much population stomping around up here these days.

Lime is a green-tasting rock.

Many dead animals of the past changed to fossils while others preferred to be oil.

A fossil is a dead bone.

Genetics explain why you should look like your father and if you don't why you should.

Although Edison was once considered a great inventor, we now know of many inventions he overlooked.

Vacuums are nothings. We only mention them to let them know we know they're there.

Some oxygen molecules help fires burn while others help make water, so sometimes it is brother against brother.

Molecules are constantly bumping against each other in the air. There is really quite an overpopulation of molecules.

A planet cannot have an axis until it can get a lion to run through it.

Some people can tell what time it is by looking at the sun. But I have never been able to make out the numbers.

Our Mother Earth has small poles and a large equator because of the tremendous speed as she hurdles through the space. Since we are along for the ride, we also get to be flat at our poles and rounded at our equators.

We say the cause of perfume disappearing is evaporation. Evaporation gets blamed for many things people forget to put the top on.

To most people solutions mean finding the answers. But to chemists solutions are things that are still all mixed up.

When the fuel in a rocket starts burning, gases rush out at the nozzel. So would anybody.

In looking at a drop of water under a microscope, we find there are twice as many H's as O's.

I am not sure how clouds get formed. But the clouds know how to do it and that is the important thing.

The highest of all clouds are the circus clouds.

Clouds just keep circling the Earth around and around. And around. There is not much else to do.

Water vapor gets together in a cloud. When it is big enough to be called a drop, it does.

When there is a fog, you might as well not mind looking at it.

When a wave rolls over on itself it is called a breaker. Of just about anything, I guess.

Humidity is the experience of looking for air and finding water.

We keep track of the humidity in the air so we won't drown when we breathe.

In making rain water, it takes everything from H to O.

When rain water strikes forest fires, it heckstingwishes them. Luckily it effects we of the humans unlike that.

Rain is often spoken of as soft water, oppositely known as hail.

Rain is saved up in cloud banks.

In some rocks you can find the fossil footprints of fishes.

Cyanide is so poisonous that one drop of it on a dog's tongue will kill the strongest man.

A blizzard is when it snows sideways.

The main value of tornadoes is yet to be discovered.

A hurricane is a breeze of a bigly size.

A monsoon is a French gentleman.

A thunderstorm is like a shower, only more so.

Thunder is a rich source of loudness.

Quite a lot of the world's supply of electricity goes into the making of lightning.

Everybody leans to the sun in summer and away in winter. We are all a little tipsy that way.

We get our temperature three different ways. Either fairinheit, cellcius or centipede.

In lightning, electrons carry the negative charge while protons take the affirmative.

Isotherms and isobars are even more important than their names sound.

It is so hot in some parts of the world that the people there have to live other places.

The wind is like the air, only pushier.

Question: In what ways are we dependent upon the sun? Answer: We can always depend on the sun for sunburns and tidal waves.

Until it is decided whether tornadoes are typhoons or hurricanes, we must continue to call them tornadoes.

ADDITIONAL RESOURCES

Books and Articles

Hofstadter, D. R., and D. C. Dennet, eds. *The Mind's I: Fantasies and Reflections on Self and Soul*. New York: Basic Books, 1981. Playful yet challenging book of essays that explores the meaning of the word *I*.

Kosslyn, S. M. *Ghosts in the Mind's Machine*. New York: Norton, 1983. Good introduction to the issues of cognitive psychology.

_____ . "Stalking the Mental Image." *Psychology Today* (May 1985): 22ff. How we see things, manipulate images, and solve problems by visualizing with our "mind's eye."

Kosslyn, Steven. *Image and Mind*. Cambridge: Harvard University Press, 1980. Presents the motorboat example and other evidence suggesting how we use mental images.

Newell, Alan, and Herbert Simon. *Human Problem Solving*. Englewood Cliffs, N.J.: Prentice-Hall, 1972. Could a "thinking machine" be made to solve problems the way humans do? Newell and Simon examine problem-solving processes.

JUDGMENT AND DECISION MAKING

If you have to make a choice and don't make it, that in itself is a choice.

William James

Unit 11 explores the decision-making process and the psychology of risk taking, revealing how people arrive at good and bad decisions. It also looks at the reasons people lapse into irrationality and how personal biases can affect judgment.

Jim Ziv/Kellogg School, Northwestern University

Outside influences and emotions often overpower our better judgment when we are faced with uncertainty.

OBJECTIVES

After viewing the television program and completing the assigned readings, you should be able to:

1. Define decision making and describe alternative rational approaches to making decisions

2. Outline heuristic approaches to decision making, and illustrate errors in decision making due to the use of the representative (similarity) and the availability heuristic

3. Discuss decision errors due to framing errors and anchoring biases

4. Define "groupthink" and discuss ways to protect group decision making from groupthink

5. Explain the causes of cognitive dissonance and how people reduce it

6. Discuss the major errors in the process of negotiation and how to guard against these errors

READING ASSIGNMENT

After viewing Program 11, read pages 368–372 in *Psychology: Science, Behavior and Life*. Your instructor may also assign the anthology selections for Unit 11.

KEY TERMS AND CONCEPTS

The following terms are used in Program 11 but are not defined in the text.

anchoring bias—a bias in judgment that due to a memory residue of information, correct or incorrect

cognitive illusion—errors in human judgment due to systematic ways of thinking

dread factor—the fear of unfamiliar or potentially catastrophic events that makes us judge them to be riskier than familiar events

framing—the way information is presented that tends to bias how it is interpreted

groupthink—the pattern of distorted reasoning in group decision making due to group dynamics

invariance—the principle that preferences between options should be independent of different representations

similarity heuristic—see representative heuristic, p. 368 in the text

PROGRAM SUMMARY

No matter how uncertain life is, we all have to think and act decisively. Every day we assess situations, take risks, and make judgments and decisions.In Program 11 we'll get a chance to participate in experiments that illustrate the psychology of making decisions and taking risks. And we'll find out what psychologists are discovering about why people make bad decisions and irrational judgments.

There are several explanations for human error and irrationality. Social psychologists point to the influence of the crowd; Freudians claim that animal passions and emotions tend to overpower our better judgment.

Amos Tversky of Stanford University and Daniel Kahneman of the University of California at Berkeley study how and why people make illogical choices. They believe that irrationality is based on the same processes that enable us to form concepts and make inferences. But we often make irrational decisions because these same mental strategies are not appropriate in all cases. Confronted with uncertainty or ambiguity, we tend to think that the most easily recalled events are the most likely. For example, when news reports are full of vivid accounts of plane crashes and hijackings, we overestimate the likelihood of these events and may avoid traveling altogether.

We make some decisions based on other mental shortcuts, often using prototypes to represent classes of objects, events, and people. These assumptions can mislead us into making poor judgments, since we may mistakenly categorize something based on one feature. How information is "framed," or presented, can also influence our decision making—in mathematics, geography, politics—virtually any subject area.

Recently, the science of risk assessment has also been attracting a lot of interest. Researchers are discovering that most people avoid risks when seeking gains. But they also choose risks to avoid sure losses. Prolonged wars are a good example of loss avoidance; it's extremely difficult for one side to accept a sure loss (and cut its losses) and admit that there's no chance of winning. So both sides end up fighting longer and losing even more.

How people perceive a risk may also depend on complex psychological factors such as the "dread" factor. For example, we may be terrified of a nuclear accident but never think twice about jaywalking. That's because jaywalking is familiar, while a nuclear accident is unfamiliar and therefore seems more potentially catastrophic. Yet the odds of a nuclear accident are a tiny fraction of the odds of getting hurt while jaywalking.

Psychologists also study group decision making and have found that rationality often turns out to have little to do with intelligence, because decision making changes in groups. Psychologist Irving Janis studied the records of John F. Kennedy's cabinet meetings at which the disastrous decision to invade the Bay of Pigs was made. He found many examples of distorted reasoning, which he has labeled *groupthink*. Janis has also outlined some procedures that decision makers can implement in order to prevent irrational group decision making.

Another new field is the psychology of negotiation. It attempts to avoid the negative effects of bad decisions among individuals, groups, and institutions. Many people, especially government and business professionals, are taking a great interest in this area in an effort to improve their own negotiating skills.

What happens after a decision is made? The act of making a decision can set other processes in motion. Psychologists have found that whenever we decide something that conflicts with our prior beliefs, a state of "cognitive dissonance" results. We often try to reduce the tension and discomfort of cognitive dissonance by changing our attitude toward the decision or changing how others think about it.

Although bright, reasonable people often make irrational decisions and take unacceptable risks, the field of psychology is helping to shed light on our behavior and even provide guidelines for helping us catch ourselves before we go astray—or redirect ourselves if we do.

REVIEW QUESTIONS

Program Questions

1. *Cognition* is a general term that refers to all forms of

   a. remembering.
   b. perceiving.
   c. interacting.
   d. knowing.

2. The movement in psychology called cognitive psychology developed primarily

   a. at the turn of the century.
   b. in the 1920s.
   c. after World War II.
   d. during the social unrest of the 1960s.

3. What analytic tool did David Broadbent use to model the process by which information is perceived and stored in memory?

   a. Statistical analysis on a computer
   b. A flow chart
   c. A set of categories
   d. An analogy to a steam engine

4. When Herbert Simon discusses the computer, he compares neurons to

   a. punched cards.
   b. display monitors.
   c. central processing units.
   d. wires.

5. When we distinguish between groups of letters on the basis of the kinds of lines that form them, we are performing the mental process of

   a. relating.
   b. categorizing.
   c. creating prototypes.
   d. activating schemas.

6. Concepts are mental representations. Which is a concept of an attribute?

   a. Bed
   b. Jumping
   c. Slow
   d. Courage

7. What is our prototype of a tree most likely to be?

   a. A maple tree
   b. A palm tree
   c. A Christmas tree
   d. A dead tree

8. According to the program, why do we assume that Montreal is farther north than Seattle?

   a. Because we have learned it
   b. Because we are less familiar with Montreal than with Seattle
   c. Because Canada is north of the United States in our mental maps
   d. Because we are not good at making such judgments

9. When Steve Kosslyn asked subjects about the picture of a motorboat, he was primarily interested in

   a. how subjects scanned a mental image.
   b. how much detail subjects noted.
   c. how subjects compared a new picture with a prototype.
   d. how sure subjects felt about what they had seen.

10. What is one way in which human problem solving appears to be quite different from the way computers solve problems?

    a. Humans can solve problems that don't involve numbers.
    b. Humans are more logical in their approach to problems.
    c. Humans have trouble when content is unfamiliar.
    d. Humans are less likely to be misled by bias.

11. What did Michael Posner find when he conducted PET scans of people reading a word and associating it with a function?

    a. Localized activity occurred, but the location varied widely.
    b. Similar localized activity was seen in all the subjects.
    c. Brain activity was general rather than localized.
    d. No general pattern of activity was observed.

12. According to Robert Glaser, what is the general purpose of the research at the University of Pittsburgh's Learning and Research Development Center?

    a. To create new types of computers
    b. To model the organic functions of the brain
    c. To classify errors and mistakes
    d. To improve the way people use their intelligence

13. What is a cognitive illusion?

    a. A mental map that we can scan for information
    b. A biased mental strategy
    c. A concept formed on the basis of a perceptual illusion
    d. A decision motivated by emotion

14. How did Freud explain the fact that human beings sometimes make irrational decisions?

    a. They are driven by primitive needs.
    b. They are influenced by the emotions of the crowd.
    c. They are basing their decisions on availability.
    d. They are using standard human mental processes.

15. Why did the people questioned assume that there were more words beginning with k than with k as the third letter?

    a. There is a general tendency to favor the initial position.
    b. The anchoring effect biased their answers.
    c. It's easier to find examples of words beginning with k.
    d. It seems less risky as an answer.

16. A heuristic is a kind of

    a. mistake.
    b. tendency.
    c. mathematical model.
    d. shortcut.

17. A researcher asks two groups of students to estimate the average price of a new car. One group is asked if the price is more or less than $9,000. The other group is asked if the price is more or less than $18,000. Each group is asked to estimate the actual average price. How will the two averages compare?

    a. They will be essentially the same.
    b. The first group will have a slightly higher average.
    c. The second group will have a slightly higher average.
    d. The second group will have a much higher average.

18. When people were confronted with a choice of a sure loss of $85 or an 85 percent chance of losing $100, how did most people react?

    a. They chose the loss.
    b. They chose the chance.
    c. They pointed out the statistical equivalence of the alternatives.
    d. They refused to make the choice.

19. Why would smokers be likely to underestimate the chance of developing lung cancer?

    a. They do not dread the disease.
    b. It is an unfamiliar risk.
    c. It is not representative.
    d. It represents a delayed consequence.

20. Irving Janis studied how the decision to invade Cuba was made during the Kennedy administration. What advice does Janis offer to promote better decision making?

    a. Encourage groupthink by team-building exercises.
    b. Appoint one group member to play devil's advocate.
    c. Restrict the size of the group.
    d. Assume that silence means consent on the part of all group members.

21. Imagine that you are a business leader who has been to a negotiating workshop led by Max Bazerman and Lawrence Susskind. Which statement shows something you should have learned from the experience?

    a. "I will escalate conflict."
    b. "I know this is a zero-sum game."
    c. "I will enlarge my frame of reference."
    d. "I am confident that I am right and will prevail."

22. How does cognitive dissonance make us feel?

    a. We are so uncomfortable that we try to reduce the dissonance.
    b. We enjoy it so much that we actively seek dissonance.
    c. Our reaction to dissonance depends largely on personality.
    d. It creates boredom, which we try to overcome.

23. In Festinger's experiment, which students felt dissonance?

    a. Both the students who got $20 and those who got $1
    b. The students who got $20 but not those who got $1
    c. The students who got $1 but not those who got $20
    d. Neither the student who got $1 nor those who got $20

Textbook Questions

24. In order to think and communicate, we must mentally group events into categories or

    a. mental images.
    b. thoughts.
    c. clusters.
    d. concepts.

25. The optimal _____ level in each concept hierarchy is the process we naturally use when we think about objects.

    a. basic
    b. higher
    c. formal
    d. thought

26. Research has supported the idea that when thinking, we rely on _____ level categories most of the time.

    a. basic
    b. lower
    c. natural
    d. formal

27. Children probably use _____ level concepts first as they name and classify events and objects.

    a. formal
    b. natural
    c. basic
    d. subordinate

28. A concept which includes or contains other concepts or classes is known as

    a. the primary concept.
    b. subordinate.
    c. superordinate.
    d. the general concept.

29. The concept of dog is _____ to the concept and class of Collie dogs.

    a. subordinate
    b. superordinate
    c. secondary
    d. less important

30. Houses, cars, boats, chairs, cats, and dogs are all examples of

    a. basic-level concepts.
    b. superordinate-level concepts.
    c. subordinate-level concepts.
    d. hierarchical-level concepts.

31. According to association theory, when you encounter a new instance of a category, you respond to it on the basis of

    a. similarities and differences.
    b. stimulus generalization.
    c. extraction of common perceptual elements.
    d. analysis of its common elements and features.

32. According to the hypothesis-testing theory, concepts are formed by

    a. stimulus generalization.
    b. identifying and testing common perceptual attributes.
    c. mental images of prototypical members of specific categories.
    d. abstract rules and laws governing membership in specific categories.

33. The natural concepts that we learn every day are represented in our memories by examples rather than by abstract rules according to the _____ theory.

    a. association
    b. hypothesis-testing
    c. exemplar
    d. Clark Hull

34. In concept formation, an active process in which we try to ferret out the meanings of concepts by testing our assumptions is called

    a. subordinating concepts.
    b. hypothesis testing.
    c. superordinating.
    d. generalizing concepts.

35. The first step in problem solving is to

    a. test the hypotheses.
    b. evaluate the situation.
    c. generate possible solutions.
    d. identify the problem.

36. One of the difficulties in solving problems of daily life is that the problems tend to

    a. be ill-defined.
    b. be overly defined.
    c. involve personal matters.
    d. require too much time.

37. Trial-and-error problem solving is most effective when

    a. there is a wide range of solutions.
    b. there is a narrow range of solutions.
    c. strategies are needed.
    d. there must be a "quick fix."

38. The problem-solving strategy that involves formulating specific guesses that generate relatively efficient approaches to solving a problem, and then tests these guesses in a systematic fashion is called

    a. trial-and-error searching.
    b. heuristic searching.
    c. algorithm testing.
    d. hypothesis testing.

39. Asking for directions when lost is an example of using _____ as the problem-solving technique.

    a. a heuristic device
    b. an algorithm
    c. means-ends analysis
    d. incubation

40. Heuristics are

    a. rules of thumb which help simplify problems.
    b. mathematical formulas.
    c. mental sets.
    d. the same as algorithms.

41. If while watching TV the picture distorts and the images vibrate, and you get up and hit the top of the set with your hand to solve the picture problem, you are using what is called

    a. trial-and-error.
    b. hypothesis testing.
    c. quick heuristics.
    d. algorithms.

42. A common heuristic problem-solving strategy that starts by defining the goal, and then defines the steps that directly precede that goal, is called

    a. trial-and-error.
    b. means-ends analysis.
    c. evaluation.
    d. working backward.

43. A tendency to respond to a new problem with an approach that was successful in the past is called

    a. heuristics.
    b. a mental set.
    c. incubation.
    d. functional fixedness.

44. The tendency to view an object in terms of its name or familar usage is defined as

    a. mental set.
    b. incubation.
    c. functional fixedness.
    d. algorithmic perception.

45. The tendency to seek out evidence that will confirm our hypothesis while overlooking contradictory evidence is known as

    a. means-ends analysis.
    b. functional fixedness.
    c. incubation.
    d. confirmation bias.

46. Reasoning in which we begin with general assumptions that apply to specific instances is called

    a. deductive reasoning.
    b. inductive reasoning.
    c. functional reasoning.
    d. common sense.

47. An argument consisting of two or more premises and a conclusion is called

    a. means-ends analysis.
    b. working backward.
    c. inductive reasoning.
    d. a syllogism.

48. According to the experts, we often face conflict between principles of logic and what we believe about the world because of

    a. faulty algorithmic effect.
    b. the heuristic effect.
    c. belief-bias effect.
    d. mental set effect.

49. When we use _____ strategy, we compare something with preconceived stereotypes.

    a. availability heuristic
    b. representative heuristic
    c. compensatory
    d. noncompensatory

50. Based on past experience, Sue decides not to take her two five-year-old grandsons to the movie at the same time. She is using which decision-making strategy?

    a. Representative heuristic
    b. Availability heuristic
    c. Compensatory
    d. Noncompensatory

QUESTIONS TO CONSIDER

1. According to the *Journal of the American Medical Association*, strep throat is one of the most common reasons that children and young adults visit the doctor. It is difficult to diagnose by history or examination only. Ten doctors working in a university health center overestimated the incidence of strep throat by 81 percent. Of the 308 patients in the study, only 15—about 5 percent—actually had strep throat. What might explain the doctor's overestimation?

2. Knowing about problem-solving strategies and using them are two different things. Based on the information in the program and in your text, what are some of the pitfalls you need to avoid in both day-to-day problem solving and decision making about major life changes?

3. The profile of a creative person involves such qualities as nonconformity, curiosity, a high degree of verbal fluency, flexibility with numbers, concepts, a sense of humor, a high energy level, impatience with routine tasks, and a vivid imagination that may take the form of wild stories or fibs. What would be the implications for this type of child in the typical school classroom?

4. How does the scientific method try to guard against an experimenter's cognitive biases?

OPTIONAL ACTIVITY

1. Go to a busy intersection and observe pedestrian street-crossing behavior. Observe the kinds of risks people take crossing the street. What do you consider risky behavior? Who is most likely to engage in it? Why do you suppose certain people take more risks than others?

ANTHOLOGY

The following selections illustrate individual and group decision making in which emotions, superstitions, or other irrational influences dominate. Think about some important decisions you may face in your own life. How will awareness of these influences help make you a better decision maker?

Reading 24

The field of risk assessment is attracting more interest than ever before. Scientists are particularly interested in the problem of assessing and communicating risks related to environmental quality and health. Based on this article, do you think the new testing methods help the decision-making process? What principles of risk taking and decision making are involved in the issues described?

Risky Business

By Michael Shodell

During the 1970s, the national coming together of two major worries—concern for the environment and concern for our health—changed the way we think about ourselves and the world we live in. While the environment was a relative new comer to our compendium of cares, health had long been a venerable veteran of our worry campaigns, with cancer just the most recent standard-bearer. It was not surprising, then, that people were particularly responsive to linking cancer with the environment and placing both on a broad national scale of action.

Our overall chance of dying from cancer, the number two killer, is approximately 20 percent. Another way of saying it is that in the grab bag of mortality, two out of every 10 of the fatal items are a kind of cancer. It was thus relatively good news when estimates indicated that perhaps 80 percent of all cancers were attributable to environmental causes—not only pollution but the foods we eat and habits such as smoking. For if cancer were largely environmental, we should be able to do something about it. Reducing our exposure to carcinogens was one obvious approach. But like many a simple solution to a complex problem, this one too has been riddled with hidden complications.

The 1970s conjunction of health and environmental worries, however, produced an amazing array of concrete results. Opening with the establishments of the Environmental Protection Agency and the celebration of Earth Day, the decade also saw the creation of the Occupational Safety and Health Ad-

ministration, the National Institute for Occupational Safety and Health, and the Consumer Product Safety Commission, as well as a great deal of sweeping legislation, such as the Clean Air Act, the Safe Drinking Water Act, and the Toxic Substances Control Act. While the public ardor for ecology was considerably dampened by the additional time for reflection afforded by the long gas lines of the mid-1970s' energy crunch, we still strongly believed in the concept that we are responsible for our environment and for our health.

The idea that health risks might be mitigated by policing the environment has ancient roots. Rome and Athens both had special inspectors to protect against illicit wine additives. In 13th-century England, King Henry III's "Pillory and Tumbrel Statute" specified punishments for adulterations of foodstuffs; an assize in 1634 extended those penalties for the selling of "any musty or corrupted meal, which may be to the hurte and infection of man's body." But it wasn't until the early 19th century that such concerns received wide public attention. In 1829, F.C. Accum published his "Treatise on Adulteration of Food and Culinary Poisons," while an anonymous manuscript, "Deadly Adulteration and Slow Poisoning Unmasked, or Disease and Death in the Pot and the Bottle..." was widely circulated in 1830. By the middle of the century, the British physician Arthur Hassall was writing regular accounts for the British journal *The Lancet* about his microscopic examination of various foods. He found alum, an agent for whitening old and discolored flour, in virtually every bread sample he tested. Other foods, from sugar to Cayenne pepper, contained foreign substances such as mites and compounds of lead—still a rather prosaic list compared to our modern PCBs, pesticides, and other organic chemicals.

Revulsion aside, how could one determine whether these sorts of things proved a real health danger? An American pioneer in answering such questions was Harvey Wiley, a turn-of-the-century crusader for the role of government in regulating food and beverages for the health protection of the consumer. As director of the Department of Agriculture's Bureau of Chemistry which was later to become the federal Food and Drug Administration, Wiley undertook a series of experiments that captured the public imagination. With the help of the "poison squad," a group of male volunteers, Wiley tested the health effects of some commonly used food preservatives of the time—borax, salicylates, sulfites, benzoic acid, and formaldehyde. Between 1902 and 1904, following approaches that were not unusual at that time, Wiley fed these substances to 12 young men who reported disturbances of appetite and digestion. However, in another study in 1908, benzoate was fed to students at Columbia, Yale, and Northwestern universities. They apparently suffered no ill effects. Similar experiments—feeding borax to children—were carried out in England around this time. Toxic effects ranged from nausea and vomiting to skin irritations, accompanied, at least in one case, by the total loss of hair.

Today the human guinea pig approach to testing is, at least officially, at an end. It may be unflattering or even inhumane, but our modern surrogates are generally rodents. These animal bioassays, as they are called, involve exposure of mice or rats to varying amounts of test substance for most of their lives. The long exposure time is essential since cancer has a long latency, progressing through many different stages from the first initiating event to the final appearance of the disease. In humans this can take anywhere from 20 to 40 years. Although not without controversy, results from animal bioassays correlate well with the relatively few known causes of cancer in humans, a list of two

dozen or so that includes arsenic, asbestos, DES, mustard gas, and vinyl chloride.

But an animal bioassay of one substance requires testing for more than two years and can cost about half a million dollars. For substances taken in by inhalation rather than in food or water, the price tag can double or even triple. The Toxic Substances Control Act of 1976 gives the EPA the power to gather information from manufacturers about chemicals already in use or proposed new ones. The Act also directs the EPA to require testing of chemicals that may present an unreasonable risk of injury to health or the environment and to ban or restrict any substances that "will present an unreasonable risk of serious or widespread injury to health or the environment," including any substances that pose a serious risk of cancer, gene mutation, or birth defects. But there are on the order of five million known chemicals, with more than 60,000 of these in general commercial use in the United States and approximately 500 to 1,000 new ones added each year. The task is clearly overwhelming. A recent review by a committee of the National Research Council concluded that "of tens of thousands of commercially important chemicals, only a few have been subjected to extensive toxicity testing and most have scarcely been tested at all." Even for drugs and pesticides, the most extensively tested substances, complete health hazard assessments are available for only 10 percent of the pesticides and 38 percent of the drugs. One-fourth of drug ingredients and 38 percent of pesticide ingredients have no available data at all.

One approach to mitigating this problem has been the introduction of a variety of short-term tests. The most prevalent is a test developed by Bruce Ames of the University of California at Berkeley. The Ames test, which uses bacteria instead of animals, takes just a few days to complete and a few hundred dollars for each substance tested. The idea behind it is that since the chemistry of DNA is basically the same for all organisms, chemicals that cause gene mutations in bacteria are also likely to do so in humans. Since gene mutations in DNA may be involved in the origin of cancer, substances that cause such changes may also be strongly suspected of being carcinogenic. Other short-term tests look for gross physical changes in chromosomes, unusual patterns in the way DNA is made in cells grown in the laboratory, and mutations produced in fruit flies, yeast, protozoa, and a variety of bacteria besides those used in the Ames test. While these tests have been very useful as a sort of grand jury indictment, to convict a substance as a carcinogen, it is still necessary to demonstrate that it really does cause cancer. And the only way to find out experimentally is by testing the substance in animals.

Aside from extremely rare information on the consequences of human exposure to a carcinogen, tumors in animals are the gold standard of carcinogen regulation—the data needed for regulatory action. The Delaney Clause of the federal Food, Drug, and Cosmetic Act, for instance, states that *any* substance that causes tumors in animals may not be added intentionally to foods.

The Delaney Clause, however, is an exception. In general, regulatory agencies must look beyond just the production of tumors in animals before they can take action. Other factors to be considered include the extent of human exposure to the substance together with a numerical estimate of the actual effects on humans that might result. This is the process known as risk assessment, central to current thinking about regulating environmental health hazards. And it is definitely a risky business. How, for example, do you accurately estimate a human's chance of getting cancer from a substance that causes excess liver tumors in one strain of mouse but only benign growths in rats?

It might be reasonable to first ask how much of the substance a person actually is exposed to, compared to how much the rodents got. Frequently the answer is that the rodents received thousands of times the level that people could possibly find even if they made a conscious effort to do so. Furthermore, with rare exceptions, even a potent carcinogen solely on its own generally does not cause very high rates of cancer. But this also means that, with mathematical certainty, the effects of most substances would likely be undetectable in a test of 100 or even several hundred experimental animals. It is experimentally and economically more manageable to greatly increase the amount of the test substance rather than the number of animals.

This is why we hear such curious reports as the one about rats getting bladder tumors after being exposed daily to an amount of saccharin found in 800 diet sodas. In striving to make this kind of information relevant to our own situations, some adjustments obviously must be made. For instance, if 10 percent of the rats had tumors, would lowering the group's intake to the equaivalent of eight sodas daily, one one-hundredth of their original exposure, cause one one-hundredth the rate of cancer? That would mean a rate, on the average, of one excess cancer case caused by saccharin in every group of 1,000 exposed to this substance for their lifetimes. The best available answer to that question is, "Maybe." There are many different ways of doing the arithmetic for risk assessment, each of which has some scientific support, but none of which can be checked experimentally.

One reason for the uncertainty in extrapolation is that humans are different from rats or mice. We are, for instance, a lot bigger—with each of us having about 2,000 times the number of cells found in a mouse. We also live about 35 times longer, have lower metabolic and respiratory rates, and have different surface areas for our different shapes. Moreover, animals used in tests are exposed to but one pure substance under carefully controlled conditions, such as control over variation from one animal to another through the use of genetically inbred strains—which hardly compares to our own relatively haphazard environment and sundry genetic backgrounds. Even after attempting to adjust for these differences with calculations based on animal experiments, a major quantitative hurdle still remains: how do you use data from the high-level exposure of animal tests to estimate the possible cancer risk to humans at real exposure levels, often thousands of time lower?

One megamouse experiment set out to evaluate which of these possible extrapolation patterns might be most appropriate. The four-year experiment, carried out in the mid-1970s at the National Center for Toxicological Research in Jefferson, Arkansas, used more than 24,000 mice and cost more than $12 million. It is known as the ED_{01} experiment since it was designed to find the effective dose of a carcinogen, in this case 2-acetylaminofluorene—developed as a pesticide but never marketed and now used only in the laboratory—that would result in a one-percent cancer incidence in experimental animals. The study involved some 90 tons of mouse food and approximately 150 personnel, including animal care staff, data collection clerks, histologists, research scientists, technicians, and computer people, and the results were published as a small book in 1980.

While the ED_{01} experiment remains an important basis for judging extrapolation procedures, it has also been invoked in the highly controversial "threshold" debate, the question of whether there might be levels of a carcinogen that are virtually without risk—that is, a threshold below which no cancer would be produced. Compelling arguments exist both for and against thresholds. While the megamouse experiment did not go all the way down to the region where such a threshold might exist, it did supply real data for exposure levels far below those previously available. The data indicated that, at least in the case of 2-acetylaminofluorene in mice, no threshold was apparent, although it should be emphasized that this interpretation too is based on extrapolation.

It is the responsibility of regulatory agencies like EPA and OSHA to use human exposure levels together with risk assessment techniques in extrapolating from animal tests to what might be the actual impact of cancer on humans. The policy of many agencies is to decide what level of risk is acceptable and then, using the extrapolation procedures that correspond to the worst possible case, set exposure limits at a level that would not exceed this risk. An acceptable risk level frequently used is not more than one additional cancer for every million people exposed to a given substance throughout their lifetimes. If this risk level is accurate, what this means is that if all 238 million of us were exposed to that substance over our entire lifetimes, three additional people would die each year from this exposure.

In some instances the establishment of acceptable levels of a given substance involves balancing benefits and risks, in others, costs and benefits. In February 1981, President Reagan issued Executive Order 12291, which requires, in the absence of contravening legislation, that regulatory action be undertaken only if "the potential benefits to society

(from) the regulation outweigh the potential costs to society." Since it is hard to compare directly the cost of reducing the level of a particular chemical in the environment with the number of lives that could be saved, dollar values are put on a human life. OSHA, for instance, has used a value of $3.5 million, and EPA estimates have ranged between $400,000 and $7 million per life. In 1978, the Federal Aviation Administration established a value of $300,000 when considering the cost-effectiveness of installing breakaway poles on airport approach lights; today the figure has risen to $650,000. The National Highway Transportation Safety Administration, in judging the comparative value of various types of highway dividers, has used $175,000 as a reasonable figure for each life saved.

The cost accounting of human life can be tricky. The Office of Management and Budget, for instance, recently challenged the EPA's use of $4 million for purposes of asbestos regulation and asked that it be reduced, pointing out that cancer from asbestos could take four decades to develop. OMB requested that the human life value be comparably reduced by prorating it over a 40-year period.

OMB has similarly requested that OSHA reduce by approximately two-thirds the $3.5 million figure it has used as the life value for construction workers. In arguing such things, there is, of course, no column in the ledger books for metaphysics. Determinations are made based solely upon such items as total loss of earnings, tax revenue that otherwise might have been generated, and how much extra pay might be needed to induce a worker to take on more risks to his life. While such standards may be expedient for placing regulatory intervention on what appears to be an objective basis, under such criteria it is interesting to note there would have been a far higher priority on saving Midas over Moses, while the cost effectiveness for intervening to save the life of Jesus could well be called into question if the price exceeded 30 pieces of silver.

In some instances a simple rule of thumb called ALARA, for "as low as reasonably achievable," is used to determine the acceptable levels of exposure to a chemical. The ALARA number fluctuates with available control technologies and their costs. In other cases the lowest level detectable may become the standard—a continually decreasing scale. Prior to 1970 only about 100 organic compounds had been detected in drinking water, but a little more than a decade later, advances in mass spectrometry and gas chromatography had increased the number nearly fivefold.

As we become better and better at detecting environmental contaminants, we will get an ever-increasing list of things to worry about. While it is still a relatively young science, risk assessment continues to develop. One newly emerging approach, referred to as molecular epidemiology, measures with extraordinary sensitivity the effects of carcinogens, not in bacteria or test animals but on the DNA and protein molecules of the very human population so exposed. This approach is helping determine directly the impact of a chemical on the genes of a person exposed to a variety of agents, at the same time showing how the impact might vary from one individual to another.

The conflict between our chemical inventiveness and concerns for our health and environment may well be indicative of a more fundamental dichotomy within us—a dynamic tension between our technological development and its regulatory restraint. We share the planet with animals of remarkable speed, strength, and agility: birds of soaring flight and extraordinary vision, insects of amazing adaptability and fecundity. Only one flabby, clumsy, near-sighted species, known as *Homo sapiens*, depends on technology for survival. We view the world around us as just so much raw material to be combined and reworked—our evolutionary ace in the hole. Working together in complex, communicating social groups, we make things, revamping the world to our own specifications. Making judgments about what those specifications should be remains a relatively underdeveloped but increasingly important ingredient in human survival. Learning how to worry together as a species may well be our next essential evolutionary turning point.

Reading 25

This article illustrates the concept of groupthink in the corporate world, citing two common tactics: collective rationalization and shared stereotypes. As you read, think of moments when you may have participated in a decision-making process that resulted in groupthink. What were the implications of the decision? Were there ways groupthink could have been prevented?

Following the Leader

By Daniel Goleman

When E.F. Hutton speaks, the famous slogan goes, everyone listens. But Hutton's trouble seems to have been a case of no one speaking and no one listening.

What was not spoken about—or at least not in a way that led anyone there to question it—was the practice of checkkiting by Hutton money mangers. And what no one listened to was the still, small voice of conscience, whispering misgivings about an unethical and illegal practice.

The scheme was simple. A branch of the company would have, say, $70,000 on deposit in a small bank in Ohio. The branch would wire a cash transfer from the account for $1 million. The bank, not wanting to lose Hutton's valuable business, would advance the money, and a day later Hutton would replace it. Hutton got the use of $1 million of the bank's money for 24 hours.

While such oversights happen from time to time in business banking, Hutton made a practice of it: on any given day, the firm overdrew its bank accounts to the tune of millions of dollars; the interest on that money became a major source of company revenue. When the Justice Department finally investigated, Hutton was cited on 2,000 counts of mail and wire fraud, received a $2 million fine, and had to set up a multi-million-dollar fund to reimburse banks for interest payments lost on their funds.

Few at Hutton seem to have questioned the practice before the federal investigation; once established among the Hutton executive echelons, it was taken for granted. In fact, an internal memo from the corporate department in charge of cash management advised, rather blandly, "If an office is overdrafting their ledger balance consistently, it is probably best not to request an account analysis." In other words, the memo said, in effect, We'd rather not know about it—and rather the bank not notice, either.

How could those in Hutton's management let such a practice persist? Quite happily, as it turned out. The group dynamic at play seems to have been one that crops up to one degree or another in groups of all kinds: the group erects barriers against ideas or information that might prove upsetting. At Hutton, presumably, the idea that was out-of-bounds was that the overdraft practice was unethical; the taboo information was that the practice was illegal.

The culture of the workplace, where people are together, day after day, is an arena ripe for implicit agreements not to bring up upsetting facts. Irving Janis, a social psychologist recently retired from Yale and now an adjunct professor at University of California, Berkeley, has done the most detailed studies of this dynamic, which he dubs groupthink. In groupthink, decision makers tactly conspire to ignore crucial information because it somehow challenges a collective view with which everyone is comfortable; members of the group cramp their attention and hobble their information-seeking to preserve a cozy unanimity. Loyalty to the group requires that members not raise embarrassing questions, attack weak arguments, or counter soft-headed thinking with hard facts. Janis sums it up: "The more amiability and esprit de corps among the members of a policy-making in-group, the greater is the danger that independent critical thinking will be replaced by groupthink." The most likely result is a faulty decision.

The notion of groupthink has been around for more than a decade, when Janis proposed it to explain such foreign policy fiascoes as the Bay of Pigs and the bombing of North Vietnam. But more recently other psychologists have used his theory to study decision making in corporate life.

Groupthink, of course, is an especially dangerous pathology for businesses. In making a marketing or product-development decision, for example, a cozy executive group can make costly mistakes. The failure of American automakers to build high quality economy cars in response to the oil crisis of the 1970s—and their subsequent loss of a market share to the Japanese—is a famous example.

Groupthink, according to other organizational experts, is a danger inherent in the structure of a corporation, where the success or failure of an employee depends to a large extent on his immediate superior's evaluation. This can make the junior employee more than happy to support the senior one's opinions, even when he sees they are wrong.

One possible way around this is a group sometimes known as a self-managed work group set up among employees to cut through red tape and let workers manage themselves. These groups could be an organizational antidote to groupthink. But some research shows them to be just as prone to groupthink as any other part of the corporation.

Charles Manz and Henry Sims, business professors at University of Minnesota and Penn State who study organizational behavior, sat in on such work groups in a battery assembly plant in the South. These groups consist of workers doing similar tasks in, for example, a maintenance group or a quality control group or a production group. They were set up to do such things as propose an annual budget, make job assignments, and evaluate job performances of fellow members. They were also encouraged to solve problems as they came up, such as how to meet special production demands, or how best to schedule overtime.

At one meeting of a group in the quality control laboratory, the issue was a recent complaint from a production team that the quality control inspections were taking too long. While the quality control team did their tests for defects, production lines were shut down; the production workers who had to wait were indignant at the inconvenience. The quality control group quickly came to their own conclusion: the workers "expect us to drop everything." and "they don't understand how long the tests take." These group members felt they were in the right, that the complaints were unreasonable and unjustified. The matter was dropped, without taking the complaint seriously or searching for a solution.

In Manz and Sims' view, that resolution was arrived at using two groupthink tactics: collective rationalization and shared stereotypes. The rationalization was that there was nothing wrong with their own work—a self-serving assumption at best. The stereotype was that stupid production workers could not be expected to understand the intricacies of quality-control work. The result: the complaint was ignored.

There is similar evidence that strong business leaders encourage groupthink, even though they are promoting frank and open discussion. Eugene Fodor, a social psychologist at Clarkson University, and graduate student Terry Smith conducted an experiment that highlights how a strong leader can unwittingly stifle free thought.

In the experiment, volunteers simulated corporate decision making by playing executives of "Modern World Electronics" during a discussion of whether that company should manufacture a microwave oven. Each group member had several items of information to contribute that were known to him or her alone.

Independent of the discussion, the experimenters had tested the "boss" in each group on how much he was motivated by the need for power. People high in this motive do things for the sake of making an impact on others, rather than to meet an inner standard of excellence (the hallmark of the achievement motive) or to enjoy the company of others (the affiliation motive). As leaders, those high in power motivation enjoy exercising authority solely for the taste of power.

In the actual discussions, those leaders high in the need for power sought fewer facts from other group members and were offered fewer proposals. Once the leader had expressed his views, members fell in line, deferring to him. It was not so much that the leaders stifled dissent—many *seemed* to be democratic in how they ran things—but that they subtly reinforced compliance with their own opinions.

The groupthink that resulted was a matter of degree: somewhat less initiative by members, a notable lack of opposition to the leader's views, a compliant falling in line behind him. It seems that if the leader went in thinking the pseudocorporation should decide to manufacture microwaves, that's what the group ended up deciding. If he went in thinking they should not, then the group's decision was that they should not. The discussion, in other words, was a charade. That falling into step behind a leader masquerades as open discussion all too often in the corporate life. Anyone in the business world will be able to recognize moments like these and to add ample examples from experience.

Of course, not all groups are victims of groupthink—although occasionally even the healthiest may exhibit symptoms. The more often the symptoms crop up, the worse the resulting illusions, and the poorer the decisions that that group will make. The healthy alternative is a group that balances unity with an openness to all relevant information—even at the risk of a fracas from time to time.

ADDITIONAL RESOURCES

Books and Articles

Janis, Irving. *Victims of Groupthink: A Psychological Study of Foreign-Policy Decisions and Fiascoes.* 2d ed. Boston: Houghton Mifflin, 1972. Decision making in highly cohesive groups can be radical and even foolhardy. A sense of esprit de corps often appears connected with shared illusions and overconfidence.

Kahneman, D., P. Slovic, and A. Tversky, eds. *Judgment Under Uncertainty: Heuristics and Biases.* Cambridge: Harvard University Press, 1982. How framing and other biases affect and often distort judgment.

Rice, Berkeley. "Performance Review: The Job Nobody Likes." *Psychology Today* (September 1985): 30–36. Explores methods used to evaluate how well workers do their jobs.

MOTIVATION AND EMOTION

We may affirm absolutely that nothing great in the world has been accomplished without passion.

Georg Wilhelm Friedrich Hegel

What moves us to act? Why do we feel the way we do? Unit 12 shows how psychologists study the continuous interactions of mind and body in an effort to explain the enormous variety and complexities of human behavior.

UPI/Bettmann Newsphotos

Psychologists are studying what motivates Olympic athletes to push the limits of human endurance. Pictured are Cornelia Buerki of Switzerland, Cindy Bremser of the United States, and Zola Budd of Great Britain.

OBJECTIVES

After viewing the television program and completing the assigned readings, you should be able to:

1. Define motivation and outline the following theoretical perspectives: instinct theory, drive reduction, Maslow's hierarchy of needs, and the cognitive perspective

2. Contrast the views of Freud and Maslow regarding the basis of human motivation

3. List the four categories of human motivation and give examples of each

4. Discuss recent research on the hunger motive and outline the different theories of hunger

5. Outline our current understanding of the causes of obesity. Discuss research on dieting and the eating disorders of bulimia and anorexia nervosa

6. Discuss the important factors in human sexual motivation

7. Define achievement motivation and discuss its causes and consequences

8. Discuss the importance of explanatory style (optimism and pessimism) in achievement and health

9. Define emotion and outline its four integral components

10. Outline Plutchik's theory of basic emotions and Ekman's work on the universality of human emotional expression

11. Explain how the James-Lange, Cannon-Bard, and Schachter-Singer theories account for emotional behavior

READING ASSIGNMENT

After viewing Program 12, read pages 273–310 and 315–328 in *Psychology: Science, Behavior and Life*. Your instructor may also assign the anthology selections for Unit 12.

KEY TERMS AND CONCEPTS

As you read the assignment, pay particular attention to these terms, which are defined on the given pages in the text.

motivation (273)
instincts (275)
drive-reduction theory (276)
primary drives (276)
secondary drives (276)
incentives (276)
Maslow's hierarchy of needs (277)
self-actualization (277)
biologically based motives (282)
sensation-seeking motives (292)

complex psychosocial motives (300)
dual hypothalamic control theory (284)
glucostatic theory (285)
lipostatic theory (286)
set point (287)
obesity (287)
anorexia nervosa (291)
bulimia (292)

arousal (293)
optimal level of arousal (293)
Yerkes-Dodson law (294)
androgens (298)
hypogonadism (299)
estrogens (299)

need for achievement (278)
emotion (273)
James-Lange theory (317)
Cannon-Bard theory (320)
Schachter-Singer theory (321)
facial feedback theory (323)

The following terms are used in Program 12 but are not defined in the text.

explanatory style—how we explain our successes and failures to ourselves with an optimistic or pessimistic style

optimism (optimistic style)—the tendency to attribute failure to external, unstable, or changeable factors and to attribute success to stable or internal factors

pessimism (pessimistic style)—the tendency to attribute failure to stable or internal factors and to attribute success to global unstable factors

PROGRAM SUMMARY

What moves people to act? What makes someone jump into freezing water, risking his or her own life, to save a stranger, or why do exhausted marathon runners stagger relentlessly toward the finish line, determined to complete a punishing race?

To explain the enormous variety and complexity of behavior, psychologists study the environment as well as the individual, the mind as well as the body, to find what moves people to take action. They have observed that we move toward some things and away from others.

When we can't help moving toward something, we have an addiction. When we have an unnatural aversion to something, we have a phobia. Between the two extremes of approach and avoidance, psychologists infer motives by noting what we choose, how intensely we involve ourselves, and how long we keep at it.

Seeking pleasure and avoiding pain explain many of our actions. But this same principle can also work against us. For example, alcohol and drugs may be pleasurable, but they are bad for us. And studying may be extremely difficult, but it can be good for us. As we grow older, we learn to do the things that will pay off in the future. But our true desires may never go away.

Freud theorized that behavior was based on our motivation to seek sexual satisfaction and to express aggressive urges against those who restrain our pursuit of pleasure. He explained that our basic sexual and aggressive desires are hidden from our conscious awareness but that they still influence our behavior and sometimes reveal themselves in dreams, fantasies, or slips of the tongue.

In contrast to Freud, Carl Rogers and Abraham Maslow, who studied normal, healthy people, saw a different side of human nature. They theorized that our lives are shaped by a basic tendency toward growth and mastery.

Sexual behavior is a good example of the complex interaction of psychological and biological forces. In contrast to the motivation of other animals, whose sexual mating behavior patterns promote the survival of the species, human sexual motivation is a readiness to experience intense pleasure and, often, romantic love. It combines physical arousal, strong emotion, and intense attraction to another person. Human sexual behavior is highly diverse and subject to a mixture of personal, social, situational, and cultural influences.

A related area of psychological interest is emotion, the complex pattern of changes involving feelings, thoughts, behavior, and physical arousal. Psychologist Robert Plutchik has proposed that there are eight basic emotions made up of four pairs of opposites, such as joy and sadness, and anger and fear, which we combine when we feel other emotions (see Figure 6).

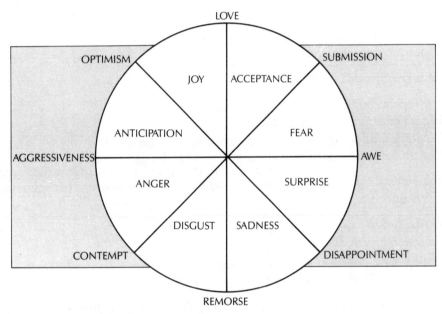

Figure 6: Wheel of Emotion
Psychologist Robert Plutchik created a wheel of emotion showing eight primary emotions and composites of adjacent emotions. According to this model, fear and surprise, when combined, become awe, and joy mixed with acceptance becomes love.

Psychologist Paul Ekman's cross-cultural studies reveal a remarkable universality in the way facial expressions communicate basic emotions. In fact, people all over the world decode emotions in much the same way. And they show similar changes in the brain, muscles, thoughts, and behavior.

Theorists such as Martin Seligman emphasize the role of cognitive appraisal in motivation and emotion. He suggests that what people do and how hard they try are influenced by basic optimism and pessimism. Our motivations and emotional states depend on how we view failure and success. An optimist failing a test would attribute the poor performance to external causes (The test was too hard) or changeable factors (I'll try harder and do better next time). The pessimist would feel doomed by stable, unchangeable factors (I guess I'm dumb and unlucky) and out of control (Nothing I do will make a difference; I'll always be this way). On the other hand, optimists take full credit for their successes, while pessimists see only luck or chance in anything good that happens to them. A person's explanatory style can influence performance in school and work and even his or her physical and mental well-being.

REVIEW QUESTIONS

Program Questions

1. What is the general term for all the physical and psychological processes that start behavior, maintain it, and stop it?

   a. Explanatory style
   b. Repression
   c. Addiction
   d. Motivation

2. Phoebe has a phobia regarding cats. What is her motivation?

   a. Environmental arousal
   b. Overwhelming fear
   c. Repressed sexual satisfaction
   d. A need for attachment with others

3. What is the role of the pleasure-pain principle in motivation?

   a. We repress our pleasure in others' pain.
   b. We seek pleasure and avoid pain.
   c. We persist in doing things even when they are painful.
   d. We are more intensely motivated by pain than by pleasure.

4. Which activity most clearly involves a "reframing" of the tension between desire and restraint?

   a. Eating before you feel hungry
   b. Seeking pleasurable physical contact with others
   c. Working long hours for an eventual goal
   d. Getting angry at someone who interferes with your plans

5. Freud thought there were two primary motivations. One of these is

   a. expressing aggression.
   b. seeking transcendence.
   c. fulfilling creativity.
   d. feeling secure.

6. Compared with Freud's view of human motivation, that of Abraham Maslow could be characterized as being more

   a. negative.
   b. hormonally based.
   c. optimistic.
   d. pathologically based.

7. Behaviors such as male peacocks displaying their feathers or male rams fighting are related to which part of sexual reproduction?

   a. Providing a safe place for mating
   b. Focusing the male's attention on mating
   c. Selecting a partner with good genes
   d. Mating at the correct time of year

8. In Norman Adler's research on mating behavior in rats, what is the function of the 10 or so mountings?

    a. To trigger hormone production
    b. To prepare the male for ejaculation
    c. To cause fertilization
    d. To impress the female

9. What kinds of emotions tend to be involved in romantic love?

    a. Mainly intense, positive emotions
    b. Mainly intense, negative emotions
    c. A mixture of intense and weak emotions that are mainly positive
    d. A mixture of positive and negative emotions that are intense

10. Darwin cited the similarity of certain expressions of emotions as evidence that

    a. all species learn emotions.
    b. emotions are innate.
    c. emotions promote survival of the fittest.
    d. genetic variability is advantageous.

11. Pictures of happy and sad American workers are shown to American college students and to Italian workers. Based on your knowledge of Paul Ekman's research, what would you predict about how well the groups would identify the emotions?

    a. Both groups will identify the emotions correctly.
    b. Only the Americans will identify the emotions correctly.
    c. Only the Italians will identify the emotions correctly.
    d. Neither group will identify the emotions correctly.

12. Theodore has an explanatory style that emphasizes the external, the unstable, and the specific. He makes a mistake at work about which his boss becomes very angry. Which statement is Theodore most likely to make to himself?

    a. "I always make such stupid mistakes."
    b. "I was just distracted by the noise outside."
    c. "All my life people have always gotten so mad at me."
    d. "If I were a better person, this wouldn't have happened."

13. Why does Martin Seligman believe that it might be appropriate to help children who develop a pessimistic explanatory style?

    a. These children are unpleasant to be around.
    b. These children lack contact with reality.
    c. These children are at risk for depression.
    d. These children seldom achieve much in life.

Textbook Questions

14. Innate and complex patterns of behavior that occur in every normally functioning member of a species under certain set conditions are called

    a. drives.
    b. reflexes.
    c. reactions.
    d. instincts.

15. According to the text, _____ tend to be species specific.

    a. drives
    b. instincts
    c. needs
    d. motives

16. Hungry animals will learn and work for saccharine, which has no nutritional value. This is a challenge for the

    a. drive-reduction theory.
    b. cognitive theory.
    c. opponent-process theory.
    d. arousal theory.

17. Money may be a(n) _____ for a person to work.

    a. incentive
    b. need
    c. motivation
    d. drive

18. Striving to become what one is capable of being and to reach one's full potential is, according to Abraham Maslow,

    a. drive reduction.
    b. instinct satisfaction.
    c. building psychic energy.
    d. self-actualization.

19. According to Maslow's theory, in a generally well-fed society such as ours, much of our frustration stems from failure to meet

    a. love and belongingness needs.
    b. safety needs.
    c. self-actualization needs.
    d. physiological needs.

20. Expectations play an important role in the _____ theory of motivation.

    a. instinct
    b. drive-reduction
    c. cognitive
    d. hierarchy

21. The brain structure involved in regulating hunger is the

    a. pons.
    b. hypothalamus.
    c. medulla.
    d. pituitary.

22. The ventromedial nucleus of the hypothalamus seems to be the control center for

    a. eating.
    b. sex.
    c. stimulation.
    d. arousal.

23. The theory that suggests structures in the hypothalamus operate together to maintain a constant state of satiety, is the

    a. dual hypothalamic control theory.
    b. lipostatic theory.
    c. set point theory.
    d. glucostatic theory.

24. The fact that weight usually stays constant is explained by the

    a. set point theory.
    b. lipostatic theory.
    c. glucostatic theory.
    d. dual-hypothalamus theory.

25. Anorexia nervosa is a disorder usually found in young _____ that is associated with a change in body image and a marked weight _____ .

    a. men; gain
    b. men; loss
    c. women; gain
    d. women; loss

26. A general level of activity, or preparedness for activity, in an organism is called

    a. arousal.
    b. novel.
    c. sensation.
    d. parasympathetic activity.

27. The principle which states that complex tasks are performed most efficiently at lower levels of arousal is hypothesized by the

    a. Cannon-Bard theory.
    b. James-Lange theory.
    c. Yerkes-Dodson law.
    d. hierarchy of desire theory.

28. Which of the following is true of participants in the sensory-deprivation experiment discussed in the text?

    a. Participants did not fall asleep.
    b. Participants had no difficulty concentrating.
    c. Participants felt very relaxed.
    d. Many reported hallucinations after two or three days.

29. The male sex hormone is

    a. androgen.
    b. estrogen.
    c. adrenaline.
    d. antiandrogen.

30. Recent studies on estrogen replacement therapy in females suggests that

    a. some estrogen is necessary to maintain normal sexual interest.
    b. estrogen is not needed.
    c. excessively high dosages are needed.
    d. it is useless.

31. The fact that there is tremendous variation in human sexual behavior across cultures gives the strongest evidence for the _____ in human sexual motivation and expression.

    a. inborn influence
    b. unconscious factor
    c. hormonal influence
    d. psychosocial factors

32. Classic studies find that people with _____ nAch earn higher grades than people of equal learning ability with _____ nAch.

    a. high; moderate
    b. high; low
    c. low; high
    d. moderate; high

33. If a person ran away from a fire for fear of an explosion, what component of emotion is represented by that person's running away?

    a. Cognitive
    b. Subjective
    c. Physiological
    d. Behavioral

34. We see a bear! We run, and then feel fear. This experience is supportive of the _____ theory.

    a. Schachter-Singer
    b. James-Lange
    c. Cannon-Bard
    d. Grizzly Adams

35. Which theory (theories) of emotion fail(s) to adequately recognize that emotions are more than automatic reactions to stimuli?

    a. Both the James-Lange and the Cannon-Bard theories
    b. The Schachter-Singer theory
    c. The James-Lange theory
    d. The cognitive theory

36. The theory which states that the same body state of arousal can lead to a variety of emotions depending on an individual's interpretation is called the

    a. James-Lange theory.
    b. Schachter-Singer theory.
    c. Cannon-Bard theory.
    d. Plutchik's theory.

37. Darwin's, as well as Ekman's, research supports the theory that
_____ are universal and have survival value.

    a. facial expressions
    b. body gestures
    c. temper tantrums
    d. secondary emotions.

QUESTIONS TO CONSIDER

1. Human sexual motivation expresses itself in sexual scripts that include attitudes, values, social norms, and expectations about patterns of behavior. Consider how males and females might develop different sexual scripts. How might lack of synchronization affect a couple? How might sexual scripts change as the bad news about sexually transmitted diseases and AIDS increases?

2. Do you consider yourself an optimist or a pessimist? Pick a recent success and a recent failure or disappointment and consider how an optimist and a pessimist would explain each experience. How did you handle each situation?

3. Does your body give away your true feelings? What is the role of emotion in nonverbal communication? When words and body language don't match, do you pay more attention to the words or to the behavior? Why?

4. Consider how eating disorders such as anorexia and bulimia contradict the pain-pleasure principle.

5. Why might both extremely sad and extremely happy events be stressful?

6. If you could choose between taking this course pass-fail (credit only) or getting a letter grade, which would you choose? How would your decision affect your study time, motivation, test-taking behavior?

OPTIONAL ACTIVITY

1. Are we sad because we cry, or do we cry because we are sad? Can making a sad face make us feel sad? Does going through the motions trigger the emotion?

   Try this: Set aside 10 or 15 minutes for this experiment. Write down the words *happy*, *sad*, *angry*, and *fearful* on slips of paper. In front of a mirror, select one of the slips, and watch yourself as you create the facial expression for it. Hold the expression for at least a minute. Note the thoughts and physical reactions that seem to accompany your facial expression. Then relax your face and repeat the exercise with another slip of paper. Which theories does your experience support or challenge?

ANTHOLOGY

Unit 12 delves into the psychological study of motives and emotions. As you read the following selections, think about the different motives people have for the same behavior. Also consider how the same behavior can evoke very different emotions at different times.

Reading 26

Do you have strong preferences for certain foods? Are there times when you can't resist them? In what ways is a craving like an addiction? As you read this article, consider the implications of explaining eating disorders, taking into account the variations in blood chemistry and hormones.

Taster's Choice

By Madeline Drexler

Food cravings are gustatory fingerprints. In those sluggish hours when there's nothing better to do than imagine a perfect one-course entree, our choices are as varied as they are precise: One mind turns to mashed potatoes, another to chocolate-covered raisins, a third to subgum chow mein. Our stomachs have stubborn reveries.

Then there are more novel yearnings. Pica, the desire to eat dirt or clay, occurs among native Africans and Southern US blacks. There are also cornstarch cravings, in which people eat whole boxes of the substance at a time. And alpine climbers are known to relish salt pork, perhaps because they need to replenish the 6,000 or more calories they burn in a day.

Where do our gastronomical urges come from? For a seemingly innocuous question, there is surprisingly heated scientific debate. Part of the disagreement is semantic. While some researchers believe there are strong physiological links to cravings, many nutritionists claim we don't really "crave" in the strict biological sense of the word (such as when a sodium-deficient deer finds a salt lick); rather, we exercise our subjective "preferences." Our protein intake, for example, is amazingly steady (12 to 15 percent of our diets) and not a frequent source of cravings. What varies wildly is fat and carbohydrate consumption—the classic pined-for foods in a pleasure-celebrating culture.

Recent research lends support to both sides. In the it's-not-in-my-head-it's-in-my-body camp, scientists have found that many female animals tend to eat more sugars, while males consume more food overall. Some suggest that this has to do with the female estrogen metabolism, also one of the reasons offered to explain why women with premenstrual syndrome crave carbohydrates. (Why pregnant women long for peculiar foods is still unclear.)

People who give up smoking crave carbohydrates. At Texas Tech University, psychology professor Bonnie Spring fed the amino acid tryptophan and a high-carbohydrate diet to those who kicked the cigarette habit—and found that they were less hostile and anxious during their withdrawal. One explanation is that since nicotine elevates our blood glucose level and carbohydrates break down into glucose, the carbo craving comes from the body's need to return to a cigarette-induced high-glucose state.

At the Massachusetts Institute of Technology, research scientist Judith Wurtman has identified a group she calls "carbohydrate cravers." According to Wurtman, these people have low levels of serotonin, a brain chemical that induces calm and has been tied to carbohydrate consumption; when their serotonin level drops, they become irritable and anxious and often end up in a cycle of overeating. Wurtman also speculates that artists and others in a high state of mental arousal crave carbos for similar effects: to help settle and focus their minds. For such carbo cravers, she prescribes low-fat carbohydrate snacks to alleviate the anxiety.

Wurtman's books and advice have become immensely popular in the past several years. But other scientists in the field believe there are methodological flaws in her work. One prominent critic is John Fernstrom, a professor of psychiatry and behavioral neuroscience at the University of Pittsburgh School of Medicine. Fernstrom contends that Wurtman doesn't define "carbohydrate food" in her experiments. "When you look at what her subjects are eating, what you in fact find is that they are not carbohydrate cravers at all, but carbohydrate and fat cravers," he says. And while carbohydrates are indeed the nutrients tied to serotonin production, the carbo-fat combination is not. It is, instead, a "hedonistically very appealing . . . sensory taste and culturally defined craving," Fernstrom says.

Studies have shown that people derive more pleasure from eating a carbo-fat mix than from eating either sugar or fat alone. Fernstrom believes that people crave that mix not for physiological reasons but because "they get a positive reinforcement from a food that they really enjoy. What they're doing is selecting a food that, out of their culture and past and taste buds, gives them a good feeling."

Other behavioral scientists agree that we learn our food fixations. Leann Birch, professor of human development, family ecology, and nutrition at the University of Illinois, found that young children must taste a new item eight to 10 times before they decide they like it. She also discovered that children, left to their own devices, self-regulate their caloric intake—unlike adults, who, in Birch's words, "have cognitive and cultural overlays."

At Johns Hopkins University, associate professor of psychiatry Barbara Rolls found that even after we are sated with a savory food such as sausage and can eat no more, we still desire a sweet taste—as in dessert. One researcher called this the "Thanksgiving phenomenon," because after three platefuls of turkey, we still manage to make room for pumpkin pie.

Many scientists contend that being over-weight has more to do with our general eating patterns than with fixating on fudge sauce. According to Tom Castonguay, assistant director of the Food Intake Laboratory at UC/Davis, obesity is related to genetic predisposition, a lifetime of poor exercise, and simply bucking dietary common sense. Sometimes, he adds, "we use food to be bad."

Despite disagreements among scientists themselves, every fad diet for "cravers" that hits the market claims to rely on scientific proof. Recently, for example, West Coast physician Douglas Hunt published a book titled *No More Cravings*, in which he prescribes heavy doses of minerals and other compounds, and speculates that food yearnings are caused by allergies and yeast infections. "Cravings are not 'all in your mind,'" he writes. "They are physiological effects stemming from physiological causes."

Not so, say most experts. "The word 'craving' conjures up an addiction, but I don't think that's the kind of thing that a person with a sweet tooth is experiencing," says Tom Castonguay. At the Obesity Research Clinic of the University of Pennsylvania, codirector Kelly Brownell takes a commonsensical approach. He likens cravings to a wave in the ocean—starting small, building steadily to a peak, then rapidly subsiding. If you track where you are in the craving cycle, or if the desire strikes at the same time each day, you can ward off the urge for a bowl of ice cream by taking a brisk walk before the craving peaks.

Brownell admits he's not sure whether cravings are in the head or in the gut. "It's possible that there's nothing physiological about it," he says. "Even if you do buy the physiological arguments, there are many foods that are high in fat—and which one you choose depends on cultural habit."

"Cravings are not that deep-rooted or overwhelming," says Tom Castonguay. "But people are making a lot of money talking about them."

Reading 27

This article looks at kissing in the workplace, exploring the complex motives and emotions involved in deciding whether, with whom, when, and where it is appropriate. As you read, think about how sexual, cultural, and situational differences affect behavior and emotional responses. Do you think motives can be misinterpreted? Consider how conflicting sexual scripts contribute to the confusion.

Kissing in the Workplace Poses Dilemma

By Kathleen A. Hughes

It happens in a split second: You've been kissed by a business associate.

Social kissing—the peck on the cheek—has become so widespread that it's spilling over into the business world. In certain corporate circles, at company parties and even in offices, some people who barely know each other exchange kisses as freely as handshakes.

Yet many people find corporate kissing awkward and confusing. Both men and women say they are often unsure about just whom to kiss, and under what circumstances. And recipients of corporate kisses often are horrified. Indeed, etiquette gurus say corporate kissing is usually a faux pas unless the participants are close friends outside the workplace.

"There's more kissing than ever before because there are more women in business than ever before," says Jerry Della Femina, chairman of Della Femina McNamee WCRS, a New York advertising agency. "Deciding whether to kiss takes up most of my waking hours."

Shifting Norms

Kissing has spread partly because the distinction between social and business etiquette has blurred. Social kissing, no longer just an upper-class phenomenon, has "gotten completely out of hand, and no one can agree on the system," says Judith Martin, who authors the syndicated Miss Manners etiquette column. And extroverts who consider someone a friend after a few business meetings or a few months on the job are taking today's looser social-kissing norms into the corporate world.

But when two people aren't close friends, the recipient of a corporate smooch often feels uncomfortable. Part of the problem is that those who have been kissed are suspicious of the motives; the kissers, they feel, are trying to sell something, ingratiate themselves or impress others.

Robert Kirby, chairman of Capital Guardian Trust in Los Angeles, recently attended a presentation by a female marketing consultant in his firm's New York office and was given a big parting hug and kiss on the cheek. The two had attended a business dinner together, but Mr. Kirby still considered the kiss inappropriate. "It leaves you with ongoing wariness, and it's kind of embarrassing," says Mr. Kirby. "There's an implication that this isn't 100% business."

The woman's presentation wasn't accepted, though Mr. Kirby says the kiss wasn't a factor. But "the next time we have occasion to meet," he adds, "I'll keep a conference table between us."

Joseph Lewis, a sales manager at Seattle Pacific Industries, says a former customer who brought her boss along on a visit gave Mr. Lewis a big kiss on the cheek. Mr. Lewis was startled, because he and the customer hadn't gotten along. "She was trying to impress her boss" with her friends in the company, he says. "She greeted me like I was her long-lost friend; and I don't even like her. I thought it was phony."

Spouses, too, often seem calculating. Morgan H. Harris Jr., Lora/Ferry International's managing director for Southern California, says that after a dinner with a job candidate and his wife, the woman kissed Mr. Harris goodbye—right on the lips. "She wanted to make sure her husband made a good impression, and she overdid it," Mr. Harris says. "I thought 'Her aim is bad.' "

Corporate kissers, however, deny any intent to manipulate. Maureen Kindel, president of Rose & Kindel, a consulting firm in Los Angeles, says she kisses at least once a day in business because it's part of her demonstrative nature. The kiss, she says, "isn't compromising because it has replaced the handshake."

Many kissers say they do it because it puts people at ease. Joann Shanley, vice president of advertising at Ticor, a financial-services firm in Los Angeles, says she kisses business associates she hasn't seen in a while. "I think it's one of the advantages women have," she says. "It puts you in a closer bond with whomever you're meeting than would be the case with a simple handshake."

As the practice spreads, business people increasingly face the dilemma of whether to kiss. Steve Hayden, chief creative officer of the advertising agency BBDO/Los Angeles, says deciding can be hard because there are "about 17 variables"—including the city, business, ages and rank of the two people—to consider before kissing, while a kiss "happens in an instant."

People who move in many different corporate circles may become especially confused. Mr. Hayden says he is unsure whether to kiss in business relationships about 10% of the time. "We go from a Japanese meeting to a meeting with passionate movie people to a meeting with staid New Yorkers. You start getting your signals mixed up."

He recently met with a female executive from a big Chicago-based company about a new business pitch and gave her a buss on the cheek. "I had just gotten out of a meeting where that was the behavior. I was in a kissing mode," Mr. Hayden recalls. But halfway into the kiss he started to regret it, remembering that the woman "had already expressed some concern that we were a bunch of L.A. hot-tub types."

The executive wasn't pleased. "Her eyes kind of widened and she drew back. She was a bit shocked. Then she smiled a little bit, as if to say, 'This is how they act in Los Angeles.'"

BBDO/Los Angeles didn't get that account. "It was all the wrong kiss," Mr. Hayden says with a sigh.

Couples often complicate the question of whom to kiss. Some men say they feel compelled in social settings to kiss the boss's wife. But female executives rarely feel compelled to kiss the husband of a female boss. Nancy Vreeland, a Los Angeles fund raiser, says she finds it awkward when she knows a wife but barely knows the husband. "The wife and I kiss. I certainly don't feel comfortable kissing the husband. I wind up shaking his hand. The whole things feels uncomfortable."

Some business associates who become friends over time say they know instinctively when it's time for a kiss. Others use formulas. Alan Landsburg, chairman of Landsburg Co., a television production company in Los Angeles, says "the rule is if they have been guests in my house, a kiss on the cheek as a greeting is valid" in a social setting, but not in the office.

Robert Sherwood, vice president of acquisitions at Lorimar Film Entertainment Group in Los Angeles, uses a rule he read somewhere: "Defer to the woman to lead. If she wants to be kissed, she will offer that."

But others use a simpler formula: Just say no. Some male executives say they try to avoid giving female colleagues a peck on the cheek under any circumstances, assuming that women would find it demeaning. "The answer to kissing is never, never," says Postmaster General Anthony Frank, a former savings and loan chief executive officer. "It accentuates the difference in gender, and I don't think you should do that."

Indeed, etiquette gurus say corporate kissing usually is a mistake. "It's ludicruous and rather obsequious to pretend you are warm, close friends in a business environment," says Ms. Martin, the columnist. "It obscures the line of rank and command." She and others recommend handshakes, except with close friends.

How often a person encounters corporate kissing depends partly on occupation. People who work in upscale businesses such as art galleries, luxury hotels and restaurants are smothered with kisses. Nicholas Mutton, general manager of Seattle's Four Seasons Hotel, says more than a third of the female guests give him a peck on the cheek before leaving. Richard Kuhlenschmidt, owner of Kuhlenschmidt/Simon Gallery in Los Angeles, says women at art openings frequently kiss him, some of them on the lips. "I'm usually shocked. They're not even women I know well."

Occupations in which kissing rarely seems to occur include investment banking, law and accounting. "I'm an accountant. I don't kiss anyone but my wife," says Hans Turner, a vice president and controller at Samuel Goldwyn Co., a Los Angeles entertainment company.

Reticent Bostonians

There are also geographical differences. Some Bostonians, for instance, won't even *talk* about kissing. Others just dismiss it. George Lodge, a professor of comparative government-business relations at Harvard, says: "I don't recall any instances of kissing at Harvard Business School."

Kissing, however, pervades the nation's capital. "People in Washington touch cheek-to-cheek quite often," says Effi Barry, wife of the city's mayor, Marion Barry Jr. That includes political opponents. Ms. Barry says she finds it disturbing when she receives a big smooch from people who haven't supported her husband's administration. When it happens, however, she simply smiles and says, "Nice to see you."

In Los Angeles, a fear of contagious diseases has boosted the popularity of the "air kiss," in which two people put their cheeks in close proximity without touching. Sometimes they make kissing sounds, and sometimes they just say, "Kiss, kiss."

Still, the city may well be the nation's kissing capital. Successful entertainment-industry gatherings often are referred to as "huggy-huggy, kissy-kissy." Those who prefer not to kiss simply suffer. "Sometimes people purse their lips and come running at you," says Thomas D. Tannenbaum, president of Viacom Productions Inc. "If someone puts their face up to be kissed, you can't just let them hang there."

Reading 28

As you read this excerpt from a story by Richard Rovere, notice the strong emotions evoked by the boy's school experience. Consider the impact the experience has on his self-concept, motivation, and performance. Do you think the boy's perceptions are exaggerated? Do you believe his pessimistic attitude contributes in part to his experience and resulting depression? How would an optimistic child have dealt with the same situation?

Wallace

By Richard H. Rovere

As a schoolboy, my relations with teachers were always tense and hostile. I disliked my studies and did very badly in them. There are, I have heard, inept students who bring out the best in teachers, who challenge their skill and move them to sympathy and affection. I seemed to bring out the worst in them. I think my personality had more to do with this than my poor classroom work. Anyway, something about me was deeply offensive to the pedagogic temperament.

Often, it took a teacher no more than a few minutes to conceive a raging dislike for me. I recall an instructor in elementary French who shied a textbook at my head the very first day I attended his class. We had never laid eyes on each other until fifteen or twenty minutes before he assaulted me. I no longer remember what, if anything, provoked him to violence. It is possible that I said something that was either insolent or intolerably stupid. I guess I often did. It is also possible that I said nothing at all. Even my silence, my humility, my acquiescence, could annoy my teachers. The very sight of me, the mere awareness of my existence on earth, could be unendurably irritating to them.

This was the case with my fourth-grade teacher, Miss Purdy. In order to make the acquaintance of her new students on the opening day of school, she had each one rise and give his name and address as she called the roll. Her voice was soft and gentle, her manner sympathetic, until she came to me. Indeed up to then I had been dreamily enter-taining the hope that I was at last about to enjoy a happy association with a teacher. When Miss Purdy's eye fell on me, however, her face suddenly twisted and darkened with revulsion. She hesitated for a few moments while she looked me up and down and thought of a suitable comment on what she saw. "Aha!" she finally said, addressing not me but my new classmates, in a voice that was now coarse and cruel. "I don't have to ask *his* name. There, boys and girls, is Mr. J. Pierpont Morgan, lounging back in his mahogany-lined office." She held each syllable of the financier's name on her lips as long as she was able to, so that my fellow-students could savor the full irony of it. I imagine my posture was a bit relaxed for the occasion, but I know well that she would not have resented anyone else's sprawl as much as she did mine. I can even hear her making some friendly, school-marmish quip about too much summer vacation to any other pupil. Friendly quips were never for me. In some unfortunate and mysterious fashion, my entire being rubbed Miss Purdy and all her breed the wrong way. Throughout the fourth grade she persisted in tormenting me with her idiotic Morgan joke. "And perhaps Mr. J. P. Rovere can tell us all about Vasco da Gama this morning," she would say, throwing in a little added insult by mispronouncing my surname.

The aversion I inspired in teachers might under certain circumstances have been turned to good account. It might have stimulated me to industry; it might have made me get high marks, just so I could prove to the world that my persecutors were motivated by prejudice and perhaps by a touch of envy; or it might have bred a monumental rebelliousness in me, a contempt for all authority, that could have become the foundation of a career as the leader of some great movement against all tyranny and oppression.

It did none of these things. Instead, I became, so far as my school life was concerned, a thoroughly browbeaten boy, and I accepted the hostility of my teachers as an inescapable condition of life. In fact, I took the absolutely disastrous view that my teachers were unquestionably right in their estimate of me as a dense and altogether noxious creature who deserved, if anything, worse than he got. These teachers were, after all, men and women who had mastered the parts of speech, the multiplication tables, and a simply staggering number of countries. They could add up columns of figures the very sight of which made me dizzy and sick to the stomach. They could read "As You Like It" with pleasure—so they said, anyway, and I believed everything they said. I felt that if such knowledgeable people told me that I was stupid, they certainly must know what they were talking about. In consequence, my grades sank lower and lower, my face became more noticeably blank, my manner more mulish, and my presence in the classroom more aggravating to whoever presided over it. To be sure, I hated my teachers for their hatred of me, and I missed no chance to abuse them behind their backs, but fundamentally I shared with them the view that I was a worthless and despicable boy, as undeserving of an education as I was incapable of absorbing one. Often, on school days, I wished that I were dead.

ADDITIONAL RESOURCES

Books and Articles

Elkman, P., and W. Friesen. *Unmasking the Face: A Guide to Recognizing Emotions from Facial Cues*. Englewood Cliffs, N.J.: Prentice-Hall, 1975. A look at how emotions are communicated through facial expressions.

Freud, Sigmund. *The Psychopathology of Everyday Life*. New York: Macmillan, 1914. How slips of the tongue, dreams, fantasies, and other phenomena manifest forces of the unconscious that motivate behavior.

Fromm, Erich. *The Art of Loving*. New York: Harper and Row, 1956. Fromm suggests that, in order truly to experience love, we must have "courage, faith, and discipline." He looks at various types of love—motherly, brotherly, erotic, religious, and the love of oneself.

Hall, E. T. *The Silent Language*. Garden City, N.Y.: Anchor Press, 1959. On intercultural communications.

Konner, Melvin. "The Enigmatic Smile." *Psychology Today* (March 1987): 42–46. The smile serves an important role both in individual development and in human society as a whole. Anthropologist Melvin Konner takes a cross-cultural look at the smile.

Maslow, Abraham. *Toward a Psychology of Being*. New York: Van Nostrand, 1968. This classic groundwork of humanistic psychology explores the human striving for self-actualization.

Miller, Laurence. "The Emotional Brain." *Psychology Today* (February 1988): 34–42. Where do emotions originate? Recent studies trace different emotions to specific parts of the brain.

Plutchik, Robert. *Emotion: A Psychoevolutionary Synthesis*. New York: Harper and Row, 1980. Discusses the evolution of eight basic emotions in human beings. Depicts these emotions as four pairs of opposites, such as joy and sadness.

Roberts, Marjory. "Baby Love." *Psychology Today* (March 1987): 60. Two recent studies suggest that the nature of early attachments with parents affects how people view romance and love.

Trotter, Robert. "Stop Blaming Yourself: A Profile of Martin E. P. Seligman." *Psychology Today* (February 1987): 30–39. Seligman's work on learned helplessness and depression has revealed that pessimists may predict their own failures. Cognitive therapy can help patients exchange the pessimistic explanatory style for a more positive one.

Zimbardo, Philip. *Shyness: What It Is, What to Do About It*. Reading, Mass.: Addison-Wesley, 1977. What causes shyness, and how can people overcome it? Philip Zimbardo looks at the often painful experience of shyness.

THE MIND AWAKE AND ASLEEP

One of the most adventurous things left us is to go to bed. For no one can lay hand on our dreams.

E. V. Lucas

Unit 13 describes how psychologists investigate the nature of sleeping, dreaming, and altered states of conscious awareness. It also explores the ways we use consciousness to interpret, analyze, even change our behavior.

NOVA/The Secrets of Sleep, WGBH Educational Foundation

We sleep for more than a third of our lives, yet researchers are just beginning to understand the nature of the unconscious mind and the meaning of dreams.

OBJECTIVES

After viewing the program and completing the reading assignment, you should be able to:

1. Compare and contrast structuralist and functionalist approaches to the study of consciousness

2. Describe the different levels of consciousness and the kinds of processing that occur at each level

3. Describe the four levels of sleep and the characteristics that differentiate them

4. Describe the results of dream deprivation sleep and discuss the theories for why people dream

5. Define Freud's concepts of a dream's manifest content and latent content

6. Explain and contrast the Freudian theory of dreaming, the Hobson-McCarley theory and the information-processing theory of dreaming

7. Describe lucid dreaming and the present controversy surrounding training people in this technique

8. List the major sleep disorders and the factors thought to be responsible for each

READING ASSIGNMENT

After viewing Program 13, read pages 167–186 in *Psychology: Science, Behavior and Life.* Your instructor may also assign the anthology selections for Unit 13.

KEY TERMS AND CONCEPTS

As you read the assignment, pay particular attention to these terms, which are defined on the given pages in the text.

electroencephalogram (169)   K complex (173)
REM (Rapid Eye Movement) (169)   stage 3 sleep (173)
NREM (Nonrapid Eye Movement)   delta waves (173)
   (169)   stage 4 sleep (173)
beta waves (171)   pontine reticular formation (170)
stage 1 sleep (172)   atonia (170)
theta waves (172)   REM rebound (179)
stage 2 sleep (173)   activation-synthesis hypothesis (181)
sleep spindles (173)   manifest content (182)

latent content (182)
sleep disorders (183)
insomnia (183)
sleep apnea (183)
SIDS (sudden infant death
  syndrome) (184)

tracheostomy (184)
continuous positive airway pressure
  (184)
narcolepsy (184)
night terrors (184)
sleepwalking (185)

The following terms are used in Program 13 but are not defined in the text.

circadian rhythm—the pattern of cyclical body activities which is determined by an internal biological clock and lasts about 24 hours

hypnagogic state—a period of reveries at the onset of the sleeping state

PROGRAM SUMMARY

Throughout the day we experience changes in our biological processes and states of consciousness. Body temperature, blood pressure, pulse rate, blood sugar, and hormone levels fluctuate over the course of a day. As we will see in Program 13 these fluctuations affect our moods, motivations, energy level, and performance.

We are rarely aware of our body's automatic "housekeeping" functions. Nor are we aware of processing sensory input. But we are able to walk down the street without bumping into things because our brains automatically estimate distances and detect obstacles. Once we have mastered the routine tasks, we no longer need to direct and monitor our efforts.

Just as some cognitive psychologists use the metaphor of the computer to describe human cognition, William James used the stream, with its constantly changing flow, to explain the concept of consciousness. He also noted that the mind is selective and is able to reduce the continual bombardment of sensory input, freeing us to attend to what is most relevant to our survival.

Interest in the conscious mind has waxed and waned throughout the history of psychology. In nineteenth-century Germany, Wilhelm Wundt conducted studies of consciousness. He looked for an underlying structure of the mind by performing experiments in which his subjects reported their sensations. In the United States, Edward Titchener also explored the contents of consciousness—the "what" instead of the "how and why." This approach became known as structuralism. William James rejected the attempts of the structuralists to reduce consciousness to component parts, focusing instead on how the mind adapts to the environment. His approach was known as functionalism.

Then, in the 1920s, a leading behaviorist named John Watson declared the study of consciousness worthless and called for an objective science that studied behavior. He influenced the focus of American psychology for the first half of the twentieth century.

The study of consciousness was reintroduced in the late 1950s by a new breed of cognitive psychologists who took an interest in how and why we pay attention to some things and not to others. One of them, British psychologist Donald Broadbent, demonstrated that our attention has a limited capacity.

Further research shows the selective aspects of attention. For example, if someone mentions your name across a crowded, noisy room, it will probably catch your attention, whereas you probably wouldn't notice other names or words that were being spoken. This demonstrates mental activity at a preconscious level. Just outside of conscious awareness, ideas and feelings that are stored in memory and external stimuli are continuously processed or filtered.

Another state of consciousness is daydreaming. Although some people consider daydreaming a waste of time, psychologists believe daydreams are quite useful. They can be a source of creativity, a way of coping with problems and overcoming boredom, and a way of stimulating the brain.

In contrast, sleep helps reduce stimulation. But until the first half of this century we knew relatively little about it. In 1937 research revealed that brain waves change in form during the entire sleep cycle. In the early 1950s studies led to the discovery of rapid eye movements, known as REM (see Figure 7). When REM was linked to dreaming, researchers had a reasonably objective index of the dream.

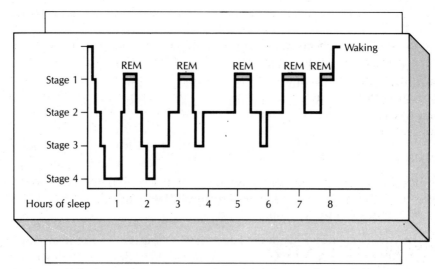

Figure 7: Sleep Cycles
For the typical sleeper, five periods of REM sleep alternate with non-REM sleep through an eight-hour night. Sleep is deeper earlier in the night, and REM sleep increases toward morning.

But what do dreams tell us about ourselves and our world? Freud claimed that they revealed the presence of deep secrets buried in the unconscious and that dreams protected the dreamer from disturbing wishes and thoughts. He believed that dreams were the key to understanding unconscious sexual and aggressive desires and fears.

Researchers Alan Hobson and Robert McCarley explain the controversial theory that dreams arise from spontaneous discharges of electrical impulses in the brain stem. They assert that REM sleep promotes brain development and does not have a psychological purpose. The electrical discharges activate the memories that appear in dreams as coherent images, but the psychological meaning is added afterward by the dreamer.

The middle view is that dreams are the result of the interplay of the physiological triggering of brain activity and the psychological function of its imaginative, interpretative parts. Electrical impulses activate concepts stored in memory, and the cerebral cortex helps to shape recall.

Steven LaBerge of Stanford University explores the power of the cerebral cortex to influence dreamers. He trains his study participants to report aloud their dreams without waking. They can also be given suggestions for directing their dreams. Some people claim this can enhance creativity and control of the unconscious; others object because such directed dreaming tampers with the unconscious. Psychologists find it fascinating because it represents a way of intentionally altering consciousness.

REVIEW QUESTIONS

Note: Review Questions for Units 13 and 14 are provided in Unit 14.

QUESTIONS TO CONSIDER

1. Donald Broadbent conceived of attention as a selective filter which acts like a tuner on a radio, selecting one message from all the others. According to Broadbent, the unattended sensory information is sent to a buffer, where it either receives attention and gets processed or is ignored and lost. How is this buffer similar to the concept of the sensory memory? What role might it play in subliminal perception?

2. What are the benefits and drawbacks of mindlessness?

3. Consider the role of culture and language in structuring consciousness or focused perception. In what ways is awareness culturally determined?

OPTIONAL ACTIVITIES

1. Keep a pad and pencil by your bed and start a dream journal. Just before you fall asleep, remind yourself to remember your dreams. Immediately upon awakening, record what you remember: images, actions, characters, emotions, events, and settings. Does your ability to recall your dreams improve over time? Does your recall become more vivid or more organized? Are there common elements, people, symbols, or themes? Can you shape your dreams by telling yourself at bedtime what you want to dream about?

2. Make a list of common examples of dissociation and divided consciousness. Do these examples support the concept of mini-minds or independent areas of the brain conducting their business? What other explanations might explain your ability to divide your consciousness?

ANTHOLOGY

The following selections offer insight into different aspects of consciousness. As you read them, consider the personal, social, and environmental influences on conscious awareness. Think about your own conscious activity. In what ways would you like to change your conscious and unconscious activities?

Reading 29

This article describes the dangers and high cost of sleep problems in the workplace. Although some industries and companies take the problem seriously, many do not. As you read, consider what you have learned about research on body rhythms, sleep, and dreams. How can this information be used to improve safety and productivity on the job? Does your own schedule match your body rhythms and sleep needs?

Firms Waking Up To Sleep Disorders

By Cynthia F. Mitchell

Unable to cope with a constantly changing work schedule, a waste-treatment plant operator at a big oil refinery dozes off in the middle of the night—and inadvertently dumps thousands of gallons of chemicals into a nearby river.

A Dallas salesman suffering from narcolepsy —a hereditary disease that causes frequent and uncontrollable bouts of sleepiness—loses several customers, then his job, after clients complain that he repeatedly falls asleep at business meetings.

Sleeping problems in the workplace— whether the result of irregular shifts or medical disorders—are costing companies an estimated $70 billion annually in lost productivity, huge medical bills, and industrial accidents, according to the Institute of Circadian Physiology, a research center in Boston.

Though some companies are starting to deal with the problem, most know little about medical or shift-related sleep disorders— much less what to do about them. And often they refuse to acknowledge that sleep problems are to blame in accidents imperiling workers and the public.

"It's kind of too ugly. How can you admit that your nuclear-power-plan operators regularly fall asleep on the job?" says Jose Gavalondo of the Center for Design of Industrial Schedules, a Harvard affiliate. The Peach Bottom Power station, operated by Philadelphia Electric Co., had to concede just that, however: Last year the plant was closed after investigators found control-room operators sleeping on night and weekend shifts.

At Least Once a Week

An estimated 20 million people work in industries that maintain round-the-clock schedules. And in sleep-disorder studies, about half of the people who regularly or occasionally work late shifts say they fall asleep on the job at least once a week. In interviews with researchers, employees from the graveyard shift report tales of seeing sleeping assembly-line workers falling off their stools, batches of defective products sliding past dozing inspectors, and exhausted forklift operators crashing their machines into walls.

Sleep researchers say the body's natural sleep-and-wake cycle prevents most people from ever fully adjusting to night shifts or irregular schedules. As a result, workers on odd shifts take more sick days and are absent more often. And researchers say that after five years, people who work late shifts are twice as prone to heart attacks, peptic ulcers, and other cardiovascular and gastrointestinal diseases than those who work regular day hours.

For workers suffering from genetic or hereditary sleep disorders—an estimated 2% of the general population—problems in the workplace are even more difficult. Most employers know little about such ailments as narcolepsy and sleep apnea, whose victims momentarily stop breathing hundreds of times a night. Every time breathing stops, the apnea victim wakes up just enough to keep from reaching the deepest, most restful stages of sleep.

Sleep disorders, of course, are particularly frightening in areas affecting public safety. Pilots, for instance, say their inconsistent schedules often force them to snooze in the cockpit in order to get enough sleep. The National Transportation Safety Board cited pilot fatigue as either the cause or a contributing factor in 69 plane accidents from 1963 through 1986 in which 67 people died.

"There have been times I've been so sleepy, I'm nodding off as we're taxiing to get into take-off position," says a pilot for Federal Express, who says other pilots have similar difficulties. "I've fallen asleep reading checklists. I've fallen asleep in the middle of a word."

Like most carriers, Federal Express is unwilling to discuss its pilots' schedules and fatigue-related problems. The Memphis, Tenn.-based overnight-delivery service has never had an aircraft accident involving crew fatigue, but pilots say the company is conducting a study of their sleep habits. The company wouldn't comment on the study.

The Federal Aviation Administration is especially worried about newer jets that can stay airborne for 18 hours straight. It is considering changing the sleep and schedule regulations for pilots on all international flights to lengthen the time that they have to rest between flights.

Nurses and doctors—especially medical-school residents—often work several days straight with little sleep. "It's clear to us it's a dangerous situation and something has to be done," says a spokesman for the New York State Department of Health. In June, the New York State Hospital Review and Planning Council adopted rules limiting medical residents to 12-hour shifts in the emergency room, with at least eight hours off between shifts. California, Hawaii, Massachusetts and Pennsylvania are considering similar measures.

For police officers, lack of sleep because of frequently changing schedules can be a matter of life or death. John Fescher, a Philadelphia policeman, says he often starts a midnight-to-6-a.m. shift already wiped out because his schedule changes so often that he can't adjust.

"I'm falling asleep at red lights," he says. "And here I have to push a car around for eight hours and do a job where you constantly have to have your senses about you." He says he knows his reaction time isn't always the sharpest—including cases in which he has to decide whether or not to shoot.

For people suffering from genetic sleep disorders, the workplace can become a nightmare. Billy Ray Thompson, the Dallas salesman whose narcolepsy cost him his job, says he has been unable to keep steady employment since 1980 because of the disease. Although he is on medication, he still shows signs of the disorder. "With the slurred speech and all, if I were to encounter a person like that the first thing *I* would think is that he was a druggie," he says.

Robert Legan, an industrial physicist for Texas Instruments Inc., hadn't slept well for several years and was no longer able to solve abstract problems as quickly as he should. "I'd be trying to construct an equation, and I'd have to go look in books," he says. "And even then, I'd have a hard time figuring out these things that I'd known two years before."

But last month Mr. Legan's physician sent him to a sleep-disorder center at a hospital in Dallas, where he was diagnosed as having sleep apnea. Now he's being outfitted with a device that pumps air through a nasal mask to hold his throat open while he sleeps, preventing him from repeatedly choking—and having to wake to breathe.

Only in recent years have employers and even medical professionals begun to respond to the impact of sleep disorders in the workplace. In the past five years, for example, health insurers have started approving workers' claims related to hereditary sleep disorders just as they do for other medical claims.

Some companies have taken steps to deal with schedule-related sleep problems among workers. Dow Chemical Co., Detroit Edison, Pennzoil Co. and Exxon Corp., for instance, have rejiggered schedules and are giving all workers several days off between shift changes. Some have added incentives that give workers bonus time off for reaching productivity goals on graveyard shifts.

Such efforts can pay off quickly. Productivity per labor-hour at Amax Coal Co., Indianapolis, for example, jumped 10% when the company switched to a schedule that rotates workers' shifts once every 28 days, with a seven-day break before going to the new shift. The increase in productivity enabled Amax to shelve plans to invest $14 million in added capital equipment and to sharply reduce overtime.

An Experiment in Philadelphia

The Philadelphia Police Department, in an 11-month experiment using fewer and less random schedule changes in one of its busiest precincts, reported a 40% decline in the rate of officers' automobile accidents on the job. Compared with the previous schedules, half as many officers reported problems with daytime fatigue, and 25% fewer said they slept poorly, compared to the previous schedules.

The city's new police commissioner, Willie Williams, says he's in favor of adopting some of the scheduling changes, but that implementing the new program citywide would be too costly. The police union, which claims that scheduling should be part of contract negotiations, has taken the matter to arbitration.

Workplace changes to accommodate sleep problems remain the exception, though. "Maybe we should worry about it more as a potential problem for us, but it's not something anyone's working on or worrying about right now," says a spokesman for Greyhound Lines Inc., which runs Greyhound and Trailways bus systems.

Researchers say that as more is learned about the economic toll of sleep disorders, companies will find that they can't afford to continue ignoring the problem. Says David Kupfer, a physician and director of sleep research at the University of Pittsburgh's Western Psychiatric Institute and Clinic: "Megabucks are involved, and sometimes, lives."

Reading 30

This article discusses the benefits of "constructive reflection" as a way of coping with the anger, pain, frustration, and helplessness of serious illness. What levels of consciousness are involved in this type of mental activity? Does the patient, David, do more than just record his conscious thoughts and daydreams? Do you think keeping a journal is useful for people going through a particularly difficult or painful time of life? Why?

The Pen Is Mightier Than . . .

By Virginia K. Lee

The day before Christmas 1974, David, my 35-year-old husband, was hospitalized with sudden abdominal pain and fever. A diagnosis of acute abdomen with possible peritonitis was made. Exploratory surgery that afternoon showed that he did in fact have peritonitis from a ruptured diverticulum; a bowel resection and temporary double-barrel colostomy were done. David was discharged a week later.

One of the gifts David received that Christmas was a blank, write-your-own-book, which he promptly titled "The First and Last Annual Surgical Journal or the Last Will and Intestine of David Lee." He drew and occasionally wrote in this journal over the next few weeks, recording his reactions to hospitalization, surgery, and the frustrations of learning to live with a colostomy.

Three months later David, with his journal, returned to the hospital for closure of his colostomy. He expected to be home again in about a week, all systems together. Instead, complications including a wound infection, an abdominal abscess, and a fistula kept him hospitalized for almost a month. Six months later he was in again, this time for repair of an incisional hernia.

That year was filled with a great deal of pain, anger, frustration, and fatigue. Used to being in control, David suddenly found himself physically and emotionally vulnerable. (As an Episcopal priest, he was used to dealing with other people's problems, not his own.)

David kept his journal with him throughout this time. He would work on it intently for a time and then ignore it for days. His humorous drawings and brief writings provided a creative outlet for his expression of the anger and frustration he felt about being ill.

He shared the journal with me and occasionally with his surgeon and nurses. Since he tended not to talk about what he was feeling, the journal was a way for me to gain some insight into how things were going for him.

He also recorded the thanksgivings and intimate moments that helped us cope with this potentially divisive experience. I often felt guilty because I hadn't recognized signs and symptoms earlier and because I didn't always have specific answers to many of David's questions about living with a colostomy. This journal helped me realize that he recognized and valued my "just being there."

As a nurse, I was struck by how David's journal helped us cope with the emotional and psychological responses to his illness. This overwhelming evidence that being able to express these responses is an essential step in working through the loss events. David's journal made this abstract concept very real to me.

David's extended illness refocused and clarified his priorities and was the beginning, at least, of a decision to alter his lifestyle and his image of himself. He began to say "No," to give up some control, delegate responsibilities and ultimately decided to change jobs.

I believe nurses should encourage more people to keep journals. Certain patient populations seem particularly appropriate: people experiencing significant changes in body image (ostomates, amputees, transplant recipients), anyone faced with long hospitalizations, recurrent treatment or prolonged pain (patients with cancer, those on kidney dialysis, patients with terminal illness), or anyone undergoing times of particular stress or change in their lives (adolescents, family members of chronic and terminally ill people). The elderly might also use journals to reflect on the past and share memories with loved ones.

Some people will not take to the empty page as quickly as David did. People are often intimidated by the idea of drawing or writing down their thoughts and feelings; in fact, some may refuse to try. Initially it may help to establish a contract with the person to keep a diary. As he becomes more comfortable recording day-to-day events, he is likely to move beyond merely factual accounts and express feelings and ideas.

It is crucial to remember that it is the individual's private journal. He must be the one to decide when, or if, it is to be shared. Of course, a journal cannot replace the personal response, caring, and emotional support of health care professionals and family members. But a journal may help distract a person during long days of recovery or provide a medium for constructive reflection as he begins to cope with his illness.

212   *Unit 13*

ADDITIONAL RESOURCES

Books and Articles

Coleman, R. *Wide Awake at 3:00 A.M. By Choice or by Chance?* New York: W. H. Freeman, 1986. Excellent treatment of biological clocks and the role they play in work, jet lag, and insomnia.

Dement, W. C. *Some Must Watch While Some Must Sleep*. San Francisco: Freeman, 1974. Dement, who has contributed the most to the understanding of sleep, has written this book about sleep research for the layperson.

Gazzaniga, Michael. *Mind Matters: How Brain and Mind Interact to Create Our Conscious Lives*. Boston: Houghton Mifflin, 1988. Insights from the field of neuropsychology can help us better understand the nature of consciousness.

Hartman, Ernest. *The Nightmare: The Psychology and Biology of Terrifying Dreams*. New York: Basic Books, 1984. Who has nightmares? Why do they happen, and what do they mean? Hartman looks at the psychological, social, and biological aspects of bad dreams.

LaBerge, Stephen. *Lucid Dreaming*. New York: Ballentine Books, 1986. Can we learn to control our dreams? LaBerge discusses lucid dreaming as a skill that can be taught.

Sacks, Oliver. *Awakenings*. New York: Dutton, 1983. A great sleeping sickness epidemic 50 years ago left many with a bizarre and debilitating disease. A new "miracle drug" allowed them to wake, but the process of recovery was far from easy. Sacks recounts the fascinating cases of several patients.

Webb, W. B. *Sleep: The Gentle Tyrant*. Englewood Cliffs, N.J.: Prentice-Hall, 1975. Borrows illustrations from Dr. Seuss's sleep book to help introduce processes of sleep.

THE MIND HIDDEN AND DIVIDED

The mind is the most capricious of insects—flitting, fluttering.

Virginia Woolf

Unit 14 considers the evidence that our moods, behavior, and even our health are largely the result of multiple mental processes, many of which are out of conscious awareness. It also looks at some of the most dramatic phenomena in psychology: hypnosis, multiple personality disorder, and the division of human consciousness into "two minds" when the brain is split in half by surgical intervention.

The Bettmann Archive

The classic film *Dr. Jekyll and Mr. Hyde* helped bring the concept of split personality into the popular media.

OBJECTIVES

After viewing the program and completing the assigned readings, you should be able to:

1. Explain meditation and list some mental and physical benefits that have been linked to meditation and relaxation

2. Define dissociation

3. Describe hypnotic techniques and some of the phenomena that have been associated with hypnosis

4. Discuss theories of hypnosis

5. Define the major drug categories of stimulants, depressants, and hallucinogens and give an example of a substance from each category. Compare the psychological and physiological effects of each category

6. Describe the phenomena of tolerance, physiological dependence, and psychological dependence

7. Explain several hypotheses about the causes of alcoholism and evaluate methods that have been used to treat alcohol addiction

8. Describe some of the physiological and psychoactive effects of nicotine and caffeine

9. Describe the symptoms, the typical patient profile, and the preferred treatment associated with the mental disorder known as multiple personality

10. Discuss the research on "split-brain" patients and what it indicates about the capabilities of each hemisphere of the brain

11. Describe the evidence that supports the theory that the brain is organized as multiminds or modules

READING ASSIGNMENT

After viewing Program 14, read pages 186–191 and 97–106 in *Psychology: Science, Behavior and Life*. Your instructor may also assign the anthology selections for Unit 14.

KEY TERMS AND CONCEPTS

As you read the assignment, pay particular attention to these terms, which are defined on the given pages in the text.

hypnosis (187)	dissociated (186)
age regression (188)	hidden observer (189)
posthypnotic suggestion (189)	psychoactive drugs (97)
dissociation theory (190)	physiological dependence (97)

psychological dependence (98)	amphetamines (101)
sedatives (98)	cocaine (102)
opiates (98)	crack (102)
alcohol (99)	hallucinogens (103)
delirium tremens (d.t.'s) (100)	LSD (104)
fetal alcohol syndrome (100)	PCP (105)
stimulants (100)	marijuana (105)
caffeine (100)	lateralization of function (86)
nicotine (101)	corpus callosum (87)

The following terms are used in Program 14 but are not defined in the text.

hypnotic analgesia—lack of pain perception while under hypnosis

posthypnotic amnesia—forgetting selected events by suggestion given while under hypnosis

PROGRAM SUMMARY

Is it possible to "know thyself"? Evidence suggests that a lot of important mental activity occurs outside our conscious awareness and that unconscious experiences can significantly alter our moods, behavior, and health. This is the subject of Program 14.

In one experiment, patients under anesthesia were given negative and positive information about their condition. Patients who received positive messages felt better, required less medication, and were discharged earlier than those who overheard upsetting news. This suggests that the unconscious brain processes stimuli and receives messages. Although the patients claimed not to be aware of what was said, many did recall the messages under hypnosis.

How does the unconscious influence our thoughts, moods, and behavior? Neuroscientists theorize that our brains are organized into separate minibrains, or modules. Each is designed to do a specific job, such as speaking or reading; there is really no single, all-powerful command center.

Since the earliest times, people have been fascinated with the idea that human behavior could be taken over by hidden identities or unknown parts of themselves. The transformation of identity is one of the major themes in world literature and myth; recall Robert Louis Stevenson's famous story *The Strange Case of Dr. Jekyll and Mr. Hyde* and Franz Kafka's *The Metamorphosis*.

We do know that there are many ways the mind can be transformed. Psychoactive drugs can change how the mind functions and how personality is expressed. Studies of different cultures reveal rituals and many other forms of altering consciousness, including drugs, fasting, and meditation.

Consciousness can also be altered by mental illness. The multiple personality is a dramatic example of dissociation in which several distinct personalities develop in the same individual. F. W. Putnam, an expert in this field, explains that the typical profile of a multiple personality is that of a woman who shut out the reality of sexual and physical childhood abuse by mentally escaping into dissociative states. The alternate personalities exist in the unconscious, often unaware of each other.

According to Freud, our most traumatic feelings are bound and gagged in the unconscious. Unacceptable desires, urges, and painful memories are hidden by the process he called repression. Freud interpreted anxiety as the alarm that warns when these feelings are about to break through into consciousness. Dreams, errors, and slips of the tongue reveal some of these otherwise repressed aspects of unconscious activity.

Hypnosis is another window into the unconscious. Under hypnosis, some people act unconsciously on ideas, thoughts, and feelings. Suggestions can direct behavior afterward, altering memory, the perception of pain, even influencing decisions about smoking and eating.

The notion that part of the mind can function separately is difficult for many people to accept. But we can't deny the evidence. Supporting data about the behavior of the divided brain come from studies of patients whose corpus callosum, the connecting nerves between the two hemispheres of the brain, has been cut to prevent epileptic seizures from spreading across both hemispheres. Although the behavior of these patients appears normal, tests of eye-hand coordination show that each hemisphere

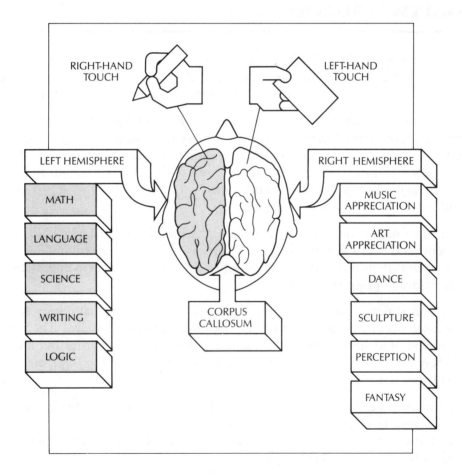

Figure 8: Left Brain/Right Brain Abilities
In this diagram, the differences between the left and right brain are exaggerated. In general, however, the left hemisphere is more involved with logic and reasoning, and the right hemisphere is more concerned with emotions and imagination.

receives and processes only certain information. The right brain is better at solving perceptual problems, pattern recognition, and spatial relationships; the left excels in language and logical analysis (see Figure 8).

A final study suggests that the left brain is the "social brain" and that each person's unique consciousness is a product of this interpretive left hemisphere. The idea that the brain has many semi-independent modules or highly specialized multiminds is supported by research with split-brain and brain lesion patients. Modularity has a real anatomical base.

REVIEW QUESTIONS

Program Questions

1. Which of the following is an example of a circadian rhythm?

   a. Eating three meals a day at approximately the same time
   b. Experiencing alternate periods of REM and non-REM sleep
   c. Having systematic changes in hormone levels during 24 hours
   d. Having changes in fertility levels during a month

2. How normal is it to experience alternate states of consciousness?

   a. It happens to most people, mainly in times of stress.
   b. It is something we all experience every day.
   c. It is rare and generally indicates a mental disorder.
   d. It is common in childhood and becomes rarer with age.

3. In the program, the part of the brain that is identified as the "interior decorator" imposing order on experience is the

   a. pons.
   b. hippocampus.
   c. limbic system.
   d. cerebral cortex.

4. Which of the following is an example of the lower-level processing of sensory input that is nonconscious?

   a. Recognizing a friend's face
   b. Detecting edges
   c. Working on an assembly line
   d. Noticing something tastes good

5. Edward Titchener was the leader of functionalism in the United States. What aspect of the concept of consciousness interested him?

   a. The contents of consciousness
   b. The material repressed from conscious awareness
   c. The uniqueness of consciousness
   d. He viewed consciousness as a scientifically worthless concept.

6. In Donald Broadbent's research, what happened when subjects heard two stories but were asked to attend to only one?

   a. They comprehended both stories.
   b. They comprehended only the attended story.
   c. They wove bits of the unattended story into the attended story.
   d. They were not able to follow either story.

7. What is a positive function of daydreaming?

   a. It focuses attention on a task.
   b. It reduces demands made on the brain.
   c. It enables us to be mentally active when we are bored.
   d. It provides delta wave activity normally gotten only in sleep.

8. Ernest Hartmann points out the logic behind Shakespeare's description of sleep. According to Hartmann, a major function of sleep is that it allows the brain to

   a. process material too threatening to be dealt with consciously.
   b. integrate the day's events with previously learned material.
   c. make plans for the day ahead.
   d. discharge a buildup of electrical activity.

9. According to Freud, dreams are significant because they

   a. permit neurotransmitters to be regenerated.
   b. reveal unconscious fears and desires.
   c. forecast the future.
   d. supply a story line to patterns of electrical charges.

10. According to McCarley and Hobson's activation synthesis theory of dreams, what activates dreams?

    a. The needs of the dreamer's unconscious
    b. The sending of electrical charges to the forebrain
    c. The memories contained in the cerebral cortex
    d. The synthesis of chemicals needed for brain function

11. In his work on lucid dreaming, why does LaBerge use a flashing light?

    a. So subjects are consciously aware of their dream and can control it
    b. So subjects can incorporate the light itself into their dream narrative
    c. So subjects get feedback about where they are in the REM sleep cycle
    d. So measurements can be made of physiological response

12. In the experiment described in the program, patients under anesthesia were exposed to a positive or negative message. What effect did getting a positive message have?

    a. It meant less anesthesia was needed.
    b. It shortened patients' hospital stays.
    c. It created more positive attitudes toward surgery.
    d. Positive messages had no effect because patients were unaware of them.

13. Which phrase sums up the traditional image of the brain in Western culture?

    a. "Master of all it surveys"
    b. "The slave of the passions"
    c. "The tip of the iceberg"
    d. "Battleground of hostile armies"

14. When societies around the world were studied, what proportion of them practiced some culturally patterned form of altering consciousness?

    a. Practically none
    b. About a third
    c. About half
    d. The vast majority

15. Harriet is a young woman with a multiple personality disorder. What was her childhood probably like?

    a. She suffered from severe abuse.
    b. She was under strong pressure to excel.
    c. She was an only child whose mother died.
    d. She had an unusually tranquil childhood.

16. According to Freud, how do we feel when painful memories or unacceptable urges threaten to break into consciousness?

    a. Relieved
    b. Guilty
    c. Sad
    d. Anxious

17. What do Freudian slips reveal?

    a. What we have dreamed about
    b. How we really feel
    c. Who we would like to be transformed into
    d. Why we make certain choices

18. What happens when a hypnotized subject smells ammonia when he expects to smell cologne?

    a. The ammonia smell wakes him from the trance.
    b. He recognizes the ammonia smell, but he remains hypnotized.
    c. He interprets the ammonia smell as a musky cologne.
    d. He overgeneralizes and finds the cologne smells like ammonia.

19. Imagine you see something with your right eye. Where is the information routed in your brain?

    a. To both hemispheres simultaneously
    b. To the right hemisphere
    c. To the left hemisphere
    d. Where it is routed depends on what kind of thing is seen

20. Michael Gazzaniga has worked with "broken-brain" patients. What has this led him to believe about our individuality?

    a. It comes from an interpreter in the left hemisphere.
    b. It is an illusion based on our emotional needs.
    c. It derives from our unique set of independent mind-modules.
    d. It is located in the corpus callosum.

Textbook Questions

21. An interesting fact about daydream cycles is that

    a. they are remarkably similar to the cycles of our dreaming when we sleep.
    b. they are always rational and practical.
    c. they are never productive.
    d. they occur rarely if ever for most people.

22. There are _____ stages of sleep, including dream sleep.

    a. two
    b. three
    c. four
    d. five

23. Dreaming is

    a. more likely to occur in REM than in NREM sleep.
    b. more likely to occur in NREM than in REM sleep.
    c. equally as likely to occur in REM as in NREM sleep.
    d. limited to REM sleep.

24. Rapid, low-amplitude brain waves that have been linked to relaxed states and pleasurable feelings are called

    a. alpha.
    b. beta.
    c. theta.
    d. delta.

25. REM periods of sleep tend to _____ as the night wears on.

    a. deepen
    b. lighten
    c. shorten
    d. lengthen

26. Sleepwalking almost invariably occurs during

    a. NREM sleep.
    b. dream sleep.
    c. nightmare stages.
    d. the early morning hours.

27. When researchers destroyed a portion of a cat's brain that produces atonia, the cats

    a. became very active during REM sleep.
    b. no longer dreamed.
    c. dreamed incessantly.
    d. became inactive during all stages of sleep.

28. As people grow older, the time spent sleeping _____ and the time spent in REM sleep _____ .

    a. increases; increases
    b. increases; decreases
    c. decreases; increases
    d. decreases; decreases

29. When deprived of REM sleep, people later show increased REM sleep activity which is called

    a. REM-depression.
    b. REM-suppression.
    c. REM-rebound.
    d. less dream-time.

30. Hobson and McCarley believe that dreams reflect _____ rather than psychological activity.

    a. unconscious
    b. conscious
    c. biological
    d. abnormal

31. The fact that older people spend less time in REM sleep seems to support the _____ theory of dreams.

    a. mental reprogramming
    b. dealing with dreams
    c. activation synthesis
    d. unconscious expression

32. Freud theorized that dreams reflected

    a. reality.
    b. unconscious wishes.
    c. the collective unconscious.
    d. normal life stresses.

33. According to Freud, the manifest content of a dream

    a. is the part of the dream that is forgotten.
    b. is the true meaning of the dream.
    c. is what the person remembers and reports about a dream.
    d. can never be known even after extensive analysis.

34. Insomnia is defined as

    a. a sleep attack.
    b. difficulty sleeping.
    c. death during sleep.
    d. cessation of breathing.

35. A sleep disorder in which people fail to breathe regularly during sleep is

    a. insomnia.
    b. sleep apnea.
    c. narcolepsy.
    d. somnambulism.

36. SIDS is an acronym for

    a. sensory indicators describing senses.
    b. sudden infant death syndrome.
    c. sudden identification of disorders.
    d. student indicating desire to sleep.

37. A minister falls alseep while preaching; he may be suffering from

    a. apnea.
    b. narcolepsy.
    c. SIDS.
    d. night terrors.

38. Which psychologist is cited by the textbook as having done credible, thoughtful research into hypnosis?

    a. Ernest Hilgard
    b. Sigmund Freud
    c. William Dement
    d. Franz Mesmer

39. Efforts to differentiate between the brain waves, heart rates, and respiration of hypnotized and nonhypnotized people

    a. have noted sex differences.
    b. have noted age differences.
    c. have largely been unsuccessful.
    d. have been highly successful.

40. Hypnosis has been successful when used to

    a. perform amazing feats of strength.
    b. regress a person in age.
    c. relieve physical pain.
    d. cause outstanding athletic performances.

41. A problem with using hypnosis for memory enhancement is that

    a. the subject may report many things that are untrue.
    b. the subject may say something he or she didn't intend to say.
    c. the subject may remember something too traumatic.
    d. the hypnotist may not be trained to interpret correctly.

42. The best available evidence suggests that age regression subjects are

    a. playing a role consistent with their present conception of their past behavior.
    b. accurately portraying the past.
    c. faking hypnosis.
    d. more suggestible than others.

43. That people can selectively focus attention on one thing (hypnotic suggestion) and still perceive other things "subconsciously" is Hilgard's _____ theory.

    a. psychoanalytic
    b. neodissociation
    c. role-playing
    d. meditation

44. Drugs which alter perceptions and behavior by changing conscious awareness are called

    a. hallucinogenic.
    b. psychoactive drugs.
    c. sedatives.
    d. depressants.

45. Dependence on a chemical substance in which a person finds the substance so pleasurable or helpful in coping with life that he or she becomes addicted to its use is known as

   a. psychological dependence.
   b. physiological dependence.
   c. social dependence.
   d. physical dependence.

46. Sedatives, opiates, and alcohol are all

   a. narcotics.
   b. hallucinogens.
   c. stimulants.
   d. depressants.

47. Morphine, codeine, and heroin are all three classed as

   a. stimulants.
   b. narcotics.
   c. hallucinogens.
   d. sedatives.

48. The number one drug problem in America is with

   a. heroin.
   b. alcohol.
   c. tranquilizers.
   d. cocaine.

49. Drugs which act by increasing the activity of the nervous system are called

   a. depressants.
   b. stimulants.
   c. narcotics.
   d. opiates.

50. Amphetamines can dramatically increase alertness and promote feelings of euphoria and well-being by

   a. enhancing dopamine and norepinephrine activity.
   b. suppressing dopamine and norepinephrine activity.
   c. keeping dopamine and norepinephrine levels constant.
   d. none of the above.

51. LSD is classified as a(n)

    a. opiate.
    b. analgesic.
    c. depressant
    d. hallucinogenic.

QUESTIONS TO CONSIDER

1. Changes in perceptions, time sense, memory, feelings of self-control, and suggestibility are aspects of an altered state of consciousness. Would you consider illness, love, or grief to be altered states of consciousness?

2. Psychoactive drugs are only partially responsible for the changes in the drug taker's consciousness. Mental sets, expectations, and the context in which the drugs are taken can also have a significant influence. What are the implications for alcohol and drug education and treatment?

3. Do you consider television a mind-altering influence? What does TV have in common with other mind-altering substances or experiences? Are children more susceptible to TV's effects than adults?

OPTIONAL ACTIVITIES

1. Use this visualization technique to achieve a state of relaxation and, perhaps, alter your consciousness. Select a quiet place where you won't be interrupted. Choose a scene in which you have been very relaxed. To help you create a good mental picture, recall all the sensations that enhance in you a feeling of deep calm. Focus on the scene for 15–30 minutes. Practice this visualization exercise several times over a period of a few weeks. With practice, calling up the visual image may trigger a sensation of calm whenever you want to.

2. Try to think of a time when you surprised yourself by having a very strong feeling in response to an incident that didn't seem to warrant such a strong response. Could nonconscious factors have played a role in your response? What did you think about your response at the time? What did you think about it later?

ANTHOLOGY

How do events perceived in different states of consciousness contribute to our sense of reality? How do different states of consciousness affect our "true" identity? As you read the following selections, think about how various altered states of consciousness can be helpful to us, while others can be quite harmful.

Reading 31

This article explores the dilemmas created by allowing testimony based on hypnosis to be used in court. As you read, consider whether juries and the judge are qualified to determine the value of testimony obtained under hypnosis. Should such testimony be permitted? What are the implications for the judicial process?

First Word

By Howard E. Goldfluss

In the spring of 1984 Vickie Loren, an Illinois housewife, fired a loaded gun at her husband, Frank Rock. The bullet lodged in Rock's chest, and he died a few hours later.

During cross-examination immediately following the incident, it was discovered that Loren failed to remember any specific details related to the shooting. To help unravel the circumstances surrounding Rock's death, Loren's attorney decided to bring in a hypnotist. While in a hypnotic trance, Loren revealed evidence crucial to her defense. She had placed her thumb on the hammer of the gun but had not pulled the trigger. A gun expert inspected the weapon and found that it was prone to fire when hit or dropped, without the trigger being pulled.

The judge, however, doubted the validity of the evidence that was revealed under hypnosis and ruled that no hypnotically induced testimony would be considered as part of the defense. He limited Loren's testimony to "matters remembered and stated to the examiner prior to being placed under hypnosis." Loren was convicted of manslaughter and sentenced to ten years in prison.

An appeal was filed with the state supreme court, but the original decision was upheld. Loren and her attorney then petitioned the United States Supreme Court to review her conviction, claiming that Loren had been denied her constitutional right to testify on her own behalf.

On June 22, 1987, the Supreme Court decided *Rock* v. *Illinois*—an opinion that is still reverberating throughout the legal community. The court held that Loren had the right to testify in her own defense and that prior statements made by an accused under hypnosis are admissible evidence. If hypnotically induced testimony were suspect, reasoned the court, its veracity could have been adequately tested by cross-examination.

Justice Harry A. Blackmun, who wrote the majority opinion, conceded that there are varied responses to hypnosis. It cannot and does not guarantee accuracy; in fact, he noted, it often has no effect on memory whatever. Hypnosis serves merely to broaden both correct and incorrect recollections.

This decision foretells a myriad of fascinating possibilities—options that may dramatically change courtroom procedure. For instance, if a defendant is allowed to submit to hypnosis, the prosecution will also request the use of hypnosis to jar the memory of a witness. It would be unfair to bar any witness from using hypnotic assistance to remember details that may solve a crime.

While the Rock decision will affect criminal trial practice, it will also create judicial dilemmas. It will become the duty of the jury to decide if the hypnotist is competent. But what standard does the jury use, and how does the judge instruct it? A hypnotist is not a licensed professional but can be anyone from a sideshow flimflam artist to a professional interested in finding out the truth. The scientific use of hypnosis is relatively recent.

The jury will have to wrestle with the possibility that a hypnotist can subtly suggest a statement to a defendant, implant it in his subconscious, and have him verbalize it during the hypnotic session. The individual subjected to hypnosis may also try to please the hypnotist by giving answers he thinks will meet with approval. "Memory hardening" can also occur during a hypnotic session. This phenomenon gives the defendant great confidence in both true and false memories, making effective cross-examination more difficult. If the results of any of the hypnotically induced statements prove beneficial to the accused, then, under the Rock decision, the full testimony must be heard.

Respected hypnotists concede that the process has an inherent weakness. A person can lie while in a hypnotic trance. Apparently the subconscious releases only that which it wishes to release. While in a hypnotic state an individual cannot be compelled to do or say anything that his subconscious knows is detrimental to his own interests. He will relate what he believes to be true only when it aids him. Confessions under hypnosis are few and far between.

Trial lawyers will have a field day with hypnosis in the courtroom, and hypnotic testimony will open up a whole new avenue of attack for prosecutors as well. Both sides will bring in hypnotists, who will undoubtedly disagree with one another's tactics. The prosecutor's hypnotist will accuse the defense's hypnotist of implanting an idea in the mind of the defendant and setting up a false testimony, while the defendant's hypnotist will demand to see evidence supporting the credibility of the prosecutor's hypnotist. Trials will become confusing, and it will become much more difficult to determine who is innocent and who is guilty.

I think it is therefore necessary to keep the Rock decision in its proper perspective. The Supreme Court did not give an unconditional seal of approval to hypnotically induced testimony. It said that in the instance of Vickie Loren, the judge denied her a fair trial when he did not permit her to testify fully on her own behalf. In effect, the court held that it was up to the jury to determine whether her testimony was self-serving or was in fact a true accounting of what had occurred at the time of the incident.

One thing is certain. Hypnotically based testimony will introduce issues the courts have never before encountered. It will be interesting to see how the issue is dealt with and if hypnosis will help or hinder the judicial process.

Reading 32

In this article, noted neuropsychologist Oliver Sacks describes the problem of defining the nature of consciousness. He offers alternatives to the metaphor of the stream and discusses why consciousness is so hard to describe in scientific language. As you read, consider which metaphor best expresses your experience of consciousness. Are the terms brain activity, mind, *and* consciousness *interchangeable?*

The Nature of Consciousness

By Oliver Sacks

There is nothing in the universe deeper or more complex than the phenomenon of consciousness. And yet there is nothing simpler and, in a way, more inevitable. Consciousness arises when life arises: consciousness is "inner life," or the inward side of being alive.

Consciousness does not yield to dissection or analysis. It needs to be grasped and studied as a whole. Similarly, it evades definition: We can never say what consciousness *is*, we can only suggest its nature by metaphors and images.

We find certain images of consciousness which recur again and again in the history of thought: images of flowing and succession and change; images of an extended space or field; and dramaturgical images of stages and arenas. Thus we speak of the "stream of consciousness," an image which William James brought into common use. Sir Charles Sherrington spoke of consciousness as a loom or a shuttle, weaving a constant succession of ever-changing patterns, each pattern different, but all related in an ultimate unity of direction and style. Leibniz described consciousness as a succession of flashes or "fulgurations." And Proust saw consciousness as a series of Moments. Visual images are crucially important. Leibniz speaks of sentient beings as "living mirrors" reflecting the world, a mirroring which is active, selective, creative; introspecting the nature of his own consciousness he wrote, "I need no telescope except my attention." The particular lens or optic of one's personal telescope may be warped by neurosis or disease, causing systematic distortions in one's consciousness or vision. Nietzsche compares these to optical illusions, calling paranoia, for example, "a moral-optical illusion." Hume sees the mind as essentially dramatic; he compares consciousness to an inner theater, in which we are simultaneously authors, actors, audience, and auditorium.

These images derive from physics and poetry. Are they merely fanciful, or are they consonant with the evidence we have? Can we properly call them scientific paradigms or hypotheses? I think that they are justified by observations we can make, and that their illuminating power can be exemplified in innumerable ways. I can only indicate this very briefly, from certain observations I have made of my patients and myself.

In my book *Awakenings* I describe something of the extraordinary inner lives of a unique group of patients, all victims of the extraordinary "sleeping-sickness" epidemic of fifty years ago and their "awakenings" when given the drug L-Dopa after years or decades of profoundly altered consciousness. The effect of disease in many of these patients was to "freeze" consciousness absolutely and completely, to arrest the inner stream or shuttle at a particular point of time years or decades in the past. In such patients (whose intellectual powers and personalities were otherwise intact), consciousness might be arrested, so to speak, in a single stroboscopic-transfixed brain-flash, a single unchanging moment of being. Such patients had no true sense of the passage of time during the years or decades of their consciousness-stasis.

In others there occurred not a stasis of consciousness, but strange dynamic distortions, so that their movements, typically, would tend to be too slow, too fast, too large, or too small. Such patients might not realize that their movements were in any way abnormal; they would feel that their movements were correct in scale, when in fact they were wildly disturbed. Such patients suffered from a peculiar sort of illusion or delusion, not psychotic or moral in quality but relating only to the judgment of space and time.

Seeing such patients with their strangely warped "inner screens" or frames of reference, one could not but admit the power and precision of Nietzsche's image.

An example from my own experience. Last year I severely injured one leg while mountain climbing. Following an operation, the leg was enclosed in a plaster cast, which served not only to prevent any movement, but also to cut it off from confirmation by sight or touch. In consequence of this I developed a peculiar hiatus in imagination or consciousness. I became unable to summon up any image of my leg; I felt as if I were an amputee (a condition sometimes called negative phantom-limb). The coming back of the leg, of the inner image of the leg, occurred in a most fascinating and instructive way. When, after some weeks, I was judged ready to walk again, when I was poised on the brink of my first step—but having lost the idea of stepping, and of a leg to step with—I was suddenly precipitated into a sort of perceptual delirium, an incontinent bursting-forth of representations and images unlike anything I had ever experienced before. Suddenly my leg and the ground before me seemed immensely far away, then under my nose, then bizarrely tilted or twisted one way and another. These wild perceptions (or perceptual hypotheses) succeeded one another at the rate of several per second, and were generated in an involuntary and incalculable way. By degrees they became less erratic and wild, until finally, after perhaps five minutes—and a thousand such flashes, a plausible image of the leg was achieved. With this the leg suddenly felt *mine* and real again, and I was forthwith able to walk. This experience provided an astonishing example of the brain-shuttle, with its rushing, involuntary generation of perceptions, hypotheses, flashes, and guesses. It showed the essentially dramatic and inventive quality of consciousness, recreating an idea which had been destroyed by injury.

Finally a brief consideration of the physical basis of consciousness. If there is exhaustion or depression of the cerebral cortex, the level of consciousness is lowered; if there is gross destruction of the cortex, consciousness is apparently extinguished. Thus it is clear that the cerebral cortex is needed to *mediate* consciousness. But this does not mean that "the cortex is the sole organ of consciousness in man," as William James described it. On the contrary, the alterations of consciousness occurring in sleeping-sickness patients, for example, arise from damage to structures below the cortex (which itself is almost always undamaged). Moreover, our appetites and emotions and sensations of pleasure and pain, which rise into consciousness and can dominate it, are strikingly uncortical in quality, and are determined by cerebral activities below the cortex. The basic "turning-on" and "turning-off" of consciousness is accomplished by arousal-systems in the lower brainstem, many levels below the cortex. The state of all our "innards," our viscera, our glands, our blood vessels, et cetera, enters into consciousness, and alters its "tone."

And, as my own example shows, the inner images which constitute consciousness can even be fundamentally altered by disturbances in the periphery of the body. The entire organism is a functional unity: thus we are not conscious with our cortex alone; we are conscious with the whole of ourselves.

One must go further. It is not merely we who are conscious. It cannot be supposed that the origination of consciousness lies in us alone. Our consciousness is like a flame or a fountain, rising up from infinite depths. We transmit and transfigure, but are not the first cause. We are vessels or funnels for what lies beyond us. Ultimately we mirror the nature which made us. Nature achieves self-consciousness through us.

ADDITIONAL RESOURCES

Books and Articles

Freud, Sigmund. *The Ego and the Id*. Edited by Joan Riviere, New York: Norton, 1923. Freud divides the human mind into three categories: id, ego, and superego. He discusses these three elements and theorizes about conscious and unconscious processes.

Gazzaniga, Michael. *The Social Brain*. New York: Basic Books, 1985. The study of split-brain patients has enlightened our understanding of the human brain. Gazzaniga deems the left side of the brain "the social brain"—the interpretive, meaning-making hemisphere.

Grinspoon, L., and J. B. Bakalar. *Psychedelic Drugs Reconsidered*. New York: Basic Books, 1979. A thoughtful scientific treatment of issues surrounding psychedelic drugs.

Hilgard, Ernest R. *Divided Consciousness: Multiple Controls in Human Thought and Action*. New York: Wiley, 1977. Examines how hypnosis can bring out information that seems hidden from the conscious mind.

Levy, Jerre. "Right Brain, Left Brain: Fact and Fiction." *Psychology Today* (May 1985): 38–44. Each hemisphere of the brain may have special abilities, but we all use both sides all the time. Levy explores facts and fallacies about the human brain.

Wilkes, J. "A Study in Hypnosis." *Psychology Today* (January 1986): 22–27. A conversation with Ernest Hilgard, an expert in hypnosis research.

Films

Sybil. Directed by Daniel Petrie; starring Sally Field. 1976. Emmy-winning study of a woman who, after being terribly abused as a child, develops 17 different personalities. Based on a true story and book.

The Three Faces of Eve. Directed by Nunnally Johnson. 1957. Joanne Woodward, in an Academy Award-winning role, plays a Southern housewife with multiple personalities. Adapted from the 1957 book by two doctors, C. H. Thigpen and H. M. Cleckley.

THE SELF

[There is need] to discover that we are capable of solitary joy and having experienced it, know that we have touched the core of self.

Barbara Lazear Ascher

What makes each of us unique? What traits and experiences make you *you*? Unit 15 describes how psychologists systematically study the origins and development of self-identity, self-esteem, and other aspects of our thoughts, feelings, and behaviors which make up our personalities.

How we feel about ourselves has a strong influence on our perceptions of the world—and on how others perceive us.

OBJECTIVES

After viewing the television program and completing the assigned readings, you should be able to:

1. Define personality and outline the main theoretical approaches to personality

2. Discuss the trait theory approach to personality and the trait vs. situation debate on the prediction of behavior

3. Outline Freud's psychoanalytic theory of the development and structure of personality; discuss the criticisms of psychoanalytic theory

4. Discuss the behavioral and social-learning approaches to personality; outline the main criticisms of these approaches

5. Outline the elements of the humanistic approaches to personality as developed by Rogers and Maslow; give the main criticisms of the humanistic approach

6. Discuss the emphasis on the conscious self in Bandura's theory of self-efficacy as an alternative to Freud's emphasis on unconscious processes in personality

7. Describe and discuss the pros and cons of the four main approaches to personality assessment: behavioral observation, interviews, questionnaires, and projective tests

8. Define creativity and discuss the importance of self-esteem in creativity

READING ASSIGNMENT

After viewing Program 15, read pages 523–555 in *Psychology: Science, Behavior and Life*. Your instructor may also assign the anthology selections for Unit 15.

KEY TERMS AND CONCEPTS

As you read the assignment, pay particular attention to these terms, which are defined on the given pages in the text.

personality (523)	id (530)
trait theories (524)	primary process thinking (530)
cardinal traits (525)	ego (530)
central trait (525)	reality principle (530)
secondary traits (526)	superego (531)
surface traits (526)	anxiety (532)
source traits (526)	defense mechanisms (532)
situational variance (528)	repression (532)
free association (529)	rationalization (533)
unconscious (mind) (529)	projection (533)
psychoanalysis (529)	displacement (533)
psychoanalytic theory (530)	sublimation (534)
libido (530)	regression (535)
pleasure principle (530)	reaction formation (535)

psychosexual development (535)
oral stage (536)
anal stage (536)
phallic stage (536)
genital stage (536)
Oedipus complex (536)
Electra complex (536)
latency period (536)
fixation (536)
behavioral theories of personality
  (543)
social-cognitive perspective (544)
reciprocal determinism (546)
self-efficacy (546)
humanistic theories of personality
  (540)

self (541)
self-actualization (541)
behavioral assessment of personality
  (548)
interview assessment of personality
  (549)
Minnesota Multiphasic Personality
  Inventory (MMPI) (550)
criterion-keyed test (550)
California Psychological Inventory
  (CPI) (552)
projective tests of personality (552)
Rorschach ink-blot test (553)
Thematic Apperception Test
  (TAT) (554)

The following terms are used in Program 15 but are not defined in the text.

behavioral confirmation—a form of social feedback in which our self-beliefs determine how we are perceived and evaluated by others

reference standard—a norm or model of behavior that we use to decide how to behave in a situation

self-concept—see the discussion of self, pages 445–446 in the text

self-handicapping—a process by which we try to explain away potential failures by blaming them on something other than our lack of ability

shyness—a form of social anxiety caused by the expectation of negative social evaluation

status transaction—a form of interpersonal communication in which we establish relative degrees of social status and power

PROGRAM SUMMARY

How do you know who you are? Are you the same person when you are alone as you are in public? Who is the real you? In Program 15 we'll find out how we develop our concept of self—the consciousness of our own identities.

Through the ages philosophers have tried to solve the puzzle of identity—to explain the consistencies and differences in human behavior that result in individual character and personality. In 1890 William James differentiated three aspects of identity: our awareness of the world, our awareness of ourselves as thinkers, and our awareness of the impression we make on others.

For much of the twentieth century, the concept of the self was considered too "fuzzy" for the behaviorists who dominated American psychology. Even Freud did not consider the conscious self to be as important as either our moral conscience or our primitive unconscious. Today, however, many psychologists are dedicated to

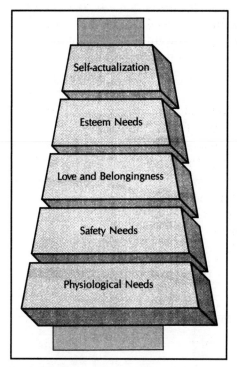

Figure 9: Maslow's Hierarchy of Needs
Humanist psychologist Abraham Maslow believed that human behavior is motivated by a hierarchy of needs. Once basic survival needs are met, we move on to higher needs, finally reaching self-actualization, fulfillment of our unique potential.

explaining our needs, fears, wishes, decisions, and expectations in an attempt to understand how self-concept affects behavior and, conversely, how behavior influences our sense of self.

The humanist movement of the 1940s, led by Carl Rogers, concentrated on the conscious self, characterizing it as a striver for personal fulfillment (see Figure 9). Rogers believed that a positive self-image enhanced personal development.

Other psychologists use the term *self-concept* to refer to an individual's awareness of a continuous identity. The self-concept shapes behavior by acting as a self-monitor and regulating behavior according to an inner standard. According to this approach, we organize our knowledge into clusters, or schemas, and make adjustments to match the way we think things ought to be. If our self-concept is good, we try to live up to our ideal standard. If it is bad, we behave and feel badly.

Still other psychologists theorize that we present ourselves so others will see us the way we see ourselves. We act and react to each other, creating and confirming the person we believe ourselves to be. Some research that that's why depressed people are often treated as if they were inadequate and why happy people tend to elicit positive responses from others.

Shy people vividly illustrate this process. Typically, they feel inadequate and anticipate failure and rejection. When they get negative reactions, their self-doubts are reinforced. Their low self-esteem makes them anxious in circumstances in which they may be judged—in meetings, at parties, or in other social and business situations.

People who fear failure need to protect their self-esteem; thus they develop strategies to avoid challenges. They also protect their self-image with cover-ups to avoid blaming themselves for failure. They tend to procrastinate, forget to show up for important appointments, even abuse alcohol or drugs to excuse poor performance—or to dull the pain caused by it.

Although people sometimes handicap themselves, society can be a handicapper too. Racism, sexism, and social prejudice discourage and inhibit a positive self-image and good behavior. Consider the high rate of alcoholism and suicide among Native Americans and the perpetual despair and rage in our urban ghettos.

On a more hopeful note, another element of personality—the creative self—testifies to our ability to invent new realities. In every civilization, men and women have left their stamp of individuality on anything that can be shaped, decorated, colored, or rearranged. Just as Carl Rogers believed that people naturally move toward fulfillment, Alfred Adler has called this phenomenon our inner striving for superiority.

But social evaluation can undermine creativity. Researcher Teresa Amabile has found that 7- to 11-year-olds were less creative when they expected their work to be judged by others. To be truly creative, people need a sense of self-esteem independent of social approval. They need the freedom to experience the world in new, unusual, and unconventional ways.

REVIEW QUESTIONS

Program Questions

1. What name did William James give to the part of the self that focuses on the images we create in the mind of others?

   a. The material self
   b. The spiritual self
   c. The social self
   d. The outer self

2. Gail is a toddler who is gradually separating from her mother. This process is called

   a. identification.
   b. individuation.
   c. self-presentation.
   d. self-consciousness.

3. In Freudian theory, the part of the person that acts as a police officer restraining drives and passions is called the

   a. superego.
   b. ego.
   c. id.
   d. libido.

4. Which statement reflects the humanistic view of the self described by Carl Rogers?

   a. Our impulses are in constant conflict with society's demands.
   b. We have a capacity for self-direction and self-understanding.
   c. We form an image of ourselves that determines what we can do.
   d. Our views of ourselves are created by how people react to us.

5. When we characterize self-image as a schema, we mean that

   a. we use it to organize information about ourselves.
   b. other people see us in terms of the image we project.
   c. it is a good predictor of performance in specific situations.
   d. we rationalize our behavior to fit into an image.

6. In Dr. Bandura's research, subjects were given the task of improving production at a model furniture factory. Subjects performed the best when they believed that performance

   a. depended on their intelligence.
   b. related mainly to how confident they felt.
   c. would be given a material reward.
   d. was based on learning an acquirable skill.

7. Which of the following behaviors signals low status in a status transaction?

   a. Maintaining eye contact
   b. Using complete sentences
   c. Moving in slow, smooth way
   d. Touching one's face or hair

8. According to the principles of behavioral confirmation, what reaction do people generally have to a person who is depressed?

   a. People sympathetically offer help to the person.
   b. People regard the person as inadequate.
   c. People act falsely cheerful to make the person happy.
   d. People treat a depressed person the same as anybody else.

9. Which statement about shyness is true?

   a. It is an uncommon condition.
   b. It can be overcome by anticipating negative consequences.
   c. It is a form of social anxiety.
   d. It accompanies an honest acceptance of oneself.

10. Peter is worried about a report. He keeps putting off doing it until the last minute. When he is told that the report is poor, he says that he needed more time. What name do psychologists give to this phenomenon?

    a. Self-efficacy
    b. Self-handicapping
    c. Confirmatory behavior
    d. Status transaction

11. In Teresa Amabile's work on creativity, how did being in a competitive situation affect creativity?

    a. It reduced creativity.
    b. It increased creativity.
    c. Its effects varied depending on the innate creativity of the subject.
    d. There was no effect.

Textbook Questions

12. According to Mischel, personality may be defined as

    a. behavior patterns that characterize a person's adaptation to life.
    b. a dominant trait.
    c. that part of us that never changes.
    d. our unconscious.

13. According to Allport, traits are

    a. instinctive.
    b. unconscious processes which cause behavior.
    c. constantly changing.
    d. aspects of personality that give rise to behavioral consistency.

14. Allport believed that the total pattern of traits is the

    a. psychic structure.
    b. collective unconscious.
    c. personality structure.
    d. private self-consciousness.

15. Critics of trait theories have suggested that traits

    a. are only descriptions, not explanations.
    b. may be situationally dependent.
    c. provide no theory of personality development.
    d. all of the above.

16. The personality theory that emphasizes the importance of unconscious motivation and conflict to personality development is

    a. behavior modification theory.
    b. trait theory.
    c. humanistic theory.
    d. psychoanalytic theory.

17. Freud considered dreams

    a. unimportant in psychoanalysis.
    b. a result of the superego.
    c. a major outlet for unconscious wishes.
    d. realistic.

18. According to psychoanalytic theory, the _____ is fully unconscious and represents the physiological drives.

    a. ego
    b. id
    c. superego
    d. preconscious

19. Freud believed that our personalities contained a sexual energy which operates according to the pleasure principle known as

    a. the Oedipus complex.
    b. the libido.
    c. Thanatos.
    d. the Electra complex.

20. A third psychic structure of Freud's theory which functions as a moral guardian and sets high standards of behavior is the

    a. id.
    b. ego.
    c. superego.
    d. alter ego.

21. According to Freud, when the ego is not able to relieve anxiety through rational methods, it resorts to tactics called

    a. impulse control.
    b. defense mechanisms.
    c. neurotic coping.
    d. displacement.

22. Many Californians who live in the earthquake zones say they are not at risk. What defense mechanism might they be using?

    a. Displacement
    b. Regression
    c. Rationalization
    d. Repression

23. A man takes out his anger on his wife, the wife spanks the child, the child kicks the dog, the dog bites the mailman, etc. This behavior is an example of

    a. reaction formation.
    b. displacement.
    c. sublimation.
    d. projection.

24. Freud believed that smoking, eating too much, drinking, chewing gum, and talking too much all represented a fixation in the _____ stage.

    a. genital
    b. oral
    c. anal
    d. phallic

25. A major criticism of Freud's theory has to do with his sample. He based his entire theory on his observations of

    a. a small number of middle- to upper-class female patients.
    b. small children.
    c. working-class males.
    d. elderly men and women.

26. B. F. Skinner wrote that we are unique individuals because

    a. we inherit unique genes.
    b. we develop differently through stages.
    c. no two people share identical reinforcement histories.
    d. we strive for superiority in unique ways.

27. According to Bandura's concept of reciprocal determinism, our personalities are shaped by

    a. the interaction between cognitive and environmental factors.
    b. our unique history of operant and classical conditioning.
    c. the unique organization of behavioral traits.
    d. the impact of childhood events and unconscious memories.

28. Children often say words they are forbidden to say. Parents seldom reinforce or shape this behavior. How then would a learning theorist explain the child's saying the words?

    a. Through inherited abilities
    b. Through modeling
    c. Through reinforcement
    d. Through classical conditioning

29. In humanistic theory, the innate tendency to strive to realize one's potential, or to be all one can be, is termed

    a. self-efficacy.
    b. self-esteem.
    c. self-actualization.
    d. compensatory striving.

30. Rogers believes that we have mental images of that which we are capable of becoming; he calls these images

    a. peak experiences.
    b. ideal-self.
    c. self-esteem.
    d. positive regard.

31. Humanistic theory has been criticized for (the)

    a. vague, subjective nature of its concepts.
    b. basing the theories on subjective, nonverifiable observations.
    c. ignoring the impact of environmental factors in shaping behavior.
    d. all of the above.

32. A limitation of the interview technique for personality evaluation is

    a. its vast quantifiability.
    b. its flexibility.
    c. interviewer bias.
    d. informality.

33. Personality tests which are developed with the underlying rationale based on psychoanalytic theory are called

    a. paper-and-pencil tests.
    b. objective tests.
    c. subjective tests.
    d. projective tests.

QUESTIONS TO CONSIDER

1. What is your impression of the speaker in the following poem? How would you describe her? What is the poet's level of self-esteem? Do you think it is better to be a somebody or a nobody?

   I'm nobody! Who are you?
   Are you—Nobody—Too?
   Then there's a pair of us!
   Don't tell! they'd advertise—you know!

   How dreary—to be—Somebody!
   How public—like a Frog—
   To tell one's name—the livelong June—
   to be an admiring Bog!

   (Emily Dickinson, poem no. 288, from *The Complete Poems of Emily Dickinson*, edited by Thomas H. Johnson. Copyright © 1914, 1929, 1935, 1942 by Martha Dickinson Bianchi. © renewed 1957, 1963 by Mary L. Hampson. Reprinted by permission of Little, Brown and Company.)

2. How is Seligman's concept of pessimism related to shyness?

3. What are some of the positive and negative aspects of the id, according to Freud?

4. Do you have higher self-esteem in some situations than in others? How do different environments and conditions affect you? Do you think that self-esteem is constant or variable?

5. Consider the Barnum effect and the techniques astrologers use to describe personality. Why are people so easily impressed?

OPTIONAL ACTIVITIES

1. How do you recognize extraverts and introverts? Observe people on television, in a public place, or at home. Rate their behavior on a continuum between the opposites of extravert and introvert. How helpful is the distinction? Do these qualities seem to be a primary dimension of personality?

2. Describe yourself by highlighting your special abilities, admirable qualities, and accomplishments. Write a brief description of your spouse, children, or a close friend. Consider how often you appreciate the positive aspects of your own or another's personality and how often you focus on the negatives. How does your focus affect your own self-esteem and your relationships?

3. Create three groups of statements about yourself which illustrate William James's three aspects of the self.

ANTHOLOGY

As you read the following selections, think about your own individuality and its various components. Consider how the different approaches to personality emphasize different thoughts, feelings, expectations, intentions, and situational factors in explaining behavior. Which theory or approach is closest to your own ideas about the self?

Reading 33

What accounts for unbridled optimism? What makes some people accept failure while others react with dogged determination? When do you call it denial and when do you call it courage? As you read this article, consider how the different theories of personality, self, and human development would explain the case of Mary Ann, a study in self-confidence and achievement against the odds.

Mary Ann—A Lesson in Determination

By Maureen Dowling

The first time an educator told me something was not possible was during my own early school years. The kindergarten teacher seated us around a long wooden table. Ominously, she cleared away all school materials and books. Meticulously, and in silence, she placed before each of us a board with various shaped holes and a packet of pegs. She told us to place the pegs in the correct holes. "And remember," she said staunchly, "it is impossible to put the wrong peg in the wrong hole." There was something about the way she said "impossible" that convinced me to prove her wrong. With dogged determination, I began to pound the round pegs into the square holes and triangular pegs into rectangular holds. When the time was up, the teacher collected each board, and, as mine was carried away, one round peg could be seen standing proudly from a partially accepting square hole.

Although I had been in my new position as Director of Pupil Personnel Services for several months, requests for services for handicapped children were still flooding my office, burying me in paperwork and details. Prioritizing children according to their needs had become my diurnal task. Mary Ann's name, however, had quickly and inevitably risen to the top of my list.

I had been told that Mary Ann, then a sophomore, would be the first student in our high school not to graduate because of her failure to meet the requirements of the New York State Regents Competency Tests. The Regents ensured that every student who received a high school diploma had met minimum standards of competency in mathematics, reading, and writing.

It wasn't that she had already failed; it was simply the general consensus of the teachers and administrators who had worked with Mary Ann that she couldn't possibly pass. As one teacher put it:

> She may pass one of the Regents, but never all three. She doesn't have the skills. The question really shouldn't be "Can she do it?" but rather, "What type of certificate can we give her other than a diploma?"

Mary Ann had been adopted in Greece at the age of six and then brought to the U.S. In 4th grade, she was referred to the Committee on the Handicapped. A psychological evaluation indicated that Mary Ann's verbal and performance levels placed her in the lowest 5th percentile nationally. Teacher assessments of Mary Ann's performance supported these results. In those days, the recommendation was usually to send the student to a special class in a state-supported school for the handicapped. Mary Ann's mother made an impassioned plea to keep her child in the mainstream. Both Mary Ann and her mother must have been very special because the committee agreed to declare Mary Ann not handicapped. She was given educational support outside of the classroom. Her teachers generally accepted her limitations and were willing to make modifications and to overlook a great deal.

A Special Dream

I was anxious to meet Mary Ann, never suspecting that she would teach me so much about the human spirit. I intended to speak first with her and then with her mother, about the near-certainty that Mary Ann could not meet the graduation requirements. I hoped to discuss the educational alternatives to an academic program in our high school.

Mary Ann was impressive. Wearing a pale pink dress, she appeared pretty and feminine. She sat down in a poised and confident manner. Her speech was halting, but her thoughts were clear and direct. "I can pass the Regents. I want to try. Please let me. I want to graduate more than anything else." Sensing my concern, she added, "I'll pass them, don't worry."

I met with her mother the next day and enumerated the many obstacles that stood in the way of Mary Ann's graduation. Her mother nodded knowingly. "I believe she can do it. I want her to have a chance—it means so much. I know you'll do everything you can to help her."

After these meetings, I referred Mary Ann to the Committee on the Handicapped. It was in May of her sophomore year. The results of the tests we conducted seemed to put a high school diploma well out of Mary Ann's reach. Her verbal and performance levels remained in the bottom 5th percentile nationally: math diagnostic tests put her grade level at 1.5. She couldn't write more than a few sentences about a single topic, and her reading was mid-3rd grade.

Yet nothing could deter Mary Ann and her mother, and no member of the committee could refuse their request to help Mary Ann graduate with her class. The committee classified Mary Ann as learning disabled. Her placement included two periods of math remediation daily—one with a special education teacher and one with a mainstream math teacher: and one period of reading/writing remediation daily, with a specialist. We had two years to bring Mary Ann's performance to minimum competency levels.[1]

Mary Ann's educational program began in September and was followed by months of hard work and seemingly little success. The teachers' refrains reverberated through my office and my conscience. . . .

She can't pass the Regents. We're not doing the right thing for her—we're setting her up for unattainable expectations.

My committee members and I questioned our judgment—it was a difficult time for us.

Mary Ann had been enrolled in a half-day BOCES (Board of Cooperative Educational Services) cosmetology program early that year to help her realize her dream of becoming a beautician. In December, I received a call from the BOCES counselor. The recommendation was familiar and expected—she should not be in the program. Even if she could manage the practicum, she could never pass the written examination. There was no reasoning with Mary Ann on this question—she was determined to be a beautician. She remained in the program.

The Turning Point

In February of her junior year, one of Mary Ann's math teachers came into my office, smiling. "I just gave Mary Ann a practice Regents math test, and she scored 20 points higher. You know something? I think you're right. I think she can do it. She works so hard." The word spread quickly, and her reading/writing teacher added to the new enthusiasm—Mary Ann was reading better. For the first time, she had a chance of passing the Regents reading exam. Writing, however, seemed the impossible obstacle. We persevered. Mary Ann's learning rate began to increase. We watched improvements in her scores on practice tests with a controlled exuberance.

In June of her junior year, Mary Ann passed the Regents math exam with a highly respectable grade of 78 percent.

The high school principal, who had been committed to helping Mary Ann, recommended to the board of education and the superintendent that Mary Ann be given additional instruction in reading and writing, after school hours, during her senior year. (Actually, unbeknownst to us, the teacher was already doing this three times a week without compensation.) They readily agreed, and this impressive young woman became a cause for many people.

In January of her senior year, Mary Ann passed the Regents reading exam with several points to spare. Again, it became painfully clear that her programs in writing seemed to be proceeding too slowly, given our deadline.

During all this, Mary Ann attended classes and fulfilled her other school responsibilities. At home, her mother and friends tutored her. Mary Ann never faltered or lost heart. She simply tried harder.

In June, three days before commencement, Mary Ann passed the Regents writing examination—barely.

The graduation ceremony took place on a warm, clear day. It was held on the lawn, and the sound of chamber music periodically filled the air. The opening speeches and other details are difficult to recall, but I will never forget the intense pride I felt as Mary Ann walked across the dais in her cap and gown. The assistant principal smiled warmly as he awarded Mary Ann a diploma. He held her hand for what seemed a long time as the applause of her admirers resounded.

There is a sequel to this. Mary Ann passed the practicum for the beautician's license with a "B" average, but for two years, and after three attempts, she failed the written exam.

I contacted a BOCES counselor and asked about tutoring. The counselor reviewed Mary Ann's records and excitedly—defensively—reported that BOCES was not responsible for her failure. For two years, the BOCES teachers had recommended that Mary Ann be withdrawn from the program. I quickly reassured her. "I know. I'm asking for over and above—the impossible." Her tone softened with compassion as she spoke and offered one-to-one tutoring without charge. I asked a question I had asked several times before, "Is there any way to provide modified testing conditions?"[2] "No," she replied, "Only foreign-born students are eligible." With a surge of hope, I exclaimed. "Mary Ann was born in Greece!" Though reserved, the counselor instilled confidence as she responded, "I'll see what I can do."

When Mary Ann was finally allowed to take the test orally, she passed. For months after, Mary Ann struggled to become a professional haircutter. She worked in several local salons but was given only menial tasks to perform. One employer told her that professional haircutting would be out of her reach. Last fall, Mary Ann was promoted to haircutter in a fine salon and has continued successfully in this position.

As I remember Mary Ann, I think of something Thoreau said:

> If one advances confidently in the direction of his dreams, and endeavors to live the life which he has imagined, he will meet with success unexpected in common hours.

[1]Minimum high school competency levels are nebulous when transferred to grade equivalents. Generally, a student must have the overall ability to perform the skills of reading, writing, and mathematics on a 7th to 9th grade level to pass these exams.

[2]Modified testing conditions are available to handicapped students under many statewide testing programs. In Mary Ann's case, her learning disability prevented her from writing her answers in the allotted time. She did, however, know the material for which she was being tested.

Reading 34

This article takes a close look at how people handle failure and disappointment. It suggests that excuses are an important mechanism for maintaining self-esteem and cites research indicating that excuse making can have both a negative and a positive side. Compare Snyder's description with Seligman's theory about the role of pessimism and optimism in personality and behavior. Think about the kinds of excuses you use in your daily life and the purposes they serve.

Excuses, Excuses

By C. R. Snyder

Excuses have a bad image. In the cartoon strip *Peanuts*, Lucy has blamed her missed fly balls on the sun, the moon, the wind, the stars and even toxic substances in her baseball glove. We laugh at this light side of excuse-making, thereby preserving the point of view that excuses are silly, transparent and weak ploys that other people use. Although we sense that there is really much more to excuses, we are reluctant to consider them in any serious, detailed way. My recent work on excuse-making has convinced me that it is not only much more common than generally realized, but that it plays a central role in how we get along in life, both with ourselves and with other people.

I have long been intrigued by the human dilemma of fallibility. We all make mistakes of one kind or another and find ourselves in predicaments in which we don't perform well.

Something has to be done with these disappointing outcomes so that they don't restrict and intimidate us; that something often takes the form of excuses.

Excuse-making has a few basic components. First, most people want to maintain a positive image of themselves. While some psychologists protest that there are other, nicer motives underlying the way people behave, self-esteem is in my estimation a driving force for most of us.

Furthermore, we like to keep our image in good shape both for an internal audience (ourselves) and for an external audience (everyone else). Although at times we are especially concerned with what others think, most of the time we simultaneously polish our positive image for both audiences.

Given this tendency in people, excuses are sparked by any situation that links a person to a bad performance—an action, that is, that does not meet either the individual's or society's standards. The more closely a person is linked to a bad performance and the more negatively that performance is regarded, the greater the probability of excuse-making. People begin to explain or to act in ways that lessen the negative implications of the bad performance in their own eyes, in the judgment of others or both.

Excuse-making takes three general routes: "I didn't do it," "It's not so bad" and "Yes, but. . . ." Since people are linked to their poor performances by information, often physical evidence, "I didn't do it" excuses aim to sever this causal connection. Wide-eyed children frequently use simple denial ("Who, me?"), the most rudimentary form of excuse-making, and even adults occasionally revert to it, as the Rev. Jesse Jackson did by initially disavowing his "Hymie" comment.

If we are not responsible, of course, someone else must be, and it helps to give some clue as to who the culprit is. We become helpful witnesses willing to "testify" regarding the culpability of someone—anyone—else. Psychologist Robert Cialdini and his colleagues uncovered this behavior among college students when they counted school identifying apparel (T-shirts, jackets and buttons showing the school mascot, nickname or name) on Mondays following Saturday football games. Students displayed their "school colors" less frequently when the team had lost than when it was victorious.

In a related study, researchers asked students to recall the results of a game that the team had won, and others to recall the results of a game the team had lost. The wins were typically recalled as "We won," the losses as "they lost." Cialdini has termed the former effect BIRGing (*B*asking *I*n *R*eflected *G*lory). I call the latter phenomenon CORFing (*C*utting *O*ff *R*eflected *F*ailure).

If excuse-makers cannot sever the ties to the bad performance, if they must admit, "I did it," then they must somehow make it seem "not so bad." Here we see what I have called "reframing maneuvers," behavior aimed at softening, bleaching and generally repackaging the bad act in a more positive light.

The simplest reframing strategy is to consciously or unconsciously hide from yourself the undesirable consequences of your actions. Since the 1964 murder of Kitty Genovese called attention to bystander apathy, there have been several studies of people's unwillingness to offer aid to victims. What I find especially intriguing are the inadequate perceptions of the people who do not render aid. Just as one witness to the Genovese murder saw it merely as a "lovers' quarrel," the participants in analogous studies "just don't seem to see anything too bad going on." For example, psychologists Bibb Latané and Judith Rodin let students overhear a staged accident in which a woman fell down and screamed, "Oh, my God, my foot . . . I . . . I . . . I can't move it. Oh, my ankle . . . I . . . can't get this . . . thing . . . off me!" The students, seated together in the next room, typically offered excuses rather than aid. Most said, "I didn't really know what happened," while others asserted that "it wasn't serious." In daily life outside the laboratory, this self-deception leads to such excuses as "Gosh, I didn't hear the baby screaming." Or, "I didn't know you needed help cleaning the bathroom." Many things, obvious to others, seem to "escape the notice" of excuse-makers.

A more complex kind of reframing involves reworking the standards related to a particular act. Children say, "No fair, you didn't tell me the rules," and a few years later they tell themselves and their teachers, "The requirements of this course were too fuzzy." Or if the clarity of the standards can't be questioned, they can certainly be lowered. A losing candidate in a Presidential primary may maintain that his 9 percent of the vote represents a victory, because it is more than he and everyone else expected. People new to a job, be it basketball coach or President, tell how bad things are and how much work will be necessary to get them back in shape in order to lower expectations of the performance to come.

A related approach is to customize the standards to fit one's purposes. The ruling pigs in George Orwell's *Animal Farm* redid the commandments to lessen their transgressions: "No animal shall sleep in a bed" became "No animal shall sleep in a bed with sheets." Or the standard may be reworked by embedding the seemingly bad act into a larger good context. The bombing of Hiroshima, it is suggested, actually saved lives by shortening World War II. We hear (and say), "I was only doing it (for your own good, to teach you a lesson . . .)" regularly, in one form or another.

If excuse-makers accept responsibility ("I did it") and concede further, "It was bad," they then need excuses of the "Yes, but" variety—excuses designed to weaken the accountability link by introducing additional information that reduces the person's sense of responsibility for the poor performance. By playing on the familiar notion of extenuating circumstancees, "Yes, but" excuses tell the audience that the excuse-maker shouldn't be held totally accountable. The consensus and consistency notions of social psychologist Harold Kelley provide a useful framework for understanding the "Yes, but" approach. For example, one way we can diminish responsibility for failure is by showing that other people would perform just as poorly as we did under the same circumstances. If many people are failing at the same task, then the situation must be the problem, not us.

Experiments in this area usually examine what people say after succeeding or failing at tasks such as college exams, anagrams and other tests of achievement. Successful people attribute the outcome to their own ability. Unsuccessful ones blame their failure on the difficulty of the task or bad luck. By claiming that the test was so difficult that anyone would flunk it, students impeach the situation and get themselves off the hook. Similarly, we all know how easily a streak of bad luck can defeat even the best of us.

Projection, the process by which a person ascribes personal failings and deficiencies to other people, is another way we explain away our failures. My colleagues David Bennett and David Holmes told one group of students they had done poorly on a vocabulary test, while a second group received no such feedback. When asked to estimate how well three friends would do on the same test, the first group judged that their friends would score at the 57th percentile; the others estimated marks at the 73rd percentile. Such projection is common in daily life as well, at all ages. The teenager notes, "Well, everyone was doing it"; grandpa snorts, "Old people just can't remember things." Indeed, such excuse-makers confirm the adage that "misery loves company."

To fail once is unpleasant, but to repeat failure is even worse. To avoid this, excuse-makers employ what I call consistency-lowering strategies to make the point that their bad performance in a given situation is unusual. And they certainly should not be held totally responsible for "just one bad performance."

There are two major forms of this excuse. One tactic involves lowered effort. To test this, experiments usually ask people, "How hard did you try?" after they have failed, succeeded or received no information on their performance. Those who know they failed consistently report lower levels of effort, subtly suggesting that in subsequent attempts they will do much better. After losing the Illinois primary to Walter Mondale, for example, Democratic Presidential candidate Gary Hart noted that because of the hectic primary schedule, he didn't have enough time to campaign properly.

The second consistency-lowering tactic is to claim lack of intent. "I didn't mean to do it" implies that some unforeseen circumstances took control just this once. The legal plea of temporary insanity is a more complex form of this excuse.

Although excuses are so common that they must be considered normal human behavior, there are certain situations in which excuse-making simply won't do. You don't, for example, give an excuse to a person who is very knowledgeable in the area in which you performed badly. The expert might see through the excuse and expose it. I remember grappling with a question on a college exam. My professor asked why I looked so perplexed, to which I muttered, "I bet nobody is getting this question right." This attempt at a consensus-raising excuse was shattered by his reply: "Actually most other people do seem to getting it."

Rick Mehlman, a graduate student, and I recently completed a project in which we documented the situational backfiring of excuses. After being told that they had failed a test, research participants were hooked up to a device that monitored physiological reactions; they were asked why they thought they had failed and were given psychological tests that measured positive and negative feelings (they had taken the same tests earlier). For those people who were told that this device "merely measured physiological responses," making excuses caused the expected decrease in negative feelings. The excuses, that is, did their psychological work by protecting the ego. But for people who were told that the device was a "lie detector that measured their true feelings," excuses increased their negative feelings. Under the scrutiny of an all-knowing audience (in this case the supposed lie detector), excuses may only serve to make us feel worse.

Certain styles of excuse-making can also be counterproductive. Some people, for example, offer excuses so elaborate and so frequent that they cause problems. People who excuse their absence at a party, for example, by saying that a close relative has died, usually are detected, and their image suffers. Chronic excuse-makers find themselves suffering from two bad performances—their original failures and their muffed attempt to excuse it.

Such excuse-makers probably have a fragile sense of personal worth to begin with, and in more and bigger excuses, they may have stumbled into a Faustian bargain: Once-moderate and perhaps effective excuses become harmful when taken too far. The concept of self-handicapping introduced by psychologists Edward Jones and Steven Berglas applies here. This is the practice of embracing a "handicap" to maintain a view of oneself as competent, intelligent and generally worthy. To preserve some semblance of self-esteem, people admit to a seemingly peripheral problem or weakness (the self-handicap) as an explanation for their failures.

I have been interested in how people employ their symptoms, especially those related to anxiety, as self-handicaps. My hunch has been that people who have major anxiety-related problems show their symptoms, in part, as self-handicaps, while people who have only minor problems in this area do not employ such symptoms as excuses. In one experiment, my colleagues and I recruited students who had earlier shown either high or low levels of test anxiety for an experiment in which they took a two-part test of various intellectual abilities. We told students in both the high- and low-anxiety groups that they had performed poorly on the very difficult first half of a test. Then, before they took the second part, we asked them to report their anxiety symptoms.

We told half the students in each group that such symptoms do not influence performance on this test, while the rest were given no such information. The highly anxious students who had not been told reported significantly more test-anxiety symptoms than did those who had been. In contrast, students with low levels of test anxiety reported the same number of test-anxiety symptoms whether they had been told or not. This suggests that the symptoms of highly anxious people appear or dissipate depending on their excuse potential. Simply put, it is better to see oneself as anxious than as dumb.

Other experiments in my laboratory suggest that such symptoms as hypochondriacal complaints and shyness may have a self-handicapping function as excuses. Craig DeGree and I have also found that people emphasize their difficult life histories as excuses for a potential failure ("What do you expect out of me, I've had a hard life!").

The insidious aspect of using symptoms as excuses is that people can increasingly become stuck with the problem they have been exploiting. My colleague Ray Higgins has conducted studies suggesting that alcohol consumption increases in circumstances in which it can serve as an excuse for poor performance. Higgins rigged an experiment so that college students who were heavy social drinkers experienced much greater success on certain problems than they could have anticipated, and he found that they significantly increased their consumption of a placebo beverage before a retest on similar problems. Uncertain of their ability to perform well again, the heavy drinkers handicapped themselves in advance, setting up alcohol as an excuse for failure if they did poorly on the retest. Indeed, part of the seductive path to alcoholism may be the excuse potential of drinking.

The best way to deal with pathological excuse-making, I have found, is, first, to point out the excuses when they are offered. In developing a model of how excuses work, I have been impressed by the many types of not-so-obvious behavior that are, in fact, excuses. Often people aren't even aware that they are making excuses, as repeated excuse-making gradually becomes automatic. Since excuse-making is considered bad form, we don't like to think we give excuses for failure. Rather, we have explanations or, better yet, good reasons for bad performances; other people give excuses. When it comes to spotting our own excuse-making, we are poor detectives.

Once excuse-makers are aware of their habit, they can begin developing skills in areas that are important to their self-esteem, thereby lessening the chance of a poor performance and the need for excuses. Finally, the chronic excuse-makers must change this maladaptive way of viewing and judging themselves; once they realize that poor performances in life are quite common and do not reflect on one's character, then the continual explanations become unnecessary.

Although excuses sometimes backfire and excuse-making can become habitual and pathological, I believe they do serve an adaptive role for most people at most times, providing a way of negotiating life's uncertain terrain. Normal excuses are often quite subtle, equally unrecognized by excuse-makers and their audience. An evident physical disability, for example, may nicely protect a person from a potential failure. In my Little League days, a bandaged sprained wrist convinced me and (I supposed) the crowd that I wasn't really a bad ballplayer; I was just hurt. I wonder now how long I wore the wrapping even after my wrist stopped hurting.

At a recent colloquium on excuse theory, a member of the audience firmly posed a rhetorical question, "Aren't excuses always just lies?" No, I don't think they are. It's true that by adopting an explanation that preserves positive self-images, people are subjectively biasing their interpretations of their world. But these biased interpretations are not always "errors" or "lies." When there are no objective yardsticks for measuring the "truth" of differing explanations of events, several explanations may fit the facts equally well. There often is not one black or white view of reality; several gray interpretations are also plausible.

Both the research I've done and work done by others suggest that excuses generally do work; they serve to preserve our self-image and reduce the stress associated with our failures. They work well enough that we pass on our implicit knowledge of excuses to our children. As parents or teachers we demand explanations from children when they make a mistake, but we also give them some hints regarding which excuse-like maneuvers will do the job. When we tell a child, "I know you didn't mean to do that," the child learns that this lack-of-intent plea works. It is only natural that we try to teach our children about excuse-making, because they go on to live in a society where even the legal system reflects grown-up excuse-making principles.

Beyond the image protection that excuses offer, they are also a social lubricant that enables us to continue interactions with friends, coworkers and bosses when we foul up. By giving an excuse, we acknowledge the validity of the standards we have violated. Lastly, excuses help us to take chances, to push the limits in a world in which we are bound to fail occasionally. To face a world of absolute accountability would be a terrifying prospect. With our excuses, we can take risks and try again.

There will always be certain things for which we will be accountable. The inexcusable will and should remain inexcusable. But from the beginning of time, we have pursued the personal and societal forgiveness that excuses bring. Adam blamed Eve, Eve blamed the serpent, and we have been blaming away happily ever since.

ADDITIONAL RESOURCES

Books and Articles

Amabile, Teresa M. *The Social Psychology of Creativity*. New York: Springer-Verlag, 1983. A sense of self-esteem not based on social approval seems critical to creativity. Students not focused on the imminent evaluation of judges perform more creatively.

Chance, Paul. "Your Child's Self Esteem." *Parents Magazine* (January 1982). Early experience can promote or hinder a child's mastery and self-esteem. The author discusses how caregivers can provide experiences that encourage competence and optimism.

Goffman, Erving. *The Presentation of Self in Everyday Life*. Garden City, N.Y.: Doubleday, 1959. Are we performers constantly managing how we present our "selves" to others? Goffman, a sociologist, uses metaphors of the theater to describe how people "act" in social situations.

Goleman, Daniel. "Who Are You Kidding." *Psychology Today* (March 1987): 24–30. Self-deception may help you avoid some of life's anxieties, but it can also involve some risks.

Kohn, Alfie. "Art for Art's Sake." *Psychology Today* (September 1987): 52–57. A profile of Teresa Amabile's work, which focuses on creativity and motivation.

Rogers, Carl. *On Personal Power: Inner Strength and Its Revolutionary Impact*. New York: Delacorte, 1977. Rogers focuses on an individual's natural tendency toward psychological health and growth.

Terkel, Studs. *Working*. New York: Pantheon Books, 1972. The stories people tell about their work reveal much about their self-concepts. This extraordinary book about ordinary people sheds light on many issues concerning identity and the self.

Williams, Juan. "The Color of Their Skin." *Parenting* (March 1988). Raising children in a race-conscious (if not always racist) society is one of the toughest challenges black parents face today. The author discusses the challenge of helping children grow up strong enough to confront the negative stereotypes and messages of inferiority.

TESTING AND INTELLIGENCE

Intelligence is not something possessed once and for all. It is in constant process of forming, and its retention requires constant alertness in observing consequences, an open-minded will to learn and courage in readjustment.

John Dewey

Just as no two fingerprints are alike, no two people have the same set of abilities, aptitudes, interests, and talents. Unit 16 explains the tools psychologists use to measure these differences. It also describes the long-standing controversy over how to define intelligence and how IQ tests have been misused and misapplied.

Arthur Grace/Stock, Boston

Is it wise, accurate, or fair to reduce intelligence to a number? Researchers are currently debating the value of intelligence and personality tests.

OBJECTIVES

After viewing the television program and completing the assigned readings, you should be able to:

3 component

1. Define intelligence and discuss the different theoretical approaches to <u>Sternberg</u>, Thurstone, <u>Spearman</u>, and Guilford to the study of intelligence

2 factors

2. Contrast the recent theory of multiple intelligences proposed by Howard <u>Gardner</u> to the theories in number one above

seven different ways to be intelligent

3. Identify the contributions of <u>Galton</u>, <u>Binet</u>, and <u>Terman</u> to the measurement of intelligence

4. Explain the concept of intelligence quotient (IQ)

5. Outline the concept of test standardization in terms of test norms, reliability and validity. Discuss different measures of reliability and validity

6. Discuss the problem of cultural bias in intelligence testing

7. Summarize the evidence for genetic and environmental contributions to scores on intelligence tests

8. Evaluate the evidence for racial differences in intelligence

READING ASSIGNMENT

After viewing Program 16, read pages 485–511 in *Psychology: Science, Behavior and Life.* Your instructor may also assign the anthology selections for Unit 16.

KEY TERMS AND CONCEPTS

As you read the assignment, pay particular attention to these terms, which are defined on the given pages in the text.

information-processing approach (Sternberg) (496–497)
two-factor theory (Spearman) (495)
primary mental abilities (Thurstone) (496)
structure of intellect (Guilford) (496)
intelligence (486)
mental age (488)
intelligence quotient (IQ) (488)

Stanford-Binet Test (489)
Wechsler Adult Intelligence Scale (489)
aptitude tests (494)
achievement tests (494)
(test) standardization procedures (492)
(test) norms (492)
(test) reliability (493)
(test) validity (494)

PROGRAM SUMMARY

From nursery school through college, in business and the military, tests are used to label and classify each of us. Information about our academic achievements and failures, personality traits, and mental health is collected in an effort to predict how we will perform in the classroom, on the job, or in society.

Defining and measuring intelligence is perhaps the best-known but most elusive goal of psychometricians, the scientists who specialize in psychological testing. Since the turn of the century when the Englishman Sir Francis Galton devised a set of mental tests, there has been an ongoing debate about what intelligence is, how to measure it, and how much heredity and environment contribute to it.

In 1905 in France, Alfred Binet set out to replace teachers' subjective opinions with an objective way to identify children who needed special help in school. His procedure included testing children individually on various reasoning tasks, then comparing each child to the average performance of children in the same age group.

In 1916 Lewis Terman of Stanford University adapted Binet's test for American schools and introduced the concept of the intelligence quotient. Terman came to believe that intelligence was an inner quality reflecting inherited differences and an unchangeable aspect of a person's makeup.

Terman's test became popular in the United States. The time was ripe for an efficient and inexpensive way to test and categorize large numbers of children. There were millions of new immigrants to be educated and a flood of army recruits enlisting for service in World War I. Assessing mental ability seemed a good way to impose order on this social chaos. Many people accepted the idea that intelligence tests could identify special abilities. Test results seemed to support the idea that there were racial and ethnic differences in intelligence.

But critics protested that intelligence tests depended too much on language ability and could not measure the competencies of non–English speakers and young children. In 1939 David Wechsler developed test problems that did not depend on English skills, a major milestone in intelligence testing.

Today, psychological testing is big business. Psychologist William Curtis Banks explains the criteria used to judge whether a test does what it is supposed to do. First, a test must predict what it was designed to predict. If it helps to identify those who will get the highest grades in the future, then it is valid as a grade predictor. Second, the test must demonstrate over time that its results are consistent. Third, everyone taking or scoring the test must do it according to the same rules. But how objective are these tests? Are they the unbiased, objective assessment device that Binet had imagined?

Banks points out that tests and testing practices can be used to discriminate against minorities in school and in the workplace. Cultural biases in many tests overlook important differences in experience and only measure attributes such as verbal ability or social conformity without acknowledging the importance of creativity, common sense, and other important skills. Some personnel screening tests are used to reject or exclude people although the tests have nothing to do with skills required for success on the job. The most serious misuse of tests is rooted in the mistaken belief that an intelligence test can somehow reveal basic unchanging qualities of mind and character. Some people have even used test results to claim that entire races are inferior.

In addition to challenging how tests are constructed and how results are used, psychologists define intelligence in different ways. Some psychometricians believe they are measuring a single ability or trait called intelligence. But recently cognitive psychologists have provided alternative views on the subject. Howard Gardner of Harvard University theorizes that there are at least seven different kinds of abilities and that it is society or culture that decides the value of a particular ability (see Figure 10). Western cultures prize verbal skills and logical thinking; in Bali, physical grace and musical talent are highly coveted skills.

1. Linguistic ability
2. Logical-mathematical ability
3. Spatial ability—navigating in space; forming, transforming, and using mental images
4. Musical ability—perceiving and creating pitch patterns
5. Bodily-kinesthetic ability—skills of motor movement, coordination
6. Interpersonal ability—understanding others
7. Intrapersonal ability—understanding one's self, developing a sense of identity

Figure 10: Gardner's Seven Intelligences
According to cognitive psychologist Howard Gardner, intelligence can be identified as seven different abilities, the value of which are culturally determined.

Some neurologists completely bypass the complications of mind and culture. They measure brain waves to detect differences in how people react and adjust to surprises. They assume that the smart brain has characteristic reaction patterns. Whether these measures are valid and what purpose they serve is not yet known. And the controversies will likely continue.

REVIEW QUESTIONS

Program Questions

1. What is the goal of psychological assessment?

    a. To derive a theory of human cognition
    b. To see how people vary in ability, behavior, and personality
    c. To measure the stages of growth in intellectual abilities
    d. To diagnose psychological problems

2. You are taking a test in which you are asked to agree or disagree with statements such as "I give up too easily when discussing things with others." Which test would this be?

   a. The Scholastic Aptitude Test
   b. The Rorschach test
   c. The Strong Interest Inventory
   d. The Minnesota Multiphasic Personality Inventory

3. What was Binet's aim in developing a measure of intelligence?

   a. To identify children in need of special help
   b. To show that intelligence was innate
   c. To weed out inferior children
   d. To provide an empirical basis for a theory of intelligence

4. How were the results of Binet's test expressed?

   a. In terms of general and specific factors
   b. As an intelligence quotient
   c. As a mental age related to a norm
   d. As a percentile score

5. What formula did Terman create to express intelligence?

   a. $MA/CA = IQ$
   b. $MA \times CA = IQ$
   c. $CA/MA \times 100 = IQ$
   d. $MA/CA \times 100 = IQ$

6. In 1939 David Wechsler designed a new intelligence test. What problem of its predecessors was the test designed to overcome?

   a. Bias against minority groups
   b. Unreliable scores
   c. Dependence on language
   d. Norms based on a restricted population

7. A test for prospective fire fighters has been shown to predict success on the job. Which statement about the test is true?

   a. The test is reliable.
   b. The test is valid.
   c. The test is standardized.
   d. The test is unbiased.

8. Cultural biases in tests can lead to the overvaluing of some attributes and the undervaluing of others. Which of the following is likely to be overvalued?

   a. Common sense
   b. Motivation
   c. Creativity
   d. Verbal ability

9. Imagine that anyone who wants a job as a hospital orderly has to take a test. The test if valid for its norm group, white men. Imagine a black woman is taking the test. Which statement about the woman's score is most likely to be accurate?

    a. It will accurately predict her job performance.
    b. It will be lower than that of white men.
    c. It may indicate she is not capable when she in fact is capable.
    d. It cannot indicate anything about her since there were no blacks or women in the norm group.

10. What new perspective does Howard Gardner bring to the study of intelligence?

    a. He wants to redefine intelligence as "practical intelligence."
    b. He wants to expand intelligence to include other dimensions.
    c. He hopes to find a biological basis for describing intelligence in terms of brain waves.
    d. He believes that the term *intelligence* should be abolished.

11. Robert Sternberg has devised a test for managers. How does its prediction of success compare with predictions from a standard IQ test?

    a. They predict equally well and are not correlated.
    b. They predict equally well, probably because they are measuring the same thing.
    c. Sternberg's test predicts twice as well as IQ and is not correlated with IQ.
    d. Sternberg's test predicts twice as well as IQ and is moderately correlated with IQ.

12. The attempt by neuroscientists to find biologically based measures of intelligence rests on the assumption that intelligence involves

    a. multiple factors.
    b. cultural learning.
    c. speed of adaptation.
    d. high excitability.

Textbook Questions

13. Laypersons and experts agree that the concept of intelligence implies

    a. high levels of creativity.
    b. adjustment in one's career.
    c. verbal ability.
    d. personal happiness.

14. One of Sternberg's most interesting findings is that people who score high on intelligence tests

    a. spend more time analyzing a question.
    b. finish in record time.
    c. answer questions quickly.
    d. ask more questions.

15. _____ is a term commonly understood to include the abilities to think rationally and abstractly, act purposefully, and deal effectively with the environment.

    a. Creativity
    b. Intelligence
    c. Aptitude
    d. Achievement

16. An IQ is a person's

    a. score on an intelligence test.
    b. intelligence.
    c. academic success.
    d. learning ability.

17. An eight-year-old child whose mental age is twelve would have a Stanford-Binet IQ of

    a. 100.
    b. 85.
    c. 125.
    d. 105.

18. The average IQ for all nine-year-olds is

    a. 85.
    b. 95.
    c. 100.
    d. 105.

19. Achievement tests are designed to

    a. predict ability to learn new information or a new skill.
    b. measure what one has already learned.
    c. determine your intelligence quotient.
    d. none of the above.

20. Mary is taking her final exam in math. She is in fact taking a(n)

    a. aptitude test.
    b. cognitive abilities test (CAT).
    c. achievement test.
    d. intelligence test.

21. A standard that reflects the normal or average performance of a particular group of people on a measure such as an IQ test is called the

    a. mean reference.
    b. range.
    c. norm.
    d. reference point.

22. The degree to which scores are dispersed around the average score (or mean) is a statistic called a

    a. norm.
    b. standard deviation.
    c. standardizing procedure.
    d. correlation coefficient.

23. Many human attributes, including intelligence, are distributed along a

    a. continuum.
    b. standard deviation.
    c. normal or bell curve.
    d. t-test.

24. If an intelligence test yields highly similar scores on separate testings, it is said to be

    a. reliable.
    b. valid.
    c. dependable.
    d. culture-fair.

25. A method for determining the reliability of a test by comparing test-takers' scores on separate occasions is known as

    a. test-retest reliability.
    b. split-half reliability.
    c. alternate-form reliability.
    d. validity reliability.

26. One of the simplest ways to assess _____ validity of a test is to compare a person's test scores with his/her scores on other measures known to be good indicators of the skill or trait being assessed.

    a. alternate
    b. predictive
    c. concurrent
    d. criterion-related

27. According to Robert Williams, intelligence tests are culturally biased because they

    a. reflect the middle-class white culture.
    b. emphasize performance skills.
    c. measure achievement.
    d. do not predict achievement in school.

28. According to the text,

    a. both heredity and environment influence intelligence.
    b. only heredity influences intelligence.
    c. only environment influences intelligence.
    d. neither heredity nor environment influences intelligence.

29. There is no relationship between IQ scores of persons who are

    a. unrelated and reared apart.
    b. unrelated and reared together.
    c. foster parent and child.
    d. foster father and daughter.

30. Identical twin studies are important because the twins have the same

    a. parents.
    b. genetic background.
    c. brother or sister.
    d. environment.

31. Studies have found a stronger relationship between IQ scores of adopted children and their _____ parents than with their _____ parents when socioeconomic status is equal.

    a. adoptive; grand-
    b. biological; grand-
    c. biological; adoptive
    d. adoptive; biological

32. According to recent research, knowing whether a person is black or white

    a. gives much information about his or her IQ.
    b. indicates a significant difference between IQs.
    c. indicates the person's level of creativity.
    d. provides little basis for predicting his or her IQ.

QUESTIONS TO CONSIDER

1. Does evidence of a genetic basis for intelligence mean that intelligence is unchangeable?

2. What would happen if everyone knew everyone else's IQ scores? How might it affect decisions about whom to marry or hire?

3. How can standardized test numbers affect you? If you took a test that indicated you were a genius, how would it change your life? If after a year, you were notified that you had been given someone else's results by mistake and that your score was lower than average, what difference would it make?

4. How are projective tests, such as the Rorschach inkblot test and the Thematic Apperception Test, related to intelligence? How are intelligence and creativity related?

5. What are some of the ethical questions related to intelligence testing and psychological assessment?

OPTIONAL ACTIVITIES

1. Pick a special interest of yours, such as cooking, baseball, woodworking, dancing, or traveling. Design a test that includes both questions and tasks that measure knowledge and ability in that area. How would you ensure the test's validity?

2. Consider the possibility that intelligence could be improved. Design a one-year plan to improve your intelligence. What would be the most important components of your plan?

ANTHOLOGY

The following selections raise questions about how intelligence is defined and measured and about the impact that testing has on individuals and society. As you read, consider the decisions that have been made about you on the basis of standardized tests. Also consider the decisions you have made based on test results.

Reading 35

Do kids who have high IQs require special treatment? The author of this article asks us to think about whether special programs for intellectually gifted children are really a good idea. Wouldn't all children benefit from special encouragement, enrichment, and extra advantages, which are often reserved for this elite group of youngsters? What are the purposes of such programs? Should they exist?

Aren't All Kids Gifted?

By John Kristofco

The lady who lives behind us has one. So does the family just down the street. In fact, three of my teaching colleagues have one, and they tell me that several of their friends do, too. I am quite impressed. My circle of acquaintances is not that large, really, that there should be within it so many children called gifted and talented.

Not long ago even I was approached by a friend who inquired about my interest in attending a meeting for the parents of gifted children. I was taken somewhat aback by the question. Although my wife and I know our boy is bright—at least, we feel he's bright, and he has struggled mightily to equip himself with the basics of written expression and mathematical computation—I asked my friend what made her feel that, indeed, we were parents so blessed. "Oh, he's bright all right. I've talked with him enough to know that," she responded. "Besides, the meetings are great. You'll enjoy them."

Surely, I imagined, there is more to it than that. So much hoopla has to add up to more. And in many ways it does. But in many ways, too, it adds up to less.

A Narrow Definition of Excellence Cheats Many

The label "gifted and talented" is most often applied to those students who by some objective measurement have been found to be exceptionally capable in some academic sense: their IQ has been assessed at 130 or higher; they have shown extraordinary capacity in language use, computational skills or art. It is measurable, academic traits like these that generally mark the boundaries of gifts and talents. And it is in part the definitions of these boundaries that raise so many questions about the concept of gifted and talented.

To what degree are other genuine gifts and talents ignored in these screening procedures? Is creativity measured in such a way that exceptionally creative students can be similarly identified? And what about precious abilities such as ingenuity, sociability, self-reflection, persistence, humor? Are these not also gifts that deserve nurturing within the system? Are talents other than general or specific academic potentials to remain unacknowledged? Is the system designed to perpetuate itself by identifying only students who excel within the traditionally described intellectual functions?

Going further, is it not reasonable to contend that all students—indeed, that all people—are gifted and talented in some way? To label only particular individuals gifted and talented argues, in fact, that all those not so identified are therefore not gifted at all.

I am hardly suggesting that all people have equal gifts. No teacher could be that blind to the obvious range of talents presented by any class of students. Every math instructor has had the frustration of trying to bring understanding to the occasionally soft mathematical lights in certain minds. And English teachers by the score will testify to the apparently bottomless well of abused pronouns at the disposal of all too many student writers. But we must be careful not to narrow our view of what is talent in a student to only those things that have been historically and culturally so viewed. If education is to serve the needs of all students, it must be as much interested in locating and nurturing the talents of each student as it is interested in locating and isolating the special talents of a few.

A prevailing educational view of "gifted and talented" maintains that after the students have been identified as such, they should be kept together with only other gifted students for classmates. These small classes are then taught by special teachers who, often, are selected because of their own academic performance or who have otherwise shown themselves to be "especially bright" individuals. This practice grows out of the beliefs that the best teachers belong with the best minds, only selective grouping can provide sufficient challenge to exceptional young people, and an enriched program must be a program for the few. Each of these assumptions, however, warrants examination—especially by parents understandably flattered that their child is being singled out so favorably.

Is It Best To Reserve the Best for the Best?

If we seek to challenge only those at the top of the academic ladder, what message do we send to those in the middle or at the bottom, to the nonelect? How do we know how a student—any student—will respond if he is not challenged? A well-respected colleague with 20 years of experience, sharp wit and unalloyed classroom savvy tells the story of how some years ago she was assigned the "reject" sophomore English class as a part of her teaching load.

In a school district light on funding, she found herself at a loss for a proper text to use with this class. Browsing through an old book room one day, she stumbled upon 30 copies of the *Complete Works of Shakespeare* in a corner collecting dust. The book had been selected originally for the college-prep seniors, but the volumes had been abandoned as no longer relevant and set aside for more updated fare. Deciding to accept fate and challenge herself as well as her students, my friend dusted off the *Complete Works* and made it her English text. The results of the experiment, she reports with a satisfied smile,

far exceeded her fondest wishes. She still mentions now and then how some of the essays submitted by those "slow" sophomores were far better pieces of writing than many by the college freshmen whose work she now grades.

This story—and countless others that all teachers can call up from personal experience—point to the important fact that good teachers do the most good for the most students. Just as it makes no sense to assign our healthiest citizens to our most capable physicians, so too it is not prudent to single out the best teachers and match them with our best students.

Good teaching is an art that, like other arts, touches people in some transcendent way. As with talent in any area, we are wisest when we direct a valuable resource toward the greater good in teaching. My friend, like most good teachers, was able to apply her substantial talents to create an opportunity for learning that was both challenging and exciting. All students need opportunities like that to realize their unique potentials, whatever those happen to be.

Selective Groups Receive Selective Goods

Similarly, the concept of homogeneous grouping of students into classes of the gifted and talented also needs to be questioned.

Too often the elect have a fascinating world of field trips and innovative curricula opened to them while the ordinary receive just that, the ordinary. Why isn't it more obvious that movement toward challenging curricula across the range of student abilities would achieve results like those of my friend with her sophomores—or like any real good teacher manages to achieve?

Not long ago the coordinator of gifted and talented education at a midwestern school district arranged for an army general to address the seniors in the gifted and talented program about the role of the military in America and the likely direction of any future military conscription in this country. Why, I wondered when I first heard of this—as I wonder now—were not all all seniors invited to such a presentation—such an opportunity? The parents of the majority of the 17- to 19-year olds in the school district—as well as the teenagers themselves—were being told, in effect, that the school was not going to spend its outside-speaker budget on those for whom such an opportunity might be wasted. Parents in such circumstances have a perfect right to yell "foul" and demand that their children be given the chance to participate in what is called the enriched program, the program packaged for the few.

The "average" and "slow" members of that senior class had a right to hear the army general. They help make up the America about which he would speak. Their lives are just as dramatically influenced by the military decisions we make as a nation. Their votes need to be just as enlightened as the votes of the "brightest." Indeed, the average high school seniors could make a good case that they should have held priority as the audience for the general's views on the draft, for if the past is any indication, it will be the average high school senior who bears the weight of any future plans for conscription. And it is those average individuals for whom the brightest will be formulating policy in years to come. It seems wise to have these people listen to each other now. There is plenty of time in the future for noncommunication between the leaders and the led.

School Should Mirror the Real World

The isolation of the brightest, which forces them to function exclusively in a world of their intellectual peers, is a problem from several vantage points. One major drawback is that we can never be sure about the constituency of that special world—who gets in, who doesn't and why.

Equally important, however, is that one of the prime functions of public school is the socialization of children—the inculcation of a sense of belonging to society and operating within it. In the broadest sense our schools should provide our children with a taste of living in the real world—a place where the bright and the fast exist side by side with the dull and the slow. If, as many educators believe, exceptionally gifted individuals have a difficult time adjusting to the world and dealing with their giftedness, it doesn't make a lot of sense to isolate them with their own kind at a time when they should be learning how to be a part of society. It does make sense to put them in a situation that is a microcosm of the larger society.

This does not mean that smart students need deny their talents and become a part of the average, whatever average means. It does mean that they should be provided an environment where they have to begin their process of adjustment sooner rather than later. That way they would have the chance to understand at an early age the society they are a part of.

In the skilled hands of the good teacher, the heterogeneous grouping of the regular classroom can become a model for integrated living. Such a setting also provides the teacher with a range of instructional options that can prove rewarding for all members of the group—experiences that mine the resources of each student.

Within such a classroom, for example, a teacher may choose to create project teams that are assigned long-range goals comprising various levels and stages of achievement. The teams, chosen to blend student abilities and interests, carry out projects that call on a range of academic, social, managerial, communicative and artistic skills, which will require the involvement of the different students through different tasks at different levels. Through this process, which is actually an amalgamation of individual efforts to produce a successful whole, school projects serve both skill-development and integrative functions. Education serves us well indeed when it can achieve such ends.

The teacher in the heterogeneous classroom that has the opportunity to work in the microcosmic setting that most closely mirrors the world beyond the chalkboard. Gaining a sense of the abilities, interests, strengths and needs of all the students, the teacher in this setting can direct the specific contributions of each into an integrated educational whole. And within this whole, everyone can grow.

A Possible Confusion of Interests

The final point about this subject is also the touchiest. There is a strong element of parental ego-building in the creation and implementation of programs for the gifted and talented. It is no accident, I think, that some of the parent groups associated with "G and T" are made up almost solely of college graduates and professional parents. Though it's true that these groups often try to offer their children stimulating environments, there's more to it than that. It seems they are somehow validated by their child's participation in enrichment programs. It seems to authenticate their own success and achievement, and they get the opportunity to bask in the radiance of their child's privileged position. The label "gifted" provides a kind of gene-pool accreditation that our society does not bestow through peerage.

The questions about gifted and talented programs need to be asked in order to clarify the assumptions, purposes and goals that exist in the public schools. When we let programs that focus on the few proliferate, we are doing far less than we must do in our schools. Rather than meeting the real challenge of education, we are avoiding it with highly visible, glossy programs that we can showcase while the needs of the majority of students are attended to in ordinary and routinized ways.

We do need to stimulate, challenge, and encourage the best to be the best, but the way to do this is to stimulate and challenge *all* students. Who knows, there may be "bests" we never dreamed of.

Reading 36

This article describes experimental efforts to find out if chimps can count and emphasizes the difficulty of isolating and measuring that ability. Could the testing method described in the article be improved? Do you think the research is useful? Why look for intelligence in monkeys at all?

Calculating Apes

By Bruce Bower

Sherman and Austin, two chimpanzees housed at the Yerkes Regional Primate Research Center in Atlanta, are fond of chocolate. Their sweet tooth, however, has led psychologists at nearby Georgia State University to a distinctly noncaloric conclusion: Sherman and Austin, when presented with two trays of chocolates, can perform a basic type of calculation that may be a precursor of more advanced arithmetic skills used by humans.

"As far as we know, these chimps can't count and do not know numbers," says psychologist Duane M. Rumbaugh. "What's important is that they can somehow combine separate piles of chocolates and, without any reinforcement other than the immediate food reward, choose the pair that nets them the greater amount."

Rumbaugh and colleagues Sue Savage-Rumbaugh and Mark T. Hegel say that this mental operation is a form of "summation." The exact way in which summation works is not clear, but the process involves joining pairs of separate quantities and determining which combination contains the most items. Rumbaugh notes that this is not addition, in which numbers that represent totals of separate sets of items are combined. Addition and other counting operations rely on several abilities, including the tagging of individual items with an ordered series of numbers and knowing that the number assigned to the last member of a counted set also represents the total number of items in the set.

Although research on language abilities of apes and controversy over the findings continue, increasing attention is being focused on whether they can carry out primitive types of calculation that might be linked to the human ability to count.

Sherman and Austin were allowed to choose between two sliding trays placed against a chain link fence enclosing their exercise yard. Each tray contained two food wells with varying amounts of chocolate chips. They could poke a finger through the fence to obtain the chocolate, but once contact with a tray was made, the other tray was immediately drawn out of reach by an experimenter. Each chimp made this type of choice 50 times a day for six days.

In experiments where each food well contained from zero to four chocolate chips, the chimpanzees chose the tray with the greater sum more than 90 percent of the time. For example, a tray with three chips in one well and three chips in the other well was nearly always picked over a tray with four chips in one well and none in the remaining well. When the maximum number of chocolates in a food well was increased to five, Sherman and Austin still chose the tray with the greater sum more than 90 percent of the time.

Their most difficult task was distinguishing between sums of seven and eight. In one such case, a tray with five chips in one well and two chips in the other was placed next to a tray with four chips in each well. The chimps chose the larger of these sums 79 percent of the time.

In the April JOURNAL OF EXPERIMENTAL PSY-CHOLOGY: ANIMAL BEHAVIOR PROCESSES, the researchers offer a preliminary explanation of Sherman and Austin's successes. The chimps may first have "subitized" the number of chocolates in each food well. Subitizing—perceiving at a glance up to five items without actually counting them—has been observed in human children and adults. How it works, and its role, if any, in the emergence of counting skills is unclear. Each pair of subitized amounts could have been combined or summated to obtain an estimate of the tray totals, with the summations then compared before a choice was made.

"This is only a model," says Rumbaugh, "but what we've observed with Sherman and Austin seems to be a rudimentary calculation system. They weren't counting, but they got beyond the limits of subitizing."

As in ape language studies, however, the significance of the chimps' performance is open to interpretation. Emil W. Menzel of the State University of New York at Stony Brook has only one objection to the model proposed by the Georgia investigators. "Calling the chimps' calculation system 'rudimentary' is putting them down," he says. "This study importantly extends previous work on ape calculation."

In 1960, Menzel reported that chimps quickly learned to distinguish between two colored plaques, one of which resulted in a larger food reward. The apes also learned to rank five opaque plaques according to the amount of food they covered.

Sherman and Austin's chocolate chip choices are an important first step in studying the ability of animals to perform operations on numbers, says Hank Davis of Guelph (Canada) University, but summation remains a murky concept. "Summation may not be a precursor to addition," he maintains. "I'm not convinced that there is a developmental link between the two abilities."

Davis and his colleagues have found that in some situations rats can discriminate between small numbers of events. For example, when three mild shocks are administered during an experimental session, the animals are less apt to press a lever previously associated with food, but they readily learn to resume lever pressing after the third and final shock. When the situation is made more complex by introducing another cue, such as a tone before and after each shock, level pressing does not rebound after the third shock.

These discriminations are more refined than judgments of "several" or "few," says Davis, but there is no solid evidence that rats, chimps or any other animals can count.

Another important study of what may be calculation without counting by an ape was reported in the May 2, 1985, NATURE. Tetsuro Matsuzawa of Kyoto (Japan) University trained a chimp to name 14 objects and 11 colors by choosing among a set of symbols. The chimp then learned to select from a keyboard an Arabic numeral, from one to six, matching the number of objects displayed. When, for example, five blue toothbrushes were shown, the animal pressed keys bearing "5" and symbols for "blue" and "toothbrush."

In this case, says Davis, although the chimp often tagged objects with an appropriate number, it may have formed associations with a "jumble of unrelated number tags" rather than demonstrating knowledge of an ordered series of numbers beginning with "1" and ending with "6."

Unlike Davis and Menzel, David Premack of the University of Pennsylvania in Philadelphia says the chocolate chip experiment with Sherman and Austin does not add up to much. "Summation has to do with quantity judgment, not counting," says Premack, who is also Matsuzawa's postdoctoral supervisor. "The discrimination [that the Georgia researchers] are looking at is so primitive, I'd be surprised if a housefly couldn't do it."

In his own experiments with a language-trained chimp named Sarah, Premack has found that she can match like proportions of objects that do not look alike. For instance, given a choice between a glass of water one-quarter full and three-quarters full, Sarah correctly matches the latter item with three separated quarters off an apple.

Premack suggests that the Georgia researchers must establish whether their chimps can distinguish between, say, three small chocolate chips that take up the same amount of space.

Rumbaugh acknowledges that Sherman and Austin may have combined what they saw as unitary amounts of food, not subitized values, based on estimates of the surface area of each pile of chips. He and his colleagues, however, have found that another language-trained chimp, Lana, appears to be able to count up to three items on a computer screen by using a joystick to control a cursor. Since the size of each item and the volume of quantities can be varied on a computer, the researchers plan to conduct further summation experiments with this technology.

Results so far with Lana are "exciting," says Rumbaugh, and indicate that she is focusing on quantity, not volume. It would be interesting, he adds, to give summation tests to chimps with no language training. Premack holds that, although he believes no important calculation abilities were uncovered in the chocolate chip experiment, language training boosts a chimp's analytical reasoning skills and ability to grasp small numbers and simple fractions (SN: 12/5/81. p. 363). Davis, on the other hand, says that language is not a requirement to use numbers or judge quantities, since human infants show "remarkable numerical ability." In one study, 7-month-olds showed a preference for looking at an array of objects that matched in number a sequence of sounds presented by experimenters.

"True" counting by children begins at around 4 to 5 years of age, but appears to develop in stages, says Brendan McGonigle of the University of Edinburgh, Scotland. For instance, many 6-year-olds cannot count above 10. At first, the number "1" is often used as an anchor to begin counting; performance falters if counting starts from a higher number. Furthermore, forward counting is mastered before counting backwards.

Summation may be a primitive link in the developmental chain of counting skills, says Rumbaugh. "It may reflect something for which chimpanzees have a need in the wild," he suggests. One possibility is that chimps use a "natural, number-related response" to decide which cluster of berries on a bush should be approached and which branch bears the greater number of buds.

"Studies of this type of behavior in the wild would be fascinating," says Rumbaugh. "But the key question is, when does formal counting become a requisite for these kinds of judgments?"

ADDITIONAL RESOURCES

Books and Articles

Coleman, Andrew. *Facts, Fallacies and Frauds in Psychology*. London: Hutchinson, 1987. In chapter 2, Coleman critically examines the concept of IQ and looks at the nature-nurture debate. Chapter 3 explores the racism behind attempts to show "scientifically" that intelligence is determined by genetics.

Coles, Gerald. *The Learning Mystique*. New York: Pantheon, 1988. In this controversial book, Coles takes a critical look at programs for children with learning disabilities. He argues that the label "learning disabled" itself is detrimental to a child's development.

Dorfman, D. D. "The Cyril Burt Question: New Findings." *Science*, September 29, 1987, p. 1117. Looks at the controversy that has surrounded the research of Cyril Burt.

Gardner, Howard. *Frames of Mind: The Theory of Multiple Intelligences*. New York: Basic Books, 1983. The definition of "intelligence" varies from culture to culture. Gardner suggests that intelligence can be understood as an array of seven different capacities, including a sense of music and a sense of oneself.

Gould, Stephen Jay. *Mismeasure of Man*. New York: Norton, 1981. Does the size and shape of your head mark you as a genius or a fool? Some scientists of the past believed so. Gould recounts incredible and often shocking stories of the measure—and mismeasure—of people.

Herrnstein, R. J. "IQ." *Atlantic Monthly* 228 (1971): 43-64. The debate over "Jensenism" (that is, that racial differences in IQ scores are inherited and not a bias of the test) can be explored in the charges and counter-charges reviewed in this work.

Keyes, D. *Flowers for Algernon*. New York: Harcourt, Brace and World, 1966. A fictitious experiment changes a man from retarded to gifted and back.

McKean, Kevin. Intelligence: New Ways to Measure the Wisdom of Man." *Discover* (October 1985): 25-41. An excellent, entertaining review of the history of IQ testing and of recent attacks on this limited measure of intelligence. Profiles the work of Howard Gardner and others currently attempting to redefine intelligence.

Oakes, Jeannie. *Keeping Track: How Schools Structure Inequality*. New Haven: Yale University Press. Students across the United States and throughout the world are put in educational tracks that can largely determine their life courses. Oakes examines the problems and possible injustices of tracking.

Simons, Carol. "A Long-Distance Ticket to Life: They Get by with a Lot of Help from Their Kyoiku Mamas." *Smithsonian* (March 1987): 44-53. Almost every high-scoring student in Japan's competitive system has a mother whose efforts seem superhuman.

Sternberg, Robert. *Beyond IQ*. Cambridge: Cambridge University Press, 1985. In this exploration of human intellectual capacities, Sternberg outlines cognitive processes used in problem solving.

Film

Stand and Deliver. Directed by Ramon Menendez. 1987. Math teacher Jaime Escalante
prepares Hispanic students from the barrios of East Los Angeles to pass the
Advanced Placement calculus test and convinces the Educational Testing Service
that the results are valid.

SEX AND GENDER

Different though the sexes are, they intermix. In every human being a vacillation from one sex to the other takes place, and often it is only the clothes that keep the male or female likeness, while underneath the sex is the very opposite of what it is above.

Virginia Woolf

Ulrike Welsch © 1989, The Boston Globe

Unit 17 looks at the similarities and differences between the sexes resulting from the complex interaction of biological and social factors. It contrasts the universal differences in anatomy and physiology with those learned and cultural, and reveals how roles are changing to reflect new values and psychological knowledge.

Psychologists study social play to determine whether differences between boys and girls are biologically innate, shaped by cultural experience, or both.

OBJECTIVES

After viewing the television program and completing the assigned readings, you should be able to:

1. Define and compare the terms *sex*, *gender*, *gender identity*, and *sex role stereotype*

2. Describe social learning theory as it applies to gender identity

3. Explain cognitive learning theory as it applies to gender identity

4. Define androgyny

5. Explain the role of hormones in determining sexual characteristics

6. Describe different gender roles in your home, classroom, or workplace

7. Explain the role that hormones play in male and female sexuality, and also discuss how these behaviors are influenced by psychosocial and cultural factors

8. Explain how the double standard, peer pressure, and sexual liberation influence sexual development in adolescence

READING ASSIGNMENT

After viewing Program 17, read pages 439–448 and 297–308 in *Psychology: Science, Behavior and Life*. Your instructor may also assign the anthology selections for Unit 17.

KEY TERMS AND CONCEPTS

As you read the assignment, pay particular attention to these terms, which are defined on the given pages in the text.

gender identity (439)   castration (298)
social learning (444)   androgen-blocking drugs (298)
gender roles (445)   hypogonadism (298)
socialization (446)   estrogens (299)
androgens (298)

The following terms are used in the program but are not defined in the text.

androgynous—having both masculine and feminine traits

cognitive developmental theory—the theory stating that children use male and female as fundamental categories and actively sex-type themselves to achieve cognitive consistency

developmental strategies—behaviors that have evolved to conform to the sex roles typical of the adult members of a species

sex typing—the psychological process by which boys and girls become masculine or feminine

stereotype—the belief that all members of a group share common traits

PROGRAM SUMMARY

From the first breath a baby takes, sex determines how he or she will be treated throughout life. Being male or female means we inhabit very different biological, psychological, and social environments. Program 17 looks at sex, the biologically based characteristic that distinguishes males from females, and gender, the cultural category that includes the psychological and social characteristics of being male or female.

From birth, life is full of gender messages and lessons that shape behavior. Boys and girls learn which behaviors are appropriate for their gender group and act accordingly. In our culture, they also dress differently, act differently, and often develop different interests and goals. These categories exist in the home, in school, in social situations, and in the workplace.

Although gender roles are often portrayed as polar opposites, psychologist Sandra Bem argues that people have both masculine and feminine characteristics, and in fact, this blend of traits she calls psychological adrogyny often results in greater behavioral adaptiveness.

Scientists have discovered that there are some universal behavioral differences between the sexes. Male children tend to engage in more rough play and gross motor activities. Female children are more likely to play mother, groom baby dolls, and engage in fine motor activities. This is true of people as well as other animals.

Neuroscientist Michael Meany explains that these sex differences in social play are evidence of how biology and psychology influence each other. Sex-role behaviors have evolved because different activities stimulate different brain regions. And the hormones affect the brain during prenatal development, causing sex-linked preferences to certain social activities. Another example of the interaction of biology and psychology in sex differences is physical health. Because men are more likely to drink, smoke, use weapons, and work in hazardous environments, they are more vulnerable to certain diseases, such as lung cancer, bronchitis, emphysema, and heart disease.

One example of sex-role behavior that has no biological basis is crying. It is acquired as part of the socialization process. Of course, both male and female babies cry. But as they grow, boys learn to hold back their tears while girls learn that crying is acceptable.

According to psychologist Jeanne Block, social gender messages affect the way children think about themselves and the world. Girls' activities are more supervised, structured, and restricted. They are raised to stay close to home, while boys are typically given more freedom to roam and discover the world.

But children also participate in shaping their own social environment. Eleanor Maccoby has studied how young boys and girls use sex as a basic category to sort themselves. In the classroom and on the playground, each group seems to have a distinct culture and style, including different language patterns. Gender identification serves as a powerful organizer of their social lives. Girls play house and boys play army. Girls play with dolls and boys play with trucks. These differences are apparent as early as nursery school.

There are positive and negative consequences to gender differences. Males have the freedom to innovate and explore, but their independence may cost them a sense of family intimacy or the security of belonging to a community. Females have the freedom to express their feelings and build a social support network, but they suffer social constraints on their intellectual and individual development. And a greater focus on their feelings and moods makes them more susceptible to depression.

Despite traditional gender stereotypes, researchers have never been able to link different social roles to innate sex differences. Any differences are more a matter of degree than a difference in kind. For example, in physical ability and sports, male and female performances overlap when their training is comparable.

It is important to recognize that our gender categories heavily influence our expectations, judgments, and behavior. These gender stereotypes narrow the options available to us. In fact, women and men are more similar than different in almost all psychological traits and abilities.

REVIEW QUESTIONS

Program Questions

1. According to research by Zella Lurin and Jeffrey Rubin, the difference in the language parents use to describe their newborn sons or daughters is primarily a reflection of

   a. actual physical differences in the newborns.
   b. differences in the way the newborns behave.
   c. the way the hospital staff responds to the babies.
   d. the parents' expectations coloring their perceptions.

2. What is gender?

   a. The biologically innate differences between male and female
   b. The psychological and social meanings attached to male and female
   c. The interplay between biologically based and psychologically based definitions of male and female
   d. The blend of masculine and feminine characteristics within an individual person

3. Which set of adjectives best characterizes the feminine gender role in the United States?

   a. Gentle, emotional, dependent
   b. Creative, intelligent, attractive
   c. Aggressive, independent, dominant
   d. Industrious, nurturing, ambitious

4. Which difference between the ways in which boys and girls play seems linked to sex hormones?

    a. Girls play with dolls.
    b. Boys engage in rough and tumble play.
    c. Boys play in larger groups than girls do.
    d. Girls build rooms, and boys build towers.

5. Michael Meany attributes the differences in the behavior of male and female rats to the fact that these behaviors "feel good" to the animals. The reason for this is that the behaviors

    a. increase hormone production.
    b. prepare the organism for its life tasks.
    c. stimulate certain brain regions.
    d. fit the preferred pattern of motor activity.

6. How does the health of men compare with the health of women through the life cycle?

    a. Men are more vulnerable throughout the life cycle.
    b. Women are more vulnerable throughout the life cycle.
    c. Women are more vulnerable only during their childbearing years.
    d. There is no consistent sex difference in health.

7. Which learned behavior in the masculine gender role poses a health risk?

    a. Having recessive genes
    b. Relying on social networks
    c. Being active in sports
    d. Drinking alcohol

8. According to Professor Zimbardo, what is the source of the behavioral difference between the sexes regarding crying?

    a. It is an innate difference.
    b. Initial innate differences are reinforced by parents.
    c. It is learned during the socialization process.
    d. We do not know the source.

9. What typically happens when a girl behaves in gender-inappropriate ways?

    a. She feels uncomfortable.
    b. She is praised.
    c. She is scolded.
    d. The behavior is not noticed.

10. According to Jeanne Block, the sociopsychological contexts for boys and girls tend to be different. One such difference is that the context for girls tends to be more

    a. home centered.
    b. achievement oriented.
    c. filled with risk.
    d. involved with same-sex peers.

11. What is one of the negative consequences of the masculine gender role?

    a. It makes men more vulnerable to depression.
    b. It imposes limits on intellectual development.
    c. It provides little sense of belonging.
    d. It encourages risk-taking behaviors.

12. According to Eleanor Maccoby, at about what age do children begin to prefer same-sex playmates?

    a. Two years old
    b. Three years old
    c. Four years old
    d. Five years old

13. Which sentence is more characteristic of girls' speech patterns than of boys'?

    a. "I can do it better than you can."
    b. "Do you want to come over to my house?"
    c. "Mr. Clark is the world's worst teacher."
    d. "Let's have a picnic."

14. Which statement about sex differences in psychological traits and abilities is best supported by research?

    a. There are no identifiable differences.
    b. The differences that exist are more a matter of degree than a difference in kind.
    c. The differences are the result of differences in brain chemistry and organization.
    d. The differences are arbitrary since they are the result of social learning.

Textbook Questions

15. A person's sense of being a male or a female is called a

    a. gender role.
    b. sexual orientation.
    c. gender identity.
    d. sexual role.

16. Sets of expected behaviors for males and for females are called

    a. gender identities.
    b. gender types.
    c. sexual norms.
    d. gender roles.

17. Although Sharon is genetically a male, her sex at birth was ambiguous. During early infancy, Sharon underwent surgery to have female-appearing genitals implanted, and she was subsequently reared as a girl. It is likely that during her development Sharon will make a

    a. satisfactory adjustment as a girl.
    b. poor adjustment, feeling like a girl but behaving like a boy.
    c. poor adjustment, feeling like a boy but behaving like a girl.
    d. poor adjustment, feeling and behaving like a boy.
    e. poor adjustment, alternating between male and female identities and behavior.

18. The social roles assigned to women and men

    a. are virtually the same in all cultures.
    b. have been virtually the same in all historical time periods.
    c. differ markedly across cultures.
    d. differ markedly across historical time periods but not across cultures.

19. Kevin, who plays with cars and trucks, knows that he "is male." Lauren and Taylor play with dolls and know they "are female." Each has established

    a. gender consciousness.
    b. sex knowledge.
    c. gender identity.
    d. gender role.

20. Societal standards appropriate for each sex are referred to as

    a. socialization.
    b. sublimation.
    c. gender role.
    d. gender identity.

21. The process by which society conveys behavioral expectations to an individual, through various agents such as parents, peers, and school, is

    a. education.
    b. acculturation.
    c. socialization.
    d. accommodation.

22. About 95 percent of the androgens secreted by the testes are in the form of

    a. progesterone.
    b. testosterone.
    c. estrogen.
    d. semen.

23. Behavioral differences between preschool boys and girls are primarily the result of

    a. different parent-child relationships.
    b. different amounts of hormones.
    c. different kinds of peer pressure.
    d. age.

24. Numerous studies have shown that castration

    a. causes diminished sexual activity.
    b. causes increased sexual activity.
    c. causes no noticeable differences in sexual activity.
    d. causes facial acne.

25. According to Bancroft and Davidson (1984), _____ play(s) an important role in male sexual motivation.

    a. progesterone
    b. antiandrogens
    c. androgens
    d. estrogen

26. The female sex hormone is

    a. progesterone.
    b. androgen.
    c. estrogen.
    d. antiandrogen.

27. Sexual arousal and expression in humans is influenced far more by
    _____ than by hormones.

    a. whether we are male or female
    b. our ages
    c. station in life
    d. psychological and cultural conditions

QUESTIONS TO CONSIDER

1. People organize their perceptions, expectations, and judgments around social schemas and scripts. How are sexual scripts related to gender roles?

2. How does gender-typing influence perceptions?

3. How do young children show that they are aware of their gender identity?

4. Research suggests that androgynous people are better adjusted than those who are traditional sex-role stereotyped. But critics contend that the masculine traits lead to higher self-esteem and better adjustment than does a combination of masculine and feminine traits. How can having masculine traits enhance a woman's self-esteem?

5. Many women writers have published under masculine-sounding names. Does the sex of the writer make a difference? Should it?

OPTIONAL ACTIVITY

1. Pick three close relatives or friends. How would your relationship with them be different if you were of the opposite sex? Which aspects of your personal identity and behavior would change? Which would stay the same?

ANTHOLOGY

When society views members of each sexual group as polar opposites, the groups are expected to be mutually exclusive. Men and women are expected to have different (and opposite) abilities, interests, and needs. As you read the following selections, think about your own character traits and abilities. Are they typically masculine or feminine?

Reading 37

This article describes the practice of testing women athletes to certify that they are female. But is the line between female and male as distinct as the testers think? Is biological femaleness being confused with femininity, as the author suggests? As you read the article, think about the implications of reevaluating not only the social categories but also the biological categories we think of as male and female.

Chromosome Count

By Alison Carlson

I am an athlete, and I am a woman. At least I think I'm a woman. But if I were among the dazzlingly gifted number of female athletes preparing to compete in Seoul, my gender, like theirs, would be considered suspect. So much so, that before any athlete is allowed to compete in women's events at the Games or in most other major international competitions, she must first submit to a "gender verification" test of her chromosomes. As a tennis pro who has competed on the regional level, I have never had to subject myself to this "Orwellian" inspection, nor contemplate the traumatic possibility of being told that I am not female. But this is precisely what has happened to other women athletes, despite the fact that gender is far too complex to be evaluated by a laboratory test.

Since 1968, the International Olympic Committee (IOC) has been screening the chromosomes of all women competitors, "to insure femininity in the competitors" and "establish equality among athletes." Passing the test, which is called the buccal smear, has nothing to do with the way a woman looks, her birth records, or her sense of self. Getting "certified feminine" depends on the results of microscopic analysis of cells, scraped from inside the athlete's cheek to determine the pattern of her sex chromosomes. Normally, the female pattern is XX, and the male is XY. But that is not always the case. And when an abnormality appears, the athlete is subjected to a battery of gynecological and clinical exams to decide whether she is "feminine" enough to compete. So far, it is estimated that a dozen women have been disqualified from Olympic competition.

Those numbers don't begin to tell the chilling story of what's happening to young girls who are being pretested today at lower levels of competition, or of the innacuracies in the test itself and the flawed assumptions about the very nature of sexuality, or the narrow definitions of femininity that its use is based upon. Neither do they reflect the havoc it wreaks in the lives of those who do not pass, or the stress the test imposes on female athletes on the eve of their competition. As Olympic high jump champion Debbie Brill, who was first "certified feminine" in 1972, says, "It is scary having to report to a 'sex control' station. You go through all these "what ifs.' You know you are a girl, but what if the test doesn't show that?"

Which is what happened to Eva Klobukowska. The Polish sprinter was the first woman to be disqualified by the test when it was used on a trial basis at the European Track and Field Championships in 1967. Klobukowska may have had some internal male organs due to a birth defect, which is not unusual. Estimates of the incidence of sex chromosomal defects range from one in 1,000 to one in 4,000 births. At one end of the spectrum are people who look female; while at the other extreme are those who can have some ambiguity in their sex organs and secondary sex characteristics and are almost always treated medically and surgically to produce as concordant a sexual identity as possible.

What the officials told the 21-year-old Klobukowska was that her test revealed an irregularity. Upon further examination, they said she showed "male-like characteristics." Despite the fact that she was neither hyper-muscular nor particularly more successful than her peers, their conclusion was that she had been competing "unwittingly as a man." Klobukowska was quoted as saying, "I know what I am and how I feel.... It's a dirty and stupid thing to do to me." After her dis-qualification, she went through severe and long-lasting depressions; it was rumored that she even submitted to surgery to try to cor-rect her internal abnormalities and retain her eligibility. Although Klobukowska was an Olympic gold medalist and world record holder in the 100-meter dash, her name was removed from the books, and all public recognition of her awards taken away. Today, she works for a Polish computer firm in Czechoslovakia and has broken off all contact with the sports world.

"What is so ridiculously sad about the whole affair is that she was probably just as much a woman as anyone else, especially if she had male internal organs that were re-moved and she was given the female hormone estrogen, which is standard procedure," says John Money, a psychologist at Johns Hop-kins who is one of the world's authorities on disorders of sexual differentiation.

So why are female athletes being subjected to this? Because of rumors about men masquerading as women, and of women "who were not really women" competing at the Games. Although these allegations were not unfounded, they were greatly exaggerated and reflected a fundamental ignorance of the biological conditions of women like Klobu-kowska, who were singled out.

There is only one documented case of a man masquerading as a woman at the Olym-pics. In 1957, Hermann, a.k.a. "Dora" Ratjen from Bremen, Germany, went public with the news that in the 1930s he had been forced to pose as a woman for three years by officials in the Nazi Youth Movement. Entered in the women's high jump in the Berlin Games in 1936, he qualified for the finals and came in fourth. And then in 1938 Ratjen went on to set a world record in the event at a lesser meet.

Other cases cited as justification for the IOC's sex-testing policy involved individuals who lived and competed as females, but later through surgery became males. Between the late thirties and the mid-sixties, there were reports that three track and field athletes and one top skier had sex-change operations after winning medals in women's competition. It was generally assumed that these athletes, described as "imposters" by the IOC, had had an unfair physical advantage.

As a result of those cases and the persistent rumors, the sex of some of the very dominant eastern bloc athletes came into question. Because of their strength and masculine appearance, suspicion focused on Tamara and Irina Press, two famous Soviet athletes who from 1959 to 1965 won five gold medals and set 26 world records between them. At the same time, men from one eastern Euro-pean nation were rumored to be binding their genitals and taking estrogen in order to develop breasts and pass for females in competition.

And so for the first time, at the 1966 European Track and Field Championships in Budapest, women were required to undress for what the press called a "nude parade" in front of a panel of gynecologists. All 234 competitors were inspected and all of them, including Klobukowska, passed. But several of those dominating eastern bloc athletes, among them the Press sisters, failed to ap-pear. Their absence was construed as confir-mation that they were afraid of failing the sex test.

By 1968, the visual check was not enough. A year after Klobukowska's very public dis-qualification, the IOC decided to adopt the newly discovered buccal smear test, which it considered a simpler, more objective, and more dignified method of distinguishing the sexes. The IOC Medical Commission further justified its use by stating, "It would be unfair in a women's competition to allow chromo-somally abnormal athletes with male-like characteristics."

From the first, concerned medical special-ists have protested using the buccal smear in this context. The American College of Physi-cians and the American College of Obste-tricians and Gynecologists recently passed resolutions calling for the test to be banned. Not surprisingly, critics are labeling the entire theory and practice of sex testing discriminatory—not just because men are not tested—but because athletes are disqualified on the basis of a postulated advantage that may not be an advantage at all. But at the very heart of the debate is the far more disturbing and complex question of whether testing should be done in the first place.

For 20 years, the Finnish geneticist Albert de la Chapelle has spearheaded a movement to get the IOC to reconsider its policy. He reasons that if the intent of the test is to exclude men and women whose body structure or muscle strength confers a "male-like" advantage, then "the buccal smear is the wrong test." He contends it catches some women with genetic abnormalities that bear no relation to any conceivable advantage in strength, while it fails to detect up to 90 percent of the women who might have such an "advantage," the majority of whom have normal chromosome patterns but increase their muscle bulk and strength by taking steroids or who have other disorders that give them a similar advantage.

Although all normal women and men produce both male and female hormones—it is their relative proportion that is important in sexual development—there are also genetically normal women with medical conditions causing an overabundance of the male hormone testosterone. One of these, congenital adrenal hyperplasia, accounts for many, if not most, innately hypermuscular women. Then there are women who have testosterone-producing tumors on their ovaries, which can induce "male-like" characteristics. Even some hermaphrodites, who are born with both male and female internal organs, have the female XX pattern. And there are men who have the XX chromosome pattern, although this is extremely rare. All of these people would pass through the chromosome screen undetected, would never be subjected to further examination, and would not be banned. Considering the IOC's standards, de la Chapelle points this out as "inconsistent" and "unfair" to those with similar characteristics who do get disqualified.

And what of those women with abnormal chromosomes who fail the test but have no hormonal or physical advantage? The most common example is a child born with the male chromosome pattern and testes but an impaired ability to either produce or respond to testosterone. Most are raised female and, if necessary, treated surgically and hormonally to correct their abnormalities.

As psychologist John Money explains in his book *Sexual Signatures: On Being a Man or a Woman,* "The easy assumption has been that there are two quite separate roads [to gender identity], one leading from XY chromosomes at conception to manhood, the other from XX chromosomes at conception to womanhood. But . . . scientists are uncovering a different picture. The fact is that there are not two roads, but one road with a number of forks where each of us turns in either the male or the female direction. You become male or female by stages. Most of us turn smoothly in the same direction at each fork."

If there is complete nonresponsivity to testosterone at each of the forks after the embryonic development of testes, the child develops as a female, except that she has no uterus or Fallopian tubes and is sterile. She has a vagina, and what is commonly perceived as female body proportions and muscle strength. Most of these people don't even know they have discordant chromosomes, and wouldn't find out unless they investigated their infertility or got tested by a sporting federation or at international competitions.

When a person is born with a high degree of apparent sexual ambiguity, it can be the result of having both ovaries and testes. According to prevailing medical opinion it is more than likely that all the historical cases of sex change cited as justification for gender testing were in fact not imposters, but hermaphrodites who were assigned to the female gender at birth.

An IOC magazine editorial asserted when the buccal smear was adopted that "the chromosome formula indicates quite definitely the sex of a person." But critics disagree, countering that a person's "genetic sex" is the least relevant parameter of gender. Once the chromosomes have given their message to the embryo to develop testes or ovaries at the first fork in the road, they never again play a role in the process of sexual differentiation. Hormone levels, internal and external organs, and overall body build all have greater influence on gender. Money, who considers psychosocial influences a major factor, says, "The label 'boy' or 'girl' has tremendous force as a self-fulfilling prophesy."

Asking, "How often do competitors wittingly seek to deceive the IOC?" an editorial in the *Journal of the American Medical Associa-*

tion took the position that genetic males raised as females universally believe they are women. "We physicians tell them so! To accuse such individuals of willful deception would be churlish."

"It is imperative that this minority of individuals not get discriminated against," added Dr. Jean Wilson, an endocrinologist who wrote a letter to the IOC in 1968 elaborating on the dangers of the buccal smear. "It would be better for individual athletes to receive a competitive advantage than for underlying diagnoses to be exposed in this cruel and heartless manner."

For a young girl, the news could be utterly devastating. In cases when a patient has to be informed of her condition, most doctors wait until she reaches her mid-twenties and is mature enough to handle it. Yet most of the athletes getting tested these days are in their teens. What Dr. de la Chapelle views as the worst consequence of the IOC's position is this testing of younger and younger girls, often in situations where there isn't even the guarantee of quality control. And technical inaccuracies in the test itself are not unusual. De la Chapelle estimates that between 6 and 15 percent of the time, individuals tested for the presence of a Y will score falsely positive, as was the case with U.S. swimmer Kirsten Wengler (see box).

Myron Genel, a pediatric endocrinologist who is an associate dean at the Yale University School of Medicine, is concerned about the philosophical implications of the test as well. Asking, "What makes a woman a woman?" Genel says, "What it comes down to is the definition of femininity. Should it be left to a handful of people at the IOC, most of whom are men, to decide who is 'feminine enough' to compete?"

The IOC Medical Commission says its intention is not to issue "ex cathedra" decisions about who is a man or a woman. Eduardo Hay, a 73-year-old gynecologist from Mexico City, is ultimately responsible for making all disqualification decisions at the Olympics. He emphasizes that the buccal smear was never meant to be more than an initial screen, and that it is always followed by more detailed chromosomal analysis, as well as gynecological and clinical exams. If the woman refuses these, she can quietly withdraw from competition. If she is disqualified, the IOC will help her invent an "injury" or some other excuse for withdrawal.

According to Hay, the IOC's aim is simply to prevent unfair competition. "At the moment when you have genetic abnormalities such as hermaphroditism, you also see anatomical differences. If there is a classically male-shaped pelvis and body configuration,

---

Y Doesn't Always Mark The Spot

The first time U.S. swimmer Kirsten Wengler went for a sex test the results went awry. In 1985 she was scheduled to compete in an international student swim meet in Japan. Gathered together for a coed team meeting, every girl but Kirsten was handed a certificate of femininity, or "fem card" as it is called. In front of the other athletes she was told by the team manager that she needed to go back to the lab.

Wengler, who was 21 at the time, said the "guys kidded me. But I knew I was a girl." At first she simply assumed it was a mistake. But when they retested her the doctors confirmed results showing the presence of a Y chromosome and said that she might not be able to have children. After some debate, she was finally allowed to compete, because the Japanese were not prepared to do the clinical and gynecological exams that are supposed to follow when the smear detects an abnormal pattern.

The full impact of the test results "really hit me on the plane home to Austin," said Wengler. "I was crying and

really freaked out. I thought I would never be able to have children and that something was wrong with me."

Fortunately, Wengler's father is a physician and her mother teaches at a medical school. They quickly arranged for more sophisticated tests at great personal expense. It took four months to get the results, and during that time Wengler was worried and depressed. "I don't know what I would have done if I hadn't been a 21-year-old biology major with doctors for parents," she said.

Wengler eventually learned that what the buccal smear had shown as a Y chromosome was in fact the presence on one of her autosomal or nonsex chromosomes of a protein that is similar to one in a Y. Although she now has her "fem card" and continues to compete at major events, Kirsten Wengler worries about other women who encounter similar results. "What about a poor girl from some backward country? She would probably go home, never find out about the mistake, and feel inadequate for the rest of her life."

then you can assume there is an advantage. You can see very well that men's records are better than women's, generally by a margin of 8 to 17 percent, depending on the sport. That difference overall is only on account of anatomical differences."

But to assert that a woman's "male-like" characteristics automatically account for her success dismisses the many interactive factors that contribute to athletic victory, such as training, intelligence, coordination, and discipline. According to Dr. Genel, not only is the assumption of advantage based on such anatomical measures scientifically unsound, but the issue of whether the presence of typically male traits creates an advantage is far from being settled.

John Money emphasizes: "The difference between male and female is not black and white; it is a biological continuum. I don't know of any statistical studies anywhere that could tell you what isn't overlap between men and women on anatomical scales.... Really, the range of difference within the same sex can be as great as that between men and women. Any dividing line is a matter of context."

Inevitably, drawing that line is a subjective decision. Just how much "male-likeness" is too much? When does it start to mean an unfair advantage?

Dr. Genel deems it absurd that the IOC is trying to guarantee such things as "physical equality," "unfair advantage," and "fair competition"—concepts that he says can't even be defined consistently in the first place. "If some women get disqualified for being extra strong, then why not also disqualify those with unusual height or more oxygen capacity?"

Or for that matter why disqualify only some women who have so-called genetic advantages? Genel cites the case of Flo Hyman, who suffered from Marfan's syndrome, a genetic disorder that causes extra height. At six feet five, she was one of the best volleyball players in the world. If anything, height is the anatomical parameter that correlates best with athletic success. Following the IOC's standards, should she have been disqualified?

If authorities begin selecting out designated bits of anatomy, John Money wonders, "What of the Masai with their huge long legs, or the Mexican-Indian tribals with their extraordinary oxygenation capacity? Who gets excluded?" He contends that "sports are

not democratic; they're elitist. The tallest play basketball, the shortest are jockeys. The ultimate would be to break the Olympics into biological classes and run them like the Westminster Dog Show."

Dr. Genel says, "If the test were applied across the board to men as well, people would quickly see how useless it is because it sure wouldn't tell which men had an unfair advantage." Although not convinced that someone who is an intersex is more successful athletically because of that condition, he concedes that if the results achieved by intersex individuals could be proven to be unattainable by "genetically normal women, then the IOC might have a leg to stand on." But the records of those athletes have consistently been superseded by women of normal genetic makeup, generally within an Olympics or two.

Not surprisingly, women athletes are divided on the subject. Long jumper Willye White had the world record she set at a U.S.-USSR meet in 1964 broken soon afterward at the same event by a Russian whose femininity was in question. Today, White unconditionally supports sex testing: "If she hadn't been a man I would have been the world record holder."

Kate Schmidt, a world-class javelin thrower who competed in the 1972 and 1976 Olympics, considers sex testing "just another us-against-them thing that is being done in the name of protecting women. It is Cold War mentality, because most of the athletes involved were eastern bloc." Schmidt would never protest the presence of people with birth defects, or make them feel bad for being good: "That is a sour grapes, ungracious, win-at-any-cost attitude. People like that are bad sports."

Heptathlete Jane Frederick says she doesn't believe the official explanation of the test. "I think they are just saying, 'You are so good, we can't believe you're a woman. So prove it.'"

The IOC's response to the debate? "If there is a better way, we would welcome suggestions," says IOC Medical Commission Chairman Prince Alexandre de Merode. After 20 years, the IOC has finally agreed to set up a "working group" to address the problem. Chairman de Merode promises that by Seoul the medical commission will have decided "how and when the IOC will look into the issue."

Dr. de la Chapelle, although a member of that group, is somewhat skeptical, saying: "For so long I have asked the IOC to reassess their policy, and every four years they tell me, 'Let us just get through these next Games, and then we will look into it.' I know the IOC means no harm, but their policy is misguided."

One of the suggestions sure to be made will be to replace the chromosome test with a simple physical exam by female doctors. Another might be the introduction of a hormone test for allowable testosterone limits, but that is fraught with the same technical and ethical inconsistencies engendered by chromosome testing. A postcompetition "appeal system" for cases where there is controversy has also been proposed. But the resulting publicity could potentially damage an unwitting athlete's psyche and reputation. Some just want to see testing dropped altogether.

Whatever is decided, the people the IOC claims it is trying to protect should be included in the discussion. To date, there has been no indication that women athletes have ever been asked.

Reading 38

Bias is subtle. When researchers analyze a situation scientifically they often come up with surprising results. This article reviews studies that have analyzed the way schools may be undermining the development of healthy self-esteem in girls. As you read, consider how you would design a study to investigate the work environment's influence on women's behavior. How would you differentiate between current and past influences?

Studies Link Subtle Sex Bias in Schools With Women's Behavior in the Workplace

By Sharon E. Epperson

What's holding women back as they climb the success ladder?

Classrooms may be partly to blame.

Overt discrimination it isn't, for schools are increasingly offering equal opportunities to girls and boys in both formal courses and extracurricular activities, including sports. But several studies suggest that, from first grade through college, female students are the victims of subtle biases. As a result, they are often given less nurturing attention than males.

Consider these findings from studies at schools in the U.S. and Britain. Compared with girls, boys are:

—Five times as likely to receive the most attention from teachers.

—Eight times as likely to call out in class, which helps to explain why they out-talk girls there by a ratio of 3 to 1. (When the teacher is female and the majority of the class is male, boys are 12 times as likely to speak up.)

—Twice as likely to demand help or attention from the teacher, to be seen as model students or to be called on or praised by teachers.

Researchers maintain that a chilly climate for women in the classroom undermines self-esteem and damages morale. They believe, too, that some of these patterns of student-teacher interaction may help set the stage for expectations and interactions later in the workplace.

Emotional Baggage

"Females aren't taught to be risk takers; they don't have the same autonomy as males," asserts Jane Ayer, associate dean of education and professor of counseling psychology at the University of Wisconsin, Madison. "And you take what you've learned about yourself in the classroom into the workplace."

In coed schools, researchers find that girls receive considerably less direct attention than boys. For instance, a study of teachers' interactions with pupils in more than a hundred fourth-, sixth- and eighth-grade math and language-arts classes found that boys receive significantly more praise, criticism and remedial help.

Reactions to both male and female teachers to their female students "aren't that great," says David Sadker, an American University professor of education who conducted the four-year study with his wife, Myra, also an education professor at American. Teachers often accept the girls' responses without offering constructive comment, Mr. Sadker explains.

"In the workplace," he argues, "women are less likely to present themselves as effective managers. A lot of it deals with passive roles" they assume at school.

In lower grades, other researchers have found, boys often also receive more attention through disciplinary action. These scoldings for disruptive activity can make boys "less sensitive to negative feedback from teachers" and may further their aggressive behavior, says Marlaine Lockheed, a senior research scientist for the World Bank who studied the matter while working for the Educational Testing Service in Princeton, N.J.

Yet another study, begun in 1981 by two researchers at the University of Illinois, has measured the self-confidence of 80 high-school valedictorians, salutatorians and honor students. The study found that, upon graduation, 23% of the men and 21% of the women believed they were "far above average" in intelligence. As college sophomores, only 4% of the women said they felt far above average, while 22% of the men rated themselves that way. By senior year in college, none of the women reported feeling far above average, compared with 25% of the men.

This apparent lack of self-esteem on the part of the women apears to be rooted in classroom interaction, says Bernice Sandler, executive director of the Association of American Colleges' project on the status and education of women. Researchers, she notes, have found that even in college classes "men receive more eye contact from their professors than women, are called on more often and receive informal coaching from their instructors."

Racial prejudice can make the situation even worse. "Minority women in higher education frequently face double discrimination—once for being female and once for being racially or ethnically different," noted a 1986 report by the college association's project on women. "For example, intellectual competence and leadership ability, along with other primary academic qualities, are associated not only with males but with white males."

A More Comfortable Setting

Researchers say sexual bias leads some women to opt for courses with a large female enrollment, where they will feel more comfortable voicing their opinions. Bertha French, a junior at the University of Virginia, Charlottesville, agrees. She notes that women usually dominate discussions in her mostly female French classes; the two or three male students don't speak up so much. "I think it's because it's not considered a masculine major," she says. In her male-dominated government classes, she adds, she and other female students sometimes feel intimidated.

At many schools, students, teachers and administrators often seem unaware of everyday inequities in the classroom. Faculty members may consider themselves too even-handed to discriminate.

For example, the Sadkers' study included a math teacher who was active in the National Organization for Women. She told the Sadkers she probably wouldn't benefit from their training sessions on sexism in the classroom because she had been concerned about the issue for years. After viewing videotapes of her classroom interaction, however, she said she was "stunned' to find that she was talking to boys more than twice as much as to girls, and praising them four times as much.

Such disparities are the reason some educators stress the usefulness of single-sex schools, which are nonetheless on the decline. All-girl schools and women's colleges "create a more positive learning environment for females, who don't have to fear failing in front of males," maintains the University of Wisconsin's Ms. Ayer. She says she believes the schools help females to get away from traditional social conditioning and give them freedom "to show what they can do."

ADDITIONAL RESOURCES

Books and Articles

Bem, Sandra. "Probing the Promise of Androgyny." In *Beyond Sex-Role Stereotypes: Readings Toward a Psychology of Androgyny*, edited by A. G. Kaplan and J. P. Bean. Boston: Little, Brown, 1976. A blend of masculinity and femininity (androgyny) may result in greater behavioral adaptiveness.

Benderly, Beryl L. *The Myth of Two Minds: What Gender Means and Doesn't Mean*. Garden City, N.Y.: Doubleday, 1987. Science writer Benderly set out to write a book on current research backing a biological basis for gender differences. Her findings, though, led her to conclude that most gender differences are rooted in cultural influences, not genes. A good synthesis of recent work on sex and gender.

Gilligan, Carol. *In a Different Voice*. Cambridge: Harvard University Press, 1982. Why do women tend to see moral dilemmas differently than men do? Are women weaker or less capable of seeing things logically? Gilligan's important work traces the moral voices of men and women to their different psychological development.

Kimura, D. "Male Brain, Female Brain: The Hidden Difference." *Psychology Today* (November 1985): 50–58. Women's brains may be organized like men's for some tasks, and more or less diffusely for others.

Kohn, Alfie. "Girl Talk, Guy Talk: How Speaking Patterns Reveal Our Gender." *Psychology Today* (February 1988): 65–66. Why do men and women speak in distinctly different styles? Is it because they relate to others and think about themselves in different ways?

Miller, Jean Baker. *Toward a New Psychology of Women*. 2d ed. Boston: Beacon Press, 1986. A book attempting to reinterpret the "weaknesses" of women as strengths.

Women on Words and Images. *Dick and Jane as Victims: Sex Stereotyping in Children's Readers*. 2d ed. Princeton, N.J.: Author, 1975. Storybooks heavily influence children's ideas about gender. This book examines how children are led to stereotype the sexes.

Films

Mona Lisa. Directed by Neil Jordan; starring Bob Hoskins, Cathy Tyson. 1986. A moving drama that explores the darker side of sexuality: the underworld of prostitution.

The Pinks and the Blues. NOVA #709, Time-Life Video. 1980. From moments after birth, baby boys and girls are treated differently. This film explores how environmental influences affect gender.

Tootsie. Directed by Sydney Pollack; starring Dustin Hoffman, Jessica Lange. 1982. An actor who disguises himself as a woman to get work sees himself and the world in a different light. Illustrates how both sexes can play both gender roles.

Victor/Victoria. Directed by Blake Edwards; starring Julie Andrews. 1982. Role-reversal, the other way round. Andrews masquerades as a man masquerading as a woman and becomes the toast of the town in 1930s Paris.

MATURING AND AGING

As a man advances in life he gets what is better than admiration—judgment to estimate things at their own value.

Samuel Johnson

Marianne Gontarz/The Picture Cube

Thanks to growing scientific interest in the elderly, research on aging has replaced many myths and fears with facts. Unit 18 focuses on what scientists are learning about life cycle development as they look at how aging is affected by biology, environment, and life-style.

Growing older can also mean psychological "adolescing"—developing psychologically to our full potential.

OBJECTIVES

After viewing the television program and completing the assigned readings, you should be able to:

1. Define adolescence and summarize the physical changes that take place in boys and girls during puberty. Compare the effects of early and late maturation on boys and girls in American society

2. Describe Lawrence Kohlberg's moral dilemma method of measuring moral reasoning and summarize his six stages of moral development

3. Describe Erikson's eight psychosocial stages and explain his concept of "life crisis"

4. Summarize the physical and cognitive changes that occur in early and middle adulthood

5. Discuss the current trends in marriage, single living, cohabitation, and childbearing and describe the societal factors that have encouraged these trends

6. Describe Levinson's periods of systematic and age-related changes in adulthood

7. Compare the research findings with the myths and stereotypes about the experience of late adulthood and aging

8. Discuss the effects of aging on health and sexuality

9. Describe the risk factors for an elderly person in a nursing home

10. Review several strategies for preventing and ameliorating some of the problems associated with old age

11. Describe the symptoms and the effects of senile dementia

12. Define thanatology and describe Elisabeth Kübler-Ross' five stages of dying

READING ASSIGNMENT

After viewing Program 18, read pages 453–481 and 437–439 in *Psychology: Science, Behavior and Life*. Your instructor may also assign the anthology selections for Unit 18.

KEY TERMS AND CONCEPTS

As you read the assignment, pay particular attention to these terms, which are defined on the given pages in the text.

puberty (454)
adolescent growth spurt (454)
gonadotrophins (454)
secondary sex characteristics (454)
secular growth trends (454)
Kohlberg's theory of moral
    development (457)

preconventional morality (457)
conventional morality (457)
postconventional morality (457)
identity formation (460)
age-based expectations (464)
climacteric (466)
menopause (466)

the double standard of aging (466)
crystallized intelligence (467)
fluid intelligence (467)
problem finding (468)
dialectic operations (468)
cohabitation (469)
the graying of America (474)
organ reserve (475)
genetic clock (programmed) theory (476)
senile dementia (477)
Alzheimer's disease (478)

activity theory (479)
disengagement theory (479)
life review (480)
trust vs. mistrust (438)
autonomy vs. shame and doubt (438)
initiative vs. guilt (438)
industry vs. inferiority (438)
identity vs. role confusion (438)
intimacy vs. isolation (438)
generativity vs. stagnation (439)
ego integrity vs. despair (439)

The following terms are used in Program 18 but are not defined in the text.

biological senescing—growing older physically, or biological aging

life-span development—developmental changes continuing throughout the life cycle

psychological adolescing—developing psychologically to full potential

selective optimization—making the most of what you have

PROGRAM SUMMARY

Until recently, many psychologists believed that there were few important developmental changes after adolescence. However, beginning in the 1950s, research on aging began to expose many myths about the extent of deterioration and despair among the elderly.

The concept of life cycle development was created by psychologist Erik Erikson. His framework describes eight psychosocial developmental stages in which individuals face specific conflicts that require balancing two opposite demands. Failure to resolve these conflicts can lead to isolation, feelings of unfulfillment, even despair (see Figure 11).

Daniel Levinson, another developmental psychologist, studies the life course of adults as a sequence of developmental stages. He has identified age-linked developmental periods and transition periods that coincide with specific age ranges.

Until we are old, most of us will have little understanding of what it is like to be old, and we rarely consider how society treats its elderly citizens. Social responses to the elderly range from indifference to fear to hostility. But although the processes of biological aging are inevitable, variables such as life-style, diet, and exercise can influence when and how fast they occur. Whether or not a person lives in a supportive community or has a sense of control over his or her life can also influence self-concept and attitude toward aging. Mental strategies may also increase an individual's self-worth and optimism.

Approximate Age	Crisis	Adequate Resolution	Inadequate Resolution
0–1½	Trust vs. mistrust	Basic sense of safety	Insecurity, anxiety
1½–3	Autonomy vs. self-doubt	Perception of self as agent capable of controlling own body and making things happen	Feeling of inadequacy to control events
3–6	Initiative vs. guilt	Confidence in oneself as initiator, creator	Feelings of lack of self-worth
6–puberty	Competence vs. inferiority	Adequacy in basic social and intellectual skills	Lack of self-confidence, feelings of failure
Adolescent	Identity vs. role confusion	Comfortable sense of self as a person	Sense of self as fragmented; shifting, unclear sense of self
Early adult	Intimacy vs. isolation	Capacity for closeness and commitment to another	Feeling of aloneness, separation; denial of need for closeness
Middle adult	Generativity vs. stagnation	Focus of concern beyond oneself to family, society, future generations	Self-indulgent concerns; lack of future orientation
Later adult	Ego-integrity vs. despair	Sense of wholeness, basic satisfaction with life	Feelings of futility, disappointment

Figure 11: Erikson's Psychosocial Stages
According to Erik Erikson, certain conflicts must be resolved at each stage in the life cycle in order for people to meet the demands of the next life stage.

(Based on Erikson, 1963; from Zimbardo—Psychology and Life, Scott Foresman and Co., 11th ed., 1985.)

Recent studies have shown that psychological deterioration is the exception not the rule of old age when there is no physical illness. Specialists have developed new strategic training methods to teach the elderly to recover earlier levels of inductive reasoning, spatial orientation, and attention. Behaviorist B. F. Skinner also believes that behavioral problems associated with aging can be overcome by learning specific strategies.

Though some problems can be overcome with training, brain injury and dementia are often permanent disabilities with devastating consequences. But they occur much less frequently than people generally think. Contrary to another popular myth, depression and anxiety are not more common among the elderly. In fact, the elderly do not show an increase in stress-related disorders despite an increase in stressful life events. And, if a person remains in good health, there is no decline in the ability to enjoy sex either.

If the latest research findings are generally optimistic about the state of the elderly, why does the stereotype of deterioration and despair persist? It may be because of the availability heuristic. Dramatic or vivid negative images are overrepresented in our memory so that we get a falsely exaggerated picture despite many examples of outstanding accomplishment and self-satisfaction among the elderly.

But there is also a very sad side of growing old in the United States. As the number of older people in the population increases, the percentage of those living in nursing homes will increase too. In many nursing homes, unfortunately, people suffer significant losses and are subjected to conditions that accelerate their physical deterioration, even death.

As we learn more about the elderly, we discover that many of these problems can be ameliorated by education, training, and environmental changes. We can also work on improving our attitudes toward aging and the elderly.

The first step is dispelling the myths and changing our culture's negative stereotypes about the elderly. Second, it is important to redesign the environment and health care delivery systems to make them more accessible and accommodating to the needs of those with limitations. Third, an early intervention program that identifies those with psychological and behavioral problems and provides psychotherapy and behavioral therapy is needed.

As older people become an increasingly powerful force in the population, we can expect the "graying of America" to bring about many positive changes.

REVIEW QUESTIONS

Program Questions

1. How has research on life-span development changed our idea of human nature?

    a. We see development as a growth process of early life.
    b. We see that a longer life span creates problems for society.
    c. We view people as continuing to develop throughout life.
    d. We regard development as a hormonally based process.

2. What does the term *psychological adolescing* mean?

    a. Coming into conflict with parents
    b. Entering into a senile state
    c. Being swept by emotional conflicts
    d. Developing to our full potential

3. What personal experience does Erik Erikson cite as leading to his redefinition of himself?

    a. Having a religious conversion
    b. Being an immigrant
    c. Surviving a major illness
    d. Getting married

4. According to Erikson, the young adult faces a conflict between

    a. isolation and intimacy.
    b. heterosexuality and homosexuality.
    c. autonomy and shame.
    d. wholeness and futility.

5. Which statement sounds most typical of someone in the throes of a midlife crisis?

    a. "I enjoy my connections with other people."
    b. "I'd like to run off to a desert island."
    c. "My work is my greatest source of satisfaction."
    d. "I accept the fact that I've made some bad decisions."

6. Daniel Levinson divides the life cycle into a series of eras. For which era is a major problem the hazard of being irrelevant?

   a. Childhood
   b. Early adulthood
   c. Middle adulthood
   d. Late adulthood

7. In her work, Diana Woodruf-Pak is studying the eyelid response and its changes in aging rabbits and people. Why has she chosen to study this particular response?

   a. The brain circuit involved is well mapped.
   b. It is typical of the cognitive deficits that occur with aging.
   c. Memory loss in this area is highly correlated with other forms of memory loss.
   d. Changes occur progressively, beginning in midlife.

8. When Pat Moore transformed herself into an 85-year-old woman, she was surprised by the

   a. compassion with which others treated her.
   b. lack of facilities designed to accommodate the aged.
   c. extent of ageism in our society.
   d. poverty faced by many older people.

9. How do psychosomatic symptoms tend to change with age?

   a. People develop more of them.
   b. The ones people develop are more severe.
   c. They tend to be more related to sleeping and less related to eating.
   d. They are less common.

10. What has Sherry Willis found about the abilities of older people with regard to spatial orientation tasks?

    a. Irreversible decline is inevitable.
    b. Training programs yield improved skills.
    c. Skills can be maintained but not improved.
    d. If memory loss occurs, other skills deteriorate.

11. About what percent of people over 65 suffer from senile dementia?

    a. 5 percent
    b. 15 percent
    c. 25 percent
    d. 40 percent

12. Assuming that a person remains healthy, what happens to the ability to derive sexual pleasure as one ages?

    a. It does not change.
    b. It gradually diminishes.
    c. It abruptly ceases.
    d. It depends on the availability of a suitable partner.

13. In general, how does the view of the elderly among the population at large compare with the actuality?

    a. It is more negative.
    b. It is more positive.
    c. It is generally accurate.
    d. It is more accurate for men than for women.

14. The results of the long-term study by Werner Schaie suggest that the people who do best in the later stages of life are people with

    a. high incomes.
    b. advanced degrees.
    c. flexible attitudes.
    d. large, close-knit families.

15. In nursing homes, the staff often behave in ways that treat the elderly like children. What is the effect of this treatment on most older people?

    a. It makes them feel more secure.
    b. It makes them behave in dependent, childlike ways.
    c. It increases their sense of autonomy and control.
    d. It improves their health by reducing their stress levels.

Textbook Questions

16. By cross-cultural standards, the prolonged period of adolescence in America is

    a. considered standard.
    b. not necessary.
    c. unusual by comparison.
    d. applicable to the "war-baby" generation only.

17. Physical traits that differentiate the sexes but are not directly involved in reproduction are called

    a. secondary sex characteristics.
    b. primary sex characteristics.
    c. homogeneous.
    d. heterogeneous.

18. Chuck is 10 years old and has already grown two inches taller than his age-mates. He has the beginnings of chest hair and his voice has deepened. We can predict that while Chuck is in school he

    a. will be less popular.
    b. will feel less secure.
    c. will be aggressive and rebellious.
    d. will be more popular and poised.

19. When compared to later-maturing girls, early-maturing girls tend to be

    a. more introverted and less social.
    b. more social.
    c. less conspicuous.
    d. shorter than boys their age.

20. When a person has cognitively matured to the point that they can explore "what if" possibilities, Piaget would say that they are in the

    a. sensorimotor stage.
    b. preoperational stage.
    c. concrete stage.
    d. formal stage of thinking.

21. According to Kohlberg, moral judgment that reflects social convention and "law and order" characterizes the

    a. preconventional level.
    b. conventional level.
    c. postconventional level.
    d. principled level.

22. _____ people look to themselves as the highest moral authority.

    a. Preconventional
    b. Conventional
    c. Postconventional
    d. Stage five

23. Which of the following will help maintain healthy parent-teen relationships?

    a. Teens should not question parents' values.
    b. Listen calmly, attentively, and nonjudgmentally.
    c. Restrict the testing of new ideas.
    d. Do not openly show love; it is too embarrassing.

24. The important role of peers in adolescent development appears to be

    a. a worldwide phenomenon.
    b. an American phenomenon only.
    c. applicable only to Western civilization.
    d. a female need only.

25. The tendency to associate certain appropriate behaviors with each phase of adult life is called

    a. social expectancies.
    b. stereotyping.
    c. developmental tasks.
    d. age-based expectations.

26. Which of our sense(s) remain(s) relatively unchanged as we move into our middle adult years?

    a. Vision
    b. Hearing
    c. Perception
    d. Smell, taste, and feel

27. Recent longitudinal studies concerning age and intelligence have found that

    a. there is no significant decline in intelligence until about age 60 or older.
    b. there is a significant intellectual decline beginning with young adulthood.
    c. intellectual decline is greatest in middle-age.
    d. a person's intelligence continues to improve throughout the life span.

28. Dan has discussed contradictory religious philosophies with friends and accepts the conflict and contradiction as natural consequences of living. Dan is cognitively operating at what Riegel calls the

    a. problem finding stage.
    b. concrete operations stage.
    c. dialectic operations stage.
    d. formal operations stage.

29. Erikson labels the life crises of the middle years

    a. midlife crisis.
    b. middle adulthood.
    c. generativity vs. stagnation.
    d. the Pepsi generation stagnation.

30. The dramatic increase in cohabitation has been attributed to

    a. economics.
    b. religious beliefs.
    c. the tendency to question traditional marriage mores.
    d. the threat of nuclear war.

31. Some studies show that marriages without children are _____ than those with children.

    a. more boring
    b. happier and more satisfying
    c. more self-centered
    d. more strife-torn

32. Which of the following is/are true of women over the past decade?

    a. There is a dramatic increase in their number in the work force.
    b. Those who enjoy their work have higher levels of self-esteem, emotional, and physical health.
    c. Those who are satisfied with their jobs also tend to be satisfied with their lives.
    d. All of the above.

33. Which sense, after its decline, can cause an older person to feel a sense of isolation?

    a. Hearing
    b. Vision
    c. Smell
    d. Taste

34. The fact that identical twins have very similar life spans seems to support the

    a. organ reserve theory.
    b. wear-and-tear theory.
    c. genetic clock theory.
    d. accumulating damages theory.

35. The most common form of senile dementia is

    a. organic amnesia.
    b. Alzheimer's disease.
    c. involutional melancholy.
    d. senility.

36. Marion Diamond (1978) suggests that brain cells can grow at any age in response to

    a. medication.
    b. vitamins.
    c. any stimulation that is novel and challenging.
    d. physical exercise.

37. Thelma is retired but she travels and occasionally takes care of her grandchildren. She is coping with aging according to the

    a. activity theory.
    b. disengagement theory.
    c. inactivity theory.
    d. drop-out theory.

38. One of the positive features of Erik Erikson's developmental theory is that it

    a. is a life span theory.
    b. deals with the unconscious mind.
    c. tries to explain abnormal behavior.
    d. is a psychosexual theory.

QUESTIONS TO CONSIDER

1. Define normal aging. How has science helped to differentiate between the normal processes of aging and the effects of illness?

2. What are the psychological themes unique to the middle years, sometimes called the midlife crisis?

3. How does intelligence change in later adult years?

4. How do changing social patterns affect adult life patterns?

5. How do social conditions help create the characteristics of adolescence and adulthood in the human life cycle?

6. How does becoming a parent help define the developmental stages of adulthood?

OPTIONAL ACTIVITIES

1. At what age will you consider yourself to be "old"? Define your personal concept of old age, and describe what you expect your life to be like. Describe the health status, activities, satisfactions, and concerns you anticipate in your late adult years.

2. Keep track of the images of people over 60, over 70, and over 80 that you encounter during an average day. Notice how older adults are depicted in television programs and advertisements. What conclusions can you draw about how popular images reflect the characteristics, abilities, concerns, and diversity of the over-60 population? What stereotypes persist? Is there evidence that images are changing?

3. Make a list of the labels used to describe people at various stages of life from infancy to old age. Which age group has the most labels? Compare the synonyms and modifiers for childhood to the words that help define adulthood. What might explain the difference?

4. Tape-record an oral history interview of a person over age 75, perhaps someone in your own family. (Be sure to obtain the person's permission for the taping.) Ask for comments about the technological and social changes he or she has observed. Ask about memories of important community, national, and global events. What have you learned that you did not know before?

ANTHOLOGY

Unit 18 emphasizes that aging is a physical, psychosocial, and cultural phenomenon. The following articles raise some of the personal problems and social questions at the heart of the process. As you read, think about your current stage of life and the various stages of members of your family. Are you optimistic about the future, both for yourself and for your family?

Reading 39

With middle age comes increasing awareness of the inevitability of aging and death. Confronting one's own mortality is one of the challenges of adulthood. Does mortality enhance life? The author of this column asks us to consider the alternative to old age—not early death but an extended life span. Consider the enormous personal and social implications.

But Would We Really Want to Live Forever?

By Chet Raymo

Why do we die? I'm not talking about death by accident, murder, war or disease, but the inevitable senescence that comes to us all, the decline into old age and death that no amount of care, wealth or connivance can delay. A lucky mayfly might survive for as long as four weeks, a turtle can live for 150 years, and a human being for a century, but when your number comes, the time is up.

Why aren't we immortal?

The question is not altogether frivolous. There is at least one good reason to wonder why we live for so short a time. Evolution should favor long life spans. The longer an animal lives the more offspring it is likely to produce (assuming no decline in reproductive capacity), and therefore the greater the chance that its genes will spread throughout a population. In Darwinian terms, the reproductively active immortal organism should be the fittest of all.

But maybe it's not that simple. Within most animal populations, predators drastically reduce the number of survivors before old age takes its toll. Among certain wild birds, for example, only a tiny fraction of the population survives into old age. A gene which causes senescence in birds will not be strongly selected against because the number of birds that reach old age is negligible.

The situation is rather different for human beings. Within the developed countries, especially, human beings are increasingly likely to die of old age rather than by violence or premature disease. In the lingo of the biolo-

gist, the survival curve for humans is becoming ever more "rectangular"—the percentage of survivors remains fairly constant with age until about age 70 and then plummets precipitously.

But what causes the rapid decline at three score and ten? Is the aging process triggered by genes? Or do cells in the body simply wear out by accumulating an unsupportable number of defects or waste products? At a recent International Genetics Congress in Toronto, Olivia Pereira Smith of Baylor College of Medicine in Houston reported data suggesting that genes do indeed cause aging and death. The work is described in the Oct. 7 issue of the journal Science.

Pereira Smith and her colleagues studied laboratory cultures of human cells (colonies of cells grown in a nutrient medium). Normal cell cultures become senescent and die after a certain fixed number of doublings. But gene mutations can lead to exceptions. Certain immortalized cell lines—cancerous cells, for example—will continue to divide forever.

By performing hybridization experiments on 26 immortalized cell lines, the Baylor group amassed evidence to suggest that as few as four genes might be responsible for senescence in normal cells. The group is now trying to identify the genes.

It's a long way from studying cell cultures in laboratory flasks to understanding entire organisms. Nevertheless, the report of the Baylor researchers inspires a bit of wide-eyed speculation. Biologists have acquired the ability to modify genes. Might it be possible someday to engineer a strain of humans who are not programmed for aging and death? Is immortality an option, not for us but for that future race of *Homo aeternus*?

Senescence in humans is a complicated mix of subtle and obvious changes, none of which scientists yet fully understand. But if aging and death are programmed by genes, then I wouldn't bet against the possibility that extravagantly long lifetimes can be engineered. Geneticists will certainly learn to tinker with the biological clock that ticks inexorably in every cell, and maybe, just maybe, postpone the alarm that announces decay and death.

The personal and social implications of immortality are staggering. If overpopulation is already a problem, what will happen in a world where individual human beings can live forever—assuming, of course, that they stay out of the way of germs, bullets, speeding automobiles and other external threats to life?

And would we want to live forever if we had the choice? Do we really envy Methuselah? Can you imagine a love affair lasting 900 years? Or 900 years of presidential debates? The Hyperboreans of Greek myth lived for a thousand years, free of ills, in a land of eternal sunshine beyond the north wind: they leaped into the sea like lemmings to escape boredom.

It is scary to contemplate what immortality might mean for the human species. I asked a friend if he would want to discover the Fountain of Youth: no, he said, but he wouldn't mind discovering the Fountain of Middle Age. For myself, I suspect that longer lifetimes would bring more grief than bliss. Natural selection had millions of years to perfect the cellular apparatus of life. The aging and death of individuals probably confers subtle adaptive advantages to a species. I doubt if the Ponce de Leons of genetic science will improve upon Mother Nature's plan.

Reading 40

Contrary to popular belief, it is not the hormonal changes of menopause that contribute to depression in midlife but the stresses of economic problems and other life demands. As you read this article, consider the implications of downplaying menopause as an important factor in women's lives.

What *Really* Bothers Women in Midlife

By Jean Dietz

An unprecedented study of women at midlife, based on five years of interviews with 2,500 Massachusetts residents, is dispelling some long-held myths and drawing a striking new picture of the stresses and strengths in this group of women.

One key conclusion that challenges conventional medical wisdom is that menopause does not precipitate depression. Contrary to the image of the Victorian woman retreating to her room with "vapors" attributed to "the change," the study indicates that menopause rarely plays a significant role in the health of women at midlife at all.

In addition, the Massachusetts Women's Health Study found that women whose husbands had recently died were no more likely than others to get sick, a finding that contradicts previous studies of the bereaved. While newly widowed women often were depressed, the study found that the physical health problems some experienced were not related to

depression but to economic factors: reduced income, loss of health insurance, loss of access to health care.

Instead of languishing by an "empty nest," it turns out that the typical woman at midlife is an extremely busy person. In the initial survey of 8,050 women from which the study sample was selected, two-thirds still had children living at home and 6 percent had an elderly parent living with them. Twenty-five percent were providing regular care for an elder relative. About 75 percent held fulltime or parttime jobs.

The federally-funded research was conducted by epidemiologists Sonja and John B. McKinlay of the newly-established New England Research Institute. The study is attracting widespread interest, in part because its findings are based on a large population of women chosen at random from street listings in 38 Massachusetts cities and towns. Earlier studies have usually been based on groups of women who had sought medical help for one reason or another, a group not representative of the population as a whole.

"For the first time, the McKinlays looked at 'normal' women instead of those you find in doctors' offices, women in an age group thought to be at greater risk for depression and heart attacks," said Dr. Isaac Schiff, chief of gynecology at Massachusetts General Hospital, in an interview. "By looking at women in the community instead of those who frequent hospital clinics because they are not feeling well, they found out that a lot of things are going on at this busy time in a woman's life, and that menopause is just a changing state.

Sonja McKinlay, who holds three master's degrees and a doctorate in mathematical statistics, is associate professor of community health at Brown University. Her husband is on leave as professor of sociology at Boston University.

Several specialists who have seen the results said the study may provide valuable understanding of issues that confront women at midlife, particularly depression, which often is attributed to hormonal changes.

Work proves to be a positive factor in the lives of most of the women, actually reducing the stress caused by family members. Although nearly all who work say that money is an important reason, most report that their jobs are interesting at least some of the time.

The study began in 1981–82 with a statewide survey of a sample of women 45 to 55 years old. Of the 8,050 women who responded to the initial written survey, 2,500 were selected for the continuing study. Each was interviewed every nine months, either by telephone or by mail, for nearly five years to monitor changes in health, work and family responsibilities.

The prevalence and origins of depression of women at midlife was a major focus of the research. Although 10 percent of the women studied were depressed at the time the study began, the researchers found that the onset of menopause, marking the end of fertility, had no effect on the rate of depression.

What did cause depression in these women was worry. And primary focus of that worry was their families, including the women's parents or parents-in-law, who were often very old; their husbands, particularly those who were sick or dying; and their children, usually teen-agers.

"There may be something in the old joke that "Insanity is hereditary—you get it from your kids," said John McKinlay, who jointly presented the findings with his wife at a recent meeting in Boston of the Society for Behavioral Medicine.

As the study continued, one new phenomenon that emerged was the return home of adult children, because of divorce or difficulty finding jobs or housing, an event found to be a source of stress and to affect the women's health.

Some factors help counteract depression, the study found. Having someone close who provides emotional support or practical help has a major effect, reducing by half the amount of depression attributed to worry.

The McKinlays, authors of a number of research reports, trained in their native New Zealand and worked in Scotland and London before coming to the United States in the early 1960s.

The couple recently left the Washington-based American Institutes for Research, a consulting firm, to start their own New England Research Institute in Watertown, which does multidisciplinary studies funded by government and private institutions.

Study Largest of Its Type

The Massachusetts Women's Health Study, described as the largest epidemiological study of a community sample of mid-aged women ever conducted, is supported by a grant from the National Institute on Aging. But it is strictly a McKinlay project.

The idea was conceived several years ago in Aberdeen, Scotland, when the couple met a researcher who had done a survey of British women who attributed no special health problems to menopause except "sweats and flashes." Sonja McKinlay decided further research was needed.

The findings of the new study strengthen the case against routine prescription of estrogen for women undergoing menopause who don't require it for specific problems such as osteoporosis.

"Estrogen replacement therapy has been viewed as a mental tonic by doctors," said John McKinlay. Instead of treating menopausal women as victims of a deficiency disease caused by lack of estrogen, the

McKinlays say, it's time for doctors to put more emphasis on seeking causes of depression independent of hormonal changes.

Dr. Malkah Notman, a Harvard professor of psychiatry at Cambridge Hospital, acknowledged the importance of the McKinlay's long-term studies. But Notman said she thinks the implication that doctors still widely prescribe estrogen as a treatment for depression in menopausal women is outdated.

"Many once shared the idea that a major source of self-esteem in women comes from their reproductive capacity. It used to be felt that if estrogen lost at midlife were replaced, women would feel more feminine. In some cultures, that's still important," Notman said.

Hormones in Combination

Some women at midlife are depressed, said Notman, but she thinks that the prescribing of estrogen as treatment for depression decreased some years ago when the use of estrogen alone was linked to uterine cancer. This risk now is avoided, she said, by using estrogen in combination with progesterone, another hormone. More frequently, she said, the hormones are prescribed in an effort to prevent osteoporosis.

But some obstetricians and gynecologists, including Schiff, suspect that the use of estrogen for a variety of reasons is on the rise again. So do some well-informed women.

"A woman in midlife who goes to a doctor complaining about not feeling well is likely to be told to take estrogen," said Diana Laskin Siegal, co-author of "Ourselves Growing Older," a new book by a group of Boston women on "aging with knowledge and power."

"It's not that some women don't need estrogen," she said in an interview. "But fatigue can look like depression. And doctors don't often think in terms of exercise or good nutrition to prevent osteoporosis, or simple things like wearing cotton nightgowns instead of nylon to help with sweats."

About 10 percent of women in the menopausal age group now take estrogen for various reasons, including treatment of depression, hot flashes and vaginal atrophy, according to Dr. Brian Walsh, a gynecologist at Brigham and Women's Hospital.

The Subject's View

Perhaps the most important point the McKinlays make is that women themselves do not look on menopause as a cause of depression.

"Persistently depressed women are repeat-users of medical care, those who regularly turn up in doctors' office," said John McKinlay. "But these visits are not because of menopause, but because of pre-existing depression. We found that those women who have been persistently depressed were twice as likely to report hot flashes, sweats and other menstrual problems."

The McKinlays said they intend to make further analyses of data and will continue the interviews until the women reach retirement age if they can obtain additional federal funding.

"Women in the middle are having a tough time of it today," he said. "Between caring for their elders, their children, and husbands who are beginning to realize they are not going to be such great shakes after all, women have got it rough. It's not surprising they feel tired and are so often misunderstood."

Reading 41

This article summarizes research that demonstrates the importance of novelty and intellectual stimulation for maintaining and improving mental capacities as we age. These studies provide crucial evidence that experience influences the brain throughout our lives. As you read, consider how these studies will change the practice of geriatric medicine.

New Evidence Points to Growth of the Brain Even Late in Life

By Daniel Goleman

Evidence is building that development and growth of the brain go on into old age. It was once thought that the brain was fixed by late childhood, according to innate genetic design.

As long ago as 1911, however, Santiago Ramón y Cajal, a pioneering neurobiologist, proposed that "cerebral exercise" could benefit the brain. But a scientific consensus that the brain continues to bloom if properly stimulated by an enriched environment was long in coming.

"Over the last decade, neuroscientists have become impressed by the degree to which the structure and chemistry of the brain is affected by experience," said Floyd Bloom, director of the division of neuroscience and endocrinology at the Scripps Clinic and Research Foundation in La Jolla, Calif. The new research seeks to provide a more detailed understanding of that phenomenon.

Investigations at several different laboratories have shown that environmental influences begin while the brain is forming in the fetus and are particularly strong in infancy and early childhood.

Among the most striking new evidence is a report published in a recent issue of Experimental Neurology showing that even in old age the cells of the cerebral cortex respond to an enriched environment by forging new connections to other cells. Marian Diamond, a professor of physiology and anatomy at the University of California at Berkeley, led the team of researchers who did the study.

In Dr. Diamond's study, rats 766 days old—the equivalent in human terms to roughly 75 years—were placed in an enriched environment and lived there until they reached the age of 904 days. For a rat, an impoverished environment is a bare wire cage a foot square with a solitary occupant; an enriched one is a cage a yard square where 12 rats share a variety of toys, such as mazes, ladders and wheels.

The elderly rats, after living in the stimulating environment, showed increased thickening of the cortex. This thickening, other research has shown, is a sign that the brain cells have increased in dimension and activity, and that the glial cells that support the brain cells have multiplied accordingly.

The brain cells also showed a lengthening of the tips of their dendrites, the branches that receive messages from other cells. This increase in the surface of the dendrites allows for more communication with other cells.

Previous studies have shown that enriched environments changed brain cells in a number of ways, these among them. While the specific effects differ from one region of the brain to another, in general the enriched environment has been generally seen to result in growth in the bodies of nerve cells, an increase in the amount of protein in these cells and an increase in the number of length of dendrites. In more fully developed dendritic spines, a part of the dendrite that receives chemical message from other brain cells is induced to further growth.

Moreover, as in the new study, the thickness of the cortex was seen to increase, in part because of an increase in the numbers of glial cells needed to support the enlarged neurons. Dr. Diamond's studies on the older rats show that many, but not all, of these effects continue into old age.

These changes, in Dr. Diamond's view, mean that the cells have become more active, forming new connections to other brain cells. One sign of what the increased brain cell activity signifies for intellectual abilities is that the rats in the enriched environment became better at learning how to make their way through a maze. Indeed, Dr. Diamond and other researchers recently examined specimens from Einstein's brain. The tissue samples, from parts of the cortex presumed critical for mathematical skills, seems to have unusually large numbers of glial cells.

More Neural Flexibility

What does this mean for the aging brain? There is much more neural flexibility in old age than we have imagined," said Roger Walsh, a psychiatrist at the University of California medical school at Irvine, who has done research similar to Dr. Diamond's. "The changes in brain cells have been found in every species investigated to date, including primates. They certain should occur in humans as well."

"In my work," Dr. Walsh added, "I've

found that an enriched environment in late life can largely compensate for brain cell deficiencies from earlier deprivations."

"We've been too negative in how we view the human brain," Dr. Diamond said in an interview. "Nerve cells can grow at any age in response to intellectual enrichment of all sorts: travel, crossword puzzles, anything that stimulates the brain with novelty and challenge."

Still, there seems to be limits to the degree to which the brain can respond to experience. Richard Lerner, in "On the Nature of Human Plasticity" (Cambridge University Press), notes, for example, that the impact of environmental enrichment on brain cells seems to diminish with age, although it continues into old age, an effect Dr. Diamond has noted in her research.

The effects of enriched environments on the brain are but part of a larger investigation of the impact of life's experiences on the brain, and the picture is not always positive.

"Brain plasticity can operate for better or for worse," said Jeannine Herron, a neuropsychologist at California Neuropsychology Services in San Rafael. Dr. Herron has organized a conference to be held later this month at which Dr. Diamond and other researchers will describe their findings.

Tests on Vision of Kittens

Perhaps the most frequently cited example of how experience—or the lack of it—can have a negative effect on the brain is the work of David Hubel. Dr. Hubel, who will also speak at the California conference, won a Nobel Prize for his research on the visual cortex.

As part of his research, Dr. Hubel showed that if the eye of a growing kitten is kept shut so that it is deprived of its normal experience, the cells that would ordinarily register what that eye sees will develop abnormally.

The notion that certain experiences go hand in hand with the growth and development of the brain has been demonstrated in other research, as well. For example, Arnold Scheibel, a professor of anatomy and psychiatry at the University of California at Los Angeles, has found that the cells in the speech centers of infants undergo a growth burst, in which they form many new connections to other cells, just at the time the infant is beginning to respond to voices, between 6 and

18 months, as the infant begins to grasp that words have meanings, this growth accelerates.

Part of this explosion of growth, Dr. Scheibel proposes, may be primed by the infant's interactions with adults, who stimulate the centers for speech by talking to the infant.

The main changes that occur during this growth in the cells of the speech centers are in the ensemble, the projecting branches of the cell that spread to send and receive messages from other cells. "The dendritic projections are like muscle tissue," Dr. Scheibel said. "They grow more the more they're used."

"Even in adulthood," he added, "if you learn a new language, it's dendritic fireworks."

Responses to Injury

The brain's ability to adapt to circumstances can also be seen in its response to injury. Patricia Goldman-Rakic, a neuroanatomist at Yale University medical school, is one of many researchers who have shown that brain cells, within limits, can rearrange themselves to compensate for a brain injury.

"The new connections that occur after an injury to the brain show that the brain's anatomy is not rigidly fixed," Dr. Goldman-Rakic said in an interview. "The uninjured cells reroute how they grow and interconnect. This ability is most prominent during infancy, when neurons are still growing. It doesn't go on forever, but we don't yet know precisely at what point in later life the brain no longer can compensate in this way. We need to more fully understand normal brain maturation first."

Norman Geschwind, a noted neuroanatomist at Harvard medical school who died [in 1985], had been pursuing evidence suggesting that the experiences of a mother can have a lasting effect on the structure of the developing fetus's brain.

In a series of articles published posthumously in the most recent issues of Archives of Neurology, Dr. Geschwind, with Albert Galaburda, a colleague at Harvard Medical School, proposes that the infant brain is shaped in crucial ways by the level of testosterone, a male sex hormone, present in the intrauterine environment at different stages of fetal development.

At crucial points in the growth of the fetus, brain cells are formed and then migrate to the part of the brain ordained by a genetic plan. In certain parts of the brain these patterns of migration can be affected by the presence of sex hormones, particularly testosterone.

Testosterone levels in the fetus can vary with such factors as the amount of psychological stress the mother feels, maternal diet and possibly even the season of the year.

The main effects of testosterone, according to Dr. Geschwind and Dr. Galaburda, are in the areas of the brain that control such skills as speech, spatial abilities and handedness. One of the key effects of testosterone is in determining the side of the brain on which the centers that control such skills will be located.

When the process goes awry, according to the theory, the result can be problems such as dyslexia, on the one hand, or unusual talents, such as mathematical giftedness, on the other.

These effects are more marked among males, in part because the brains of males develop more slowly than those of females, and in part because testosterone plays a direct role in the growth of certain areas of the male brain. The unusual patterns of brain formation are most common, the theory holds, among left-handed males.

Before his death, Dr. Geschwind found from autopsies of people who had severe dyslexia in childhood that the parts of the cortex that control speech had abnormal cell development along the lines predicted by his theory.

ADDITIONAL RESOURCES

Books and Articles

Blythe, R. *The View in Winter: Reflections on Old Age*. New York: Harcourt Brace Jovanovich, 1979. First-person accounts of how individuals experience the process of aging.

Daniels, Pamela, and Kathy Weingarten. *Sooner or Later: The Timing of Parenthood in Adult Lives*. New York: Norton, 1982. The characteristic issues, advantages, and drawbacks of having children at different stages of adult life.

Erikson, Erik. *The Life Cycle Completed: A Review*. New York: Norton, 1982. A compact explanation of Erikson's psychosocial theory.

Erikson, Erik, Joan M. Erikson, and Helen Kivirich. *Vital Involvement in Old Age*. New York: Norton, 1986. Interviews with older people show that vitality is possible in the last stage of psychosocial development.

Kübler-Ross, Elisabeth. *Death: The Final Stage of Growth*. New York: Simon & Schuster, 1975. Why is death treated as a taboo subject? How do we accept the deaths of those close to us—or prepare for our own? This book explores how different cultures answer such universal questions.

Levinson, D. *Seasons of a Man's Life*. New York: Knopf, 1978. Presents a stage theory of adult development through individual case studies.

Moore, Pat. *Disguised*. Waco, Tex.: Word Books, 1985. The true story of a young reporter who assumed various disguises in order to study the obstacles and frustrations experienced by old women.

Neugarten, Bernice, and Dale Neugarten. "The Changing Meanings of Age." *Psychology Today* (May 1987): 29–33. What does it mean to "act your age"? Past assumptions about aging are being challenged.

Schanback, Mindy. "No Patience for Elder Patients." *Psychology Today* (February 1987): 22. A study of how physicians interact with older patients reveals ageism—a system of false, destructive beliefs about the elderly.

Sekuler, Robert, and Randolph Blake. "Sensory Underload." *Psychology Today* (December 1987): 48–51. Experts describe how perception changes with age, and provide suggestions for modifying the physical and social environment to improve safety and quality of life for people with various sensory losses.

Sheehy, Gail. *Passages: Predictable Crises of Adult Life*. New York: Dutton, 1976. A book based on interviews that reveal the life patterns of adult men and women.

Simon, Cheryl. "Age-Proofing the Home." *Psychology Today* (December 1987): 52–53. Suggestions for adapting environments to enhance vision, hearing, and mobility.

Films

To Live Until You Die: The Work of Elisabeth Kübler-Ross. NOVA #1013, distributed by Time-Life Video. 1983. A profile of Elisabeth Kübler-Ross, a psychiatrist who challenges prevalent attitudes about aging and death.

The following popular films illustrate the diversity and vitality of older people:

Cocoon. Directed by Ron Howard. 1985.

Harold and Maude. Directed by Hal Ashby. 1972.

On Golden Pond. Directed by Mark Rydell. 1981.

The Trip to Bountiful. Directed by Peter Masterson. 1985.

The Whales of August. Directed by Lindsay Anderson. 1987.

THE POWER OF THE SITUATION

This man is dangerous. He believes what he says.

Joesph Goebbels on Adolf Hitler

UPI/Bertmann Newsphotos

Is everyone capable of evil? Unit 19 investigates the social and situational forces that influence our individual and group behavior and how our beliefs can be manipulated by other people.

Adolf Hitler created a social-political structure that transformed rational individuals into blindly obedient masses.

OBJECTIVES

After viewing Program 19 and completing the assigned readings you should be able to:

1. Compare the effects of the different leadership styles studied in Lewin's experiment

2. Discuss the principles of social perception with particular reference to first impressions, attribution theory, and the fundamental attribution error

3. Discuss the principles of social conformity with particular reference to Asch's research

4. Discuss the situational conditions that promote obedience with particular reference to Milgram's research

5. Describe Zimbardo's prison experiment and discuss his conclusions about how people are trapped by roles and situations

6. Outline the factors that contribute to interpersonal attraction

7. Describe the different theoretical approaches to the understanding of interpersonal aggression

8. Describe and evaluate the different views on the effects of exposure to reports and portrayals of violence in mass media

9. Discuss the ethical issues posed by experimental research such as Zimbardo's prison experiment and Milgram's obedience experiment

READING ASSIGNMENT

After viewing Program 19, read pages 660–700 in *Psychology: Science, Behavior and Life*. This textbook reading covers Units 19 and 20. Your instructor may also assign the anthology selections for Unit 19.

KEY TERMS AND CONCEPTS

As you read the assignment, pay particular attention to these terms, which are defined on the given pages in the text.

diffusion of responsibility (661)
bystander apathy (661)
social psychology (661)
social perception (662)
implicit personality theories (664)
central traits (665)
halo effect (665)
attribution theory (665)

correspondent inference theory (667)
covariation principle (667)
fundamental attribution error (668)
false consensus bias (670)
illusion of control (670)
attitudes (671)

balance theory (677)
cognitive dissonance theory (677)
persuasion (678)
conformity (685)
compliance (687)
foot-in-the-door technique (688)
door-in-the-face technique (688)
obedience (688)

prejudice (681)
stereotypes (682)
discrimination (682)
ingroup bias (682)
outgroup (682)
sociobiology (693)
frustration-aggression hypothesis
  (695)

The following terms are used in Program 19 but are not defined in the text.

autocratic—governed by one person with unlimited power

blind obedience—an unquestioning compliance with authority

democratic—practicing social equality

laissez-faire—allowing complete freedom, with little or no interference or guidance

legitimate authority—a form of power exercised by someone in a superior role such as a teacher or president

PROGRAM SUMMARY

During the 1930s and 1940s, evil seemed to have taken over much of the world. Millions of ordinary people became willing agents of fascist governments dedicated to genocide. The Holocaust took place almost 50 years ago, but accounts of massacres, terrorism, torture, and cruelty are still in the news every day. Are these horrors the work of sadists and madmen? Or are they perpetrated by ordinary people, people like us? Program 19 attempts to provide some answers to these questions.

While most of psychology tries to understand the individual, social psychology looks at human behavior within its broader social context. Efforts to understand how dictators mold the behavior of individuals gave birth to this field. Its practitioners began to analyze how leaders, groups, and culture shaped individual perceptions, attitudes, and actions.

One group of social psychologists began by studying the power of persuasive speeches. Another group looked at the nature of prejudice and the authoritarian personality. A third team, headed by Kurt Lewin, studied how leaders directly influence group dynamics. Lewin's team trained men to lead groups of boys, using one of three styles of leadership: autocratic, laissez-faire, and democratic. The results suggested that the leader's style, not personality, determined how the boys behaved.

Understanding conformity is another important goal of social psychologists. In a series of visual perception tests, Solomon Asch discovered that nearly a third of the subjects were willing to go along with the majority's wrong judgment to avoid seeming "different" (see Figure 12).

Another researcher, Stanley Milgram, concluded that virtually all of us are capable of blind obedience to authority. In various versions of an experiment, hundreds of subjects—men and women, young and old—delivered what they believed were severe

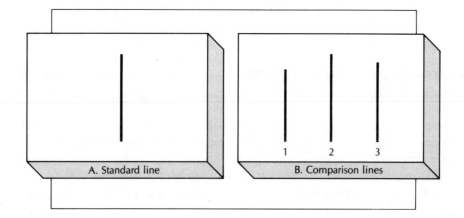

Figure 12: Asch's Study on Conformity
When test subjects were asked which line on Card B was the same length as the line on Card A, nearly a third chose a line that was obviously incorrect to avoid seeming different from the group.

shocks to innocent people rather than disobey authority. Milgram demonstrated that anyone has the capacity for evil if the situation is powerful enough.

Philip Zimbardo's Stanford Prison Experiment also demonstrated the effect of social situations on human behavior. In the study, college students were assigned to play the roles of either prison guards or prisoners. The situation was so powerful that these bright, healthy students actually took on the personalities of sadistic guards and despondent prisoners. In fact, the experiment, which was meant to last two weeks, had to be terminated after six days because of the extremely disturbing results.

Social influence can be positive as well. Researcher Tom Moriarity showed how apathy can be turned into action simply by asking for assistance from another person, even a total stranger. And Ellen Langer, in her experiments with ROTC cadets training to be fighter pilots, demonstrated that treating people with greater respect and professionalism can actually improve their performance.

Clearly, manipulating even small or seemingly minor aspects of social situations can bring out the best or worst in human nature. But most of us are too quick to blame people for their problems and to give them credit for their successes. We tend to overemphasize the importance of personality traits and to discount how easily people are influenced by the power of situations.

The experiments in Program 19 reveal much about human nature, but they also raise an important ethical question: how far can researchers go when a study calls for deceiving, manipulating, or humiliating their subjects? Research goals and procedures must meet ethical standards to protect study participants from distress or unnecessary deception. They must also maintain the integrity of psychological research. Many of the experiments in this program would not be permitted under today's strict guidelines.

REVIEW QUESTIONS

Note: Review Questions for Units 19 and 20 are provided in Unit 20.

QUESTIONS TO CONSIDER

1. Some psychologists have suggested that Milgram's subjects must have suffered guilt and loss of dignity and self-esteem, although they were told later that they hadn't actually harmed the learner. Follow-up studies to the prison experiment revealed that the subjects had not suffered long-term ill effects. What psychological principle might explain these outcomes? Did the value of the research outweigh the risks for the subjects? Would you participate in such experiments?

2. The doctor-patient relationship is one in which many people feel trapped by situational power. The idea of patients' playing a more active role in their own medical care threatens the power of many doctors and contradicts the stereotype of the patient who passively obeys orders. Think about the relationship you have with your doctor. Imagine a situation in which you would question your doctor's authority. How would you do it? How would you feel about it? What might inhibit you? And how might you overcome your hesitations?

3. In Zimbardo's prison experiment, students were randomly assigned the role of guard or prisoner. All participants in the study were surprised when the true identities of the guards and prisoners were erased during the course of the experiment. Each of us plays many roles: child, spouse, friend, student, parent, boss, employee, citizen, consumer, sibling. Do you feel that any of the roles you play conflict with your "true identity"? How do you know what your true identity is?

4. Think about your own experiences in school, at work, and in group situations. Consider which factors bring out the best and worst in you. Recall and compare examples of how teachers, bosses, or leaders brought out positive and negative aspects of your personality.

5. What is the difference between respect for authority and blind obedience? How do you tell the difference? How would you explain the difference to a child?

OPTIONAL ACTIVITIES

1. Architects and interior designers use specific elements—furnishings, lighting, color, seating arrangements—to encourage certain behaviors and to discourage others. Compare the comfort level of chairs in various public places. Which chairs are designed to encourage lingering or to discourage loitering? What types of people use the spaces? What physical changes would influence who uses the space and how they behave there?

2. Norms of social behavior include "social distances" that we place between ourselves and friends, acquaintances, and strangers. Observe and compare the social distance you maintain between yourself and family members, friends, and strangers. Purposely change how close to them you would normally stand. Observe their responses. Does anyone mention it? Do others adjust their positions to achieve normal distances?

ANTHOLOGY

The following readings illustrate the issues of obedience, conformity, and social influence. As you read, look for the situational factors that influence individual and group behavior. Think about how you might react in similar situations.

Reading 42

This selection describes one person's experience when he decided to blow the whistle on corporate wrongdoing. Like many who choose not to conform, he was criticized and ostracized. The author suggests that his biggest crime was not being a team player. Imagine that you are a loyal, hard-working employee of a large corporation and you discover that something corrupt or dangerous is going on. What do you do? What forces would you have to resist?

A Whistle-Blower

By Don Rosendale

We passed on 52d Street like strangers, avoiding each other's gaze. He had once recruited me as vice president of a major American corporation and then moved on. I, too, had left the company, but under decidedly less pleasant circumstances.

I backtracked, caught his elbow and reminded him of the junction where our lives had crossed. We chatted pleasantly until he blurted out: "You should have *known* better. You should have known you can't blow the whistle in a major corporation and survive."

It started innocently enough, on a blustery April Wednesday: One of the men who worked for me came to my office, asking me to approve routine bills. Some of the bills didn't seem right. I asked questions. I didn't like the answers. Each evasion led to another question that had to be asked. The other man sat fidgeting on my couch; he clutched at the bills and broke into a sweat.

I spent the next 48 hours poring over computer printouts. I found that almost a million dollars had been paid to a firm I had never heard of, for work that I seriously doubted had ever been performed. By the weekend, I felt compelled to go to the home of the corporation's chairman. I apologized for bothering him away from the office (a major sin in that corporation) but, spreading invoices and canceled checks across his living room carpet, I took him through what I'd discovered. He seemed concerned. He promised he'd help me get to the bottom of the matter. He put his hand on my shoulder and lent me a raincoat to ward off a spring shower. A few weeks later, I was out of a job.

I always realized that whistle-blowing could lose me my job, yet an irrational part of my brain kept telling me that I would, in fact, be commended for stanching a torrent of cash pouring from a corporation that could ill afford to lose it. I knew, too, that if I didn't report what I suspected and thus end the scheme, I would be breaching my responsibilities as an officer of the company; from that day forward, anyone who confronted me with the fact would *own* me. I had no choice but to press on.

The company's internal auditors were reluctant at first, but, when forced to investigate, they acted like terriers after a cornered fox. One about whom I'd raised questions came to me. It was pointless to continue the audit, he said; he would readily admit that he'd made a duplicate payment, in the high five figures, to a company supplier. He'd done so, he said, with the intent of "helping to keep a valuable supplier in business." I went to a senior manager of the company and asked that the man be fired on the spot. No, came the answer. The man's admission was not enough; the company believed in due process, and a thorough investigation was still warranted.

Grown men, seasoned executives, people who could tear an aide to pieces in a moment, sat around polished boardroom tables and argued, with straight faces, that though large sums of money were missing, there was no evidence that anyone had actually done anything wrong, no proof that any employee had "personally benefited" from the expenditures. There has been massive "bad judgment," but certainly no grounds to dismiss anyone. A lawsuit to recover some of the funds? It would cost too much and bring bad publicity.

Within weeks, one of my closest associates, a man who had diligently helped me unravel the trail of invoices, was chastising me for having blown the whistle. The company was in trouble, he said, survival was paramount, my actions had only distracted top management from more important tasks.

The company's internal auditors turned on me next. The whole cancer was *my* fault, they contended. I should have caught it sooner. I had been too lenient. This should not have surprised me. By uncovering practices that had gone unnoticed for a decade, I had caused them a major embarrassment.

There was a final showdown. I could have stormed from the office and headed for the Securities and Exchange Commission, but I neither felt nor acted like a hero. I negotiated a year's "golden handshake" and left quietly. (I had, it should be noted, by this time consulted with a law firm, which counseled me that I had fulfilled my duty by telling the chairman, and had no obligation to take the matter further.)

The path I chose was brutal on my family and cost me tens of thousands in lost income. It also meant that I'd never again work in a corporate environment. You can negotiate a "golden handshake," but it doesn't guarantee a reference. There is always the nuance, the raised eyebrow, the inflection that means, "Well, if you really want to know. . . ." But I've learned there is life outside the corporate world, life without corporate jets and stock options, limousines and expense accounts, and I've built a new career without them.

Last Christmas, I received a letter from one of my oldest friends, an Englishman with whom I often share thoughts and experiences. He and his wife remained baffled, he wrote, by what had gone wrong: "We still can't understand. You report a major shortage of funds at a corporation, and it's *you* who has to leave?"

I tried to explain it to him: Corporations, most of them anyway, are male-bonding fraternities made up of team players, men who blend in, men who don't rock the boat. I had been the antithesis of all those things. The term "whistle-blower" has no gender, but to snitch is not considered manly; "one of the boys" is never a tattletale.

I have a recurring dream: It's a dark and nasty night; I'm at one of those roadside telephone booths, with an important call to make, but the person inside won't give up the phone. When he does, I have only one quarter; I drop it, pick it up and put it into the slot; the phone malfunctions. I press the buttons futilely, some times garbling the number I want, sometimes getting a wrong number—but no matter what I do, my call won't go through.

Having learned, the painful way, that there are no "right" choices for a whistle-blower—only a series of choices that are all "heads they win, tails I lose"—would I, confronted with the choice again, make the same decision? I'd like to think that I would, but I'd also like to think that, this time, someone would answer the phone.

Reading 43

Psychologists are interested in the human capacity for good as well as the potential for evil. This article describes research into the sources of altruism. As you read, consider how different researchers define altruism and what personal and situational factors they believe contribute to its expression.

Great Altruists: Science Ponders Soul of Goodness

By Daniel Goleman

It was still dark that morning in 1942 when the Gestapo rousted from bed the Jews of Bobawa, a Polish village. In the confusion, 12-year-old Samuel Oliner slipped away and hid on a roof, still in his pajamas. The next afternoon, when he dared to look around, the ghetto was silent. The Jews of Bobawa, murdered that day, then were lying in a mass grave in the nearby countryside.

Samuel found some clothes in an empty house and, skirting German patrols and Polish looters, fled to the country. There, after walking for two days, he found his way to the farmhouse of Balwina Piecuch, a peasant woman who had been friendly with his family. Mrs. Piecuch knew, when Samuel knocked at the door, that she would be shot if the Germans found her harboring a Jew. Without hesitating, she took Samuel in.

Balwina Piecuch taught Samuel the rituals of Polish Catholic life—how to go to confession, how to pray, catechism. With her help, Samuel posed as an impoverished Polish stable boy in search of work and a place to live. Thus Samuel survived the war.

Exemplars of Human Goodness

By some estimates, there were as many as 200,000 Jews who, like Samuel Oliner, were saved from the Nazis by non-Jewish rescuers. In Berlin 5,000 Jews survived through the combined efforts of tens of thousands of Germans, many of whom fooled the Gestapo by moving Jews from hiding place to hiding place.

Now, in a remarkable project, researchers are reaching into the caldron of good and evil that was World War II to retrieve for study those examplars of human goodness, the non-Jews who, like Mrs. Piecuch, risked their lives to help Jews survive the Nazis.

The director of the project is Samuel Oliner, now a sociologist at Humboldt State University in Arcata, Calif.

"We want to find the common threads among those few who helped, and the differences between the rescuers and those others who might have helped but chose to look the other way," Dr. Oliner said in an interview. He heads the Altruistic Personality Project, in which researchers working in the United States, Canada, Europe and Israel will conduct, if funds allow, detailed interviews with 400 people who rescued Jews during the war.

Strong Sense of Self-Worth

Dr. Oliner and his associates, who have already interviewed 140 rescuers, believe they are racing the clock to reach the rest before they die. On the basis of the interviews he has conducted already, however, he has reached some preliminary conclusions about the characteristics of the rescuers.

Study Suggests Self-Love Underlies Ability to Reach Out to Others Despite Personal Risk

In broad strokes, his findings are in accord with the views of such humanist psycholo-

gists as Abraham Maslow and Erich Fromm, who saw a strong sense of self-worth and security as the psychological base from which people could reach out to help others.

To be sure, there is no single, all-encompassing explanation for the rescuers' acts. Indeed, some saved Jews for selfish reasons: They were paid or bribed. Most sheltered people they knew or with whom they had ties. But many rescued complete strangers.

Dr. Oliner's research project is part of a broad search under way to understand what leads an individual to help when others turn their backs on a person in need. While that question is one that theologians and philosophers have sought to answer for thousands of years, psychologists of late have made intensive efforts to provide their own insights.

Spurred by Murder of Kitty Genovese

Ironically, the current research on altruism was spurred, in large part, by a tragic instance of its absence: the 1964 murder of Kitty Genovese as 38 neighbors in Kew Gardens, Queens, looked on without calling the police for help. The incident galvanized psychologists, who realized that they had no ready explanation for why these neighbors refused to help, or for contrasting acts of human kindness.

Psychoanalysts have proposed several psychological motives for altruism. One view, for example, holds that those who help others to their own detriment are masochistic. Another sees altruism as an effort to expiate unconscious guilt or shame. For example, Erik Erikson attributed Mohandas Ghandi's humanitarianism, in part, to such guilt.

Behaviorists, on the other hand, have explained altruism in terms of the reinforcement people get from making themselves feel good by doing good. Behavior geneticists have studied twins to see if there is an inherited temperament that predisposes some toward acts of kindness.

Sociobiologists offer an entirely different analysis of altruism, noting that it is seen, too, in animals. For example, in several species of primates, members of one troop will raise an orphaned youngster from another troop. Some sociobiologists argue that altruism is a survival strategy in evolution, since helping others who share one's genes is a form of reproductive success. But such theories, in Dr. Oliner's view, do little to explain what impelled the rescuers he is studying to risk their lives—and often their families' lives, too.

What can be said, for example, of the motives of the S.S. officer who concealed a Jewish couple until the end of the war in his living quarters directly above the S.S. Center in Berlin? Or, for that matter, what drove the Belgian countess who not only hid 100 women and children on her estate, but also cooked kosher food for them?

Of most interest to the researchers is the contrast between these rescuers and the vast majority of non-Jews who also could have saved Jews, but did not. Dr. Oliner has so far interviewed 20 non-rescuers, and plans to talk to 180 more.

The preliminary findings from his project, and results from a variety of other studies, converge on the formative experiences people have in childhood, which seem to make them, many years later, more predisposed than others to come to the aid of the distressed.

On the basis of his preliminary data, Dr. Oliner has identified a key cluster of the factors that seem to be at play in the rescuers as a group. There were, in his view, three elements that combined to lead the rescuers to their acts of kindness and heroism.

Foremost among them was having compassionate values. In most cases, these values seem to have come from someone in the person's childhood who embodied them. Perry London, a psychologist at Harvard University who studied a group of rescuers now living in Israel, concluded that "almost all the rescuers" had a strong identification with a parent who was a "very strong moralist."

But, Dr. Oliner points out, espousing such values was in itself not enough. The rescuers were also distinguished by a sense of competence. They saw themselves as in control of their lives. Moreover, they also seemed inclined to take calculated risks.

And, finally, the rescuers had to have at their disposal the wherewithal to put their values and sense of competence into action. For some that meant a special expertise, such as being an expert skier who could escort Jews across the snow-covered Alps to Switzerland; for others, it simply meant having a home large enough to have a hiding place and having family and friends who supported the rescue effort.

Though Dr. Oliner cautions that these findings are preliminary, they dovetail with results from several other diverse studies of altruists.

In an approach similar to that taken by Dr. Oliner, Nancy McWilliams, a psychoanalyst, has conducted intensive clinical interviews with five people who have dedicated their lives to helping others. Although exploratory, Dr. McWilliams's research is instructive because her subjects represent an extreme of altruism: they include a woman who cares for the children of lepers in the Far East, and a man who runs an international adoption agency for crippled or otherwise unwanted children.

She began her study because she was dissatisfied with the psychoanalytic theories of altruism that saw it as pathological. "These are the kind of people who don't show up in psychotherapists' offices," she said. "They're not neurotic or depressed, they have good relationships and a sense of humor about themselves."

She found a common pattern in the early development of those she studied. Most had suffered the loss in early childhood of a warm and nurturant caretaker, such as the death of a mother. And in every case there was a "rescue" by someone in their lives who they felt saved them by replacing the lost person.

"As children they idealized that person," Dr. McWilliams said. "He or she became their model for altruism."

One of the most detailed theories of the roots of altruism is that proposed by Ervin Straub, a psychologist at the University of Massachusetts. Writing in *The Biological and Social Origins of Altruism and Aggression*, a collection of articles by several experts to be published later this year by Cambridge University Press, Dr. Staub reports evidence that altruism requires more than just compassionate values and the psychologial and practical competence to put them into effect.

"Goodness, like evil, often begins in small steps," Dr. Staub said in an interview. "Heroes evolve; they aren't born. Very often the rescuers made only a small commitment at the start—to hide someone for a day or two. But once they had taken that step, they began to see themselves differently, as someone who helps. What starts as mere willingness becomes intense involvement."

Dr. Staub cites the example of Raoul Wallenberg, the Swedish diplomat who used his status to save hundreds of Hungarian Jews. "The first person Wallenberg rescued was a business partner, who was a Hungarian Jew. Soon, though, Wallenberg was manufacturing passes that made Jews candidates for Swedish citizenship, and so protected them from the Germans. As his involvement grew, it got to the point that he was exposing himself to great risks by giving out the passes to Jews waiting in line for Nazi deportation trains."

But there is a special kind of person who is more likely than most to take the first step to help, and to stay with the effort to the end: the altruist.

"There is a pattern of childrearing that seems to encourage altruism in later years," said Dr. Straub, who is studying the roots of altruism in childhood. "A warm and nurturant relationship between parent and child is essential, but not enough in itself. The same holds for having parents who espouse altruistic values—it's important, but not sufficient."

"The parents who transmit altruism most effectively," he said, "exert a firm control over their children. Although they are nurturant, they are not permissive. They use a combination of firmness, warmth and reasoning. They point out to children the consequences to others of misbehavior—and good behavior. And they actively guide the child to do good, to share, to be helpful."

Children who have been coached to be helpful, or who engaged in altruistic projects such as making toys for poor, hospitalized children, Dr. Staub has found, are later more altruistic when a spontaneous situation in which they can help others arises.

There may be quite specific interactions between parents and children that cultivate such altruism, according to results from a major series of studies by Carolyn Zahn-Waxler and her colleagues at the National Institute of Mental Health.

The beginnings of altruism, her research shows, can be seen in toddlers as young as 2 years.

Whether a child displays altruism seems tied to how the mother or other caretakers treat the child in key moments, particularly times when another person is in distress. For example, according to Dr. Zahn-Waxler, children who were more often altruistic had mothers who tended to explain to them the consequences of hurting other children, and to do so with great feeling, with an admonition such as, "I don't like to be with you when you act like that."

When the mothers gave a calm, unemotional admonition, it did not seem to lead the children to be altruistic.

Some mothers Dr. Zahn-Waxler studied, particularly those who blamed their children for mistreating playmates, induced a guilt-ridden altruism in their young children. These children often feel they have caused hurts that were not their doing.

On the other hand, the young children of chronically depressed mothers seem to be particularly sensitive to the distress of other children. Dr. Zahn-Waxler finds. While they are not overly guilty about the distress, they are preoccupied by it.

A healthier kind of altruism, she believes, is that produced by "the nurturant but moralizing parent who arouses the child to concerned action."

Reading 44

Torturers are not necessarily evil, sick people. This article demonstrates that more often they are ordinary, intelligent people who are educated in torture. As you read, consider how the knowledge of psychological principles can be used to influence people—for good or evil. Can understanding the principles of social influence protect an individual from becoming a victim of it?

The Education of a Torturer

By Janice T. Gibson and Mika Haritos-Fatourous

Torture—for whatever purpose and in whatever name—requires a torturer, an individual responsible for planning and causing pain to others. "A man's hands are shackled behind him, his eyes blindfolded," wrote Argentine journalist Jacobo Timerman about his torture by Argentine army extremists. "No one says a word. Blows are showered. . . . [He is] stripped, doused with water, tied. . . . And the application of electric shocks begins. It's impossible to shout—you howl." The governments of at least 90 countries use similar methods to torture people all over the world, Amnesty International reports.

What kind of person can behave so monstrously to another human being? A sadist or a sexual deviant? Someone with an authoritarian upbringing or who was abused by parents? A disturbed personality affected somehow by hereditary characteristics?

On the contrary, the Nazis who tortured and killed millions during World War II "weren't sadists or killers by nature," Hannah Arendt reported in her book *Eichmann In Jerusalem*. Many studies of Nazi behavior concluded that monstrous acts, despite their horrors, were often simply a matter of faithful bureaucrats slavishly following orders.

In a 1976 study, University of Florida psychologist Molly Harrower asked 15 Rorschach experts to examine inkblot test reports from Adolph Eichmann, Rudolf Hess, Hermann Goering and five other Nazi war criminals, made just before their trials at Nuremburg. She also sent the specialists Rorshach reports from eight Americans, some with well-adjusted personalities and some who were severely disturbed, without revealing the individuals' identities. The experts were unable to distinguish the Nazis from the Americans and judged an equal number of both to be well-adjusted. The horror that emerges is the likelihood that torturers are not freaks; they are ordinary people.

Obedience to what we call the "authority of violence" often plays an important role in pushing ordinary people to commit cruel, violent and even fatal acts. During wartime, for example, soldiers will follow orders to kill unarmed civilians. Here, we will look at the way obedience and other factors combine to produce willing torturers.

Twenty-five years ago, the late psychologist Stanley Milgram demonstrated convincingly that people unlikely to be cruel in everyday life will administer pain if they are told to by someone in authority. In a famous experiment, Milgrim had men wearing laboratory coats direct average American adults to inflict a series of electric shocks to other people. No real shocks were given and the "victims" were acting, but the people didn't know this. They were told that the purpose of the study was to measure the effects of punishment on learning. Obediently, 65 percent of them used what they thought were dangerously high levels of shocks when the experimenter told them to. While they were less likely to administer these supposed shocks as they were moved closer to their victims, almost one-third of them continued to shock when they were close enough to touch.

This readiness to torture is not limited to Americans. Following Milgram's lead, other researchers found the people of all ages, from a wide range of countries were willing to shock others even when they had nothing to gain by complying with the command or nothing to lose by refusing it. So long as someone else, an authority figure, was responsible for the final outcome of the experiment, almost no one absolutely refused to administer shocks. Each study also found, as Milgram had, that some people would give shocks even when the decision was left up to them.

Milgram proposed that the reasons people obey or disobey authority fall into three categories. The first is personal history: family or school backgrounds that encourage obedience or defiance. The second, which he called "binding," is made up of ongoing experiences that make people feel comfortable when they obey authority. Strain, the third category, consists of bad feelings from unpleasant experiences connected with obedience. Milgram argued that when the binding factors are more powerful than the strain of cooperating, people will do as they are told. When the strain is greater, they are more likely to disobey.

This may explain short-term obedience in the laboratory, but it doesn't explain prolonged patterns of torture during wartime or under some political regimes. Repeatedly, torturers in Argentina and elsewhere performed acts that most of us consider repugnant, and in time this should have placed enough strain on them to prevent their obedience. It didn't. Nor does Milgram's theory explain undirected cruel or violent acts, which occur even when no authority orders them. For this, we have developed a more comprehensive learning model; for torture, we discovered, can be taught (see "Teaching to Torment," this article).

TEACHING TO TORMENT

There are several ways to teach people to do the unthinkable, and we have developed a model to explain how they are used. We have also found that college fraternities, although they are far removed from the grim world of torture and violent combat, use similar methods for initiating new members, to ensure their faithfulness to the fraternity's rules and values. However, this unthinking loyalty can sometimes lead to dangerous actions: Over the past 10 years, there have been countless injuries during fraternity initiations and 39 deaths. These training techniques are designed to install unquestioning obedience in people, but they can easily be a guide for an intensive course in torture.

1) Screening to find the best prospects: normal, well-adjusted people with the physical, intellectual and, in some cases, political attributes necessary for the task.

2) Techniques to increase binding among these prospects:
● Initiation rites to isolate people from society and introduce them to a new social order, with different rules and values.
● Elitist attitudes and "in-group" language, which highlight the differences between the group and the rest of society.

3) Techniques to reduce the strain of obedience:
● Blaming and dehumanizing the victims, so it is less disturbing to harm them.
● Harassment, the constant physical and psychological intimidation that prevents logical thinking and promotes the instinctive responses needed for acts of inhuman cruelty.
● Rewards for obedience and punishments for not cooperating.
●Social modeling by watching other group members commit violent acts and then receive rewards.
●Systematic desensitization to repugnant acts by gradual exposure to them, so they appear routine and normal despite conflicts with previous moral standards.

We studied the procedures used to train Greek military police as torturers during that country's military regime from 1967 through 1974. We examined the official testimonies of 21 former soldiers in the ESA (Army Police Corps) given at their 1975 criminal trials in Athens; in addition, Haritos-Fatouros conducted in-depth interviews with 16 of them after their trials. In many cases, these men had been convicted and had completed prison sentences. They were all leading normal lives when interviewed. One was a university graduate, five were graduates of higher technical institutes, nine had completed at least their second year of high school and only one had no more than a primary school education.

All of these men had been drafted, first into regular military service and then into specialized units that required servicemen to torture prisoners. We found no record of delinquent or disturbed behavior before their military service. However, we did find several features of the soldiers' training that helped to turn them into willing and able torturers.

The initial screening for torturers was primarily based on physical strength and "appropriate" political beliefs, which simply meant that the recruits and their families were anticommunists. This ensured that the men had hostile attitudes toward potential victims from the very beginning.

Once they were actually serving as military police, the men were also screened for other attributes. According to former torturer Michaelis Petrou, "The most important criterion was that you had to keep your mouth shut. Second, you had to show aggression. Third, you had to be intelligent and strong. Fourth, you had to be 'their man,' which meant that you would report on the others serving with you, that [the officers] could trust you and that you would follow their orders blindly."

Binding the recruits to the authority of ESA began in basic training, with physically brutal initiation rites. Recruits themselves were cursed, punched, kicked and flogged. They were forced to run until they collapsed and prevented from relieving themselves for long stretches of time. They were required to swear allegiance to a symbol of authority used by the regime (a poster of a soldier superimposed on a large phoenix rising from its own ashes), and they had to promise on their knees to obey their commander-in-chief and the military revolution.

While being harassed and beaten by their officers, servicemen were repeatedly told how fortunate they were to have joined the ESA, the strongest and most important support of the regime. They were told that an ESA serviceman's action is never questioned: "You can even flog a major." In-group language helped the men to develop elitist attitudes. Servicemen used nicknames for one another and, later, they used them for victims and for the different methods of torture. "Tea party" meant the beating of a prisoner by a group of military police using their fists, and "tea party with toast" meant more severe group beatings using clubs. Gradually, the recruits came to speak of all people who were not in their group, parents and families included, as belonging to the "outside world."

The strain of obedience on the recruits was reduced in several ways. During basic training, they were given daily "national ethical education" lectures that included indoctrination against communism and enemies of the state. During more advanced training, the recruits were constantly reminded that the prisoners were "worms," and that they had to "crush" them. One man reported that when he was torturing prisoners later, he caught himself repeating phrases like "bloody communists!" that he had heard in the lectures.

The military police used a carrot-and-stick method to further diminish the recruits' uneasiness about torture. There were many rewards, such as relaxed military rules after training was completed, and torturers often weren't punished for leaving camp without permission. They were allowed to wear civilian clothes, to keep their hair long and to drive military police cars for their personal use. Torturers were frequently given a leave of absence after they forced a confession from a prisoner. They had many economic benefits as well, including free bus rides and restaurant meals and job placement when military service was over. These were the carrots.

The sticks consisted of the constant harassment, threats and punishment for disobedience. The men were threatened and intimidated, first by their trainers, then later by senior servicemen. "An officer used to tell us that if a warder helps a prisoner, he will take the prisoner's place and the whole platoon will flog him," one man recalled. Soldiers spied on one another, and even the most successful torturers said that they were constantly afraid.

"You will learn to love pain," one officer promised a recruit. Sensitivity to torture was blunted in several steps. First, the men had to endure it themselves, as if torture were a normal act. The beatings and other torments inflicted on them continued and became worse. Next, the servicemen chosen for the Persecution Section, the unit that tortured political prisoners, were brought into contact with the prisoners by carrying food to their cells. The new men watched veteran soldiers torture prisoners, while they stood guard. Occasionally, the veterans would order them to give the prisoners "some blows."

At the next step, the men were required to participate in group beatings. Later, they were told to use a variety of torture methods on the prisoners. The final step, the appointment to prison warder or chief torturer, was announced suddenly by the commander-in-chief, leaving the men no time to reflect on their new duties.

The Greek example illustrates how the ability to torture can be taught. Training that increases binding and reduces strain can cause decent people to commit acts, often over long periods of time, that otherwise would be unthinkable for them. Similar techniques can be found in military training all over the world, when the intent is to teach soldiers to kill or perform some other repellent act. We conducted extensive interviews with soldiers and exsoldiers in the U.S. Marines and the Green Berets, and we found that all the steps in our training model were part and parcel of elite American military training. Soldiers are screened for intellectual and physical ability, achievement and mental health. Binding begins in basic training, with initiation rites that isolate trainees from society, introduce them to new rules and values and leave them little time for clear thinking after exhausting physical exercise and scant sleep. Harassment plays an important role, and soldiers are severely punished for disobedience, with demerits, verbal abuse, hours of calisthenics and loss of eating, sleeping and other privileges.

Military training gradually desensitizes soldiers to violence and reduces the strain normally created by repugnant acts. Their revulsion is diminished by screaming chants and songs about violence and killing during marches and runs. The enemy is given derogatory names and portrayed as less than human; this makes it easier to kill them. Completing the toughest possible training and being rewarded by "making it" in an elite corps, bring the soldiers confidence and pride, and those who accomplish this feel they can do anything. "Although I tried to avoid killing, I learned to have confidence in myself and was never afraid," said a former Green Beret who served in Vietnam. "It was part of the job. . . . Anyone who goes through that kind of training could do it."

The effectiveness of these techniques, as several researchers have shown, is not limited to the army. History teacher Ronald Jones started what he called the Third Wave movement as a classroom experiment to show his high school students how people might have become Nazis in World War II. Jones began the Third Wave demonstration by requiring students to stand at attention in a unique new posture and follow strict new rules. He required students to stand beside their desks when asking or answering questions and to begin each statement by saying, "Mr. Jones." The students obeyed. He then required them to shout slogans, "Strength through discipline!" and "Strength through community!" Jones created a salute for class members that he called the Third Wave: the right hand raised to the shoulder with fingers curled. The salute had no meaning, but it served as a symbol of group belonging and a way of isolating members from outsiders.

The organization expanded quickly from 20 original members to 100. The teacher issued membership cards and assigned students to report members who didn't comply with the new rules. Dutifully, 20 students pointed accusing fingers at their classmates.

Then Jones announced that the Third Wave was a "nationwide movement to find students willing to fight for political change," and he organized a rally, which drew a crowd of 200 students. At the rally, after getting students to salute and shout slogans on command, Jones explained the true reasons behind the Third Wave demonstration. Like the Nazis before them, Jones pointed out, "You bargained your freedom for the comfort of discipline."

The students, at an age when group belonging was very important to them, made good candidates for training. Jones didn't teach his students to commit atrocities, and the Third Wave lasted for only five days; in that time, however, Jones created an obedient group that resembled in many ways the Nazi youth groups of World War II (see "The Third Wave: Nazism in a High School," *Psychology Today*, July 1976).

Psychologists Craig Haney, W. Curtis Banks and Philip Zimbardo went even further in a remarkable simulation of prison life done at Stanford University. With no special training and in only six days' time, they changed typical university students into controlling, abusive guards and servile prisoners.

The students who agreed to participate were chosen randomly to be guards or prisoners. The mock guards were given uniforms and nightsticks and told to act as guards. Prisoners were treated as dangerous criminals: Local police rounded them up, fingerprinted and booked them and brought them to a simulated cellblock in the basement of the university psychology department. Uniformed guards made them remove their clothing, deloused them, gave them prison uniforms and put them in cells.

The two groups of students, originally found to be very similar in most respects, showed striking changes within one week. Prisoners became passive, dependent and helpless. In contrast, guards expressed feelings of power, status and group belonging. They were aggressive and abusive within the prison, insulting and bullying the prisoners. Some guards reported later that they had enjoyed their power, while others said they had not thought they were capable of behaving as they had. They were surprised and dismayed at what they had done: "It was degrading. . . . To me, those things are sick. But they [the prisoners] did everything I said. They abused each other because I requested them to. No one questioned my authority at all."

The guards' behavior was similar in two important ways to that of the Greek torturers. First, they dehumanized their victims. Second, like the torturers, the guards were abusive only when they were within the prison walls. They could act reasonably outside the prisons because the two prison influences of binding and reduced strain were absent.

All these changes at Stanford occurred with no special training, but the techniques we have outlined were still present. Even without training, the student guards "knew" from television and movies that they were supposed to punish prisoners; they "knew" they were supposed to feel superior; and they "knew" they were supposed to blame their victims. Their own behavior and that of their peers gradually numbed their sensitivity to what they were doing, and they were rewarded by the power they had over their prisoners.

There is no evidence that such short-term experiments produce lasting effects. None were reported from either the Third Wave demonstration or the Stanford University simulation. The Stanford study, however, was cut short when depression, crying and psychosomatic illnesses began to appear among the students. And studies of Vietnam veterans have revealed that committing abhorrent acts, even under the extreme conditions of war, can lead to long-term problems. In one study of 130 Vietnam veterans who came to a therapist for help, almost 30 percent of them were concerned about violent acts they had committed while in the service. The veterans reported feelings of anxiety, guilt, depression and an inability to carry on intimate relationships. In a similar fashion, after the fall of the Greek dictatorship in 1974, former torturers began to report nightmares, irritability and episodes of depression.

"Torturing became a job," said former Greek torturer Petrou. "If the officers ordered you to beat, you beat. If they ordered you to stop, you stopped. You never thought you could do otherwise." His comments bear a disturbing resemblance to the feelings expressed by a Stanford guard: "When I was doing it, I didn't feel regret.... I didn't feel guilt. Only afterwards, when I began to reflect ... did it begin to dawn on me that this was a part of me I hadn't known before."

We do not believe that torture came naturally to any of these young men. Haritos-Fatouros found no evidence of sadistic, abusive or authoritarian behavior in the Greek soldiers' histories prior to their training. This, together with our study of Marine training and the Stanford and Third Wave studies, leads to the conclusion that torturers have normal personalities. Any of us, in a similar situation, might be capable of the same cruelty. One probably cannot train a deranged sadist to be an effective torturer or killer. He must be in complete control of himself while on the job.

ADDITIONAL RESOURCES

Books and Articles

Festinger, L., H. Riecken, and S. Schachter. *When Prophecy Fails*. Minneapolis: University of Minnesota Press, 1956. What happens to a follower's faith when a leader's predictions fail to come true? This analysis of fanatical followings reads like a novel.

Glazer, M. P., and P. M. Glazer. "Whistleblowing." *Psychology Today* (August 1986): 37. The costs are high, the results uncertain. So why do some people risk all to reveal fraud and waste in their organization?

Hunt, Morton. "Research Through Deception." *New York Times Magazine*, September 12, 1982, pp. 66–67. Where should the boundaries be for research on human beings? Morton Hunt believes the Zimbardo prison experiment goes too far.

Kelman, H. C., and V. L. Hamilton. *Crimes of Obedience*. New Haven: Yale University Press, 1989. Explores examples of the tendency of people to commit illegal or immoral acts when so ordered by authority and of others later to excuse them. Includes discussion of the My Lai massacre, Watergate, and the Iran-contra affair.

Langer, Ellen. *Mindfulness*. Reading, Mass.: Addison-Wesley, 1989. Causes and consequences of "mindlessness," with implications for mindful alternatives. Includes study done on ROTC cadets' vision.

Soaken, Donald R. "J'accuse." *Psychology Today* (August 1986): 44. A therapist and a whistleblower himself, the author works to bring peace to those who dare to speak out.

Films

The Great Dictator. Directed by and starring Charlie Chaplin. 1940. The theme of murder on a grand scale contrasted with individual crime. Is murder by a government normal and legal? Chaplin challenges us to question accepted definitions of "crime," "normality," and "insanity."

Lacombe Lucien. Directed by Louis Malle. 1974. A chilling investigation of the banality of evil. A rough farm boy becomes a vicious brute—a Nazi collaborator who casually tortures people.

Trading Places. Directed by John Landis; starring Dan Ackroyd and Eddie Murphy. 1983. This popular movie is another version of the prince and the pauper reversal. Will heredity and character or environment prove to be the major influence?

CONSTRUCTING SOCIAL REALITY

Everything that deceives may be said to enchant.

Plato

Unit 20 explores our subjective view of reality and how it influences social behavior. It reveals how your perceptions and reasoning ability can be influenced in positive and negative ways, and it increases our understanding of how psychological processes govern interpretation of reality.

The Guyana tragedy in 1978, when more than 900 members of a religious cult committed mass suicide, was a shocking case of the subjective constructions of reality.

OBJECTIVES

After viewing the television program and completing the assigned readings, you should be able to:

1. Describe how our attitudes are formed and how they affect our behavior

2. Discuss theories of attitude change such as Heider's balance theory and Festinger's cognitive dissonance theory

3. Define prejudice and explain the cognitive and emotional basis for stereotyping

4. Discuss the various theoretical approaches to the understanding of prejudice: ingroups and outgroups, frustration theory, social learning and the prejudiced personality

5. Discuss Jane Elliot's classroom experiment on brown eyes and blue eyes in terms of the above approaches to prejudice

6. Summarize Rosenthal's research on the Pygmalian effect

7. Compare Cialdini's categories of social influence used by advertisers with Hovland's elements of persuasive communication

8. Describe research aimed at decreasing prejudice such as Sherif's Robber's Cave study, Aronson's Jigsaw Technique study, and social and school integration studies; outline the important social psychological principles used in these studies

READING ASSIGNMENT

After viewing Program 20, read pages 662–684 in *Psychology: Science, Behavior and Life*. Your instructor may also assign the anthology selections for Unit 20.

KEY TERMS AND CONCEPTS

To review textbook terms, refer to the Key Terms and Concepts in Unit 19.

The following terms are used in Program 20 but are not defined in the text.

cognitive control—the power of beliefs to give meaning to a situation

Pygmalion effect—the effect of positive and negative expectations on behavior

PROGRAM SUMMARY

In 1978, 900 members of a religious cult committed murder and mass suicide in a remote jungle settlement in Jonestown, Guyana. What kind of people would participate in a mass suicide? What kind of people would murder their own children? Beware of making the fundamental attribution error! Program 20 explains how social forces can distort reality and exert tremendous power on apparently rational people. So the question "What kind of people?" may not be the right question.

Our beliefs can be so powerful that they can, in fact, influence our perceptions and interpretation of reality. The power to create subjective realities is known to psychologists as cognitive control. When individuals and nations believe that their own perception is the only valid one, hostility and prejudice can result and an "us versus them" mentality develops.

Even our most minor differences can trigger prejudice, as we see in Jane Elliot's fourth-grade classroom experiment. Elliot demonstrated how easy it is to alter reality by providing an arbitrary reason to think in adversarial terms. She divided the children into two groups: the "inferior" brown-eyed students and the "superior" blue-eyed ones. This superficial difference provided the basis for institutionalizing discrimination. Those who were seen as inferior began to feel and act that way. And the blue-eyed students took on superior airs.

Another classroom experiment demonstrated that positive expectations can dramatically influence perceptions and behavior. When psychologist Robert Rosenthal and school principal Lenore Jacobson randomly labeled some students as academically superior, those students were given more attention, support, and praise by their teachers. They had created a climate of approval and acceptance that transformed ordinary kids into extraordinary students. The teachers' expectations became a self-fulfilling prophecy.

Both classroom experiments illustrate how social feedback influences the way we see ourselves and the way we behave. In another school, Elliot Aronson and Alex Gonzales created the "Jigsaw Classroom," a class divided into several expert groups that reported on specific topics. Aronson and Gonzales wanted to test their theory that cooperation, not competition, increases achievement and instills self-esteem in all students. The Jigsaw Classroom proved to be a great success, demonstrating that situational forces include not only objective characteristics but the participants' subjective realities too.

Manipulating our perceptions is also the specialty of advertising professionals. They are experts in manipulating the decisions we make as consumers and voters. Their goal is to get us to say yes to their products without thinking or critically evaluating what we are doing.

Psychologist Robert Cialdini has studied thousands of tactics used by salespeople, fund-raisers, public relations practitioners, and advertisers. Their tactics fall into categories, each governed by a basic psychological principle (see Figure 13). Cialdini's

---

1. *Commitment-Consistency*—Public commitment engages the need to be or appear consistent with others and/or oneself.

2. *Authority-Credibility*—Conferring authority status on others by virtue of their roles and appearances simplifies information processing by increasing credibility.

3. *Obligation-Reciprocity*—When someone does us a favor or gives us a gift or compliment, a context of obligation is created which induces a social need to respond politely—to reciprocate.

4. *Scarcity-Competition*—When anything is perceived as scarce, demand for it escalates, and individuals will compete against potential rivals to get it.

5. *Social Validation-Consensus*—We use the behavior of similar others or the majority as guidelines for what we do, especially in novel or ambiguous situations.

6. *Friendship-Liking*—Contexts that encourage the perception of familiarity and similarity increase liking and effectiveness.

Figure 13: Cialdini's Six Influence Strategies
Psychologist Robert Cialdini of Arizona State University spent three years examining advertising strategies and tactics as a professional in the field. He found six central categories of influence strategies, each based on a basic psychological principle.

research shows how easy it is for us to behave in conforming, prejudiced, or competitive ways. Social psychologists hope to use these same principles of influence to develop new strategies that will help people become more independent, more tolerant, and more cooperative.

REVIEW QUESTIONS

Program Questions

1. What do social psychologists study?

   a. How people are influenced by other people
   b. How people act in different societies
   c. Why some people are more socially successful than others
   d. What happens to isolated individuals

2. What precipitated Kurt Lewin's interest in leadership roles?

   a. The rise of social psychology
   b. The trial of Adolf Eichmann
   c. Hitler's ascent to power
   d. The creation of the United Nations after World War II

3. In Lewin's study, how did the boys behave when they had autocratic leaders?

   a. They had fun but got little accomplished.
   b. They were playful and did motivated, original work.
   c. They were hostile toward each other and got nothing done.
   d. They worked hard but acted aggressively toward each other.

4. In Solomon Asch's experiments, about what percent of subjects went along with the group's obviously mistaken judgment?

   a. 30 percent
   b. 50 percent
   c. 70 percent
   d. 90 percent

5. Before Stanley Milgram did his experiments on obedience, experts were asked to predict the results. The experts

   a. overestimated the subjects' willingness to administer shocks.
   b. underestimated the subjects' willingness to administer shocks.
   c. gave accurate estimates of the subjects' performance.
   d. believed most subjects would refuse to continue with the experiment.

6. Which light did Milgram's experiment shed on the behavior of citizens in Nazi Germany?

   a. Situational forces can bring about blind obedience.
   b. Personal traits of individuals are most important in determining behavior.
   c. Cultural factors unique to Germany account for the rise of the Nazis.
   d. Human beings enjoy being cruel when they have the opportunity.

7. Which statement most clearly reflects the fundamental attribution error?

   a. Everyone is entitled to good medical care.
   b. Ethical guidelines are essential to conducting responsible research.
   c. People who are unemployed are too lazy to work.
   d. Everyone who reads about the Milgram experiment is shocked by the results.

8. Why did the prison study conducted by Professor Zimbardo and his colleagues have to be called off?

   a. A review committee felt that it violated ethical guidelines.
   b. It consumed too much of the students' time.
   c. The main hypothesis was supported so there was no need to continue.
   d. The situation that had been created was too dangerous to maintain.

9. How do you imagine Kurt Lewin's reaction to his experimental results compared to Professor Zimbardo's reaction to the results of the prison study?

   a. Both men were pleased that their ideas were confirmed.
   b. Both men were disappointed by the subjects' performance.
   c. Lewin was pleased, but Zimbardo was shocked.
   d. Lewin was disappointed, and Zimbardo felt neutral.

10. How did Tom Moriarity get people on a beach to intervene during a robbery?

    a. By creating a human bond through a simple request
    b. By reminding people of their social responsibility
    c. By making the thief look less threatening
    d. By providing a model of responsible behavior

11. How did the situation of being involved in an active flight simulation affect the vision of the Air Force ROTC cadets that Ellen Langer studied?

    a. It made them so nervous they saw less well.
    b. It stimulated them to see better.
    c. It had no effect.
    d. It improved the performance of female cadets but not male cadets.

12. According to the program, the behavior of the people who died in Jonestown was a function of

    a. their mental state, as created by Jim Jones.
    b. their moral weakness in getting involved in a cult.
    c. the situation in which they found themselves.
    d. the human tendency toward self-destruction.

13. Psychologists refer to the power to create subjective realities as the power of

    a. social reinforcement.
    b. prejudice.
    c. cognitive control.
    d. the Pygmalion effect.

14. When Jane Elliot divided her classroom of third-graders into the inferior brown-eyed people and the superior blue-eyed people, what did she observe?

    a. The students were too young to understand what was expected.
    b. The students refused to behave badly toward their friends and classmates.
    c. The boys tended to go along with the categorization, but the girls did not.
    d. The blue-eyed students acted superior and were cruel to the brown-eyed, who acted inferior.

15. In the research carried out by Robert Rosenthal and Lenore Jacobsen, what caused the performance of some students to improve dramatically?

    a. Teachers were led to expect such improvement and so changed the way they treated these students.
    b. These students performed exceptionally well on a special test designed to predict improved performance.
    c. Teachers gave these students higher grades because they knew the researchers were expecting the improvement.
    d. The students felt honored to be included in the experiment and so were motivated to improve.

16. Imagine you are a teacher who wants to use the results of the Rosenthal study to improve the performance of your students. What step would be in line with the study results?

    a. Praise students no matter how they do.
    b. Provide differentiated feedback.
    c. Keep the input as simple as possible.
    d. Provide for more group response and less individual response.

17. What happens to low-achieving students in the Jigsaw Classroom?

    a. They tend to fall further behind.
    b. They are given an opportunity to work at a lower level, thus increasing the chance of success.
    c. By becoming "experts," they improve their performance and their self-respect.
    d. By learning to compete more aggressively, they become more actively involved in their own learning.

18. When Robert Cialdini cites the example of the Hare Krishnas' behavior in giving people at airports a flower or other small gift, he is illustrating the principle of

    a. commitment.
    b. reciprocation.
    c. scarcity.
    d. consensus.

Textbook Questions

19. Bystanders are more likely to help another in time of need

    a. when many people are present.
    b. if the victim is the same sex.
    c. when few people are present.
    d. when the risk is high.

20. Darley and Latane (1968) found that we would be more likely to help a person in trouble if

    a. we were paid to do so.
    b. they were the same sex.
    c. we felt we were the only ones present.
    d. there were several other bystanders.

21. If we meet a person that we perceive as being warm and friendly, we will probably expect that person to also be generous and to have a good sense of humor. These expectancies are based on our

    a. social attributions.
    b. interpersonal stereotypes.
    c. normative influences.
    d. implicit personality theories.

22. Janice is rather cold and unsociable and because of this we expect her to also be humorless and lack popularity because

    a. of our keen sense of perception.
    b. of our assumptions or implicit personality theories about her.
    c. of our ability to be correct on first impressions.
    d. we always know others better than we know ourselves.

23. Which of the following statements reflects a clear dispositional attribution?

    a. "Something got the best of him."
    b. "He did what he thought was right."
    c. "He did it that way because of the weather."
    d. "He could not refuse the money."

24. We tend to attribute our own successes to

    a. external factors.
    b. dispositional factors.
    c. mostly luck.
    d. determinations.

25. When a person's behavior fits with what we expect, we tend to discount it as a clue to that person's true nature according to

    a. correspondent inference theory.
    b. social-learning theory.
    c. the primacy effect.
    d. the halo effect.

26. We tend to make external attribution for behavior when that behavior is low in

    a. distinctiveness.
    b. dissonance.
    c. consensus.
    d. consistency.

27. A tendency to overestimate dispositional or internal causes and to underestimate external causes for other people's behavior is called a(n)

    a. fundamental attribution error.
    b. illusion of control.
    c. attributional bias.
    d. discrimination error.

28. When people believe they actually can influence all the events (external, internal) in their lives, the belief is referred to as

    a. false consensus.
    b. illusion of control.
    c. fundamental error.
    d. noncommon effects.

29. An enduring system of beliefs, feelings, and behavioral tendencies defines

    a. personality.
    b. values.
    c. stereotype.
    d. attitudes.

30. Attitudes are particularly strong predictors of behavior when

    a. an attitude is highly relevant to the behavior being considered.
    b. we are conscious of our attitudes when we act.
    c. both of the above.
    d. attitudes are not strong predictors of behavior under any conditions.

31. By trying a new soft drink yourself, you are more likely to develop a strong attitude toward it than just seeing it advertised on TV because of

    a. illusion of control.
    b. classical conditioning.
    c. operant conditioning.
    d. direct experience.

32. A characteristic of people who are readily persuaded by others is

    a. low social anxiety.
    b. low self-esteem.
    c. individuation.
    d. diffusion of personality.

33. The key word in cognitive-dissonance theory is

    a. imbalance.
    b. persuasion.
    c. inconsistency.
    d. operant conditioning.

34. Ads for aspirin boast that nine out of ten doctors recommend their product because _____ makes the ad more persuasive.

    a. attractiveness
    b. similarity to the audience
    c. expertise
    d. trustworthiness

35. Politicians eating the foods that are characteristic of the various ethnic neighborhoods in which they visit are examples of which persuasion technique?

    a. Trustworthiness
    b. Similarity to the audience
    c. Attractiveness
    d. Expertise

36. We would be more likely to believe that exhaust fumes are harmful if the claim came from

    a. a politician running for office.
    b. an environmental group.
    c. the president of General Motors.
    d. the President of the United States.

37. A two-sided argument tends to be more effective if the audience is

    a. well-educated.
    b. well-informed.
    c. both of the above.
    d. none of the above.

38. Persons in groups will not usually conform to incorrect judgments if at least _____ other person(s) in the group agree(s) with him or her.

    a. one
    b. two
    c. three
    d. eight

39. Conformity and compliance are similar except that compliance has

    a. an unconscious motivation.
    b. a smoother change process.
    c. an element of coercion as well.
    d. indirect pressure applied.

40. A car salesman who persuades you to come into the office to "get a look at the bottom price" is using the

    a. obedience technique.
    b. foot-in-the-door technique.
    c. door-in-the-face technique.
    d. low self-esteem approach.

41. According to the Stanley Milgram findings, the Watergate cover-up was made possible because of the compliance of people who were

    a. not moral people.
    b. innocent of wrongdoing.
    c. more concerned about the approval of their superiors than about their own morality.
    d. basically a bunch of criminals.

42. Why do people sometimes succumb to destructive instances of obedience to authority?

    a. Personal accountability is diminished.
    b. Authority figures often possess highly visible symbols of power.
    c. People are "sucked in" by a series of gradual demands beforehand.
    d. For all the above reasons.

43. Cognitively, prejudice is associated with

    a. expectations to behave badly.
    b. avoidance behavior or discrimination.
    c. facts and logic.
    d. negative feelings such as hatred or dislike.

44. We divide our world into two groups of people, "us" and "them." You and I belong to the

    a. outgroup.
    b. ingroup.
    c. minority group.
    d. known group.

45. A personality characterized by intolerance, coolness, rigidity, stereotyped thinking, and unquestioning submission to higher authority is called a(n)

    a. permissive personality.
    b. stereotyped personality.
    c. foot-in-the-door type person.
    d. authoritarian personality.

46. Homeowners are more likely to develop friendships with

    a. next-door neighbors.
    b. people across the street.
    c. people across the backyard fence.
    d. people two doors away.

47. Judith Langlois (1987) at the University of Texas at Austin found that two- to eight-month-old infants demonstrated _____ for attractive faces.

    a. marked preferences
    b. fear
    c. less preferences
    d. no preference

48. The theory that suggests aggressive behavior is learned by reinforcement for being aggressive and by observing aggression is

    a. psychoanalytic theory.
    b. behavior theory.
    c. social-learning theory.
    d. social biology theory.

QUESTIONS TO CONSIDER

1. How do social power and personal power contribute to behavior?

2. How is nationalism used to structure social reality?

3. Would Rosenthal's experiment meet today's ethical standards?

4. What do dissonance reduction, the self-serving bias, and the defense mechanism of rationalization all have in common?

5. How do programs on television construct a distorted reality for children?

OPTIONAL ACTIVITIES

1. Look for editorials, news stories, or political cartoons that portray an international situation. Which words, labels, and images promote "us versus them" thinking? How might someone with opposite views have written the articles or drawn the cartoons differently?

2. Think of norms of proper dress or social behavior that you can violate. For example, what would happen if you wore shorts to a formal gathering? Or asked a stranger an extremely personal question? Or arrived at work in your bedroom slippers? Pay attention to your feelings as you think about carrying out these activities. What fears or inhibitions do you have? How likely is it that you could actually carry out these activities?

ANTHOLOGY

The following selections highlight the social forces that shape personal and social behavior. As you read, consider the interaction between personal needs and group demands, especially in public places, such as at school, in the workplace, at social gatherings, and in the military. How have social forces shaped your identity, attitudes, and behavior?

Reading 45

The same techniques used to persuade people to vote for a candidate or buy a certain brand of coffee can be used to alert the public to the dangers of drunk driving or to promote cancer checkups. This article describes how advertisers attempt to influence attitudes about potentially sensitive or offensive ideas and products. As you read, compare your reactions to the ad campaigns with those of the psychologists and professional consultants. Which principles of perception and social influence do the advertisers use? Are you more likely to be persuaded by a soft sell or a hard sell?

Advertisers Struggle to Portray Subject of Death in Commercials

By Ronald Alsop

The American Cancer Society has always tried to be as upbeat as possible in its public-service announcements. Rarely has there been any mention of surgery or chemotherapy. And blatant references to death have been absolutely taboo.

But such soft selling hasn't drawn hordes of people into doctors' offices for checkups. So later this week, the cancer society will get deadly serious in a new television spot about colorectal cancer.

The ad will run in reverse sequence, with scenes of mourners at a cemetery, a hearse carrying a casket and a woman weeping by her husband's hospital bed. The flashback ends with the doomed spurning his wife's suggestion that they get a checkup for colon cancer.

Jolting People

"It was risky for us to deal so honestly with death, but we believe scare tactics will jolt people more than an intellectual appeal," says Peter Hirsch, executive creative director of Calet, Hirsch & Spector, the volunteer agency from the Advertising Council that created the cancer spot.

Other advertisers also face the prickly issue of depicting death in their commercials. The life insurance and funeral industries constantly wrestle with how best to market their death-related products. While they want to make a forceful sales pitch, they certainly don't want their ads to come across as macabre or distasteful.

Organizations trying to awaken people to the dangers of AIDS, drug abuse and drunk driving also debate how morbid their ads should be. A few years ago, a drunk-driving spot showed a car full of teen-age beer drinkers being transformed into gruesome skeletons. The ad agency that created the spot feared it was too grisly, but teen-agers in focus groups told the agency that they considered the ad tame compared with the special effects in slasher-type horror movies.

"Some people deal quite well with their mortality, but most Americans are death avoiders," says David Wills, vice president of marketing at Service Corp. International, an operator of funeral homes and cemeteries. In a consumer study a few years ago, the company found that 35% of respondents said they become frightened when they contemplate their own deaths.

Service Corp., therefore, plays it low-key. A new commercial for its funeral preplanning service shows a family packing up dishes, books and memorabilia following the father's death. The mother informs her children that like her husband, she too has already made her funeral arrangements. "We wanted the ad to ring true but be nonthreatening," says Murray Brauman, chief executive officer of Moss & Co., the agency that produced the commercial. "We don't want people visualizing themselves lying in a box."

According to Service Corp., only 21% of consumers say they're offended by funeral-home advertising. But some funeral-industry ads are so subtle, consumers might be hard-pressed to figure out what's being promoted. Consider, for instance, a funeral ad showing a little boy holding another child up to a drinking fountain. The message: "Sometimes we all need a little help."

"We would never show coffins in ads because that wouldn't be humane or dignified," says Glenn Gould, a marketing consultant for the funeral industry. "But we also don't want to hem and haw with phrases like 'passed away' or 'no longer with us.' Our copy testing shows that consumers don't like those euphemisms."

Lately, the insurance industry has dealt much more frankly with the unpleasant reason that people buy life insurance. Allstate Insurance Co. bluntly uses the word "dying" in its ads and has created "visual euphemisms" for death. In some commercials, the insurer has superimposed a black box over the victim's face. In another ad, a woman and her husband are admiring a new clock on the mantel until—poof!—she vanishes into thin air.

One of the most memorable life insurance campaigns was Prudential Insurance Co.'s takeoff on the movie "Heaven Can Wait." In the commercials, angels in white three-piece suits fetch their victims at golf courses and bowling alleys and escort them up an escalator to heaven.

Prudential tested the angel spots carefully with consumers because it wasn't sure how they would react to a whimsical treatment of death. Only about 15% of the people disliked the approach. "I was terrified when we first put the angel commercials on the air because we were breaking new ground," says Connie Sartain, a Prudential vice president. "But most people felt it was a hard subject for us and thought we handled it with charm."

Still, after one focus group session, Prudential reluctantly scrapped one of the commercials. It showed a man escaping from the angels and the angels fretting about how they would explain it to their boss. "Consumers in the focus group went nuts when they saw that storyboard," Ms. Sartain recalls. "They said that when it's your time, it's your time and you can't avoid it. They had real sympathy for the angels who were just doing their job."

The Calet Hirsch ad agency didn't test its new colorectal cancer ad with consumers, but the agency's executives say they're confident that it won't make people squeamish. What helps keep the spot from being depressing is its lively music. The agency decided to use an early '60s rhythm-and-blues sound both to lighten up the spot and to appeal to the target audience of consumers over 40 years old.

The ad opens with a shot of mourners huddled around an open grave. Suddenly, a casket rises out of the ground and is deposited back in a hearse. As the flashback continues, doctors remove a white sheet from the dead man's face, and an oscilloscope monitoring his heartbeat changes from flat line to a wave. The final scene shows him working at a personal computer in his den, while his wife reads an article saying that 90% of colon cancer cases are curable if detected early enough. "Maybe we should get a checkup," she suggests. His reply: "I have more important things to worry about right now."

Raising Awareness

"The cancer society has reservations about a shock technique like this, but Americans simply aren't aware that colon cancer claims 60,000 lives a year," says Irving Rimer, vice president of public relations for the society. "Our previous ads were too pedestrian and didn't have enough dramatic value."

One of the earlier commercials, for example, had a much warmer tone, showing a recovered colon cancer patient returning home to a cake and hugs from family and friends. Another featured a tightrope walker discussing the risks of cancer.

Despite the images of death, some marketing consultants question how much more effective the new cancer spot will be in motivating people to visit their physician. In fact, Carol Moog, a psychologist and advertising consultant, says the coffin rising out of the ground may be reassuring because it subconsciously reinforces religious beliefs about rising from the dead. "I'm not sure people will be persuaded to go for a colorectal test," Ms. Moog says, "because the ad turns back the clock in such a magical way and makes death seem unreal."

Reading 46

This article illustrates many issues: group influence and the pressure to conform, intergroup relations, prejudice and stereotyping, social perception, mob psychology, and individual resistance. As you read, consider how the pressure to conform would have affected your ability to stick to your opinion.

The Jury System on Trial

By Linda Cox

This summer, in my first jury duty, I served on a criminal case that ended in a mistrial. After deliberating for nine hours, the jury was deadlocked 11 to one. I was the "one." What happened in that room shattered my faith in our jury system.

The defendant was a young Hispanic accused of possessing cocaine and carrying an illegal firearm. A police officer testified that the defendant was the man who had dropped a gun and fled from an apartment where drugs were found. He had been picked up an hour after the crime, standing on a street corner. The gun and the drug packets were not fingerprinted.

After hearing testimony for three days, I was convinced that the defendant had not been proved guilty and that it was probably a case of mistaken identity. When we began to deliberate on Friday morning, all but two other jurors were ready to convict. Soon those two changed their minds and urged me to change mine. I was alone.

We wrangled for hours in that hot room, barely cooled by an ancient air conditioner. The others could not understand my doubts about the testimony of the accusing officer, the only witness who identified the defendant. "The cop saw him!" was repeated like a mantra. But that witness did not seem credible to me. He could not remember the time of any of the events, his testimony was at odds with the incident and arrest reports, and two other officers contradicted him on several points.

"Why don't you believe the cop?" the others asked me again and again. When I tried to answer, they shouted me down: "You're dwelling on little things, just like the defense attorney did."

No one but me believed the defendant's testimony, backed up by witnesses, that he had been playing pool all evening and had stepped outside for a breath of air when he was taken into custody. The other jurors were

suspicious of all the defense witnesses, who spoke only Spanish and used a translator: "You can't trust them. They're his friends and relatives."

They saw proof of his guilt in everything. "The guy's out of work, so where does he get his money? Wasn't that a silk suit he was wearing?" "Looked like it to me. And his girlfriend was carrying a Gucci bag." "He can't remember the year he went back to Puerto Rico." (This seemed particularly significant to everyone.) "What was he doing with a 50-dollar bill when he was picked up? I never carry a fifty." They glared at me when I asked what these things had to do with the charges.

By midafternoon, with only a short break for a catered lunch whose main ingredient was mayonnaise, we were clearly deadlocked. The foreman sent a note to the judge: "One juror is adamantly entrenched in an opposing view." A few minutes later, the court officer returned and told us to keep deliberating.

More wrangling, more shouting. "Why are you being so unreasonable? What makes you so sure you're not wrong?" Exhausted, I answered as best I could: "I may be wrong, but I cannot vote to convict on the evidence presented to us. There are too many doubts in my mind." I felt as much on trial as the defendant and, like him, presumed guilty.

At 4 o'clock, we were called back to the courtroom. Instead of dismissing us—as we all must have been hoping—the judge instructed us to return on Monday morning, "refreshed and with open minds."

Over the weekend, I thought of nothing else and could hardly sleep or eat. I had flashes of insight about the evidence and testimony, even dreamt about it, and found more and more holes in the prosecution's case. By Sunday night, I thought I could prove the defendant innocent. With my notes on index cards, my ducks in a row, I saw myself as Henry Fonda in "Twelve Angry Men," blowing the prosecution out of the water.

My arguments on Monday persuaded no one. They had an answer for everything. The suspect had been described as having greasy ringlets—"a Michael Jackson hairdo." The defendant was arrested an hour after the crime; in the mug shot, his hair was rather short with no ringlets. Answers: "He cut his hair." "He used mousse to make the ringlets, and the mousse dried, shrinking the ringlets."

Fear was on the mound, the logic struck out. Nothing could change their picture of the defendant as a criminal. One juror saw a menace: "I don't want drugs and guns on my street." Another dreamt about the defendant: "He was chasing me with a gun and threatening to kill me." Another's words still haunt me: "I have to go with our side."

We were at exactly the same impasse as Friday afternoon—11 against one. They exchanged looks of disgust when I made my final declaration: "I cannot vote to convict. We have a hung jury." Little was said as I wrote a note to the judge. While we waited for his response, the others began to talk.

They took turns, almost like a ritual stoning. One man spoke at length. "It's not right that one person can keep us from reaching a verdict. You just feel sorry for him. You're blinded by emotion and can't see the truth." He angrily tapped his juror's handbook. "You're wearing a blindfold just like she is!" He was pointing to the portrait of Justice.

About 3 o'clock, we were called to the courtroom, and the judge reluctantly declared a mistrial. A few jurors clustered around the prosecutor; others walked straight to the elevators. I headed for the stairs and home.

I was one juror on one trial, but I cannot write off my experience as a fluke. I keep hearing stories about remorseful jurors who have been pressured into convicting. In all these stories, the defendant is not white.

My fellow jurors automatically believed the policeman and distrusted the dark-skinned Other who could not speak their language. In their eyes, the defendant could only be a criminal, and I was a defector who would not go with "our side." I saw in that jury room a classic mob scene: townspeople hounding the outsider.

How many jury rooms do they take over?

ADDITIONAL RESOURCES

Books and Articles

Bettelheim, Bruno. *Surviving and Other Essays*. New York: Vintage Books, 1979. Beautifully written and insightful essays by a psychologist who survived life in a concentration camp. Some of the essays deal with how both prisoners and persecutors behave in extreme situations.

Cialdini, Robert. *Influence: Science and Practice*. Glenview, Ill.: Scott, Foresman, 1985. An engaging book that describes six central strategies of influence and their application in advertising and other arts of persuasion.

Goffman, Erving. *Behavior in Public Places*. New York: Free Press of Glencoe, 1966. Uncovers the behavioral order found in all peopled places, whether an organized social occasion or merely a routinized social setting.

Orwell, George. *1984*. New York: Harcourt Brace and World, 1949. Imagine if every aspect of your life were planned for you and every move you made were watched by a "Big Brother." Orwell's frightening vision of the future shows how behavior can be molded in a totalitarian society.

Osherow, N. "Making Sense of the Nonsensical: An Analysis of Jonestown." In *Readings About the Social Animal*, edited by E. Aronson. San Francisco: Freeman, 1981. How can we begin to understand the tragic mass suicide led by Jim Jones? This article tries to piece together and explain what happened.

Rosenthal, Robert, and Lenore F. Jacobson. *Pygmalion in the Classroom*. New York: Holt, 1968. Classroom studies show that the expectations teachers have about their students greatly influence how the students perform.

Turnbull, C. M. *The Mountain People*. New York: Simon & Schuster, 1972. Social crises and the breakdown of social structures can be devastating to individuals. In one African tribe, conditions of extreme deprivation led to drastic changes in personality and behavior.

Film

Twelve Angry Men. Directed by Sidney Lumet; starring Henry Fonda. 1957. The jury deliberations in a murder case illustrate principles of social influence, conformity, and persuasion.

PSYCHOPATHOLOGY

Life begins on the other side of despair.

Jean-Paul Sartre

Unit 21 describes the major types of mental illnesses and some of the factors that influence them—both biological and psychological. It also reports on several approaches to classifying and treating mental illness and explains the difficulties of defining abnormal behavior.

Michael Weisbrot and Family/Stock, Boston

Recent studies indicate that one in every five Americans—20 percent—may suffer from some form of mental disorder, and that mild forms of depression, the "common cold" of psychopathology, are experienced by almost everyone.

OBJECTIVES

After viewing the television program and completing the assigned readings, you should be able to:

1. Identify the criteria commonly used to determine mental illness
2. Describe the Diagnostic Statistical Manual and how it is used
3. Explain how psychological disorders are classified
4. Identify sources of personal, social, and cultural bias in definitions of mental illness
5. Define and identify the different categories of anxiety disorders. Discuss the different theories as to the cause of anxiety disorders
6. Define and identify the different categories of somatoform disorder. Discuss the different theories as to the cause of somatoform disorders
7. Define and identify the different categories of dissociative disorder. Discuss the different theories as to the cause of dissociative disorders
8. Define and identify the different categories of mood disorder. Discuss the different theories as to the cause of mood disorders
9. Define and identify the different categories of schizophrenic disorder. Discuss the different theories as to the cause of schizophrenic disorders
10. Define and identify the different categories of personality disorder. Discuss the different theories as to the cause of personality disorders

phobias

READING ASSIGNMENT

After viewing Program 21, read pages 563-608 in *Psychology: Science, Behavior and Life*. Your instructor may also assign the anthology selections for Unit 21.

KEY TERMS AND CONCEPTS

As you read the assignment, pay particular attention to these terms, which are defined on the given pages in the text.

maladaptive (565)
Diagnostic and Statistical Manual (DSM) (566)
neurosis (566)
psychosis (566)
anxiety disorders (567-577)
panic disorder (567-568)
agoraphobia (568)
phobias (568-569)
social phobia (568-569)

simple phobias (569)
obsessive-compulsive disorder (569-570)
posttraumatic stress disorder (PTSD) (570-571)
generalized anxiety disorder (571)
autonomic lability (574)
somatoform disorders (577)
somatization disorder (577)
hypochondriasis (578)

don't need to know names of drugs.
different symptoms of schizophrenic

conversion disorder (578)
sensory conversion (578)
motor conversion (578)
primary gain (580)
secondary gain (580)
dissociative disorders (580)
dissociative amnesia (580)
dissociative fugue (581)
dissociative personality (581)
mood disorders (582)
major depression (unipolar
   disorder) (584)
manic-depressive (bipolar
   disorder) (584)
mania (584)

not too much

delusions (585)
hallucinations (585)
learned helplessness (589)
monoamine oxidase inhibitors
   (MAO inhibitors) (592)
tricyclics (592)
norepinephrine (592)
serotonin (592)
amine theory (593)
premenstrual syndrome (PMS) (595)
schizophrenic disorder (595)
dementia praecox (596)
disturbances of thought (597)

not too much

disturbances of content (597)
disturbances of form (597)
neologisms (598)
disturbance of perception (598)
disturbance in emotional perception
   (598)
blunted or flat effect (598)
disturbances in speech (599)
mutism (599)
echolalia (599)
social withdrawal (599)
diminished motivation (599)
prodromal stage (599)
active stage (599)
residual phase (599)
disorganized schizophrenia (600)
clang (600)
word salad (600)
catatonic schizophrenia (600)
waxy flexibility (600)
paranoid schizophrenia (601)
undifferentiated schizophrenia (601)
residual schizophrenia (601)
regressive symptoms (601)
restitutional symptoms (601)
dopamine hypothesis (603)
personality disorders (604)
antisocial personality disorder (606)

don't need to know clusters

know

PROGRAM SUMMARY

Hearing voices, fear of public places, and pervasive feelings of inadequacy are just a few examples of how the powers of the brain distort our perceptions, thoughts, and feelings. Psychopathology, the subject of Program 21, is the study of these distortions, the mental disorders that affect personality and normal functioning.

One in every five Americans suffers from some form of mental disorder. It is difficult to measure the true extent of the problem because many mental disorders resemble typical everyday problems that we all experience. Mental health specialists trained to make these judgments rely on observations of behavior, diagnostic tests, and complaints from the individual who is suffering and from others.

Mental illnesses need to be classified for many different reasons. When a problem is identified and classified, appropriate treatment can be planned. Mental health and stability can also have important legal implications. For example, a psychiatric diagnosis may determine whether a person is able to stand trial. Classification also aids research, furthering the study of pathology and the effectiveness of various treatments. And insurance companies need classification for economic reasons; they provide payments based on the type of mental disorder and its accepted treatment.

Years ago, people with psychological problems were lumped with society's outcasts and punished without compassion. In the eighteenth century, Phillippe Pinel, a French physician, suggested that mental problems should be viewed as sickness. The treatment of people with mental disorders has changed and continues to improve—but not fast enough.

Psychiatrist Thomas Szasz argues that mental illness is a myth used as an excuse for authorities to repress people who violate social norms. It has been used by the Soviet Union to justify imprisoning social and political dissidents. It was also used to justify the treatment of slaves in the United States.

Stanford psychologist David Rosenhan explains that behavior is always interpreted within a context. In an experiment, he and seven other sane people gained admission to a mental hospital, having convinced authorities that they were suffering from hallucinations. Although they behaved normally once they were admitted, virtually everything they did was interpreted as abnormal. His experiment teaches us that virtually anyone can be diagnosed as mentally ill in certain situations.

But mental illness is not simply a social label. Anxiety disorders such as phobias, affective disorders such as depression of mania, and schizophrenia account for an estimated 25 million cases in the United States.

Freud labeled anxiety states *neuroses*, a term considered too general today. He believed that neurotic individuals, unaware of the underlying infantile conflicts, showed a pattern of self-defeating behavior. According to his theory, the difference between neurotic and normal behavior is one of degree.

Although almost everyone has been depressed at one time or another, an individual with extreme and chronic depression may require hospitalization and drug therapy. In fact, depression accounts for most mental hospital admissions. But about 80 percent of those suffering from clinical depression never receive any treatment.

The label *psychosis* describes a class of disorders that are not on the continuum of normal behavior. People with psychotic disorders suffer from impaired perception, thinking, and emotional responses. Schizophrenic disorders, a major subclass, are characterized by a complete break with reality.

The two primary approaches to understanding schizophrenia are biological and psychological. The biological approach traces the disorder to abnormal brain structure or functioning. The psychological approach assumes that the key to understanding lies in the patient's personal experiences, traumas, and conflicts.

Because schizophrenia and depression are so varied, most researchers believe that the disorders are the result of complex interactions between biological and psychosocial factors. Irving Gottesman, a leading expert on the genetics of schizophrenia, concludes that there is a genetic path for some forms of the disease. The results of his research with pairs of identical twins who are discordant for schizophrenia sheds light on other psychosocial factors, such as family communication patterns and social isolation.

Other scientists, such as Teresa La Framboise, are trying to understand the origins of psychopathology by looking at cultural factors in the Native American population. La Framboise explains that because Native American values conflict with those that predominate in the culture around them, mental problems have become common in their culture.

Mental illness may be caused by a combination of physical and psychological variables, and its diagnosis may be biased by cultural or social factors. But the suffering of the afflicted is real.

REVIEW QUESTIONS

Program Questions

1. Psychopathology is defined as the study of

    a. organic brain disease.
    b. perceptual and cognitive illusions.
    c. clinical measures of abnormal functioning.
    d. mental disorders.

2. What is the key criterion for identifying a person as having a mental disorder?

    a. The person has problems.
    b. The person's functioning is clearly abnormal.
    c. The person's ideas challenge the status quo.
    d. The person makes other people feel uncomfortable.

3. Frannie is a mental health specialist who has a Ph.D. in psychology. She would be classified as a

    a. psychiatrist.
    b. clinical psychologist.
    c. social psychologist.
    d. psychoanalyst.

4. What happened after David Rosenhan and his colleagues were admitted to mental hospitals by pretending to have hallucinations and then behaved normally?

    a. Their sanity was quickly observed by the staff.
    b. It took several days for their deception to be uncovered.
    c. In most cases, the staff disagreed with each other about these "patients."
    d. Nobody ever detected their sanity.

5. Olivia is experiencing dizziness, muscle tightness, shaking, and tremors. She is feeling apprehensive. These symptoms most resemble those found in cases of

    a. anxiety disorders.
    b. affective disorders.
    c. psychoses.
    d. schizophrenia.

6. Agoraphobia is the most common of the phobias. What does a person with this condition fear?

   a. Being at the top of a tall building
   b. Going out in public
   c. Being violently attacked
   d. In this condition, people have a generalized fear of experience.

7. When Freud studied patients with anxiety, he determined that their symptoms were caused by

   a. childhood abuse, both physical and sexual.
   b. imbalances in body chemistry.
   c. childhood conflicts that had been repressed.
   d. cognitive errors in the way patients viewed the world.

8. Vincent Van Gogh's paintings reflect his mental disorder. He suffered from

   a. alternate episodes of mania and depression.
   b. an anxiety state unrelated to any specific phobia.
   c. an extreme fear of open spaces.
   d. impaired perception, thinking, and emotion.

9. What happens to most people who are suffering from serious clinical depression?

   a. They commit suicide.
   b. They are hospitalized.
   c. They receive treatment outside a hospital.
   d. They receive no treatment at all.

10. People lose touch with reality in cases of

    a. neurosis but not psychosis.
    b. psychosis but not neurosis.
    c. both psychosis and neurosis.
    d. all psychoses and some neuroses.

11. When Hans Strupp speaks of the importance of psychological factors in schizophrenia, he specifically cites the role of

    a. feelings of inadequacy.
    b. antisocial personality.
    c. delayed development.
    d. early childhood experiences.

12. Irving Gottesman and Fuller Torrey have been studying twins to learn more about schizophrenia. If the brain of a twin with schizophrenia is compared with the brain of a normal twin, the former has

    a. less cerebrospinal fluid.
    b. larger ventricles.
    c. a larger left hemisphere.
    d. exactly the same configuration as the latter.

13. For Teresa La Framboise, the major issue in the treatment of mental disorders among Native Americans is

    a. the prevalence of genetic disorders.
    b. alcohol's impact on family structure.
    c. the effect of imposing white American culture.
    d. isolation due to rural settings.

Textbook Questions

14. Behavior that impairs a person's ability to function adequately in everyday social and occupational roles is considered

    a. atypical.
    b. psychologically discomforting.
    c. socially unacceptable.
    d. maladaptive.

15. A person who would stand on a street corner dressed only in a necktie and scream obscenities at passing motorists would fit which of the four criteria of abnormality?

    a. Socially unacceptable behavior
    b. Atypical behavior
    c. Maladaptive behavior
    d. Psychologically discomforting behavior

16. When compared to the DSM-II, the DSM-III has the advantage of

    a. specifying more precisely when a diagnosis should be made.
    b. greater diagnostic validity.
    c. being based completely on the social-learning model.
    d. addressing disorders that have only psychological causes.

17. On the morning of his chemistry exam, Jeff suddenly felt an intense apprehension and overwhelming terror, causing his heart to pound and his breathing to become labored. Jeff is probably experiencing a

    a. heart attack.
    b. panic attack.
    c. hysterical reaction.
    d. compulsion.

18. Maria is afraid to leave her home to go shopping or even to go to work; she avoids all public places. Maria suffers from a panic disorder known as

    a. agoraphobia.
    b. social phobia.
    c. simple phobia.
    d. claustrophobia.

19. A fear that is out of proportion to the real danger is labeled _____ by the DSM-III-R.

    a. a natural fear
    b. neurotic
    c. psychotic
    d. a phobia

20. The anxiety disorder characterized by persistent, unwanted, and unshakable thoughts and/or irresistible repeated actions is

    a. posttraumatic anxiety.
    b. obsessive-compulsive disorder.
    c. agoraphobia.
    d. simple phobia.

21. Many Vietnam veterans have flashbacks of traumatic war experiences and experience severe stress as a result of the memories. These veterans are experiencing _____ according to the DSM-III-R.

    a. phobic disorder
    b. posttraumatic stress
    c. generalized anxiety
    d. obsessive-compulsive disorders

22. Excessive vigilance, dread, foreboding, tension, insomnia, and impatience are symptoms of

    a. phobic disorder.
    b. generalized anxiety disorder.
    c. obsessive-compulsive disorder.
    d. dissociative disorder.

23. Freud explained phobias in terms of

    a. unresolved separation anxiety.
    b. anal fixations.
    c. unresolved oral fixation.
    d. displacement.

24. Behaviorists explain anxiety disorders as a result of

    a. conflicts involving sexual or aggressive impulses.
    b. classically conditioned emotional responses.
    c. loss of control over life's rewards and punishments.
    d. an unusually responsive nervous system.

25. Three-year-old Patricia sees her mother react fearfully to a dog, which causes Patricia to develop a fear of dogs. Her fear is a result of

    a. repressed hostility.
    b. modeling/imitation.
    c. an unresolved anal fixation.
    d. reinforcement.

26. _____ is the persistent belief that one has a medical problem despite lack of medical findings.

    a. Conversion disorder
    b. Hypochondriasis
    c. Malingering
    d. Dissociative disorder

27. A somatoform disorder that is manifested as a sensory or motor system disorder for which there is no known organic cause is called a(n)

    a. hypochondriasis.
    b. conversion disorder.
    c. somatoform conversion.
    d. dissociative disorder.

28. According to the behaviorist, somatoform disorders

    a. allow a person to escape from or avoid the negative reinforcer.
    b. resolve fixations in the anal stage.
    c. resolve sexual impulses.
    d. redirect hostility.

29. Disorders in which the thoughts and feelings that generate anxiety are separated from consciousness by memory loss or a change in identity are called

    a. dissociative disorders.
    b. somatoform disorders.
    c. conversion disorders.
    d. anxiety disorders.

30. If amnesia is not caused by organic problems, such as a blow to the head or alcoholic intoxication, it is called

    a. retrograde amnesia.
    b. obsessive-compulsive.
    c. dissociative amnesia.
    d. a panic disorder.

31. A dissociative disorder in which a person experiences several "personalities," each with distinct traits and memories, is referred to as

    a. dissociative personality.
    b. malingering.
    c. schizophrenia.
    d. somatoform disorder.

32. According to _____ theory, dissociative disorders involve massive repression.

    a. psychoanalytic
    b. behavior
    c. social-learning
    d. cognitive

33. Both major depression and bipolar disorders are classified as _____ disorders.

    a. schizophrenic
    b. mood
    c. conversion
    d. somatoform

34. A type of mood disorder characterized by deep and persistent depression is

    a. traumatic depression.
    b. conversion disorder.
    c. bipolar disorder.
    d. major depression.

35. In the _____ disorder, moods swing from elation to depression.

    a. manic
    b. paranoid
    c. schizoid
    d. bipolar

36. Nelda is a 45-year-old attorney who is divorced and is going through a prolonged depression. What would accurately describe her situation?

    a. Her situation is fairly typical.
    b. She will become schizophrenic.
    c. She is dissociative.
    d. She is highly at risk to attempt suicide.

37. According to the behavioral and learning theorists' perspective, mood disorders are

    a. caused by repressed love-hate relationships.
    b. the result of the loss of a primary source of reinforcement, such as the loss of a loved one or of loss of any kind.
    c. because of feelings of loss of control over rewards and punishments.
    d. caused from a deficiency in brain chemicals.

38. A patient whose behavior is characterized by withdrawal and a severe confusion of self-identity and thought processes would probably be classified as a

    a. multiple personality.
    b. schizophrenic.
    c. manic-depressive.
    d. hypochondriac.

39. Schizophrenics who show disorganized delusions, regression, and vivid hallucinations are labeled _____ schizophrenics.

    a. catatonic
    b. disorganized
    c. paranoid
    d. autistic

40. Schizophrenics who show striking impairment of psychomotor activity are label _____ type.

    a. catatonic
    b. paranoid
    c. disorganized
    d. simple

41. The "catch-all" category for schizophrenics who may possess disturbances of thought, perception, or emotional expression but none of the specific symptoms is called

    a. withdrawal.
    b. residual.
    c. catatonic.
    d. undifferentiated.

42. According to Freud, the schizophrenic regresses to the _____ stage.

    a. phallic
    b. genital
    c. oral
    d. anal

43. Research by Gottesman (1987) demonstrated that identical twins' concordance rates were two to four times higher for schizophrenia than that of fraternal twins, thus giving evidence for

    a. a psychoanalytic explanation.
    b. genetic influence.
    c. a learning theory explanation.
    d. a cognitive theory explanation.

44. Psychopath is another label for

    a. antisocial personality.
    b. paranoid schizophrenic.
    c. schizotypal personality.
    d. disorganized personality.

45. Recent research suggests that antisocial personalities are undeterred by punishment because

    a. they have lower IQs.
    b. they are used to it.
    c. they have lower than normal levels of arousal.
    d. crime pays.

46. The learning/behavioral perspective sees the antisocial personality as

    a. having an ill-developed superego.
    b. not learning to avoid punishment.
    c. inheriting the disorder.
    d. having brain chemistry disorders.

QUESTIONS TO CONSIDER

1. Is the insanity defense legitimate?

2. Why has the DSM been criticized?

3. Is homosexuality a deviant behavior?

4. Are standards for psychological health the same for men and women? Why are most patients women?

5. How can you tell whether your own behavior, anxieties, and moods are within normal limits or whether they signal mental illness?

6. Explain why the term *split personality* is not an accurate way to describe schizophrenia.

OPTIONAL ACTIVITIES

1. Collect the advice columns in the daily papers for a week or two (such as "Dear Ann Landers" or "Dear Abby"). What kinds of problems do people write about? How often does the columnist refer people to a psychologist, psychiatrist, or other profressional for counseling? Why do people write to an anonymous person for advice about their problems?

2. Ask several people (who are not psychology professionals) to define the terms *emotionally ill*, *mentally ill*, *crazy*, *insane*, and *mad*. Ask them to describe behaviors that characterize each term. Do some terms indicate more extreme behavior than others? How do their definitions compare with the ones in your text? What can you conclude about the attitudes and understanding of mental illness shown by the people you interviewed?

ANTHOLOGY

The following selections highlight the problem of identifying and explaining mental illness. As you read, ask yourself these questions: When does a behavior become clinically significant? Are some forms of mental illness more socially or culturally acceptable than others? What does each approach to diagnosis, classification, and treatment add to our understanding of normal and abnormal behavior?

Reading 47

When does a behavior qualify as a mental disorder? This article raises a number of medical, social, and political issues about the American Psychiatric Association's diagnostic and statistical manual. As you read, consider the advantages and disadvantages of the classification system and how the labels shape our views of mental illness.

A Last Dance With Freud

By Stuart A. Kirk

Perhaps I always had a secret desire to be a dancer. I do enjoy seeing people dance. I love the elegance of the ballet, the exuberance of a big Broadway musical and, I confess, the tacky routines on television dance shows. Occasionally, I, too, can be coaxed onto a dance floor—but only after a few drinks in an appropriately anonymous situation. I had never before reflected on these pastimes nor thought much about them in relation to a peculiar late-night habit of mine. A report issued by the American Psychiatric Association changed that.

I want you to know that writing about this is embarrassing, but for the sake of science and personal catharsis, I'll divulge my secret. Sometimes in the middle of the night, I get this restless feeling in my legs; they just want to move. This is not ordinary fidgetiness. On these occasions, they won't let me sleep and they won't let me rest. I can't seem to talk them out of doing what they do. It's as if my legs have a will of their own; as if they're dancing to a different nighttime drummer. It can be annoying, of course, but in the greater scheme of things, it's not something I thought very much about. In fact, it's not something I even spoke about before. I certainly didn't place it in the same category as war, famine or cancer. It paled by comparison to death and taxes.

That is, until I discovered that I was suffering from a new mental disorder, coded 780.52 by the committee charged with updating the American Psychiatric Association's diagnostic and statistical manual. Tucked right into their first-draft report, and listed with more familiar illnesses like schizophrenia, depression and addiction, was my nocturnal affliction. Called Restless Legs Sleep Disorder, this bedtime nuisance had been given an authoritative label and a diagnostic description as well: "The sensations . . . are rarely painful, but agonizingly relentless, and cause an almost irresistible urge to move the legs."

My first reaction was shock. Then laughter. Then quiet resignation to my undeniable affliction. Still, I kept wondering—could it be a mistake? Do I really have the correct symptomatology?

Such a discovery, I suppose, brings about a new and profound sense of self-knowledge. It's certainly a relief to know there is a name for my quirk, and that it attracted the attention of the best and brightest of psychiatric scientists. That sort of dignifies it; gives it a place above my other idiosyncrasies, a special status in the medical world it heretofore was without. But it also can bring the burden of sharing such a diagnosis with loved ones.

"Hello, Mom, this is Stuart. Now don't get upset. I'm going to be OK, I think, but I'm mentally ill. I'm suffering from Restless Legs Sleep Disorder.

"No, Mom, I don't know when or how I got it. Yes, I have been eating properly. No, you shouldn't feel guilty; I don't think it's related to enforced bedtimes during childhood. I don't know yet if it's treatable. It's not terminal. Thank God I have good medical insurance."

There was some solace in reading other chapters in the revised version of the psychiatrists' bible. I learned that lots of other people also have mental disorders, some of them brand new, too. Those who are drowsy in the daytime, or awake at night, or who frequently change their sleeping schedule now have their very own labels. And the old standbys were curiously comforting, as well. If you don't like your gender, or get sexually aroused by unusual but harmless things, have orgasms too easily or with difficulty, there is a code for you. Having trouble with cigarettes or caffeine? You're in luck, too.

Children were at a special disadvantage, perhaps because there is no child's version of the manual—a Dr. Seuss-compatible. But there are lots of labels for kids. Trouble reading, young fella? Code 315.00: Reading Disorder. Don't like math, young lady? Code 315.10: Arithmetic Disorder. Can't wait your turn in line? Code 314.01: Attention Deficit-Hyperactivity Disorder. Don't talk back to me! You little code 313.81 (Oppositional-Defiant Disorder). They're all in the book—most of the kids who don't meet our middle-class expectations, or who are a little too slow or a little too fast, or who are simply a pain in the butt.

Controversial categories: I began to read all that I could about the manual and learned that the number of psychiatric diagnoses officially recognized by the APA had increased from 60 in 1952 to 230—before the latest round of revisions began. In keeping with our democratic traditions, there may yet be one for every man, woman and child.

In fact, women are already eligible for a special, new mental disorder and they don't like it one bit. It's called Periluteal Phase Dysphoric Disorder, an extremely severe form of premenstrual syndrome (PMS), which feminists fear can be used as a scientific excuse for job discrimination. How did the shrinks handle the conflict? They moved it to the back of the book, to an appendix aptly titled "new controversial categories."

Which brings me back to my own restless legs. I had considered using my special syndrome as an all-purpose excuse, even as a valid claim on my medical insurance. After all, I could have been a code 315.40 (Coordination Disorder) as a kid. Embarrassed and frustrated, maybe I repressed my secret desire to glide like Fred Astaire. Who knows what this did to my head? These are serious clinical questions for the Freudians, who, by the way, seem harmless when compared to the more behaviorally inclined. But that is a discussion for another time—especially since I've discovered that my disorder has disappeared from the book. Sure, I can still find it in the old manual, in a semiofficial spot in an appendix. It's also there in plain English in a draft of the updated edition. But it's gone from the latest revision.

What happened to my disease? Now I'm told that it's just a neurological aberration. If I think about *that*, I will surely earn a code 307.45: disorganized Sleep-Wake Schedule Disorder. So I am going off to bed where I can have a mentally healthy night of dance, dance, dance.

Reading 48

This article raises a lot of important questions about the long-held belief in the link between madness and creativity. Do you agree with the author's premise? Are the artists and writers diagnosed as having mental disorders a representative sampling of the "creative" population? Do you think creative people would sacrifice their supposed extreme sensitivity for a more "normal" emotional life?

Exploring the Link Between Art and Madness

By Alfie Kohn

"All who have been famous for their genius ... have been inclined to insanity."

Aristotle wrote that more than 2,000 years ago, and the belief that creativity requires a touch of madness remains popular to this day.

Indeed, researchers have recently begun to find associations between certain psychiatric disorders and some measures of artistic success. But many psychologists insist that the capacity to create depends on personality features that read like a textbook profile of mental health.

It is a paradox that specialists continue to grapple with.

"How can the maladjustment of many great creative minds be reconciled with the assertion that they are in some respects unusually healthy?" asks Robert Prentky, a Boston University psychologist and the author of "Creativity and Psychopathology."

Part of the answer seems to be that while a disproportionate number of creative writers and artists have been diagnosed as having a mood disorder, it is their reservoir of psychological strength that allows them to turn these emotional difficulties into something that can move or inspire others.

In fact, when specialists look closely at the small group of manic-depressives who are especially creative, they find that it is during the periods of relative normality that these individuals usually do their best work.

Besides depression, the major disturbance of affect or mood is called "bipolar" disorder, in which depression alternates with periods of mania—that is, euphoria and frenzied activity. New studies have documented a statistical relationship between this disorder and certain forms of creative accomplishment, particularly in writing and the visual arts.

Last fall, psychiatrist Nancy Andreasen of the University of Iowa published an update of her 15-year-long survey of faculty members at the school's Writers' Workshop. Of 30 established creative writers, 24 had at some time been diagnosed with an affective, or mood, disorder—nearly three times the rate in a matched group of 30 professionals in other fields.

Equally remarkable was Andreasen's finding that the writers' parents and siblings were also much more likely than the general population to have had a psychological disorder as well as to have reached an impressive level of creative achievement. "The families of the writers were riddled with both creativity, and mental illness," said Andreasen.

These results echo a 1983 study of 47 leading British artists and writers conducted by Kay Jamison, a psychologist at Johns Hopkins Medical School. Eighteen of them, or 38 percent, had been treated for an affective disorder. Fully half the poets had been

hospitalized or received medication for such a problem.

By contrast, about one percent of the general population will be diagnosed as having bipolar disorder at some point, and at least 5 percent will be diagnosed as seriously depressed.

A similar association was found in yet another research project, this one by Hagop Akiskal, professor of psychiatry at the University of Tennessee. Seventy percent of his sample of famous contemporary Persian painters, musicians and writers were prone to mood swings, and more than half had been treated for the problem.

Such studies seem to bear out the pattern of creative individuals whose breakdowns or suicides have become legend. Composers such as Robert Schumann and George Frideric Handel, and poets such as Anne Sexton and Robert Lowell are but a few.

Several reasons have been proposed for the connection between mood disorders and creativity. First, manic states can heighten the senses, accelerate the flow of ideas and reduce the need for sleep. "Such people have a higher energy level," Jamison said in an interview. "They think faster."

Second, elation and depression can provide good material for creative work—a variety of sensations to be explored artistically. "Extreme affective experience might, if there's talent and motivation, be grist for the creative mill," said Teresa Amabile, a Brandeis University psychologist who studies creativity.

Third, there might be a genetic link. While this is highly speculative—and there is surely no gene for poetry or sculpture, per se—researchers are excited by findings that relatives of creative subjects are themselves very creative.

While Andreasen and Jamison found high rates of psychological disorders among those known to be creative, McLean Hospital researchers Ruth Richards and Dennis Kinney found higher creativity among those known to have psychological disorders.

Richards and Kinney recently gave a newly devised pencil-and-paper test for creativity to 33 people with mood disorders and 11 of their normal relatives. All, including the relatives, scored slightly higher than a control group.

"Since it runs in families, and the form of creativity is different [between writers and their relatives], that suggests that what you're seeing is not learned behavior," Andreasen said. "It's probably genetically transmitted."

But what is the "it" that may have a genetic component? Andreasen emphasizes that psychological disorders in themselves don't lead to higher creativity. "It's not the illness that makes people more creative. It's that they have a fundamental cognitive style that makes them more creative and also makes them more susceptible to illness."

Researchers use words like openness, sensitivity and intensity to describe that style.

Ernest Hartmann, a Tufts University psychiatrist, calls it "thin boundaries." In the course of studying hundreds of nightmare sufferers, he found that those who experienced more than their share of unpleasant dreams are "especially vulnerable to stress, loss and rejection—which are known as precipitants of mental illness." Thin boundaries are also found in people who "would tend to become artists if they had any talent," he said in an interview.

Because creativity and manic-depressive disorder seem only indirectly related, with each being connected to a third factor, virtually all researchers join Andreasen in denying any necessary connection between madness and art.

"I don't believe that the vast proportion of creative people are or were psychotic," said Prentky.

Conversely, noted Frank Barron, a psychologist at the University of California at Santa Cruz who has studied creativity for nearly three decades, "There are lots of manic depressives who don't manifest any creativity. If you go into a hospital, you don't find eccentric people, you find apathetic, pathetic sick people."

When Barron gives personality tests to original thinkers, he finds that they sometimes score high on measures of abnormality but also on measures of "ego strength."

Mood swings and health, in other words, are not mutually exclusive. Andreasen believes creative people "are fundamentally rather healthy, neat, well-put-together people who happen to be vulnerable to mood disorders. Between episodes [of mania and depression], they are very normal."

In fact, she added, it is during healthy periods that creative people do the best work.

"They don't do well when their mood isn't normal. They're too disorganized when they're high and too despondent when they're depressed."

Even disturbed creators like Schumann "were not psychotic at the time they were highly creative," said Prentky.

Psychoanalysts have made this point for years: Artists must be able to leave the world of rationality and inhibitions behind in order to tap the primitive, unconscious realm. But they must also be able to return to the "real world," to shape, integrate and evaluate what they have done.

There are still other caveats. First, said Jamison, "There's no evidence for an association with other kinds of mental illness"—including schizophrenia.

Second, many types of creativity, such as original scientific thinking, seem unrelated to mood disorders.

Third, creativity is more likely to be found among people whose mood disorders are relatively mild. "After a certain point in mania, you're not producing," said Jamison. "You're just nuts."

Some suggest the eccentricity of creative people may lead to their being misdiagnosed as manic-depressive. Mood swings, they argue, don't always imply mental illness. It may be "an intense sensibility rather than psychopathology," said Barron.

In another soon-to-be published study, Tennessee's Akiskal looked at 750 psychiatric patients. Of those with mild mood swings, 8 percent turned out to be relatively well-known artists. Virtually no artists turned up among the patients who were treated for more serious bipolar disorder, simple depression or schizophrenia.

Finally, there is the possibility that being a creator, particularly in a society that doesn't always value the process or the product, can cause or at least worsen, psychological problems.

"Artists are often mavericks whose pursuits isolate them from the mainstream," said Peter Ostwald, a San Francisco psychiatrist and author of a study of Robert Schumann. "I see a close relationship between the difficult lifestyle of a person and the development of anger, frustration, and depression.

Andreasen, too, mused that rather than mental illness causing artistic talent, "The relationship is often in the opposite direction.

Being creative may make one more susceptible to depression."

Asked what psychological profile is most likely to produce creativity, Boston-area psychologist and author Howard Gardner said, "I'd bet on health—especially in the long run."

Reading 49

There are problems with all the methods used to define mental illness. This article points out some of those weaknesses. As you read, think about your own definition of a psychologically fit individual. Who has the right to decide who is psychologically fit and who is not?

I'm OK, You're a Bit Odd

By Paul Chance

The new groom was happy with his bride, and everything, he explained, was fine. There was just this one peculiarity his wife had. During lovemaking she insisted that he wear his motorcycle helmet. He found it uncomfortable, and he felt just a tad foolish. Is it normal to want someone to wear a helmet during amorous activities? Does a quirk of this sort keep one off the rolls of the mentally fit? The answer depends on how you define mental fitness. There are several ways of going about it.

One model calls to mind the Platonic ideal. Somewhere in the heavens there exists a person who is the perfect specimen of psychological health. (Or maybe there are two of them: The perfect man may be different from the perfect woman. At least, one would hope so.) We all fall short of this ideal, of course, but it provides a model that we can emulate. Unfortunately, the Platonic answer merely begs the question, since somebody has to describe what the ideal is like. And how do we do that?

The everyday way of defining mental health is more subjective: If I do it, it's healthy; if I don't do it, it's sick. Is it crazy to spend Saturdays jumping out of airplanes or canoeing down rapids? Not to skydivers and whitewater canoers. Is it sick to hear voices when no one is there? Not if you're the one who hears the voices—and you welcome their company.

This commonsense way of defining mental health sets ourselves up as the standard against which to make comparisons. There's nothing wrong with this, except that it's just possible that some of us—not me, you understand—are a bit odd ourselves. And you can't measure accurately with a bent ruler.

The psychodynamic model of mental health suggests that psychological fitness is a kind of balancing act. There are, according to this view, impulses in all of us that society cannot tolerate. The healthy person is not the one who always keeps these impulses under lock and key but the one who lets them out once in awhile when nobody's looking. If you run around the house smashing delicate things with a hammer, for example, someone's apt to object. But if you hammer a nail into a board, and seem to have a good excuse for it, nobody minds. So the healthy person with violent impulses builds a deck behind the house.

The chief problem with the psychodynamic model is that it doesn't define the standard by which balance is to be measured. Building a deck may be an acceptable outlet for violent impulses, but what if every time a person feels like slugging someone he adds on to the deck until his entire backyard is covered in redwood? He's directing his impulses constructively, but his family might find him easier to live with if he just broke something once in awhile.

Behaviorists offer a different solution. They focus on behavior, naturally, and decide whether behavior is healthy on the basis of its consequences. If the results are good, the behavior is good. In this view, there is nothing nuts about building a two-acre redwood deck so long as the person enjoys it and it doesn't get him or her into trouble. Normal behavior, then, is whatever works.

The behavioral approach appears to offer an objective and rational way of defining mental health. Alas, appearances are deceiving. We may agree that a person enjoys an activity, but is that enough? A sadist and a masochist may work out a mutually rewarding relationship, but does that make them healthy? A psychopath may flimflam oldsters out of their life savings and do it with such charm that they love him for it, but should the rest of us emulate the psychopath?

An alternative is to let society decide. What is healthy then becomes what society finds acceptable; what is unhealthy is whatever society dislikes. Thus, aggression is abnormal among the gentle Tasaday of the Philippines but normal among the fierce Yanomamo of Venezuela.

The societal model has a lot of appeal, but it troubles some mental-health workers. There is something about fixing mental health to a mailing address that they find unsettling. They think that there ought to be some sort of universal standard toward which we might all strive. Besides, does it really make sense to say that murder and cannibalism are OK just because some society has approved them? And if it is, then why not apply the same standards to communities within a society? Murder is a popular activity among Baltimore youth. Shall we say that, in that city, murder is healthy?

A similar problem exists with the statistical model of mental health. In this case, being mentally healthy means falling close to average. Take the frequency of sexual activity among married couples, for example. Let's say that, on average, married people your age have intercourse about twice a week. That's the norm. If you indulge more or less often than that, you're abnormal—with or without a helmet.

There's some logic to this view. The further people deviate from the average, the more likely they are to seem strange. You may think, for instance, that limiting sex to two times a week is a bit prudish, but almost everyone is likely to think that once an hour is excessive. Again, however, there are problems.

Does it really make sense to hold up the average person as the paragon of mental health? This logic would have everyone cultivate a few phobias just because they happen to be commonplace; even the best students would strive to earn Cs; and all couples in the country would be frustrated by their inability to have exactly 1.8 children.

We can all agree that there are a lot of weirdos around, but there seems no way for us to agree about who's weird. And so there's no way for us to agree about what mental health is. That's unfortunate, because it gives us no clear goal toward which to strive and no stable benchmark against which to gauge our progress. Even so, I'm damned if I'm gonna wear a helmet to bed.

ADDITIONAL RESOURCES

Books and Articles

Axline, Virginia. *Dibs, in Search of Self*. Boston: Houghton Mifflin, 1963. The story of a young boy—judged mentally ill by doctors, teachers, and even his own parents—who breaks out of his prison of silence and rage with the help of psychotherapy and love.

Bettelheim, Bruno. "Joey: A 'Mechanical Boy.'" *Scientific American* 200 (1959): 116–27. A compelling look at an autistic boy and at childhood schizophrenia.

Capote, Truman. *In Cold Blood*. New York: Random House, 1966. Murder is often thought of as a crime of hot-blooded passion. This gripping novel tells the true story of two psychopathic men who commit a set of senseless murders without remorse.

Green, H. *I Never Promised You a Rose Garden*. New York: Holt, Rinehart & Winston, 1964. A based-on-fact account of a young woman's experience with a schizophrenic disorder. Includes descriptions of her inner world and an account of her psychotherapy.

Hall, Holly. "The Homeless: A Mental-Health Debate." *Psychology Today* (February 1987): 65–66. Does mental illness lead to homelessness, or does living on the streets cause mental illness? A look at mental illness among the homeless helps point out the interaction between mental health and environment.

Rosenhan, David L. "On Being Sane in Insane Places." *Science* 179 (1973): 250–58. Rosenhan and several colleagues gained admission to mental hospitals by feigning mental illness. Their subsequent "sane" behavior was interpreted within a context of illness.

Rubin, Theodore I. *Lisa and David*. New York: Macmillan, 1961. A love story about two troubled adolescents, one suffering from multiple personality disorder, the other fearing the slightest human touch. Together they develop a trusting relationship that helps them recover.

Sheehan, Susan. *Is There No Place on Earth for Me?* Introduction by Robert Coles. New York: Vintage Books, 1982. This biography of a young schizophrenic woman offers insights both into the disease and the mental health care system. A moving novel that won the Pulitzer Prize for nonfiction.

Vonnegut, Mark. *The Eden Express*. New York: Praeger, 1975. An autobiographical account of the author's schizophrenic breakdown and recovery.

Winokur, G. *Depression: The Facts*. New York: Oxford University Press, 1981. A thorough summary of the issues of and research on depression.

Films

Best Boy. Directed by Ira Wohl. 1979. A poignant documentary about the director's 52-year-old, mentally retarded cousin Philly. It illustrates the many struggles faced by mentally impaired people and their families.

I Never Promised You a Rose Garden. Directed by Anthony Page. 1977. The story of a young schizophrenic, focusing on her relationship with one dedicated psychiatrist. Based on the book by Hannah Green.

In Cold Blood. Directed by Richard Brooks. 1967. A gripping adaptation of Truman Capote's novel about two methodical murderers.

One Flew over the Cuckoo's Nest. Directed by Milos Forman; starring Jack Nicholson. 1975. This Oscar award-winning adaptation of Ken Kesey's novel takes a critical look at mental institutions. When a high-spirited—but hardly mentally ill—individual is admitted for treatment, he enlightens fellow patients to paths of recovery. His help, though, is considered a threat to the system.

Rain Man. Starring Dustin Hoffman and Tom Cruise. 1988. Dustin Hoffman accurately and sensitively portrays an individual with a remarkable mental disorder. While able to perform extraordinary feats of memorization and mental arithmetic, he cannot process simple information necessary for functioning alone in the outside world.

Silent Snow, Secret Snow. (Macmillan, 20 min.) An adaptation of Conrad Aiken's short story about a little boy's gradual descent into schizophrenia.

PSYCHOTHERAPY

To say that a particular psychiatric condition is incurable or irreversible is to say more about the state of our ignorance than about the state of the patient.

Milton Rokeach

© Richard Sobol/Stock, Boston

Therapists help people sort through painful and disordered thoughts and feelings, and to understand and change self-defeating behaviors.

Unit 22 looks at the field of psychotherapy and therapists, the professionals trained to help us solve some of our most critical problems. You will learn about different approaches to the treatment of mental, emotional, and behavioral disorders and the special kind of helping relationships that therapists provide.

OBJECTIVES Freud

After viewing the television program and completing the assigned readings, you should be able to:

1. Describe early approaches to identifying and treating mental illness

2. Explain the theory and the basic technique of psychoanalysis

3. Explain the theory and the various types of humanistic therapy

4. Explain the basic premise of most types of cognitive therapies and describe the different types

5. Describe the different types of behavior therapy and the techniques used in each

6. Discuss the uses and advantages of group and family therapy

7. Identify the common forms of drug therapy and how each has changed the mental health system

8. Describe the use of psychosurgery and electroconvulsive shock in the treatment of mental illness

9. Summarize research by Eysenck and others on the effectiveness of psychotherapy

READING ASSIGNMENT

After viewing Program 22, read pages 621–653 in *Psychology: Science, Behavior and Life*. Your instructor may also assign the anthology selections for Unit 22.

KEY TERMS AND CONCEPTS

As you read the assignment, pay particular attention to these terms, which are defined on the given pages in the text.

psychotherapy (621)
psychoanalysis (621)
insight (621)
free association (622)
dream analysis (622)
resistance (622)
transference (623)
countertransference (623)
humanistic therapies (624)
person-centered therapies (624)
genuineness (625)
unconditional positive regard (625)
empathic understanding (625)
active listening (625)
Gestalt therapy (626)

coexplorer (626)
role playing (626)
cognitive therapies (628)
rational emotive therapy (628)
cognitive restructuring therapy (631)
behavior therapy (632)
classical conditioning therapies (632)
systematic desensitization (633)
aversive conditioning (634)
operant conditioning therapies (635)
positive reinforcement therapy (635)
extinction technique (636)

punishment (636)
modeling (637)
group therapy (638)
family therapy (638)
couple therapy (640)
psychosurgery (645)
lobotomy (645)

electroconvulsive therapy (ECT)
(647)
psychoactive drugs (649)
antipsychotic drugs (651)
antidepressants (651)
antimanics (652)
antianxiety drugs (652)

The following terms are used in Program 22 but are not defined in the text.

biological biasing—a genetic predisposition that increases the likelihood of getting a disorder with exposure to prolonged or intense stress

time-limited dynamic psychotherapy—a form of short-term therapy

PROGRAM SUMMARY

When you have a problem, to whom do you turn for comfort and advice? For most of us, the answer is a family member or a friend. But when problems cause prolonged or severe distress, friends and relatives may not have the interest or skills to help us resolve them. Then it may be time to seek professional help. Program 22 considers the range of treatments available, how they developed, and the types of problems they are effective in treating.

Therapies can be divided into two major groups: biomedical therapies, which focus on physical causes, and psychological therapies, which focus on helping us to change the way we think, feel, and behave.

The biomedical approach looks at mental disorders as the result of biochemical events that disrupt the delicate ecology of the mind. Psychiatrists and neurobiologists specialize in identifying disease states or syndromes believed to underlie the disorders.

One of the most radical biomedical treatments is psychosurgery. The prefrontal lobotomy, used only in extreme cases, cuts the nerve fibers connecting the brain's frontal lobes. Although the operation eliminates agitated schizophrenia or extreme compulsions, many people consider the cure to be worse than the illness. After a lobotomy, the patient cannot remember clearly or plan ahead and may no longer feel the normal range of emotions.

Electroconvulsive shock therapy, which alters the brain's electrical and chemical activity, is also controversial. Its proponents claim that, for depressed patients who can't tolerate medication, it can be an effective treatment. But its misuse has prompted legal restrictions in many states.

The real revolution in biomedical therapy began in the 1950s with the use of tranquilizing and antipsychotic drugs. Drug therapies not only relieved suffering but also made psychotherapy possible. The danger with drugs, however, is that they may be misused by overworked or poorly trained hospital staff or by patients overmedicating themselves.

Another great revolution in biomedical therapy is currently under way. Scientists are already making significant breakthroughs in identifying genetic sources of schizophrenia, depression, and Alzheimer's disease. They are also learning how these genetic predispositions interact with environmental influences to affect the development of the disease.

Psychotherapists deal with psychological problems in very different ways. Although there are at least 250 different approaches, they can be divided into four general categories. Psychodynamic (or psychoanalytic) therapy sees all behavior as being driven by inner forces, including early life traumas and unresolved conflicts. This perspective was developed by Sigmund Freud around the turn of the century.

In psychoanalysis, the patient's therapy is based on talking things out. Change comes from analyzing and resolving unconscious tensions by using various techniques, including free association, dream analysis, achieving insight and ultimately catharsis.

Over the years, psychoanalysts have modified Freud's techniques, but the goal has always been to change the patient's personality structure, not just to cure the symptoms. It can take years and requires a lot of participation by the patient. Shorter, time-limited, and less intensive treatment can also be effective in helping many patients.

Another approach, behavior therapy, ignores unconscious motives, the past, and personality, and instead concentrates on problem behaviors. Behavior therapists apply principles of conditioning and reinforcement in an effort to eliminate symptoms and teach patients new and healthier behaviors.

Cognitive therapists teach their clients how to change problem attitudes, irrational beliefs, and negative thoughts that trigger anxiety or low self-esteem. They also teach clients to change the way they perceive significant life events. In rational-emotive therapy, a form of cognitive therapy developed by Albert Ellis in the 1960s, the therapist teaches clients to recognize the "shoulds," "oughts," and "musts" that control them so that they can choose the life they wish to lead.

In contrast to the therapies that focus on problem behaviors and psychological disorders, humanistic therapies focus on normal people who wish to be more productive, creative, or fulfilled. They emphasize the psychological growth of the total person in the social context and have expanded treatment to include therapy for groups, couples, and families.

REVIEW QUESTIONS

Program Questions

1. What are the two main approaches to therapies for mental disorders?

   a. The Freudian and the behavioral
   b. The client-centered and the patient-centered
   c. The biomedical and the psychological
   d. The chemical and the psychosomatic

2. The prefrontal lobotomy is a form of psychosurgery. Though no longer widely used, it was at one time used in cases in which a patient

   a. was an agitated schizophrenic.
   b. had committed a violent crime.
   c. showed little emotional response.
   d. had a disease of the thalamus.

3. Elinor had electroconvulsive shock therapy a number of years ago. She is now suffering a side effect of that therapy. What is she most likely to be suffering from?

   a. Tardive dyskinesia
   b. The loss of her ability to plan ahead
   c. Depression
   d. Memory loss

4. Vinnie suffers from manic-depressive disorder, but his mood swings are kept under control because he takes the drug

   a. chlorpromazine.
   b. lithium.
   c. Valium.
   d. tetracycline.

5. The Woodruff family is receiving genetic counseling because a particular kind of mental retardation runs in their family. What is the purpose of such counseling?

   a. To explain the probability of passing on defective genes
   b. To help eliminate the attitudes of biological biasing
   c. To repair specific chromosomes
   d. To prescribe drugs that will keep problems from developing

6. In psychodynamic theory, what is the source of mental disorders?

   a. Biochemical imbalances in the brain
   b. Unresolved conflicts in childhood experiences
   c. The learning and reinforcement of nonproductive behaviors
   d. Unreasonable attitudes, false beliefs, and unrealistic expectations

7. Imagine you are observing a therapy session in which a patient is lying on a couch, talking. The therapist is listening and asking occasional questions. What is most likely to be the therapist's goal?

   a. To determine what drug the patient should be given
   b. To change the symptoms that cause distress
   c. To explain how to change false ideas
   d. To help the patient develop insight

8. Rinaldo is a patient in psychotherapy. The therapist asks him to free associate. What would Rinaldo do?

   a. Describe a dream
   b. Release his feelings
   c. Talk about anything that comes to mind
   d. Understand the origin of his present guilt feelings

9. According to Hans Strupp, what is an important way in which psychodynamic therapies have changed?

   a. Less emphasis is now placed on the ego.
   b. Patients no longer need to develop a relationship with the therapist.
   c. Shorter courses of treatment can be used.
   d. The concept of aggression has become more important.

10. In the program, a therapist helped a girl learn to control her epileptic seizures. What use did the therapist make of the pen?

   a. To record data
   b. To signal the onset of an attack
   c. To reduce the girl's fear
   d. To reinforce the correct reaction

11. When Albert Ellis discusses with the young woman her fear of hurting others, what point is he making?

   a. It is the belief system that creates the "hurt."
   b. Every normal person strives to achieve fulfillment.
   c. Developing a fear-reduction strategy will reduce the problem.
   d. It is the use of self-fulfilling prophecies that cause others to be hurt.

12. What point does Enrico Jones make about investigating the effectiveness of different therapies in treating depression?

   a. All therapies are equally effective.
   b. It is impossible to assess how effective any one therapy is.
   c. The job is complicated by the different types of depression.
   d. The most important variable is individual versus group therapy.

Textbook Questions

13. According to Freud, the primary theme in many patients' conflict(s) is

   a. social demands.
   b. environmental pressures.
   c. the struggle between the id's sexual and aggressive impulses and the superego's moral demands.
   d. genetic inheritance.

14. Psychoanalysis does not appear to be successful with _____ clients.

   a. well-educated
   b. psychotic
   c. verbally expressive
   d. highly motivated

15. The popularity and influence of psychoanalysis since the early 1950s has

   a. tremendously increased.
   b. remains the same.
   c. steadily increased.
   d. steadily declined.

16. Humanistic therapists see their main therapeutic goal as

    a. resolving unconscious conflicts and repressed urges.
    b. confronting self-defeating, irrational beliefs.
    c. fostering psychological growth.
    d. correcting distortions in a person's cognitions or thoughts.

17. According to person-centered therapy, the acceptance of clients out of respect for them as important human beings is referred to as

    a. phenomenological.
    b. unconditional positive regard.
    c. genuineness.
    d. frame of reference.

18. Gestalt therapy strives to help a person

    a. resolve unconscious conflicts and repressed urges.
    b. confront self-defeating, irrational beliefs.
    c. interpret the meaning of dreams.
    d. bring together the alienated fragments of self.

19. A client is asked to role play his or her parent while the therapist role plays the client. The therapy being practiced is probably that of

    a. psychoanalysis.
    b. Gestalt therapy.
    c. person-centered therapy.
    d. rational-emotive therapy.

20. The premise that most psychological disorders result from distortions in a person's awareness and thoughts describes the basis of

    a. psychoanalysis.
    b. humanistic therapy.
    c. Gestalt therapy.
    d. cognitive therapy.

21. Rational-emotive therapy is based on the belief that psychological problems result from

    a. unconscious conflicts and repressed urges.
    b. self-defeating, irrational beliefs.
    c. alienated fragmentation of the self.
    d. traumatic childhood experiences.

22. Cognitive therapists focus on _____ changes while behavior therapists focus on _____ changes.

    a. temporary; permanent
    b. systematic; general
    c. behavior; cognitive
    d. cognitive; behavior

23. The central thesis of behavior therapy is that maladaptive behavior

    a. is based on unconscious conflicts and repressed urges.
    b. is due to self-defeating, irrational beliefs.
    c. has been learned and can be unlearned.
    d. is based on distortions in a person's thoughts.

24. Systematic desensitization involves

    a. training to relax when confronted with fearful stimuli.
    b. interpreting fearful stimuli so they are less fearful.
    c. changing misconceptions regarding fearful stimuli.
    d. uncovering repressed feelings regarding fearful events.

25. The type of therapy in which a chronic drinker is given a drug that induces nausea when combined with alcohol is called

    a. systematic desensitization.
    b. aversive conditioning.
    c. chemotherapy.
    d. counterconditioning.

26. The technique of letting a child watch TV only after successfully completing his or her homework is called

    a. positive reinforcement.
    b. negative reinforcement.
    c. modeling.
    d. desensitization.

27. By ignoring misbehavior, a parent or teacher is using the _____ technique of behavior modification.

    a. positive reinforcement
    b. extinction
    c. punishment
    d. shaping

28. By watching a person handle a live snake, a person who has a phobia of snakes may reduce his or her fear. This technique is called

    a. positive reinforcement.
    b. aversive training.
    c. punishment.
    d. modeling.

29. The goal of group therapy is to

    a. analyze transactions.
    b. analyze dreams of others.
    c. heighten awareness of needs and feelings of oneself and others.
    d. provide a warm therapeutic climate.

30. Family therapy is based on the idea that an individual's problems stem from

    a. patterns of social interaction within the family unit.
    b. unconscious family conflicts and repressed urges.
    c. self-defeating, irrational family beliefs.
    d. distortions in a person's cognitions or thoughts.

31. The couple therapist attempts to

    a. improve communication.
    b. probe for "hidden agendas."
    c. help clarify goals and attitudes.
    d. do all the above.

32. Luborsky (1975) reported that 80 percent of the studies on the effects of psychotherapy found

    a. women improved but men did not.
    b. that therapy was detrimental.
    c. significant benefits associated with psychotherapy.
    d. that psychotherapy did not benefit the client.

33. Research has clearly demonstrated that in most cases, improvement rates for people undergoing psychotherapy

    a. are markedly better than those for untreated individuals.
    b. are the same as for untreated individuals.
    c. are markedly worse than those for untreated individuals.
    d. the research evidence is not clear.

34. Certain common features shared by almost all styles of therapy include

    a. combating the client's symptoms.
    b. treatment of the client's symptoms.
    c. providing a warm, supportive relationship.
    d. all of the above.

35. A surgical procedure called the lobotomy is performed by

    a. severing the nerve tracts from the frontal lobes and the lower regions of the brain.
    b. severing the corpus callosum.
    c. using cryosurgery in the area of the thalamus.
    d. separating the occipital lobe from the parietal lobe.

36. One of the most perplexing questions about electroconvulsive therapy is

    a. what it does do.
    b. how it works.
    c. how to administer the treatment.
    d. whether to administer the treatment.

37. It is widely held that antidepressants work by

    a. increasing the neurotransmitters norepinephrine and serotonin at sites in the brain.
    b. increasing the sensitivity of the receptors in the brain for norepinephrine and serotonin.
    c. doing what both answer a and b describe.
    d. providing a placebo effect.

38. The drug lithium is the most effective drug for controlling _____ symptoms of _____ disorder.

   a. manic; bipolar
   b. manic; unipolar
   c. anxiety; anxiety
   d. schizophrenic; psychotic

QUESTIONS TO CONSIDER

1. How do the placebo effect and the spontaneous recovery effect make evaluating the success of therapy difficult?

2. Why is it so difficult to evaluate and compare the relative effectiveness of therapies?

3. How does someone decide on an appropriate therapy?

4. Can everyone benefit from psychotherapy, or do you think it is only for people with serious problems?

5. Why is there a stigma sometimes associated with seeking professional help for psychological problems?

OPTIONAL ACTIVITIES

1. Identify the services and resources available in your community in case you ever need emotional support in a crisis, want to seek therapy, or know someone who needs this information. How much do these services cost? Look for names of accredited professional therapists and counselors, support groups, hotlines, medical and educational services, and programs in church and community programs. Is it difficult to find information? How accessible are mental health services?

2. Do you have any self-defeating expectations? Do you feel that you might benefit from cognitive therapy? Write out statements of positive self-expectations. For a week, rehearse them. Then try to use them in situations in which you feel anxious or insecure. Do they have any effect?

3. Speculate on how you would feel upon receiving a computer printout of all your genetic biases.

ANTHOLOGY

The individual seeking professional help for psychological problems has a wide variety of specialists from which to choose. The following selections illustrate different approaches to treatment and therapy. Each approach is based on different assumptions about the causes of psychological problems and may provide very different benefits. As you read, think about the therapies that seem to be in tune with your own approach to mental health.

Reading 50

This article illustrates an eclectic approach to short-term therapy developed by two people who specialize in work-related problems. As you read, try to identify aspects of different theoretical roots, approaches, and techniques you have learned about in Program 22 and in your text.

Breaking Loose

By Bob Anderson

Jack O'Conner's career was stalled.

A tall, ruggedly handsome man with a reddish mustache, the 33-year-old O'Conner (a pseudonym) had recently taken a temporary leave of absence from his $50,000-a-year job as an engineer at a nuclear power plant. He was now carrying a full schedule of classes at the University of Chicago's Graduate School of Business and working weekends as an engineering consultant for General Motors.

O'Conner recognized that something was missing from his life, some connection that his academic courses were not making. He needed help—and thought he knew what kind. O'Conner had been inspired by an article in the October SUCCESS about one executive's experiences at the magazine's Career Clinic, which resulted in a promotion. "What I need to learn," O'Conner told his wife Beth, "is how to present myself in an interview the way he did." She shrugged, saying, "I don't know what you mean. You seem pretty persuasive and in control. Of course, I haven't seen you in a job interview." After wrestling with his decision—O'Conner felt concern about seeing even less of his wife and their sons, David, 6, and Jim, 3, if he should enter—he finally took the step last October and applied for the Career Clinic; two weeks later he was accepted.

* * *

Certain patterns spring out when the SUCCESS counselors review O'Conner's questionnaire. It indicates, for example, that he does not communicate well with bosses. He says they think he is uncooperative, a loner. It was, in fact, this difficulty that led him to take a leave of absence and return to school.

O'Conner needs help, the counselors agree, but their recommendation is not what he expects. Joseph C. McIntyre of Communispond, Inc., a New York executive communications training and consulting firm that has been crucially involved in past Career Clinics, feels that O'Conner already possesses most of the business skills he needs. His difficulties lie elsewhere. It is agreed that O'Conner should be referred to husband-and-wife psychologists Robert L. Powers and Jane Griffith of America's Institute of Adlerian Studies in Chicago.

O'Conner has possible self-image and attitude problems that could be causing the trouble he has in dealing with superiors. That's an early conclusion Powers and Griffith reach, as they interpret his questionnaire in light of his family history. "Here we have an obviously successful engineer," says Powers. "He was making $45,000 a year by the time he was 30. Then he moved to a better job at the nuclear power plant, which he was good at, but it was strictly technical work. Note his response to the question 'What has been your greatest career accomplishment to date?' It describes skill with people on his previous job. When the plant manager asked him to bring order to the chaotic overlapping of four separate departments, he established an activities-coordination team. He set up a program that relieved the confusion and helped get the plant licensed. He loved that. My guess is that he relies too much on his technical and analytical skills, while underestimating the value he places on human relationships and the pleasure he takes in maintaining them."

Back in 1971, when O'Conner finished college with a degree in engineering, his goal was to become a systems design engineer. Now he thinks "the commercial aspects of running a business may hold more allure for me." O'Conner faces a serious dilemma, however. He doesn't want to change to a different industry and waste 11 years of experience. But the utility company that employed him has abandoned construction of the plant where he worked, so the option of returning there is now gone.

"He won't have any problem getting another job," says Powers. "But unless he learns more about himself, he's not likely to land the kind of job he will enjoy and that will call on a fuller range of his capabilities. He probably has much more going for him than he realizes."

Still ambivalent, O'Conner frees up two days in mid-November to meet with Powers and Griffith. He makes no bones about his skepticism toward the type of counseling chosen. "I don't put much stock in psychoanalysis," he says. "Neither do I, because I don't believe a person can be divided into bits a pieces," Powers replies. "You have a unique style. Our goal is to understand that style and to clarify your way of being effective."

Powers and Griffith decide that she will conduct the first interview. O'Conner does not object to having a reporter present. Turning on the tape recorder, Griffith asks O'Conner to describe his early childhood. He was the firstborn of a middle-level oil-company executive, who died of cancer in 1978. He has four sisters, and his mother still lives in the family home in a New York suburb. For nearly two hours O'Conner recalls memories of boyhood scrapes and the resulting discipline. He was "full of hell," constantly doing things that upset his mother. A devout Catholic, she was always understanding though; she has "the patience of a saint." His father spent little time with the family. "He was strong and had high principles, and to provide for us he spent most evenings and weekends on the job."

Talking about his father is obviously painful for O'Conner. Tears come to his eyes when he recalls quarrels they had when he was in high school over the music he listened to, or the movies he went to that his father considered immoral. "I'm sorry I never got a chance to tell him I admired him," he says.

Griffith ends the session, and tells O'Conner to take a break for a couple of hours. After he leaves, she explains that she wants his emotional turmoil to subside: "As it does, he will remember a lot of other things to tell us." The responses to her questions, she says, are "openings to a private album of past events. I am looking for a pattern of attitudes and values. If the pattern can be discerned and reconsidered, it need not be repeated in the future."

A person's rank in family birth order is of major interest to Adlerian psychologists, comments Griffith. They believe it establishes an initial vantage point from which we form our view of ourselves. The young child sizes up his own successes and failures by comparing them with those of the other children in the family. Gradually he learns to practice the behavior that works for him. Eventually, Adler said, "the person arrives at a style which is his own, and in accordance with which we see him thinking, feeling, and acting throughout his whole life."

Upon returning, O'Conner is more vocal the rest of that day, and the next. Memories rush in. Powers joins Griffith periodically and she briefs him on what's been said. He then writes an interpretation which he gives to O'Conner for verification. "The firstborn is in many ways like an only child," Powers explains. "You are self-reliant and independent. Because you did not recognize any peer among the children, you have a difficult time negotiating. There was no equal with whom you had to practice give and take. You were in a class by yourself. It may be that you still feel that way, that no one can understand you. But," he tells O'Conner, "you can learn negotiation. Think of it as absolute monarchs making a treaty!

"The picture of your father as devoted, self-sacrificing, but also unhappy, cautions you against allowing yourself to emulate him. On the other hand, your admiration of your father's principled manner of dealing with others and your imitation of that manner leave you frightened that you won't live up to his example. This pessimistic expectation handicaps you and your career." O'Conner agrees with this assessment, though he is surprised and somewhat upset by the remark about his hidden pessimism.

Before leaving, O'Conner says he thinks the sessions probably have been helpful. "They have opened my eyes to some things. But I wonder if this is a luxury I can afford. I came here hoping to decide where I should focus my resources. I wanted to get some tips on interviewing, too. I have an interview coming up for a job in Pennsylvania, and I'm concerned about how I'll do."

His comments lead to a discussion of an interview he had just before taking his last job. It was with a company that has a fine reputation in the nuclear power industry, and he was eager to work for the man who runs it. But at lunch the man threw out a particularly tough engineering question. "I realized that he was putting me under pressure to see how I would react," says O'Conner, "but I just froze. I should have been able to answer the question, but I wasn't able to do that."

Powers asks if he told the man how he felt. "No. I couldn't say anything," O'Conner replies. "Next time you're in that kind of situation, say what is in your mind," suggests Powers. "Blurt it out. Say, 'I realize you intend to put me on the spot, and I know the answer to your question.' Then you'll probably find you can answer. Because unless you can say what you are thinking, it will block everything else out—that which is unspeakable becomes unthinkable. It's like the lecturer who loses his train of thought. You've probably seen this. The audience knows from the look on his face what's happened. If he says, 'I've lost my train of thought, where was I going with that?' the thought will probably come back to him, and then he can continue."

O'Conner returns the next week, saying the interview had resulted in a tentative job offer, dependent on the firm's decision to establish a branch office which he would manage. "I'm doubtful," he says, "because the office would be an experiment for them, and they may be just using it as a carrot. They aren't committed to it. The money is right, $55,000 plus a bonus, but the office would be in Pittsburgh, and I'm not too crazy about living there." Asked if he feels better now after the counseling, O'Conner replies, "I

guess so. I think it has helped me raise my sights. But I still don't see the target."

The interviews continue for the next two days, now centering on O'Conner's youth, his courtship of Beth, and their marriage. He was considered a real party man by his college classmates. But when he met Beth at a senior dance, O'Conner decided to change. "I knew she wouldn't like my wild side." Later, he says he would like to retire at 50 and be able to "let go" and enjoy life. He wouldn't feel right about doing so until his sons were on their own, however.

Powers breaks in to point out that if he subjects himself to the same self-sacrificing regime his father followed, he might wind up equally unhappy. O'Conner goes rigid and silent. "How do you feel?" Powers asks. No answer. "Your attitude seems to be that showing emotion is somehow feminine and weak and that it is embarrassing to be cared for by others. Do you think that this may be shutting off communication and intimacy?" "Maybe," says O'Conner.

Powers and Griffith next direct the questioning toward the future. O'Conner now feels that a job combining technical and human-relations skills would be best. His ideal is a franchise where he and Beth would work together. She is an experienced accountant and could keep the books. In the next breath, however, he says that neither he nor Beth would be willing to risk an entrepreneurial venture. They are too cautious.

Powers returns to this at the end of the session. "You have held on too long to the fiction that if you are curious, enthusiastic, and eager you will come across as juvenile. It's in keeping with your gray picture of what is required of you as a 'grown man.' At age 18, you decided to put away childish things. That idea is exaggerated, developed from your impressions of your father's life which allowed no time for himself. Your idea seems to be: Either I am grown-up—sober, cautious, constricted—or I am juvenile. This polarized thinking is no longer useful to you. You are disciplined, loyal, reliable, and straight-dealing. Other people recognize it in you. It's time for you to recognize it in yourself. Break loose! Allow yourself to enjoy life."

Good news follows fast. Before another session can be arranged following O'Conner's graduation from business school in December, he has already landed a job with a nuclear power utility in Atlanta. "I'm just delighted about it," he says over dinner. "We really like the area. The housing there is less expensive, and the schools seem to be great. The best thing is that I will have supervisory responsibilities, too. I'm really looking forward to that. My salary will be $60,000 plus a bonus, another $10,000 at least." Asked whether the counseling was helpful, O'Conner replies, "Oh yes. I'm sure it was, though it's hard to say exactly how." Beth says that she thinks it was really a waste of time. "I couldn't believe it when he told me the questions they asked. I still don't know why he went along with it."

Powers and Griffith are disappointed when they learn of Beth's attitude. They would like to meet with the O'Conners as a couple. The four days of counseling have pointed Jack in the right direction, they feel, but creating any lasting effect is going to require quite a bit more work.

Contacted several months later, however, O'Conner appears to have found himself— and a life that suits him. "I feel that the sessions reinforced my feeling that I had the ability to work well with people. That is a major aspect of the job I'm in now. It's a liaison job, and I coordinate the work of many different people. I am more confident about person-to-person relationships, and, on balance, I am much happier. Though there are some things I haven't yet sorted out about my role, I feel I am in a job that has a future for me. I know where I'm going at last."

Reading 51

This article is a first-person account of how meditation and the relaxation response are used to relieve symptoms such as back pain, headaches, and other stress-related disorders. What long- and short-term benefits could a person gain from learning these self-healing techniques? What characteristics does this approach share with traditional psychodynamic and biomedical approaches?

In the Stillness of Our Minds

By Linda Weltner

My husband comes home from work and takes me by the hand. He leads me upstairs to a small room at the back of the house. He lowers me to a mattress placed on the floor expressly for this purpose and gives me time to remove my shoes. Then he turns off the light, starts incense burning, and lights a candle on a small table under the window.

At some other time, in some other place, this might be a setting for seduction, but not tonight. He's brought me here for another purpose.

To meditate.

My husband has to bring me because I'd never come of my own free will. My instincts lead me everywhere but to peace and quiet.

This is the shape of my resistance: My mind is far too busy solving problems to turn it off for 20 minutes at a stretch. My thoughts are fully occupied coping with problems. I'm making lists, finishing projects, taking care of business. I am a purposeful person. I don't have time to sit and close my eyes, breathe deeply, and repeat "Ham-sha" until my ego disappears.

I'd like to go on doing exactly what I have been doing, but I don't want to pay the price that goes with business as usual any longer. The medication that helped my migraines for nearly a year has begun to lose its effectiveness, and my headaches are back with a vengeance. I've ended up in a hospital emergency room with the last two, seeking relief in shots of Demerol when all other pain killers failed.

So in January I enrolled in Deaconess Hospital's Body/Mind Program and now, midway through the course, I'm trying to reduce the amount of tension in my body through daily meditation. I'm committed to giving the "relaxation response" a chance to work its magic. Recent research seems to show that among the healthful effects of deep relaxation are a strengthening of the immune system, lowered blood pressure, improved blood flow to the heart, relief from asthma attacks, and a lessening of pain. I'm learning to heal myself.

I sit in our meditation room, legs crossed. My lungs filled with my breath, feel like a great white bird raising its wings; as I exhale, the bird settles back within my chest. I breathe, feeling a warmth pressing upon my eyes and rushing through my limbs. I become a pleasurable rhythm that feels like rocking in my mother's arms.

There are many of us caught in a vicious spiral of tension and disease. Our worries make us ill; our illness makes us worry. We have back pain or gastrointestinal problems, anxiety and insomnia, panic attacks, hypertension, or chronic pain. We've tried doctors and drugs, hoping to rid ourselves of these unwanted visitors who have invaded our bodies and threaten our habitual way of dealing with life. Then there comes a time, as it has for me, when we shift perspective, choosing to view our symptoms as loving messengers who are urging us to modify our diets, to exercise, to relax our grueling demands upon ourselves, to live more consciously.

It's amazing to think of my headaches as spirit guides, though I'm not sure "spirit guides" is the right phrase to describe the forces to which I'm finally listening. Unlike Shirley Maclaine and Elizabeth Kubler-Ross, my spirit guides don't come from another era or communicate in words that I can understand. Their messages are symbolic and hard to decipher, yet as simple and as devastating as blinding pain in one temple, a problem sleeping, and a constant stiff neck. My symptoms are telling me to let go, to loosen up, and to listen.

I sit on the bed beside my husband, back against the wall, listening to waves as I sit upon a tropical beach in my mind. As I inhale, the wave

breaks upon me, bathing me in warm water. As I exhale, the wave ebbs, drawing me down to the edge of the sea. I breathe the wave back, banishing the thoughts that interrupt my concentration, returning to an inner universe that feels like it is breathing me.

My symptoms have led me to meditate; my meditation has led me to new depths within myself. This fits in with something I learned from Ira Progoff years ago when I took his course in Intensive Journal Keeping. He described the origins of our creativity as an underground stream that feeds the deep well of our imagination. This underground stream flows from some universal source we can barely comprehend, yet it is available to us in the stillness of our minds when it speaks to us in the images which rise to consciousness, in fantasies and in dreams.

I sit listening to a meditation tape. A soft voice weaves a fantasy as I follow its soothing directions. I am walking barefoot down a path, following a stream into the deep forest. I feel the moss under my feet and hear the sound of the wind in my breath. I come to a deep quiet pool which frightens me. Taking courage, I dive into it, the I who is witnessing my fantasy disappears. Time vanishes until the voice summons me back to reality.

There is more to life than analytical thinking and accomplishing things. I have always known that. There may be within us a "self-balancing wisdom," as Progoff puts it, a capacity to integrate and heal ourselves by encountering the reality of our inner life.

During this one short break in my daily activities, I set off to find it.

Reading 52

This article looks at a special application of the psychotherapist's analytical skills: the psychological autopsy of a suicide. It presents several points of view on how the information is gathered and the inferences that can be drawn from it. As you read, consider the theoretical, legal, and social implications of psychological autopsies.

Experts Debate Value of 'Autopsy' on Suicide's Mind

By Alison Bass

When Boston psychiatrist Douglas Jacobs testified two months ago that a 40-year-old Florida woman was responsible for her teenage daughter's suicide, he sent shudders through other parents whose children have killed themselves.

He also upset many mental health profes-sionals. Dr. Jacobs had based much of his testimony against Theresa Jackson on a little-known technique—the psychological autopsy—in an effort to reconstruct the mental state of the daughter when she shot herself to death at the age of 17. Some mental health professionals believe Jacobs went beyond the technique's scientific capability to determine the psychological causes of death and entered the murky world of speculation.

"None of us who are experts in suicide understand enough about the causes and precipitants of suicide to make a definitive statement about why someone committed suicide," says Dr. David Clark, director of the Center for Suicide Research and Prevention at the Rush-Presbyterian St. Lukes Medical Center in Chicago. "To say that a family member was responsible for that suicide is beyond the ability of psychiatrists. It's way ahead of the science at this point."

Jacobs, an assistant clinical professor of psychiatry at Harvard Medical School who is widely considered an expert on teenage suicide, insists he overstepped no scientific bounds.

"You can never know with 100 percent certainty what's going on in just anybody's mind, but her [the daughter's] mind was the mind of a suicidal person, and I know what goes on in the mind of a suicidal person," Jacobs said in a recent interview at his Newton office. "The suicidal mind has certain consistencies."

Psychological autopsies have been around since the late 1950s: they were first used in Los Angeles to determine whether unexplained deaths were accidents, suicides or homicides. Such psychological detective work has also been used to settle estate questions and worker compensation claims, and in malpractice suits to determine if there had been negligence on the part of psychiatrists whose patients killed themselves.

Defense for Battered Women

More recently, psychological autopsies have been employed in criminal cases, in the defense of battered women accused of killing their husbands. In one landmark case in Arizona, for instance, defense attorneys reconstructed a psychological profile of the slain husband to show that he had been a "sadistic, paranoid psychopath" who beat his wife and threatened his entire family.

Jacobs' testimony in the trial of Theresa Jackson, however, marks the first time a psychological autopsy has been used by the prosecution in a criminal case. Jackson is facing up to 25 years in prison largely on the strength of Jacobs' opinion that she compelled her daughter to dance nude in strip

joints, until finally, out of unbearable rage and humiliation, the teenager was driven to kill herself.

Jacobs says he was able to reconstruct the daughter's mental state at the time of her death by examining her school, hospital and employment records and by reading pretrial depositions taken of her family, friends and coworkers.

At Jackson's well-publicized trial in October, Jacobs testified that the mother had created an unbearable psychological climate from which the daughter, Tina Mancini, felt there was no escape—except through suicide. He said Mancini must have found herself in a "psychological straitjacket" because of her mother's demands, even though the mother knew her daughter found nude dancing "degrading."

"A murderous rage built up inside of her that is literally painful," Jacobs testified at the Florida trial. "It can make anyone want to burst." Unable to convey that intolerable rage to any of her friends or family, Mancini finally turned it on herself. She shot herself with a .357 caliber Magnum on March 24, 1986.

"In my mind, I know what she was thinking and feeling at the time of her death," Jacobs told the jury. Shortly afterwards, that jury convicted Theresa Jackson of aggravated child abuse, procuring a sexual performance by a child and forgery (Jackson was charged with forging a birth certificate so her daughter could get a job as a stripper).

Preciseness Questioned

Leading mental health professionals who use psychological autopsies in their work don't doubt that Theresa Jackson was a rotten mother. But they question Jacobs' ability as a psychological detective to say so precisely why Tina Mancini killed herself.

"You can make inferences about the state of someone's mind, and the more experienced you are, the better your guesses," says Dr. Avery Weisman, a Massachusetts General Hospital psychiatrist who, like Jacobs, teaches at Harvard Medical School. Weisman, a highly respected thanatologist (specialist in the medical, psychological and social problems of dying), wrote a book in the 1970s about the use of psychological autopsies to understand why terminally ill patients end their lives. "But for someone to to say that they know what's going on in someone else's mind is arrogance in my opinion. It's hard enough when you talk to someone to know if they're suicidal."

Some psychologists are concerned that Jacobs' autopsy was not as thorough as it could have been. In attempting to reconstruct a suicide's mental state, they say, a mental health professional must go out and interview everyone who knew the deceased person, including family members, friends, neighbors and coworkers, a process that can take weeks.

Jacobs, however, relied totally on depositions taken by the Broward state attorney's office. From these pretrial interviews, and Tina Mancini's school, hospital and employment records, he says he was able to formulate a preliminary opinion about the girl's mental state in 20 to 30 hours.

"That's not a psychological autopsy in my book," says Theodore H. Blau, a psychologist and consultant to the Manatee County sheriff's office in Tampa, Fla., who routinely does such autopsies for civil and criminal suits. Blau is a former president of the American Psychological Association (APA).

"You need at least a month to conduct long, laborious interviews with everyone who knew the person for a month prior to the death," Blau says.

Raymond Fowler, a University of Tennessee psychologist who is incoming president of the American Psychological Association, says it took him years to complete a psychological autopsy of billionaire Howard Hughes. Attorneys representing Hughes' estate had asked Fowler to do the autopsy because so many people were contesting his will, and they felt it was "important to know what his mental state was at various periods of his life."

"Even after I had talked to everyone I could and compiled more than 50,000 documents on Howard Hughes, all I had were some highly educated guesses about his mental condition," Fowler says.

Some Say Interviews Not Vital

Some psychologists, however, don't think personal interviews are always necessary.

"Records may be sufficient," says Gerald Koocher, director of psychology at Children's Hospital in Boston. "It depends on how rich a picture you can get of the person. Apparently he [Jacobs] has a rich enough picture to convince the jury beyond a reasonable doubt."

Jacobs agrees. "I don't think interviewing people would have given me any more information than I already had," he says. "I've done a lot of psychological autopsies for malpractice cases, and I felt I was able to come up with an opinion about her mental state that is as clinically precise as possible. It's usually pretty clear why people killed themselves."

Other psychologists argue that pretrial depositions are not sufficient because they are not done by skilled psychological interviewers who follow specific guidelines for eliciting information about the dead person's state of mind.

Edwin Shneidman, the Los Angeles psychologist who first developed the psychological autopsy as a formal forensics tool in 1958, lists 16 specific facts that must be obtained in interviews with people close to the dead person. These range from the "death history" of the victim's family (suicides of other members, etc.), to any dreams or premonitions the victim may have had about death or suicide, to observing the reaction of the interviewees to the victim's death.

As a number of psychologists point out, people who were close to a suicide victim do not always tell the truth, and it's up to the interviewer to gauge the accuracy of their statements.

"The key survivors deny, repress, dissemble and just don't know," Shneidman said in a telephone interview from Los Angeles. "So one would not necessarily believe what they say."

Shneidman, however, says he considers Jacobs a highly skilled clinician who may have been able to make accurate inferences from the pretrial depositions in this case. "Interviewing people is preferred, but it may be that he had enough information from the records the state of Florida presented," Shneidman says.

Shneidman and most of the other psychologists interviewed agreed that psychological autopsies do have a valid place in the criminal justice system—as long as they are done properly.

In a 1981 article for the American Criminal Law Review, Attorney David Lichter expressed another concern: that a jury might be overly impressed by the testifying psychiatrist's credentials. As a result, the jury might overemphasize the importance of the psychiatrist's testimony at the expense of other, less-compelling evidence in the trial, wrote Lichter, now an assistant US attorney in Miami.

However, as Jacobs and other psychologists point out, such prejudicial evidence can and should be countered by the opposing testimony of psychiatric witnesses for the defense. In the course of Jackson's trial, the defense attorney did bring in other mental health professionals to testify. But none of

them matched Jacobs' credentials.

Shneidman agrees that "it's the job of the defense attorney to bring in equally credentialed witnesses."

Theresa Jackson would probably concur. She has since fired the attorney that represented her in October and hired a new one. The Fort Lauderdale woman will be sentenced Jan. 7, but she is planning to appeal the conviction.

If and when her case is retried, the validity of Douglas Jacobs' psychological autopsy will almost certainly go on trial with her.

ADDITIONAL RESOURCES

Books and Articles

Albee, G. "The Answer Is Prevention." *Psychology Today* (February 1985): 60–62. Asserts that prevention through social change is the best and most effective method of dealing with the major causes of mental illness.

Basch, Michael F. *Understanding Psychotherapy: The Science Behind the Art*. New York: Basic Books, 1988. Through compelling case histories, Basch explores both the processes of psychotherapy and human nature. His perspective draws from many branches and schools of psychology.

Bettelheim, Bruno. *The Empty Fortess*. New York: Free Press, 1967. A child psychologist recounts three case histories of autism and his efforts to help each child through therapy.

Frankl, Victor E. *Man's Search for Meaning*. New York: Pocket Books, 1963. Frankl's brand of therapy, logotherapy, grew out of his experiences in a Nazi death camp. Frankl also discusses several clinical applications of his theory.

Freud, S. *The Question of Lay Analysis*. New York: Norton, 1969. Freud explains psychoanalysis through arguing with an imaginary "impartial person."

Garfield, S. L., and A. E. Bergen, eds. *Handbook of Psychotherapy and Behavior Change*. 3d ed. New York: Wiley, 1986. Contributed chapters review the substantive technical and methodological issues in psychotherapy research.

Maslow, A. *Religions, Values, and Peak Experiences*. New York: Viking, 1964. Conveys Maslow's humanistic approach to psychology.

Turner, S. M., K. S. Calhoun, and H. E. Adams, eds. *Handbook of Clinical Behavior Therapy*. New York: Wiley, 1981. Chapters in the book are arranged around specific disorders or syndromes, with the emphasis placed on providing descriptions of comprehensive behavioral treatments of psychological dysfunctions.

Watts, A. W. *Psychotherapy East and West*. New York: Random House, 1975. How differences in values and beliefs between Eastern and Western cultures affect their approaches to therapy.

Wood, Clive. "Therapy: Their Own Worst Enemy." *Psychology Today* (February 1987): 18. Albert Ellis, the father of rational-emotive therapy, believes many patients sabotoge their own efforts to help themselves.

HEALTH, MIND, AND BEHAVIOR

Suffering isn't enobling, recovery is.

Christiaan Barnard

A profound rethinking of the relationship between mind and body has led to the holistic concept in which mental and physical processes are seen as constantly interacting. Unit 23 looks at what health psychologists know about the factors that increase our chances of becoming ill and what we can do to improve and maintain our health.

Courtesy Museum of New Mexico, negative no. 42220

Navajo sandpainters create images of *hozho*, the Navajo concept of beauty, peace of mind, goodness, and health, all inextricably entwined.

OBJECTIVES

After viewing the television program and completing the assigned readings, you should be ble to:

1. Discuss the concepts of health psychology, psychosomatic medicine and behavioral medicine in the context of the bio-psycho-social model of health and illness

2. Outline the relationship between stress and illness in terms of Selye's general adaptation syndrome (GAS)

3. Discuss the psychological factors linked with the etiology of disease

4. Describe the effects of cognitive appraisal on our reactions to stress

5. Outline the psychological factors that contribute to the stressfulness of a situation

6. Describe the relation of Type A and Type B behavior patterns to coronary heart disease (CHD)

7. Describe the relationship of stress to the immune system

8. Discuss psychological methods for managing stress such as biofeedback, relaxation training, exercise, and modifying the cognitive and behavioral antecedents of stress

READING ASSIGNMENT

After viewing Program 23, read pages 328–345 in *Psychology: Science, Behavior and Life*. Your instructor may also assign the anthology selections for Unit 23.

KEY TERMS AND CONCEPTS

As you read the assignment, pay particular attention to these terms, which are defined on the given pages in the text.

stress (329)
stressors (335)
general adaptation syndrome (GAS) (329)
alarm, resistance, and exhaustion (330)
primary and secondary appraisal (333)

biofeedback (343)
relaxation training (343)
Type A and Type B behavior patterns (339)
coronary heart disease (CHD) (338)
hypertension (340)
immune system (342)

The following terms are used in Program 23 but are not defined in the text.

bio-psycho-social model—a new holistic approach to health that treats not just the body but the whole person in his or her social context

cognitive appraisal—see primary and secondary appraisal on page 605 in the text

psychic numbing—being emotionally unaffected by an upsetting or alarming event

psychogenic—organic malfunction or tissue damage caused by an anxiety, tension, or depression

PROGRAM SUMMARY

Noise, smoke, overcrowding, pollution, divorce, violence—how much can one person tolerate? Program 23 focuses on the work of health psychologists who study the social and environmental conditions that put people at risk for physical and psychological disorders.

The field of health psychology has grown out of a profound rethinking of the mind-body relationship. In contrast to the traditional biomedical model, health psychology is based on a new holistic approach that recognizes each person as a whole system in which the emotional, cognitive, and physical processes constantly interact and affect each other.

Mind and body affect one another in a number of ways. Ulcers and hypertension can be caused by anxiety or depression. Headache and exhaustion may be signs of underlying tension. Evidence suggests that psychological factors may suppress or support the body's immune system. And psychological factors certainly contribute to smoking, drinking, and taking drugs.

Judith Rodin of Yale University studies mind-body relationships in the hope of finding ways to improve our health. Her work reveals the link between a person's sense of control and the functioning of the immune system. Rodin has discovered that psychological factors affect complex biological systems that in turn can affect health, fertility, even the life span.

There are many other ways in which the mind can influence the body. Skin temperature, blood pressure, and muscle tension can be influenced by mere thinking. Psychologist Neal Miller discovered that the mind can have a powerful influence on biological systems. Using the psychology of biofeedback, he has helped many people learn to manage chronic pain and to lower their blood pressure.

Another important area of health psychology is stress control. When we feel stressed, our heart beats faster and our blood pressure and blood sugar levels change. The physical state of alertness, called the fight-or-flight response, is the body's answer to anything that disturbs our equilibrium or taxes our ability to cope. Any change in our lives, good or bad, causes stress because it demands an adjustment to new circumstances. But even life's little hassles, like sitting in traffic or searching endlessly for a parking space, can create stress (see Figure 14).

As stress accumulates, the chance of becoming ill increases. Some experts believe that stress contributes to more than half of all cases of disease.

Life Event	Life-Change Units
Death of one's spouse	100
Divorce	73
Marital separation	65
Jail term	63
Death of a close family member	63
Personal injury or illness	53
Marriage	50
Being fired at work	47
Marital reconciliation	45
Retirement	45
Change in the health of a family member	44
Pregnancy	40
Sex difficulties	39
Gain of a new family member	39
Business readjustment	39
Change in one's financial state	38
Death of a close friend	37
Change to a different line of work	36
Change in number of arguments with one's spouse	35
Mortgage over $10,000*	31
Foreclosure of a mortgage or loan	30
Change in responsibilities at work	29
Son or daughter leaving home	29
Trouble with in-laws	29
Outstanding personal achievement	28
Wife beginning or stopping work	26
Beginning or ending school	26
Change in living conditions	25
Revision of personal habits	24
Trouble with one's boss	23
Change in work hours or conditions	20
Change in residence	20
Change in schools	20
Change in recreation	19
Change in church activities	19
Change in social activities	18
Mortgage or loan of less than $10,000	17
Change in sleeping habits	16
Change in number of family get-togethers	15
Change in eating habits	15
Vacation	13
Christmas	12
Minor violations of the law	11

Figure 14: Scale of Life-Change Units
Researchers Thomas Holmes and Richard Rahe assigned units to both positive and negative life changes. They found that people who accumulated more than 300 units within a year were at greater risk for illness.

Source: Holmes and Rahe (1967).

*This figure was appropriate in 1967, when the Life-Change Units Scale was constructed. Today, sad to say, inflation probably puffs this figure up to at least $50,000.

The Canadian physician Hans Selye identified two types of stress reactions in animals. One type is a specific response to a specific stressor. Blood vessels constrict in response to cold, for example. The second type is a pattern of responses known as the general adaptation syndrome, which begins with the body's alarm reaction, mobilizing the body's ability to defend itself. In the resistance stage, hormonal secretions are activated, and the body seems to return to normal. Finally, the body may express a state of exhaustion caused by chronic stress.

Selye's work helped point out the role stress plays in the origin of many disorders. However, because he worked mainly with animals, he neglected one factor—how individuals perceive and interpret an event is often more important than the event itself. We know that what one person perceives as a stressful situation another person may consider to be a challenge. Richard Lazarus calls this personalized perception of stress "cognitive appraisal."

As relative newcomers to the field, health psychologists help people develop strategies for coping with stress, preventing illness, and promoting good health. They teach behaviors that encourage wellness and help condition our bodies to be less vulnerable to disease.

One illness combines psychological and medical issues in an explosive way: AIDS. Thomas Coates is part of a health psychology team studying the AIDS epidemic from the psychological perspective. He calls for combining medical, epidemiological, psychological, and social knowledge to improve what we know about risk factors, incidence, and progression of the disease.

Health psychologists, as scientists and advocates, study how psychological and social processes contribute to disease and then apply their knowledge to the prevention and treatment of illness. Coates emphasizes the need for messages that inform and motivate educational, social, and medical interventions at a variety of levels in the fight against AIDS. It is evident that the role of health psychologists will increase as we acknowledge the importance of psychological factors in health.

REVIEW QUESTIONS

Program Questions

1. How are the biopsychosocial model and the Navaho concept of *hozho* alike?

    a. Both are dualistic.
    b. Both assume individual responsibility for illness.
    c. Both represent holistic approaches to health.
    d. Both are several centuries old.

2. Dr. Wizanski told Thad that his illness was psychogenic. This means that

    a. Thad is not really sick.
    b. Thad's illness was caused by his psychological state.
    c. Thad has a psychological disorder, not a physical one.
    d. Thad's life-style puts him at risk.

3. Judith Rodin and Ellen Langer have studied mind-body relationships among older people. What independent variable did they investigate?

    a. The role of exercise
    b. Increased social contacts
    c. Decreased mortality rates
    d. Increased sense of control

4. When Judith Rodin talks about "wet" connections to the immune system, she is referring to connections to the

    a. individual nerve cells.
    b. endocrine system.
    c. sensory receptors.
    d. skin.

5. What mind-body question is Judith Rodin investigating in her work with infertile couples?

    a. How do psychological factors affect fertility?
    b. Can infertility be cured by psychological counseling?
    c. What effect does infertility have on marital relationships?
    d. Can stress cause rejection of in-vitro fertilization?

6. When Professor Zimbardo lowers his heart rate, he is demonstrating the process of

    a. mental relaxation.
    b. stress reduction.
    c. biofeedback.
    d. the general adaptation syndrome.

7. Psychologist Neal Miller uses the example of the blindfolded basketball player to explain

    a. the need for information to improve performance.
    b. how chance variations lead to evolutionary advantage.
    c. the correlation between life-change events and illness.
    d. how successive approximations can shape behavior.

8. In which area of health psychology has the most research been done?

    a. The definition of health
    b. Stress
    c. Biofeedback
    d. Changes in life-style

9. Imagine a family is moving to a new and larger home in a safer neighborhood with better schools. Will this situation be a source of stress for the family?

    a. No, because the change is a positive one.
    b. No, because moving is not really stressful.
    c. Yes, because any change requires adjustment.
    d. Yes, because it provokes guilt that the family does not really deserve this good fortune.

10. Which response shows the stages of the general adaptation syndrome in the correct order?

    a. Alarm reaction, exhaustion, resistance
    b. Resistance, alarm reaction, exhaustion
    c. Exhaustion, resistance, alarm reaction
    d. Alarm reaction, resistance, exhaustion

11. What important factor in stress did Hans Selye not consider?

    a. The role of hormones in mobilizing the body's defenses
    b. The subjective interpretation of a stressor
    c. The length of exposure to a stressor
    d. The body's vulnerability to new stressors during the resistance stage

12. Today, the major causes of death in the United States are

    a. accidents.
    b. infectious diseases.
    c. sexually transmitted diseases.
    d. diseases related to life-style.

13. When Thomas Coates and his colleagues studying AIDS carry out interview studies, they want to gain information that will help them

    a. design interventions at a variety of levels.
    b. determine how effective mass media advertisements are.
    c. motivate AIDS victims to take good care of themselves.
    d. stop people from using intravenous drugs.

Textbook Questions

14. The text authors define stress as the process of

    a. appraising events, assessing potential responses, and responding.
    b. metabolic breakdown of the body under threat or pressure.
    c. responding with reduced ability to concentrate.
    d. a tendency to have morbid and disruptive thoughts.

15. Hans Selye's term for a hypothesized three-stage response to stress is

    a. the alarm reaction.
    b. the general adaptation syndrome.
    c. the fight-or-flight reaction.
    d. the resistance/recovery reaction.

16. Which of the following is a component of the alarm reaction?

    a. Muscles relax.
    b. Adrenaline is secreted.
    c. Blood coagulability decreases.
    d. Heart rate decreases.

17. The term for a hypothesized innate adaptive response to a perceived danger is the

    a. fight-or-flight reaction.
    b. mental stress syndrome.
    c. general adaptation syndrome.
    d. alarm reaction syndrome.

18. During an emergency, we may be able to perform with high levels of strength and ability because of the

    a. resistance stage of the GAS.
    b. parasympathetic nervous system.
    c. somatic nervous system.
    d. fight-or-flight reaction.

19. The exhaustion stage of the general adaptation syndrome (GAS) is characterized by

    a. a flood of stress hormones that prepare the body for "fight or flight."
    b. a return to a less aroused state, but one which continues to draw upon resources at an above normal rate.
    c. a stage of fatigue in which body tissues begin to show signs of wear and tear and susceptibility to disease.
    d. b combined with c above.

20. The stage of the GAS characterized by weakened resistance and possible deterioration is the

    a. adaptation stage.
    b. resistance stage.
    c. alarm stage.
    d. exhaustion stage.

21. According to Lazarus and Folkman (1984), when confronted with stress we must engage in a cognitive process which they call

    a. damage appraisal.
    b. emotional appraisal.
    c. primary appraisal.
    d. secondary appraisal.

22. _____ provides individuals with information about their bodily processes that they can use to modify these processes.

    a. Relaxation training
    b. Biofeedback
    c. Exercise
    d. A regular checkup

23. Virtually every form of stress management program teaches some form of

    a. relaxation technique.
    b. biofeedback technique.
    c. hypnosis.
    d. meditation technique.

24. Progressive relaxation involves

   a. alternately tensing and relaxing muscles.
   b. learning biofeedback techniques.
   c. rational restructuring.
   d. using hypnosis.

25. A student has learned to deal with the stress of an exam by using positive self-talk such as "There's no point in imagining the worst; I've prepared as well as anyone and I'll do the best I can." This method of therapy is called

   a. stress inoculation.
   b. relaxation training.
   c. biofeedback.
   d. going it alone.

26. One criticism of Holme and Rahe's life-change scale is that

   a. it is experimental rather than correlational.
   b. real people do not have many of these things happen to them.
   c. positive events may be less disturbing than negative events.
   d. all people respond in the same way to stress.

27. What are the criticisms of the Holmes and Rahe's life-change and stress scale?

   a. The scale does not consider the individual's cognitive appraisal of the event.
   b. There are too many items listed on the scale.
   c. There are not enough items listed on the scale.
   d. The items are not "real-life" items.

28. The first step in coping with Type A behavior is to

   a. confront the value system that supports it.
   b. use biofeedback.
   c. use hypnosis.
   d. make a list of things not to do.

29. Friedman and Rosenman found that Type A men were _____ as vulnerable as Type B.

   a. less than one-half times
   b. equally
   c. five times
   d. more than twice

30. Type A patients undergoing surgery manifested _____ of blood pressure than Type Bs undergoing the same procedure.

   a. greater fluctuation
   b. the same
   c. a greater elevation
   d. a lower elevation

31. Josey has a history of becoming ill during final exams. Jemmott and others (1983) have found that

    a. the increased stress lowers immunocompetence.
    b. people like Josey unconsciously fear failure.
    c. Josey's illness has become an excuse not to take finals.
    d. the illness is psychosomatic.

32. There are some indications of the existence of a cancer-prone personality characterized by the tendency to be

    a. hard-driving, ambitious, and competitive.

    b. angry, combative, and driven to achieve perfection.
    c. inhibited, compliant, and depressed.
    d. anxious, irritable, and easily embarrassed.

QUESTIONS TO CONSIDER

1. How can you help another person cope with stress?

2. How can a voodoo curse cause sudden death?

3. How do defense mechanisms help you deal with stress?

4. How can self-deprecating thoughts and behavior increase stress?

5. How might perfectionism lead to stress?

OPTIONAL ACTIVITY

1. Sort the following behaviors into two categories: Category A, Stress Warning Signals; and Category B, Signs of Successful Coping. (You may add others from your own experience.)

Indigestion	Ability to sleep
Fatigue	Tolerance for frustration
Loss of appetite	Constipation
Indecision	Overeating
Sense of belonging	Overuse of drugs or alcohol
Sense of humor	Adaptability to change
Irritability	Optimism
Reliability	Cold hands
Sexual problems	Ulcers
Frequent urination	Sleep problems
Migraine headaches	Difficulty concentrating
Boredom	Free-floating anxiety
Temper tantrums	Frequent colds

ANTHOLOGY

The following readings explore how an individual's psychological attitude can affect health. As you read, consider your reactions to stress and whether your feelings toward a distressing event have ever resulted in illness. Think about what you can do to handle stressful situations more effectively.

Reading 53

Studies have demonstrated that people under a great deal of stress tend to get sick more often than those under less stress. Yet some individuals who experience high stress levels seldom get sick. The researchers quoted in this article point to psychological "hardiness" as a critical factor influencing a person's ability to resist illness. What do you think of their argument? How do you assess the charges of their detractors? Do you think it is possible to train oneself to become more disease-resistant?

Getting Tough

By Joshua Fischman

Salvatore Maddi thinks he can teach you to be tough. But not to break legs, humiliate beach bullies or catch bullets in your teeth. Maddi teaches a different kind of tough: toughness against disease. And like karate and many other forms of self-defense, this toughness is first and foremost a way of thinking about your life. It's called the hardy personality.

Hardiness is a set of beliefs about oneself, the world and how they interact. It takes shape as a sense of personal commitment to what you are doing, a sense of control over your life and a feeling of challenge. The concept is based on more than a decade of research by Maddi, a University of Chicago psychologist, and Suzanne C. Ouelette Kobasa, a psychologist now at the City University of New York. They found that people who hold these beliefs are unusually resistant to many kinds of illness.

The idea that personality characteristics could be buffers against physical illness grew out of the wave of research linking sickness to emotional stress during the 1970s. Study after study showed that people experiencing stressful life events fell victim to colds, flus and other maladies more frequently than did people who reported less stress. Divorce, family illness, job pressure and many other problems all added up to an attack on the body's defense systems, it was thought, leaving people vulnerable and weak.

Kobasa and Maddi felt this view was rather pessimistic. "We could not believe that the same human imagination responsible for urbanization and industrialization was somehow incapable of coping with the . . . ensuing pressures and disruptions," Maddi remembers. The researchers took a close look at the stress-illness studies and noticed that a few people in these studies did not get sick, despite their high stress levels. "It seemed obvious," says Maddi, "that individual differences in response to stress were important."

Hoping to bring some of these differences to light, Kobasa and Maddi began a seven-year-long study of illness patterns and stress among middle-aged managers, both men and women, at the Illinois Bell Telephone Company. The managers were tested every year, with questionnaires, interviews and medical examinations. The researchers found that some of these people were much more likely to become sick after a stressful event than others were. The healthier people, in contrast to the more sickly group, showed higher levels of commitment, challenge, and control. Kobasa and Maddi dubbed these characteristics "the three C's" and believe they form the basis of the hardy personality.

"If you feel self-confident, and that the world is rather benign, you have commitment, or the knack of finding something important about whatever it is you are doing," Maddi says. "You also have control, or the belief that you can influence what is going on around you. . . . Further, you think your life is best led in pursuit of development. Pressures and disruptions, however painful, appear to be something you can learn from and grow." These people stay healthy, according to Maddi, because they hold a worldview that allows them to transcend stressful circumstances.

The two psychologists found that the presence or absence of the hardy personality could actually predict whether the managers got sick. Hardiness was unrelated to health habits, so it could not simply be a result of the "glow" of physical exercise, nor was it related to a family history of health or illness. Further studies done with bus drivers, printers and lawyers confirmed these findings. They also indicated that the healthy effects of hardiness cut across a variety of economic and educational boundaries. What the mind actually does to the body to enhance health is still being debated; Maddi, however, is sure that hardiness works.

Other stress researchers are not quite convinced. Psychologist Richard Lazarus of the University of California, Berkeley, has argued that Kobasa and Maddi had no actual measure of hardiness in these studies but only inferred the presence of the hardy personality from low scores on tests of "unhardy" traits, such as powerlessness or alienation. The relative absence of these traits did not prove that something called "hardiness" existed.

Maddi pleads guilty to this charge but with an explanation and a rebuttal: "I don't want to do a lot of psychometric work [and devise a new test] before I know that the idea is important, and that there is something there to measure." Once the early studies indicated that there was an effect worth investigating, Maddi and Kobasa developed an independent, definitive measure for hardiness that Maddi describes as "highly reliable." He says that results using this test conform closely to results using the earlier measures, although these later studies have not been published yet.

Not only is Maddi confident that hardiness has a real effect, he also thinks that it can be taught. In a 15-week course at Illinois Bell, male and female managers met with Maddi in small groups of seven or eight, for one hour at a time, and discussed various problems encountered on the job and in their personal lives. Maddi instructed them in a number of coping strategies designed to enhance their hardiness. The trainees were scored on the new hardiness test before the course; when it was over and they were retested, their scores more than doubled.

In addition to improving their hardiness scores, the Illinois Bell trainees reported more job satisfaction. Their levels of anxiety, depression and obsessiveness dropped quite noticeably, as did some physical symptoms of mental strain such as headaches and loss of sleep. Their blood pressure dropped as well, from an average of 130/82 to 120/77. "We did not expect to demonstrate a decrease in illness over the short period of the course," Maddi says, "though the changes we did find should lower illness over the long run." None of these changes occurred in a comparison group of managers who did not take the course.

Hardiness training centers around three techniques: "situational reconstruction," "focusing" and "compensatory self-improvement." Mastery of these strategies gives trainees a taste of successfully influencing events in their lives, and they can build on this experience outside of class.

Situational reconstruction. This technique emphasizes problem-solving and stretches the imagination to set stressful circumstances in a broader perspective. Trainees learn to recognize underlying assumptions that determine how stressful a situation is, and can then think about alternative courses of action.

For example, Arthur, a manager at Illinois Bell, was very upset over a mediocre performance appraisal from his supervisor that cost him a promotion, although it did net him a small raise. Maddi encouraged Arthur to imagine a number of ways the situation could be worse, such as getting fired or not getting a raise, and ways it could be better, such as the corporate officers not believing the evaluation and promoting him despite it.

Arthur realized that the worst-case scenarios would have required a worse performance than he had actually turned in or perhaps an attempt to "get him" by his supervisor. Since he had not performed that badly, he began to regain a sense of control and self-worth, and the realization that his boss was not trying to do him in helped defuse some of Arthur's anger.

He also realized that the better outcome he imagined would be possible only if the higher-ups were more aware of him and what he did. This gave him a goal and a plan of action: to become more involved in his work and to make sure that those above him knew it. Arthur initiated a series of conferences with his supervisor, who was impressed enough to offer him more challenging opportunities within the department.

Focusing. Sometimes people are only vaguely aware that they feel unhappy or distressed and are unable to locate the specific cause of such feelings. In these cases, Maddi encourages trainees to try focusing: concentrating on various bodily sensations and trying to recall the circumstances under which they usually occur. By using physical reactions as clues, trainees may get a clearer idea of the cause of their distress.

An example might be Roger, another executive, who tried the focusing technique when he was having difficulty completing a report by his assigned deadline. Roger couldn't figure out what was holding him up, but he was becoming quite upset about it.

Roger began by sitting quietly and reflecting. His first thought was: "They never give you enough time to do anything in this place." He felt angry at his boss and depressed at his own plight, but then he noticed a tightening in his chest and discomfort in his stomach that felt like fear.

"Why am I so afraid?" he wondered. Once he began to think about it, the answer came: He was afraid of losing his job. This fit in a pattern with other times he felt fear, Roger realized, such as in grammar school when he didn't do his homework because he was afraid of failing. By not turning in work, he couldn't be judged on it.

Through focusing, Roger was able to take a nameless blockage and transform it into a problem with personal meaning, something he could work on. This renewed his sense of control, and using and mastering the focusing technique created a sense of challenge and commitment. Armed with new faith in himself, Roger was prepared to work on a strategy to deal with the problem.

Compensatory self-improvement. If focusing also fails, Maddi concludes that a person has run up against a genuine roadblock, a situation that truly cannot be changed. Then compensatory self-improvement comes into play. People identify another stressful situation in their lives that does appear changeable and work to find some positive aspects of it. At the same time, they try to accept the unchangeable nature of the original problem.

Barbara, another of Maddi's clients, was in this position. Her husband had fallen deeply in love with another woman and wanted a divorce. Barbara tried desperately to win him back, making changes in their relationship and in herself to accommodate him, but to no avail. She saw herself as a failure and became very depressed.

Barbara felt her marital failure was but one instance of her general inability to meet challenges. So with Maddi's help, she decided to tackle another area of her life: learning to ski. Skiing appears trivial next to a broken marriage, but to Barbara her lack of competence was more evidence of her timidity. She lived in northern Michigan, where winter sports dominate the social scene, but Barbara had avoided any gathering that involved skiing and kept her inability a secret.

With her heart in her mouth, Barbara signed up for skiing lessons on weekends. It took a while, but her anxiety began to subside as her uncertain progress became steady development. She started looking forward to the lessons and the social contact they provided and made plans to incorporate skiing into her life.

"This developing sense of possibility began to spill over into other areas of her life," Maddi remembers. There was no magical remedy for her dissolving marriage, but Barbara's growing sense of herself as an individual enabled her to view her husband with more equanimity and gave her energy to do many things she had been avoiding. There was much more going on than self-improvement, Maddi says; Barbara was taking aspects of her life into her own hands and beginning to fashion a future.

Maddi thinks that, in time, learned hardiness will become second nature to people who use the techniques. And there are hints that he may be right: "When tested two and six months after the Illinois Bell course, the managers still scored high on the hardiness scale, even improving slightly over time. Their personal responses have been even more encouraging," Maddi says. Many trainees told him that "the course changed my life" and spoke of tremendous improvements in their work and personal relationships.

Of course, the success isn't universal. A few of the trainees—those who missed a number of the sessions and were reluctant participants in the sessions they did attend—showed little improvement in their hardiness scores and the other measures. "You get out of a course what you put into it," Maddi says.

Maddi has formed a consulting group that offers hardiness training to interested companies, and he plans to market the new hardiness test commercially. He is very highly regarded as a therapist, but this approach has created some unease among other psychologists who feel that Maddi may have jumped the gun by offering hardiness training before it has been critically evaluated by other researchers. Recent reports have questioned the accuracy of statistical techniques that Maddi and Kobasa used, and have claimed that the three different components of hardiness real-ly have separate effects, and that some don't affect health at all. "I'm sympathetic to the idea of hardiness," says psychologist Donald Meichenbaum of the University of Waterloo in Ontario, Canada, who also studies stress and coping, "but I just wish we knew a little more about it."

Maddi's faith in the power of hardiness remains unshaken. "You may remember the old prayer: 'God grant me the courage to change that which can be changed, the serenity to accept that which cannot be changed and the wisdom to know the difference,' " he says. "Hardiness training provides the secular attitudes and skills that used to be treated as a state of grace for which one had to pray."

Reading 54

This reading explores one aspect of the mind's impact on the body—specifically, how anxiety and perception affect the immune system. What does the author suggest about the effect of depression on illness? Consider the research implications for controlling sickness.

The Immune System Reacts to Stress

By Sally Squires

People who lose their jobs seem to lose something more as well: some of their immune system's ability to fight disease.

A new study, reported last week at the Society of Behavioral Medicine annual meeting here, found that men and women who lose their jobs also lost for a short period of time some of their body's ability to fight infection.

The study involved 24 people ages 30 to 60, recruited from unemployment offices in Maryland. Blood tests showed that their immune systems had lower numbers of white blood cells, known as T- and B-lymphocytes, which are important in fighting infectious agents and the growth of tumors. Urine tests indicated that they had increased levels of the hormone cortisol, which also suppresses the immune system.

At the same time, researchers found that unemployed people seem to adapt to the stress of losing their jobs because their immune systems eventually returned to normal.

"The most important finding is that there was recovery of the immune system function and the hormonal levels," said Dr. Andrew Baum, associate professor of medical psychology at the Uniformed University of the

---

SIGNS OF STRESS

The signs of stress are as varied as the people who experience it. But some of the symptoms are:

- Tense muscles. Backaches.
- Cold hands or feet.
- Pounding or racing heart. Shortness of breath.
- Irritability or edginess.
- Increased use of alcohol, tobacco, caffeine or other drugs.
- Forgetfulness. Lack of concentration.
- Nail biting or teeth grinding.

Health Sciences in Bethesda and the author of the study. "They tended to go back to the same level as the control subjects, whether or not those who lost their jobs got another job."

"The biological effects of that kind of stress are not necessarily long-lasting," he said.

Important differences also emerged in the study between people who found jobs within six months of becoming unemployed and those who did not. To begin with, people whose immune systems were stronger, according to blood tests, tended to find new positions within one to two months.

Whether this difference was due to less stress, greater confidence or knowledge of a good job lead is still unknown, he said. But once on the job again, the re-employed participants had another dip in their immune function for about a month—a result, Baum says, of the stress encountered in their new position. Recovery was swift.

The study is the latest in a series of reports showing that stress can affect the body's immune system and may take a toll on health. In recent years, evidence has been accumulating of a strong connection between the mind and the body in controlling disease—whether the stress stems from losing a job, living in the shadow of the Three Mile Island Nuclear Power Plant, or caring for a spouse with Alzheimer's disease.

Today, medical investigators are examining these situations in an attempt to find out what enables some people under stress to remain healthy while others become ill.

At Three Mile Island, Baum and his colleagues found, even six years after the nuclear reactor accident many residents still have suppressed immune function compared with a control group living in Frederick, Md.

"The health significance of these differences is unknown right now," Baum said. "These people are still under stress. We don't know how much, but it does seem to be affecting their immune system. We don't know if that has any clinical significance. It will be a matter of time before we can tell."

To medical researchers, the study suggests that the stress from the nuclear plant accident may be having more effect on the residents than actual exposure to radiation. "Whatever is going on in these people is probably more related to stress than any radiation exposure," Baum says.

Some of the TMI study participants indicated that they are "more concerned about what happened to them [during the accident] than what might happen to them in the future," Baum said. "That kind of stress, being worried about something that has already happened, is harder to tackle."

How is it that stress can exert such strong health effects? The answers are coming from a variety of animal and human studies that examine both short-term and chronic stressful situations. A large part of the answer seems to come from the interplay between mind and body.

At the National Cancer Institute, for example, an ongoing AIDS-stress study of 5,000 men is providing some evidence of the strong effect the mind can have on the immune system. Known as the Multicenter AIDS Cohort Study—or MACS—preliminary results show that a person's belief about their risk of AIDS can produce changes in the immune system.

Since 1983, when the study began, the 5,000 participants—all bisexual or homosexual men—have been examined and undergone psychological testing every six months.

"What we found is that those participants who believed that they were ill, were depressed," says Dr. Andrew Monjan, acting associate director of the neuroscience and neuropsychology of aging program at the National Institute of Aging and an investigator of the NCI study.

As part of the study, the investigators asked participants if they had had swollen glands in the past two weeks—one indication of an infection. Each participant also underwent a physical exam to check for swollen glands and other physical symptoms of disease.

Men who mistakenly believed they were ill also mistakenly reported having swollen glands. When researchers tested their blood, they found that these men had lowered—but still normal—levels of white blood cells, known as helper and suppressor T-cells. By comparison, men who did not believe they were ill had higher levels of these same cells.

Men who actually had swollen glands, whether or not they thought they had them, had blood levels of lymphocytes that were similar to the men who believed their glands were swollen.

"The point here is that if someone was free from disease, the psychological component may have an effect on the immune system," Monjan says. "But if they had evidence of illness—swollen glands or evidence of HIV [the virus that causes AIDS] infection—the disease overwhelmed the psychological effect."

Other studies suggest that age may also play an important role in immune function. At Mt. Sinai School of Medicine in New York, Dr. Steven Keller and his colleagues have shown that depression also affects the immune system, especially among older individuals.

The study, which included 88 men and women with manic depression and a group of controls found that "older depressed people are at particular risk for consequences of the immune systems," Keller said. "These changes are most striking after age 60."

Scientists are working toward understanding how stress influences the neurobiological processes of the mind that in turn influence a person's health.

"Each one of these studies is slightly different," Keller said. "But together they are giving us more evidence of the nature of behavioral effects on the immune system."

Reading 55

This article suggests that a feeling of helplessness can affect the resistance of an individual infected by the HIV virus, believed to cause AIDS. How can the research described in this reading be used to improve the coping strategies of people with AIDS?

AIDS and Personality

By Eleanor Smith

People who "take the bull by the horns" and actively try to solve their problems may be better able to resist the AIDS virus than those who are passive in their approach to life. That's the implication of some preliminary findings by University of Miami researchers who are studying links between the immune system and the different ways people typically deal with life's ups and downs.

The researchers are examining a group of gay men in the early stages of infection by the human immunodeficiency virus (HIV), which is believed to cause AIDS. Psychologist Nancy T. Blaney and her colleagues asked 49 infected men questions about their present moods and their typical strategies for coping with problems. They also tested the responses of various components of the men's immune system, such as the ability of lymphocytes to respond to stimulation. In results similar to those in studies by other researchers showing that cancer patients with a "fighting spirit"

live longer, Blaney's team learned that men who showed anger and a sense of vigor had better immune functions than men who reacted to hardship with depression, anxiety or loneliness.

High immunoglobulin, or antibody, levels are a hallmark of HIV infection, and Blaney found that men who "were characterized by withdrawing, giving up and feeling helpless when faced with a problem" had higher immunoglobulin levels than men who actively try to cope with their troubles.

One form of active coping, focusing on a problem and taking steps to find a solution, was linked to greater natural killer cell activity and lymphocyte—white blood cell—response. So was a strategy dubbed "positive reinterpretation and growth." Blaney explains: "A lot of men had this coping style. They were making the best of their situation; they viewed their infection as an opportunity for self-growth."

ADDITIONAL RESOURCES

Books and Articles

Benson, H. *The Relaxation Response*. New York: Morrow, 1975. An introduction to the relationships among heart disease, hypertension, and stress. Contains guidelines on how to meditate.

Benson, H., and W. Proctor. *Beyond the Relaxation Response: How to Harness the Healing Power of Your Personal Beliefs*. New York: Times Books, 1984. Further advice on managing stress.

Lazarus, R. S. "Little Hassles Can Be Hazardous to Your Health." *Psychology Today* (July 1981): 58–62. Stress can come from accumulated small stressors as well as from major crises.

Lazarus, R. S., and S. Folkman. *Stress, Appraisal, and Coping*. New York: Springer, 1984. A comprehensive analysis of stress and stress reactions.

Ornstein, Robert, and David Sobel. "The Healing Brain." *Psychology Today* (March 1987): 48. Attitudes about ourselves and others may affect our ability to resist disease.

Rodin, Judith. "A Sense of Control." *Psychology Today* (December 1984): 38–45. A leading figure in the field of health psychology, Rodin discusses the importance of having a sense of control, in everything from losing weight to being productive in old age.

Selye, Hans. *The Stress of Life*. New York: McGraw-Hill, 1956. Explores the stressors that threaten the physiological function of animals and proposes a "general adaptation syndrome."

IN SPACE, TOWARD PEACE

It will free man from the remaining chains, the chains of gravity which still tie him to this planet.

Wernher von Braun

Unit 24 concentrates on how psychologists from a variety of fields put their knowledge, research skills, and insights to work in space travel, arms negotiations, and peacemaking.

Applied psychologists are making a difference in diverse areas, from travel in space to peace on Earth.

OBJECTIVES

After viewing Program 24 and completing the assigned readings, you should be able to:

1. Outline the effects of environmental conditions such as noise, heat, and toxins on behavior

2. Define the concepts of territoriality and personal space and outline the effects of personal space on behavior

3. Discuss stress factors for space travel and methods for engineering the environment to alleviate stress

4. Describe how industrial/organizational (I/O) psychology applies basic psychological principles to aid in personnel selection and in evaluating job satisfaction

5. Discuss the effects of different management styles on worker response

6. Describe research by psychologists on the psychology of peace—including the factors that lead to suspicion and conflict and the work on negotiation and conflict resolution

There is no reading assignment from the text. Your instructor may assign the anthology selections for Unit 24.

KEY TERMS AND CONCEPTS

As you read the assignment, pay particular attention to these terms.

environmental psychology
behavioral toxicology
architectural psychology
territoriality
primary and secondary territories
personal space and interpersonal distance
intimate, personal, and social distance
density and crowding

industrial/organizational (I/O) psychology
job analysis
assessment centers
leaderless group discussions
job satisfaction
job description index (JDI)
participant management
Theory X and Theory Y management

PROGRAM SUMMARY

In the preceding programs we have seen how psychologists study neurons and hormones, motives and needs, perception and decision making, communication, intelligence, creativity, critical thinking, and stress. In Program 24 we will see how psychologists put their insights to work to solve global problems and improve the quality of life for individuals and nations.

Two areas of great interest to applied psychologists today are space travel and peacemaking. Both fields incorporate knowledge gleaned from many areas of study, from behavioral and social psychology to biochemistry and environmental engineering.

As the duration of space travel lengthens and the crews become larger and more diverse, psychologists will play an increasingly important role in addressing the psychological and physiological dimensions of spaceflight. There are a variety of stressors in space that could cause medical and psychological problems such as anxiety, depression, boredom, loneliness, and hostility. These problems threaten the well-being, morale, and performance of astronauts and future space travelers.

The limitations in space are not as much medical as psychological. Taking into account human reactions to the unique features of space travel, psychologists are helping to design the spacecraft environment and to teach personal and group adjustment strategies. Yvonne Clearwater of NASA provides evidence of the many ways confinement and isolation affect astronauts. There is often a rise in stress hormones, some intellectual impairment, a decline in motivation, an increase in tension and hostility, and social withdrawal.

Another psychologist, Pat Cowings, teaches astronauts how to overcome motion sickness in space using individualized psychological techniques. In a laboratory setting, she uses rotating devices and linear accelerators actually to make them sick. Then she shows them how to control voluntarily specific symptoms, such as heart rate, temperature changes, and blood flow.

In order to create a socially comfortable spacecraft environment, psychologists are working on techniques for overcoming the inevitable distortions of voice, facial expression, and movement which affect interpersonal communication. They are also researching techniques to help space travelers overcome boredom. And with larger, more diversified crews on board, they will need to help solve the problems caused by conflicts in professional status, language styles, even cultural differences.

Just as the psychology of space travel brings together many different disciplines, the study of peace demands the involvement of psychologists, sociologists, political scientists, and others concerned with preventing nuclear war and promoting peace among nations. Research ranges from studies of arms negotiations to how people respond to the possibility of nuclear war.

Psychologist Scott Plous, who has explored the attitudes of American and Soviet leaders, has discovered that both sides are suspicious of the other's intentions. Max Bazerman of Northwestern University explains the problems of negotiation when participants mistrust each other. He explores ways of finding areas of shared self-interest which both sides can agree on.

John Mack specializes in understanding the obstacles to international conflict resolution. At his center, researchers study the psychosocial forces that lead many

Soviets and Americans to see each other as demons. No matter what the society, nations portray each other in similar, dehumanizing ways. When each side pictures its enemies as monsters, madmen, or vicious animals to be eradicated, preparing for nuclear war seems reasonable and justified. Researchers are now investigating new strategies for changing how people perceive their traditional enemies.

REVIEW QUESTIONS

Program Questions

1. Why is there more concern about psychological factors in spaceflight now than there was several years ago?

   a. Psychologists' shift toward cognitive science has increased interest in what happens in space.
   b. Longer flights and larger crews make greater psychological demands.
   c. The severe psychological problems of previous astronauts has demonstrated the need for more research.
   d. As funding has become available, psychologists have become interested in doing research.

2. Dr. Millie Hughes-Fulford points out that as part of the preselection process potential astronauts are tested for

   a. anxiety disorders.
   b. antisocial personality disorder.
   c. paraphilias.
   d. claustrophobia.

3. What causes the motion sickness astronauts experience?

   a. The speed at which their craft is moving
   b. The restricted diet they eat
   c. The conflict between vision and position
   d. The rotational pattern in which their craft is orbiting

4. What physical problem has emerged on flights of long duration?

   a. Kidney failure
   b. Hearing loss
   c. Hormone imbalances
   d. Bone loss

5. What effect does living in close quarters have on the likelihood of interpersonal conflict?

   a. The likelihood increases.
   b. The likelihood decreases.
   c. The likelihood does not change.
   d. It depends on the nationality of the crew.

6. What is meant by the term *cocooning*?

    a. Making one's living quarters comfortable
    b. Ignoring the demands of the job to concentrate on oneself
    c. Becoming psychologically adjusted to a new environment
    d. Withdrawing from social contacts by creating private space

7. According to Yvonne Clearwater, the people on the submarine may have spent so much of their time alone because of their need to

    a. reflect on their experiences.
    b. get away from an environment that was too stimulating.
    c. limit the possibility of hostile interactions.
    d. escape into books and other forms of entertainment.

8. What is Pat Cowings's purpose in using rotating rooms and linear accelerators to induce motion sickness?

    a. To select as astronauts those least likely to develop motion sickness
    b. To work with ex-astronauts who suffer from recurrent motion sickness
    c. To find personality variables that are correlated with developing motion sickness
    d. To train potential astronauts to control their motion sickness

9. According to the program, why are astronauts at risk for sleep disorders?

    a. Their circadian rhythms are out of sync with shipboard time.
    b. Their lack of exercise makes it harder for them to fall asleep.
    c. They must be restrained during sleep.
    d. Inner ear disturbances from lack of spatial orientation disrupt sleep.

10. Scott Fisher takes us on an imaginary escalator ride using the virtual interactive environment work station. What is the purpose of this device?

    a. To generate images of objects astronauts are working with
    b. To provide recreation in a simulated environment
    c. To calculate designs that fit human measurements
    d. To visualize objects hidden in the darkness of space

11. Imagine you are a crew member on a space mission. How would your voice sound?

    a. Higher in pitch
    b. Lower in pitch
    c. As if you had laryngitis
    d. As if you had a cold

12. The program points out that the Soviet ground control monitors cosmonauts' stress levels through

    a. checking blood hormone levels.
    b. recording interactions between cosmonauts.
    c. measuring performance levels.
    d. analyzing speech patterns.

13. Yvonne Clearwater shows us a mock-up of a crew member's living quarters. What is the purpose of the wall treatment?

    a. To cue spatial orientation
    b. To relieve boredom
    c. To create opportunities for individual choice
    d. To lessen muscle fatigue

14. What does research by Scott Plous on the attitude of Soviet and American leaders suggest?

    a. Each side really wants to take advantage of the other.
    b. Each side realizes that the other wants disarmament.
    c. Each side is suspicious of the other's intentions.
    d. Each side believes the other is trustworthy.

15. Max Bazerman cites the example of the recent progress in negotiations between the United States and the Soviet Union as the result of

    a. breaking out of a zero-sum situation.
    b. escalating the level of conflict.
    c. using psychological principles to promote trust.
    d. giving the "enemy" a more human face.

16. What is the effect of portraying enemies as demons, vermin, liars, and rapists?

    a. It makes us fearful enough to take action.
    b. It dehumanizes them so we can kill them.
    c. It projects our own feelings of shame so we feel better about ourselves.
    d. It makes them seem easier to defeat.

17. According to John Mack, one of the aims of the Center for Psychological Studies in the Nuclear Age is to challenge the norm of

    a. accepting war as inevitable.
    b. seeing the other side as people like ourselves.
    c. viewing conflict as the basis of political life.
    d. blaming the enemy.

QUESTIONS TO CONSIDER

1. Contrast and compare the contributions of basic research with those of applied research.

2. Organizational and industrial psychologists focus on how individuals and organizations influence each other. One of their interests is increasing the compatibility between people and machines. Many computer companies claim their machines and programs are "user friendly." What does this mean?

3. Can psychological principles and knowledge be applied for evil purposes as well as good?

OPTIONAL ACTIVITIES

1. Collect political cartoons and analyze how individuals, countries, and opposition parties are characterized. Do you see any evidence of stereotyping or dehumanizing?

2. Interview a few people about their attitudes about countries in the news: China, the Soviet Union, South Africa, Cuba, Libya, and Iran. Ask them to give you two or three adjectives to describe the traits they associate with each. Ask your survey participants how they feel their associations have been shaped. By the media? By experience?

ANTHOLOGY

Unit 24 shows how psychologists are helping to solve real-world problems of global harmony and survival in outer space. Note how advances in technology and improved methodology help psychologists study important issues, with broad applications in many areas. As you read the following selections, consider the personal as well as the global implications of these areas of basic and applied research.

Reading 56

In this editorial, John Mack describes a survey that investigated how the threat of nuclear war affects American and Soviet teenagers. Besides providing important data, the survey overcomes the limits of earlier attempts to document the impact of the nuclear threat on children. As you read, think about your own concerns and attitudes toward nuclear war. Has the threat of nuclear war influenced your outlook on the future?

American and Soviet Teenagers and Nuclear War

By John E. Mack, M.D.

In a study that is a model of scientific collaboration between the United States and the Soviet Union, Eric Chivian and his Soviet and American colleagues in this issue of the *Journal*[1] provide a methodologically sophisticated comparison of the attitudes toward nuclear war and the future of teenagers in the U.S.S.R. with those of teenagers in the United States. The article stems from an international survey of adolescent attitudes toward these and other matters. Except for more realism in the American sample about the likelihood of surviving a large-scale nuclear war—probably the result of public education on this issue—the study's findings affirm the observations offered tentatively in a report published three years ago.[2]

Questions about the psychological effect of the threat of nuclear war on children and adolescents have stirred considerable professional and public interest in recent years, and studies of the subject have proliferated. There are several reasons for this. First we are understandably concerned if large numbers of young people are growing up worried, afraid, or otherwise troubled by the perception of a global or other large-scale threat, especially one of our own making. Second, we wonder about the effect on children and adolescents of living with the constant possibility of annihilation. In particular, we are interested in the effect of growing up in such a context on many developmental issues: impulse control and the capacity to delay gratification, the formation of long-term

ideals, the ability and willingness to form relationships, views of death, the capacity for intergenerational trust, the development of social responsibility, and interest in planning for the future.[3] How does the nuclear threat, or any major event or pervasive situation in the larger environment, affect personality development or structure?

Finally, the matter has political importance, inasmuch as evidence that young people are adversely affected psychologically by a threat that stems from international conflict and governmental policy may stand as a potential challenge to that policy. It is for this last reason, over and above the complex and difficult scientific questions that surround this subject, that the issue of the effect of the nuclear threat on young people aroused so much public interest and controversy after initial studies in the early 1980s showed that some children and adolescents were seriously troubled by the threat of nuclear war.[4, 5] The shortcomings of early studies, which suffered from limitations of sampling methods and size and from the distortions that follow from asking direct, leading questions about nuclear matters, became the focus of professional criticism and political challenge.[6, 7]

It is against this background that the study of Chivian et al. needs to be seen and that it acquires such importance. Because the investigators have gone to great lengths to avoid the methodologic deficiencies of previous studies and to anticipate future criticisms, their findings—which confirm, by and large, those of other studies—must be taken seriously. The sample is large for a questionnaire of such complexity (2148 Russian students from the Rostov-Tambov region, 11 to 17 years of age, and 3370 Maryland students, 12 to 18); the threat of nuclear war is buried among 19 potential adolescent worries; the investigators made a great effort to address differences in language and meaning within the two cultures; and they took pains to administer the questionnaires at the same time in the Soviet Union and the United States. Since study of the American sample was unintentionally delayed and data collection not begun until after the Chernobyl accident, the entire Soviet survey, which had been completed before Chernobyl, was repeated in order to eliminate the biasing influence of that event. The authors are appropriately self-critical about the ways in which nuances of language or culturally determined differences of attitude toward filling out questionnaires may nevertheless affect their results.

Keeping these limitations in mind, the authors observe that for both Soviet and American teenagers, "nuclear war," along with "your mother or father dying," ranks highest among the worries, ahead of such other global concerns as environmental pollution or overpopulation and such personal preoccupations as one's own death or "people not liking me." Few teenagers believed survival after a nuclear war to be possible. The Soviet adolescents were more worried about global threats than personal ones and more optimistic about the future than their American counterparts, which the authors suggest reflects the characteristics of the Soviet system—the greater emphasis on the good of the collective as compared with that of the individual, the shielding of young people (at least before the advent of Gorbachev) from the worst domestic and global problems, and the generally positive attitude about the future that is communicated through the Soviet media and educational system. This study is important because, together with other recent research,[8] it does a good deal to lay to rest the claims, offered repeatedly in the United States without much supporting data, that the fears of American teenagers have been exaggerated by the researchers themselves or that fears of nuclear war are largely the preoccupation of the children of socially advantaged, concerned parents. In this study,

worry about nuclear war was found to cut across class, racial, sex, and religious lines.

Chivian et al. have helped to establish with greater authority the basic facts about the concern of many teenagers over nuclear war. But important questions about the meaning of this information for young people in America and abroad, for our society as a whole, and for the global community remain largely unanswered. Our notions of the effect of the nuclear threat on child development and mental health, personality formation, vocational choice, social and political thinking, and our attitudes toward the future are still speculative. We know little about how the fears of nuclear war expressed by children and adolescents affect other developmental problems and needs. Nor have we addressed through responsible professional and public debate the implications of young people's concerns about the nuclear threat for parents, primary and secondary education, and mental health care.[9] Finally, we have yet to look forthrightly at the military and political implications of findings such as these. It is to be hoped that the work of Chivian and his colleagues will now enable us to get on with these important tasks.

References

1. Chivian, E, Robinson JP, Tudge JRH, Popov NP, Andreyenkov VG. American and Soviet teenagers' concerns about nuclear war and the future. N Engl J Med 1988; 319:407-13.

2. Chivian E, Mach JE, Waletzky JP, Lazaroff C, Doctor R, Godenring JM. Soviet children and the threat of nuclear war: a preliminary study. Am J Orthopsychiatry 1983; 55: 484-502.

3. Hesse P. Children's and adolescents' fears of nuclear war: is our sense of the future disappearing? Int J Ment Health 1986; 15:93-113.

4. Beardslee W, Mack JE. The impact of nuclear advances on children and adolescents. In: Rogers R, ed. The psychosocial aspects of nuclear developments. Task force report no 20. Washington, D.C.: American Psychiatric Association. 1982: 64-93.

5. Bachman J. American high school seniors view the military: 1976-1982. Armed Forces Society. Fall 1983:86-104.

6. Terr LC. Treatment of psychic trauma in children. In: Noshpitz JD, ed. Basic handbook of child psychiatry. Vol. 5. New York: Basic Books. 1987:262-72.

7. Mack JE. The psychological impact of the nuclear arms competition on children and adolescents. Testimony: children's fears of war. Hearing before the Select Committee on Children, Youth, and Families. House of Representatives, Ninety-Eighth Congress. First Session, September 20, 1983. Washington, D.C.: Government Printing Office, 1984.

8. Diamond G, Bachman J. High-school seniors and the nuclear threat. 1975-1984: political and mental health implications of concern and despair. Int J Ment Health 1986; 15:210-41.

9. Stoddard F, Mack JE. Children, adolescents, and the threat of nuclear war. Noshpitz JD, ed. Basic handbook of child psychiatry. Vol. 5. New York: Basic Books, 1987:616-27.

Reading 57

Teamwork is important not only on space missions but also in the cockpit of commercial airliners. Technical competence has traditionally been the only criteria for pilot selection. This article suggests that the degree of cooperation and communication in the cockpit can mean the difference between life and death. As you read, consider why some pilots object to the training. Why is the impact or success of the training so hard to measure?

Wild Blue Blunders

By Elizabeth Stark

Ever since Tom Wolfe coined the term "the right stuff" the universal image of a pilot has been of a fearless, brash and macho maverick who makes seat-of-the-pants decisions and dares fate to tamper with his plane. Conversation is not his strong suit. Silence, grunts and commands are more his style.

While this may be the right attitude for flying an F-16, it is not the best way to manage the crew of a commercial carrier. The amount of information flight crews must process demands a highly coordinated team performance. Former top guns need to be effective managers willing to delegate responsibility and take advice from subordinates. Unfortunately, aircraft captains are usually chosen for their "stick and rudder" skills, not their management style.

Better communication and teamwork are not just a matter of improved performance among the cockpit crew; they are literally matters of life and death. The Federal Aviation Administration (FAA) estimates that between 60 and 80 percent of all accidents are due, at least partially, to "human factors." In other words, someone in the cockpit made a mistake.

The rash of near misses and accidents at Delta Airlines last year were largely due to human error. In its report on Delta's problems, the FAA concluded its investigators had "observed instances of a breakdown of communications, a lack of crew coordination and lapses of discipline in Delta's cockpit." Crew members were not necessarily unprofessional or purposely negligent, the FAA said, but they were "frequently acting as individuals rather than as members of smoothly functioning teams."

No lives were lost in the Delta mishaps, but poor cockpit management has resulted in fatal accidents. One of the most notorious examples was a 1972 Eastern Airlines crash in which more than half the passengers died.

As the plane was approaching Miami International Airport, the captain, first officer and flight engineer were so preoccupied with a minor problem involving an indicator light that none of them noticed that the plane was making an unplanned descent. By the time the first officer asked, "We're still at two thousand, right?" they were seconds away from impact.

In many accidents due to human error a junior member of the crew knew about a problem but either didn't mention it or was ignored. Copilots are often hesitant to forcefully contradict or question the captain, according to H. Clayton Foushee, an aviation psychologist at the National Aeronautics and Space Administration's Ames Research Center.

In a study of group interaction in the cockpit, subordinate crew members told Foushee that captains could be so intimidating and gruff they were often reluctant to speak up, even in critical situations. In one instance a captain barked back to a copilot's reminder that they were exceeding a speed limit, "I'll do what I want." When the copilot advised him again, the captain ordered him to "just look out the damn window."

Although captains who are this curt and domineering may be rare, a run-in with just one may intimidate a subordinate forever, Foushee explains. A copilot who was reluctant to correct a captain during a simulated flight admitted, "This captain is very 'approachable' and I had no reason to hold back. It is just a bad habit that I think a lot of copilots have."

Even air traffic controllers, who direct pilots, often handle them with kid gloves. In the Eastern crash a ground controller was aware that the plane was descending, but only managed to muster up the vague comment, "How are things comin' along out there?"

When subordinates do question the captain, their advice is sometimes dismissed. The voice recording from a 1982 Air Florida accident, in which 78 people lost their lives after the plane hit Washington, D.C.'s 14th Street Bridge and plunged into the Potomac River, revealed that the copilot had warned the captain four times before takeoff that something was wrong.

But blame for mismanagement does not lie completely with authoritative captains and insecure junior officers. Part of the problem is that flight crews often don't have much time to get to know each other. Some meet for the first time only an hour before takeoff.

How a crew will interact hinges largely on the tone the captain sets in the first few minutes, according to Robert Ginnett, a psychologist and lieutenant colonel at the U.S. Air Force Academy in Colorado Springs. During the preflight briefing, crew members notice subtle cues that tell them what the captain will be like to work with. "Crews know the captain meets FAA requirements regarding technical proficiency; what they don't know is how this guy will work with people," he says.

Ginnett has found that a careful mix of authority and receptiveness to advice seems to be the winning combination. Since most pilots have had no reason to develop this cooperative attitude before they become commercial pilots, they have to learn it on the job. And many people in the airline industry think that a program called Cockpit Resource Management (CRM) is the way to teach it.

Most CRM courses involve a modified version of typical management-training programs that include role playing, psychological inventories, accident case studies, peer and professional feedback, videotaping and self-analysis. Many programs also include a session on a flight simulator, in which a crew actually simulates an entire flight from takeoff to landing. Along the way they encounter varius problems, such as an on-board fire or bad weather conditions, that can only be handled through teamwork and cooperation. One of the most popular and well-known simulator programs is LOFT (Line Oriented Flight Training).

United Airlines was one of the first airlines to mandate special training for cockpit crews. CRM was adopted after a United plane ran out of fuel near the Portland International Airport in 1978, crashing and leaving 10

dead and 23 seriously injured. The captain had insisted on maintaining a holding pattern for about an hour to check out the landing gear, despite warnings from the other officers that they were low on fuel.

Through its program United hopes to prevent this sort of destructive and disastrous management style from occurring in the future. "We don't encourage crews to mutiny or take over the ship," explains Steve Davis, a technical specialist for United, "just to be able to make assertive statements."

Over the past few years many other CRM programs have sprung up throughout the industry—at least 16 airlines offer some type of training. "It's almost become a fad," Foushee says. A true sign of CRM's popularity is that even branches of the military—the procurer and instructor of "the right stuff"—have adopted the training method.

Pan American, Continental, Alaska Air and Delta have begun or are about to begin mandatory CRM courses that will be evaluated over the next two to three years, along with United's, by Foushee and psychologist Robert Helmreich of the University of Texas. "We're interested in long-term behavioral change, not just religious conversion," Helmreich says.

Not surprisingly, CRM programs have encountered initial resistance among crews reluctant to attend what, according to Foushee, many considered "charm school." When United first sent out its preprogram homework to pilots, one returned the packet with the words "Burn this" scrawled across the top, says Bill Taggart, a program director with Resource Management Associates, which offers CRM training to Pan Am.

"The longer you've been flying without any training on how to fly as a team, the harder it is to give up your old ways," says Conrad S. Biegalski, a lieutenant colonel with the 349th MAW reserve wing at Travis Air Force Base. Biegalski, who's been flying in the military for 25 years, cites himself as a former prime offender. But with a convert's fervor he now runs a CRM-type training program for the Military Airlift Wing.

Long-term results of Helmreich and Foushee's evaluations of CRM won't be available for a while, but the researchers have preliminary evidence of a positive change among pilots after attending a CRM course. Unfortunately, they have also found that somewhere between 5 percent and 10 percent of those attending CRM courses get worse, at least initially. Pilots with poor social skills are often threatened by the communication and cooperation exercises and become more dictatorial and rigid. Ironically, those who need the training the most may actually be put off by it. Helmreich hopes this backlash can be overcome during future training sessions.

Follow-up is crucial to CRM programs. "It's not a one-shot trip to Lourdes where you get sprinkled with the holy waters of CRM," Taggart says. CRM specialists recommend that crews come back in 6 to 12 months for a refresher course and then return yearly. "You may see the effects of CRM for a short time, but there is probably not much impact without some kind of follow-up," says Richard Jensen, a psychologist at Ohio State University who has studied various CRM programs.

The long-term effects of CRM training are obviously the major question for everyone involved. Some airlines are reluctant to strain their budgets and schedules by taking their pilots out of the sky for three or four extra days a year if there's no proof that training will improve their safety records. United points to its low accident record since the early 1980s as proof that CRM is making a difference. But, as Jensen points out, "it's hard to say if that is due to the course or the whole environment."

Other companies using the program believe that it is working. According to Taggart, junior crews are more willing to speak up and captains are more open to questions and disagreement as a result of the training. "Most of the self-reports are very favorable," Helmreich says. "My gut feeling is that CRM works." But for now there is mostly anecdotal evidence to attest to CRM's benefits.

Despite the lack of hard evidence, the FAA seems convinced that it makes a difference. By the end of the year it plans to issue an advisory promoting CRM training. And, according to Guice Tinsley, acting manager of the Flight Technical Program Branch at the FAA, "a regulatory requirement is not far off."

Once that happens, Jensen says, evaluation will become a crucial and probably controversial issue as the FAA and the pilots' unions fight over how the evaluations should be used. The holders of "the right stuff," who have so solidly mastered their technical skills, may soon have to prove to the FAA that they can perform as effective managers as well.

Reading 58

This newspaper report expands the idea of using virtual reality devices beyond helping astronauts to overcome their sense of confinement and isolation. How many other applications can you think of? What kind of virtual reality experience would you enjoy?

You Are About to Enter Another Reality . . .

By Tom Ashbrook

It's the year 2010, and you're going to a party. An otherworldly party.

You rustle up a herd of winged elephants, mount the lead bull and make your entrance over a flaming rainbow. Frankie comes as a wailing saxophone in tennis shoes, Jennifer comes as a blue blast furnace, Jason shows as a dancing double image—Gandhi and Godzilla.

Daffy Duck strikes up the band on a Maui beach at sunset. The music goes up-tempo and the party rolls into the belly of a translucent whale. For an hour you dance on the Statue of Liberty's torch, then on Red Square, then on Saturn's rings. After midnight, you play billiards with the planets, blow popcorn over the Himalayas and sail ruby slippers down the Amazon until dawn.

Welcome to the looming world of "virtual reality"—a malleable, computer-generated wonderland that may, just may, turn 21st-century Hollywood, Wall Street and your living room upside down and dazzlingly inside out.

Already, research scientists are slipping on wired clothing that allows an electronic image of their bodies to step into and interact with a rapidly expanding university of computer-animated graphics.

As advances in supercomputers and software continue, the long two-dimensional reign of television and movies looks set to be challenged by full-scale, hands-on, 3-D "feel-ies"—electronic environments that "viewers" have the sensation of diving completely into, creating, surveying and manipulating as they go.

If a "Who Framed Roger Rabbit? IV" comes out in 1999, the price of admission may put you smack dab into the middle of a "Toonland" that can be explored at will, an enveloping universe of cartoon characters that walk, talk and respond to human visitors. Kick these electronic critters and you may be kicked back: WHAM!

"It's like we've just hit the coast of a whole new continent," says Jaron Lanier, a prominent California figure in the emerging universe of alternate electronic realities. "There will be enormous uses that we can't predict now at all. Nobody can. It's a new medium. It will hold an entire new world."

Sometime in the next century—and much sooner for those with access to new equipment, scientists say—people at home in their living room will be able to step into a sensor-wired body suit, strap on a computer-linked headset, and dial themselves into almost any "virtual reality" their heart desires.

"In a sense it's the ultimate drug," says Jeffrey Deutsch, a California researcher specializing in investing computer creations with the laws of real-world physics. "The '60s and taking acid were nothing. This has the potential to be that, but much, much more."

Instead of sensing the physical world, the virtual reality voyager will sense computer-generated input—visual, aural, tactile and eventually more—via a body suit with what researchers predict will be ever-increasing persuasiveness, subtlety and capacity for interaction.

"The kinds of worlds you could build might be much more interesting or exciting than the physical world," says Marvin Minsky, artificial intelligence don at MIT. "It will happen. It's sort of waiting for people to see how rewarding it can be."

The notion of artificial planes of reality is far from new to science fiction writers and film makers. In recent films from "Tron" and "Brainstorm" to this summer's smash "Roger Rabbit," Hollywood has toyed with the theme of humans thrown convincingly beyond the physical realm.

Now, at a new nexus of art, science and high imagination, Hollywood's fantasy is fast becoming high-tech fact. At NASA's Ames Research Center in California, researchers are already strapping on headsets and body gear that convincingly transport the wearer into "virtual environments" created by computer simulation.

Tiny head-mounted video screens throw up three-dimensional, wrap-around renderings of outer space, replete with huge space stations, circling shuttles and distant satellites. Signals from sophisticated wired gloves put images of the wearer's own hands into the simulated environment, where they can manipulate simulated tools. A verbal command or hand signal from the virtual space traveler sends him or her soaring through the scene, complete with the sensation of jet pack flight.

"You feel like you are literally immersed in this computer environment," says Scott Fisher, principal investigator for NASA's Virtual Environment Workstation Project.

For NASA, advances in "virtual reality" research have both practical and recreational applications. Astronauts in training can use the gear for highly versatile, realistic simulation sessions. Astronauts in space are expected to enter the look-alike netherworld to manipulate distant robots that will precisely mimic their motions to make real repairs outside space stations or on satellites miles away.

Astronauts stuck for months in cramped space quarters may also use their "virtual environment" kits for relaxation, dialing up parameters for tennis, squash or adventure games—the kind of application that may first give the general public a hint of things to come.

"We've got virtual worlds kind of coming up on us," says NASA's Fisher. "It's going to have tremendous social impact."

A unique feature of computer-generated environments is the ability of people separated by many miles to share the same electronic reality.

Children in schools across the country could scamper electronically through the same vast "virtual reality" museums, where super computers spew out an endless array of 3-D, electronic "hands-on" exhibits of natural history, science or sculpture. Families separated by miles could hold virtual reunions around virtual tables—a format that could also give immediacy to business teleconferencing.... "Beam me over, Rockefeller, and we'll talk."

And then there is play and party time, a rich field for masquerade and invention in virtual reality. Without ever leaving home, Jaron Lanier says, partygoers will be able to assume whatever electronic form they like, dial up a common line and converge on the shared "virtual environment" of their choice.

"Imagine yourself going into virtual reality and calling up a floating image of Earth," says Lanier, president of VPL Research Inc. of Redwood City, Calif., the company that makes the electronic gloves used in NASA's Ames lab and that now produces a full electronic body suit. "You pick up the Amazon, plunk it down, it gets big and you can crawl around in it. Buzz a friend, and you can crawl around together."

One distant day, Lanier says, so much commerce, recreation and daily life may be shifted to the electronic realm that "I guess I kind of see the physical plane becoming a national park—all of it."

Already, exasperated brokers on Wall Street's crowded trading floors, says Lanier, have inquired about "virtual reality" stock trading centers that brokers could electronically inhabit from dispersed locations. Scientific American has published work on the expanding horizons of artificial reality. So has the National Enquirer, which added its own twist, suggesting that remote control of Lanier's sensor gloves could send robotic hands on dangerous espionage missions "breaking into fortified enemy headquarters and taking files."

That article, says Lanier, brought repeated calls from the US State Department, demand-

ing to know which government agency was funding the imagined "spy glove."

"Can you imagine a robot glove trudging across the Sahara toward Libya or something?" says Lanier, noting wryly that the State Department appeared more attuned to the National Enquirer than to Scientific American.

For all the potential of "virtual realities," at least two large concerns remain. One, says James Foley, chairman of the electrical engineering and computer science department at George Washington University, is that commercial applications of the technology may not be immediately apparent enough to attract the substantial funds required for its full development and dissemination.

Another concern, Foley says, is that if the technology does become widely available, users could become deeply hooked, withdrawing into the exotic thrills of "virtual reality" entertainment.

"Our kids have already become less aware of the world around them, more captivated by passive entertainment," says Foley. "This kind of technology could dwarf the impact of television."

But Foley and others see worlds approaching in "virtual reality" that may be too compelling not to tap—a universe that might ultimately leave the human mind free to create and manipulate its creations without physical constraint, a universe in which the limits of human imagination might be the only boundaries.

"This technology will show us more of ourselves than any technology ever has," Lanier says. "I, for one, am optimistic about what we will see."

ADDITIONAL RESOURCES

Books and Articles

Chevian, Eric, et al. "American and Soviet Teenagers' Concerns about Nuclear War." *New England Journal of Medicine* (August 18, 1988). A large-scale survey assesses the attitudes of American and Soviet teenagers about the future and the possibility of nuclear war.

Kull, Steven. "Feeling Good about Hard-Target Kill Capability." *Bulletin of the Atomic Scientists* (July/August 1988): 30–35. Policymakers offer elaborate military and political rationales for building nuclear weapons. But in-depth studies of key policies reveal flaws in their arguments.

Sterba, James P. *The Ethics of War and Nuclear Deterrence*. Belmont, Calif.: Wadsworth, 1985. Can nuclear weapons ever be legitimately used? Is threatening the use of nuclear weapons morally justified? This book of readings looks at the moral assessment of nuclear war and nuclear deterrence, helping readers make responsible, informed decisions.

White, K. Ralph. *Psychology and the Prevention of Nuclear War*. New York: New York University Press, 1986. A collection of readings addressing the psychological effects of nuclear threat, means of deterrence, perceptions and misperceptions regarding nuclear war, and how government officials negotiate in the arms race.

A UNION OF OPPOSITES

The closing of a door can bring blessed privacy and comfort—the opening, terror. Conversely, the closing of a door can be a sad and final thing—the opening, a wonderfully joyous moment.

Andy Rooney

Courtesy of Boston Symphony Orchestra, Inc.

Masterpieces of music and art attest to the power of the creative mind. Pictured: Seiji Ozawa conducting the Boston Symphony Orchestra.

Unit 25 reviews the psychological principles, studies, and theories that psychologists use in their quest to solve the puzzle of human nature. This knowledge, organized as a set of complementary opposites, helps us make sense of the many approaches to studying the enormous complexity of behavior.

OBJECTIVES—COURSE REVIEW

1. List the major complementary opposites that represent the main organizational issues and themes of psychology

2. Summarize the history of the major theoretical approaches to psychology

3. Identify important milestones in the history of psychology

4. Describe the role of the critical thinking in the advancement of science

5. Describe some of the tools that psychologists use to measure behavior

6. Explain how statistics help psychologists describe what they observe and determine the significance of their findings

READING ASSIGNMENT

Review the program summaries for each unit and the chapter summaries from each chapter of *Psychology: Science, Behavior and Life*. Your instructor may also assign the anthology selections for Unit 25.

KEY TERMS AND CONCEPTS

As you reexamine the course material, be sure the review the Key Terms and Concepts in each unit.

PROGRAM SUMMARY

Psychologists are trained people watchers dedicated to understanding how we function and why we think, feel, and act as we do. As scientists they are trained to challenge their assumptions. They analyze common, everyday experiences such as perception, memory, and language and try to make sense of the infinite variations in our everyday functioning.

Not all psychologists work in the same way or come up with the same results. In fact, many studies seem to contradict each other. Program 25 reviews some of the most significant insights and principles of human nature and animal behavior, organizing the various approaches into complementary opposites. Like the Chinese principles of yin and yang, the psychological opposites are inextricably entwined, each influencing the other.

The most basic pair of opposites is nature versus nurture as determinants of behavior. On the side of nature, our genes and brain chemistry exert constraints on what is possible at a given stage of development. Research has made us increasingly aware that much of our behavior is determined by inherited traits. On the other side, we have environmental influences. Nurture—our physical, cultural, and social environment— can be extraordinarily powerful, affecting not only our perceptions and social roles but also our physical growth and even brain chemistry. Understanding how nature and nurture interact to shape human behavior is one of psychology's most important challenges.

Another task is understanding how the physical and conceptual worlds interact. What we think, feel, and know are all products of the complex activities of billions of nerve cells. Our consciousness emerges from these activities. While the brain can control the mind by altering behavior, the mind can also alter the brain by responding to the environment. There is no dualism of brain versus mind, but rather a continual interplay of two inseparable systems.

The principles of learning raise another important question: Are we objects of deterministic forces or creators of our own limitless universe? Is our behavior merely a set of conditioned responses, or are we free to make our own choices? Throughout this series we have seen how the same principles of learning that help us profit from experience allow us to create new realities and free us from behavioral constraints.

One of psychology's most rewarding endeavors has been the study of life-span development. Advances in developmental psychology have shown how precocious babies really are, and have revealed the wisdom and previously unrecognized abilities of older people. As a result, we have a more sophisticated view of life as a continuum of new challenges. As a society we are able to overcome the myths about youth and aging and have become more responsive to the needs of people at all stages of life.

Cognitive competence and irrationality are another pair of opposites of great interest, especially to cognitive psychologists. The origins of bad decisions, foolish actions, and irrational beliefs are found within the basic processes of the human intellect that ordinarily works so well for us. Clearly, the power and fallibility of the human mind are two sides of the same coin.

Psychologists have discovered the interplay of opposite roles as we function both as individuals and as members of social groups. In Western culture there is an emphasis on individuality and self-reliance. A person earns praise for initiative and accomplishment but also bears the burden of failure alone. In other cultures the group is more important than any one individual. It offers comfort and social support. But its influence can also lead to intolerance and rigid conformity.

Psychologists strive to understand the balance of human needs and the influence of situational forces that can cause us to be gregarious or shy, independent or conforming, selfish or altruistic.

REVIEW QUESTIONS

Note: Review Questions for Units 25 and 26 are provided in Unit 26.

QUESTIONS TO CONSIDER

Note: Because these questions are open-ended and require answers based on your own experience and personal opinions, an answer key has not been included in the Appendix.

1. Apply the nature-nurture dynamic to your own development. In what ways can you contribute to your future identity?

2. Why study human behavior? Why look for understanding and insight into the sources of your own beliefs, motives, and behaviors? Compare your ideas to those expressed in the paragraph below.

> For the self-renewing man the development of his own potentialities and the process of self-discovery never end. It is a sad but unarguable fact that most human beings go through their lives only partially aware of the full range of their abilities. As a boy in California I spent a good deal of time in the Mother Lode country, and like every boy of my age I listened raptly to the tales told by the old-time prospectors in that area, some of them veterans of the Klondike gold rush. Every one of them had at least one good campfire story of a lost gold mine. The details varied: the original discoverer had died in the mine, or had gone crazy, or had been killed in a shooting scrape, or had just walked off thinking the mine worthless. But the central theme was constant: riches left untapped. I have come to believe that those tales offer a paradigm of education as most of us experience it. The mine is worked for a little while and then abandoned. (From John W. Gardner, *Self-Renewal* [New York: Harper Colophon books, Harper & Row, 1983], p. 10)

3. One of the goals of *Discovering Psychology* is to increase our understanding and tolerance of the behavior of others. How can you know whether you have achieved that goal? One way might be to think about the judgments you make about individual differences and the behavior of others. Read the following excerpt from *On Becoming a Person*, by Carl R. Rogers (Boston: Houghton Mifflin Sentry Edition, 1961), which suggests that understanding and tolerance come from eliminating those automatic judgments. What other questions might you ask yourself? As you read, consider the contribution that humanism has made to psychology and its impact on society.

> Our first reaction to most of the statements which we hear from other people is an immediate evaluation, or judgment, rather than an understanding of it. When someone expresses some feeling or attitude or belief, our tendency is, almost immediately, to feel "That's right" or "That's stupid"; "That's abnormal"; "That's unreasonable"; "That's incorrect"; "That's not nice." Very rarely do we permit ourselves to understand precisely what the meaning of the statement is to him.
>
>   I have found that to truly accept another person and his feelings is by no means an easy thing, any more than is understanding. Can I really permit another person to feel hostile toward me? Can I accept his anger as a real and legitimate part of himself? Can I accept him when he views life and its problems in a way quite different from mine? (p. 18)

OPTIONAL ACTIVITIES

1. Identify and analyze the strategies used in a specific political election or an advertising campaign. Does understanding techniques of influence weaken some of their persuasive power? Why or why not?

2. Imagine that you had the chance to live the last 10 years of your life over again. What would you do differently? What different choices would you have made? Discuss how your identity would be different as a result.

ANTHOLOGY

The following selections bring together many different approaches to understanding human behavior. As you read, consider the roots of psychological knowledge and the impact psychology has had on education, on society, on the media, and on promotion of health and treatment of disease. Have you become a better consumer of psychological information, a more informed member of society, or a better learner? How has your newly acquired knowledge changed your feelings about yourself, your family, your past, and your future?

Reading 59

This article demonstrates the biological, psychological, developmental, and social aspects of a rare neurological condition: Tourette syndrome. As you read, consider the psychological impact of the disease and what psychologists might have to offer afflicted individuals and their friends and families.

Taming Tourette's Tics & Twitches

By Evelyn Zamula

Poor Danny. In the doghouse again. Teacher sent him out of the room because he's disrupted his second-grade class just once too often this morning. She knows he's being treated for hyperactivity—and she can cope with his occasional frenetic outbursts—but lately something new has been added. He blinks his eyes and twitches his nose continually, and his feet are never still. Every once in a while he'll let out a series of yelps, which the children find hilarious, but which also makes it impossible for her to teach. He has told her he can't help making these noises. She is beginning to wonder. Can it be that Danny has the disease she heard about on TV a few years ago? The one in which the victims uncontrollably bark like dogs and curse and scream?

The disease she's thinking of is called Tourette syndrome, and her suspicions about Danny are correct.

People with Tourette syndrome have recurrent involuntary muscle contractions called tics, such as eye-blinking, nose-twitching, facial grimacing, head-shaking, or shoulder shrugging. TS usually begins in childhood, between the ages of 2 and 15, with most cases clustered around the age of 7.

TS is seen throughout the world, in all races. Because TS often is not diagnosed correctly, accurate figures are hard to come by, but experts estimate that as many as one in 2,000 persons may be affected by the disorder, with males outnumbering females approximately three to one. It is believed that about 100,000 people in the United States have the disease.

Although childhood tics are common—about a fourth of all children have them at one time or another—they usually disappear spontaneously within a year. In patients with TS, however, the tics usually persist for life, except for a lucky few who experience complete remission during adolescence.

The tics may affect different parts of the body at different times, and get better or worse over weeks or months. The first tics to appear are motor tics, usually in the face, with eye-blinking the most common. The facial tics may vanish, only to be replaced by new ones that may involve the neck, arms and legs in the form of head-tossing, neck-stretching, arm flailing, shoulder-shrugging, jumping, or similar purposeless movements. The motor tics may either go away or be joined by vocal tics—grunts, throat-clearing, barks, sniffs, whistles. About a third of the victims feel compelled to use explicit four-letter words. This is called coprolalia, which means "babbling about feces." Some people with Tourette syndrome repeatedly echo other people's words (echolalia) or imitate others' movements (echopraxia).

Those with severe cases may practice self-mutilating behavior, such as lip-biting or head-banging, while others may be caught up in obsessive-compulsive behavior such as excessive handwashing or elaborate bedtime rituals. Their lot is not a happy one.

TS people can sometimes control their tics for minutes to hours, but sooner or later the urge becomes irresistible, and the tics must be allowed to play themselves out. Tics get worse when TS patients are anxious and improve when they concentrate on something. Since many patients try to keep a tight rein on their tics at school or work, they are inclined to "let it all hang out" at home where they're comfortable.

The cause of TS is unknown. For years some scientists argued that the disease was a psychiatric disorder. Freud himself believed that tics were a neurosis, resembling hysteria, but that TS was hereditary. Psychoanalysts who came after him used familiar Freudian terms to explain TS, in which words like eroticism, sadism, aggression, anal, narcissism and the like figured prominently.

Other scientists, including Gilles de la Tourette, the physician who described the disease definitely in 1885 and after whom the disorder is named, believed TS had a physiological basis, which is also the current thinking. No doubts at all existed in the minds of a group of inquisitors in 1489, when a priest with motor and vocal tics was diagnosed as being possessed by the devil and was subjected to the rite of exorcism.

The story goes that he was cured and thus avoided being burned at the stake. But, as Arthur K. Shapiro, M.D., and Elaine Shapiro, Ph.D., point out (in a July 1982 article in the *American Journal of Psychotherapy*), exorcism seems to have lost its clout through the ages. Inspired by the book and movie "The Exorcist," about two dozen people with TS symptoms have undergone exorcism in the last few years, but no cures have been reported. The Shapiros and others believe that "The Exorcist" was an exaggerated description of an actual TS patient. The young girl in the story displayed a number of TS symptoms: vocal tics (animal sounds, like barking and mewing); purposeless movements (whirling and flinging); obscene language; self-mutilation (scratching and biting); and an abnormal degree of neck-stretching, culminating in that hair-raising scene in the movie where her head appears to completely turn around.

The best evidence suggests that, although TS has psychological manifestations, the disease is a neurological disorder. Researchers believe that there is a chemical abnormality in the part of the brain called the basal ganglia. This affects the neurotransmitter systems used by the brain to regulate movement and behavior. (Neurotransmitters are chemicals that carry signals between nerve cells.) Many people with TS show signs of neurologic abnormalities, such as hyperactivity, poor coordination, and attention deficit disorder (characterized by impulsiveness, hyperactivity, poor concentration, and inattention).

A certain type of TS is inherited. A high percentage of Tourette patients have relatives with motor tics, and some families have more than one member with TS. Recent genetic studies indicate that the three types of tic disorders (childhood tics, chronic tics, and Tourette syndrome) are all genetically related, making TS a common hereditary illness. Scientists do not yet know why some people get milder forms while others get the full-blown syndrome with its motor and vocal symptoms.

Just as the world of psychiatry was turned upside down when it was discovered that many disorders presumed to be "psychiatric" in fact had a physiological basis and could be treated with drugs, so was the argument that TS had an organic, rather than a psychologic, basis made more compelling by the fact that certain drugs were also found that controlled tics in a large number of cases.

But a disease in which the body is made to do things it doesn't want to do is bound to cause psychological problems, too. Though many Tourette people with mild symptoms adjust quite well to their disability and can hold jobs, marry, and live normal lives, those with more serious symptoms that interfere with normal relationships may need psychological help to cope with this socially crippling illness.

This is especially true for Tourette people who demonstrate obsessive-compulsive behavior, an example of a classic psychiatric symptom arising, in this case, from neurological disease. It may be almost impossible for obsessive-compulsive people to keep a job. People who arrange or rearrange papers on their desks all day long or touch their toes repeatedly are not likely to get much work done.

Some TS people never make it out the

front door in the morning. They spend the day taking innumerable showers, or feel compelled to touch and retouch certain objects in the house a certain number of times before leaving. Acting out the compulsions gives them no pleasure, because they know the behavior is senseless. Some obsessive-compulsive patients have recurrent, protracted thoughts about death or sex that haunt them night and day. Depression, embarrassment, and despair are an everyday part of life for these unfortunate people. A small number of people with severe TS symptoms have been institutionalized, either because they've been incorrectly diagnosed or ineffectively treated.

TS children often have problems in school because other children may make fun of them or are even afraid of them. As a result, TS students are often forced to use all of their energy and concentration trying to control or mask their symptoms. Teachers may become exasperated by TS students' tendency to perseverate—that is, to ask the same question over and over again, even though they know the answer. Some teachers incorrectly interpret the motor and vocal tics as misbehavior or attention-getting devices, and may punish a child for symptoms he or she can't control.

Parents, to their dismay, often make the same mistake. "From the time I was 7 until I was 11, I spent a lot of time in my room," says Michelle. "My parents thought my eye-blinking was deliberate, so they punished me by sending me up to my room. Relations between me and my parents were very bad at that time. It was only by chance that we discovered what the real problem was. We were at a party with some other families, when I noticed one of my father's friends staring at me. By this time, I was not only blinking my eyes, I was twitching my nose, jerking my arms, and doing some grunting. He told my father that his partner's son was making the same kinds of movements, and when they took him to the doctor, his parents found out he had Tourette syndrome. I was taken to a neurologist a week later and I was diagnosed with the same thing. My parents felt terrible, but I was kind of relieved. At least I had something that had a name."

Many TS children have difficulty fitting in socially. Many simply have no friends. Some, like Michelle, miss so much school because of twitching, that they don't get a chance to form close relationships. Many are left out of social activities, and tend not to be chosen for team sports, or elected class officers, or asked out on dates. To avoid psychological damage, it is important that the disease be diagnosed and treated early. When a child is told often enough that he's crazy, in time he'll begin to believe it. Educating classmates of TS children about the disorder also helps lessen teasing and ridicule. Videotapes and pamphlets can be used to teach children to be more tolerant of TS symptoms.

Tourette children are usually of normal intelligence, and most can attend regular school. But some may need to be in special classes, or smaller classes, because besides motor and vocal tics, they often have attention-deficit disorder, learning disorders, and speech problems, such as stuttering. Children with more severe TS may become such behavior problems that they must go to special schools.

Most need the help of compassionate teachers, who will allow for some flexibility in the normal school routine. This may include a private study area, extra time to complete assignments, privately held exams, or oral exams if the child has difficulty writing. Reading disorders are six to seven times more common in TS children than in the general population, so timed tests often throw them into a panic.

In the past, all kinds of treatments were tried on Tourette patients, including acupuncture, shock treatment, insulin shock therapy, psychotherapy—even frontal lobotomy. The modern era of treatment began in 1961 when Italian and French researchers discovered that haloperidol, a major tranquilizer used to treat severe mental disorders such as schizophrenia, also suppressed tics. Haloperidol is believed to block transmission of dopamine, a neurotransmitter. It is not clear to researchers whether the brain's dopamine systems are overactive in TS or whether the dopamine receptors in the brain are hypersensitive. Other neurotransmitters (serotonin and norepinephrine) may also be involved.

Haloperidol reduces tics in as many as 86 percent of Tourette patients, but has to be stopped in most cases because of formidable side effects—depression, weight gain, difficulty in concentration, drowsiness, a feeling of being "spaced out," and Parkinsonian symptoms of tremor, rigidity, lack of facial expression, and slow movement. (Since

Parkinson's disease is characterized by abnormally low levels of brain dopamine, there's obviously a fine line between too much and too little dopamine.)

Those who can't tolerate haloperidol may be switched to other drugs, among them pimozide, another major tranquilizer, or clonidine, a blood pressure medication that is used experimentally in treating the obsessive-compulsive symptoms of TS. Side effects of pimozide are similar to, though not as severe as those of, haloperidol, and clonidine may cause dry mouth.

Pimozide, incidentally, played a major role in the passage in 1983 of the Orphan Drug Act, a law that made it easier to get drugs for rare disorders on the market in the United States. (See "Medicine's 'Orphans': Drugs for Rare Diseases" in the February 1988 *FDA Consumer*.) Though approved in Canada, pimozide was unavailable here because the manufacturer, McNeil Laboratories, did not find it economically feasible to go through the tests required for FDA to approve the drug. Consequently, about 100 patients were illegally smuggling the drug in from Canada. The unavailability of "legal" pimozide was called to the attention of several congressmen by families of TS patients and the Tourette Syndrome Association. After a series of congressional hearings investigating the plight of those with so-called "orphan diseases"—diseases affecting fewer than 200,000 people—Congress passed the Orphan Drug Act in 1983. Under this law, drug companies receive special incentives to develop unprofitable drugs for small patient populations. The law also added a fast-track drug approval system in FDA. Pimozide was approved in 1984.

When Tourette patients start drug therapy, they usually must see their physicians often, because considerable fine-tuning of medications is necessary. A drug that works initially may lose its effectiveness, so another drug may have to be tried. Dosage may be increased when symptoms worsen or decreased when the disease is in remission. However, many patients find significant relief in drug therapy, with few or no side effects, and may see their doctors only once a year. Others with mild symptoms may require no medication. Very often, if a patient can cope psychologically—even with severe symptoms—drug therapy is not necessary.

Michelle has had her ups and downs with drug therapy. "In the 10th grade I was out a whole semester because I was ticcing like mad. My doctor took me off Haldol [haloperidol] for two weeks to see if it was the drug that was making me tic so much. Those two weeks were unbearable. You know, Haldol is a major tranquilizer, and when I was off the drug, I just couldn't sleep. My tics would keep me up until 4 in the morning. The doctor put me back on a half-dose of Haldol and I was O.K. until last summer when I developed blepharospasm [rapid twitching of the eyelids] that was so bad that I couldn't see. Altogether, I was on Haldol for 10 years. Now I'm on Orap [pimozide] and Prolixin [fluphenazine, a drug used experimentally in the treatment of TS]. My doctor is gradually decreasing the Orap and increasing the Prolixin. He wants me to be off drugs completely by this summer, though, but he's doing it very slowly so that I don't get withdrawal symptoms. He thinks my body is becoming immune to drugs and I need a 'drug vacation.' Besides, he wants to see if TS is causing the tics or maybe it's the drugs. I'm scared witless about going off drugs completely."

Maybe Michelle has less to fear than she thinks. Consider Danny's story. Danny is 10 now and has been through some rough times. His tics became worse, eventually involving his upper arms and shoulders and then progressing to complex tics that caused him to leap from his desk and throw himself on the floor. In addition to yelping and screaming, he began using obscene language.

But by that time, Danny's disorder was finally diagnosed correctly. The stimulant medication that he was given in the mistaken belief that he was simply hyperactive was withdrawn. (Some TS experts believe that stimulant medication, such as methylphenidate or pemoline, used to treat children with hyperactivity and attention-deficit disorder, may actually bring on tics in those genetically vulnerable to TS. The labeling of both drugs warns about giving them to children with tics or children who have relatives with tics.) Drug therapy effectively controlled his symptoms, but made him a "zombie" in school, to use his own description. All medication was then stopped. Danny's tics and hyperactivity continue, but supportive counseling has taught him to cope with these problems.

At his physician's recommendations, Danny's teachers are trying to minimize stress in the classoom and provide special education services. His schoolmates have been shown a videotape about TS and are much more sympathetic. Members of his family have also undergone counseling and have a better understanding of his illness. They maintain close contact with his teachers. Changes in the home and school environment have made all the difference in the world for Danny, who is now a happy, well-adjusted child.

Research on TS has been neglected until recent years. One difficulty is that there is no diagnostic test for TS. It is recognized only when certain symptoms occur together. But interest in this unique disease has revived because biomedical researchers feel there's much to be learned about TS that will cast light on other neurological disorders affecting movement behavior. Major medical institutions throughout the country are participating in TS research, which is being supported by the National Institute of Neurological and Communicative Disorders and Stroke, the National Institute of Child Health and Human Development, and the National Institute of Mental Health.

Because very few autopsies have been done on TS victims, studies of brain tissue have been unavailable until recently. Now, with the help of sophisticated new diagnostic tools, such as positron emission tomography (PET scans) and magnetic resonance imaging, it may be possible to locate more precisely areas of the living brain that are malfunctioning.

Researchers also are conducting genetic studies, including some using twins, to identify families at risk for TS, and to determine exactly how the gene is transmitted. Also, because many TS victims do not respond to haloperidol or cannot tolerate its side effects, investigators are searching for other drugs that may help. At least half of TS research money is being devoted to projects focusing on neurotransmitters and the operation of the synapses—the junction where neurotransmitter chemicals carry impulses from one nerve to another.

For more information, readers may contact the Tourette Syndrome Association, a nonprofit organization located at 42-40F Bell Boulevard, Bayside, N.Y. 11361. The telephone number is 1–800–237–0717, except for residents of New York state, who can phone 718–224–2999.

Reading 60

This article discusses how cultural biases determine variations in the incidence, diagnosis, and treatment of various conditions. As you read, consider how beliefs, values, and social labels shape our lives. Is health care based more on tradition than science? What are the implications for medical and psychological treatment in a pluralistic, multicultural society like that of the United States?

Cultures Shape Our Medical Views

By Richard Saltus

An American visiting France is startled when he's told that germs can be beneficial, or that his migraine headaches stem from a "liver crisis."

Germans, the traveler might notice, consume a remarkable number of drugs, especially for the heart. Unlike Americans, they also have a bent for natural remedies, like herbal and arcane water-therapies. Residents of West Germany can even take a biennial *kur*, or health vacation, at a spa—courtesy of the government.

And in the United Kingdom, doctors are noted for their conservatism: fewer checkups and drugs, less surgery (especially bypass surgery), and large doses of skepticism about radical treatments.

According to a new book that compares medicine in America and three European countries, medical practices vary more widely than most people—even doctors themselves —realize. What's considered a normal physical condition in one country may be labeled a disease in another; doctors on one side of the border may operate for a given problem while those on the other prefer to prescribe a medicine and keep a watch on the patient's problem. Customary doses of drugs can be 10 times higher in one country than in its neighbor. And, contends the author, much of the variability has nothing to do with biological reality.

"Values are important in medical decisions," said Lynn Payer, a medical journalist and author of "Medicine and Culture."

"When your doctor recommends a certain treatment, it's a mixture of fact and opinion," she said in an interview.

The author, a freelance medical journalist, began noticing differences in medical styles while living in Europe and writing for US-based doctors' magazines. She then undertook her informal study of medical variations by interviewing doctors in several countries and reviewing scientific studies of country-to-country practices.

Payer's book reflects a growing interest among social scientists in the influence of cultural factors on the development of medicine. In the past, medicine was usually described in histories of the field as if it were an objective science, in part because the chroniclers were usually doctors.

But, especially since the 1960s and '70s, historians have become increasingly interested in uncovering the cultural factors—political agendas, economics, social class, race, gender, folk beliefs, and so forth—that have shaped medical notions and practices. While there have now been some academic studies on these issues, much of what Payer and others discuss is based on impressions and anecdotes.

For example, Dr. Leon Eisenberg of Harvard Medical School said US doctors may order sophisticated and potentially risky diagnostic tests where a British doctor would "sit back and wait awhile." The US doctors, he explained, "are reflecting an American culture that believes that everything can be potentially fixed. The British are much less impressed with human powers as against the healing powers of nature."

In her book, Payer reports finding a lower rate of caesarian sections and hysterectomies in Europe than in the United States; a marked reluctance in Germany to use antibiotics, and a strong bent for aggressive, high-tech treatments in America. In France, she says, doctors favor medical procedures that spare the reproductive organs, out of concern over the country's low birth rate. And in both France and Germany, there is a trend toward "gentle" treatments like those offered by homeopathy,

a type of medicine considered by most US doctors to be the next thing to quackery.

Though diagnoses have been increasingly standardized by international groups such as the World Health Organization, disagreements remain, said Dr. Jack Froom of the State University of New York at Stony Brook. Members at an international meeting of family physicians argued over "hypotension," or low blood pressure.

"We don't make the diagnosis here," he said, "but our German colleague was most adamant that we include it," because in Germany low blood pressure is considered a problem needing treatment.

French Blame the Liver

The French, for obscure reasons, attribute many more health problems to the liver. Germans are obsessed with functions of the heart and circulatory system. Payer believes the latter may be a lingering influence of German romanticism, which viewed the heart as an emotional organ of central importance, not simply a machine-like pump.

"Often, all one must do to acquire a disease is to enter a country where that disease is recognized," writes Payer. "Leaving the country will either cure the malady or turn it into something else."

"Every society constructs its own diseases," said Dr. Guenter Risse, a medical historian at the University of California at San Francisco. "The way you write it [a disease] up, define it, believe who has it—these all depend very much on ideas that are floating around in the culture."

In his book, "The Illness Narratives," Dr. Arthur Kleinman, a Harvard psychiatrist and medical anthropologist, writes: "Illness complaints are what patients and their families bring to the practitioner."

"Disease, however, is what the practitioner creates in the recasting of illness in terms of theories of disorder." And the doctor or healer recasts the illness by peering through the "theoretical lenses" of the particular form of practice in which he has been trained, added Kleinman.

Even within countries, Kleinman pointed out, there are regional or class variations: Rural American blacks, for example, have distinctive complaints, such as "high blood" and "nerves," that are not mentioned by other people; working-class Mexicans in Los Angeles speak of "soul loss;" Puerto Ricans in New York believe in spirit possession, and Nigerian psychiatric patients have a unique symptom of feeling "like ants are crawling in their heads," wrote Kleinman.

These complaints seem exotic. But elusive conditions have been diagnosed for centuries among Americans in middle- and upper-class society. The varying terms—"vapours," "hysteria," "neurasthenia," and so forth—reflect then-current notions of medicine, but generally they refer to a cluster of symptoms, such as nervousness and fatigue, that are difficult to link to any physical abnormalities.

Today there may be a similar category, Risse said, in the mysterious pattern of symptoms—fatigue, slight fevers, mental depression—first called "chronic mono" and now called "chronic fatigue syndrome." Though some physical findings have been observed, they are inconsistent.

The victims are usually very fit, active, professional types, and Risse offered a psychosocial explanation for the condition: "It's not socially acceptable in this active, upwardly mobile society to be fatigued or unproductive. You need a label to allow you to seek help with dignity."

Payer said that when she first began noticing the American-European differences, such as the French idea that exposure to germs is beneficial because it builds resistance, or that gentler, natural remedies can sometimes be as helpful as aggressive treatments, she thought that European medical practices were simply less advanced than those she was accustomed to in the United States.

Investigation, however, convinced her that foreign ways were not necessarily inferior, and in some respects were better. For instance, the French reluctance to use intrauterine devices for contraception proved well-advised when later, in the United States, they were found responsible for much infertility.

While historians say there is much to be learned about society and culture by comparing medical tendencies, medical scientists say there are also benefits for patients and doctors. It may be possible, they say, to learn which of several approaches to treatment is more effective by looking at results in different countries.

One such international comparison is soon to report results, however. Headed by Froom of Stony Brook, the International Primary Care Network, an organization of physicians in nine countries, compared treatments for otitis media, a common inner ear infection. There are marked differences in how this infection is treated, said Froom, and even in the United States the rationale is not necessarily based on science.

"There are studies showing that giving antibiotics for two days, three days, or five days are all about as good as giving them for 10 days, yet most doctors give them for 10 days simply out of tradition," he said.

The nine-country study will show some striking differences in treating otitis media, along with the results of each treatment method, he said.

Comparisons of the international variations in medical practice, he said, "in the long run help us to understand better what we're doing, because much of what we do is based on tradition, and for much of that tradition there are no hard data that indicate that's the best way to do it."

NEW DIRECTIONS

There's only one corner of the universe you can be certain of improving, and that's your own self.

Aldous Huxley

Where is psychology headed? In Unit 26, leading theorists and researchers in many areas of psychology predict future directions for psychological research, theory, and application.

NASA

The future of psychology may go in any number of directions, but its ultimate goal is the betterment of humankind.

OBJECTIVES

After viewing the television program and completing the assigned readings, you should be able to:

1. Describe possible directions in psychological research

2. Suggest ways in which cognitive science will influence other areas of psychology

3. Describe how the computer has changed the field of psychology

4. Describe how new approaches to individual assessment will influence education

5. Discuss the implications of turning from the old emphasis on abnormality and therapy to a new psychology based on a model of health and prevention

6. Cite evidence that psychology can help solve some of society's most perplexing problems and cite evidence to the contrary

7. Describe Professor Zimbardo's concept of the "new psychology"

READING ASSIGNMENT

There is no textbook reading for this unit. Your instructor may assign the anthology selections for Unit 26.

PROGRAM SUMMARY

The goals of today's psychological researchers are very much the same as those of their predecessors. Unit 26 presents the views of some of the leading psychologists who are engaged in the effort to explain human nature and behavior. They were asked to speculate on where the field of psychology is headed.

The leading cognitive psychologist Howard Gardner sees increased specialization in the future. He believes that researchers will branch off into areas such as cognitive science and neuroscience, while other psychologists will merge with philosophy, sociology, anthropology, and other disciplines.

Psycholinguist Jean Berko Gleason speculates that psychology will become less fragmented because humans can only be understood as complex systems. Researchers must take into consideration the interactive effects of all the physical and social systems—family, cognitive development, language, sex roles, and so on. In agreement with Gleason, Steve Suomi sees fewer barriers between specific areas and predicts the growing integration of interests.

Richard Thompson anticipates an increased emphasis on the brain. Researchers will not only study the physiology of the brain but will also look at behavior, awareness, and consciousness as expressions of the brain itself. He foresees the increasing overlap of brain science, psychology, and artificial intelligence.

No one model of psychology will dominate the future, predicts Dan Slobin. He points out that psychological research is going on all over the world at hundreds of universities and on all levels. Increased cross-fertilization of ideas and methodologies will likely result.

Behaviorist B. F. Skinner deplores the growth of cognitive psychology, claiming that it will not help us explain anything about the behaving organism. He believes that in forsaking observable behavior in favor of metapsychology, intention, and mental processes, psychology is going down the wrong path.

F. W. Putman, an expert on multiple personality, suggests that there are expanded ways of defining behavioral and mental disorders. He contrasts the concept of the "unified self" with the concept of "separate selves."

Stanford psychologist David Rosenhan sees an increasing sensitivity to the effects of the social environment on individual behavior. This will have implications for how we understand behavior, perception, and judgment.

Teresa Amabile favors a more personal, inward-looking approach that combines cognitive and emotional areas of psychology.

The computer has offered psychology new tools for studying behavior and has also created new areas of interest. E. Roy John discusses how new measurement techniques will contribute original information about the brain and behavior. Jean Berko Gleason points out how computers have provided access to enormous data banks that have revolutionized the amount of information researchers can tap.

Dan Slobin sees increased interest in individual patterns of behavior and styles of learning. Explaining how the complex human machine has such amazing flexibility in response to the environment will be one of the next big challenges in the field.

Testing expert Curtis Banks believes that psychology should assess individuals in more narrow contexts. He points out that individuals within groups, such as blacks or women, must be conceptualized, assessed, and understood on different terms.

A number of psychologists were also asked how psychology will change or improve the quality of life in the future. Judith Rodin predicts an intense collaboration between the geneticists and the environmentalists as the importance of the interaction between biology and environment becomes increasingly recognized.

Martin Seligman contrasts the bywords of the past, "illness and therapy," with those of the future, "health and prevention." The new model will be based on helping people to fulfill their potential. But B. F. Skinner doubts that psychological knowledge will be enough to prevent disasters such as global pollution or nuclear holocaust.

In conclusion, *Discovering Psychology*'s host Philip Zimbardo declares his optimism about the future, believing that psychology will help alleviate and even prevent some problems. But he stresses that it must be a new psychology that includes social, economic, and political realities. The psychology of the future must incorporate many complex, interacting factors and go beyond the traditional focus on individual actions and mental processes.

REVIEW QUESTIONS

Course Review

1. What is the basic goal of psychology?

   a. To improve human nature by understanding its strengths and weaknesses
   b. To integrate biological and sociological knowledge to form a complete picture of the individual
   c. To determine the relative roles of nature and nurture in shaping a person
   d. To describe, explain, predict, and control behavior

2. In Steven Suomi's work on shyness in monkeys, what seems to be the basis of shyness?

   a. Traumatic experiences in early life
   b. A genetic predisposition
   c. Inadequate mothering
   d. Biological weakness due to prematurity

3. Research on the mother's touch in baby rats has shown that

   a. the need for touch is brain based.
   b. maternal touch is helpful but not essential to development.
   c. sex differences exist in the need for touch.
   d. baby rats use behaviors that trigger maternal touch.

4. Imagine you were studying the biological basis of remembering and forgetting. You would be especially interested in the chemical substances called

   a. androgens.
   b. steroids.
   c. fatty acids.
   d. neurotransmitters.

5. In a perfume ad, a product becomes associated with positive stimuli. This process is most comparable to

   a. classical conditioning.
   b. operant conditioning.
   c. reasoning by representativeness.
   d. consensual validation.

6. How have recent advances in developmental psychology changed the way we view babies?

   a. We now see them as more vulnerable to environmental hazards.
   b. We understand their adherence to a biologically determined timetable.
   c. We realize their need for attachment to a single, full-time caretaker.
   d. We recognize their strengths in understanding their worlds.

7. Imagine that in 1990 you are a graduate student in psychology involved in studies of intelligence. You would be likely to base your work on the idea that

   a. an IQ test provides a valid measure of intelligence.
   b. intelligence is determined solely by environmental factors.
   c. there are actually multiple intelligences.
   d. cognitive bias keeps people from manifesting their true intelligence.

8. You would be most likely to rely on the research of Amos Tversky and Daniel Kahneman if you were investigating

   a. why people were suddenly worried about the greenhouse effect.
   b. how childhood abuse led to adult personality disorders.
   c. under what conditions bystanders would help a victim.
   d. at what age children developed the idea of object permanence.

9. What fundamental assumption of Western culture profoundly affects how we assign responsibility?

   a. Situations alter our perceptions.
   b. Each individual determines his or her own fate.
   c. Human nature is fundamentally aggressive.
   d. The mind controls the body.

10. Psychological research suggests that when a person is isolated, then he or she

    a. achieves greater mastery of the environment.
    b. becomes more actively involved in seeking personal fulfillment.
    c. is at risk of developing mental and physical disorders.
    d. ceases to function normally.

11. When William James published *Principles of Psychology* in 1890, his vision of the future of psychology was one in which

    a. only the observable would be investigated.
    b. a synthesis of knowledge would be investigated.
    c. therapy would be based on psychodynamic theory.
    d. the application of psychological knowledge would improve human lives.

12. Most psychologists seem ready to welcome cognitive studies as part of their discipline. Someone who actually deplores this development is

    a. F. W. Putman.
    b. B. F. Skinner.
    c. Dan Slobin.
    d. Richard Thompson.

13. Testing is likely to change over the next decade by becoming more concerned with

    a. ranking individuals for selection purposes.
    b. assessing individual strengths and weaknesses.
    c. comparing characteristics of different population groups.
    d. developing tests for college admission.

14. According to Martin Seligman, who has studied explanatory style, psychology can contribute greatly to human well-being by shifting to a model that emphasizes

    a. Freudian psychodynamics.
    b. behavioral management.
    c. social context rather than individual responsibility.
    d. prevention rather than therapy.

15. Today psychologists have very different approaches to what to study and how. When, in the history of psychology, did such differences first appear?

    a. They have been present since the beginning.
    b. They arose in the 1920s.
    c. They arose in the 1950s.
    d. They are a very recent development.

16. Why would an experimenter employ a double-blind procedure?

    a. To keep the placebo effect from occurring
    b. To check the accuracy of measurements
    c. To make results easier to replicate
    d. To avoid biasing the results

17. Imagine that you read about a survey of American plumbers which suggested that most had very negative attitudes toward children. What question should you ask about the research?

    a. Did the people surveyed understand the questions?
    b. Was the sample representative of the population?
    c. Was there a cause-effect relationship or just a correlation?
    d. Was the placebo effect at work?

18. The two hemispheres of the brain are connected by the

    a. cerebral cortex.
    b. hippocampus.
    c. pons.
    d. corpus callosum.

19. Runners and other athletes report experiencing a natural "high" that elevates mood and decreases perception of pain. This effect is caused by a category of neurotransmitters called

    a. corticosteroids.
    b. endorphins.
    c. androgens.
    d. stimulants.

20. The modern world is full of stress, and stress is known to harm health. Michael Meany has shown that young rats cope with stress better if they have

    a. been raised on a low-fat diet.
    b. mothers who were subjected to high stress levels in pregnancy.
    c. had regular handling as newborns.
    d. environments that are enriched.

21. Which of the following ways of studying the brain and behavior is most clearly a field study?

    a. Studies of brain wave patterns of people in different countries
    b. Studies of people in REM and non-REM sleep
    c. Studies of grafts of fetal brain tissue
    d. Studies relating social rank and health in baboon colonies

22. Imagine you are the parent of a shy young child. If you asked Jerome Kagan, who has done extensive work on shyness in children, he would probably tell you,

    a. "Children are born shy or bold, and nothing can change it."
    b. "Shyness is a stage most children go through, so don't worry about it."
    c. "Shyness is genetic, but it can be modified by sensitive parenting."
    d. "Children learn shyness from parents, so the parents must overcome it first themselves."

23. How is Piaget's theory of development most like Erikson's?

    a. Both theories cover the entire life span.
    b. Both theories set up a series of stages.
    c. Both theories concentrate on cognitive growth.
    d. Both theories were based mainly on research with male subjects.

24. If language development is considered in the light of the nature-nurture debate, then the evidence suggests that the growth of language competence depends

    a. mainly on the maturation of the brain and the muscles in the mouth and tongue.
    b. mainly on the language acquisition device that children are born with.
    c. primarily on the interaction with parents and other caregivers.
    d. on the interplay of biological and environmental factors.

25. What is the main reason that psychologists study perceptual illusions?

    a. To learn how normal perception works
    b. To help people correct the errors that they make
    c. To analyze the difference between "top-down" and "bottom-up" processing
    d. To study the relation between sensation and perception

26. What does the term *habituation* mean?

    a. The development of a behavior pattern that is applied in different situations
    b. A decrease in responding when a stimulus is presented repeatedly
    c. A false sensory perception produced by a variety of conditions, including mental disorders, brain diseases, and some drugs
    d. A cognitive strategy used as a shortcut in solving a complex inferential task

27. What is a fundamental tenet of the behaviorist approach in psychology?

    a. Cognition is the key causal factor in behavior.
    b. Unconscious drives provide the motivational energy for behavior.
    c. Behavior can be explained by understanding brain processes.
    d. Behavior is determined by conditions in the environment.

28. B. F. Skinner developed the Skinner box to study behavior that was based on

    a. classical conditioning.
    b. social learning.
    c. operant conditioning.
    d. trial-and-error learning.

29. Current ideas of memory are based on an analogy that compares the mind to

    a. a computer.
    b. an electromagnet.
    c. a hydraulic machine.
    d. a steam engine.

30. Robin is a subject in an experiment on short-term memory. If she wants to remember more items, what should she do?

    a. There is nothing she can do, since short-term memory can contain only seven items.
    b. She should visualize the name of each item.
    c. She should chunk items together in a way she finds meaningful.
    d. She should rely on procedural memory rather than semantic memory.

31. When we hear a word like *prom*, we can easily imagine what people will wear and do. This cluster of knowledge is an example of

    a. an engram.
    b. an evoked potential.
    c. a heuristic.
    d. a schema.

32. Lorraine feels annoyed with herself for agreeing to go out with somebody she doesn't really like. But when she does go out, she finds she likes the person much better. This result might well be predicted by the theory of

    a. cognitive dissonance.
    b. the self-fulfilling prophecy.
    c. the availability heuristic.
    d. psychic numbing.

33. Carl Rogers and Abraham Maslow are thinkers in the humanistic tradition in psychology. What did they see as the motivation underlying human action?

    a. People seek pleasure and avoid pain.
    b. People are motivated by sexual and aggressive desires hidden from conscious awareness.
    c. People try to fulfill their potential.
    d. People follow fixed action patterns in response to environmental forces.

34. Your friend Carlotta tells you that she never dreams. Based on your knowledge of dream research, what would you tell her?

    a. She must be under so much stress that she doesn't dream.
    b. Everybody dreams several times a night, but not everybody remembers his or her dreams.
    c. The latent content on her dreams must be very threatening to make her forget her dreams.
    d. She is perfectly normal because a certain percentage of the population doesn't dream.

35. How is hypnosis like multiple personality disorder?

    a. Both involve dissociation.
    b. Both are caused by an outside agent acting on the individual.
    c. Both alter the perception of physical reality.
    d. Both are more likely to occur in introverted people.

36. Which theory of personality emphasizes the role of early experience and the importance of the unconscious?

    a. Freudian
    b. Cognitive
    c. Humanistic
    d. Behaviorist

37. Imagine that you are a school principal who wants to help students become more creative. What would tend to promote that goal?

    a. Having creativity contests where the best entries get prizes
    b. Emphasizing freedom in creative work
    c. Having students use models of great works to copy from
    d. Arranging students into "Jigsaw Classrooms"

38. A researcher is concerned about the reliability of one of the measurements she is using in her work. This means she is concerned that the instrument

    a. gives consistent scores.
    b. is not biased against certain population groups.
    c. measures what it is supposed to.
    d. has been standarized on an appropriate population.

39. How does the masculine gender role in the United States affect the health of American men?

    a. Positively, by encouraging good health practices
    b. Positively, by stressing the importance of physical well-being
    c. Negatively, by emphasizing feelings and thus leading to depression
    d. Negatively, by encouraging behaviors that put men at risk for diseases and accidents

40. What life crisis does Erikson see as occurring at the end of the life cycle?

    a. Initiative versus guilt
    b. Ego-integrity versus despair
    c. Intimacy versus isolation
    d. Generativity versus stagnation

41. Zelda has little patience with people who feel depressed. She believes the depression is their own fault for giving in to their feelings. This way of thinking can be termed

    a. the stereotype effect.
    b. reasoning by representativeness.
    c. the fundamental attribution error.
    d. cognitive appraisal.

42. In general, how does being anonymous change people's behavior?

    a. They behave in more antisocial ways.
    b. They are less likely to conform to group pressure.
    c. They act in ways that tend to individuate them.
    d. They are more likely to behave altruistically.

43. Models of mental disorder that emphasize an individual's perceptions and interpretations of experience are called

    a. biologically oriented models.
    b. psychodynamic models.
    c. behaviorist models.
    d. cognitive models.

44. Vincent Van Gogh's paintings reflect the fact that he suffered from manic-depressive disorder. How would he probably be treated for this disorder today?

    a. Through psychosurgery
    b. With lithium
    c. With psychoanalysis
    d. Through group therapy

45. What is the basic principle underlying biofeedback?

    a. The body's response to stress is to fight or flee.
    b. Medical problems can have psychological origins.
    c. The mind can learn to control biological functions.
    d. Optimism and pessimism influence the response to stress.

QUESTIONS TO CONSIDER

Note: These questions are designed to promote personal reflection and speculation. Because there are no right or wrong answers, an answer key has not been included in the Appendix.

1. Who will you be in the year 2000? Describe yourself. What personal, family, social, and cultural changes do you anticipate? How will the work of psychologists affect you?

2. If you had the power to distribute $10 million in research grants, what three areas of psychology would be highest on your list of possible recipients? Why?

3. Are human beings responsible for their behavior? Or are they victims of environment, their personal history, or biological determinants? Consider what psychologists and psychiatrists can contribute to our understanding of criminal

behavior. Does the "psychologizing" of American culture complicate the judicial process? How might the "new psychology" influence the value of expert testimony? What would B. F. Skinner say about the ability of psychologists to testify about what a defendant was thinking?

4. If Martin Seligman is correct, the future of psychology will increasingly include efforts to prevent psychological problems and enhance human potential. How will this work be carried out? Who should decide who needs preventive intervention?

5. Management consultant Peter Drucker has raised questions about the legal and ethical basis of requiring corporate employees to attend psychologically oriented seminars (*Wall Street Journal*, February 9, 1989). His concerns also apply to schools and other settings in which participants are involved in training and educational programs. How can students and employees be protected against involuntary participation? How would you feel if you were required to attend a personal growth group as a condition of passing this course?

OPTIONAL ACTIVITIES

1. Observe children in a kindergarten classroom, shoppers in a store, students taking an examination, or people standing in line outside a theater. Make a list of questions that illustrate the different types of behavior of interest to psychologists. Compare your questions with those you generated for activities in previous units. Do they reflect a more sophisticated awareness of the internal and external determinants of behavior?

2. Choose one of your personal habits or typical behaviors. Speculate how psychologists from different areas of psychology might describe and explain it.

ANTHOLOGY

Will psychology become more generalized, blending many disparate areas of interest? Or is it destined to become more specialized, with knowledge expanding so fast that only a few specialists will be able to keep track of new development? The following articles illustrate controversies and dilemmas that we encounter every day in our own lives. Are you optimistic or pessimistic about psychology's ability to help us cope and improve the quality of our lives?

Reading 61

Advances in genetic testing challenge long-standing ideas about what it is to be human and about how much control people have over their lives. As you read this article, consider the links between genetic research and its impact on individuals and on society as a whole. What are the benefits and drawbacks of genetic predestination? How does the study of psychology help us to understand and resolve some of these questions?

To Test or Not to Test

By Madeline Drexler

Genetic testing has been called a latter-day Manhattan Project, and for good reason. Like the atom bomb, the new technology will shake up our most cherished ideas about what it means to be human. It will provoke a public debate about where it should and shouldn't be applied. And like the bomb, it will be visited upon us before we have a chance to contemplate its consequences. In fact, this has already happened.

Cystic fibrosis, Huntington's disease, manic-depression, muscular dystrophy, Alzheimer's disease, and predisposition to heart disease and colon cancer are just a few of the conditions now traced to a specific gene. And although we now know of an estimated 3,500 genetically linked diseases, many more will turn up as researchers study the mechanics of biological inheritance.

Individuals, families, employers, insurers, government—all can make a moral case for knowing, or not knowing, the results of such tests. Indeed, genetic testing has given rise to almost science-fiction-like speculations about the future. If we could prevent the birth of seriously handicapped babies through pre-natal screening, would that diminish our tolerance for disability, or even diversity? Would our concept of a sound body shift, so that what is now considered a problem to be treated with compassion, such as deafness or a learning impairment, would be viewed more cynically as an embarrassing preventable handicap? How would society decide what diseases should be eliminated? And how confidential should genetic information be?

If these questions sound unfamiliar, it may be because the science of genetics has largely progressed outside the spotlight of public awareness. Just a decade ago, scientists couldn't do much more than examine the frequency of inherited diseases and warn patients about their risks. Today, they are starting to locate the genes for simple, hereditary diseases.

Genes are the chemical blueprints each person inherits from his or her parents, determining how we look, how we grow, and whether we will be susceptible or resistant to diseases. Many genes merely reveal the predisposition for disease, meaning that environment and lifestyle play an important role. Still, finding a gene is important, because when scientists know the approximate site of the gene on one of our 23 pairs of chromosomes, they can diagnose a genetic disease (if there is a previous family history) before the appearance of symptoms—as early as the fetal stage, and as late as old age. If researchers know the precise location of a gene, they can screen whole populations to identify carriers of the disease. Finding the gene doesn't cure a a disorder. But analyzing the biochemical function of the gene can point the way to new, effective treatments.

Today, gene testing is largely used by couples who are at risk of having a baby with birth defects and want to find out if they are carrying a genetic disorder or if their fetus is affected. Some adults are also tested in order to learn their chances of developing a disorder for which the gene has been located, such as Huntington's disease, which strikes in middle-age. But it is not farfetched to imagine a day when genetic testing would be offered as a routine diagnostic service, both for babies in the womb and for anxious adults.

Geneticists often paint an upbeat picture of the future, where science helps create healthy, happy lives by predicting and, in many cases, eliminating disease. But other observers are concerned about the subtle social implications of such a capability.

"One of the things that troubles me is that scientists and molecular biologists have the right to develop these tests. But once they're out there, not to use it is to make a choice," says Ruth Hubbard, professor of biology at Harvard University and a member of the Committee for Responsible Genetics, a Boston-based group dedicated to raising ethical issues in biotechnology. Some scientists have a stake in keeping the public in the dark about advances in genetics. After all, a fierce community debate could lead to a moratorium on research. Hubbard laments that "with scientists, there's the constant refrain: We must educate the public. But what that means is that we must educate the public to trust our decisions."

The most salient concern about gene testing revolves around eugenics—the questionable goal of improving the human species by controlling heredity. Though scientists insist that that is not their goal, the mere existence of the technology introduces the possibility of selecting healthy babies. Barbara Katz Rothman, a sociologist at the City University of New York and author of *The Tentative Pregnancy*, points out that, with prenatal tests, "it's not, 'Here's a kid with his mother's nose and a crooked toe.' Instead, it's, 'What's coming is Down's syndrome.' The child becomes the embodiment of a disease category."

Marsha Saxton, a disability rights activist in Boston, notes that women in West Germany are particularly outspoken in their concerns about genetic testing—probably because of the legacy of the Holocaust. 'I think there's a pervasive numbness in our culture that it can't happen here," she says. But Saxton, who was born with spina bifida, understands the threat intimately. "At a very gut level, genetic testing feels like eugenics. It feels like an effort by society to eliminate people with my disability."

Prenatal testing places a new and unique burden on mothers. Suddenly, through the ability to carry on or terminate a life based on genetic information, they become responsible for what used to be considered the caprices of fate. "I spoke to women who were grieving deeply about the loss of a baby," says Barbara Katz Rothman. "But their feeling was, 'How could I let my child be ill after I'm dead and gone?'"

Most women who decide to undergo tests have already decided they would abort a seriously disabled fetus. But what if the test results are ambiguous? Or what if a woman wants to forgo the screening altogether? Or decide to carry a disabled child to term? "Chromosomes aren't the issue. To me, the woman who is pregnant is the most important person involved," Rothman says. Robin Blatt, a local genetics educator, adds that "women need to be supported, no matter what decision they make."

Another peril is that gene testing might create a new kind of social outcast. "As more things become diagnosable, being handicapped will be a mark of social class. Children will be marked because their parents presumably didn't have the education or money to have a test," says Dorothy Wertz, a research professor in Boston University's School of Public Health. "There may be attempts to divert funds away from helping the handicapped to preventing their birth or preventing handicapped persons from having their own children."

Even today, class defines who uses prenatal genetic screening. Except in New York City and California, where outreach efforts are strong, it is largely a middle-class and upper-middle-class option. "What you see, as couples have fewer and fewer children and wait longer and longer to have them, is that those one or two children become important. There's a kind of emphasis on 'quality control,'" explains Carol Levine, formerly an ethicist with the Hastings Center in New York and now executive director of the Citizens Commission on AIDS in New York City.

Employers also have a stake in the new technology. Genetic monitoring—tracking the occurrence of chromosome changes over time—is already in place in some companies. It can reveal susceptibilities to certain workplace hazards, in which case the area could be cleaned up, or an employee could be transferred to a safer environnment. At Johnson & Johnson and the American Hospital Supply Corporation, monitoring showed that some workers were suffering chromosome changes from high levels of ethylene oxide—even though the levels were within government regulations. In response, the US Occupational Health and Safety Administration revised its guidelines for exposure to the chemical.

But genetic tests in a job setting could also be applied unfairly. What if an employer refused to hire anyone with a genetic vulnerability to chemicals in the workplace? Or what if a company based placement decisions on genetic information completely unrelated to work, such as the presence of a gene for manic-depression or alcoholism? Most important, what if a company refused to clean up the workplace and instead tried to fill it with genetically hardy employees? "Employers love to say they can't make the workplace cleaner. And they love to blame the employee," says Dorothy Wertz.

Insurance is another area where moral questions will have practical consequences. If companies know their policy-holders' genetic profiles, they could either provide preventive treatments—or deny coverage to high-risk individuals. Jonathan Beckwith, who teaches genetics at Harvard Medical School, says he has heard of an insurance company in Indiana that pays for amniocentesis—but if the fetus has one of a list of genetic diseases specified by the company, the mother must abort or face cancellation of her policy.

There's been conjecture that an insurance company which did not take into account genetic information would attract so many high-risk individuals it would go out of business. On the other hand, some say that if genetic screening produced huge disparities in insurance premiums, it could lead to federally financed risk pools and, eventually, a more equitable system: national health insurance.

All these visions prompt the question of how confidential genetic information should be. Many observers insist that only those of us who are screened should know the outcomes of our tests, because society has been known to misuse such information. Carriers of sickle-cell anemia, for instance, who are mostly black, once faced employment discrimination in the US Air Force and in private airlines—even though carrier status merely signals the possibility of handing down the disease, and does not affect the carrier's own health. But the most telling precedent may be set by AIDS testing. AIDS sufferers have faced tremendous emotional and economic hardships after their test results were leaked: loss of jobs, insurance, and housing; removal from schools; banishment by family and friends.

Genetic screening is fraught with so many moral implications, even the person tested may choose not to know the results. The saddest aspect of the technology is that, at least in the near future, scientists will be able to predict disease without being able to cure it. The current test for Huntington's disease, the degenerative neurological disorder that killed folk singer Woody Guthrie, is a poignant illustration. Children who have seen their parents waste away in their prime can now learn if they, too, can expect that fate—there's a 50-50 chance they would. Many choose to preview their deaths; others refuse, because they say the knowledge would cast a cloud over their lives.

"Some people say, 'It's always better to know than not to know. After all, we're not telling people what to do, we're giving them knowledge,'" says Ruth Hubbard. "But I ask people: 'If there were a test available that would tell you the exact moment when you were going to die, would you want to know? Most people would not."

Just as Copernicus, Darwin, and Freud uprooted our philosophical moorings, gene testing will prompt another round of introspection. "Genetic predestination" could become a fashionable idea. But ultimately, we will always be more than the sum of our genes. Thomas Murray, director of the

Center for Biomedical Ethics at Case Western Reserve University in Cleveland, compares a gene profile to a piece of music. Reducing a great symphony to a musical score doesn't diminish the grandeur of the work.

Likewise, our 50,000 to 100,000 genes "need in no way diminish the performance of our symphony," he says. "The performance is us."

Reading 62

This excerpt analyzes the policy of deinstitutionalization and its role in the growing problem of the homeless mentally ill, criticizing the profession of psychiatry for turning its back on the problem. As you read, consider how public attitudes and public policy have changed. Why has deinstitutionalization failed? What advances in prevention, diagnosis, and treatment might alleviate the problem? Speculate on how the new psychology, as envisioned by Professor Zimbardo, might help policymakers who must face the political and economic realities of these problems.

Human Jetsam

By E. Fuller Torrey, M. D., Sidney M. Wolfe, M. D., and Laurie M. Flynn

More than any other single factor in the past two years, the homeless mentally ill have focused public attention on the failures of the public psychiatric care system. Once sporadic apparitions in our cities, the homeless mentally ill have become ubiquitous and daily reminders of the chasm which separates intent from actuality in psychiatric services. Not only have bag lady chic clothing styles infiltrated our culture, but the problem of homelessness has infiltrated our dinner conversations, vying with AIDS and chicken cordon bleu for pre-eminence.

It has also become clear that the population of the homeless is a varied group. In addition to the mentally ill the homeless includes alcoholics, drug abusers, individuals who have lost their jobs, individuals forced into homelessness by the reduction of low income housing, and individuals who are lazy and simply refuse to work. It is the mentally ill homeless who are most visible and vulnerable, however, as they sit halluncinating in a park or cower in an alley to escape the psychic terrors of their disease.

The percentage of the homeless population with serious mental illness has varied considerably in different studies. A 1986 survey of cities by the United States Conference of Mayors reported that the percentage of the homeless with "chronic mental illness" (excluding alcohol or drug abuse) varied from 60 percent in Louisville and 45 percent in San Francisco and Salt Lake City to 25 percent in New York and Phoenix and 15 percent in Philadelphia and Los Angeles. Detailed assessments of homeless individuals living in public shelters have been more consistent with most studies reporting that approximately one-third of them have a serious mental illness, mostly schizophrenia. A study of homeless individuals sleeping on heating grates, in doorways, and in abandoned buildings in New York City found "that 60 percent exhibit evidence of schizophrenia as manifested by disorganized behavior and chronic delusional thinking." Thus, those homeless people not able to get to the shelters are even more likely to have a serious mental illness than those who can.

The quality of life for homeless individuals with serious mental illness varies from harsh to brutal. Disease, muggings, rat bites, and rapes are common concomitants of their daily rounds as they seek food and shelter. According to *U. S. News* and *World Report*, T-shirts are for sale in California reading "troll buster" in honor of the young men who beat up homeless individuals living beneath bridges.

Where did the homeless mentally ill come from? Why have they suddenly appeared in such large numbers in the 1980s? The answer, quite simply, is that the homeless mentally ill are products of the era of deinstitutionalization, human jetsam from the good ship mental health which promised to sail to a wonderful new land.

The Debacle of Deinstitutionalization

Deinstituionalization has been a social policy designed with the best of intentions but operationalized with the least of competence. It was an attempt to counteract the brutality and inhumane conditions of public mental hospitals by restoring mentally ill individuals to their own communities where they would, in theory, live happily ever after. As phrased by President John F. Kennedy in his historic 1963 special message to Congress concerning passage of the Community Mental Health Center Act, "reliance on the cold mercy of custodial isolation will be supplanted by the open warmth of community concern and capability." If deinstitutionalization is judged solely on the number of seriously mentally ill individuals emptied out of state hospitals, it was a resounding success. In 1955 there were 552,150 patients in state mental hospitals; 30 years later there were just 118,647 patients, a 79 percent reduction.

Deinstitutionalization went wrong for a variety of reasons. One reason was shortage of low income housing which could be used for the released patients, many living on a fixed and minimum income. Another reason was that civil rights lawyers, anxious to protect the rights of mentally ill patients, effected changes in state commitment laws so that patients did not have to take medication if they did not wish to and could not be rehospitalized until they became overtly dangerous to themselves or others; such laws assume that seriously mentally ill individuals are capable of making rational decisions about their own needs when in fact, because of their brain disease, many seriously mentally ill individuals are not capable of doing so.

A third reason that deinstitutionalization has failed is the system of economic incentives which accompanied it. Prior to 1963 each state was almost completely responsible economically for its own seriously mentally ill patients. Following 1963, however, the mentally ill were made eligible for federal support programs including Supplemental Security Income, Social Security Disability Income, Medicaid, and Medicare. The consequence was that states suddenly had a strong economic incentive to get mental patients out of the state hospitals, where the state was paying the costs, and into community boarding houses, nursing homes, or other facilities where the patients would be eligible for the federal programs. In 1963 state governments paid approximately 96 percent of the total costs of the care of the seriously mentally ill, whereas by 1985 state governments were paying only 53 percent of the total cost. In some states the directors of the state hospitals were promoted primarily on the basis of how many patients they had gotten out of the hospital. The question of primary concern to state administrators was *how many* patients had gone, not *where* they had gone.

The fourth, and probably most important reason that deinstitutionalization has failed is that community facilities and follow-up of deinstitutionalized patients were never developed. The cornerstone of community care was to be the community mental health centers, and the failure of these centers has been an essential ingredient in the debacle of deinstitutionalization.

The Failure of Community Mental Health Centers

When President Kennedy in 1963 proposed the creation of a federally-funded community mental health center (CMHC) network, he said that the mentally ill would no longer have to undergo "a prolonged or permanent confinement in huge unhappy mental hospitals." Similarly during congressional hearings on the CMHC proposal spokespersons for the administration stated specifically that "the basic purpose of the President's program is to redirect the focus of treatment of the seriously mentally ill from state mental hospitals into community mental health centers." Since 1963 the federal government has spent over $3 billion dollars to fund 789 community mental health centers. Despite the originally stated purpose of these centers, however, most have never assumed responsibility for more than a handful of seriously mentally ill patients being deinstitutionalized from state mental hospitals. From 1968 to 1978 the National Institute of Mental Health (NIMH) issued annual reports on the CMHCs; the reports showed that an average of less than 5 percent of center patients came from state mental hospitals despite the fact that hundreds of thousands of patients were being deinstitutionalized during those years. Even more disturbing was a trend among CMHCs to accept *fewer* state hospital patients the longer the center was in operation.

Another measure of the failure of community mental health centers to assume responsibility for the seriously mentally ill was the percentage of CMHC admissions with a diagnosis of schizophrenia. From 1970 to 1978, the years for which such information is available from NIMH, the percentage of CMHC admissions with schizophrenia dropped steadily from 19.1 percent to 10.6 percent. During those same years the number of CMHC admissions with a diagnosis "social maladjustment" or "no mental disorder" increased steadily from 4.6 percent in 1970 to 20.8 percent in 1978.

In summary, what took place was that community mental health centers, originally conceived and funded as alternatives to state mental hospitals, never assumed that function. They became instead psychotherapy and counseling centers for individuals with problems communicating with a spouse, feelings of low self-esteem, difficulties with teenage children, inability to find meaning in life—in short the whole panoply of life's problems which trouble the worried well and the existentially unhappy. Such troubles are deserving of attention and have traditionally been "treated" by friends, clergy, bartenders, hairdressers, and less often by psychotherapists. CMHCs were not originally intended to assume this function but rather to care for the seriously mentally ill, especially those who had been, or would likely be, patients in state mental hospitals. The fact that community mental health centers focused their resources primarily on the worried well rather than the seriously mentally ill was, therefore, a major reason for the failure of deinstitutionalization.

Although NIMH no longer collects annual data from community mental health centers, there is evidence that little has changed in the 1980s. There are of course a few centers which have done an excellent job of providing *care* for the seriously mentally ill but such centers are rare. Overall the percentage of patients with serious mental illness seen in CMHCs averages under 20 percent. A 1987 survey by the National Council of Community Mental Health Centers—the lobbying group for CMHCs—claimed that 44 percent of CMHC patients had a serious mental illness but the survey defined serious mental illness very broadly to include personality disorders (e.g. dependent, narcissistic, antiso-

cial), a group of patients which was almost never treated by state mental hospitals. The failure of most community mental health centers to care for a substantial number of seriously mentally ill continues to the present despite the fact that 75 percent of their revenues still comes from federal, state, and local public funds; these funds are allocated to CMHCs with the assumption that they will be used primarily for the seriously mentally ill.

The Scandal of American Medicine

At the end of World War II it was estimated that there were approximately 3,000 psychiatrists, 4,200 psychologists, and 2,000 psychiatric social workers in the United States, a total of just over 9,000 mental health professionals. There was widespread agreement that more professionals were needed to provide treatment and rehabilitation for the seriously mentally ill, and for this reason federal training funds were included in the legislation which created the National Institute of Mental Health. At the hearings on the legislation one congressman raised a question whether psychiatrists trained with federal funds would serve in public mental hospitals and clinics where they were most needed or whether they would go directly into private practice; both the director of NIMH and a representative of the American Psychiatric Association assured the congressman that some sort of mandatory payback obligation would be included in the program so that such abdication of professional psychiatric responsibility would not take place.

Forty years later, after the federal government has spent over $2 billion and state governments uncounted billions more to train psychiatrists, psychologists, and psychiatric social workers, there are now a total of over 150,000 of them. Despite this 16-fold increase in numbers, there continues to be a critical shortage of mental health professionals in public psychiatric hospitals, community mental health centers, and public psychiatric outpatient clinics. Although Congress had been assured in 1945 that some sort of payback obligation in public service would be attached to the federal training funds, this was never implemented until 1981. Predictably, without any obligation to a specified period of public service, most mental health professionals whose training had been partially or totally subsidized with federal and state funds went directly into private practice leaving the public psychiatric facilities little better off than they had been in 1945. Psychiatrists in particular continued to be desperately needed in public mental hospitals over the years; states, forced to fill vacancies with anybody with a medical degree and a pulse, turned increasingly to foreign medical graduates who flooded the U. S. following liberalization of immigration regulations for professionals in the 1960s.

The staffing of public psychiatric facilities in America with foreign-trained psychiatrists, while private psychiatric facilities have continued to be staffed with American-trained psychiatrists, is without question one of the scandals of American medicine. Over half of psychiatrists currently employed in state mental hospitals are foreign-trained, and in some states (e.g. Arizona, Delaware, Florida, Kansas, and North Dakota) the percentage is over three-quarters. Many of the foreign-trained psychiatrists staffing America's public sector are excellent psychiatrists. Many others, however, are considerably less competent and a significant number are clearly incompetent because of their inability to speak or understand English, their poor training in psychiatry, or their poor training in medicine. Many of these less competent psychiatrists are unable to pass state licensing examinations; in order to fill empty positions in state mental hospitals all except seven states modified their state licensing requirements so that the less competent psychiatrists could practice in these institutions despite the fact that they were unlicensed. Data from the 1970s showed that in New York and Ohio 40 percent of psychiatrists in state mental hospitals were unlicensed while in West Virginia the number was 90 percent. In 1988 over one-quarter of psychiatrists in the state hospitals in Delaware, Mississippi, and Kansas are still unlicensed.

Meanwhile America's university medical school departments of psychiatry have continued training psychiatrists using both federal and state public funds. A few of the departments have attempted to interest their trainees in public sector psychiatry by having the psychiatric residents spend a few weeks working in a state mental hospital. But the fact of the matter is that most of America's

115 university departments of psychiatry, and therefore most American-trained psychiatrists, have no interest whatsoever in patients with serious mental illness or in public sector jobs. Status accrues only to private practice, most of which consists of counseling and psychotherapy for the worried well, and to academic sector jobs. Despite the fact that large amounts of public (state and federal) funds support these training programs, there is virtually no service payoff for the public sector. Representative of the vast majority of such programs is the psychiatric residency program at the University of New Mexico; since 1966 a total of 68 psychiatrists have completed their training in the program yet as of 1986 only 1 of the 31 psychiatrists still in the state was working in public sector psychiatry.

The American Psychiatric Association, as might be expected, shares the disinterest of its members with public psychiatry. This is ironic since the organization was originally begun in 1844 by 13 superintendents of state mental hospitals and was known as the Association of Medical Superintendents of American Institutions for the Insane. At that time American psychiatry was public psychiatry and the concern of psychiatrists was almost exclusively patients with serious mental illness. That focus has virtually disappeared; in 1988 the only evidence of public psychiatry in the American Psychiatric Association is a Committee on State Mental Health Systems, which is one of 115 committees and task forces of the APA and on the same administrative plane and status as committees and task forces on Problems of Americans Overseas, Psychosocial Aspects of the Middle East Process. Religion and Psychiatry, and Prospective Payment Issues.

Psychologists and psychiatric social workers have usually followed the lead of psychiatrists in deciding how to spend their professional time, and as psychiatrists abandoned the public sector most psychologists and social workers did likewise. There are to be certain a few outstanding exceptions in which academic departments of psychology (e.g. University of Vermont, University of Nebraska, University of Houston) or social work (e.g. University of Kansas, University of Cincinnati, University of Connecticut) have oriented their training programs to public sector jobs, but they stand in sharp contrast to most departments whose training programs are focused on producing private psychotherapists for the private sector. The consequence of this private practice orientation is predictable and was demonstrated in a 1980 study of psychiatrists, psychologists, and psychiatric social workers in which practitioners of all three professions were found to be concentrated in areas with "higher income, higher education, more urbanization, (and) more insurance availability" which is used to pay the fees of the private mental health professionals.

In summary, given the problems and resources described above, it is remarkable that care of the seriously mentally ill in public facilities in the United States is not worse than it is. Most patients who receive treatment must rely on inadequate facilities and incompetent psychiatric professionals; many of others receive no treatment at all and have joined the legion of the homeless mentally ill. Individuals with less serious problems who are covered by insurance, meanwhile, avail themselves of comfortable private hospitals and more competent professionals. A two-class system of psychiatric care has emerged which is, quite simply, a disgrace to a democratic nation.

ADDITIONAL RESOURCES

Books and Articles

The following readings touch upon current issues in psychology or speculate about the future of the field.

Drexler, Madeline. "The Couch and the Courtroom." *Boston Globe Magazine,* October 3, 1988, pp. 72–73. Drexler looks at how psychiatrists are used to provide expert testimony in the courtroom.

Drucker, Peter F. "New Age Sessions are Same Old Brainwashing," *Wall Street Journal,* February 9, 1989, p. A22. Drucker describes potential abuses of preventive psychology and personal growth programs.

Gazzaniga, Michael. *Mind Matters: How Brain and Mind Interact to Create Our Conscious Lives.* Boston: Houghton Mifflin, 1988. Insights from the field of neuropsychology can help us better understand the nature of consciousness.

Hall, Holly. "The Homeless: A Mental-Health Debate." *Psychology Today* (February 1987): 65–66. Does mental illness lead to homelessness, or does living on the streets cause mental illness? A look at mental illness among the homeless helps point out the connection between mental health and environment.

Hurley, Dan. "Getting Help from Helping." *Psychology Today* (January 1988): 62–67. Mutual-help groups such as Alcoholics Anonymous have been around for years, but mental health professionals have only recently recognized and studied their programs of therapy. More professionals are now contributing to these organizations, and the groups themselves are growing rapidly.

Joyce, Christopher. "This Machine Wants to Help You." *Psychology Today* (February 1988): 44–50. They haven't yet replaced human therapists, but computers are increasingly being relied on by mental health professionals. Though generally used to help therapists test and diagnose patients, some software programs even help patients run their own therapy sessions.

Knight, Pamela. "ARC: Life in Limbo." *Psychology Today* (March 1987): 18. The psychological strains for individuals diagnosed with AIDS-related complex (ARC) are tremendous. Not only must they cope with the hardships of physical illness, but they also often face discrimination and scorn. Psychologists are being called on to help these people and should be prepared for the challenge.

Miller, Laurence. "The Emotional Brain." *Psychology Today* (February 1988): 34ff. In the near future we may be able to link a variety of mood disorders to different patterns of cerebral disorganization. Miller describes how this could lead to more effective, custom-tailored therapies.

Puckett, Sam B. "When a Worker Gets AIDS." *Psychology Today* (January 1988): 26–27. Misconceptions and anxiety about AIDS can lead to panic at the workplace when a worker is infected with the HIV virus. Although a cure for the disease has not yet been found, education can help managers and workers work together in preventing such fear and panic.

Roberts, M., and T. G. Harris. "Wellness at Work: How Corporations Help Employees Fight Stress and Stay Healthy." *Psychology Today* (May 1989): 54–58. In providing fitness plans and structuring other ways to reduce stress on the job, employers help workers stay healthy . . . and productive. This new trend may have been influenced by the insights of health psychology.

APPENDIX

ANSWER KEY: REVIEW QUESTIONS

Unit 1

1 c	7 b	13 c	19 c 9	25 a 11	30 d 17
2 b	8 b	14 d 4	20 a 10	26 b 11	31 b 14
3 a	9 b	15 d 6-7	21 d 10	27 b 13	
4 c	10 a	16 c/d 6-7	22 c 11	28 d 13	
5 b	11 d	17 b 8	23 d 12	29 b 16	
6 d	12 c	18 b 9	24 d 10-11		

Unit 2

1 a	7 a	13 d 34	19 a 46	25 c 41	31 a 52
2 c	8 d	14 a 35	20 b 47	26 c 43	32 d 52
3 b	9 a	15 b 45	21 c 40	27 a 38	33 b 54
4 b	10 c	16 d 46	22 b 40	28 a 44	
5 d	11 b	17 a 46	23 b 41	29 b 45	
6 b	12 c	18 b 46	24 a 41	30 c 50-51	

Units 3/4

1 d	11 a	21 b 62	31 c 65	41 a 78	51 d 87
2 a	12 d	22 c 62	32 a 66	42 b 79	52 a 86
3 b	13 a	23 c 62	33 c 67	43 c 80	53 d 90
4 c	14 b	24 b 64	34 c 68	44 d 81	54 b 74
5 c	15 c	25 b 64	35 b 68	45 a 82	55 a 73-74
6 c	16 d	26 b 64	36 d 68	46 b 82	56 b 74
7 b	17 a	27 d 64	37 a 69	47 c 82	57 c 94
8 b	18 c	28 b 64	38 b 72	48 a 85	58 c 95
9 a	19 b	29 c 65	39 d 78	49 b 86	59 a 97
10 c	20 b	30 b 65	40 d 78	50 a 87	

Unit 5

1 b	7 b	13 b	19 a 413	25 a 423	31 c 436
2 a	8 a	14 d 403	20 c 414	26 a 424	32 c 439
3 c	9 d	15 b 406	21 a 417	27 a 424	33 b 438
4 d	10 c	16 d 407	22 d 421	28 c 426	
5 c	11 d	17 c 410	23 d 423	29 c 428	
6 d	12 a	18 d 410	24 c 423	30 a 428	

Unit 6

1 c	6 b	11 b	16 a	21 b 374	26 b 378
2 d	7 c	12 a	17 c	22 b 374	27 c 378
3 b	8 d	13 b	18 a 374	23 c 375	28 b 379
4 a	9 a	14 d	19 b 374	24 c 375	29 b/c 384
5 b	10 a	15 c	20 b 374	25 d 375	30 c 384

Unit 7

1 d	8 a	14 a 112	20 c 122	26 a 134	32 a 148
2 c	9 c	15 d 113	21 a 123	27 a 137	33 d 151
3 c	10 c	16 d 115	22 d 122	28 b 138	34 a 152–153
4 a	11 b	17 b 121	23 a 129	29 b 140	35 d 152
5 d	12 c	18 c 113	24 b 131	30 d 145	36 a 155
6 a	13 d	19 b 122	25 d 133	31 a 148	37 d 157
7 a					

Unit 8

1 b	8 a	14 a 198	20 b 205	26 a 211	32 b 216
2 d	9 d	15 a 199	21 a 207	27 b 215	33 a 207
3 d	10 c	16 b 201	22 b 207	28 c 212	34 c 217
4 a	11 b	17 c 202	23 b 209	29 b 212	35 c 218
5 b	12 d	18 c 205	24 d 209	30 a 212	36 c 218
6 d	13 c	19 a 205	25 b 210	31 b 213	37 a 202
7 c					

Unit 9

1 d	8 a	15 d 236	21 a 243	27 b 258	33 c 258
2 c	9 b	16 c 237	22 d 244	28 a 256	34 a/b 258
3 b	10 b	17 d 239	23 b 245	29 c 256	35 b 259
4 b	11 c	18 c 240	24 a 245	30 c 251	36 d 260
5 d	12 d	19 d 242	25 a 247	31 a 252	37 b 260
6 a	13 c 234	20 b/d 243–244	26 b 247	32 a 257	38 a 262
7 b	14 b 235				

Units 10/11

1 d	10 c	19 d	27 c 353	35 d 356	43 b 362
2 c	11 b	20 b	28 c 353	36 a 359	44 c 363
3 b	12 d	21 c	29 b 353	37 b 359	45 d 364
4 a	13 b	22 a	30 a 353	38 d 359	46 a 365
5 b	14 a	23 c	31 b 354	39 b 360	47 d 366
6 c	15 c	24 d 352	32 b 354	40 a 360	48 c 367
7 a	16 d	25 a 353	33 c 354	41 c 360–361	49 b 368
8 c	17 d	26 a 353	34 b 354	42 d 361	50 b 369
9 a	18 b				

Unit 12

1 d	8 a	14 d 275	20 c 278	26 a 293	32 b 278
2 b	9 d	15 b 276	21 b 284	27 c 294	33 d 316
3 b	10 b	16 a 276	22 a 284	28 d 296	34 b 319
4 c	11 a	17 a 276	23 a 284	29 a 298	35 a 320
5 a	12 b	18 d 277	24 b 287	30 a 299	36 b 321
6 c	13 c	19 a 277	25 d 291	31 d 300	37 a 323
7 c					

Units 13/14

1 c	10 b	19 a	28 d 174	36 b 184	44 b 97
2 b	11 a	20 a	29 c 179	37 b 184	45 a 98
3 d	12 b	21 a 167	30 c 180-181	38 a 186	46 d 98
4 b	13 a	22 d 171	31 a 182	39 c 186	47 b 98
5 a	14 d	23 a 170	32 b 182	40 c 188	48 b 99
6 b	15 a	24 a 171	33 c 182	41 a 188	49 b 100
7 c	16 d	25 d 173	34 b 183	42 a 189	50 a 101
8 b	17 b	26 a 185	35 b 183	43 b 189	51 d 104
9 b	18 c	27 a 170			

Unit 15

1 c	7 d	13 d 525	19 b 530	25 a 537	30 b 541
2 b	8 b	14 c 525	20 c 531	26 c 543	31 d 542-543
3 a	9 c	15 d 527-528	21 b 532	27 a 546	32 c 549
4 b	10 b	16 d 528	22 d 532	28 b 546	33 d 552
5 a	11 a	17 c 529	23 b 533	29 c 541	
6 d	12 a 524	18 b 530	24 b 536		

Unit 16

1 b	7 b	13 c 486	19 b 494	25 a 493	30 b 503
2 d	8 d	14 a 497	20 c 494	26 d 494	31 c 504
3 a	9 c	15 b 486	21 c 492	27 a 500	32 d 510
4 c	10 b	16 a 488	22 b 492	28 a 502	
5 d	11 c	17 c 488	23 c 493	29 a 501	
6 c	12 c	18 c 488	24 a 493		

Unit 17

1 d	6 a	11 c	16 d 446	20 c 446	24 a 298
2 b	7 d	12 a	17 a 442	21 c 446	25 c 299
3 a	8 c	13 d	18 c 445	22 b 298	26 c 299
4 b	9 c	14 b	19 c 439	23 a/c 446-447	27 d 300
5 c	10 a	15 c 439			

Unit 18

1 c	8 c	15 b	21 b 457	27 a 467	33 a 475
2 d	9 d	16 c 453	22 c 457	28 c 468	34 c 476
3 b	10 b	17 a 454	23 b 461	29 c 439	35 b 478
4 a	11 a	18 d 455	24 a 462	30 c 469	36 c 477
5 b	12 a	19 a 455	25 d 464	31 b 472	37 a 479
6 d	13 a	20 d 456	26 d 465	32 d 472-474	38 a 437
7 a	14 c				

Units 19/20

1 a	9 c	17 c	25 a 667	33 c 677	41 c 689
2 c	10 a	18 b	26 d 668	34 c 679	42 d 689
3 d	11 b	19 c 661	27 a 668	35 b 678	43 a 681
4 a	12 c	20 c 661	28 b 670	36 d 679	44 b 682
5 b	13 c	21 d 664	29 d 671	37 a 680	45 d 684
6 a	14 d	22 b 664	30 c 676	38 a 687	46 a 690
7 c	15 a	23 b 665	31 d 676	39 c 687	47 a 693
8 d	16 b	24 b 668	32 b 680	40 b 688	48 c 696

Unit 21

1 d	9 d	17 b 567	25 b 574	33 b 583	41 d 601
2 b	10 b	18 a 568	26 b 578	34 d 584	42 c 601
3 b	11 d	19 d 569	27 b 578	35 d 584	43 b 602
4 d	12 b	20 b 569	28 a 580	36 a 583	44 a 606
5 a	13 c	21 b 570	29 a 580	37 b/c 588	45 c 607
6 b	14 d 565	22 b 571	30 c 580	38 b 596	46 b 607
7 c	15 a/b 565	23 d 572	31 a 581	39 b 600	
8 a	16 a 566	24 b 572	32 a 582	40 a 600	

Unit 22

1 c	8 c	15 d 624	21 b 628	27 b 636	33 a 642
2 a	9 c	16 c 624	22 d 628	28 d 637	34 d 644
3 d	10 d	17 b 625	23 c 632	29 c 638	35 a 645
4 b	11 a	18 d 626	24 a 633	30 a 639	36 b 649
5 a	12 c	19 b 626	25 b 634	31 d 641	37 c 652
6 b	13 c 621	20 d 628	26 a 635	32 c 642	38 a 625
7 d	14 b 624				

Unit 23

1 c	6 c	11 b	16 b 330	21 c 332	26 c 336
2 b	7 a	12 d	17 a 330	22 b 343	27 a 337
3 d	8 b	13 a	18 d 330	23 a 343	28 a 339
4 b	9 c	14 a 329	19 c 331	24 a 343	29 d 339
5 d	10 d	15 b 329	20 d 331	25 a 344	

Unit 24

1 b	4 d	7 c	10 b	13 a	16 b
2 d	5 a	8 d	11 a	14 c	17 d
3 c	6 d	9 a	12 d	15 a	

Units 25/26

1 d	9 b	17 b	25 a	32 a	39 d
2 b	10 c	18 d	26 b	33 c	40 b
3 a	11 b	19 b	27 d	34 b	41 c
4 d	12 b	20 c	28 c	35 a	42 a
5 a	13 b	21 d	29 a	36 a	43 d
6 d	14 d	22 c	30 c	37 b	44 b
7 c	15 a	23 b	31 d	38 a	45 c
8 a	16 d	24 d			

ANSWER KEY: QUESTIONS TO CONSIDER

Note: There are not always clear-cut right or wrong answers to these questions, but it may be helpful to compare your ideas to the ideas provided in this Answer Key.

UNIT 1. PAST, PRESENT, AND PROMISE

1. The fundamental issues of psychology include: the relationship of mind and body, the role of heredity and environment in determining personality and behavior, the role of the conscious and the unconscious in determining behavior, the influence of individual dispositional and external social and situational forces in behavior, the influence of early experience on later life, and the significance of individual differences and similarities.

2. Many people are not aware of the many different kinds of work that psychologists do. A popular stereotype is that of the slightly nutty Freudian-style analyst depicted in popular movies of the 1930s and 1940s. As you will learn, the treatment of mental illness is only one part of psychology. Psychologists are scientists who can also help people teach more effectively and learn more efficiently. They help people improve their physical and emotional well-being, enhance communication, find the right job, quit smoking, make decisions, improve social relations, understand child development, promote world peace, and fight poverty and prejudice.

3. The media are filled with claims, myths, and biased conclusions. We need to be open-minded but skeptical of what we read or see on television. We need to learn how to evaluate the validity of claims and enhance our sensitivity to sources of bias. Our understanding of human behavior influences the decisions we make as learners, consumers, voters, policymakers, friends, and parents.

4. Observer bias influences our choices about what is relevant and what isn't. Our values, interests, and expectations can even influence our perceptions, leading us to see things that are not there and overlook things that are.

5. Thinking (perceiving, remembering, imagining) is now an accepted focus of psychological study. There have been various approaches to studying thinking behavior. Subjects are asked to think out loud while solving problems or to report their reactions to internal or external events. Mental processes can also be inferred from such measurable behaviors as reaction times in decision making, problem-solving strategies, changes in brain waves or eye movements, body language, and speech patterns.

UNIT 2. UNDERSTANDING RESEARCH

1. For every person who is supposedly healed, there are many more who are not. Faith healing is big business, and desperate people are purposely deceived in money-making

scams. The sick not only lose money to faith healers for empty promises, but they may not follow proven medical treatments that might help them.

2. The results of being graded on a curve depend on how the test is constructed, what percentage of the students do well, and whether you perform at the top of the class or are an average student. The distribution of scores around the mean would have different impacts on the A student and the C student.

3. Objections to the study of mental processes (dreams, judgment, perceptions) include the claim that they rely on self-reports, are too personal, and cannot be verified. Because mental events cannot be observed directly, they are difficult to study scientifically. But psychologists believe that by defining terms carefully, they can draw inferences from measurable behaviors. Personal experiences such as sensations, emotions, and reactions to internal and external events can be inferred from changes in heart rate, brain waves, eye movements, speech patterns, and body language—all of which can be measured.

4. The subject matter, human beings and their behavior, is very complicated and variable. The behaviors change from day to day and from situation to situation. No two people are exactly alike. In addition, virtually every behavior has multiple causes.

5. A person's subjective experience of illness or pain is difficult to measure objectively. Not all drugs work for all patients. A person can still feel ill even when all measurable indicators of illness (fever, tumor, and so forth) are gone.

6. Scientists use animal subjects to conduct research that cannot be done with humans. When research includes harming animals, it creates ethical dilemmas. You might consider an experiment justified if its findings were of direct benefit to humans. The APA's guidelines represent an attempt to prevent mistreatment and to inform the public of its professional standards.

7. People who volunteer are a self-selected group; they are not representative of the general population. Volunteers may be less inhibited or more strongly opinionated about a particular topic. For example, the results of a magazine survey may depend on a group of readers with specific characteristics not represented in the general population.

UNIT 3. THE BEHAVING BRAIN

1. If we know what causes a problem, we can avoid spending a lot of time and money on useless treatments. Even though many conditions are not correctible, knowing the cause gives us a sense of control. For example, some drugs are used to treat depressed and schizophrenic patients. Sometimes the doctors don't even know why the drugs have the desired effect. Nevertheless, these drugs clearly relieve the patients' symptoms.

2. Although early research by Delgado and others showed that electrical stimulation of the brain could produce certain results, such as initiating or inhibiting aggressive behavior, the explanation for its effects has been questioned by other research. Elliot Valenstein's analysis points out that repeated stimulation to the same spot may not predictably elicit the same feeling or action. Although electrical stimulation has been used to relieve cancer patients of pain by blocking messages in the spinal cord, most doctors consider electrode implants too radical a treatment for healthy patients with weight problems.

3. There are many unknowns in the complex chemical system in the body. And there are many side effects or long-term consequences of taking megadoses of vitamins, hormones, home remedies, folk medicines, and self-treatments. Many people believe that if a little is good, more is better. They do not understand the toxic properties of some substances. These claims are characteristic of overly simplistic approaches to complex problems and may do more harm than good. Consumers should be very skeptical about advertisements that promote these products or claim miracle cures.

4. Techniques such as the EEG, CAT, MRI, and PET provide information that can be used to help distinguish between normal and abnormal brain structures and functions. The process of mapping or imaging the brain promises to help identify the chemical or structural abnormalities underlying such problems as Alzheimer's disease, schizophrenia, learning disabilities, and depression.

UNIT 4. THE RESPONSIVE BRAIN

1. Does an athlete who takes steroids have an unfair advantage over his or her competitors? Most organizations and competitions prohibit competitors from taking drugs to enhance performance. In noncompetive situations, the issue of taking drugs should involve consideration of the unintended side effects or the individual's long-term health effects.

2. For premature infants, sessions that included touching and movement stimulation caused significant weight gain and advances in organized behavior over the control group of premature infants. You might conclude that in general, infants receiving a lot of contact and stimulation would be more advanced physically, perhaps healthier, and more alert than low-touch infants. (However, there are many other factors that influence later development.) Observation studies of people in different cultures have suggested that some European cultures are more demonstrative and more expressive than that of Americans, for example. You might assume that high-touch families would create more expressive individuals.

3. You may be able to cite specific examples of how circumstances interact with biological variables to enhance or detract from a person's life. For example, research has shown that an attractive person is more likely to be hired for certain jobs. Tall people and first-borns tend to be more successful than shorter people and those in different birth positions. Healthy people may be more active (which often leads to a healthier pattern of exercise) than people with chronic or serious health problems (which may lead to inactivity).

4. Federal and state governments sponsor many nutrition programs as well as drug and alcohol prevention, treatment, and education programs. In some states legislation has been proposed that would regulate a pregnant woman's behavior if it were judged dangerous to the fetus.

UNIT 5. THE DEVELOPING CHILD

1. The trait of boldness is expressed differently by each individual. Its advantages or disadvantages depend on the extent of the trait and the context in which it is

expressed. In most situations, boldness is influenced by social expectations about appropriate gender-related behavior. For a girl, boldness may have a negative connotation, while the same behavior in a boy might be considered masculine or attractive.

2. Watson was devoted to behaviorism. He possessed a rather cold, objective view of the child, emphasized shaping and training, and discounted the importance of inherited traits and personality. Gesell emphasized that development depended on maturation. He contended that there was no point in training children or trying to speed up learning because they couldn't learn until they were biologically ready.

3. Lack of knowledge or inappropriate expectations can cause unnecessary frustration and misunderstanding. Some child abuse may be related to unrealistic expectations, especially in toilet training and bed-wetting. In the past, parents were warned not to spoil their children by handling them too much. This was followed by a period of attentive indulgence. Currently, childrearing advice falls somewhere between these two extremes.

4. "Body language" of an adult primarily refers to facial expressions, movements, and gestures. The body language of an infant includes these as well as physiological measures. A change in arousal level could be used in infants or adults to measure a response to a stimuli. These might include a change in temperature, heart rate, or brain wave activity. Adults also tend to look at what interests them. Tracking eye movements can reveal what a person notices, prefers, or recognizes.

5. Today, researchers and writers, such as Erik Erikson, believe that infants' needs for contact, comfort, and stimulation should be met as fully as possible within the constraints of the caregiver's schedule. Positive contact with a caregiver promotes trust and initiative in the baby.

UNIT 6. LANGUAGE DEVELOPMENT

1. Whether gorillas or chimps are truly capable of language is still hotly debated. It really depends on your definition of language. Your textbook definition may include such characteristics as: specialization, arbitrariness, displacement, productivity and novelty, and iteration and recursion. Although animals do use symbols, no animal consistently and naturally organizes symbols according to specific rules. Human language seems to be unique, and humans appear to be uniquely "programmed" to acquire it. Recent research studies have suggested that there is higher-level communication between gorillas and chimps, and mothers trained in signs and symbols can transfer their learning to their offspring. The debate goes on.

2. Language helps structure thought, and people use words to think, solve problems, and define and use concepts. But thinking also involves visual and sensory images. Certain cognitive operations, but not all, are dependent on language.

3. Nonverbal communication includes body movements, postures, gestures, eye contact, and use of physical space. Other important elements of communication include such verbal features as voice intonation, hesitation, and volume. Nonlinguistic and nonverbal elements account for a significant portion of the total message.

4. The pitch and intonations of baby talk elicit the same attention response in some pets as they do in infants. Some people anthropomorphize their animals and thus speak to them as they do to infants. "Baby talk" expresses the warm, nurturing feelings that people have for their pets. Animals may also be sensitive to simple cues in structured interactions, so their responsiveness may reinforce their owners for talking to them in a certain way.

5. Parentese is characterized by a responsiveness to the child's levl of language development. A parent whose speech does not adapt to the infant might not provide the cues he or she needs to discriminate sounds, recognize important intonations of the language, or practice social interaction patterns. It might suggest the parent's inability to respond appropriately to the child. The child's language development might be somewhat delayed if there are no other sources of interaction.

6. By the age of six, most children have a skillful and functional command of their own language. However, people refine their use of language throughout their lives, including, but not limited to, expanding vocabulary and improving grammar.

UNIT 7. SENSATION AND PERCEPTION

1. To improve the environment for individuals with visual deficits, one could print large labels on medicine bottles and other containers. For people with impaired balance, handrails in hallways and safety rails in bathrooms could be installed. To adjust for hearing loss, background noise could be reduced by better insulation, and blinking lights that indicate when the phone is ringing could be installed. For those with a loss of sensitivity to smells, smoke detectors or fire alarms could be installed. And, if loss of smell is affecting appetite, special effort should go into planning a diet to enhance flavors and ensure adequate nutrition.

2. Some people assert that those who practice and promote ESP are abusing science, particularly at a time when public decisions depend on the application of good science. Others decry the spending of money on worthless books and gadgets. Admittedly, science cannot fully explain many phenomena, and people turn in frustration to miracle cures, often accepting irrational explanations that do not hold up under rigorous and repeated scientific testing. Yet people continue to support those who promote belief in the paranormal.

3. The eye is constantly organizing and interpreting visual information. Graphic artists use proximity, similarity, closure, and continuity to create associations and meaning. For example, a car ad may suggest dependability, safety, or excitement, depending on who is driving the car, its color, and where it is. A cereal ad may establish it as a fun food or health food. Notice the people who are eating the cereal, their age, and the way they are dressed. You should be able to use Gestalt principles in interpreting the purpose and effect of the ad.

4. By training yourself to pay close attention to visual and aural elements, you can become increasingly aware of the purposeful choices directors make and how they use and combine various techniques to influence your perceptions. For example, children's toys are frequently photographed in ads so that they appear larger or sturdier than they really are. In films and television programs, dim lighting, a low camera angle, and shadows are used to create suspense or danger. Music is often used in television and film to evoke certain emotions.

UNIT 8. LEARNING

1. Compulsive gambling could be considered a disease and a learned behavior. There is an organization called Gamblers Anonymous that is based on the same principles as Alcoholics Anonymous. However, analyzing compulsive gambling in terms of antecedents and consequences might suggest ways to eliminate cues that lead to gambling, thereby leading to extinction. The best policy might be to avoid all settings where gambling takes place. Because any winning would serve to reinforce gambling, the best goal for a behavior change program is no gambling. Gambling is reinforced intermittently, and may be very resistant to extinction.

2. Some states are requiring companies to provide incentives such as free gasoline and choice parking spots for car pools, cash bonuses, free or discounted bus passes, and showers for bicyclists. Many communities are increasing parking fees and cracking down on parking violations. And in some major cities, tolls on bridges and in tunnels are reduced or eliminated during rush hours for vehicles carrying three or more passengers.

3. Intention is not always a prerequisite for learning. We learn many behaviors without setting out to do so. However, if intention can help us focus attention, learning is enhanced. To date, there is little evidence that we can learn while sleeping. When the claims for sleep learning tapes have been investigated by independent researchers, they have not been substantiated.

UNIT 9. REMEMBERING AND FORGETTING

1. Helpful memory strategies include paying attention, minimizing distractions and interference, and encoding information in more than one way, such as reading out loud, outlining important points, or chunking information in some personally meaningful way. It is also helpful to add meaning by linking new facts and ideas to familiar information, to use visual imagery, to review material distributed in study sessions, to study before going to sleep, and to overlearn material.

2. Recall of childhood memories is often difficult if not impossible. The schemas we used as children are very different from the ones we have developed as adults. Most people reconstruct memories from family stories or photographs. Language helps us label and organize memories. There is also evidence that early memories may be lost due to physiological maturation.

3. The ABC song offers many devices to aid retention. The letters are chunked or grouped in units that conform to the capacity of short-term memory. The letters at the end of each phrase rhyme, which is a mnemonic device. The song encodes the information in sounds as well as in movements. And the fun of it also motivates multiple rehearsals and performances.

4. Most of us are justifiably impressed with the capacity of our long-term memory. Society esteems and rewards people for good memories, starting in early childhood. Playing trivia games can set off a host of associations to events and ideas that we often don't even know we have in memory.

5. There is substantial controversy over what "leading" questions do to memories. The way a person perceives and recalls an event depends on perceptual and cognitive biases that even the eyewitness may not be aware of. Jury members are subject to their own biases when they hear and judge testimony. Jury members need to be especially alert to leading questions that might introduce details or prompt a witness to report an event in a particular way. The more informed a jury member is about how memory works, the better he or she may be able to weigh the value of testimony.

UNIT 10. COGNITIVE PROCESSES

1. To interpret the poem you need to consider language rules and underlying structure—word order, forms, endings, and sounds and language patterns. Although there are many strange and made-up words, some clearly echo familiar words—so that there are some built-in associations that imply meaning.

2. Scripts might include types of activities and dress, level of education, achievement, income, social status, family patterns, interests, vacation ideas, restaurant preferences, and health status.

3. Political cartoons juxtapose well-known people and well-known symbols to exaggerate, ridicule, or emphasize a specific quality. Cartoonists use a visual language. They depend on the reader's concepts and schemas, a shared knowledge of common symbols and their associations within a particular society or culture.

4. Definitions of common sense may include the ability to do multilevel processing, to generalize from experience, and to learn. Computers approach tasks in a logical, orderly way according to a specific routine. No computer is self-aware, curious, or interested in a topic. The computer cannot feel happy or good or care about anything. Therefore, it can only calculate; it cannot make the value judgments involved in commonsense decision making.

5. Children have scripts—expectations built on their knowledge of routine experiences. They are also able to learn procedural information and can store and manipulate visual information.

UNIT 11. JUDGMENT AND DECISION MAKING

1. Doctors might be basing their diagnosis on their experience with a biased sample of the population. They may also have a tendency to err on the side of caution, assuming a person has a strep throat and treating it rather than not treating a possibly seriously ill patient. In addition, doctors know that test results are not always 100 percent accurate, and they may have difficulty accepting a result that differs from their own opinion.

2. Pitfalls of problem solving include the inability to define the problem, to be illogical in situations in which emotions are involved, and reluctance to consider opposing points of view. People also depend on certain familiar approaches and strategies and often do not recognize when these are no longer useful. Cognitive bias and mental shortcuts also cause people to draw false conclusions or make bad decisions.

3. A child with these qualities might easily be considered precocious, disruptive, or difficult. Although most teachers respond positively to children with good verbal skills, schools typically put more emphasis on following the rules. This may be difficult for the creative, independent child.

4. The experimental method requires exploring alternate possibilities to the hypothesis. It also requires searching for other possible explanations for the conclusions and setting up double-blind situations. Good researchers are always interested in challenging their assumptions and replicating their findings.

UNIT 12. MOTIVATION AND EMOTION

1. An individual's sexual script is based on a unique combination of personal, social, and cultural beliefs and attitudes. Scripts are influenced by family role models, the media, and feedback from social experiences. Boys and girls are typically treated differently during development. Cultural stereotypes tend to reinforce some personal choices and not others. Sexual scripts are often not overtly expressed and may be a source of friction and disappointment in a relationship. If a couple can talk about mismatched role expectations and values they may be able to negotiate a shared script. The threat of AIDS and other sexually transmitted diseases may change the norms governing sexual activity and thereby rewrite the social scripts that guide sexual behavior. Expect to see changes in what characterizes an acceptable mate, dating patterns, and other relationship issues.

2. The optimist tends to emphasize global, external, and changeable or unstable reasons for failure, while claiming all the credit for success. The pessimist attributes success to luck or other random events out of his or her control and tends to take personal blame for failure.

3. In general, position, movement, and gestures provide clues to emotional states. Some people are more controlled than others, and some are better at picking up body language or clues than others. Being able to infer meaning or spot a discrepancy between words and body language is easier if you know the person well. For example, a mother can read subtle signs in her child. One spouse can sometimes tell if something is bothering the other. Although generalizations can be made, it is very difficult to interpret gestures or other forms of nonverbal communication when you are not familiar with a person or his or her culture.

4. The principle of motivation states that, typically, people are motivated to approach those activities or goals that increase pleasure and to avoid those that cause pain. Although food is generally thought of as something pleasurable, even as a reward or incentive, people with eating disorders see food as something to avoid. They distort or inhibit their eating behavior in an attempt to achieve an idealized body shape.

5. Both extreme happiness and sadness create physiological changes. Stress occurs when the body attempts to adapt to these changes. If adaptation results in prolonged arousal, the body becomes exhausted and illness may even occur.

6. How you respond might be determined by your need for achievement. If you believed you could get an A, you probably would want a grade. Your motivation to study might be reduced by the less rewarding pass-fail option. If you thought you could only earn a C, a pass-fail option might be more appealing. You would eliminate

the potentially handicapping stress of working for a grade. Working for a grade might also interfere with your intrinsic motivation to learn. If you were very interested in the course but didn't want the pressure of working hard, you would not need the incentive of being graded, and a pass-fail option would be more appealing.

UNIT 13. THE MIND AWAKE AND ASLEEP

1. Filter theory states that there are limits on early stages of perception. Other sensory information is held briefly but not processed. Although attention reduces confusion and sensory overload, it is not an all or nothing situation. There is some screening of the sensory input for meaningful information and some partial analysis below a level of conscious awareness.

2. Mindlessness enables us to deal with far more information than we could handle if sensory inputs had to go through conscious processing item by item. But mindlessness can be maladaptive if a situation requires new discriminations and new adaptations.

3. In the sense that perception is influenced by norms and expectations, our selective attention can be said to be determined by cultural context. We form concepts based on experience and language. Our perceptual habits are influenced by the environment and by the culture, which communicates what is important to notice and remember. Language helps to categorize elements of experience. But personal motivation and individual characteristics also create enormous variation within cultures.

UNIT 14. THE MIND HIDDEN AND DIVIDED

1. Illness, love, and grief can cause many changes in mental functioning typically associated with altered consciousness. Love and grief particularly can cause people to experience intense or extensive changes in consciousness and behavior.

2. Treatment should take into account the social and psychological factors as well as the chemical effects and physiological factors. Drug education programs must prepare students to evaluate the social and psychological components of drug use that lead to dependence and addiction. Some drug education programs aimed at children attempt to establish a certain mind-set that counteracts peer and cultural pressures and promotes critical thinking about prodrug messages.

3. Effects of extensive television viewing include heightened arousal and suggestibility, depression, and lowered motivation, as well as a distorted sense of time, disorientation, impulsivity, and hyperactivity, especially in children. Studies tend to be contradictory. Prolonged inactivity can lead to a kind of stimulus deprivation. Young children do not have the intellectual ability or sufficient experience and information to distinguish fantasy from reality, so they may be confused by the distortions of reality they see on television.

UNIT 15. THE SELF

1. One interpretation of the poem is that the speaker has a poor self-image, is lonely, and feels unappreciated. However, the speaker seems to use the self-serving bias to suggest that people who are popular are always bragging and croaking about themselves. So being a nobody may be better than being a somebody.

2. Shy people tend to be pessimistic. They have more social anxieties than those who are not shy. Shy people also tend to anticipate rejection and social failure and to interpret social encounters negatively, thus confirming their sense of inadequacy and helplessness.

3. The id is the driving energy of our passion, curiosity, and excitement. According to Freud, it is the life force that operates on the pleasure principle. On the positive side, it is the drive for self-preservation. It is also the place where sexual urges arise, thus ensuring the survival of the species. The fantasies of the id are the basis for imagination and creative endeavors. The id also contains aggressive and destructive drives that can be turned against the self or against society.

4. Your answer is probably yes, that different experiences of success or failure can change your sense of efficacy and your level of self-esteem. But success and failure are relative. If a task is too easy, it doesn't help a person with a low self-esteem. Also, research has suggested that self-esteem is often affected by a social referent. An extremely attractive person sitting next to you before a job interview might make you feel dissatisfied with yourself. But a disheveled or unattractive person might make you feel better about yourself.

5. The information is so universal that anyone can see him- or herself in the description. The information is usually easy to accept because it is so general. Anyone can think of a time when he or she was generous or selfish, gregarious or shy.

UNIT 16. TESTING AND INTELLIGENCE

1. No. Environment still has an important influence on the expression of any trait or ability. This is obvious from studies of development in enriched and impoverished environments. Impoverished environments lower a person's test performance. Both heredity *and* environment play a role.

2. Some might say that people already tend to sort and segregate themselves according to intelligence, even if judgments are based on informal, personal assessments. If IQs become public knowledge, this might have the largest effect on those at the top and bottom of the scale, leading to institutionalized forms of discrimination.

3. Educational systems tend to classify children, and the labels can last a lifetime. Some standardized tests determine whether a child has access to a particular school curriculum, training program, or college. For a student with a very high test score everything he or she does is cast in a favorable light. On the other hand, there can be considerable pressure to perform well. Test results can also lead to a narrowing of expectations. People who do not perform well on intelligence tests may lose motivation as well as their sense of self-efficacy and self-esteem. The results become part of a self-fulfilling prophecy.

4. Projective tests use ambiguous images to elicit information thought to reveal inner feelings, concerns, values, needs, conflicts, and personality traits. This information is combined with data gathered in other ways to obtain a complete personality description. Intelligence test performance may be one of those additional assessments used to build a rounded picture of a person. Intelligence is usually considered to be independent of creativity. Studies show that people who score high on intelligence tests are not necessarily creative. Projective tests have been used to assess creativity. Both tests of intelligence and creativity may include measures of cognitive style.

5. Intelligence tests and psychological assessments attempt to avoid personal bias and to obtain an objective measure of a person's abilities. However, the tests can be used as a short-cut in place of a more thorough and personalized evaluation. Tests are often misunderstood and misapplied. People have an inappropriate reverence for scores. Few people question the authority of a computer printout. Objections to the tests include claims that they are not objective and that they do not measure what they are intended to measure. People often use tests to focus on what is wrong with the individual instead of considering what is wrong with the system. Test scores have been used to argue for the heritability of intelligence, which has important public policy implications for immigration, education, employment, and affirmative action.

UNIT 17. SEX AND GENDER

1. A person's sexual script includes knowing which behaviors are acceptable and unacceptable. It includes personal and social norms that prescribe what to do, when, where, how, and with whom. This may include rules that dictate who opens doors and who picks up the check. Gender roles are an important part of the scripts that influence interpersonal and sexual behavior. When people share complementary scripts they may be more compatible than people whose expectations and preferences do not mesh.

2. Merely knowing if someone is male or female leads to an exaggeration of gender differences. From the beginning, infants are perceived to be female or male although differences in appearance and behavior are negligible. Research shows how the same behavior may be judged differently depending on whether it is done by a man or a woman. A man's protest, say, over a course grade, may be perceived as assertive, but the same behavior by a woman may be judged pushy. Judgments about the suitability of people for particular jobs and occupations sometimes ignore individual traits and are based solely on gender.

3. Children show different play and toy preferences. Research has shown that as early as four years of age children choose to play with members of their own sex and in same-sex play groups.

4. Male traits are often perceived as more desirable by both men and women. Being assertive, achieving, and independent seems related to a better self-concept for both men and women. In general, the labels used to describe male traits are more positive. However, in judging the relative merits of masculine and feminine traits for adjustment, it is important to specify exactly what that means. For example, one study suggests that feminine traits contribute to happier marriages.

5. Some people insist that it doesn't make a difference, but many past studies have shown that both men and women make different judgments based on the sex of the

author. In general, articles are viewed more favorably when study participants believed they were written by a man. However, recent evidence suggests that this effect has diminished, and ratings of works by men and women are converging in the 1990s.

UNIT 18. MATURING AND AGING

1. Until recently, the study of aging was dominated by pathology, studies of the sick elderly. Now that there are large numbers of healthy, active older people, the focus of research has changed. Statistics show that most older people do not fit the stereotype of the frail elderly. Some of the psychological problems and memory loss can be attributed to drug interactions, lack of stimulation, or the feeling of a loss of control. Studies can show the effects of life-style and environment. Problems of depression, for example, might affect anyone who suffered the loss of loved ones, a job, intellectual stimulation, or control over his or her own life. Also, it shouldn't be considered an oddity that elderly people talk more about the past; they have more past than future. Comparing the status of the elderly in different cultures reveals the influence of cultural attitudes and social patterns.

2. The midlife crisis, an emotional upheaval or disorientation, is a process of self-assessment in which individuals confront such issues as the value of their lives, their social roles and relationships, the gap between their dreams and accomplishments, and the realities of aging and death. Of course not everyone goes through a crisis. In fact, some experts believe that "crisis" is too strong a word.

3. Any changes in intelligence depend on how one defines and measures intelligence. Not all cognitive abilities change at the same rate. Some decline, some improve, and some stay the same. Data on IQs collected using the cross-sectional method show more decline than results obtained from longitudinal studies. There is also some evidence that shows that fluid intelligence primarily related to speed of CNS functioning tends to decline in adult years, while crystallized intelligence, primarily related to the application of knowledge, tends to increase.

4. The social conditions and economic constraints and opportunities of every generation shape the attitudes, expectations, and values characteristic of different age groups in society. For example, increasing the ethnic and cultural diversity of the cities, the growing number of women who delay marriage and childbearing, changing sexual attitudes and values, and the rise in the divorce rate will all affect the social characteristics of the adult and elderly population of the future. The increase in the numbers of healthy, active older adults will change the way young people view older people and how older people view themselves. The need for older people to contribute to the economic system has already begun to change policies and attitudes about early retirement.

5. Social attitudes and economic conditions determine which changes and responsibilities are considered appropriate for adult roles. For example, the age at which marriage is acceptable or at which children are expected to become self-supporting is often set by economic and social conditions in the larger society.

6. Being a parent was once the norm. Taking on the responsibilities of parenthood was one of the major milestones in adult development and was considered the step that moved a person from a stage of selfishness to a stage in which nurturing and intimacy

become a priority. However, not everyone accepts the idea that having children is the only way to be productive, creative, and nurturing.

UNIT 19. THE POWER OF THE SITUATION

1. Milgram's subjects could avoid blaming themselves if they reasoned that the situation was influencing their behavior. They could rationalize that they were only following orders and did not have to accept responsibility for their behavior. Thus they could avoid guilt, much as the Nazis did when they claimed they were only following orders.

2. Many patients are intimidated by their doctor's expertise. They defer to the doctor's greater medical knowledge and stifle their doubts and fears. Because patients assume that doctors have the education and training to handle medical problems, many patients do not feel qualified to question the doctor's judgments. If patients disagree with their doctors they may not fill a prescription or take prescribed medication. They may change doctors without notice or explanation. Or they make seek out a second opinion. Today, movements to promote patients' rights and advances in patient education make questioning medical authority more acceptable.

3. Roles involve expectations about behavior. Roles and social obligations are sometimes perceived as social traps, especially when behavior is dictated by social expectations and norms rather than by personal feelings and individual taste. You may conform only to win approval or to avoid social rejection. For example, being respected in the community might require church attendance, even if you are not a believer. When social expectations conflict with feelings, alienation or resentment may result. When behavior coincides with role expectations, it reinforces a sense of true identity.

4. Everyone has had good and bad teachers and bosses. Choose specific situations and analyze the style of authority or leadership. Analyze your participation and performance. In which situation did you learn or accomplish the most? In which situation did people support and help each other the most? Which situations were most relaxed?

5. Although extreme examples of blind obedience, such as Nazi Germany or even Milgram's experiment, are easy to identify, there are many ambiguous situations in which the difference is not so clear. In schools, churches, and the workplace, cooperation is highly esteemed and compliance is usually rewarded. Efforts to undermine authority are typically considered to be a threat by the leader of the group. Parents and teachers tend to reinforce compliant behavior in children. It may be useful to cite examples of people who buck authority and to help illustrate possibilities for legitimate dissent. However, most research on social influence shows that unquestioning obedience is the norm.

UNIT 20. CONSTRUCTING SOCIAL REALITY

1. Individuals do not respond to situations identically. Some individuals have such strong personal values and self-confidence that they do not seek social approval as

much as others. Also, people usually choose what they hear and watch. They can turn off the television, ignore a program, or walk out of the movie theater. They can read selectively, actively looking for articles that support their ideas or challenge them. They can associate with people who share their beliefs and opinions or purposely expose themselves to new ideas and experiences.

2. Nationalism can be a source of pride and cohesiveness for a population. However, this is all too often gained at the expense of making certain classes of people into internal or external enemies. These out-groups are used to divert attention from national problems and often become a target for anger. Nationalism can encourage "us versus them" thinking and escalate conflicts. An "us versus them" mentality is simple to create. It depends only on drawing some distinction—meaningless and arbitrary, or meaningful—between groups of people.

3. Rosenthal's experiment would probably not meet today's ethical standards. Children cannot legally give their consent. Therefore, they would not be willing participants according to ethical guidelines. Also, there might be some harm done to a child's self-esteem by the arbitrary manipulation of the success of some of the children and not others.

4. Dissonance reduction, the self-serving bias, and defense mechanisms are very similar. They are all efforts to reduce anxiety or resolve an apparent conflict between desirable self-perceptions and unacceptable attitudes and actions.

5. Children who watch television tend to think that there is more violence in the streets than there really is. At the same time, they rarely experience the true impact of violence. They tend to see men and women in stereotyped roles and relationships. In most situation comedies, problems get resolved in 30 minutes.

UNIT 21. PSYCHOPATHOLOGY

1. Courts differ on how they deal with the insanity defense. In order for a person to be excused from legal responsibility for criminal actions, the defense must demonstrate severely impaired judgment and lack of self-control. A person is not considered legally responsible if he or she is unable to distinguish right from wrong. The definition may vary from country to country, from state to state, even from court to court. It is a highly controversial issue.

2. The Diagnostic and Statistical Manual has been criticized for inflating disorders, basing some criteria on myth rather than on empirical evidence, and for stigmatizing people. It is also, clearly, a relative assessment guide subject to cultural forces. For example, homosexuality was once characterized as a disorder. Today, the self-defeating personality has been proposed as a disorder to be included. Women's groups and others are very concerned that such a label will lead to a blaming of the victim.

3. Statistically, homosexuality is unusual. However, cultural standards are relative. Psychological assessments show no differences in personality or adjustment between heterosexuals and homosexuals. Today, the DSM III does not list homosexuality as a disorder. It is considered a problem only if it causes guilt or self-hate. However, at one time homosexuality was considered a disorder.

4. Women may be more willing to talk about distress and emotional problems. They are more often denied opportunities for independence and achievement and may feel angry, hopeless, or helpless, justifiably. There is a male bias toward traditional concepts of mental health.

5. Many psychological problems are just extreme instances of behavior that most of us exhibit at one time or another. If you are extremely worried about a certain behavior, if the behavior is disruptive to relationships, or if it has become a persistent problem, you might consider getting a professional evaluation.

6. Split personality, which is a dissociative disorder, is commonly confused with schizophrenia, a term that was often used as a grab-bag definition for any condition that did not fit neatly into other classifications. Today, psychologists define schizophrenia as the breakdown of integrated personality functioning, withdrawal from reality, emotional distortions, and a disturbed thought process.

UNIT 22. PSYCHOTHERAPY

1. It is difficult to determine the success of a particular therapy because faith in the effectiveness of any treatment may be enough to bring about changes in a patient's feelings or behavior. Also, some problems resolve themselves over time without professional intervention.

2. Comparison of therapies is difficult. There is enormous variation among patients and the intensity and duration of their problems, so that therapies are very individualized. There are also differences in the training, expertise, and personality of individual therapists. Criteria for successful outcomes will vary with the specific problem and type of therapy.

3. Finding the right match between a problem and an approach to therapy starts with how you define the problem and your attitude or beliefs about the kind of help you need. A person might seek assistance in making the decision from a physician or person in the community who is familiar with available resources and services.

4. Unit 22 describes therapies that focus on illness and problem solving, as well as on those designed to address life management issues, self-esteem, relationships, and potential. Most people, at some time, could benefit from professional intervention.

5. In American culture, there is typically a stigma associated with seeking help of any kind. Our culture emphasizes individuality, self-sufficiency, and strength, especially for men. That makes it harder to admit weakness or the need for support.

UNIT 23. HEALTH, MIND, AND BEHAVIOR

1. Friends can help reduce stress in several ways. They can offer practical help. For example, when there is illness or a crisis in a family, friends can relieve temporary concerns about money, child care, food, or transportation needs. They can also offer emotional support, being there to listen and empathize with you about what you are going through and reassuring you that you are not going crazy even when you feel most vulnerable and confused. Friends may also offer advice in an unfamiliar situation, helping you to think through decisions. Social support makes people less vulnerable to

stress-related problems. Social networks counteract a sense of isolation by providing a sense of belonging. In support groups, individuals help each other by providing a social reference group. They share advice, feelings, and information specific to the situation.

2. Victims of a curse may feel such intense or prolonged fear that it wears down the body's ability to cope. One theory suggests that the body's attempt to counteract an extreme emotional reaction may go too far, slowing down important systems and processes to the point of death.

3. Most people use defense mechanisms at times. Some defenses help us gain time to adjust to a trauma or other type of problem. Rationalization may be a stress-reducing strategy in the face of frustration or failure. Any defense mechanism can be part of a coping approach, but it may prevent us from confronting and solving our real problems if it becomes habitual.

4. Self-defeating thoughts undermine a person's sense of self-esteem, optimism, efficacy, and control—all necessary for adequate coping.

5. Perfectionists unnecessarily stress themselves by setting impossible goals and standards. They may compare themselves with inappropriate models of achievement, never being satisfied with their own accomplishments. They may feel they have inadequate resources to measure up to their unreasonably high standards. These attitudes can create stress and can undermine their ability to perform.

UNIT 24. IN SPACE, TOWARD PEACE

1. Basic or pure research is done for the sake of knowledge, while applied research is designed to solve concrete problems. For example, investigators doing basic research that focuses on the genetic influences on brain chemistry may simply be interested in defining, understanding, and predicting the effects of chemical reactions in the brain. Eventually the information may be applied. It may be used to plan treatment to correct abnormal brain conditions or to alter brain chemistry in an attempt to cure certain diseases.

2. When we call a machine "user friendly" we mean that it is easy to use. Its controls and displays are designed with human comfort and sensory and motor abilities in mind. The design of the machine minimizes mistakes and may even anticipate and correct mistakes. Organizational psychologists also address practical concerns and quality of life issues in the workplace. They influence organization effectiveness by applying their skills and insights to solving problems of human relations, communication, mediation, employee selection and training, leadership, job satisfaction, and stress.

3. Yes. People can use principles of persuasion and coercion to influence the behavior of others. For example, cults use carefully structured methods to recruit and convert new members. Advertisers might design campaigns to persuade people to buy things they don't need. Con artists use principles and techniques to sell products and to enlist cooperation from people.

CUMULATIVE GLOSSARY OF PROGRAM TERMS

agonist—a chemical or drug that mimics the action of a neurotransmitter

amnesia—partial or complete loss of memory of information or past events

androgynous—having both masculine and feminine traits

antagonist—a chemical or drug that blocks the action of a neurotransmitter

applied psychology—the practical application of psychological knowledge and principles to concrete problems

arousal—a heightened level of excitation or activation

autocratic—governed by one person with unlimited power

behavioral confirmation—a form of social feedback in which our self-beliefs determine how we are perceived and evaluated by others

beta-endorphin—a type of opioid which, under conditions of maternal deprivation, can block the action of the early regulators of insulin and growth hormone

biological biasing—a genetic predisposition that increases the likelihood of getting a disorder if exposed to prolonged or intense stress

biological senescing—growing older physically, or biological aging

blind obedience—an unquestioning compliance with authority

cognitive control—the power of beliefs to give meaning to a situation

cognitive developmental theory—the theory stating that children use male and female as fundamental categories and actively sex-type themselves to achieve cognitive consistency

democratic—practicing social equality

developmental strategies—behaviors that have evolved to conform to the sex roles typical of the adult members of a species

disposition—a person's internal or personal characteristics

double-blind procedure—an experimental procedure in which neither the researcher nor the subject knows which subjects are receiving the real treatment and which are getting the placebo

dread factor—the fear of unfamiliar or potentially catastrophic events which make us judge them to be riskier than familiar events

enzymes—protein molecules that act as catalysts in body chemistry by facilitating chemical reactions

ERP (Event-Related Potentials)—variations in brain waves as recorded by the electroencephalogram (EEG) which are triggered by specific internal or external events

field study—research carried on outside the laboratory where naturally occurring, ongoing behavior can be observed

framing—the way information is presented which tends to bias how it is interpreted

genetic counseling—counseling that advises a person about the probability of passing on defective genes to offspring

glucocorticoids—substances produced by the adrenal cortex that act on the hippocampus to alter the stress response

Heisenberg indeterminacy principle—principle stating that our impressions of other people are distorted by how we observe and assess them

hierarchies—an ordered arrangement of ranked series of items

hynagogic state—a period of reveries at the onset of the sleeping state

hypnotic analgesia—lack of pain perception while under hypnosis

invariance—the principle stating that preferences between options should be independent of different representations

jet lag—a sense of disorientation caused by disruption of internal circadian rhythms

laissez-faire—allowing complete freedom, with little or no interference or guidance

language acquisition device—the innate ability to acquire language, a hypothesis put forth by Noam Chomsky

legitimate authority—a form of power exercised by someone in a superior role such as a teacher or president

life-span development—developmental changes continuing throughout the life cycle

LSD—lysergic acid diethylamide, a hallucinogen

lucid dreaming—the awareness of dreaming without awakening, and sometimes the ability to control the content of a dream

maternal deprivation—the lack of adequate affection and stimulation from the mother or mother substitute

micro level—the smallest unit of analysis in psychology; for example, studying P-300 brain waves or other neural or biochemical changes

molar level—the analysis of larger units of behavior of the whole person in complex situations, taking into account cultural background and social experiences

molecular level—the analysis of discrete, observable behaviors such as body language, crying, or laughing

morpheme—the smallest unit of language that has meaning

optimism—the tendency to attribute failure to external, unstable, or changeable factors and to attribute success to stable factors

parentese—modified speech that parallels children's level of language development

pessimism—the tendency to attribute failure to stable or internal factors and to attribute success to global variables

phoneme—the smallest unit of sound that affects the meaning of speech

posthypnotic amnesia—forgetting selected events by suggestion

prejudice—a bias for or against someone formed without sufficient information

psychic numbing—being emotionally unaffected by an upsetting or alarming event

psychogenic—organic malfunction or tissue damage caused by anxiety, tension, or depression

psycholinguists—scientists who study how the structure of language is related to speaking and listening

psychological adolescing—developing psychologically to full potential

psychosurgery—a surgical procedure that destroys selected areas of the brain

Pygmalion effect—the effect of positive and negative expectations on behavior

random sample—an unbiased population selected at random

receptor—a specialized nerve cell sensitive to particular kinds of stimulus energy

reference standard—a norm or model of behavior that is used to decide how to behave in a particular situation

selective optimization—making the most of what you have

self-handicapping—a process by which we try to explain away potential failures by blaming them on something other than our lack of ability

semantics—a set of rules that govern the meaning of words and sentences

senile dementia—biochemical and neuronal changes in the brain that lead to a gradual reduction in mental efficiency

sex typing—the psychological process by which boys and girls become masculine or feminine

shyness—a form of social anxiety caused by the expectation of negative social evaluation

similarity heuristic—an error based on the tendency to see a connection between belonging to a certain category and having the characteristics considered typical of members of that category

social learning theory—the theory stating that children are socialized by observing role models and are rewarded or punished for behaving appropriately

stage theory—a theory that describes development as a fixed sequence of distinct periods of life

status transaction—a form of interpersonal communication in which we establish relative degrees of social status and power

stereotype—the belief that all members of a group share common traits

subjective reality—the perceptions and beliefs that we accept without question

syntax—a set of rules for combining words into phrases and sentences

time-limited dynamic psychotherapy—a form of short-term therapy

CREDITS AND PERMISSIONS

Unit 1. Past, Present, and Promise

1. Pat Brady, "Rose Is Rose," *Boston Globe*, October 4, 1988, p. 83. Reprinted by permission of UFS, Inc.

2. Lyn Johnston, "For Better or for Worse," *Boston Globe*, October 4, 1988, p. 83. Copyright © 1988 Universal Press Syndicate. Reprinted with permission. All rights reserved.

3. John Pfeiffer (science writer and consultant), "Striking the Right Trade Posture," *Science 85* (September 1985): 80-81. Copyright ©1985 by the AAAS. Reprinted by permission.

4. Susan Seliger, "What Is Best for the Children?" *Working Mother* (April 1986): 77-78. Reprinted with permission from *Working Mother* magazine. Copyright © 1986 by The McCall Publishing Company.

Unit 2. Understanding Research

1. Martha Vetter White, "Ask Dr. White," *The MA Report* 3:11 (September 1988): 6. Martha White is a pediatric allergist in Bethesda, Maryland, and medical editor, Mothers of Asthmatics, Inc., Fairfax, Virginia. Reprinted by permission.

2. Douglas J. Besharov, "The Child-Abuse Numbers Game," *Wall Street Journal*, August 4, 1988, p. 20. Reprinted with permission of *The Wall Street Journal* © 1989 Dow Jones & Company, Inc. All rights reserved.

Unit 3. The Behaving Brain

1. Ellen Goodman, "When Alcohol Is the Excuse," *Boston Globe*, December 3, 1987, p. 21. © 1987 The Boston Globe Newspaper Company/Washington Post Writers Group. Reprinted with permission.

2. Julius Segal and Zelda Segal, "When the Body Affects the Mind," *Parents* (March 1986): 178. Reprinted with permission of the authors.

3. Alison Bass, "Head Injuries Found in Young Killers," *Boston Globe*, June 20, 1988, pp. 53-55. Reprinted courtesy of the *Boston Globe*.

4. From *Psychology and Life Instructor's Resource Book*, by Philip G. Zimbardo. Copyright © 1988 by Scott, Foresman and Company. Reprinted by permission.

Unit 4. The Responsive Brain

1. Kathleen McAuliffe, "The Making of a Mind," *OMNI* (October 1985): 62-66, 74. Copyright © 1985 by Kathleen McAuliffe, and reprinted with permission of OMNI Publications International, Ltd.

2. J. Greenberg, "Early Hearing Loss and Brain Development," *Science News*, March 7, 1987, p. 149. Reprinted with permission from *Science News*, the weekly newsmagazine of science, copyright © 1987 by Science Service, Inc.

3. Christine Gorman, "A Balancing Act of Life and Death," *Time*, February 1, 1988, p. 49. Copyright © 1988 Time, Inc. Reprinted by permission.

4. Susan Seliger, "Stress Can Be Good for You," *New York Magazine*, August 2, 1982, p. 20. Article also appeared in *Stop Killing Yourself: Make Stress Work for You* (New York: Putnam) by the author. Copyright © 1989 by News Group Publications, Inc. Reprinted by permission. All rights reserved.

Unit 5. The Developing Child

1. Daniel G. Freedman, "Ethnic Differences in Babies," *Human Nature* (January 1979): 36. Reprinted by permission of the author.

2. Janet K. Black, "Are Young Children Really Egocentric?" *Young Children* (September 1981): 51-55. Reprinted by permission.

Unit 13. The Mind Awake and Asleep

1. Cynthia F. Mitchell, "Firms Waking Up to Sleep Disorders," *Wall Street Journal*, July 7, 1988, p. 25. Reprinted by permission of *The Wall Street Journal*, © Dow Jones & Company 1988. All rights reserved worldwide.

2. Virginia K. Lee, "The Pen Is Mightier Than…" Reprinted from *American Journal of Nursing* 85:9 (September 1985): 1040. Copyright © 1985 American Journal of Nursing Company. Used with permission. All rights reserved.

Unit 14. The Mind Hidden and Divided

1. Howard E. Goldfluss, "First Word," *OMNI* (January 1988): 8. Copyright © 1988 by *OMNI* Magazine and reprinted with permission of OMNI Publications International, Ltd.

2. Oliver Sacks, "The Nature of Consciousness," *Harper's Magazine* (December 1975): 5. Copyright © 1975 by *Harper's Magazine*. All rights reserved. Reprinted from the December issue by special permission.

Unit 15. The Self

1. Maureen Dowling, "Mary-Ann—A Lesson in Determination," *Educational Leadership* (September 1985): 72-74. Copyright © 1985 by the Association for Supervision and Curriculum Development. All rights reserved. Reprinted with permission.

2. C. R. Snyder, "Excuses, Excuses," *Psychology Today* (September 1984): 50-55. Reprinted with permission from *Psychology Today* Magazine. Copyright © 1984 (PT Partners, L.P.).

Unit 16. Testing and Intelligence

1. John Kristofco, "Aren't All Kids Gifted," *Family Learning* (May/June 1984): 57-59. John P. Kristofco, Chairperson, Educational Services Division, Clark State Community College, Springfield, Ohio. Reprinted with permission.

2. Bruce Bower, "Calculating Apes," *Science News*, May 31, 1987, pp. 334-35. Reprinted with permission from *Science News*, the weekly magazine of science, copyright © 1987 by Science Service, Inc.

Unit 17. Sex and Gender

1. Alison Carlson, "Chromosome Count," *MS.* (October 1988): 40-44. Reprinted with permission.

2. Sharon E. Epperson, "Students Link Subtle Sex Bias in School with Women's Behavior in the Workplace," *Wall Street Journal*, September 16, 1988, p. 27. Reprinted by permission of *The Wall Street Journal*, © Dow Jones & Company 1988. All rights reserved worldwide.

Unit 18. Maturing and Aging

1. Chet Raymo, "But Would We Really Want to Live Forever?" *Boston Globe*, November 7, 1988, p. 38. Reprinted by permission of the author.

2. Jean Dietz, "What Really Bothers Women in Midlife," *Boston Globe*, May 30, 1988, p. 33. Reprinted courtesy of *The Boston Globe*.

3. Daniel Goleman, "New Evidence Points to Growth of the Brain Even Late in Life," *New York Times*, July 30, 1985, sec. 3, p. 1. Copyright © 1985 by The New York Times Company. Reprinted by permission.

Unit 19. The Power of the Situation

1. Don Rosendale, "A Whistle-Blower," *New York Times Magazine*, June 7, 1986, p. 56. Copyright © 1986 by The New York Times Company. Reprinted by permission.

2. Daniel Goleman, "Great Altruists: Science Ponders Soul of Goodness," *New York Times*, March 5, 1985, sec. 3, p. 1. Copyright © 1985 by The New York Times Company. Reprinted by permission.

3. Janice T. Gibson and Mika Haritos-Fatourous, "The Education of a Torturer," *Psychology Today* (November 1986): 50-58. Reprinted with permission from *Psychology Today* Magazine, Copyright © 1988 (PT Partners, L.P.).

Unit 20. Constructing Social Reality

1. Ronald Alsop, "Advertisers Struggle to Portray Subject of Death in Commercials," *Wall Street Journal*, January 27, 1988, p. 27.

2. Jean Dietz, "The Jury System on Trial," *Boston Sunday Globe*, October 23, 1988, p. A26. Reprinted courtesy of *The Boston Globe*.

Unit 21. Psychopathology

1. Stuart A. Kirk, "A Last Dance with Freud," *Newsweek*, October 13, 1986, p. 15. © 1986 Newsweek, Inc. All rights reserved. Reprinted by permission.

2. Alfie Kohn, "Exploring the Link Between Art and Madness," *Boston Globe* July 4, 1988, p. 30–31. Copyright © 1988 by Alfie Kohn. Reprinted with the author's permission. Alfie Kohn is the author of *Beyond Selfishness* (New York: Basic Books, 1990) and *No Contest: The Case Against Competition* (Boston: Houghton Mifflin, 1986).

3. Paul Chance, "I'm O.K., You're a Bit Odd," *Psychology Today* (July/August 1988): 18–19. Reprinted with permission from *Psychology Today* Magazine, copyright © 1988 (PT Partners, L.P.).

Unit 22. Psychotherapy

1. Bob Anderson, "Breaking Loose," *SUCCESS* (May 1985): 44–48. Reprinted with permission from *SUCCESS* Magazine. Copyright © 1985 by SUCCESS Magazine Company. All rights reserved.

2. Linda Weltner, "In the Stillness of Our Minds," *Boston Globe*. Linda Weltner is the author of *No Place Like Home: Rooms and Reflections from One Family's Life*. Reprinted with permission of the author.

3. Alison Bass, "Experts Debate Value of 'Autopsy' on Suicide's Mind," *Boston Globe*, December 7, 1987, p. 49. Reprinted courtesy of *The Boston Globe*.

Unit 23. Health, Mind, and Behavior

1. Joshua Fischman, "Getting Tough," *Psychology Today* (December 1987): 26–28. Reprinted with permission from *Psychology Today* Magazine, copyright © 1987 (PT Partners, L.P.).

2. Sally Squires, "The Immune System Reacts to Stress," *Washington Post*, March 31, 1987, p. 9. © 1987 *The Washington Post*. Reprinted by permission.

3. Eleanor Smith, "AIDS and Personality," *Psychology Today* (March 1989). Reprinted with permission from *Psychology Today* Magazine, copyright © 1989 (PT Partners, L.P.).

Unit 24. In Space, Toward Peace

1. John E. Mack, "American and Soviet Teenagers and Nuclear War," *New England Journal of Medicine* 319:7 (1988): 437–38. Copyright © 1988 Massachusetts Medical Society. Reprinted with permission.

2. Elizabeth Stark, "Wild Blue Blunders," *Psychology Today* (October 1988): 30–32. Reprinted with permission from *Psychology Today* Magazine, copyright © 1988 (PT Partners, L.P.).

3. Tom Ashbrook, "You Are about to Enter Another Reality," *Boston Globe*, July 28, 1988, p. 65. Reprinted courtesy of *The Boston Globe*.

Unit 25. A Union of Opposites

1. Evelyn Zamula, "Taming Tourette's Tics and Twitches," *FDA Consumer* (September 1988): 27–28, 30. Reprinted by permission.

2. Richard Saltus, "Cultures Shape Our Medical Views," *Boston Globe*, August 29, 1988, pp. 25–27. Reprinted courtesy of *The Boston Globe*.

3. James Gorman, "Whose Brain Is It Anyway?" *Discovery* (November 1987): 38–41. Copyright © 1987 by James Gorman.

Unit 26. New Directions

1. Madeline Drexler, "To Test or Not to Test," *Boston Sunday Globe Magazine*, 1988. Reprinted by permission of the author.

2. E. Fuller Torrey, Sidney M. Wolfe, and Laurie M. Flynn, "Human Jetsam," *Public Citizen* (November/December 1988): 8–10, 18. Abridged and excerpted from *Care of the Seriously Mentally Ill: A Ranking of State Programs* (1988), a joint publication of the Public Citizen Health Research Group and The National Alliance for the Mentally Ill, available for $10 from the Public Citizen Health Research Group, 2000 P Street, NW, #1700, Washington, DC 20036. Reprinted with permission.